WORLD POLITICS THIRD EDITION

INTERNATIONAL POLITICS ON THE WORLD STAGE, BRIEF

CONNEC**TEXT**

JOHN T. ROURKE
University of Connecticut

MARK A. BOYER
University of Connecticut

Dushkin/McGraw-Hill

A Division of The **McGraw-Hill** *Companies*

Dushkin/McGraw-Hill

A Division of The McGraw-Hill Companies

World Politics: International Politics on the World Stage, Brief, Third Edition

Copyright © 2000 by Dushkin/McGraw-Hill, a division of The McGraw-Hill Companies, Inc. All rights reserved. Printed in the United States of America. Except as permitted under the United States Copyright Act of 1976, no part of this publication may be reproduced in any form or by any means, or stored in a database or retrieval system, without the prior written permission of the publisher.

 This book is printed on acid-free paper
ISBN 0-07-236792-X

VP and Publisher	Jeffrey L. Hahn
List Manager	Theodore Knight
Production Manager	Brenda S. Filley
Editor	Ava Suntoke
Director of Technology	Jonathan Stowe
Technology Development Editor	Shawn Callahan
Photo Researcher	Pamela Carley
Designer	Charles Vitelli
Typesetting Supervisor	Juliana Arbo
Proofreader	Diane Barker
Copier Coordinator	Larry Killian

Cover   © 2000 PhotoDisc, Inc.
Cover Design   Lara M. Johnson

The credit section for this book begins on page 479 and is considered an extension of this copyright page.

Library of Congress Catalog Card Number: 99-74551

Printed in the United States of America

23456 QPF/QPF 0543210
http://www.mhhe.com

Preface

World Politics: International Politics on the World Stage, Brief, Third Edition, has been developed as a shorter international relations text in order to provide students and teachers with the opportunity to explore international relations in a variety of ways. In contrast to a course that centers on the original, longer edition of this text, this brief edition allows for the use of more supplemental materials (such as cases, simulations, special topical approaches to the field, or computer applications) in a course. Thus the course can be tailored to fit a variety of teaching and learning styles.

The brief edition is, however, more than just an abridged version of the longer edition. It has been updated both in terms of substantive examples and scholarly research. This edition also has four fewer chapters than the longer one and has been reorganized considerably to reflect the needs of a shorter approach to the field. Still it does not lose the sense of international political drama portrayed in the original *International Politics on the World Stage,* Seventh Edition.

Being a ConnecText means that this book makes extensive use of the growth in information technologies and provides the student and teacher with a well-developed Web site of resources to aid in student learning. The Web-based resources, all flagged with a Web icon in the chapters, augment the material in the book itself. The book can be used without them, but we have endeavored to make this Web site something new and different. In particular, we have created interactive exercises for each chapter of the book. Some of these activities allow students to compare their ideas with others who are accessing the Web site, while others are focused on in-class activities. In each case, they emphasize the active learning orientation of the authors of this book and of the book itself. In essence, we developed this Web site on the firm conviction that students learn and retain more by *doing* rather than by reading alone. We welcome your feedback on this initiative, so if you have thoughts or ideas about this material (or anything else related to the book), please contact World Politics: International Politics on the World Stage, Brief, Dushkin/McGraw-Hill, Sluice Dock, Guilford, CT 06437.

The text is organized in the following way: Chapters 1, 2, and 3 focus on approaches to the study of international relations. Chapter 1 makes the case that international relations do matter to the average student and that the individual student can have an impact on international relations. It also lays out the basically theoretical and conceptual debates, in particular the recurrent divide between realist and idealist approaches to analysis and prescription in world affairs.

Chapter 2 is primarily historical. It traces the evolution of the international system, concentrating on how the contemporary international system has its roots in the past and the degree to which there are both centralizing and decentralizing tendencies coexisting in world affairs today. Chapter 3 lays out the conceptual framework of the levels of analysis to show students the different perspectives that can be used to structure our study of international relations.

The second section of the book comprises chapters 4 through 9 and follows the structure of examining the traditional versus the alternative approaches to world politics. Chapters 4 and 5 examine the forces of nationalism and transnationalism, respectively. Chapters 6 and 7 focus on the traditional dominance of national states in international affairs and the rising role and influence of international organizations. And chapters 8 and 9 lead the reader through the traditional role of power and diplomacy in the world to the impact of international law on constraining behavior by actors on the world stage.

The last portion of the book, chapters 10 through 14, discusses an array of the substantive issues of world affairs. Chapter 10 focuses on the traditional high politics issues of war and peace, military influence and arms control. Chapters 11 and 12 highlight the importance and rising influence of economic issues in the world. Chapter 12 in particular discusses the dual tendencies of competition and cooperation in the international political economy. Chapter 13 examines the human condition internationally, showing how culture, economics, and power impact the ways people live and are treated around the world. And lastly, chapter 14 elucidates the issues of ecological quality and sustainable development as well as the challenges that are emerging in that substantive area.

Even with all these changes, *World Politics: International Politics on the World Stage, Brief,* maintains the conceptual and theoretical sophistication of the longer edition and employs the same standards of timeliness and readability found therein. *World Politics* presents the student and teacher with the most up-to-date coverage of the substance of current international relations, including the expanding roles of the UN and NATO in crises such as Kosovo and East Timor and so provides the student with stronger ties to the real world of international relations. In other words, current events illustrations make the concepts and theory of the textbook come alive in demonstrative ways.

The brief edition also seeks to be student-friendly. Its wide use of graphics such as photographs, figures, cartoons, and maps gives visual life to the text ideas. A glossary, chapter outlines and summaries, and an extensive bibliography are also included to aid the student in studying and the faculty member in teaching.

Finally, this edition maintains the standards of the longer edition in continuously accessing scholarly research. We have included the insights of newly published research, even material that has been published since the last edition of the parent text came out. This means that the student today is reading a state-of-the-art discussion in international relations.

Before closing, we would like to acknowledge a number of the scholars who took the time to review our initial plan to condense the material of the longer edition. Their input and ideas were invaluable in the process that we have undertaken over the past years. They are

Russell Bova, Dickinson College

William K. Callum, Daytona Beach Community College

Neal Coates, Abilene Christian University

Rodney Grubb, St. Olaf College

Charles F. Gruber, Marshall University

Clinton Hewan, Northern Kentucky University

Diddy Hitchins, University of Alaska–Anchorage

Henry Louis, Kansas City Kansas Community College

Christine Nahau Patrinos, Holy Names College

Marek Payerhin, University of Connecticut

Daniel C. Sanford, Whitworth College

Sanford Silverburg, Catawba College

Michael Sonnleitner, Portland Community College

The time and effort they put into reviewing our approach is greatly appreciated.

Last, but most certainly not least, we would like to thank James Allan, University of Connecticut, for the tireless work he has done to help keep this book's Web site current, interesting, and engaging for students. The high quality of his work over the past two editions is much appreciated and is a key to the success of this project in the classroom.

Along those same lines and to close, we ask that you please let us know if you have any comments on what we have done in this volume. We hope that you will write to us with any insights you have on how we can make this volume more student-friendly and teacher-useful while continuing its lively mix of contemporary substance and scholarly research. We are in the business of teaching about world affairs, but we can do our job well only if we hear how we are doing from both teachers and students.

John T. Rourke
Mark A. Boyer

CONNEC**TEXT**

Visit the Web site of
*World Politics: International Politics
on the World Stage, Brief,* Third Edition,

http://www.dushkin.com/connectext/wp/

to access the Web connections
that complement the text.

Contents in Brief

Contents

Chapter **4**

Nationalism: The Traditional Orientation   **89**

Chapter **7**

International Organization: The Alternative Structure

Chapter **9**

International Law and Morality:
The Alternative Approach   **229**

Chapter **13**

Preserving and Enhancing Human Rights and Dignity **375**

Countries of the World

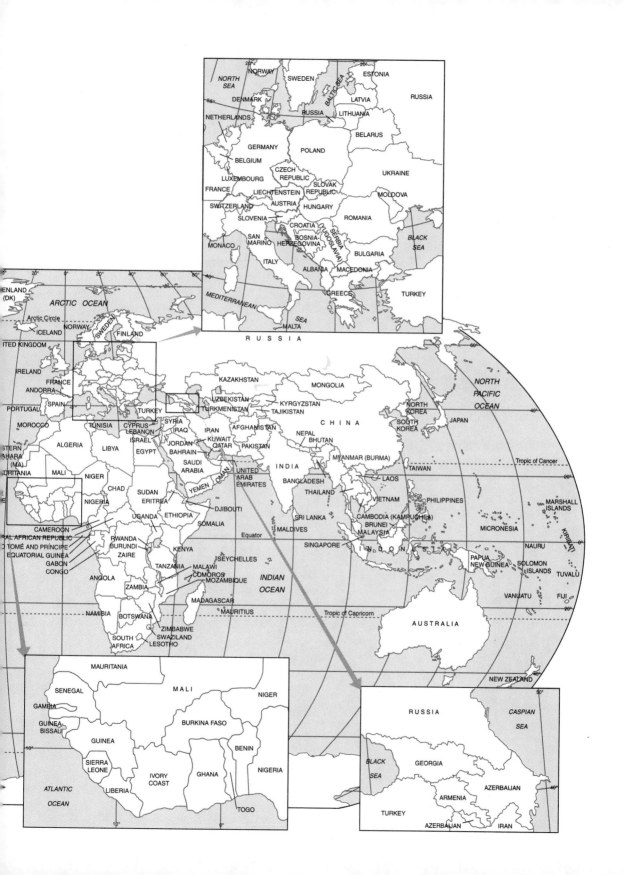

Thinking and Caring about World Politics

An honest tale speeds best being plainly told.

Shakespeare, *Richard III*

We must be more than an audience, more even than actors. We must be authors of the history of our age.

Secretary of State Madeleine K. Albright,
Senate confirmation hearings, 1997

All the world's a stage, and all the men and women merely players," William Shakespeare (1564–1616) wrote in *As You Like It*. The Bard of Avon was a wise political commentator as well as a literary giant (Alulis & Sullivan, 1996). Shakespeare's lines are used here because they help convey the drama of world politics. The characters are different, of course, with Canada, China, Germany, Japan, Russia, and the United States replacing those of his time and imagination. Beyond that, though, there are remarkable parallels between international relations and the master's plays. Both are cosmic and complex. The characters are sometimes heroic; at other times they are petty. The action is always dramatic and often tragic. As with any good play, the audience was

Chapter Outline

drawn into the action at The Globe, the London theater where Shakespeare staged his works. Similarly, the global theater of international politics draws us in. Indeed, we are seated on the stage, no matter how remote the action may seem or how much we may want to ignore it. Like it or not, we and the world are stuck with each other. The progress of the play, whether it continues its long run or closes early, is something we will all enjoy or endure.

Another quotation from Shakespeare—this time from *Macbeth*—is also worth pondering. Macbeth despairs that life "struts and frets his hour upon the stage" in a tale "full of sound and fury." Again the playwright hits the mark! The global drama has a cast of national actors (countries) that are often at odds with one another. It is true that many examples of cooperation and humanity can be found in them. But they are also full of ambition, self-serving righteousness, and greed, and it is a rare day when some of the countries are not in open conflict. And even when they are not threatening one another, they are forever calculating what is good for themselves and taking action based on their national interests.

The Importance of Studying World Politics

The last line from Macbeth's soliloquy is where this text and Shakespeare part company. The Bard pessimistically pronounces the action of life as "signifying nothing." That thought has a certain fatalistic appeal that allows us to ignore our responsibility. "What the hell," we can say, "why bother with a complicated subject about faraway places that have little to do with me?"

Many people take this "why bother" approach. A study of the political views of first-year university students found that only 27 percent of the members of the class of 2002 said they thought "keeping up with political affairs" is important. This was a decline from 58 percent in 1966 and the lowest percentage in the survey's 31-year history. The study also indicated that a mere 14 percent of students discussed politics and only 17 percent expressed any interest in influencing politics.[1] It is also the case that when Americans do pay attention to politics at all, they are mostly concerned about domestic political issues and believe that the government should concentrate on domestic affairs.

Is this widespread lack of information about or interest in world events justifiable? The answer is, No! This text does not often try to tell you what to think or do. But one message *is* stressed here: The world drama is important and deserves our careful attention. We are more than mere observers. We are all on the stage along with everybody else, and, whether we like it or not, we are all caught up in the tidal ebb and flow of global events.

This does not mean, though, that you are stuck with the world as it exists or as it is evolving. The important message of this text is that your efforts to become knowledgeable about the world and to try to shape its course to your liking are worthwhile because international politics does matter. It plays an important role in your life, and you should be concerned. To understand that further, let us turn to a number of ways, some dramatic, some mundane, in which international politics affects your economic life, your living space, and, potentially, your very existence. Then we will turn to the pivotal question: Can we make a difference?

World Politics and Your Pocketbook

World politics affects the personal economic conditions of each of us. The impact of international economics on domestic societies continues to expand as world industrial and financial structures become increasingly intertwined. Trade wins and loses jobs. We are dependent on foreign sources for vital resources. The rise and fall of inflation is influenced by foreign economic tides, as is the domestic allocation of our own resources. People in one country invest in and even own companies in other countries. The ties between national and international affairs are so close that many social scientists now use the term **intermestic** to symbolize the merger of *inter*national and do*mestic* concerns.

The intertwining of your personal economic circumstances and the world is extensive and complex. We will explore that first by looking at how the international economy affects your job and how it affects some other aspects of your financial security. Then we will examine how defense spending affects you.

The International Economy and Your Job

There is a steadily mounting interrelationship between the international economy and your employment opportunities. Trade, international investment, and tourism are just three ways that the world economy affects jobs.

Trade is a key factor that affects employment. Exports create jobs. The United States is the world's largest exporter, providing other countries with $848.8 billion worth of U.S. goods and services in 1996. Creating these exports employed some 16 million Americans (about 13 percent of the total U.S. workforce). Employment in many other countries is even more reliant on exports. For example, about 25 percent of Canadian workers depend on exports for their jobs.

Other jobs are lost to exports of both goods and services. The textiles, clothes, toys, electronics, and many other items that Americans buy were once produced extensively in the United States by American workers. Now most of these items are produced overseas by workers whose wages are substantially lower.

Lost jobs are a serious matter, but before you cry "Buy American!" and demand barriers to exclude foreign goods, it is important to realize that your standard of living is improved by the availability of inexpensive foreign products. The United States annually imports over $54 billion worth of clothes and footwear, and what Americans pay for those shirts, sneakers, and other items of apparel would be much higher if they were made by American workers earning American wages and bore the label, "Made in the U.S.A."

Foreign investment also influences the job market. The flow of investment capital around the world affects you in more ways than you probably imagine.

One way is that many familiar U.S. companies that provide jobs for Americans are owned by foreign investors and the product and marketing decisions that they make have a wide impact. For example, the textbooks that are available to American college students are, in part, produced by foreign corporations. Among the large academic presses, Simon & Schuster is owned by Pearson Education of Great Britain, St. Martin's is a subsidiary of Macmillan of Great Britain, whose largest shareholder is Holtzbrinck of Germany, and Grolier is part of the Lagardère Groupe of France.

**MAP
Dependence
on Trade**

International financial markets are yet another connection between your pocketbook and the global economy. More than 43 percent of adult Americans own stock, either directly or through personal or pension-related mutual funds holdings. This means that the stock and bond markets are no longer the concern of just the rich. One indicator is that in 1997, stock holdings made up 28 percent of the assets owned by Americans. This was an increase from 12 percent in 1990. There are a number of ways this is related to the world economy. One way is that the companies that make up the Standard & Poor's 500, a key index of the U.S. stock market, do 40 percent of their business overseas. When the world economy is good, the profits they earn result in part in dividends and capital gains for American investors.

Furthermore, many individuals, retirement funds, colleges, and other institutions also invest heavily in stocks and bonds in other countries. From 1993 through April 1996 alone, American investments in mutual funds that specialize in foreign stocks and bonds increased by $116 billion. Most of this is invested in Japan and the industrialized countries of Europe, but Americans have also been increasingly buying shares in what are known as "emerging market" funds that specialize in Latin America, Southeast Asia, and elsewhere. As of mid-1997, Americans had $22.4 billion invested in these emerging markets. This means that the state of other countries' economies and the rises and falls of their stock markets have a significant impact on the assets and incomes of a growing number of Americans. They found that out to their dismay during the Asian financial crises in late 1997 when the stock markets in Asia plummeted. Percentage declines for 1997 were −29.3 percent for Hong Kong, −42.5 percent for Singapore, and −69.7 percent for South Korea, and American investors lost billions.

**A SITE TO SURF
Yahoo! Finance**

Defense Spending and Your Economic Circumstances

Your government's *distribution of economic resources* is yet another way that world politics affect you economically. At the very least, you pay taxes to support your country's involvement in world affairs. In FY1997 the U.S. government spent 1.6 trillion (that's right, trillion, not billion) dollars. Spending on general foreign affairs (such as foreign aid) was minor, accounting for only $14 billion, or less than 1 percent of the budget. Defense spending was considerably more important. It amounted to $268 billion, about 16.6 percent of the U.S. budget. This equals about $1,010 per American for national defense.

Table 1.1

Comparative Military Expenditures

Country	Total (US$ Billions)	As Percent of Budget	As Percent of GDP	Per Capita (US$)
Canada	8.4	7.9	1.5	295
India	10.2	14.6	2.8	11
Israel	9.4	17.7	12.1	1,624
Japan	43.6	5.3	1.0	348
Mexico	2.6	4.9	0.8	28
Nigeria	1.5	11.0	3.5	15
Russia	69.5	18.4	6.5	470
Sweden	5.9	4.0	2.9	674
United States	265.8	17.0	3.6	1,001

Data sources: Wall Street Journal/Almanac (1997).

Data is for 1996. Because nearly all governments maintain some secrecy in their defense budgets, the data should be considered an estimate.

The more of a country's wealth that is devoted to military spending, the less is available for private use and for domestic government spending. Table 1.1 compares countries by a number of defense spending criteria. As you can see, some countries devote huge sums to defense; others spend little. Countries also vary widely in their defense expenditures compared to such economic measures as their **gross domestic product** (GDP: a measure of all goods and services produced within a country).

Although there is no one-to-one relationship between reduced defense spending and increased higher education spending, it is worth thinking about what would be possible if some defense spending were reallocated to higher education. There were in 1997 about 14 million students enrolled in U.S. colleges. The cost of room, board, and tuition at the average, four-year private college was $17,613; at the average public college it was $7,013. If, for example, the Pentagon deleted just one B-2 bomber (a saving of $2.1 billion), that money would be enough to give an all-expenses-paid scholarship at the average private college to 119,230 students or at the average state university to 299,444 students.

Yet the reallocation of defense spending that might bring economic relief to some people, such as college students, would harm the economic circumstances of other people. Many national economies, industries, and workers are heavily dependent on defense spending. Defense spending in the United States declined from about 6.4 percent of the GDP in 1985 to 3.5 percent in 1997. Many jobs have been lost. In the mid-1980s there were some 4 million such workers, plus 1 million civilian employees of the Department of Defense and almost 2 million uniformed personnel. That combined civilian and uniformed U.S. workforce has now declined by about 20 percent.

MAP
Military Expenditures as Percent of Gross Domestic Product

That has created tremendous pressure from negatively affected individuals, communities, and businesses to maintain defense spending. As former assistant secretary of defense Lawrence J. Korb has commented, "Both the administration and Congress increasingly view defense as a federal jobs program."[2]

World Politics and Your Living Space

International politics can affect far more than your pocketbook. It can determine the quality of the air you breathe, the water you drink, and many other aspects of the globe you inhabit.

The growth of the world's population and its pressure on resources threaten to change the quality of life as we know it. It took 100,000 years of human existence for the world to reach its 1997 population of 5.85 billion people. The increase of 80 million people in 1996 alone is the equivalent of a new U.S. population every 3.4 years or a new Canadian population every 138 days. The UN Population Fund (UNFPA) predicts that by the year 2000 the world population will reach 6.3 billion and by 2050 will have exploded to 10 billion people. This would double in less than a century the already-bulging population that existed when it reached 5 billion in 1987. Figure 1.1 depicts the population explosion.

**A SITE TO SURF
The UN Population
Fund (UNFPA)**

Americans and Canadians will not be immune to this avalanche of humanity. The burning of fossil fuels (6.1 billion tons in 1995) to warm and propel this mass and to supply it with material goods is raising the world carbon dioxide level and, most scientists worry, causing global warming. The 1980s were the warmest decade in recorded history, and 1997, at an average of 62.45 degrees Fahrenheit, was the warmest year since records were first kept in 1856. Many scientists claim that this is warming the atmosphere and threatening to melt ice caps and flood coastal areas of the world. Scientists project that global warming will also increase violent weather. One scientist estimates that an increase in the average world temperature of 3 to 4 degrees Celsius could spawn hurricanes with winds up to 220 miles per hour, thereby increasing their destructive potential by 50 percent. Adding weight to that projection, a UN panel has identified a remarkable "frequency and intensity of extremes of weather and climate" over the last quarter of a century.[3] Among other evidence that the UN panel noted was the increase in hurricanes and other violent windstorms that reached catastrophic levels from 8 in the 1960s, to 14 in the 1970s, to 29 in the 1980s.

The chemicals we spew into the air also cause disease. For example, they attack the Earth's ozone layer, which helps shield the Earth from the Sun's deadly ultraviolet rays. It is well established that the ozone layer has thinned considerably during recent decades. Concomitantly, the rate of new cases of the deadly skin cancer, melanoma, has grown dramatically from 1,168 of every 100,000 Americans to 3,650. This 213 percent increase means that 40,300 Americans were diagnosed with melanoma in 1997 and 3,650 died of the disease.

Figure 1.1

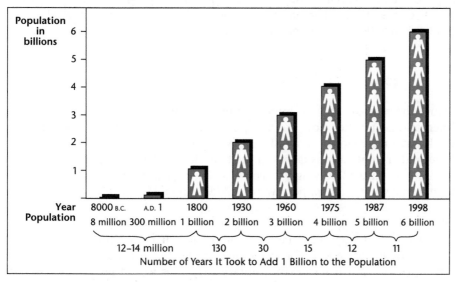

Number of Years It Took to Add One Billion to the Population, 800 B.C. to A.D. 2000

Data sources: Preston (1990); United Nations Population Fund (1992).

The world population is growing at an alarming rate. In July 1987 it passed 5 billion and in 1994 reached 5.6 billion. We reached 6 billion people in 1998. This means that the world population is growing at a rate of 265,735 per day, 11,072 per hour, 186 per minute, 3 per second.

There are some scientists who believe that pollution is even threatening the ability of humans to reproduce. Chemicals categorized as PCBs (polychlorinated biphenyls), which are used to make pesticides, plastic, and other products, are finding their way into the human food chain through fish and even through breast milk. Studies of male alligators in waters with high concentrations of the PCBs found reptiles that have "feminized hormones and half-male, half-female genitals" and are sterile.[4] Some scientists link such findings to those of Danish endocrinologist Niels Shakkebaek, who has reported that the sperm count of males in 21 countries has plunged by an average of 50 percent since 1938. Other preliminary studies have also found that the size of human genitalia may be affected among men whose mothers had been exposed to high levels of PCBs.[5]

There are numerous other proven or suspected deleterious environmental trends that are despoiling our living space. The United Nations Environmental Program (UNEP) reports that in addition to the perils already mentioned, erosion destroys 25 billion tons of topsoil each year, 900 million urban dwellers breathe dangerous levels of sulfur dioxide, and 25 percent of the Earth's animal and plant species may become extinct by the year 2020. "The environment is worse now than 20 years ago," declared UNEP head Mustafa K. Tolba. "Time is running out. Critical thresholds may already have been breached."[6]

It is true that most environmental problems have not been caused by world politics. It is also true, however, that we humans are unlikely to be able to stem, much less reverse, the degradation of the biosphere without global cooperation. That has begun, but only slowly and somewhat uncertainly, as detailed in chapter 14.

World Politics and Your Life

Plants and animals may be joined by humans on the endangered species list. International politics now has the potential of extinguishing most or all of the human race. Unlike most of history, when the vast majority of war deaths were soldiers, civilian casualties in the twentieth century have risen drastically as civilians have increasingly become a target of military operations. Nearly as many civilians as soldiers were killed during World War II. Now more civilians than soldiers are killed. According to the UN, the percentage of civilians killed during wars was 75 percent in the 1980s and 90 percent during the 1990s. Most tragically, these casualties included 2 million children, who died from wounds and other war-related causes (UNICEF, 1996). In a nuclear war or act of nuclear terrorism, military casualties would be a mere footnote to the overall death toll.

The possibility of war is a special concern for college-age adults. They are among the likeliest victims of war because they are also of prime military age. An examination of the ages of U.S. Marines killed during the Vietnam War shows that of those who died, 84 percent were aged 18 to 22. Some soldiers killed in war are volunteers, but not all are. Many countries have a draft to staff their military services. The United States abandoned the draft in the early 1970s, but draft registration is still required of all military-age males.

It is also the case that military combat is a matter that increasingly affects women directly as well as men. In the United States and elsewhere, the types of combat units in which women are allowed to serve is expanding. Either by volunteering or by being required to go, many more women may fight and die in future wars.

Even if they are now allowed into ground combat units, women are serving in military roles that bring more of them ever closer to the fighting. Thirty-five thousand women served in the Persian Gulf during the war against Iraq in 1991. Thirteen of them were killed in action, accounting for 9 percent of U.S. battle deaths. It may be a statistical anomaly because of the relatively low casualty rate during the war, but it is worth noting that women experienced a higher per capita death rate in the war zone than did men. Of every 10,000 troops of their gender there, 3.7 women died, compared to 2.6 men. The story of one of those women, Cindy Beaudoin, is told on this book's Web site.

A FURTHER NOTE
Cindy Beaudoin

War doesn't impact just the lives of soldiers. These children, forced from their homes in Kosovo, attend class in a makeshift school in Macedonia. Deprived of traditional learning materials, they must pursue their education in the face of much adversity and disruption.

World politics, then, does count. We are all involved economically and environmentally. Furthermore, it can threaten our very lives. Wars have continued and will continue to happen. Young men—and probably young women—have been and will be drafted. Some will die—perhaps you. In the worst possible circumstance, nuclear war, it will not matter whether you were drafted or not.

Can We Make a Difference?

The next logical question is, Can I make a difference? The answer is, Yes, you can make a difference! It is true that we cannot all be president or secretary of state, but we can take action and we can make our views known. Furthermore, as the Web site box, Making a Difference, illustrates, there are many parts that you can play to help shape the world more to your liking.

Direct action, such as protests, is one way to influence policy. Students, for example, have often been important agents of political change through direct action. The sum of millions of individual actions—ranging from burning draft cards, to massive demonstrations in front of the White House, to students protesting and even dying on U.S. campuses—helped end American involvement

Many citizens of established democracies take the right to vote for granted. But these black South Africans, waiting in very long voting lines, demonstrate how much they cherish their hard-won right to vote in only the second post-apartheid election in that country.

A FURTHER NOTE
Making a Difference

in Vietnam. More recently, student activists on campuses in the 1980s successfully pressed their schools to disinvest in South Africa. Such sanctions were part of the economic and moral pressure that helped end apartheid and white minority rule in that country.

Voting for candidates is another way to affect policy. It is clear that elected leaders do not always follow their campaign promises, but, in a broad sense, who gets elected does influence policy (Verdier, 1994). It made a difference in Israeli foreign policy and, potentially in global politics, when in 1996 the conservative candidate, Benjamin Netanyahu, defeated the liberal candidate, Shimon Peres, for the prime ministership of Israel. The course of Israeli politics changed yet again in May 1999 when Ehud Barak defeated Netanyahu to become prime minister. The change in policy course consequent to the election renewed optimism, though cautiously, about the prospects for peace in the region. One report made the striking statement that Palestinian leader Yasir Arafat was left "speechless" by the result.[7]

Direct voting on international questions is also possible in some countries (Rourke, Hiskes, Zirakzadeh, 1992). During the 1990s, Croatians, Ukrainians, and several other nationalities have voted to declare independence from the countries of which they had been a part. Also during the decade, and taking an opposite view, Puerto Ricans rejected independence (or statehood), and citizens of Quebec also voted against autonomy (Conley, 1997). The Swiss voted by referendum to join the World Bank and the International Monetary Fund, but they have rejected proposals to join the UN. Citizens in Austria, Finland, and Sweden voted in favor of joining the European Union; voters in Norway rejected membership (Fitzmaurice, 1995).

The point is that you count—by voting, protesting, joining issue-oriented groups, donating money to causes you support, or even by having your thoughts recorded in a political poll. Few individual actions are dramatic, and by themselves few significantly change world politics, but the sum of many smaller actions can and does make a difference. Do not consider politics a spectator sport. It is more important than that. Treat politics as a participant— even a contact—sport.

The World Tomorrow: Two Roads Diverge

The imperative to be active is particularly important as the world approaches the beginning of a new millennium. It is not too strong to argue that we have arrived at a crucial junction in the paths by which we organize and conduct our global politics. Contemplation of that junction brings to mind Robert Frost and his famous poem, *The Road Not Taken* (1916). Frost concluded his poem with the thought that

> I shall be telling this with a sigh
> Somewhere ages and ages hence:
> Two roads diverged in a wood, and I—
> I took the one less traveled by,
> And that has made all the difference.

Like the works of Shakespeare, Frost's lines are timeless and challenge the reader's intellect and emotions. We can build on Frost's imagery of two roads, one the traditional, "more traveled by" road, the other an alternative, "less traveled by" road, to discuss two possible paths for the future. The traditional road is a continuation of the path that world politics has mostly followed for at least five centuries. This route has been characterized by self-interested states struggling to secure their self-interests in a largely anarchistic international system.

The alternative direction entails significant changes in the way that politics is organized and conducted. Those who favor the alternative path argue that states need to abandon the pursuit of short-term self-interest and take a more cooperative, globalist approach. From this perspective, the advent of nuclear weapons, the deterioration of the global environment, and other looming problems create worries that, unless the world finds a new way to govern itself, there is not time to wait until "ages and ages hence" to evaluate the proper path.

Frost leaves his reader with the thought that choosing the less familiar road "made all the difference." What is unknown is whether Frost's "sigh" was one of contentment or regret. Frost wisely left that to the reader's imagination and judgment. Similarly, a major challenge that this text presents to you is deciding which road you think the world should travel by.

Realism and Idealism: Some Travel Notes on Two Roads

To help you begin to make your choice, the following section describes and contrasts the two paths and discusses those who advocate each direction. Those who favor adhering to the traditional road are often associated with the philosophical approach to politics called realism. Those who favor charting a new course along the alternative road are frequently identified with the philosophical approach to politics called idealism.

Before we detail these two approaches, some comments on the terms are appropriate. First, realism and idealism are broad categories that necessarily ignore subtle variations in complex ideas. In reality, there are multitudinous views about the nature of politics and about what that portends for the future. One reflection of this complexity is that political scientists use disparate terms to describe the ideas. The traditional path is variously associated with words such as realist (realism, realpolitik), balance of power, national (nationalist), conservative, and state-centered (state-centric, state-based). The alternative approach is associated with such words as idealism (idealist), globalism, (new) world order, liberal, liberal institutionalism, and internationalist. You will also find the prefix "neo" sometimes attached to some of these words (as in neorealism or neoliberalism) to designate recent variations on the more classic concepts (Vasquez, 1998; Beer & Harriman, 1996; Niou & Odershook, 1994a).

Second, do not get fooled by the connotations of the designations realism and idealism. The terms are used here because they are the common names for their schools of thought in international relations theory. But the sobriquets are flawed. "Realists" are not necessarily those who see things as they "really" are. Nor are "idealists" a bunch of fuzzy-headed dreamers. As you will see, perhaps a better name for realists would be "pessimists." Conversely, "optimists" is probably a more enlightening, if not more precise, label for idealists. The point is not to prejudge books by covers or theories by labels.

INTERACTIVE EXERCISE
Identify Your Perspective on World Politics

Third, it is possible to consider realism and idealism from three perspectives: descriptive, predictive, and prescriptive. The descriptive approach is concerned with "what is." Political scientists who follow this approach use empirical evidence to determine the degree to which realism or idealism influences policy (Fozouni, 1995; Griffiths, 1995; Frankel, 1994). The predictive approach tries to estimate "what will be." If one's theory is valid, then it should be possible not only to explain what has occurred, but also to predict what is likely to occur.

The prescriptive approach to realism and idealism asks the normative question, "What ought to be?" To help decide this question, the following sections compare realism and idealism according to their respective views about the fundamental nature of politics, the roles of power and justice in the conduct of political affairs, and the prospects for international competition and cooperation (Sterling-Folker, 1997; Rosenau & Durfee, 1995).

And fourth, it is also often useful to remember that most scholars and policy-makers—and maybe even you—view the world using both perspectives. At some points in time, the world might better be described as the realists see it, but at others as do the idealists. In fact, many argue that a middle ground between the two approaches may be a more appropriate vision of the world than either approach by itself (Bobrow & Boyer, 1998).

The Nature of Politics: Realism and Idealism

The disagreement between **realists** and **idealists** about the nature of politics is perhaps the most fundamental division in all of political discourse. The two schools of thought disagree over the very nature of *Homo politicus* (political humankind), and their respective views govern their approaches to domestic as well as to international politics. At root, realists are pessimists about human nature; idealists are optimists about human nature. The following sections will explore various schools of thought about the nature of politics.

Realism and the Nature of Politics

Realism portrays politics in somber hues (Spegele, 1996). Realists believe that political struggle among humans is probably inevitable because people have an inherent dark side. Many realists would trace their intellectual heritage to such political philosophers as Thomas Hobbes (1588–1679). He believed that humans possess an inherent urge to dominate, an *animus dominandi* (Thompson, 1994). Hobbes argued in his most famous work, *Leviathan,* that "if any two men desire the same thing, which nevertheless they cannot both enjoy, they become enemies and . . . endeavor to destroy or subdue one another." Taking the same point of view, one of the leading realist scholars, Hans Morgenthau, wrote that an "ubiquity of evil in human actions" inevitably turns "churches into political organizations . . . revolutions into dictatorships . . . and love of country into imperialism" (Zakaria, 1993:22).

Morgenthau represents what might be called the classic realist school. That is joined in the realist camp by a more recent neorealist school of thought (Schweller & Priess, 1997). *Neorealists* focus on the anarchic nature of a world system based on competition among sovereign states, rather than on human nature, as the factor that shapes world politics. As one neorealist puts it, the international system based on sovereign actors (states), which answer to no higher authority, is "anarchic, with no overarching authority providing security and order." The result of such a self-help system is that "each state must rely on its own resources to survive and flourish." But because "there is no authoritative, impartial method of settling these disputes—i.e., no world government—states are their own judges, juries, and hangmen, and often resort to force to achieve their security interests" (Zakaria, 1993:22).

Idealism and the Nature of Politics

Idealists reject the notion that all or most humans are inherently political predators. Instead, idealists are prone to believe that humans and their countries are capable of achieving more cooperative, less conflictive relations. In this sense, idealists might trace their intellectual lineage to political philosophers such as Jean-Jacques Rousseau (1712–1778). He argued in *The Social Contract* (1762) that humans had joined together in civil societies because they "reached the point at which the obstacles [to bettering their existence were] greater than the resources at the disposal of each individual." Having come to that point, Rousseau reasoned that people realized that "the primitive condition can then subsist no longer; and the human race would perish unless it changed its manner of existence." Like Rousseau, contemporary idealists not only believe that in the past people joined together in civil societies to better their existence; they are confident that now and in the future people can join together to build a cooperative and peaceful global society.

There is also a neoidealist school of thought (Mansbach, 1996). Thus, it is reasonable to ask, "If neoidealists and neorealists both focus on the impact of the system on political relations, what is the difference between the two?" The answer is what the two schools of thought believe can be done about the current state of affairs. Neorealists and neoidealists may agree that the anarchistic nature of the system is the cause of most international conflict, but they disagree about what can get done.

Like all idealists, neoidealists believe that humans can cooperate in order to achieve mutual benefits. Therefore, since neoidealists also hold that the anarchic system hinders cooperation, they further believe that the best path to cooperation is through building effective international organizations. This prescription is why neoidealists are often also called liberal institutionalists (Keohane & Martin, 1995).

What leaves neorealists firmly in the realist camp is that they doubt that there is any escape from the anarchistic world. Both types of realist scholars are, for example, skeptical about the ability of international organizations to promote cooperation (Cox, 1997). Instead, one scholar argues, "the most powerful states in the system create and shape [international] institutions so that [the states] can maintain their share of world power, or even increase it." Therefore, he concludes gloomily, whatever cooperation that does occur "takes place in a world that is competitive at its core—one where states have powerful incentives to take advantage of other states" (Mearsheimer, 1995:7, 12, 13).

The Roles of Power and Justice: Realism and Idealism

Realists and idealists also disagree in their descriptions of and, especially, their prescriptions about the roles of power and justice as standards of international conduct. Realists could be styled the "might makes right" school of thought. Idealists would contend that "right makes right."

Realism: An Emphasis on Power

Realists believe that struggles between states to secure their frequently conflicting national interests are the main action on the world stage. Since realists also believe that power determines which country prevails, they hold that politics is aimed at increasing power, keeping power, or demonstrating power. This is hardly a new thought. Over 2,000 years ago, Kautilya, minister to the first Maurya emperor of India, wrote, "The possession of power in a greater degree makes a king superior to another; in a lesser degree, inferior; and in an equal degree, equal. Hence a king shall always endeavor to augment his own power."

Given the view that the essence of politics is the struggle for power, realists maintain that countries and their leaders, if prudent, are virtually compelled to base their foreign policy on the existence of what realists see as a Darwinian, country-eat-country world in which power is the key to the national survival of the fittest.

This does not mean that realists are amoral (Murray, 1996). Indeed, they argue that the highest moral duty of the state is to do good for its citizens. Morgenthau (1986:39), for one, reasoned that it is unconscionable for a state to follow policy based on morality because "while the individual has a moral right to sacrifice himself" in defense of a moral principle, "the state has no right to let its moral disapprobation . . . get in the way of successful political action, itself inspired by the moral principle of national survival." More moderately, many other realists argue that surviving and prospering in a dangerous world requires that morality be weighed prudently against national interest. One scholar has summed up this realist rule of action with the maxim, "Do 'good' if the price is low" (Gray, 1994:8).

Idealism: An Emphasis on Justice

Idealists do not believe that acquiring, preserving, and applying power must be the essence of international relations (Forde, 1995). Idealists argue that, instead of being based on power, foreign policy should be formulated according to cooperative and ethical standards. President Jimmy Carter is an idealist. As president, Carter (1979:2) declared himself in favor of pursuing human rights as "part of a broad effort to use our great power and our tremendous influence in the service of creating a better world in which human beings can live in peace, in freedom, and with their basic needs met. Human rights is the soul of our foreign policy." President Clinton is also an idealist in terms of his basic philosophy. That was evident when he asked Americans to support sending U.S. troops to Bosnia because "it is the right thing to do." He called

Although as presidents Jimmy Carter and Bill Clinton sometimes followed realpolitik policies, both men are idealists. Symbolizing that orientation, the two are seen here in 1992 working together to construct low-income housing as part of a Habitat for Humanity project in Atlanta, Georgia.

up images of "skeletal prisoners caged behind barbed-wire fences, women and girls raped as a tool of war, [and] defenseless men and boys shot down in mass graves." "We cannot save all these people," Clinton declared, "but we can save many of them . . . , [so] we must do what we can."[8]

The views of Carter, Clinton, and other idealists do not mean that they are out of touch with reality. Carter himself admitted that "seldom do circumstances permit me . . . to take actions that are wholly satisfactory," but he tried. Clinton, too, has had to moderate his fundamental idealist predilections with the realpolitik demanded of presidents.

Idealists also dismiss the charge of some realists that pursuing ethical policy works against the national interest. The wisest course, idealists contend, is for Americans and others to redefine their concepts of interests to take into account the inextricable ties between the future of their country and the global pattern of human development.

Prospects for Competition and Cooperation: Realism and Idealism

The previous two sections have examined how realists describe the nature of politics and the respective roles of power and justice. This section takes up an issue introduced in the last section: should countries follow the dictates of realpolitik or strive to establish a new world based on greater international cooperation?

Realism and the Competitive Future

There are many political implications to the view of most realists that the drive for power and conflict are at the heart of politics and that there is "little hope for progress in international relations" (Brooks, 1997:473). Based on this view, realists advocate a relatively pragmatic approach to world politics, sometimes called *realpolitik*. One principle of realpolitik is to secure your own country's interests first on the assumption that other countries will not help you unless it is in their own interest.

A second tenet of realpolitik holds that countries should practice *balance-of-power* politics, which is explained further in chapter 3. This tenet counsels diplomats to strive to achieve an equilibrium of power in the world in order to prevent any other country or coalition of countries from dominating the system. This can be done through a variety of methods, including building up your own strength, allying yourself with others, or dividing your opponents.

A third realist policy prescription is that the best way to maintain the peace is to be powerful. Realists believe that it is necessary for a country to be armed because the world is dangerous. Idealists would reply that the world is dangerous because so many countries are so heavily armed.

It is important to say that this does not cast realists as warmongers. Instead, a fourth realist tenet is that you should neither waste power on peripheral goals nor pursue goals that you do not have the power to achieve. This frequently makes realists reluctant warriors. It is worth noting, for instance, that Morgenthau was an early critic of U.S. involvement in the war in Vietnam. He thought it was a waste of U.S. resources in a tangential area: the wrong war, with the wrong enemy, in the wrong place. Prudence, then, is a watchword for realists.

Idealism and the Cooperative Future

Idealists believe that humanity can and must successfully seek a new system of world order. They have never been comfortable with a world system based on sovereignty, but they now argue that it is imperative to find new organizational paths to cooperation. Idealists are convinced that the spread of nuclear weapons, the increase in economic interdependence among countries, the decline of world resources, the daunting gap between rich and poor, and the mounting damage to our ecosphere mean that humans must learn to cooperate more fully because they are in grave danger of suffering a catastrophe of unparalleled proportions.

Idealists are divided, however, in terms of how far the need for cooperation can and should go. Classic idealists believe that just as humans learned to form cooperative societies without giving up their individuality, so too can states learn to cooperate without surrendering their independence. These idealists believe that the growth of international economic interdependence or the spread of global culture will create a much greater spirit of cooperation among the world countries.

Neoidealists are more dubious about a world in which countries retain full sovereignty. These analysts believe that countries will have to surrender some of their sovereignty to international organizations in order to promote greater cooperation and, if necessary, to enforce good behavior. "The fundamental right of existence," Pope John Paul II told the UN General Assembly in 1995, "does not necessarily call for sovereignty as a state." Instead, the pontiff said, "there can be historical circumstances in which aggregations different from single state sovereignty can . . . prove advisable."[9] This point of view holds that humans have found advancement by being nonsovereign members of domestic societies governed through central authority. Similarly, states may well benefit from giving up some or all of their sovereignty to form hierarchically structured regional and global organizations.

The world has not become what idealists believe it could be but they are encouraged by some trends in recent years. One of these is the growth of interdependence as favoring their goals. Idealists also support their case by pointing to the willingness of countries to surrender some of their sovereignty to improve themselves. The European Union (EU), for instance, now exercises considerable economic and even political authority over its member-countries.

In the most demonstrative step toward European Union authority to date, the euro became a convertible and truly European currency on January 2, 1999. European Union leaders are hoping that the new currency will be one of the primary forces in creating a more prosperous and united continent in the coming years.

They were not forced into the EU; they joined it freely. This and other diminutions of sovereignty will be discussed at length later in the text.

Idealists also condemn the practice of realpolitik. Idealists further assert that the pursuit of power in the nuclear age may one day lead to ultimate destruction. This does not mean that idealists are unwilling to use military force, economic sanctions, and other forms of coercion. They are not so naive as to think that the potential for conflict can be eliminated, at least in the foreseeable future. Therefore most idealists are willing to use coercion when necessary to halt aggression or to end oppression. The use of might to restore right is especially acceptable to idealists if it is accomplished through cooperative efforts such as UN peacekeeping forces or sanctions.

Assessing Reality: Realism and Idealism

Before we leave our discussion of realism and idealism, it is worth stopping briefly to ask which theory better explains how the world has operated and how it operates now. On balance, it is safe to say that throughout history competition rather than cooperation has dominated international relations. Even when countries were at peace, it was most often because they were not clashing rather than because they were positively cooperating.

It is also the case that realpolitik is still usually the order of the day, especially where important national interests are involved. Most political leaders tend toward realism in their policies, and even those who lean toward idealism often take the realpolitik road (Elman, 1996; Nolan, 1995). The idealist in President Bill Clinton prompted him as a presidential candidate to object to China's human rights policies and to charge that the unwillingness of President George Bush to punish China demonstrated that Bush had an "unconscionable" propensity to "coddle tyrants."[10] Once he became president, though, Clinton changed his policy to a realpolitik policy that dealt with China as a major power (Rourke & Clark, 1998). As Clinton summarized his newfound strategic view, "China has an atomic arsenal and a vote and a veto in the UN Security Council. It is a major factor in Asian and global security. We share important interests, such as in a nuclear-free Korean peninsula and in sustaining the global environment."[11]

The short answer to the "what is" question is almost certainly that both realism and idealism influence policy (Miller, 1995; Wayman & Diehl, 1994). Realpolitik self-interest has been the dominant impulse of countries. Still, it is also true that countries can be cooperative and even altruistic at times. Moreover, it may well be that the idealist approach is gaining ground as states recognize that competition and conflict are increasingly dangerous and destructive and that peaceful cooperation is in everyone's self-interest. It would be naive to argue that the world is anywhere near the point of concluding that self-interest and global interests are usually synonymous. But it is not fatuous to say that an increasing number of people have come to the conclusion that working toward the long-term goal of a safe and prosperous world is preferable to seeking short-term national advantage. Thus, while the question "what is" should engage our attention, the far more important questions are "what should be" and "what will be." What should be is for you to decide after reading this book and consulting other sources of information. What will be is for all of us to see and experience.

How to Study World Politics

"Well, OK," you may say, "international politics is important and it affects me. And, yes, there are important choices to make. So I'll agree that I should know more about it and get active in the world drama. But where do I start?" Ah, we're glad you asked!

The first thing you should do, if you have not already, is to read the preface. This will tell you how we have structured this text and will help you understand what follows. The next chapter will give you more help in establishing a base to understanding world politics by laying out a brief history of and the current trends in the world system.

Political Scientists and World Politics

Before getting to the chapter on global history and trends, it is important that you understand something about what political scientists are attempting to do and how they go about doing it. This knowledge is important to help understand the efforts and goals of the many studies that are cited in this text and others that you may read. Evaluating the research of scholars may also help you construct and conduct your own studies of international relations or any other subject.

Why Political Scientists Study World Politics

The history of international relations as an intellectual focus extends far back into history, and concepts such as anarchy and sovereignty were at its core long before realism, idealism, and other schools of thought were articulated and labeled (Schmidt, 1997). Like all political scientists, scholars study world politics in order to formulate theories—generalizations—about politics. Therefore, what concerns political scientists is understanding patterns that occur over time or that occur in many places at the same times. Theory is at the heart of political science.

Within this emphasis on theory, international relations scholars have three subsidiary goals in mind: description, prediction, and prescription. *Description* is the oldest and most fundamental of these three goals. This task sounds a whole lot easier than it is. Not only are events complex and information often difficult to obtain, but political science description should focus on patterns. When a political scientist studies a single event (a case study) or, better yet, a series of events across time or over space, the object is not to just describe the event(s). Instead, the goal is to relate them to a pattern of other events. One recent and illustrative area of political science research has been to try to prove or disprove the hypothesis, "Democracies do not fight each other" (Caprioli, 1999; Gartzke, 1998; Thompson & Tucker, 1997; Kacowicz, 1995). By studying history, many political scientists have concluded that, indeed, democracies tend not to go to war with one another. This research is discussed fully in chapter 6.

Prediction is even more difficult than description because of the complexity of human nature. Nevertheless, political scientists can use careful research as a basis for "analytical forecasting [by which to] give a reasoned argument for what they expect to happen" (George, 1994:172). If, for instance, we believe the descriptive studies that conclude that democracies are peaceful toward one another, then it is possible to predict that a democratic Russia will be less likely to be antagonistic toward the United States and other democracies than was the nondemocratic Soviet Union.

Prescription is a third goal. Some political scientists go beyond their objective studies and come to normative (what is right or wrong) conclusions and prescribe policy. Those who believe that democracies have not been (description) and will not be (prediction) aggressive toward one another, may wish to advocate (prescription) policies that promote the adoption or preservation of democracy. Such advocates might, for example, urge extending massive economic aid to Russia in order to avoid the economic turmoil that is so often associated with a slide toward authoritarian government.

Political scientists, it can be added, do more than talk to students and write about their theories. Some political scientists enter directly into the policy-making realm. Among them is former Georgetown University professor and now U.S. secretary of state Madeleine K. Albright. Other political scientists try to influence policy indirectly through such methods as serving in so-called think tanks dedicated to policy advocacy, writing op-ed pieces in newspapers, and testifying before legislatures.

How Political Scientists Conduct Research

The most fundamental thing that political scientists need to gather is evidence. They gather evidence by three basic *methodologies:* logic, traditional observation, and quantitative analysis. All research should apply logic, but valuable contributions can be made by relatively pure logical analysis. Aristotle and the other great political philosophers who are mentioned in this book relied primarily on logical analysis to support their political observations. This technique is still important. Some of the best work on nuclear deterrence has been done by analysts who employ *deductive logic* (from the general to the specific) to reason from the general nature of nuclear weapons and fear to suggest specifically how nuclear deterrence works or could be improved.

A second methodology, traditional observation, uses a variety of techniques to study political phenomena. One method is historical analysis, using sources such as archives, interviews, and participant observation. Traditional observation is an old and still valuable methodology. There are many modern studies of why wars occur, but we can all still learn much by reading *The Peloponnesian War,* written by the Greek historian Thucydides in about 410 B.C.

Quantitative analysis is a third methodology. Political scientists who use this method are interested in measurable phenomena and use mathematical techniques. The studies on war and democracy cited in chapter 6 are able to use quantitative methods because countries and wars are relatively measurable.

The Analytical Orientations of Political Scientists

The seemingly bewildering array of analytical orientations that political scientists have toward their subject often confuses beginning students of political science. At the risk of overly simplifying a diverse discipline, the view here is that these orientations, perhaps all political analysis, inevitably can trace its roots back to realism and idealism.

Realism, as we have already seen, is a pessimistic view. Realists believe that politics is a struggle for power. Therefore, the norm of politics is conflict.

Idealism is a very different, more optimistic approach. Idealists believe that politics is a struggle for human betterment. Therefore, the norm of politics is (or perhaps can be) cooperation.

Beyond classic realism and idealism, there are, as noted, many variations, such as neorealism and neoidealism. Furthermore, there are a number of orientations that some political scientists have toward their subject that, depending on the theorist, either combine elements of realism and idealism or are rooted in realism or idealism. Feminism and political economy are two such orientations that deserve particular mention. They vary from general realism and idealism in part because they stress very specific units of analysis. "Most contemporary feminist scholarship," one such scholar notes, "takes gender—which embodies relationships of power inequality—as its central category of analysis" (Tickner, 1997:614). For economic theorists the unit of analysis is wealth (Burch & Denemark,1997).

Each of these two theoretical orientations is important and multifaceted, and each deservedly receives extended attention later in this text. If you wish to learn more about them now, you can turn to chapter 5 to read about feminist international relations theory and to chapter 11 to find more the various aspects of **international political economy (IPE)** theory.

What to Study: Levels of Analysis

Another major division among analytical approaches used by political scientists has to do with the level of focus. The essential question here is "what do we study?" One approach by political scientists has been to divide the study into **levels of analysis**. These refer to levels of the factors that affect international politics. Scholars have suggested a range from two to six in the number of levels at which world politics can be analyzed. The most widely used scheme utilizes three levels, and they will be employed herein. There are, for example, scholars who have explored the democratic peace debate by examining three levels of analysis (Gleditsch & Hegre, 1997). The three levels are:

System-level analysis—a worldview that takes a "top-down" approach to analyzing global politics. This level theorizes that the world's social-economic-political structure and pattern of interaction (the international system) strongly influence the policies of states and other international actors. Therefore, understanding the structure and pattern of the international system will lead to understanding how international politics operates.

State-level analysis—a view in which the concern is with the characteristics of an individual country and the impact of those traits on the country's behavior. This level theorizes that states (countries) are the key international actors. Therefore, understanding how states as complex organizations decide policy will lead to understanding how international politics operates.

Individual-level analysis—a view in which the focus is on people. This level argues that in the end people make policy. Therefore, understanding how people (individually, in groups, or as a species) decide policy will lead to understanding how international politics operates.

Focus on one level of analysis does not mean exclusion of the others. Indeed, it would be best to think of the levels as occurring along a scale from the general (system-level analysis) to the specific (individual-level analysis). It is possible to focus on one level and still use elements of the others. In the following two chapters, we will examine extensively the implications of each of these levels. After chapter 2 and its discussion of the history of and current trends in the international system, chapter 3 takes up all three levels of analysis in order from system- to state- to individual-level analysis.

Chapter Summary

1. This book's primary message is captured by Shakespeare's line, "All the world's a stage, and all the men and women merely players." This means that we are all part of the world drama and are affected by it. It also means that we should try to play a role in determining the course of the dramatic events that affect our lives.

2. Economics is one way that we are all affected. The word *intermestic* has been coined to symbolize the merging of *inter*national and do*mestic* concerns, especially in the area of economics. Countries and their citizens have become increasingly interdependent.

3. Economically, trade both creates and causes the loss of jobs. International investment practices may affect your standard of living in such diverse ways as determining how much college tuition is, what income you have, what interest rate you pay for auto loans and mortgages, and how much you can look forward to in retirement. The global economy also supplies vital resources, such as oil. Exchange rates between different currencies affect the prices we pay for imported goods, the general rate of inflation, and our country's international trade balance.

4. Our country's role in the world also affects decisions about the allocation of budget funds. Some countries spend a great deal on military functions. Other countries spend relatively little on the military and devote almost all of their budget resources to domestic spending.

5. Your life may also be affected by world politics. You may be called on to serve in the military. Whether or not you are, war can kill you.

6. World politics also plays an important role in determining the condition of your living space. Politics has, for the most part, not created environmental degradation, but political cooperation will almost certainly be needed to halt and reverse the despoiling of the biosphere.

7. There are many things any one of us can do, individually or in cooperation with others, to play a part in shaping the future of our world. Think, vote, protest, support, write letters, join organizations, make speeches, run for office—do something!

8. There are demands for and predictions of a new world order. The future path of the world can be thought about as analogous to Robert Frost's poem about two roads diverging in a wood. The poet wrote that the path he chose made all the difference. So, too, will the road that the world chooses make all the difference. Therefore it is important to think about the direction in which you want the world to go.

9. One road is the traditionalist approach, which focuses on the continuing sovereign role of the state as the primary actor in the international system. The traditionalist approach is associated with many terms; "realism" is perhaps the best known. Realism focuses on the self-interested promotion of the state and nation. Realists believe that power politics is the driving force behind international relations. Therefore, realists believe that both safety and wisdom lie in promoting the national interest through the preservation and, if necessary, the application of the state's power.

10. The second, alternative road is advocated by those who stress the need for significant change, including both a restructuring of power within states and international cooperation and global interests. Of the terms associated with this approach, "idealism" is used herein. Idealists believe that realpolitik is dangerous and outmoded. They believe that idealpolitik should be given greater emphasis and that everyone's "real" interest lies in a more orderly, more humane, more egalitarian world.

11. Political scientists have numerous orientations, including realist, idealist, feminist, and economic.

12. Political scientists study international relations to describe and predict political phenomena and to prescribe courses of action. In their studies, scholars use a variety of methodologies, including logic, traditional observation, and quantitative techniques, to analyze phenomena and test hypotheses. Scholars also have several orientations, which include focusing on power, human social relations, and economics.

13. Feminist theory contains some elements of realism and significant elements of idealism. Feminist theorists believe that politics is characterized by males keeping power by oppressing females. Feminists also believe that power should and can be distributed on a gender-equal basis and that this will result in worthwhile changes in world politics.

14. There are three levels of analysis from which world politics can be studied. They are system-level analysis, state-level analysis, and individual-level analysis. They are not mutually exclusive. Each of these levels is discussed in detail in the next several chapters.

Chapter 2

The Evolution of World Politics

I am amazed, methinks, and lose my way among the thorns and dangers of the world.

Shakespeare, *King John*

We have it in our power to begin the world over again.

Thomas Paine, *Common Sense*

This chapter has two purposes. The first is to establish a historical foundation on which to build our analysis of international relations. To this end the following pages give a brief historical narrative that emphasizes the themes and events you will encounter repeatedly in this book.

The second goal of this chapter is to sketch the evolution of the current, rapidly evolving world political system (Robertson, 1997; Puchala, 1995). The concept of an **international system** represents the notion that the world is more than just a sum of its parts, such as countries or international organizations, and that world politics is more than just the sum of the individual interactions among those parts. The idea of an international system is based on the belief that there are general patterns of actions among the system's

Chapter Outline

actors. These patterns can be explained in part by the distribution of power and several other factors that we will explore in chapter 3.

It would be wise to keep your mind open to the concept of change as you read this chapter. The international system evolved relatively slowly for several centuries, then shifted rapidly during this century. Warp-speed technological innovation is the most important source of change. It has brought benefits such as nearly instantaneous global communications, rapid travel, less disease and longer lives, and enhanced material well-being. Breakneck technological change has also created or intensified many new problems, such as global warming, the expanding population, and nuclear weapons. Whether these changes are good or bad, there can be little doubt that, as one scholar has written, there is "turbulence in world politics" as "Spaceship Earth daily encounters squalls, downdrafts, and windshears as it careens into changing and uncharted realms of experience" (Rosenau, 1990:4, 7).

The Evolving World System: Early Development

The evolution of the current world political system began in about the fifteenth century. It was then that modern states (countries) began to coalesce. The emergence of states as the focus of political authority involved two contradictory trends—one of integration, the other of disintegration—that transfigured the system that had existed for the preceding millennium.

The *integration process* began in part due to the weakening of small feudal units (such as baronies, dukedoms, and principalities) and city-states (such as Venice), which could no longer maintain their political viability and autonomy. They declined because of a series of changes in technology and economics that diminished their military and economic self-sufficiency. As these small units faltered, kings gained enough power to consolidate their authority and to end the virtual independence of the feudal states and city-states.

The *disintegration process* involved the unwillingness of people to accept distant, overarching authority. Some of this had to do with the secularization of politics, especially the resistance in Europe to the political authority of the pope and the Roman Catholic Church. Disintegration also included revolts against and the eventual collapse of huge multinational empires. This was a long process that began in Europe with the decline and fall of the Holy Roman Empire in the sixteenth and seventeenth centuries and arguably also includes the collapse of the Soviet Union in 1991. More than any other event, the Treaty of Westphalia (1648) has come to symbolize this eclipse of overarching authority and the founding of modern states. This treaty ended the Thirty Years' War and recognized the independence of the Netherlands, several German states, and a number of other Protestant political entities from the secular authority of the Holy Roman Empire and its Roman Catholic dynasty (the Hapsburgs) and, by extension, from the religious authority of the pope in Rome.

Even though many believe the state is declining in importance as a political actor internationally, these Palestinians still view statehood as an important goal for their nation to achieve. The possibility that their leader, Yasir Arafat, might declare Palestinian statehood unilaterally has been a concern for all involved in the Israeli-Palestinian peace talks.

The story of the origins of the modern state is told in greater detail in chapter 6, but it is appropriate to make a few essential points here about the growth of states and their place in the international system. First, in the post-Westphalian system, states became the primary **actors** in the international system. This leading role remains today. A great deal, although not all, of the action on the world stage is about states and groups of states interacting with one another.

Second, the operation of the post-Westphalian system is partly the result of the fact that states came to possess **sovereignty**. This means that they do not recognize any higher legitimate authority (Bartelson, 1995). The pivotal place of the sovereign state in the international system has had a defining influence on it because the system has no central authority to maintain order and dispense justice. As such, international relations occur within an **anarchical political system**. This does not mean that the international system is a scene of unchecked chaos. To the contrary, the system operates with a great deal of regularity. It exists, however, mostly because countries find it in their interest to act according to expectations. But when a state decides that it is in its interests to break the largely informal rules of the system, as Iraq did in 1990 when it invaded Kuwait, there is little to stop it except countervailing power. The point is that in any political system, anarchy does not mean chaos; it means the lack of a central authority.

The Evolving World System: The Eighteenth and Nineteenth Centuries

The solidification of the dominance of the sovereign state as the primary actor was just the beginning of the evolution of the modern international system. The pace of change began to quicken in the eighteenth century. Many of the events that occurred between 1700 and 1900 and many of the attitudes that developed during this time helped shape the structure and operation of the international system as it exists currently. Three themes stand out: the coming of popular sovereignty, the Westernization of the international system, and the culmination of the multipolar system.

The establishment of the concept of **popular sovereignty** marked a major change in the notion of who owned the state and how it should be governed. Prior to the late 1700s and early 1800s, when this new idea began to take hold, the theory of the divine right of kings held that the monarch was the sovereign and that the people in the sovereign's realm were subjects. The political identification of individuals tended to have a local orientation. It was the monarch, not the people, who owned the state and in whom legitimate political authority rested (Guibernau, 1996). The American (1776) and French (1789) Revolutions challenged this philosophy.

Democracies were established on the principle that sovereign political power rests with the people rather than with the monarch. The notion of popular sovereignty also changed and expanded the concept of *nationalism* to include mass identification with and participation in the affairs of the state (country). If the people owned the state, then they had both a greater emotional attachment to it and a greater responsibility to support it. One symbol of this change was that Napoleonic France (1799–1815) was the first country to have a true patriotic draft that raised an army of a million strong.

The domination and shaping of the international system by the **West** was a second important characteristic of the eighteenth and nineteenth centuries. Somewhat earlier, the growth of European power had enabled Great Britain, France, and other European countries to thrust outward and take control of North and South America and some other regions. The Arab, Aztec, Chinese, Incan, Mogul (Indian), Persian, and other non-European empires or dynasties began to decline or fell. The domination and shaping of the international system by the West accelerated in the nineteenth century. The result of the transformation of the international "scene . . . by the expansion of the Europeans over the rest of the globe," as two scholars have observed, is that "a cardinal rule" of the system was that the European states came "to conceive [of] themselves as forming an exclusive club enjoying rights superior to those of other political communities" (Bull & Watson, 1982:425).

One reason for the Westernization of the international system was the scientific and technological advances that sprang from the Renaissance (about 1400–1650) in Europe. This sparked the *industrial revolution,* which began in the mid-1700s in Great Britain and then spread to the rest of Europe, Canada, and the United States. Industrialization and associated advances in weaponry and other technology had a profound impact on world politics. The European powers gained in strength compared with nonindustrialized Asia and Africa. Since the industrialized countries needed to find resources and markets to fuel and fund their capitalist expansion, economic expansion promoted colonialism. Many industrialized countries also coveted colonies as a matter of prestige. The result was an era of Euro-American *imperialism* that subjected many people to colonial domination. The fate of Africa is graphically displayed in the Web site map that depicts the geographical division of Africa among the colonial powers (1910) until independence (1997).

MAP
**Africa: Colonialism
to Independence,
1910–1997**

Many Asian cultures were similarly subjected to **Eurowhite** domination. China, it should be noted, was never technically colonized, but after the 1840s it was divided into spheres of influence among the Western powers and lost substantial territories to Great Britain (Hong Kong), Japan (Taiwan/Formosa), and Russia (about 1 million square miles.) Americans also joined in the scramble for colonial possessions with the acquisition of such Pacific territories as Hawaii and Samoa in the 1890s, and victory in the Spanish-American War (1898) added Guam, Puerto Rico, and the Philippines. The imperialist subjugation of Asians, Africans, and others by Europeans and Americans set the stage for what became the North-South axis.

A third characteristic of the 1700s and 1800s is that the **multipolar system** reached its zenith. The multipolar system, which governed political relations among the major European powers beginning with the Treaty of Westphalia in 1648 and extending into the mid-twentieth century, peaked in the 1700s and 1800s because of the global dominance of the European powers. The international system was multipolar in the sense that political affairs were dominated by numerous major powers.

The balance-of-power system that existed between 1648 and 1945 was characterized by shifting alliances designed to prevent any single power or combination of powers from dominating the European continent and, by extension, the world. Prime Minister Winston Churchill once clearly enunciated balance-of-power politics as a governing principle of British foreign policy when he explained that "for four hundred years the foreign policy of England has been to oppose the strongest, most aggressive, most dominating power on the Continent.... It would have been easy ... and tempting to join with the stronger [power] and share the fruits of his conquest. However, we have always [taken] the harder course, joined with the less strong powers, ... and thus defeated the Continental military tyrant whoever he was" (Walt, 1996:109).

The balance-of-power process succeeded for three centuries in preventing any single power or coalition from controlling Europe and perhaps the world. It did not, however, persist or keep Great Britain and the other dominant European countries from falling from the ranks of major powers.

The Evolving World System: The Twentieth Century

The twentieth century was a time of momentous and rapid global change (Keylor, 1996, Rosenau, 1990). The *rapid pace of change* in our time is an important theme for you to keep in mind as you read the balance of this chapter and, indeed, of this book. It is hard for almost any of us to grasp how rapidly things are changing compared to the former pace of social, political, and technological evolution throughout history. When the twentieth century began there were no airplanes; monarchs ruled Russia, Germany, Italy, and most other countries; there were no important, ongoing global organizations; uranium was a little-known, unused metallic element; and there were about 1.5 billion people in the world. Now humans can rocket into space and deliver their weapons by intercontinental ballistic missile; elected officials govern most countries; the United Nations, World Bank, World Trade Organization, and other international organizations play important and continuing roles in the world; nuclear energy lights our cities and fuels our industries while simultaneously threatening the environment and our very lives through nuclear weapons; and the world population has quadrupled to 6 billion people. All this has happened in just one century, a time period that represents only about 3 percent of the approximately 3,500 years of recorded human history.

Technology has been the prime mover of this rapid change. This century has seen the creation of radio and television communications, nuclear power, computers, power chain saws, air and space travel, intercontinental ballistic missiles, effective birth control, antibiotics, crack cocaine, and a host of other innovations that can benefit or bedevil us—keep us together or tear us apart. The world's economy has expanded vastly. Some of the changes have been positive. Many of us have material possessions that a person living in the last century would not have been able even to imagine. But economic expansion has also brought ills, including pollution, deforestation, ozone buildup, and the extinction of untold animal and plant species.

It seems that the world is evolving much faster than ever before. That is evident in part in Fig. 2.1, which shows the increased pace of technological and scientific innovation. Technology is both creating and solving problems. Whether the positive or negative results predominate depends in part on our ability to address the issues in a politically responsible way. But with the accelerated pace of change, there is not time for a leisurely, evolutionary search for solutions.

The Twentieth Century: The Years to World War II

The pace of world political evolution began to speed up even more by the beginning of the 1900s. Democracy was rapidly eroding the legitimacy of dynastic monarchs. *Nationalism* was similarly continuing to undermine the foundations of multiethnic empires. World War I was a pivotal point. Two major empires, the Austro-Hungarian and Ottoman, were among the losers.

Figure 2.1

The Increased Pace of Technological and Scientific Innovation

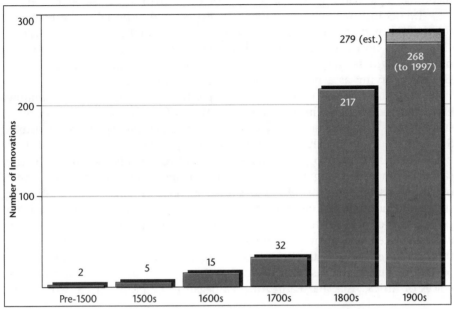

*The total number of 279 innovations for the 1900s is estimated based on 268 innovations through 1997.

Data source: World Almanac (1997).

The escalating pace of technological and scientific change has had a major impact on human beings in general and on world politics in particular. This figure depicts important innovations whose dates of discovery or invention are known. As you can see, only about 10 percent of these occurred before 1800. Another 40 percent occurred in the 1800s, and about 50 percent have occurred during this century alone.

The result was the (re)establishment of countries such as Czechoslovakia, Poland, and Yugoslavia. Other countries like Jordan, Lebanon, Syria, and Palestine/Israel came under the mandate (control) of the League of Nations and finally became independent after World War II.

The end of the *balance of power* that governed European relations during the 1800s was marked by the tragedies of two world wars. The reasons for the end of the multipolar system are still subject to dispute. We can say, however, that the European system changed from being one that was fluid and permitted shifting alliances and pragmatic cooperation to a system dominated by two increasingly rigid and hostile alliances. In World War I (1914–1918) the Central Powers included Germany, Austria-Hungary, and Turkey. The Allied Powers consisted of France, Russia, and Great Britain, which were joined by Italy just after the outbreak of the war. After its defeat in the war, Germany was initially treated severely, but the multipolar system soon led to a **realpolitik** attempt to reestablish balance by allowing Germany in the 1930s to rebuild its strength. With Germany defeated, the British worried that France might once again dominate Europe and threaten them as it had under Napoleon. Therefore, the British tried to offset French power by acquiescing to German rearmament and diplomatic demands. It was, for the British, a near-fatal mistake.

Events in Russia also prompted the British and, especially, the French to tolerate German revitalization. The seizure of power by Lenin's Bolsheviks in 1918 evoked horror in the West. Communist ideology combined with Russian military might seemed to threaten the Western powers. Some saw a rearmed Germany serving as a bulwark against the "Red menace."

While all this was occurring in Europe, the rest of the world community expanded and changed during the first 40 years of the twentieth century. Some states gained independence; other existing states, especially Japan and the United States, that had previously been on the periphery of European-dominated diplomacy gradually began to play a more significant role. China began the century saddled with a decaying imperial government and foreign domination, but it overthrew its emperor in 1911 and started a long, in some cases continuing, struggle to rid itself of foreign domination and to reestablish its role as a major power. Also during the first four decades of the century, the League of Nations was established, and many other non-European countries joined world diplomacy through membership in the League. Although international relations still focused on Europe during the first four decades of the 1900s, a shift was under way. The voices of Africa, Asia, and Latin America began to be heard on the world stage.

The Twentieth Century: The Cold War Begins and Ends

World War II was a tragedy of unequaled proportions. It also marked major changes in the nature and operation of the world political system. This section will focus on the shifts in the polar structure of the system through the end of the cold war. There are a number of other changes that began or accelerated during this period, which continue to affect us all as we move into the twenty-first century. These issues will be taken up in the following section that discusses the issues and choices that lie before us.

On the political front, a series of shifts in the system occurred in the decades after 1945 that involved the actors and, indeed, the polar structure of the system itself. World War II finally destroyed the long-decaying, mostly European-based multipolar structure. It was replaced by a bipolar system dominated by the Soviet Union and the United States. To those who experienced its anguished intensity, East-West hostility seemed to augur an unending future of bipolar confrontation and peril. As it often is, the view that the present will also be the future proved shortsighted. The bipolar era was brief. Significant cracks in the structure were evident by the 1960s; by 1992 the bipolar system was history.

The Rise and Decline of the Bipolar System

World War II devastated most of the existing major actors. In their place, the United States emerged as a military and economic *superpower* and the leader of one power pole. The Soviet Union, though incredibly damaged, emerged as leader of the other pole. The USSR never matched the United States economically, but the Soviets possessed a huge conventional armed force, a seemingly threatening ideology, and, by 1949, atomic weapons. The East-West Axis was established.

MAP
The Age of
Bipolarity:
The Cold War
ca. 1970

The exact causes of the confrontation, termed the *cold war,* are complex and controversial. It is safe to say, however, that varying economic and political interests and the power vacuum created by the collapse of the old balance-of-power structure created a bipolar system in which a great deal of world politics was centered on the confrontation between the two superpowers.

The American reaction to the perceived world Soviet/communist threat was the *containment doctrine.* This principle transformed U.S. foreign policy from a prewar norm of isolationism to a postwar globalism, opposing the Soviet Union (and later Communist China) diplomatically and militarily around the world. The United States sponsored a number of regional alliances, most notably the North Atlantic Treaty Organization (NATO, established in 1949). The Soviets responded in 1955 with the Warsaw Treaty Organization (or Warsaw Pact). Both sides also vied for power in the developing countries, and both Soviet and American arms and money flowed to various governments and rebel groups in the ongoing communist-anticommunist contest.

Despite intense rivalry marked by mutual fear and hatred, the reality that both superpowers possessed nuclear weapons usually led them to avoid direct confrontations. There were a few, however, including the scariest moment of the bipolar era, the *Cuban missile crisis* of 1962. The Soviets had begun building nuclear missile sites in Cuba, and President John F. Kennedy risked nuclear war to force them out.

The containment doctrine also led to the U.S. involvement in *Vietnam.* Vietnamese forces led by nationalist/communist Ho Chi Minh defeated France's colonial army in 1954 and achieved independence. But the country was divided between Ho's forces in the north and a pro-Western government in the south. The struggle for a unified Vietnam soon resumed, and the United States intervened militarily in 1964. The war, though popular at first, quickly became a domestic trauma for Americans as casualties mounted on both sides. Perhaps the most poignant symbol of opposition to the war was the death on May 4, 1970, of four students at Kent State University during clashes between antiwar demonstrators and Ohio National Guardsmen. War-weariness finally led to a complete U.S. disengagement. Within a short time Ho's forces triumphed and Vietnam was unified in 1975.

The involvement in Vietnam caused a number of important changes in American attitudes. One was increased resistance to the cold war urge to fight communism everywhere. Second, Americans saw more clearly that the bipolar system was crumbling, especially as relations between the Soviet Union and China deteriorated.

Beginning approximately with the administrations of Soviet leader Leonid I. Brezhnev (1964–1982) and American president Richard M. Nixon (1969–1974), East-West relations began to improve, albeit fitfully. Nixon accurately assessed

Once a superpower, Russia now struggles for economic solvency and its right to play a role in international political decisions. Who will eventually succeed President Yeltsin is also a question that concerns many in world politics, as that person will likely decide Russia's course in the coming decades.

the changing balance of power, especially the rise of China, and he moved to better relations through a policy of *détente* with Moscow and a simultaneous opening of relations with Beijing. They came to similar realpolitik conclusions based on their own international perspectives and sought better relations with Washington.

The End of the Bipolar System

During the 1970s and early 1980s, East-West relations continued to warm, although there were cool periods. Then in 1985 relations began to change more rapidly. Mikhail S. Gorbachev became the Soviet leader in 1985 and moved to reform the Soviet Union's oppressive political system by allowing a greater degree of openness *(glasnost)*. He also sought to restructure *(perestroika)* the Soviets' cumbersome bureaucratic and economic system. While Gorbachev's goals were limited, he opened a Pandora's box for the communist Soviet Union and unleashed forces that were beyond his control.

Although almost no one then could believe it might be true, the Soviet Union itself was doomed. Old-guard communists tried and failed to seize power in mid-1991 in an effort to reverse the tide of history. Within six months the USSR collapsed as its constituent republics declared their independence. On December 25 Gorbachev resigned his presidency of a country that no longer existed. Soon thereafter, at 7:32 P.M., the red hammer-and-sickle Soviet flag was lowered for the last time from the Kremlin's spires and replaced

MAP
The Breakup of the Soviet Empire

by the red, white, and blue Russian flag. Few novelists could have created a story of such sweep and drama. The Soviet Union was no more.

Toward the Twenty-First Century: Changes and Choices

"What is past is prologue," Shakespeare comments in *The Tempest*. That is as true for the real world of today and tomorrow as it was for the Bard's literary world of yesterday. One hopes that no future historian will be able to write a history of the coming century under the title *The Tempest*. Titles such as *As You Like It* or *All's Well That Ends Well* are more appealing possibilities for histories yet to be.

Whatever the future will bring, we are in a position similar to that of Banquo in *Macbeth*. He sought to know the future, and we can sympathize with him when he pleads with the Witches of Endore, "If you can look into the seeds of time, And say which grain will grow and which will not, Speak then to me." In Banquo's case, the witches gave him a veiled prophecy that he neither understood nor was able to escape. We are luckier; we have an ability to shape the harvest if we mind another bit of advice that Shakespeare gives, this time in *Much Ado about Nothing*. Our ability to achieve a favorable future, he advises, is determined "by the fair weather that you make yourself: it is needful that you frame the season for your own harvest."

The sections that follow are meant to help you determine your harvest during the coming decades by examining the factors and trends that will benefit or beset the world as it passes into the next century and the next millennium. To facilitate the discussion here, these topics are divided into four areas of changes and choices: political structure and orientation, security, international economics, and the quality of life.

Political Structure and Orientation: Changes and Choices

There are a number of important changes occurring in the political orientation and organization of the international system. A new polar structure is emerging, the Western orientation of the system is weakening, and the authority of the state is being challenged from without and from within.

The Emerging Polar Structure

For all the excitement of the events associated with the collapse of the Soviet Union and the bipolar structure, an equally riveting and even more important question is the future shape of the now-evolving international system. The most likely possibility is a renewed *multipolar system.*

The countries that are most likely to play a polar role include the United States, China, Germany, Japan, and Russia. A few other countries, most notably India, with its huge population and nuclear weapons, might join that group.

As chapter 3 will explain, a future multipolar system, like past multipolar configurations, will be characterized by patterns of alliances and enmity that will be more fluid and complicated than the relationships in the bipolar system. "It is no longer the simple world it once was," one adviser to President Bill Clinton has commented. "It is a complex world and we've got to deal with it the way it is."[1] Who is allied with whom and in opposition to whom will depend more on individual issues and on shifting circumstances than on fixed alliance systems. Old enemies are finding new accommodation. The United States has extended aid to Russia. Old friends have experienced new or intensified tensions. Trade relations among countries of the West are strained, and one scholar predicts that the twenty-first century could experience "capitalist cold war."[2]

Yet even if the coming international system is multipolar, most scholars agree that the system will not look or operate like the multipolar system that existed prior to World War II. Instead, they believe that a likely scenario is what we can call a *modified multipolar system*. This suggests a system in which states are not the only poles, or a system in which the power of even the major states is considerably restrained by international organizations, international law, and interdependence.

One modification is that the United Nations or some successive global organization might become a more independent and potent actor. Another possibility is that regional poles, such as the European Union (EU), could develop. Even if no global or regional organization becomes a pole, they and other types of global actors will play a more important role on the world stage. As a result, even the most powerful countries are not as free as they once were to pursue their unilateral national interests. This change of cast is modifying the political script, and the dynamics of the modified multipolar system that is emerging will differ from that of a traditional multipolar system.

The Weakening Western Orientation of the International System

The dominant Western orientation of the international system is weakening as a result of the expansion of the number and power of non-Western states. The colonial empires established by the imperial Western powers collapsed after World War II, and in the ensuing years over 100 new countries have gained independence (more than tripling the previous number). The vast majority of these new countries are located in Africa, Asia, and other non-Western regions. Wherever they are, non-Western countries have become a stronger voice in international affairs, and a few, especially China and at some points collections of states like the Group of 77 in the United Nations General Assembly (UNGA), have achieved enough power to command center stage.

While such countries have many differences, they share several commonalities. Most are less well-off economically, earning them the commonly used sobriquet of less developed countries (LDCs). Most of these countries have an ethnic or racial makeup that is not Eurowhite, and they share a history of being colonies of or being dominated by Eurowhites. Furthermore, many of these countries have value systems that differ from the Westernized values

A SITE TO SURF
The Group of 77

that form the basis of current international law, concepts of human rights, and other standards in the international system (Neuman, 1998).

It should not be surprising, then, that many of these new or newly empowered countries support extensive changes in the international system. The result of all this is that the perspectives and demands of these countries are considerably changing the focus and tone of world political and economic debate.

MAP
Polar Structures

Challenges to the Authority of the State

While the dynamics of the emerging international system are being determined in part by the changing polar configuration of states and by the rise in importance of non-Western states, the system is also being affected by the fact that states are no longer virtually the only important actors in the world drama. Instead, as Benjamin Barber (1995) contends in a book entitled *Jihad vs. McWorld*, national states and the state-based structure of the world are being eroded by antithetical forces, some of which are splintering states into fragments (Jihad) and others of which are merging states into an integrated world (McWorld). As Barber (p. 4) puts it, if the first set of forces prevail, there is a "grim prospect of a retribalization of large swaths of humankind by war and bloodshed: a threatened balkanization of nation-states in which culture is pitted against culture, people against people, tribe against tribe, a Jihad in the name of a hundred narrowly conceived [identifications and loyalties]." The other trend, if it triumphs, melds "nations into one homogeneous global theme park, one McWorld tied together by communications, information, entertainment, and commerce." For now, Barber believes, "Caught between Babel and Disneyland, the planet is falling precipitously apart and coming reluctantly together at the very same moment."

The Forces of McWorld   Many analysts believe that there are political, economic, and social forces that are breaking down the importance and authority of states and moving the world toward a much higher degree of political, economic, and social integration. *Political integration*, for example, is evident in the increasing number and importance of other international actors, such as the United Nations and the World Trade Organization (WTO). When there are trade disputes, countries are no longer free to impose unilateral decisions. Instead, they are under heavy pressure to submit disputes to the WTO for arbitration.

Economic interdependence, the intertwining of national economies in the global economy means that countries are increasingly less self-sufficient. As we noted in the last chapter, national governments have a decreasing ability to manage national economies. Instead, global trade, international monetary exchange, and other financial flows in the global marketplace play a strong part in determining the jobs we have, whether our investments rise or fall, our country's inflation rate, and many other economic matters. This loss of economic controls diminishes the general authority of a state. There is a lively debate over what this will mean for the future of states (Hout, 1997; Strange,

1997; Hirst & Thompson, 1996). But some scholars believe, as one puts it, "Globalization will markedly constrain the autonomy and effectiveness of states and, at a minimum, raise serious questions about the meaning of internal and external sovereignty" (Korbin, 1996:26).

Social integration is also well under way in the view of many scholars. They believe that the world is being integrated—even homogenized—by the habits of cooperation and cross-cultural understanding that result from rapid travel and communication and from increased economic interchange of goods and services. People of different countries buy and sell each other's products at an ever-increasing rate; Cable News Network (CNN) is watched worldwide; English is becoming something of a lingua franca for diplomacy, business, and other forms of international interaction; and it is possible, with McDonald's operating 22,000 outlets in 106 countries, to travel around the world dining only on Big Macs, fries, and shakes. Thus, amid some worrisome culinary trends, there are indications that we, the world's people, are moving toward living in a more culturally homogenized global village. This outward trend works to weaken inward-looking nationalism, the primary basis of identification with and loyalty to one's country.

The Forces of Jihad   States are also being tested by a number of internal challenges, which Barber refers to as Jihad (the Arabic word that means defending the faith). There are many indications that states are fragmenting. Ethnic rivalries threaten the unity of many countries. The Soviet Union dissolved into 15 independent countries in 1991, and some of them are ethnically unstable. Similarly, Yugoslavia broke apart, and one of its new republics, Bosnia, itself collapsed in ethnic warfare. In 1998 what was left of Serb-dominated Yugoslavia further convulsed when ethnic Albanians, who are a majority in Kosovo Province, rose up against Serb control and were met with bloody retaliation. The Serb offensive in Kosovo was in turn met with military force from NATO, in a U.S.-led multilateral effort to quash the bloodshed and bring peace to the troubled region. Elsewhere, what was Czechoslovakia is now two countries; Somalia exists as a unified state in name only; Turkey's army wages war against separatist Kurds in the eastern part of that country; the Hutu massacre of Tutsis exposed the myth of a single Rwandan people; the list could go on. Moreover, fragmentation and refugees are not faraway phenomena. In the Western Hemisphere, for example, there is a persistent movement in Quebec to achieve autonomy, perhaps even independence, from Canada.

Security: Changes and Choices

Military security in today's world is provided primarily by individual countries. Each state is responsible for its own protection and as best as it can maintains a military capability to defend its national interests. Other countries normally come to the aid of a country that has been attacked only if they have found it in their national interest to become allies of that country or to

This icy soldier in Bosnia likely obeys orders quite well regardless of the nationality of the superior officer. But in a world where military security increasingly demands multilateral solutions, governments must find ways to coordinate international military operations that reduce national costs and also reconcile divergent national goals. UN and NATO operations in Bosnia, Kosovo, and elsewhere constantly confront such economic and political challenges.

otherwise support the beset country. Kuwait provides a good example. The United States came to Kuwait's aid mostly because of oil. If Kuwait produced tropical fruit, it is unlikely that a half million U.S. troops would have rushed to defend the world's banana supply.

Whatever the advantages of national security based on self-reliance, there are also disadvantages. One is the cost. During the decade 1987–1996, total world military expenditures amounted to $9.3 trillion, of which Americans paid about one-third. A second drawback to the traditional way of providing security, many critics point out, is that it is hard to say that it works very well when, during this century alone, over 111 million people have been killed in wars. That is almost 6 times as many people as those killed in the previous century and approximately 16 times the number of people slain during the century before that (Wallensteen & Sollenberg, 1995).

In the face of these realities, the world is beginning to work toward new ways of providing security, as chapter 10 will detail. *Arms control* is one trend. The high cost of conventional war and the probable cataclysmic result of a war using weapons of mass destruction (nuclear, biological, chemical) have forced the political system toward trying to avert Armageddon. During the past five years alone new or revised treaties have been concluded to deal with strategic nuclear weapons, chemical weapons, land mines, nuclear weapons proliferation, and several other weapons issues.

International security forces are another relatively new thrust in the quest for security. United Nations peacekeeping forces provide the most prominent

INTERACTIVE EXERCISE
You Are the Policy Maker: Who Should Be in Charge of Peacekeeping— The UN or NATO?

example of this alternative approach to security. Fifty years ago there were none and there never had been a UN peacekeeping mission. In 1988 there were 5; in 1998 there were 16 under way. Using such forces is in its infancy, but they may eventually offer an alternative to nationally based security. There are even calls for a permanent UN army that would be available for immediate use by the UN (Haynes & Stanley, 1995).

International Economics: Changes and Choices

The years since World War II have included a number of trends in international economics that will continue to affect the international system as it moves into the next century. Economic interdependence and economic disparity between the wealthy North and the relatively less developed South are two matters of particular note.

Economic Interdependence

One important economic change in the international system that has gained momentum since World War II is the growth of economic **interdependence**. Merchandise trade during 1997 exceeded $11 billion and merchandise exports during 1997 exceeded $5.4 trillion; Americans alone own more than $2.5 trillion in the assets (companies, property, stock, bonds) located in other countries and foreigners own more than $1.8 trillion in U.S. assets; the flow of currencies among countries now exceeds $1.5 trillion every day.

This increasingly free flow of trade, investment capital, and national currencies across national borders has created such a high level of economic interdependence among countries that it is arguably misleading to talk of national economies in a singular sense. The impact of the continuing Asian financial crisis has been obvious on the U.S. economy. To cite one example, South Korea experienced one of the worst economic meltdowns, and as a result the U.S. trade balance with South Korea changed from a $181 million surplus for the month of January 1997 to an $856 million deficit for January 1998. Such negative figures are somewhat impersonal in the aggregate, but, as U.S. secretary of the treasury Robert Rubin points out, "The financial crisis in Asia is likely to impact the lives and residents and business in states across the country."[3]

To deal with this interdependence, the world during the last half-century has created and strengthened a host of global and regional economic organizations. The three most important global economic organizations are the World Bank, the International Monetary Fund (IMF), and the World Trade Organization (WTO), originally called the General Agreement on Tariffs and Trade. There are also numerous economic agencies associated with the UN. Regionally, such initiatives as the Association of Southeast Asian Nations (ASEAN), the European Union (EU), and the North American Free Trade Agreement (NAFTA) are also both dealing with and furthering interdependence.

Before leaving our discussion of economic interdependence, it should be noted that the road to integration is neither smooth nor is its future certain.

There are numerous difficulties. Trade and monetary tensions exist among countries. Many people are opposed to surrendering any of their country's sovereignty to the UN, the WTO, or any other international organization. Others concerned about workers' rights, product safety, and the environment, worry that free trade has allowed multinational corporations to escape effective regulation. Indeed, these and other worries had sparked something of a countermove against further interdependence. There are, in short, significant choices to be made in how to order financial relations among countries.

Economic Disparity between North and South

There is a wide disparity in economic circumstance between the relatively affluent life of a small percentage of the world population who live in a few countries and the majority of humanity who live in most countries. The terms North and South are used to designate the two economic spheres. The North symbolizes the wealthy and industrialized **economically developed countries (EDCs)**, which lie mainly in the Northern Hemisphere. By contrast, the South represents the **less developed countries (LDCs)**, the majority of which are near or in the Southern Hemisphere. The acronyms EDC, LDC, and associated designations are discussed in Technical Explanations and Matters of Terminology on page 433.

The economic and political ramifications of the North-South divide are discussed extensively in chapters 11 and 12, but a few basic points are appropriate here. One is that the economic circumstances of countries are not truly dichotomized. Instead they range from general opulence (the United States) to unbelievable poverty (Bangladesh). There are some countries of the South that have achieved substantial industrialization and whose standards of living have risen rapidly. These countries are called **newly industrializing countries (NICs)**. Moreover, there are some wealthy people in LDCs and numerous poor people in EDCs.

Yet, it is also the case that such details cannot disguise the fact that there is a vast economic gap between North and South. The per capita **gross national product (GNP)** in 1995 of the North was $24,930. At $1,090, the per capita wealth of those in the South was a mere 4.4 percent of that of their contemporaries in the North. This immense gulf in wealth has devastating consequences for the poor. Their children, for instance, suffer an unconscionable mortality rate that is almost seven times greater than the infant mortality rate in the wealthiest countries.

One ramification of the weakening Western orientation of the international system discussed earlier is that this economic inequity is causing increased tension along the so-called **North-South Axis**. The LDCs are no longer willing to accept a world system in which wealth is so unevenly distributed.

They blame much of their poverty on past colonialist suppression and on what they believe are current efforts by the EDCs to keep the LDCs economically and politically weak—as sources of cheap raw materials and labor. They also rebel against the North's control of the IMF and other international financial organizations. When the economies of several Asian nations collapsed in late 1997, some people in that region suspected the EDCs had conspired to thwart their booming development. The demands of the North-dominated

**MAP
Economic
Development**

IMF that Asian recipients of assistance adopt the North's model of economic development led one major newspaper in Thailand to editorialize in 1998 that, "Just as the fall of the Berlin wall represents a political and ideological victory for the U.S. over socialism, the collapse of the economies in Asia marks another, more subtle triumph of U.S. financial imperialism over this region."[4]

Whether or not one accepts this conspiracy theory is not the issue here. The point is that choices must be made in the face of the changes that are occurring. One option for the wealthy countries is to ignore the vast difference in economic circumstances between themselves and the LDCs. The other option is to do more, much more, to help. Both options carry substantial costs.

The Quality of Life: Changes and Choices

The last few decades have spawned several changes involving the quality of human life that will continue to affect world politics into the next century and that present choices we must face. Preserving human rights and the environment are two matters of particular note.

Human Rights

It borders on tautology to observe that violations of human rights have existed as far back into history as we can see. What is different is that the world is beginning to take notice across borders of human rights violations and beginning to react negatively to them.

The change involves the *norms of behavior* that help regulate and characterize any political system. Behavior in virtually all political systems is governed by a mix of coercion and voluntary compliance. Norms, or values, are what determine voluntary compliance. For example, the values about the conduct of war are changing and attacks on civilians are losing whatever legitimacy they may once have had. The international tribunal trying war crimes in Bosnia exemplifies this. Unpunished mistreatment of some or all of one's citizens under the guise of sovereignty has also lost considerable legitimacy. The international community played a strong part in forcing the all-white government in South Africa to allow all the people in the country to vote and hold office. A black, Nelson Mandela, left office as president in June 1999 and is succeeded by another black, Thabo Mbeki.

There are numerous other areas in which the demand for the protection of human rights is louder and stronger. The rights of women are just one of the subjects that have recently become a focus of international concern and action. The largest and most widely noted in a series of international conferences on the status of women met in 1995 in Beijing. Gertrude Mongella, a Tanzanian serving as secretary-general of the UN Fourth World Conference on Women, brought the global conclave into session with the ringing declaration that women are "no longer guests on this planet. This planet belongs to us too. A revolution has begun."[5] It is a revolution that will almost certainly

Once a reservoir for the town of Hermosillo in Mexico, this parched lake bed is evidence of the dramatic climate and environmental changes taking place in the world today. Permanent solutions to such transboundary problems require coordinated decisions by many states.

have a profound impact on the conduct of international as well as domestic policy in the twenty-first century.

In a similar vein, human rights conferences, once perceived primarily as window-dressing for power politics, are no longer unnoticed, peripheral affairs. A significant number of human rights treaties have been signed by a majority of the world's countries. In sum, what was once mostly the domain of do-gooders has increasingly become the province of presidents and prime ministers.

The Environment

The mounting degradation of the biosphere has its origins in the industrial revolution and, therefore, like the abuse of human rights, is not new to the world stage. But, again, like human rights, what has changed is the attention that is now being paid to the subject and the international efforts to protect the environment that have begun.

The greatest challenge is to achieve *sustainable development,* that is to (a) continue to develop economically while (b) simultaneously protecting the environment. As with human rights, you will see in a later chapter that progress on the environment has been slow. Yet, also like human rights, you will see that progress is being made. Among other advances, the subject has shifted from the political periphery to presidential palaces. What leaders have come to realize is that their national interests are endangered by environmental degradation,

Figure 2.2

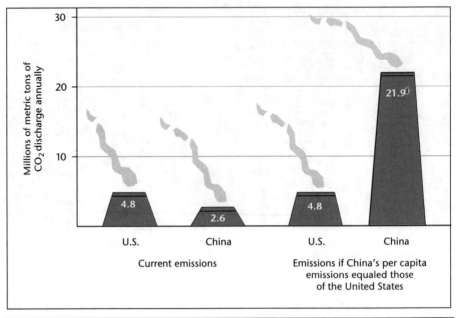

CO₂ Emissions and the Conundrum of Sustainable Development

Millions of metric tons of CO₂ discharge annually

U.S. 4.8	China 2.6
Current emissions	

U.S. 4.8	China 21.9
Emissions if China's per capita emissions equaled those of the United States	

China will develop economically. If it also reaches the per capita CO₂ emissions of the United States, then it will produce more than eight times the CO₂ it now emits and one-third more CO₂ than the combined current annual emissions (15.2 million metric tons) of the ten countries with the greatest discharges. That would be an environmental disaster. The question of sustainable development is how to help China to develop in an environmentally acceptable way.

as well as by military and economic threats. This view was expressed by President Bill Clinton when he told President Jiang Zemin of China that:

> I think the greatest threat to our security [that] you present is . . . that all of your people will want to get rich in exactly the same way we got rich. Unless we try to triple automobile mileage and to reduce greenhouse gas emission, if you all get rich in that way we won't be breathing very well . . . [because] you will do irrevocable damage to the global environment. I hope we will be cooperating on [the environment] in the years ahead, because I think that other countries will support your development more if they don't feel threatened by the environment.[6]

The need to balance economic development and environmental protection is recognized, even by those countries that are struggling to alleviate widespread poverty and its associated ills in their countries. "Family planning and environmental protection are of vital importance to sustainable economic growth," President Jiang acknowledged to reporters in 1998.[7]

Yet for China and all other countries, achieving sustainable development will not be easy. Among other challenges, the LDCs will need extensive assistance to develop in an environmentally responsible way. UN officials have placed that cost as high as $125 billion a year, and many observers believe that the North should bear a great deal of the cost for two reasons. One is that the North is much wealthier than the South. The second reason is because the North has historically emitted 70 percent of the carbon dioxide (CO_2) and a majority of most other pollutants, despite having less than one quarter of the world population. "You can't have an environmentally healthy planet in a world that is socially unjust," Brazil's president Fernando Collor de Mello noted at one point.[8]

Even if you do not agree with the social justice argument, it is arguable that the North should assist the South out of sheer self-interest. To better understand Clinton's point about China's development, consider Figure 2.2. On the left you can see that with almost four times as many people, China only produces a little more than half as much CO_2 as the United States. On the right you can see that if the Chinese produced on a per capita basis the same amount of CO_2 as the Americans, then China's annual discharges would soar to 21.9 million tons, an environmental disaster. China's discharges will be even higher if it continues to develop with its current reliance on coal for energy and its use of other less expensive, but environmentally dangerous, development strategies.

Chapter Summary

1. This chapter has two primary goals. One is to establish a reference framework from which the historical examples used to illustrate the theoretical points made in this book can be understood in context. The second goal is to sketch the evolution of the current world political system.

2. The current world system began to develop in about the fifteenth century, when modern states began to form due to a process marked by both integration and disintegration of earlier political authority. The Treaty of Westphalia (1648), more than any other event, demarcated the change between the old and new systems. With the sovereign state at its center, the newly evolving system was anarchical.

3. Several changes occurred during the 1700s and 1800s that continued to have an important impact on the international system. The coming of the concept of popular sovereignty involved a shift in the idea of who legitimately controls the state. The divine right of kings gave way to the notion that political power does, or ought to, come from the people. During these two centuries, the system also became Westernized and the multipolar configuration reached its apogee.

4. The twentieth century has witnessed the most rapid evolution of the system. The multipolar system tottered, then fell. The bipolar system declined as other countries and transnational actors became more important, as the expense of continuing confrontation strained American and Soviet budget resources, and as the relative

power of the two superpowers declined. The bipolar system ended in 1991 when the Soviet Union collapsed.

5. During this century, nationalism also undermined the foundations of multiethnic empires. European contiguous empires, such as the Austro-Hungarian Empire, disintegrated. The colonial empires dominated by Great Britain, France, and other Eurowhite countries also dissolved.

6. There are numerous new trends, uncertainties, and choices to make as we approach the twenty-first century. One significant question is, What will follow the bipolar system? The most likely possibility is some form of modified multipolar system. But even though there are likely to be four or more major powers, the system is unlikely to parallel earlier multipolar systems because of the other significant changes that have occurred in the international system. One such change is that international organizations have become much more numerous and more central to the operation of the international system.

7. Another shift in the international system is its weakening Western orientation. The number and strength of non-Western countries have grown substantially, and the strength of these states will almost certainly continue to grow in the next century. These countries often have values that differ from those of the Western countries.

8. Challenges to the authority of the state represent a third shift in the international system, which has strong implications for the next century. There are both disintegrative internal challenges to the state and integrative external challenges.

9. The pursuit of peace is also at something of a crossroads. The destructiveness of modern weaponry has made the quest for peace even more imperative. The issue is whether to follow traditional national security approaches or alternative international security approaches.

10. The international economy is also changing in ways that have important implications for the twenty-first century. Economic interdependence has progressed rapidly. The transnational flow of trade, investment capital, and currencies has economically entwined all countries. There are, however, counterpressures, and an important issue in the near future is whether to continue down the newer path to economic integration or to halt that process and follow more traditional national economic policies.

11. The effort to resolve the wide, and in many ways growing, gulf between the economic circumstances of the countries of the economically developed North and the less economically developed South is also a mounting issue as the next century approaches.

12. A final set of issues that must be addressed in the new century that is upon us involves the quality of life: human rights and the environment. Both issues are the subject of much greater international awareness and interaction. Yet the ending of abuses of human rights and the protection of the environment will be difficult in the face of national resistance to international solutions.

Levels of Analysis

Mad world! Mad kings! Mad composition!

Shakespeare, *King John*

Toughness doesn't have to come in a pinstripe suit.

U.S. senator Dianne Feinstein

The preceding chapter began our survey of system-level analysis through a brief survey of the evolution of the current world system. This chapter expands our examination of analytical perspectives on international relations first by continuing our discussion of system-level forces or the system level of analysis. Later in the chapter we move onto the two other most commonly used levels of analysis: state-level analysis (focusing on the nation-state as the traditional primary unit of analysis) and individual-level analysis (focusing on humans as the decision-making unit).

Chapter Outline

47

System-Level Analysis

System-level analysis adopts essentially a "top down" approach to studying world politics. It begins with the view that countries and other international actors operate in a global social-economic-political-geographic environment and that the specific characteristics of the system help determine the pattern of interaction among the actors. Systems analysts believe that any system operates in somewhat predictable ways—that there are behavioral tendencies that the actor countries usually follow.

Most people do not think much about systems, but they are an ever-present part of our lives. Although each of us has free will, each of us is also part of many overlapping systems that influence our behavior and make it reasonably predictable. These systems range from very local ones, such as your family and school classroom, to much larger systems, such as your country and the world. Whatever their size, though, how each of these systems operates is based on four factors: structural characteristics, power relationships, economic realities, and norms.

Structural Characteristics

All systems have identifiable structural characteristics. These include how authority is organized, who the actors are, and what the scope and level of interaction among the actors is.

The Organization of Authority

The authority structure of a system for making and enforcing rules, for allocating assets, and for conducting other authoritative tasks can range from very hierarchical to anarchical. Most systems, like your university or your country, are hierarchical. They have a *vertical authority structure* in which subordinate units answer to higher levels of authority. Vertical systems have central authorities that are responsible for making, enforcing, and adjudicating rules and that restrain subordinate actors. Other systems have a *horizontal authority structure* in which authority is fragmented. The international system is one such system with a mostly horizontal authority structure. It is based on the sovereignty of states. Sovereignty means that countries are not legally answerable to any higher authority for their international or domestic conduct. As such, the international system is anarchic; it has no overarching authority to make rules, settle disputes, and provide protection.

To see how horizontal and vertical structures operate differently, ask yourself why all countries are armed and why few students bring guns to class. The reason is that states in the international system (unlike students in a domestic system) depend on themselves for protection. If a state is threatened, there is no international 911 number that it can call for help. Given this self-help system, each state feels compelled to be armed.

Change in the authority structure of the international system is, however, under way. Many analysts believe that sovereignty is declining and that even the most powerful states are subject to an increasing number of authoritative rules made by international organizations and by international law. In 1997, for example, the United States threatened to place barriers against Fuji film and other Japanese film and argued before the WTO that Japan was discriminating against Kodak film. The United States lost its case and had to abandon the threatened retaliation. The sting of that loss was offset two months later in February 1998, when the WTO found in favor of a U.S. complaint that the European Union was illegally barring certain U.S. computer technology in an effort to protect Europe's software companies. Countries still resist and often even reject IGO governance when it touches on sensitive political issues, but that does not negate the slowly growing authority of IGOs in the international system.

The Actors

Another characteristic of any system is its actors. What organizations operate in the system, and what impact do they have on the course of international relations? We can answer these questions by dividing actors into three general categories: national actors, international actors, and transnational actors.

National Actors: States   States are the principal actors on the world stage. The leading role that states play in the international system is determined by several factors, including state sovereignty, the state's status as the primary focus of people's political loyalty, and the state's command of the preponderance of economic and military power.

Inasmuch as the nature and operation of states will be dealt with extensively in chapters 6 and 8, we will not detail them here. What is important for this discussion, though, is that states dominate the action and act with independence. Yet for all this talk of the pivotal role of sovereign states in a horizontal, largely anarchical international system, it is also true that states are not the only system-level actors and that there are significant centralizing forces in the system.

International Governmental Actors   A second group of system-level actors are made up of international organizations. These actors are also called **intergovernmental organizations (IGOs)**. The key defining characteristic of an IGO is that it has individual countries as members. The membership of the UN, for instance, consists of 185 countries. Almost all IGOs also have a central administrative structure. The UN is headquartered in New York City and has an administrative staff headed by a secretary-general.

A significant thing to remember about IGOs is that more and more in this century, states have come to share the stage with this relatively new type of actor. One indication of the enhanced role of IGOs is the steep rise in their number. In 1900 there were 30 IGOs. That number has increased some 900 percent: there are now 272. We will examine IGOs and the roles they play in world politics in much more detail in chapter 7. You can also read about the

A FURTHER NOTE
The Metamorphosis
of NATO

changes taking place in the role, membership, and activities of another IGO, NATO, in the Web Site box The Metamorphosis of NATO.

Transnational Actors   A third category of actors in the international system is **transnational actors,** organizations that operate internationally, but whose membership, unlike IGOs, is private. To provide an introduction to transnational actors, we can briefly examine the two most numerous and most organized types: nongovernmental organizations and multinational corporations.

Nongovernmental Organizations   This type of organization, like an IGO, operates across borders but is different from IGOs in that it has individuals as members. Amnesty International and Greenpeace are examples. **Nongovernmental organizations (NGOs)** also have organizational structures. Both the number and importance of NGOs on the world stage is increasing. In 1900 there were 69 NGOs. Since then the number of NGOs has expanded 70-fold to approximately 5,000. Furthermore, the influence and range of activities of transnational actors are growing as their numbers increase and as technological advances allow them to operate and communicate more effectively across political boundaries. The most important aspect of NGOs, according to one analyst, is that their "role in global negotiations and global governance has been emerging stealthily and slowly over the last quarter century" (Phan, 1996:2; Gordenker & Weiss, 1995).

Multinational Corporations   A second type of transnational actor consists of **multinational corporations (MNCs),** also sometimes referred to as **transnational corporations (TNCs).** By whatever name, the expansion of international trade, investment, and other financial interactions has brought with it the rise of huge MNCs. These businesses have operations in more than one country that extend beyond merely sales to production and other functions. The role of MNCs is discussed in detail in chapters 11 and 12, but suffice it to say here that the economic power of these corporate giants gives them a substantial role in international affairs (Barnet & Cavanagh, 1994). Some idea of the economic power of the MNCs can be gained from comparing their gross corporate product (GCP: sales and other revenues) to the **gross domestic product** (GDP: a measure of all goods and services produced within a country) of various countries (Figure 3.1). The biggest 1998 MNC, General Motors, had a GCP of $161.3 billion that was slightly larger than the GDP of Greece ($137.4 billion), about one and a half times larger than Israel's ($96.7 billion), about two and a half times larger than Ireland's ($59.9 billion), eight times larger than Slovenia's ($19.5 billion), and seventeen times larger than Nicaragua's ($9.3 billion).

Scope and Level of Interaction

A third structural characteristic of any political system is the range (scope) of areas in which the actors interact and the frequency and intensity (level) of those interactions. One key to understanding the evolution of the international system is to see that the scope and level of international interaction

(Continued on page 51)

Figure 3.1

Gross Corporate Product of General Motors Related to Gross Domestic Product of Selected Countries (in US$ billions)

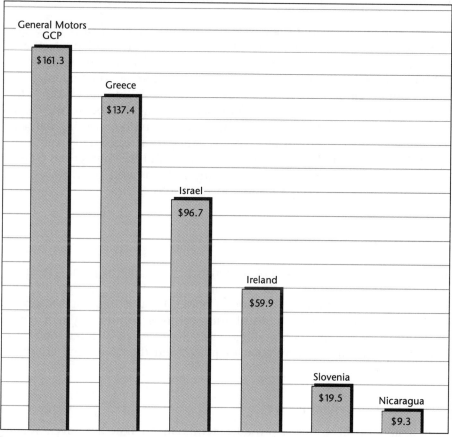

Data sources: GM data: www.pathfinder.com/fortune/fortune500/index.html; country data: *CIA World Factbook,* 1998.

Multinational corporations (MNCs) are one category of NGO. Some idea of the enormous economic power of MNCs can be illustrated by comparing General Motors' gross corporate product to the gross domestic product of selected countries.

are very much higher now than they were during the 1800s or even in the first half of the 1900s.

Economic interdependence provides the most obvious example of the escalating scope and level of interaction. Whether it was ever true, it is nonsense today to imagine that any country can go it alone in splendid isolation. Even for a powerful country like the United States, a "fortress America" policy is impossible. Without foreign oil, to pick one obvious illustration, U.S. transportation and industry would literally soon come to a halt. Without extensive trade, the U.S. economy would stagger because exports are a key factor in economic growth. American exports in 1996 grew 8.6 percent, more than three times faster than the 2.8 percent growth rate of the U.S. GDP. This is not atypical. Since 1987, exports have grown more than 4.3 times as fast as the GDP and have accounted for more than half of the growth in the U.S. economy.

Data about expanding trade does not, however, capture fully the degree to which the widening scope and intensifying level of global interaction is increasing transnational contacts among people. Modern telecommunications and travel, for example, are making once relatively rare personal international interactions commonplace. Foreign travel is just one telling indication of this change. Between 1988 and 1995 the number of foreign visitors to the United States jumped 28 percent from 33.9 million to 43.3 million. During the same period, the number of Americans traveling overseas increased 25 percent from 40.7 million to 50.8 million. People used to talk about the "mysterious Orient" or "darkest Africa." Now Americans by the millions visit these places, and people from there are regular visitors to the United States.

Power Relationships

Having examined the structural characteristics of the international system, we can turn our attention to another key set of factors: power relationships. We will in chapter 10 examine the nature of power. What is important to understand here, though, is that the distribution of power within a system affects the way that the system operates. To see this, we can look at three topics: the number of poles, the concentration of power, and the causes and effects of changes in power.

Number of System Poles

Many analysts believe that a pivotal determinant of how any given system operates is the number of major power poles that it has. Traditionally, a system pole has consisted of either (1) a single country or empire or (2) a group of countries that form an alliance or a bloc. It is possible that in the future a global IGO, such as the UN, or a regional IGO, such as the EU, might acquire enough power and independence from its member states to constitute a pole. While we will concentrate on global polar relations, it is worth noting that regions also have more localized polar structures. In the words of one recent study, "the international system is composed of multiple, overlapping systems. The global system encompasses all the states in the world, while regional systems comprise only local members" (Lemke & Warner, 1996:237). China, Russia, Japan, and the United States, for instance, constitute what one author calls a strategic quadrangle in East Asia (Mandelbaum, 1995). It also may be that a country such as India can be a regional pole without being a global power.

A FURTHER NOTE
Balance of Power

There are several ways that the number of poles affects the conduct of the international system. The **balance of power** that is sought by most actors in the system is discussed at length in the Web site box Balance of Power. To further understand this concept and the likelihood that it will be achieved in the international system, we can examine two factors. One is the rules of the game of power politics. The second is the propensity of a system for instability and war. Both relate to the number of system poles that exists at any point in time.

Some political scientists believe that the pattern of interaction varies according to the number of poles that a system has. It is possible, for example, to identify patterns or rules of the game for unipolar, bipolar, tripolar, and multipolar systems. It is especially interesting to compare bipolar and multipolar systems in order to contrast the rules of the system that has just passed with the rules of the system that is now evolving. Figure 3.2 displays these four types of system structures and ways in which the patterns of interaction differ across them.

A second possible impact of the number of poles is the propensity of a system for instability and war. There is a lively academic debate about whether or not the number of poles in a system has an impact on the likelihood of war. Some scholars have found that unipolar systems are relatively peaceful; that a system with two poles (bipolar) has a medium chance of war; that a three-pole (tripolar) system has a relatively low propensity toward war; and that systems with four or more poles (multipolar) have the highest probability of war. Systems with five poles were found to be the most unstable (Rasler & Thompson, 1992; Ostrom & Aldrich, 1978).

Concentration of Power

A pole is a major power center, but not all major powers are equal. This inequality affects how the system operates, one recent study has concluded, because system stability varies in part according to the degree to which power is concentrated or diffused among the various poles (Kegley & Raymond, 1994). The finding leads to questions about the stability of the system when two poles (countries or alliances) are in a condition of relative *power equality* or *power inequality* (Gochman & Hoffman, 1996; Schampel, 1996; Wayman, 1994).

Some scholars argue that war is more likely when antagonistic poles have relatively equal power, creating "a situation in which both sides can perceive the potential for successful use of force" (Geller, 1993:173). By this logic, war is less likely when power is concentrated in one camp, because the weaker side will be deferential. Other scholars disagree. They believe that conflict is more likely between countries of unequal power. The reasoning is that when two antagonists are equal in power, they are deterred from war by the fear of being defeated or by the mauling they will take even if they are victorious (Morgan, 1994). Why, you might ask, would an obviously weaker country fight rather than compromise or give way? One reason is that an aggressor may attack and leave the country no choice. Many countries have fought when they were invaded, even if there was no hope of winning. Emotions are

(Continued on page 55)

Figure 3.2

Models of Various International System Structures

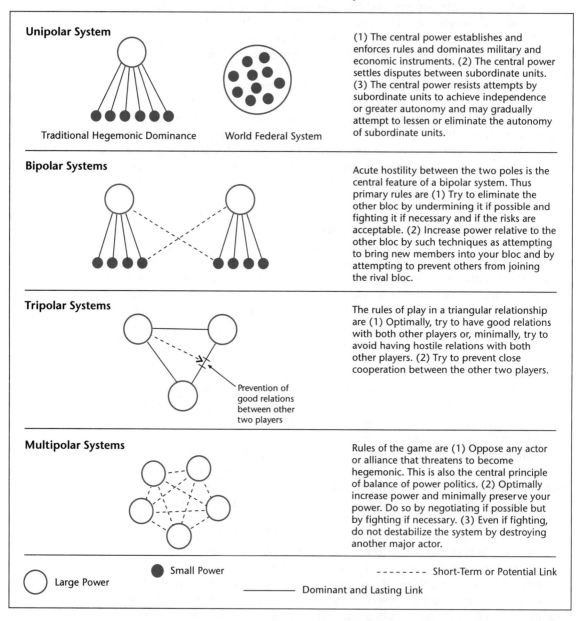

Unipolar System

Traditional Hegemonic Dominance   World Federal System

(1) The central power establishes and enforces rules and dominates military and economic instruments. (2) The central power settles disputes between subordinate units. (3) The central power resists attempts by subordinate units to achieve independence or greater autonomy and may gradually attempt to lessen or eliminate the autonomy of subordinate units.

Bipolar Systems

Acute hostility between the two poles is the central feature of a bipolar system. Thus primary rules are (1) Try to eliminate the other bloc by undermining it if possible and fighting it if necessary and if the risks are acceptable. (2) Increase power relative to the other bloc by such techniques as attempting to bring new members into your bloc and by attempting to prevent others from joining the rival bloc.

Tripolar Systems

Prevention of good relations between other two players

The rules of play in a triangular relationship are (1) Optimally, try to have good relations with both other players or, minimally, try to avoid having hostile relations with both other players. (2) Try to prevent close cooperation between the other two players.

Multipolar Systems

Rules of the game are (1) Oppose any actor or alliance that threatens to become hegemonic. This is also the central principle of balance of power politics. (2) Optimally increase power and minimally preserve your power. Do so by negotiating if possible but by fighting if necessary. (3) Even if fighting, do not destabilize the system by destroying another major actor.

◯ Large Power   ● Small Power   - - - - - - - Short-Term or Potential Link
—————— Dominant and Lasting Link

The relationships that exist among the actors in a particular type of international system structure vary because of the number of powerful actors, the relative power of each, and the permitted interactions within that system. This figure displays potential international system structures and the basic rules that govern relationships within each system. After looking at these models, which one do you think best describes the contemporary international system? This is a subject of some debate.

another reason: Live Free Or Die, as the New Hampshire license plate proclaims. What occurs, research shows, is that decision makers are willing to accept much greater risks to prevent losses than to gain an advantage (Farnham, 1994).

Still other scholars conclude that conflict is least likely when power is equal or very unequal and most likely when there are moderate power differences between antagonists (Powell, 1996; Mansfield, 1994). Less dramatic differences may lead countries either to miscalculate their power relative to that of their opponent or to gamble.

Power Changes: Causes and Effects

The power equation in the international system is seldom stable for very long. Powerful countries rise and fall in their relative power to one another. Major powers sometimes decline to the point that they are no longer a pole, and they may even cease to exist, as did the USSR. Other countries may come into existence and later rise to the rank of major power, as did the United States.

There are a number of highly debated general theories about power-based changes in the international system. Some scholars propound "cycle theories" (Pollins, 1996). Some of these theories hold that cycles occur over a period of a few decades; others suggest as much as a century. The cycles are demarcated by great-power or "systemic" wars that reflect strains created by power shifts within the system. They might be equated to earthquakes in the geological system. The systemic wars, in turn, further alter the system by destroying the major power status of declining powers and elevating rising powers to pole status. Then the process of power decay and formation begins anew. Another study uses the idea of "chaos theory" to argue that while there is an evolution to power in the system, "this evolution is *chaotic* [in that] the patterns of global power are not strict chronological cycles, but variable patterns influenced by . . . small random . . . effects" that can change the timing and impact of the cycle (Richards, 1993:71).

Whatever their view, analysts agree that the international system does change and that the shifts are important. Therefore, how power changes is a key concern. Since the current polar structure of the international system is clearly in flux, you will see throughout this book that the patterns of relationships among all actors in the system are changing and that we cannot yet determine the exact structural formula for the new polar era. The Web site box Japan: A Rising Sun? explores a possible evolutionary trajectory for one of the major actors in the current world system.

A FURTHER NOTE
Japan: A Rising Sun?

Economic Patterns

The operation of the international system is a product in part of its economic patterns. We can gain a sense of the impact of these patterns by touching on just three of them: interdependence, natural resource location and use, and the maldistribution of development.

Even though we often hear of the equalizing effects of globalization throughout the world, the developed countries are still perceived as lands of plenty, offering opportunity for a better life. In this picture, a Ugandan mother and her daughter wait to become Canadian citizens in Halifax, Nova Scotia, and begin a new life in the North.

MAP
Flows of Oil

Economic interdependence is one pattern that we have noted repeatedly. There is some controversy over whether or under what conditions interdependence promotes peace or creates tensions. One study concludes, for instance, that established powerful states (status quo powers) are most likely to join together to deter aggression "when there are extensive ties among the status quo powers *and* few or no such links between them and the perceived threatening powers." By contrast, "When economic interdependence is not strong between status quo powers or if the status quo powers have significant links with threatening powers, [status quo] leaders' capacities to balance are limited," which leads to "weak responses" and "a greater likelihood of aggression by the [threatening] power" (Papayoanou, 1997:135).

The pattern of where *natural resources* are produced and consumed also influences the operation of the system. The strong reaction of the industrialized (and petroleum import–dependent) countries to Iraq's aggression in 1990 was based significantly on the distribution of resources. Turmoil in the Persian Gulf region threatened needed oil supplies. While the Bush administration could have decided not to intervene, a system-level analyst would point out that it had little choice. American presidents as far back as Harry S. Truman had pledged U.S. protection of the West's primary petroleum source. Even the usually conciliatory Jimmy Carter had declared during his January 1980 State of the Union message that any attempt "to gain control of the Persian Gulf will be regarded as an assault on the vital interests of the United States of America." Given the distribution of system resources, then, Iraq's invasion of Kuwait and threat to Saudi Arabia and other oil producers brought what a system-level analyst would say was a predictable reaction from the powerful petroleum-importing states. Led by the United States, they moved militarily to end the threat to their supplies because, as U.S. secretary of state James A. Baker III explained to reporters, "The economic lifeline of the industrial world runs from the gulf, and we cannot permit a dictator . . . to sit astride that economic lifeline."[1]

The *maldistribution of development* is a third economic pattern that has consequences for the international system. The main actors, the states, in the system are divided into relative haves and have-nots. At the most general level, this economic division pits the less developed countries (LDCs) of the South and their demands for equity against the economically developed countries (EDCs) of the North along the North-South Axis. More specifically, as we shall see at various points in the chapters to come, there is a connection between the poor economic conditions in LDCs and such problems as rapid political oppression and instability, population growth, and environmental degradation. These problems harm the people of the South and, by their spillover effect, are detrimental for the people of the North as well. An economic pattern in which a small minority of people and countries enjoy high standards of living while the vast majority of people and countries are relatively impoverished both creates a drag on the world economy and is morally questionable. The disparity also creates resentments rooted in desperation, fertile ground that could one day yield systemic violence—a reminder of Abraham Lincoln's maxim that "a house divided against itself cannot stand."

Norms of Behavior

The widely accepted standards of behavior that help regulate behavior are the fourth major element of any system. These standards, or values, constitute the **norms** of a system. A caveat is that to be valid, norms must be generally recognized and followed, but they need not be either accepted or practiced universally. Systems develop norms for two reasons. First, various psychological and social factors prompt humans to adopt values to define what is ethical and moral. Second, humans tend to favor regularized patterns of behavior because of the pragmatic need to interact and to avoid the anxiety and disruption caused by the random or unwanted behavior of others. Over the centuries, for instance, pragmatism led to norms (now supplemented by treaties) about how countries treat each others' diplomats even in times of war. When conflict broke out in the Persian Gulf in 1991, U.S. and other enemy diplomats in Baghdad were not rounded up and executed. Iraqi diplomats in Washington, D.C., London, Paris, and elsewhere were similarly safe from official reprisal.

Changes that occur in the norms of the international system are an important aspect of how the system evolves. What is evident in the current system is that norms are becoming more universal while they are simultaneously being challenged.

The uniformity of norms is the result of the McWorld effect, the increasing homogenization of global culture because of economic interdependence, global communications, and other factors. It would be a vast overstatement to say that capitalist (free-market) economies, democracy, and the precepts of individual human rights reign triumphant throughout the world. But these and other beliefs about the "right way" to do things have certainly become the dominant theme.

Yet it is also true that the exact nature of these precepts is being modified as a result of the de-Westernization of the international system. Norms that have heretofore influenced the system were established by the dominant countries of the North. Now the South has become more assertive, and it disagrees with some of the established values. This has led in recent years to an increased number of challenges to the prevailing norms of the system.

Another important change in the nature and role of norms is that the international cast of actors is also more willing than it used to be to take action to enforce changing norms. The strengthening norms of democracy and human rights, for one, prompted global economic sanctions and other pressures that eventually forced South Africa's white government to end apartheid and eventually to turn political power over to the black majority (Klotz, 1997). Changing norms about how we use the biosphere also persuaded Japan to pledge to end drift-net fishing for squid. After a debate in the UN on the issue, a Japanese official explained that his country gave way because, "Since no other country sided with us, we have to consider Japan's position in international society and yield."[2]

The willingness to countenance war, especially unilateral action by an individual country, is also weakening. Wars still occur, but they are being perceived as less legitimate and are more widely condemned in principle. The U.S. invasion of Panama in 1989 was, for example, condemned by both the UN and the Organization of American States (OAS). During the more recent crisis over government repression in Haiti, the United States was careful to garner UN and OAS support for economic sanctions and for military intervention. The intervention in Bosnia was not the act of a single country, but an international effort sanctioned by the UN and conducted by NATO.

System-Level Analysis: Predicting Tomorrow

We have, in the preceding pages, examined the international system and how it is shaped by its characteristics: global authority structure, power relationships, economic patterns, and norms of behavior. We have also seen that all these factors are in flux. The question is, then, whether system-level analysis can give us some clues about the world we will experience tomorrow. What do these changes portend for the system during the rapidly approaching twenty-first century?

The changes that we have been discussing seem to be simultaneously pulling the international system in three directions. One direction is along the traditional, state-centric road that the system has traveled for centuries. Nationalism, as we shall see, remains the most potent political idea in the world today, and the number of sovereign states has tripled since 1945.

Then there is the alternative road. For all the strength of states as the principal actors in the international system, many scholars conclude that the dominance of states as the focus of political authority is in decline. The issue is what will fill this power vacuum. For the moment, one scholar sees "a ramshackle assembly of conflicting sources of authority" and argues that, "The diffusion of authority away from national governments has left a yawning hole of nonauthority" (Strange, 1997:199,14). If this is true, where does the alternative road take us?

The answer is uncertain because there are pressures on the state-centric system from two directions (Kaufman, 1997). Some pressures are pushing the system toward greater international cooperation and even supranational governance. This movement toward more global structures is the "McWorld" tendency that we explored in chapter 2 (Barber, 1995). It is based on the buildup of economic and ecological forces that demand cooperation and integration and, thus, are pressing us all into one commercially homogenous global network tied together by technology, ecology, communications, and commerce.

Other pressures, the Jihad tendency, are promoting subnational or transnational political organizations that are vying for the loyalty of individuals and, therefore, undermining the state. Most obviously, there is also a marked strengthening of subnational movements such as multitudinous **ethnonational groups** that demand autonomy or even independence from the states in which they reside. This is evident in the breakups of Czechoslovakia, the Soviet Union, and Yugoslavia, the separatist movement in Quebec, and ethnic conflict in Burundi, Chechnya, and elsewhere. There is also, as we shall see in chapter 5, an increase in the appeal of such transnational identifications as religion and even gender for the primary political identification of individuals.

Where will all this lead? Perhaps the most common estimation of scholars straddles these views. According to this synthesis, states will still be important, but so will be supranational and subnational structures. Scholars have not settled on a name for what they foresee. Chapter 2 used the term "modified multipolar." The term "modified" reflects the belief of many scholars that the state will, at the very least, no longer be the unchallenged core of the international system. Instead it will have to compete for political legitimacy and power with rising subnational, transnational, and international actors (Rosenau, 1997). One study uses "polyarchy" to describe such a system, one made up of "many communities, spheres of influence, hegemonic imperiums, interdependencies, trans-state loyalties" but with "no clearly dominant axis of alignment and antagonism and [with] no central steering group or agency" (Brown, 1988:242). Like Barber, Brown (pp. 260, 263) thinks that the future could hold either a system of "anarchy, where raw power is the principal social arbiter" or a hierarchical system dominated by "international and transnational webs of political accountability, many of them global in scope." Unlike Barber, Brown is unsure about which will prevail. Brown (p. 243) can only tell us that the future "has not been predetermined" and that "which of the variants does emerge will depend on the choices and commitments made by politically influential groups in the years ahead." On that we can all agree.

State-Level Analysis

State-level analysis, a second approach to understanding world politics, emphasizes the national states and their internal processes as the primary determinants of the course of world affairs. As such, this approach focuses on midrange factors that are less general than the macroanalysis of the international system but less individualistic than the microanalytical focus of human-level analysis.

Understanding State-Level Analysis

One way to understand state-level analysis is to contrast it with system-level analysis. Both state-level analysts and system-level analysts recognize that states have long been and continue to be the most powerful actors on the world stage.

Unlike system-level analysts, however, who believe that the international system pressures states to behave in certain ways, state-level analysts contend that states are relatively free to decide what policies to follow. A state-level analyst would say, "Yes, all countries must deal with the realities of the world system," but, "No, not even the least powerful state is a puppet on the string of the international system" (Elman, 1995). In sum, state-level analysts concentrate on what countries do and how they decide which policy to follow.

Studying *what countries do* is based on the view, as one study puts it, that "much of what goes on in world politics evolves around interactions between governments—two or more states trying to gauge the rationales behind the other's actions and anticipate its next move" (Hermann & Hagan, 1998:133). These interactions are called events. Country A does something (an event), country B reacts (another event), country A responds (a third event), and so on. Such simple dyadic (two-sided) relationships, as well as the more common ones involving many countries, are studied through *event data analysis* (Schrodt, 1995), which uses quantitative methodology to depict and analyze international relations as a series of events. Event data analysis is useful for analyzing matters such as reciprocity between countries. For example, if country A makes a conciliatory gesture (event) during a dispute with country B, how will country B respond (event)? By analyzing many such actions and reactions, it is possible, in this case, to determine whether acts of good will are likely to engender responding acts of good will (as idealists contend) or whether acts of good will are apt to be perceived as weakness to be taken advantage of by opponents (as realists suspect).

Analyzing *how countries decide* to adopt one or another policy is the second concern of state-level analysts. Once again to contrast system- and state-level analyses, a system-level analyst would contend that, for example, the U.S. military response to Iraq's invasion of Kuwait was almost inevitable, given the realities of where oil was produced and consumed in the system. A state-level analyst would differ strongly and insist that the U.S. response depended on the presidential-congressional relations, the strength of public opinion, and other factors internal to the United States. Therefore, state-level analysts would conclude that to understand the foreign policy of any country, it is necessary to understand that country's domestic factors and its decision-making processes (Milner, 1997; Maoz, 1996). These factors, state-level analysts say, combine to determine how states act and, by extension, how the international system works as a sum of these actions.

Making Foreign Policy: Types of Government, Situations, and Policy

If you were to ask people how foreign policy is made, many would reply that presidents or prime ministers decide, and it is done. In reality, decision making is usually a complex process. Sometimes the national leader may be pivotal, but more often the leader does not play a decisive role (Hudson & Vore, 1995). One way to begin to see the limits of even powerful leaders is to examine the authority of President Franklin Delano Roosevelt and the power of Lilliputians.

Roosevelt was an epic leader who led his country to victory over both the Great Depression and Hitler. Historians have rated him as one of the three best American presidents. To us, FDR seems to have been very much in charge. Roosevelt was, however, less assured. He often felt fettered by the restraints put on him by the bureaucracy, Congress, public opinion, and other factors.

FDR grumbled often about the bureaucracy, especially the N-A-A-A-V-Y, as he sometimes pronounced it derisively. "To change anything in the N-A-A-A-V-Y," Roosevelt once lamented, "is like punching a feather bed. You punch it with your right and you punch it with your left until you are finally exhausted, and then you find the damn bed just as you left it before you started punching" (DiClerico, 1979:107). Sometimes the Navy would not even tell him what it was up to. "When I woke up this morning," FDR fumed on another occasion, "the first thing I saw was a headline . . . that our Navy was going to spend two billion dollars on a shipbuilding program. Here I am, the Commander-in-Chief of the Navy, having to read about that for the first time in the press" (Sherill, 1979:217).

Congress also restrained Roosevelt. Isolationist legislators hampered his attempts to aid the Allies against the Axis powers before Pearl Harbor. Toward the end of the war, Congress threatened to block his dream of a United Nations. Diplomat Charles Bohlen (1973:210) has recalled FDR bitterly denouncing senators as "a bunch of obstructionists" and declaring that "the only way to do anything in the American government [is] to bypass the Senate."

Public opinion was also isolationist and further restrained Roosevelt in his desire to help the Allied powers. When one adviser urged FDR to take stronger action, he demurred, "I am doing everything possible, although I am not talking very much about it because a certain element in the press . . . would undoubtedly pervert it, attack it, and confuse the public mind" (Paterson, Clifford, & Hagan, 1995:215).

Roosevelt did not see himself, then, as the dominant figure that we remember him to be. He knew that to lead the country he had to get it to follow him. "I dream dreams," he once said, "but [I] am, at the same time, an intensely practical person" (Paterson, Clifford, & Hagan, 1995:209). Indeed, he might have compared himself to Gulliver in Jonathan Swift's classic tale.

The shipwrecked Gulliver was washed ashore in Lilliput. Although the Lilliputians were only a few inches high, Gulliver awoke to find himself bound by countless tiny ropes. He could have broken any one of them, but he could not free himself from all of them.

The point is that, like Gulliver, the freedom of all foreign policy decision makers, whether in democratic or dictatorial states, is limited by an intricate web of governmental and societal restraints (Siverson & Starr, 1994). To understand this web, we will explore three general aspects of foreign policy making. This section focuses on how differences in the type of government, the type of policy, or the type of situation influence the policy process. Then the next two sections will deal with the impact of political culture on foreign policy and the roles of the various political actors in making foreign policy.

Types of Government

One variable that affects the foreign policy process is a country's type of domestic political system. Classifying political systems, such as democratic and authoritarian governments, is important as a preliminary step to studying how they vary in policy and process. Doing this is important because there is strong evidence that differences in the process (how policy is decided) will result in differences in policy substance (which policy is adopted).

Democratic and Authoritarian Governments   There is no precise line between democracy and authoritarianism. There are, for example, degrees of democracy, with one scholar distinguishing between "consensual domination" democracies, "in which a small group actually rules and mass participation in decision making is confined to leadership choice in elections carefully managed by competing elites," and "popular democracies," in which there is "a dispersal through society of political power" that can be used for effective change (Robinson, 1996:49, 57). Many scholars believe that the two types of government are apt to make different foreign policy choices (Cohen, 1995). One standard is *how many and what types of people can participate* in making political decisions. In countries such as Canada, political participation is extensive, with few adults formally excluded from the political process. In other countries, such as China, participation is limited to an elite based on an individual's political party, economic standing, or some other factor (Nathan, 1998).

How many forms of participation are available is a second criterion for judging forms of government. Political dissent in the United States is public, frequent, often strident, and touches on issues ranging from the president's foreign and domestic policies through his personal life. The travails of President Clinton with Paula Jones, Monica Lewinsky, and other women certainly demonstrate this. China, by contrast, tolerates very little open disagreement with policy (Fewsmith, 1994). This was illustrated dramatically in 1989, when students led protest demonstrations in Beijing's Tiananmen Square and elsewhere in China. Soon tanks rolled into the square and crushed the students—politically and literally.

These ultra-Orthodox Jews are holding a protest rally against what they view as antireligious rulings by the Israeli Supreme Court. In a democratic state, such as Israel, sectarian differences at times cause significant cleavages in the domestic political scene, but they can be openly expressed.

Democracy and Foreign Policy Choices   Differences between democracy and autocracy are important to international relations because they can have a foreign policy impact. We noted earlier that how many and what types of people can participate effectively in making political decisions is one standard by which to judge whether or not a country is democratic and, if so, how democratic it is. There are a number of ways to explore the impact of expanding policy making to allow more people and types of people to have an important voice. One way, which you will see later in this chapter, is to examine differences between average citizens and leaders. There frequently is a gap.

   Gender provides another relevant standard of democracy. Despite some progress by women, males continue to dominate political decision making globally (Jeffreys-Jones, 1995). Some scholars argue that the underrepresentation of women in the political process has substantive impacts on policy. There is, for example, the view that aggression is associated with maleness. The feminist perspective, in the words of one advocate, "strips the [state] security core naked so that we can see its masculine-serving guises." These, the analyst comments, are "all gussied up with holsters bristling nuclear weapons, spittoons ready to catch the waste (maybe)," and other affectations that strike her as a macho effort to "continually restage the oft-caricatured OK Corral scene in Tombstone, Arizona, where believers now gather to hear soulful renditions of a shoot-out in a lawless place" (Sylvester, 1993:823). If this

FIGURE
Use of Military Force and the Gender Gap: The Persian Gulf War

gender gap is the case, then the greater the role of women in policy making, the less likely a country is to be bellicose.

Such theorizing and examination of data has led one scholar to conclude that women were more averse to supporting military action because "in international conflict situations, females may tend to perceive more negative risk, more potential harm, and they also may view such losses as more certain than do males" (Brandes, 1993:5).

Types of Situations

Whether in democracies or nondemocracies, policy is not always made the same way. Situation is one variable that determines the exact nature of the foreign policy process. **Crisis situations** are one factor that affects how policy is made (Haney, 1995). A crisis is a circumstance in which decision makers are surprised by an event, feel threatened, and believe that they have only a short time in which to make a decision. One trait of the policy process during a crisis is that decisions tend to be made by relatively small groups made up of high-level political leaders. Public opinion is apt to rally in support of whatever action the political leaders take. During noncrisis policy making, other subnational actors (such as the legislature, interest groups, and the public) are more likely to be active and influential.

Also, during a crisis leaders usually strive to make rational decisions. But the leaders' ability to gather and analyze information is hampered by the exigency of time. This and the anxiety or anger engendered by a crisis often also increase the emotional content of decisions. With limited information and time to think, and with elevated emotions, decision makers rely heavily on preexisting images. "During fast-moving events those at the center of decision are overwhelmed by floods of reports compounded of conjecture, knowledge, hope, and worry," Henry A. Kissinger (1979:627) has recalled from his years as national security adviser and secretary of state. "These must then be sieved through [the decision makers'] preconceptions. Only rarely does a coherent picture emerge."

Another situational variable that scholars have explored distinguishes between whether the situation fits the existing pattern of relations or portends a radical change. **Status quo situations** are those that fall within existing world patterns. Since there is an inertia in all large organizations, governments are likely to analyze problems in terms of the conventional wisdom and to choose policies that follow established precedent or make only minor changes. This is called incremental policy. It tends to evoke little dissent and to rest with the executive. **Non–status quo situations**, by contrast, occur when a country faces circumstances that diverge markedly from previous, familiar patterns. Such situations require significant changes in policy direction and tend to evoke much stronger debate and to involve a wider array of subnational actors, such as legislatures.

Types of Policy

How foreign policy is decided also varies according to the nature of the **issue area** involved. This type of analysis rests on the idea that issues that address different subject areas will be decided by different decision makers and by different processes (Hey, 1995a). One theory about policy making holds that presidents, premiers, and other leaders have greater power to decide foreign policy than they do to determine domestic policy. The latter area is one in which legislatures, interest groups, and even public opinion play a greater role. Agreement on whether this theory is true or not has so far eluded scholars (Parsons, 1994).

One explanation for this lack of consensus may be that many policies are neither purely domestic nor purely foreign. Instead they have elements of both policy types and constitute a third type called **intermestic** policy. Foreign trade is a classic example of an intermestic issue because it affects both international relations and the domestic economy in terms of jobs, prices, and other factors (Lohmann & O'Halloran, 1994; Nolan & Quinn, 1994; Verdier, 1994). The influence of political leaders is less on such intermestic issues because such concerns, like domestic issues, directly impact and activate interest groups, legislators, and other subnational actors more than do foreign policy issues. It follows that presidential leadership is strongest on pure foreign/defense policy issues, weaker on mixed (intermestic) issues, and weakest on pure domestic issues.

The difference between foreign and intermestic policy is evident in the contrasting reactions of Americans in two instances. One is an indisputable foreign policy issue—expanding NATO membership to include three East European countries. The other, an equally clear intermestic issue—President Clinton's request that Congress give him "fast-track" authority to increase free trade and other forms of economic interchange with other countries, with Congress only getting to approve or disapprove, not amend, the agreements. These contrasting policy processes are detailed in the Web site box A Tale of Two Policies.

A FURTHER NOTE
A Tale of
Two Policies

Making Foreign Policy: Political Culture

To repeat an important point, the state is not a unitary structure. Even authoritarian states are complex political organisms. Therefore, as one scholar notes, "All foreign policy decisions occur in a particular domestic context. This environment includes the . . . political culture . . . of a society" (Gerner, 1995:21).

Political culture refers to a society's general, long-held, and fundamental practices and attitudes. It has two main sources. One is the *national historical experience:* the sum of events and practices that have shaped a country and its citizens. The fact that the United States has been invaded only once (in 1812) while China has been invaded many times makes American and Chinese attitudes about the external world very different. The second source of political culture is the *national belief system:* the ideas and ideologies that a people hold. Whether it is capitalism in the United States, Shiism in Iran, Sinocentrism in China, or Zionism in Israel, these intellectual orientations are important determinants of how a country defines what is good and bad and decides its policy (Hudson, 1997; Lapid & Kratochwil, 1996).

A number of things should be noted about the impact of political culture on foreign policy. First, political culture does not usually create specific policy. Instead, political culture is apt to pressure leaders or allow them to move or not move in a general direction (Breuning, 1995). In this sense, political culture is important in establishing a country's broad sense of its national interest. Second, political culture changes. Shifts are usually evolutionary, though, because much of a country's political culture is rooted far back in its history and is resistant to change.

Third, a society's political culture is not monolithic (Shamir & Arian, 1994). American political culture, for example, includes both liberal humanitarian and isolationist impulses. These have created inconsistency in American feelings about whether or not to intervene in such places as Bosnia. Moreover, the leadership of a country may come from a limited segment of the society that does not have the same values as the general public. Some people question, for instance, how accurately American political culture is reflected in the U.S. government.

Making Foreign Policy: Actors in the Process

No state (national actor) is a unitary structure, a so-called black box. Instead, the state is more of a "shell" that encapsulates a foreign policy process in which many **subnational actors** take part. These subnational actors include political executives, bureaucracies, legislatures, political opposition, interest groups, and the people. It is the pattern of cooperation and conflict among these subnational actors that constitutes the internal foreign policy-making process.

Political Executives

The beginning of this chapter showed President Franklin Roosevelt's frustrations with the limitations on his authority. Yet it can also be said that **political executives** (officials whose tenure is variable and dependent on the political contest for power in their country) are normally the strongest subnational actors in the foreign policy process. These leaders are located in the executive branch and are called president, prime minister, premier, chancellor, or perhaps king or emir.

Whatever their specific title, political executives have important legal, or *formal,* powers. Most chief executives are, for example, designated as the commanders in chief of their countries' armed forces. This gives them important and often unilateral authority to use the military. Political executives also frequently possess important *informal* powers. Their personal prestige is often immense, and skillful leaders can use their public standing to win political support for their policies.

The foreign policy-making predominance of political executives even in democratic countries has many causes. First, kings traditionally directed foreign and military affairs, and they kept that authority long after they began

As the torch of South African political leadership is passed from Nelson Mandela to Thabo Mbeki, so too is the power of black majority rule in this once racially segregated society.

to lose control of domestic affairs to parliaments. Second, there is a widespread (albeit controversial) feeling, one analysis contends, that "the [successful] conduct of foreign policy . . . requires a concentration of executive power" (Spanier & Uslaner, 1993:1). Third, foreign policy often sparks only limited activity by other subnational actors, who tend to concentrate instead on domestic issues that affect them directly. The growing intermestic nature of issues is, however, encouraging wider subnational-actor participation in foreign policy making. Fourth, most political leaders have important advantages over other subnational actors. One edge that presidents have is the ability to act, while legislatures can only debate and vote. Another advantage is that heads of government can command much greater information-gathering and analysis resources than any other actor.

Yet it is also true that presidents and premiers are not absolute monarchs. The spread of democracy and the increasingly intermestic nature of policy in an independent world mean that political leaders must often be in a **two-level game** (Boyer, 1999; Mo, 1994). The idea of a two-level game is that in order to be successful diplomats have to negotiate with other countries at the international level and with legislators, bureaucrats, interest groups, and the public on the domestic level. Reflecting this reality, one former U.S. official has recalled that "during my tenure as Special Trade Representative, I spent as much time negotiating with domestic constituents (both industry and labor) and members of the U.S. Congress as I did negotiating with our foreign trading partners" (Lindsay, 1994:292).

Bureaucracies

Every state, whatever its strength or type of government, is heavily influenced by its **bureaucracy**. Although the dividing line between decision makers and bureaucrats is often hazy, we can say that bureaucrats are career governmental personnel, as distinguished from those who are political appointees or elected officials.

Although political leaders legally command the bureaucracy, they frequently complain that it is difficult to control the vast understructure of their governments. "One of the hardest things" about being president, Ronald Reagan grumbled, "is to know that down there, underneath, is a permanent structure that's resisting everything you're doing." Similarly, Mikhail Gorbachev lashed out against a bureaucracy dominated by "conservative sentiments, inertia, [and] a tendency to brush aside everything that does not fit into conventional patterns." And China's Zhao Ziyang agreed that the "unwieldiness of government organs, confusion of their responsibilities, and buck-passing" are "a serious problem in the political life of our party and state" (Rourke, 1990:131). Each of these leaders cast a long shadow on the world stage in his day; each also felt beset by his supposedly subordinate bureaucracy.

An organization's perceptions will cause it, consciously or not, to try to shape policy according to its views. Bureaucracies influence policy decisions by advocating particular policy choices, filtering information, tailoring recommendations to fit the bureaucracy's preference, and implementing policy in ways that alter policy direction.

Policy advocacy is evident when a bureaucratic organization favors one policy option over another based on their general sense of their unit's mission and how they should conduct themselves. How any given policy will affect the organization is also an important factor in creating bureaucratic perspective. Often what a given bureaucracy will or will not favor makes intuitive sense. The military of any country will almost certainly oppose arms reductions or defense-spending cuts because such policies reduce the military bureaucracy's resources and influence. But the stereotypic view that the military is always gung ho to go to war is not accurate. Whether the area was Bosnia, Haiti, or elsewhere, the U.S. military has been a main center of opposition within the Clinton administration to intervention. A common view, expressed by former chairman of the Joint Chiefs of Staff General Colin Powell, is that "politicians start wars. Soldiers fight and die in them."[3]

Filtering information is one method that bureaucracies use to influence policy. Decision makers depend on supporting organizations for information, but what facts they are told depends on what subordinates believe and what they choose, consciously or not, to pass on. Occasionally, for example, bureaucrats are reluctant to give their superiors upsetting or discordant information. National security adviser Henry Kissinger urged the secretaries of state and defense at one point "to talk affirmatively to the President [Nixon], stop discouraging him. Above all, don't . . . take big problems to the President" (Ambrose, 1991:32). Subordinates also may be afraid that unwelcome news will endanger their careers. In the 1960s, amid the anticommunist consensus of the cold war, one U.S. official recalls, "candid reporting of the strengths of the Viet Cong and the weaknesses of the [U.S.-backed South Vietnamese] Diem government was inhibited" by the fear that any diplomat or intelligence analyst who suggested that the communists might win would be dismissed as weak-minded or, worse, as "soft on communism" (Thompson, 1989:593).

Recommendations are another source of bureaucratic influence on foreign policy. Bureaucracies are the source of considerable expertise, which they use to push the agency's preferred position. One scholar, after analyzing bureaucratic recommendations in several countries, concluded that leaders often faced an "option funnel." This means that advisers narrow the range of options available to leaders by presenting to them only those options that the adviser's bureaucratic organization favors. The options and capabilities developed according to the bureaucracy's "cultural penchant," the analyst continued, "often decided what national leaders would do even before they considered a situation" (Legro, 1996:133).

Implementation is another powerful bureaucratic tool. There are a variety of ways that bureaucrats can influence policy by the way that they carry it out. Most often, bureaucrats misunderstand or unconsciously misinterpret policy, based on their own preferences. Sometimes they consciously attempt to delay, change, or ignore a decision or try to seize the initiative and act on their own. The world teetered closer to nuclear war during the Cuban missile crisis of 1962, and an implementation decision by a relatively low-level bureaucrat almost pushed the world over the edge. At one point during the tense two-week period, a Soviet surface-to-air (SAM) missile battery in Cuba shot down a U.S. U-2 intelligence-gathering plane. President John F. Kennedy and other decision makers in the White House were convinced that such a bellicose and dangerous act could only be a deliberate escalation ordered from the very highest level in Moscow. The Soviets have upped "the price," and they've escalated "the action," one of Kennedy's advisers told him. "This is much of an escalation by them, isn't it?" the president agreed (Chang, 1992:145). As it turns out, the perilous missile launch had not been ordered by Soviet leader Nikita Khrushchev or anyone else in Moscow. It had not even come at the command of the Soviet military commander in Cuba, General Issa Pliyev. Instead, the authority to fire was given to the battery commander by a subordinate officer on General Pliyev's staff when the general could not be found. Because the White House interpreted the shooting down of the U-2 as a deliberate escalation directed by the Kremlin, Washington warned Moscow that another attack on a U-2 would bring about a retaliatory military strike. That strike would have almost certainly been against a SAM site in Cuba, with U.S. warplanes bombing Soviet battery personnel. World War III might have resulted "all because a relatively junior Soviet officer took it upon himself to act."

Legislatures

In all countries, the foreign policy role of legislatures is less than that of executive-branch decision makers and bureaucrats. That does not mean that all legislatures are powerless. They are not, but their exact influence varies greatly among countries. Legislatures in nondemocratic systems generally rubber-stamp the decisions of the political leadership. China's National People's Congress, for example, does not play a significant role in foreign policy making.

Even in democratic countries, however, legislatures are inhibited by many factors. One of these is tradition. The leadership has historically run foreign policy in virtually all countries, especially in time of war or other crises. Second, there is the axiom that "politics should stop at the water's edge." The belief is that a unified national voice is important to a successful foreign policy. This is particularly true during a crisis, when there is the aforementioned tendency to support the political leaders and to view dissent as bordering on treason. This rally effect applies to more than specific issues; it extends to a more general support of presidential foreign policy, at least for a short time. Third, the tradition of executive dominance has led to executives normally being given extensive constitutional power over foreign policy. In Great Britain, for example, a declaration of war does not require the consent of Parliament. Fourth, legislators tend to focus on domestic affairs because, accurately or not, voters perceive domestic issues as more important and make voting decisions based in part on the legislator's domestic record rather than on his or her foreign policy stands. Indeed, paying too much attention to international affairs leaves legislators open to the electoral charge that they are not sufficiently minding their constituents' interests.

None of this means that legislatures do not sometimes play an important role in foreign affairs and have a range of potent powers, such as the ability to appropriate or withhold funds (Bacchus, 1997). Legislative activity is especially likely and important when a high-profile issue captures public attention and public opinion opposes the president's policy. Congress was one of the factors that pushed the Nixon administration to get out of Vietnam and the Clinton administration to withdraw from Somalia. In the earlier case, as is typical, members of the president's own political party were worried that continuing the war would spell disaster to Republican electoral fortunes. "We have got to have the people of the United States convinced that the war is over by this fall, or we [Republicans] are out of business," the Republican Senate leader, Howard Baker, told President Nixon in 1971. "I agree with your political assessment," Nixon replied. "I am keenly aware of the problem."[4]

Even more commonly, intermestic issues are involved that directly affect constituents and interest groups in the legislators' electoral districts and spark legislative activity. As one member of the U.S. Congress put it, "Increasingly all foreign policy issues are becoming domestic issues. As a reflection of the public input, Congress is demanding to play a greater role."[5]

Political Opposition

In every political system, those who are in power face rivals who would replace them, either to change policy or to gain power. In democratic systems, this opposition is legitimate and is organized into political parties (Breuning, 1996; Noël & Thérien, 1996). Rival politicians may also exist in the leader's own party. Opposition is less overt and/or less peaceful in nondemocratic systems, but it exists nonetheless and in many varied forms. One distinction divides opposition between those who merely want to change policy and those who want to gain control of the government. A second division is between those who are located inside and outside of the government. Just one example of how political opposition can influence foreign policy is contained in the Web site box entitled Frustration-Aggression Analysis and Russia's Future.

A FURTHER NOTE
Frustration-Aggression
Analysis and
Russia's Future

Interest Groups

Interest groups are private (nongovernmental) associations of people who have similar policy views and who pressure the government to adopt those views as policy. Traditionally, interest groups were generally considered to be less active and influential on foreign policy than on domestic policy issues because foreign policy often had only a limited effect on the groups' domestic-oriented concerns. The increasingly intermestic nature of policy is changing that, and interest groups are becoming a more important part of the foreign policy–making process. We can see this by looking at several types of interest groups.

Cultural groups are one type. Many countries have ethnic, racial, religious, or other cultural groups that have emotional or political ties to another country. For instance, as a country made up mostly of immigrants, the United States is populated by many who maintain a level of identification with their African, Cuban, Irish, Mexican, Polish, and other heritages and who are active on behalf of policies that favor their ancestral homes. The continuing U.S. pressure on Cuba, for instance, is partly the result of the sentiment in the Cuban community in Florida against the communist government of Fidel Castro. Florida is a key state in U.S. presidential elections and, as a Clinton administration official explains, "There are no votes riding on how we deal with Indonesia, . . . [but] Castro is still political dynamite."[6]

Economic groups are another prominent form of interest activity. They make contradictory demands for both protection from foreign competition and for pressure on other governments to open up their markets. As international trade increases, both sales overseas and competition from other countries are vital matters to many companies. They lobby their home governments for favorable domestic legislation and for support when a company is having a dispute with the government of a host country in which it is operating. Strong pressure from a generally united business community, for example, has repeatedly helped persuade President Clinton not to order trade sanctions on China for such transgressions as violations of human rights and shipping missiles and nuclear weapons-applicable technology to other countries. "Profit Motive Gets the Nod," a newspaper headline explained at one such juncture.[7]

Issue-oriented groups make up another category. Groups of this type are not based on any narrow socioeconomic category such as ethnicity or economics. Instead they draw their membership from people who have a common policy goal. The concerns of issue-oriented groups run the gamut from the very general to the specific. Some groups concentrate on one or a few specific issues. The United Nations Association of the United States brings together

Americans who support the UN. At the general end of the spectrum, the Council on Foreign Relations draws together some 1,500 influential (elite) Americans who hold an internationalist point of view, and the council's journal, *Foreign Affairs,* serves as a forum for circulating the view of the elite. As Deputy Secretary of State Strobe Talbott says of the journal, "Virtually everyone I know in the foreign policy/national security area of government is attentive to it."[8]

Transnational interest groups also deserve mention. Some of these are nongovernmental organizations (NGOs) of like-minded individuals from many countries who pool their resources to press their own and other governments to adopt policies desired by the group. Transnational corporations also conduct extensive lobbying efforts in countries where they have interests (Mitchell, 1995; Rehbein, 1995). Many foreign countries also try to influence specific policy in other countries or, more generally, to project a positive image (Schoenbaum, 1993).

FIGURE
Leaders and the Public: Percentage Saying "Yes"

The People

The vast majority of citizens in any country do not have a direct say in policy making. Yet they play a role. This role is obviously more important in democratic systems than in authoritarian systems, but there is no system in which the public is totally ignored by leaders. To discuss the people's role, we will look at three factors: variations in opinion interest and opinion, the quality of public opinion, and the influence of public opinion on foreign policy (Powlick & Katz, 1998).

Variations in Opinion and Opinion Interest International events and issues do not consistently command the attention of most citizens. Insofar as people are concerned with politics, they are normally focused on domestic pocketbook issues such as unemployment and taxes or social issues such as abortion. One study of the interest expressed by Americans in various news stories during 1997, found that of the top 25 stories, there was only one (the crisis with Iraq over UN inspections) related to international affairs.[9]

Also, foreign affairs issues are not normally the determining factor in how the average citizen votes. For example, an exit poll of Russians during the presidential election in 1996 found that only 2 percent of the voters said that foreign policy was the most important issue that influenced their choice.[10]

Sometimes, however, the broad public focus is on foreign policy. There is also a segment of the public, the "attentive public," that regularly pays attention to world events (Krosnick & Telhami, 1995). It is accurate to say, then, that public opinion runs the gamut from being interested in to being oblivious to foreign policy, depending on the situation and the issues. Crises will engage a significant segment of the population's attention. So will intermestic policies. Pure foreign policy issues that are not crises will engender much less attention.

The Influence of Public Opinion on Foreign Policy Whatever the divisions or quality of public opinion may be, the key matter is its impact on foreign policy. To a degree, the interest of the public and impact of its opinion rise and fall according to the situation and the policy issue, as discussed earlier. It is also the case that the impact of public opinion varies among countries. One study of public opinion in four democracies found that it had the greatest impact on policy in the United States, with progressively declining influence in then-West Germany, Japan, and France (Risse-Kappen, 1991).

INTERACTIVE EXERCISE
Attitudes in Foreign Policy–Decision Making

There are direct and indirect channels, as noted in chapter 1, of public influence on policy. Occasionally, the public gets to decide an issue directly through the use of referendums. Use of **direct democracy** is still limited, but it is growing. In 1994, for example, voters in Austria, Finland, and Sweden voted to join the EU; Norwegian voters rejected membership.

Indirect influence is more common and occurs in several ways. Most foreign policy makers, especially those in democratic countries, are politicians. First, voters sometimes get to choose among candidates who have different foreign policy goals and priorities (Jackman & Miller, 1995). The decision by Israeli voters in 1999 to replace Benjamin Netanyahu with Ehud Barak as prime minister had a great deal to do with the candidates' divergent views about how to deal with security and with the Arab world. Second, whatever the exact level of public interest may be, politicians are prone to believe that the public is watching and that if they ignore it or have it turn against them, they will suffer during the next election. Secretary of State James A. Baker III recalls in his 1995 memoirs that during the Persian Gulf crisis in 1990 he told President Bush that it "has all the ingredients that brought down three of the last five presidents: a hostage crisis, body bags, and a full-fledged recession caused by $40 [a barrel] oil."[11] Third, policy makers believe that the chances of foreign policy success overseas are enhanced by public opinion support at home. Fourth, in democracies, most policy makers believe that public opinion is a legitimate factor that should be considered when determining which policy is to be adopted. For all these reasons, public opinion does count, particularly when the people are strongly for or against a policy (Foyle, 1997; Powlick, 1995).

Individual-Level Analysis

The fundamental task of the remainder of this chapter is to identify the general characteristics of human **decision making**, to seek to elucidate patterns in the way that humans make decisions. This includes gathering information, analyzing that information, establishing goals, pondering options, and making policy choices. Decision making is a complex process that relates to many of the human traits and organizational settings that we have explored or will examine in this and other chapters.

The human role in the world drama can be addressed from three different perspectives. One is to consider human nature, to examine fundamental human characteristics that affect decisions. Organizational behavior is the second perspective. This looks at how humans interact within organized settings, such as a decision-making group. Third, the human behavior perspective explores how the idiosyncratic motivations and perceptions of specific humans affect foreign policy.

Individual-Level Analysis: Human Nature

The central concern of the human nature perspective is how fundamental human characteristics influence policy. The basic fact to begin with is that humans have limited and flawed decision-making abilities because they are unable intellectually and physically to learn and process all the information required to make fully rational decisions. Moreover, we humans have emotions that warp our judgment. These human limits apply to political leaders, as well as to the rest of us. Sometimes, for instance, presidents simply get angry. President Jimmy Carter was frustrated over his inability to free the hostages whom Iran seized in 1979. His anger was compounded by protesting Iranian students who had traveled from their U.S. colleges to Washington. Carter fumed at having "to sit here and bite my lip . . . and look impotent" while "those bastards [are] humiliating our country in front of the White House." If I "wasn't president," Carter growled to an aide, I would go "out on the streets myself" and "take a swing" at any demonstrator "I could get my hands on" (Vandenbroucke, 1991:364). Of course Carter was president and could not punch out an Iranian demonstrator. Instead, he sent the ill-fated hostage rescue mission. Pent-up anger was certainly part of that decision. The point is that there is no such thing as a truly rational decision, be it your decision about which college to attend or President Carter's plan to rescue the hostages in Tehran. To study the limits on rationality, we can examine cognitive, psychological, and biological factors in decision making.

Cognitive Factors

Decision making is one of the most complex things that political scientists study. At its most abstract, decision-making analysis is involved with *cybernetics,* which is the study of control and communications systems. Since no human even approaches a perfect cybernetic system, another important term is **cognitive decision making.** This means that humans necessarily make decisions within the limits of what they consciously know and are willing to consider (Geva & Mintz, 1997; Rosati, 1995). Since there are many external and internal barriers or boundaries to what a decision maker knows or even can know, cognitive decision making is also called "bounded rationality." External boundaries include such factors as missing or erroneous information and the inability of any decision maker to know for sure what decision makers in another country are thinking or how they will react to various policy options. Internal boundaries that account for cognitive limits on decision makers include their intellectual and physical limits. No decision maker has the vast intellectual or physical capacity to analyze completely the mass and complexity of information that is available. Emotions are another all-too-human internal restraint on rational decision making. People regularly ignore unwelcome information or reject a policy option that they find emotionally unacceptable.

To see the difficulty of making a purely rational decision, recall your decision about which college to attend. Surely you did not just flip a coin, but did you consider all colleges worldwide, analyzing each according to cost, location, social atmosphere, class size, faculty qualifications, living arrangements, and program requirements? Did you consult a wide range of experts? Did you ignore such emotional factors as how far away from home the school was and how that interacted with your desire to be near, or perhaps far away from, your family, friends, or romantic partner? The answer, of course, is that you did not do all these things fully. Instead, you probably conducted a relatively limited rational review of information and options, then factored in irrational emotional considerations. You also relied on fate, because part of your happiness and success at college would depend on things (such as with whom you would share your dorm room) that were unknowable when you applied. Thus you made one of the more important decisions of your life with a significant degree of bounded rationality.

Foreign policy decisions are also made within the limits of bounded rationality. Therefore, a key issue involves how policy makers cope with various cognitive limits on rational decision making. Four of the many mental strategies to cope with cognitive limits are seeking cognitive consistency (trying to fit information into your own frame of reference), wishful thinking (believing that a policy choice will work because of the emotional stake you have in the decision once made), limiting the scope of the decision (making small or incremental decisions to avoid big mistakes), and using heuristic devices (such as stereotypes or historical analogies to simplify the world around you).

Psychological Factors

Theories that focus on the common psychological traits of humankind also help to explain political behavior. *Frustration-aggression theory* is one such approach. It contends that frustrated societies sometimes become collectively aggressive. It is possible to argue, for example, that mass frustration promoted the rise of Adolf Hitler and German aggression in World War II. Germany's capitulation at the end of World War I left many Germans bewildered. They had defeated Russia earlier, and their army was still in France when the war ended. Germans were embittered further by the harsh economic and political terms imposed by victors, the resulting 1,700 percent inflation and economic devastation of Germany during the 1920s, and the treatment of the country as a political pariah. Hitler seized on the Germans' pent-up anger by telling them that their plight was the fault of Jewish and Bolshevik conspirators who had ruined Germany's economy and capacity to carry on the war. Rearm and reclaim your proud heritage! Hitler told the Germans. There are only two choices, he proclaimed in *Mein Kampf:* "Germany will be either a world power or it will not be at all." The frustrated German people believed in and rallied behind the prophecy—one that Hitler helped Germany nearly fulfill in both senses.

Similarities between today's Russia and that interwar Germany are worrisome. Russians find it hard to understand how they can have fallen so fast and so far from the rank of an envied superpower to that of an international hardship case. "We've become a Third World country—nobody looks at us with respect any more. Why should they?" one Russian worker frets.[12] Also, as occurred earlier in Germany, many Russians were cast into poverty by many forms of economic turmoil, including sky-high inflation that at one point rose to an annual rate of 2,525 percent and annually averaged (1991–1997) 554 percent. Inflation has now subsided, but many Russians, especially retirees and others on fixed incomes, have been impoverished. One-third of all Russians aged 65 or more have monthly incomes under $20. Russians are also plagued by violent crime, vast corruption, and other socially destabilizing forces (Yavlinsky, 1998). Partly out of despair, the suicide rate in Russia has soared, as has the death rate (often from alcohol abuse) among Russians under 60 years of age. Concomitantly, the birth rate has dropped to one of the world's lowest, and there are many other signs of a sick society. Will frustration engendered by the collapse of Russia's global power, its domestic economy, and many of its social structures lead to aggression? As the Web site box, Frustration-Aggression Analysis and Russia's Future, which we cited earlier, discussed, the answer is uncertain.

Biological Factors

Various biological theories provide yet another way to explain human behavior (Somit & Peterson, 1997). One of the most important issues in human behavior is the so-called "nature versus nurture" controversy. The question is the degree to which human actions are based on animal instinct and other innate emotional and physical drives (nature) or based on socialization and intellect (nurture). With specific regard to politics, *biopolitics* examines the relationship between the physical nature and political behavior of humans. There are a number of biopolitical approaches that can be illustrated by examining two: ethology and gender.

Ethology   The comparison of animal and human behavior is called ethology. Konrad Lorenz (*On Aggression,* 1969), Desmond Morris (*The Naked Ape,* 1967), Robert Ardrey (*The Territorial Imperative,* 1961), and some other ethologists argue that like animals, humans behave in a way that is based partly on innate characteristics. Ardrey (pp. 12–14), for example, has written that "territoriality—the drive to gain, maintain, and defend the exclusive right to a piece of property—is an animal instinct" and that "if man is a part of the natural world, then he possesses as do all other species a genetic . . . territorial drive as one ancient animal foundation for that human conduct known as war."

It is clear that territorial disputes are a common cause of war. To begin with, one study points out, "Most interstate wars are fought or begin between neighbors" (Vasquez, 1995:277). Furthermore, another study concludes that while "the presence of never-resolved territorial disputes does not account for all the interstate wars . . . since 1945, . . . war is a highly probable event in cases where contiguous states . . . disagree about the location of their shared boundary" (Kocs, 1995:173).

There are some territorial clashes that might seem rational to an outsider, but other disputes defy rational explanation. Peru and Ecuador fought a short, inconclusive war in 1995 over a tiny region near the headwaters of the Amazon River. The area is thinly populated, of no strategic and little economic value, and so remote and mountainous that the two sides had trouble getting troops and weapons to the scene of combat. Similarly hard to comprehend to anyone but those involved was the fighting in 1998 between two disparately poor countries, Ethiopia and Eritrea, over tiny bits of territory along their border. It was, said one observer, "like two bald men fighting over a comb."[13]

Gender   A second biopolitical factor that interests many analysts is the possibility that some differences in political behavior are related to gender. An adviser to President Lyndon Johnson has recalled that once when reporters pressed him to explain why the United States was waging war in Vietnam, the president "unzipped his fly, drew out his substantial organ, and declared, 'That is why.' "[14] Such earthy sexual explanations by male leaders are far from rare in private, and they lead some scholars to wonder whether they represent gender-based aggressiveness to policy making or are merely rhetorical and in bad taste.

Political scientists are just beginning to examine the questions of whether or not gender makes a difference in political attitudes and actions of policy makers. A related, more general question is whether any gender differences that do exist are inherent (biological, genetic) or the product of differences in male and female socialization (Togeby, 1994). The ultimate question is whether an equal representation of women among policy makers or, even more radically, a reversal of tradition that would put women firmly in charge of foreign and defense policy would make an appreciable difference in global affairs. Many scholars, especially of the feminist school of thought, answer yes and say that the change would be for the good. Certainly there is good evidence, as noted earlier in this chapter, that women in the mass public are less likely to countenance war than men. The attitudes of women who are in positions of authority may be much different, though. So far only about two dozen of them have been elected to lead countries, although that number is slowly growing, as is evident in the map on the Web site. Yet, even when past queens who had real power—such as Elizabeth I of England and Catherine the Great of Russia—are included, the relative scarcity of female international leaders makes comparisons with their male counterparts difficult. There can be no doubt, though, that able, sometimes aggressive, leadership has been evident in such modern heads of government as Israel's Golda Meir and India's Indira Gandhi (Caprioli & Boyer, 1999).

MAP
Female Heads
of State or
Government
1990–1998

It may also be that violence is particularly likely in some males but not in other males or in females. Work by geneticists on a Dutch extended family with a history of rape, arson, and other violent behaviors by some male family members isolated a mutant gene that was present in the violent males, not present in the nonviolent males, and (for complex genetic reasons) not possible in females. The gene is associated with the body's production of an enzyme, monoamine oxidase-a, that helps regulate the chemicals that allow brain cells to interact. While it is true, as geneticist Hans G. Brunner concedes, that "human behavior like aggression is very complex," his conclusion that "in certain instances a biological factor clearly influences [aggressive] behavior" is provocative.[15]

In sum, then, studies of biopolitics, ethology, gender genetics, and other related approaches are just beginning to probe the connection between biology and politics, and there is still wide disagreement. For example, the idea that maternal instincts may make women more peace-minded is put forward by a study that comments that "if reproductive success is defined in sociobiological terms . . . then females have an interest in the survival and well-being of not only immediate offspring" but, by emotional extension, humanity in general (Schubert, 1993:29). Not correct, concludes another study. It finds that while there are gender differences in attitudes about violence, the differences are "socially constructed and contextually driven" and that "the 'maternalist' hypothesis . . . failed—spectacularly" to explain gender differences (Conover & Sapiro, 1993:1096). From this perspective, the way that males are socialized may help account for both international and interpersonal violence (Ember & Ember, 1996).

**INTERACTIVE
EXERCISE
"So Say the Mamas":
A Feminist World**

The so-called "nature versus nurture" debate continues and presents some fascinating questions, one of which is the basis of the Web site interactive exercise, "So Say the Mamas": A Feminist World. Whatever the exact role of biological factors may be, though, it is important to bear in mind that no one argues that biology is the sole cause of behavior or even that most human behavior is instinctual rather than learned. Furthermore, learning can modify behavior even if it is partly genetic. The basically peaceful conduct of interpersonal relations in domestic societies demonstrates this.

Individual-Level Analysis: Organizational Behavior

A second approach within the general individual-level of analysis is to examine how people act in organizations. Just as our overall cultural setting influences how we behave, so do the more specific pressures of our positions and the dynamics of group interaction affect how we behave. As you will see, organizational behavior significantly influences the decision-making process of the state, which we examined earlier in this chapter. But how humans interact in organizations is a field of study that is also applicable to clubs, business, or any other type of group and is thus more closely related to the study of human nature than to politics as such. Two concepts, "role behavior" and "decision-making group behavior," are useful to discuss how humans act in organizational settings.

Role Behavior

We all play a variety of roles. They are attitudes and behaviors that we adopt depending on the position that we hold. How you act varies depending on whether you are in class, on the job, or in a family situation. You may be a leader in one role, a follower in another. Roles also influence how you think. As a worker you may grouse about high taxes; as a student at a state college you may think the government should put more money into higher education.

Presidents and other policy makers also play roles. The script for a **role** is derived from two sets of expectations about how an actor should think and behave. *Self-expectations* are one important source of a role. Behavior in a given position is based partly on what an individual expects of himself or herself. *Expectations of others* are the second important source of role behavior. We behave in certain ways because of what others expect of us in a particular role. Such expectations are transmitted by cues, or messages, that leaders receive from advisers, critics, and public opinion about how they, in the role of leader, should act. One common role expectation is that leaders be decisive and do things. A leader who approaches a problem by saying "I don't know what to do" or "we can't do anything" will be accused of weakness. Therefore, leaders tend to take action even when it might be better to wait or temporize. Reflecting this role motivation, former secretary of state Dean Rusk (1990:137) has pointed out that "we tended then—and now—to exaggerate the necessity to take action. Given time, many problems work themselves out or disappear."

The Iranian hostage crisis (1979–1981) provides an informative case study of the impact of roles. The positions of most of the principal Washington decision makers influenced their respective views about whether or not to attempt an armed rescue of the hostages. National security adviser Zbigniew Brzezinski told President Carter that "your greater responsibility [than protecting the hostages] is to protect the honor and dignity of our country" (Glad, 1989:47). Carter agreed that this was his presidential role. "I am the president of a great country. I would like to continue to be patient, but it is difficult to do so," he said (Vandenbroucke, 1991:366). Therefore, as president, Carter felt he had to do something, even if it imperiled the hostages. The secretary of defense, the CIA director, and the chairman of the Joint Chiefs of Staff (JCS) were also, as might be expected, proponents of using force to free the hostages. The president's press secretary and his chief of staff also supported the fateful rescue attempt, but for a different reason. They defined their roles as boosting the president's political popularity; the rescue of the hostages would have been a political bonus—one that might have even gotten Carter reelected. The only opposition to action came from the secretary and deputy secretary of state, who cast themselves in the roles of diplomats instead of warriors. It was role-playing that helped determine the course of action that each of the players advocated.

A last point about role is that it is not immutable for any given position. Instead, there is "a more complex, less rigid relationship between role and issue position" than is implied in the old maxim "Where you stand depends on where you sit." Just one of the many variables is that "a powerful individual may bring his or her own well-developed personal style to a position" (Ripley, 1995:91). Several recent studies have highlighted this varying fluid impact of role (Rhodes, 1994). For example, an analysis of decision making in the Dutch government found that while "some ministers consistently took positions that can be explained by their bureaucratic interest [which helps define role]," the views of other ministers "could be better understood in terms of [such factors as] moral commitment. . . . It is therefore not possible to portray Cabinet decision making as simply a clash between diverging bureaucratic interests" (Metselaar & Verbeek, 1996:25).

Group Decision-Making Behavior

People behave differently in organizations than they would act if they were alone. There are complex and extensive theories about decision making in a group setting, but for our purposes here, the most important aspect of organizational decision making is the tendency toward **groupthink** (Hart & Stern, 1997).

Causes of Groupthink The primary cause of groupthink is pressure within decision-making groups to *achieve consensus*. Consensus may be a true meeting of minds, but it also may be the product of leaders and groups ignoring or suppressing dissidents and discordant information and policy options or of the reluctance of subordinates to offer discordant opinions or information.

Ignoring or suppressing dissidents, discordant information, and policy options. Groupthink creates an atmosphere in which discordant information or advice is rejected or ignored. Furthermore, those who dissent are at risk of rejection by the group and its leaders. This pattern was evident in the Carter administration during the hostage crisis with Iran. Carter and his aides waited to make their decision to attempt an armed rescue mission until that option's chief opponent, Secretary of State Cyrus Vance, was out of town. When he learned that he had been left out, Vance insisted on another meeting to press his case. He persuaded no one; he only engendered derision. White House chief of staff Hamilton Jordan has remembered that when Vance finished talking there was an "awkward silence" while the secretary scanned the room, "his eyes begging for support. I fidgeted, feeling sorry for Cy" (Glad, 1989:50–56).

Reluctance of subordinates to offer discordant opinions. While the Vance case shows that overt suppression of dissent occurs, it is not the norm because subordinates are often careful not to contradict what they know or think to be the preferences of the group and, especially, their superiors (Vertzberger, 1994). Experienced officials understand that dissenting, especially once the leader has taken a position, is risky. Therefore, they avoid it in anticipation of negative consequences.

Effects of Groupthink The urge for consensus that characterizes groupthink limits the policy choices available. It also decreases the chances that the policy chosen will prove successful.

Limited policy choices. Anthony Lake, national security adviser to President Clinton, recognizes that "there is a danger that when people work well together [that] you can take the edge off options." This can lead, Lake says, to "groupthink . . . [with] not enough options reaching the president."[16] One way that groupthink may limit policy choices is through **incremental decision making**, which adheres to established policy or makes only marginal changes. One of Lake's predecessors, Zbigniew Brzezinski, has compared foreign policy to "an aircraft carrier. You simply don't send it into a 180-degree turn; at most you move it a few degrees to port or starboard" (Paterson, Clifford, & Hagan, 1995:488).

Another way that groupthink's drive for consensus limits policy choices is that decision makers often adopt the *lowest common denominator* policy. This is the policy that is least objectionable rather than the optimal policy. During the Cuban missile crisis, President Kennedy and his advisers did not decide to blockade Cuba because they thought it was the best thing to do. In fact, few of the decision makers really liked the idea of a blockade. Instead, it was a compromise between those who wanted to use military force to destroy the missiles and those who preferred to use diplomacy to persuade Moscow to withdraw the missiles.

The quality of policy choices. A review of the decisional inadequacies brought on by groupthink leads to the question, *Do poor decisions result in policy failures?* According to one study of nineteen crisis decisions, the answer is Yes. Decision making that falls victim to groupthink invariably does not achieve optimal foreign policy (Herek, Janis, & Huth, 1987). Thus, developing strategies to avoid such decision-making pathologies should improve the quality of policy outputs.

Individual-Level Analysis: Idiosyncratic Behavior

A third approach to individual-level analysis focuses on humans as individuals (Walsh, Best, & Rai, 1995). This approach emphasizes the idiosyncratic characteristics of political leaders (May, 1994). Note that idiosyncratic means individual, not odd. The idiosyncratic approach assumes that individuals make foreign policy decisions and that different individuals are likely to make different decisions. In its simplest form, this approach includes examining biographies and memoirs as political histories. More recently, political scientists, psychologists, and others have written sophisticated "psychobiographies" that explore the motivations of decision makers. Scholars are also using increasingly sophisticated methodologies such as content analysis, which involves analyzing the content of a decision maker's statements and writings to understand the basic ways he or she views the world.

Whatever the specific methodology of such studies, the point is not *what* a leader decided. Rather, the fundamental question is *why* the leader chose certain paths. What are the internal, psychological factors that motivated the decision maker? The list of possible psychological factors is long and varies from analyst to analyst. For our discussion, though, we will consider five basic characteristics of individual decision makers: their personality, their physical and mental health, their egos and ambitions, their sense of political history and personal experiences, and their perceptions.

Personality

The study of this characteristic stems from the belief as one scholar puts it that "the personalities of the leaders—have often been decisive. . . . In all [the studied] cases, a fatal flaw or character weakness in a leader's personality was of critical importance. It may, in fact, have spelled the difference between the outbreak of war and the maintenance of peace" (Stoessinger, 1998:210). There is a substantial body of scholarship on personality types and attributes and their impact on policy. What scholars are interested in is a leader's basic orientations toward self and toward others, behavioral patterns, and attitudes about such politically relevant concepts as authority.

There are numerous categorization schemes. The most well-known of these categorizes political personality along an active-passive scale and a positive-negative scale (Barber, 1985). Active leaders are policy innovators; passive leaders are reactors. Positive personalities have egos strong enough to enjoy (or at least endure equably) the contentious political environment; negative personalities are apt to feel burdened, even abused, by political criticism. Many scholars favor active-positive presidents, but all four types have drawbacks. Activists, for example, may feel compelled to try to solve every problem even though *not* doing something might be preferable. That could be true of President Clinton, whom most political psychology studies categorize as an extremely activist personality, and who himself admits to being "almost compulsively overactive" (Renshon, 1995:59; Greenstein, 1995).

Whatever the best combination may be, there is wide agreement that the worst is active-negative. The more active a leader, the more criticism he or she encounters. Rather than taking criticism in stride, though, the leader assumes that opponents are enemies and may withdraw into an inner circle of subordinates who are supportive and who give an unreal view of events and domestic and international opinion. Adolf Hitler and Josef Stalin and, to a lesser degree, Lyndon Johnson and Richard Nixon were all active-negative personalities who showed symptoms of delusion, struck out at their enemies, and generally developed bunker mentalities.

Physical and Mental Health

A leader's physical and mental health can be important factors in decision making (Park, 1994). For example, President Woodrow Wilson's physical health and associated psychological symptoms may have influenced the Treaty of Versailles that ended World War I. The U.S. Senate rejected the treaty, and many historians believe that Wilson's obdurate refusal to compromise with senators doomed the ratification effort. That in turn blocked U.S. membership in the League of Nations, which might have led to a stabilizing U.S. participation in world events during the 1920s and 1930s. While the causes of

Jesse Jackson is shown here making a personal appeal to Yugoslavian president Slobodan Milosevic for the release of three American prisoners captured during the NATO campaign against Yugoslavia in 1999. Jackson's successful personal diplomacy and Milosevic's decision to oppose NATO in the Balkans illustrate clearly that individuals do matter in world politics.

Wilson's actions are widely debated, it is certain that from childhood to his cataclysmic stroke in October 1919 amid the ratification fight, Wilson suffered cardiovascular difficulties (Saunders, 1994). These, in the estimate of some historians and physicians, caused the president to exhibit the "diminished emotional control, greater egocentricity, increased suspicion and secrecy, and lapses in judgment and memory [that] are common manifestations of cerebral arteriosclerosis" (Weinstein, 1981:323).

Ego and Ambition

The egos and personal ambitions of political leaders also can influence policy. Ego, especially the male variety, which sometimes works to make leaders want to appear tough, may well have figured in the onset of the Persian Gulf War (Renshon, 1993). President George Bush came to office with a reputation for being wishy-washy. Soon the "wimp factor" had become a regular subject of journalistic comment. *Newsweek* magazine, for example, ran a picture of Bush and a banner about the wimp factor on the cover of a 1989 issue. It is possible that an ego-wounded Bush responded by being too tough. He soon invaded Panama, and the following year, during the Persian Gulf crisis, some analysts argued that Bush's fierce determination not to negotiate with Iraq left Baghdad little choice but to fight or capitulate. Certainly, it would be outrageous to claim that Bush decided on war only to assuage his ego, but to ignore the possible role of this factor would be naive. In fact, even after defeating Panama and Iraq, Bush remained testy about the wimp image. Addressing a California audience in June 1991, Bush could expostulate with prickly pride, "You're talking to the wimp . . . to the guy that had a cover of a national magazine, that I'll never forgive, put that label on me" (Rourke, 1993:31).

Political History and Personal Experiences

The past is a fourth factor that shapes a political leader's approach to world problems. Philosopher George Santayana wrote in *The Life of Reason* (1905) that "Those who cannot remember the past are condemned to repeat it." Contemporary policy makers frequently echo that sentiment. "History is a strange teacher," Secretary of State Madeleine Albright has written. "It never repeats itself exactly, but you ignore its general lessons at your peril."[17] The trick of letting history be one's teacher is learning the right lesson. The ability of decision makers to wisely apply the lessons of history is not, however, always evident, as we will see by examining lessons from two types of past: political history and personal experience.

Political History   Historical analogies based on how individuals or even nations interpret historical events and apply their supposed lessons are a regular part of policy making (Houghton, 1994; Lefebvre, 1994). The **Munich analogy** is one such history lesson that figures frequently in policy debates and rationale. When Germany threatened Czechoslovakia in 1938, France and Great Britain were unwilling to confront Hitler to risk war on behalf of what Prime Minister Neville Chamberlain told the British was "a faraway country about which we know little." The British and French therefore agreed at the Munich Conference to appease the Germans by letting them annex the Sudetenland region of Czechoslovakia. The traumatic events of World War II followed, and that experience "taught" that compromise with aggressive dictators would only encourage them.

During the intervening years leaders have repeatedly cited the lesson of the 1930s as justification for confronting international opponents and, if necessary, going to war. "If history teaches us anything, it is that . . . appeasement does not work," President Bush declared to the American people when Saddam Hussein's forces attacked Kuwait. "As was the case in the 1930s," Bush instructed, "we see in Saddam Hussein an aggressive dictator threatening his neighbors. Half a century ago the world had a chance to stop a ruthless aggressor and missed it. I pledge to you: We will not make that mistake again" (Rourke, 1993:30). War followed.

Lessons of history often fade as those who remember them become fewer and as more recent history teaches new lessons. One such new lesson for Americans is the **Vietnam analogy**. This is almost the antithesis of the Munich syndrome. Now when there is the possibility of an intervention, especially in a civil war, the cry "no more Vietnams" is heard (Simons, 1998). The image of Vietnam was, for instance, raised frequently by those who opposed U.S. intervention in Bosnia. "Most of us hark back to Vietnam and have faint enthusiasm for punching somebody to see what happens," one senior U.S. military officer commented on the possibility of sending U.S. troops to the Balkans.[18] Similar concerns were raised about the subsequent U.S. and NATO involvement in Kosovo.

Two subsidiary comments about the use of historical analogies are important. First, as a heuristic device, historical analogies are too often used to avoid thinking rather than to inform decisions. The second comment is that policy makers sometimes make a decision, then select a likely historical analogy to justify their position (Taylor & Rourke, 1995:467).

Personal Experiences   Decision makers are also affected by their personal experiences. Sometimes those experiences create negative impulses. It is impossible to excuse the atrocities committed by the Serbs during the Bosnian civil war against the Muslims and Croats in the earlier 1990s. It is possible, however, to understand some of the causes by considering the bitter personal history that the military commander, General Ratko Mladic, shares in a general way with many Serbs. Mladic was born in the Bosnian village of Bozinovici in 1943. Two years later, his father was one of the hundreds of thousands of Serbs murdered by German Nazi and Croatian fascist forces. "My son is the first in many generations to know his father," Mladic told a UN officer at one point, "because there have been so many attacks on the Serbian people, children do not know their fathers."[19]

Perceptions

What decision makers perceive to be true is a fifth idiosyncratic element that influences their approach to foreign policy. There is the real world, and there is the world we perceive. These two worlds may be the same; they may be dramatically different. Some factors in world politics, such as the financial assistance extended to Russia through the IMF and bilateral aid, are in the realm of objective reality. Other factors are subjective. The West perceives its aid to Russia as an effort to improve the country's economy and to solidify democracy; some Russians perceive the aid as part of a plot to gain control of their country. Since both perceptions cannot be completely accurate, it follows that perceptions sometimes distort reality.

Perceptions have a multitude of sources; myriad inputs crystallize into what we know (or think we know) to be true and how we apply moral and other standards to evaluate what we perceive. Many of these sources, such as belief systems and historical analogies, are related to the cognitive limits discussed earlier in this chapter or to the idiosyncratic characteristics of decision makers that we have been analyzing in this section. The information that decision makers receive from their bureaucracies or elsewhere, as discussed earlier, is another important source of perceptions. Whatever their source, though, perceptions have a number of characteristics and impacts that are important to world politics (Blanton, 1996).

The link between perception and world politics is the concept of **operational reality**. Policy makers tend to act, or operate, based on perceptions, whether they are accurate or not. We noted earlier in this chapter that American perceptions of communist hostility dominated U.S. policy making during the cold war and led, among other things, to the U.S. government supporting numerous right-wing dictatorships whose internal practices contravened American political culture core values about democracy, human rights, and other matters. As one critic put it, while criticizing the hostile policy of Ronald Reagan toward Nicaragua, if the U.S. government "hated tyranny enough to invade or attempt to overthrow" numerous "presumably tyrannical" left-wing regimes, "one might wonder why [the United States] never moved against Chile, South Africa, Indonesia, Zaire, Paraguay, Turkey, and a host of other terribly repressive [rightist] regimes" (Parenti, 1992:187). Another critic charges that U.S. policy was too ready to commit vast resources to defend strategically remote places against communism. A prime example is Vietnam, where the United States spent billions of dollars and tens-of-thousands of lives in a war over what President Lyndon Johnson once called "a raggedy-ass fourth rate country."

There is a related perceptual phenomenon called an *operational code*. This idea describes how an individual acts when faced with specific types of situations, given a "leader's philosophical propensities for diagnosing" how politics works and the "leader's instrumental propensities for choosing" rewards, threats, force, and other methods of diplomacy as the best way to be successful (Walker, Schafer, & Young, 1998:176). Because of their different operational codes, decision makers differ, for example, in their responses to situations. President Nixon, for instance, believed that foreign relations "are a lot like poker—stud poker with a hole card. The hole card is all-important because without it your opponent . . . has perfect knowledge of whether he can beat you. If he knows he will win he will raise you. If he cannot, he will fold and get out of the game." Nixon thought, therefore, that a diplomatic strategy of keeping an opponent uncertain was necessary because "the United States is an open society. We have all but one of our cards face up on the table. Our only covered card is the will, nerve, and unpredictability of the President—his ability to make the enemy think twice about raising the ante" (Rogers, 1987:31).

That poker image helps explain why Nixon raised the ante in Vietnam by, for example, unleashing in 1972 such a tremendous "Christmas bombing" offensive against North Vietnam's cities that one U.S. official described it as "calculated barbarism" (Paterson, Clifford, & Hagan, 1995:464). Nixon believed that these actions would help persuade the North Vietnamese and their Soviet backers to cash in their chips and agree to more serious negotiations. Actually, the terms Nixon got after the bombing were not much different from those offered before. Be that as it may, the point is that the president's crisis-operational code caused his violent reaction, which he later claimed was a major turning point to end the war.

Chapter Summary

1. System-level analysis is an approach to the study of world politics that argues that factors external to countries and the world political environment combine to determine the pattern of interaction among countries and other transnational actors. Countries are often compelled to take certain courses of action by the realities of the world in which they exist.

2. Many factors determine the nature of any given system. Systemic factors include its structural characteristics, power relationships, economic patterns, and norms of behavior.

3. It is clear that there are significant changes occurring in all the determining elements (structural characteristics, power relationships, economic patterns, and norms of behavior) of the international system. What is not clear is exactly what the new system will look like and how it will operate. Scholars use terms such as mixed multipolar, and polyarchal to describe the system that is currently evolving.

4. State-level analysis focuses on states as the primary actors in international relations. States are political organizations that enjoy at least some degree of sovereignty. States, nations, and governments are distinct entities.

5. Foreign policy is not formulated by a single decision-making process. Instead, the exact nature of that process changes according to a number of variables, including the type of political system, the type of situation, the type of issue, and the internal factors involved.

6. Many scholars believe that the fact that democracies include a greater diversity of subnational actors in the foreign policy arena has an impact on policy. It is also the case that as current democracies become more democratic, for example, by ensuring more and more authoritative participation of women, this will affect policy.

7. States are complex organizations, and their internal, or domestic, dynamics influence their international actions.

8. One set of internal factors centers on political culture, which is the fundamental, long-term beliefs of a political system.

9. Another set of internal factors centers on the policy-making impact of various subnational actors. These include political leaders, bureaucratic organizations, legislatures, political parties and opposition, interest groups, and the public. Each of these influences foreign policy, but their influence varies according to the type of government, the situation, and the policy at issue. Overall, political leaders and bureaucratic organizations are consistently (though not always) the strongest subnational actors.

10. Individual-level analysis studies international politics by examining the role of humans as actors on the world stage.

11. Individual-level analysis can be conducted from three different perspectives. One is to examine fundamental human nature. The second is to study how people act in organizations. The third is to examine the motivations and actions of specific persons.

12. Perceptions are especially important to understanding how leaders react to the world. Perceptions spring from such sources as a group's or an individual's belief system, an individual's values, and the information available to the individual.

13. How a group or an individual perceives a situation, another individual, or another country is often a distortion of reality. Distorted perceptions are important because leaders act on what they perceive to be true rather than on what is objectively true. This phenomenon is called operational reality.

Nationalism: The Traditional Orientation

I do love My country's good with a respect more tender, More holy and profound, than mine own life.

Shakespeare, *Coriolanus*

You're not supposed to be so blind with patriotism that you can't face reality. Wrong is wrong, no matter who does it or who says it.

Malcolm X, *Malcolm X Speaks*, 1965

Aliens fascinate us. Not the aliens that immigration officials worry about, but the ones that come from other planets. Whether it is the comical others in *3rd Rock from the Sun* or the aggressive aliens in the sci-fi thriller *Independence Day*, our entertainment media are filled with "others." These others can do more than amuse or scare us; they can tell us something. For instance, take E.T.—the extraterrestrial being. Now, there was one strange-looking character. He—she?—had a squat body, no legs to speak of, a large shriveled head, saucer eyes, and a telescopic neck. And the color! Yes, E.T. was definitely weird. Not only that; there was presumably a whole planet full of E.T.'s—all looking alike, waddling along, with their necks going up and down.

Or did they all look alike? They did to us, but probably not to one another. Perhaps on their planet there were different countries, ethnic groups, and races of E.T.'s. Maybe they had different-length necks, were varied shades of greenish-brown, and squeaked and hummed with different tonal qualities.

Chapter Outline

It could even be that darker-green E.T.'s with longer necks from the country of Urghor felt superior to lighter-green, short-necked E.T.'s from faraway and little-known Sytica across the red Barovian Sea. If E.T. was a Sytican, would the Urghorans have responded to the plaintive call, "E.T., phone home"?

We can also wonder whether E.T. could tell Earthlings apart. Was he aware that some of his human protectors were boys and some were girls and that a cross section of racial and ethnic Americans chased him with equal-opportunity abandon? Maybe we all looked pretty much the same to E.T. If he had been on a biological specimen-gathering expedition and had collected a Canadian, a Nigerian, and a Laotian, he might have thrown two of the three away as duplicates.

The point of this whimsy is to get us thinking about our world, how different from and similar to one another we humans are, and how we categorize ourselves. What we will see is that we do not have an image of ourselves as humans. Rather, we divide up ethnically into Chinese, Irish, Poles, and a host of other "we-groups." Despite our manifest human similarities, we usually identify and organize ourselves politically around some "we-group" subdivision of humanity. If you think about it, you see yourself politically as a citizen of the United States, or some other country. You might even be willing to fight and die for your country. Would you do the same for your hometown? Or Earth?

Nationalism is the country-level focus that makes most people feel patriotic about their country, but not their hometown or their planet. This identification is our traditional political orientation. It has helped configure world politics for several centuries and will continue to shape people's minds and affairs in the foreseeable future. Few would argue with the observation that "nationalism has been . . . the nineteenth and twentieth centuries' most powerful political idea" (Taras & Ganguly, 1998:xi). Despite its strength, however, nationalism is not as unchallenged today as it once was. Some scholars question whether it will or should continue and predict or advocate various transnational alternative orientations. Others argue that the way an individual defines his or her political identity depends on the political setting and the issue at hand and that identity may not be as "nationally" based as scholarly tradition would have us believe (Ferguson & Mansbach, 1996).

This juxtaposition of the traditional nationalist orientation and the alternative transnational orientation represents one of this book's main themes: that the world is at or is approaching a critical juncture where two roads diverge in the political wood. The two paths to the political future—traditional and alternative—were mapped out briefly in chapter 1.

This chapter and those that follow focus on this theme by exploring the divergent political orientations of the two roads, usually by comparing them in successive chapters. This chapter, for example, takes up traditional nationalism. Then, in chapter 5, we will turn to alternative, transnationalist orientations.

Understanding Nations, Nation-States, and Nationalism

To understand the roots of world division that characterize traditional global politics requires that we understand three concepts: nation, nation-state, and nationalism (Barrington, 1997; Kedourie, 1994).

Nations

A **nation** is a people who mutually identify culturally and politically to such a degree that they want to be separate and to control themselves politically. As such, a nation is an intangible phenomenon. A nation, of course, includes tangible people, but the essence of a nation is its less tangible elements, such as similarities among the people, a sense of connection, and a desire of the people to govern themselves. A state is an institution; a nation is "a soul, a spiritual quality," a French scholar once wrote (Renan, 1995:7).

Demographic and Cultural Similarities   One set of elements that creates a nation stems from similarities that the people of the nation share. These similarities may be demographic characteristics, such as language, race, and religion. Or the similarities may be a common culture or historical experiences. When such factors are strongly present, the formation of the nation precedes that of the state. In Europe, nations generally came together first and only later coalesced into states. Germans, for instance, existed long before they came together as Germany in the 1860s and 1870s. Germany was again divided in 1945, but Germans, east and west, felt that there should be *ein Deutschland,* one Germany. Eventually the East German Communist regime collapsed because its legitimacy among the East German people evaporated. Beginning on October 3, 1990, there was once again *ein Deutschland.*

MAPS
World Religions

World Languages

In other regions and circumstances, the formation of the state comes first. In such cases, a critical task of the state is to promote internal loyalty and to create a process whereby its diverse citizens gradually acquire their nationalism through such similarities as their common historical experiences and the regular social/economic/political interaction and cooperation that occur among people living within the same state (Barkey & von Hagen, 1997). This is very difficult. For example, many states in Africa are the result of boundaries that were drawn earlier by colonial powers and that took in people of different tribal and ethnic backgrounds. These former colonial states often do not contain a single, cohesive nation, and the diverse cultural groups find little to bind them to one another once independence has been achieved. Rwanda and Burundi are neighboring states in which Hutu and Tutsi people were thrown together by colonial boundaries that, with independence, became national boundaries. The difficulty is that the primary political identifications of these people have not become Rwandan or Burundian. They have remained Hutu or Tutsi, and that has led to repeated, sometimes horrific, violence.

It should be added that nation-building and state-building are not necessarily locked in a strict sequential interaction, where one fully precedes the other (Cederman, 1997). Sometimes they evolve together. This approximates what occurred in the United States, where the idea of being American and the unity of the state began in the 1700s and grew, despite a civil war, immigration inflows, racial and ethnic diversity, and other potentially divisive factors. The point is that being within a state sometimes allows a demographically diverse people to come together as a nation through a process of *e pluribus unum* (out of many, one), as the U.S. motto says. It could be said that the American nation is the outcome of fast food, CBS, Valley Forge, Martin Luther King, interstate commerce, the Super Bowl, Gloria Estefan, and a host of other factors.

Feeling of Community   A second element that helps define a nation is its feeling of community. Perception is the key here. For all the similarities a group might have, it is not a nation unless it feels like one. What this means is that those within a group must perceive that they share similarities and are bound together by them. Unfortunately, groups too often define themselves not by reference to their own characteristics but by comparison to those of "strangers" (Guibernau, 1996:49). Whether a group's sense of connection comes from feeling akin to one another or different from others, it is highly subjective.

Desire to Be Politically Separate   The third element that defines a nation is its desire to be politically separate. What distinguishes a nation from an ethnic group is that the nation, unlike the ethnic group, has a desire to be self-governing or at least autonomous. Sometimes the line between ethnic groups and nations is not clear (Farnen, 1994). In many countries there are so-called *ethnonationalist* groups that either teeter on the edge of having true nationalist (separatist) sentiment or that have some members who are nationalists and others who are not. Canada is one such country where the line between ethnic group and nation is uncertain. There is an ongoing dissatisfaction among many

Jubilant pro-independence supporters on the night of October 29, 1995, believed that they and other Quebec citizens had won the vote for secession from Canada. In fact, the outcome went against them, although by the slimmest of margins (50.6 *non* to 49.4 *oui*). Those who voted for independence emphasized the uniqueness of the French culture in Quebec and the need to maintain Quebec's particular character. Those who voted for unity seemed to be more concerned with the potentially negative economic and political impacts that might be generated by an independent but far from self-sufficient Quebec. The closeness of the election ensures that the issue of Québécois independence will remain high on the political agenda of Canada for years to come.

French Canadians in the province of Quebec about their status in the Canadian states. Some Québécois favor separation, as we will see in a later section of this chapter.

Nation-States

A second element of our traditional political orientation is the **nation-state**. This conceptually combines the idea of a nation with that of a state.

A state, or country, is a tangible entity. It has territory, people, organization, and other reasonably objective characteristics. Angola, Canada, China, and Russia are states. Chapter 6 will give a detailed analysis of the state, but it is important to briefly introduce the idea of the state at this point in order to understand the nation-state concept.

The nation-state is the ideal joining of nation and state, the notion of a unified people in a unified country. There are two ways in which this can occur. One is where a state is created as the result of a nation's desire to have its own state and to govern itself independently. A second scenario for the creation of a nation-state is when once diverse people within a state learn to identify with one another and with the country in which they reside.

In practice the nation-state concept diverges from the ideal in two ways. The first is that many states contain more than one nation. Canada, as just mentioned, is an example. Second, many nations overlap one or more international borders and may not even have a state of their own. The presence of Palestinians in Egypt, Israel, Jordan, and elsewhere is a current illustration. This lack of "fit" between nations and states is often a source of international conflict, as discussed later. Indeed the gap between the theory of nation-states and the reality of ethnically and nationally divided states is so great that some scholars prefer the term *national state* to emphasize the idea of a state driven by nationalism.

Nationalism

The third aspect of our traditional political orientation is **nationalism** itself. It is hard to overstate the importance of nationalism to the structure and conduct of world politics. Nationalism is an ideology that, at its core, holds that the nation, embodied in its agent, the sovereign nation-state, should be the *only* object of the political loyalty of individuals. As such, nationalism is a central part of the traditional path down which the world has traveled.

Nationalism grows from the sense of community in that it "feeds on cultural differences" and "turns them into a principle of political loyalty and social identity" (Gellner, 1995:2). As such, nationalism merges the concepts of state, nation, and nation-state in a way that is personally related to citizens. This occurs, according to another study, when individuals (1) "become sentimentally attached to the homeland," (2) "gain a sense of identity and self-esteem through their national identification," and (3) are "motivated to help their country" (Druckman, 1994:44).

A SITE TO SURF
UN Members

INTERACTIVE
EXERCISE
How Do You
Define Your
International
Identity?

This motivation to help one's country implies that nationalism dictates action internally and externally. There are many varieties (or some might say faces) of nationalism, and they promote different actions. Some of them are cohesive and positive; others are divisive and destructive. We will presently examine the pluses and minuses of nationalism, but before doing that a brief review of the evolution of nationalism is in order.

The Evolution of Nationalism

The evolution of nationalism and the development of the state-centric international system are intimately intertwined. Neither states nor nationalism nor the state-centric system have always existed. This is important because what has not always been does not necessarily always have to be. It is also important to note that nationalism has evolved and continues to do so. Understanding the historical dynamics of nationalism will assist you to evaluate its current status and value and will help you to form preferences about the future of nationalism.

The Rise of Nationalism

Nationalism is such a pervasive mindset in the world today, that it may be difficult to believe that it has not always existed. It has not, however, and, indeed, most scholars contend that nationalism is a relatively modern phenomenon. It is certainly the case, one scholar notes, that "there have always . . . been distinctive cultures." It is also the case that in some very old societies the "upper classes have had some sense of shared ethnic solidarity." What is modern, the scholar continues, is the "nationalist idea," the belief that people who share a culture should "be ruled only by someone co-cultural with themselves" (Hall, 1995:10).

Early Nationalism It may be impossible to precisely establish when nationalism began to evolve, but one likely point of origin is Europe in the ninth century and the death of the Emperor Charlemagne in 814. After his death, his empire—and the unity it constituted across Europe—deteriorated.

The growth of nationalism became gradually intertwined with the development of states and with their synthesis, the national state. We will review the history of states in chapter 6, but we can say here that some of the earliest evidence of broad-based nationalism occurred in England by the time of King Henry VIII (1491–1547). His break with the centralizing authority of the Roman Catholic Church and his establishment of a national Anglican Church headed by the king were pivotal events. The conversion of English commoners to Anglicanism helped spread nationalism to the masses, as did the nationalist sentiments in popular literature. In an age when most people could not read, plays were an important vehicle of culture, and one scholar has characterized the works of William Shakespeare (1564–1616) as "propagandist plays about English history" (Hobsbawm, 1990:75). "This blessed plot, this earth, this realm, this England," Shakespeare has his *King Richard II* exalt; "God and King Henry govern England," Shakespeare's Queen Margaret instructs in *Henry VI* to note the end of the authority of the pope in Rome over the king in London (Alulis & Sullivan, 1996).

Modern Nationalism   The evolution of nationalism took an important turn in the 1700s and began to change into its modern form based on the close association of the people and the state. This occurred most decidedly when the American and French Revolutions dramatically shifted the basis of theoretical political authority in states away from the divine right of kings and toward the idea, as the American Declaration of Independence proclaimed, that governments derive their "just powers from the consent of the governed." **Popular sovereignty** had been evolving slowly in Switzerland, England, and a few other places. Still, most people remained emotionally unconnected to the state in which they lived until the revolutions of 1776 and 1789. As one study points out, "The Medieval Frenchman was a *subject* of the . . . monarch, not a *citizen* of France" (Guibernau, 1996:52).

From these beginnings in and around the French Revolution of 1787, the idea of popular sovereignty and the belief in the right to national self-determination began to spread around the globe. Some countries were formed when a nation coalesced into a national state. This was true for Germany and Italy in the 1860s and 1870s. In other cases, national states were established on the ashes of empire. The Spanish empire fell apart in the 1800s, and the Austro-Hungarian and Ottoman empires collapsed after World War I. By the mid-twentieth century, nearly all of Europe and the Western Hemisphere had been divided into nation-states, and the colonies of Africa and Asia were beginning to demand independence. The doomed British and French empires soon vanished also. Only the Russian-Soviet empire survived. Nationalism reigned virtually supreme around the world.

These developments, it should be added, were widely welcomed. An image of "populist-romantic nationalism" appealed to liberals on two grounds (Gellner, 1995:6). First, the idea of a nation contains an implied equality for all members. Liberal philosophers such as Thomas Paine in *The Rights of Man* (1791) depicted the nation and democracy as inherently linked in the popularly governed nation-state. Liberals also welcomed nationalism as a destroyer of empires. One well-known expression of this view was the call in 1918 of President Woodrow Wilson for the recognition of the right of people within empires to choose independence, if they wished, through a process of self-determination.

MAP
Sovereign States:
Duration of
Independence

The Predicted Demise of Nationalism

World War II marked a sharp change in liberal philosophy about nationalism. Fascism and other forms of virulently aggressive nationalism helped bring about the horrors of the war and cast a pall on the whole concept of nationalism. Some observers believed that the war demonstrated that the state system was not only anachronistic but dangerous. The development of nuclear weapons, in particular, led some observers to conclude that the sovereign state could no longer carry out the primary task of protecting the nation and therefore was doomed. The emphasis on free trade and growing economic interdependence also seemed to augur an end to the nationalist age. Indeed, the newly established (1945) United Nations symbolized the desire to progress away from conflictive nationalism and toward cooperative universalism.

The thrust of this thinking led numerous scholars to predict the imminent demise of the national state or, at least, its gradual withering away. As it turned out, such retirement announcements and obituaries proved reminiscent of the day in 1897 when an astonished Mark Twain read in the paper that he had died. Reasonably sure that he was still alive, Twain hastened to assure the world: "The reports of my death are greatly exaggerated." Rather than retire or die, nationalism gained strength as a world force.

Persistent Nationalism

The continued strength of nationalism is summarized in Figure 4.1, which shows that between 1940 and 1999 the number of states increased 170 percent. For most of this time, the primary force behind the surge of nationalism was the anti-imperialist independence movement in Africa, Asia, and elsewhere. More recently, nationalism has reasserted itself in Europe. Germany reemerged as West Germany and East Germany became reunited. More commonly, existing states disintegrated into 2 or more newly independent countries. Yugoslavia dissolved into 5 countries, Czechoslovakia became 2 states, and the former USSR became 15 states. Except for Eritrea, Namibia, and Palau, all of the states that have achieved independence since 1989 are in Eastern Europe or are former Soviet republics (FSRs). There are also nationalist stirrings—in some cases demands—among the Scots, Irish, and Welsh in Great Britain, the Basques and Catalans in Spain, and among other ethnonational groups elsewhere in Europe, such as, most recently, in Kosovo (Caplan & Feffer, 1996).

If anything, nationalism in the new states is stronger than in the older countries. The recent independence of these new states tends to make them especially prickly about their sovereignty. These countries are often ethnically divided, and their governments stress nationalism in an attempt to foster political unity. Also, many of the new countries have to struggle with dreary economic prospects, and their governments sometimes promote nationalistic sentiments in order to divert attention from economic woes and to maintain political support.

It may seem contradictory, but the continuing strength of nationalism does not mean that those who earlier predicted its demise were wrong. It may only mean that they were premature. For all the continuing strength of nationalism, there are numerous signs that nationalism is waning and that states are weakening. In the last section of this chapter we will turn to the future course of nationalism. To help evaluate the current role of nationalism and

(Continued on page 97)

Figure 4.1

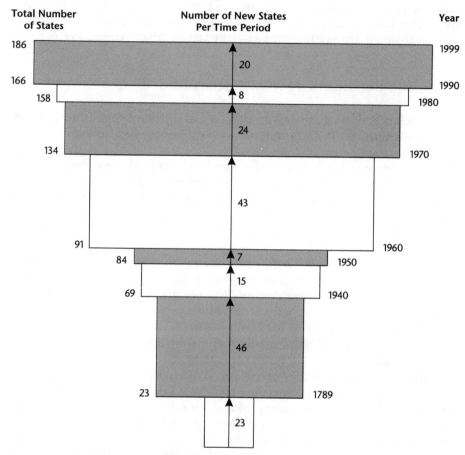

The Expanding Number of States

Total Number of States	Number of New States Per Time Period	Year
186		1999
	20	
166		1990
158	8	1980
	24	
134		1970
	43	
91		1960
84	7	1950
69	15	1940
	46	
23		1789
	23	

Data sources: CIA (1997); authors' calculations. The numbers should be taken as approximate because of controversies about how to count countries that merge, divide, or lose and regain independence.

One important change in the international system has been the rapid growth in the number of countries. It took all of political history through 1940 for 69 states to evolve, but then only a little more than 50 years for that figure to nearly triple.

to decide whether it is a good standard for the future, we should consider the positive and negative roles that nationalism plays in world politics.

Nationalism: Builder and Destroyer

When Pope John Paul II addressed the UN General Assembly in 1995, he spoke of the "need to clarify the essential difference between an unhealthy form of nationalism which teaches contempt for other nations or cultures, and . . . proper love of one's country."[1] What the pope could see about nationalism is that, like the Roman god Janus, it has two faces. Nationalism has been a positive force for political democratization and integration. It has also brought despair and destruction to the world. It is, in essence, both a uniting and a dividing force in international politics (McKim & McMahan, 1997; Hardin, 1995).

The Beneficent Face of Nationalism

Most scholars agree that in its philosophical and historical genesis, nationalism was a positive force. It has a number of possible beneficial effects.

Nationalism promotes democracy. The idea that the state is the property of its citizens is a key element of nationalism. This idea received a strong boost from the American and French Revolutions. If the state is the agent of the people, then the people should decide what policies the state should pursue. This is democracy, and, in the words of one scholar, "Nationalism is the major form in which democratic consciousness expresses itself in the modern world" (O'Leary, 1997:222).

Nationalism encourages self-determination. In modern times, the notion that nationalities ought to be able to preserve their cultures and govern themselves according to their own customs has become widely accepted. The English utilitarian philosopher John Stuart Mill's essay *On Liberty* (1859) argued that "where the sentiment of nationality exists . . . there is a prima facie case for unity of all the members of the nationality under . . . a government to themselves apart."

Nationalism discourages imperialism. A related impact of nationalism is that it strengthens newly independent countries' resistance to renewed outside occupation. Although Iraq's army routed Kuwait's defense forces in August 1990, a brave and persistent Kuwaiti resistance movement quickly arose. Also, Iraq's efforts to create a pro-Baghdad Kuwaiti government failed when Saddam Hussein's agents could not find any prominent Kuwaitis willing to collaborate. Even an unpopular government can usually whip a country's citizenry into fierce national unity in the face of a foreign invader.

Nationalism allows for economic development. Many scholars see nationalism as both a facilitator and a product of modernization. Nationalism created larger political units in which commerce could expand. The prohibition of interstate tariffs and the control of interstate commerce by the national government in the 1787 American Constitution are examples of that development. With the advent of industrialization and urbanization, the parochial loyalties of the masses were loosened and were replaced by a loyalty to the nation-state.

Nationalism allows diversity and experimentation. It has been argued that regional or world political organization might lead to an amalgamation of cultures or, worse, the suppression of the cultural uniqueness of the weak by the strong. By contrast, diversity of culture and government promotes experimentation. Democracy, for instance, was an experiment in America in 1776 that might not have occurred in a one-world system dominated by monarchs. Diversity also allows different cultures to maintain their own values. Political culture varies, for example, along a continuum on which the good of the individuals is on one end and the good of the society is on the other end. No society is at either extreme of the continuum, but Americans and people in some other nations tend toward the individualism end and its belief that the rights of individuals are more important than the welfare of the society. Chinese and people in yet other countries tend more toward the communitarian end of the continuum and hold that the rights of the individual must be balanced against those of the society and sometimes even be subordinated to the common good.

The Troubled Face of Nationalism

The benevolent view of nationalism that dominated the earlier part of this century is no longer commonly held. Where an earlier U.S. president, Woodrow Wilson, promoted national self-determination as a basic political principle, recent American presidents have warned of the ills of unrestrained nationalism. "Militant nationalism is on the rise," President Clinton has cautioned, "transforming the healthy pride of nations, tribes, religious, and ethnic groups into cancerous prejudice, eating away at states and leaving their people addicted to the political painkillers of violence and demagoguery."[2] As the figure on the Web site shows, Clinton's warning is based on fact; there has been a steep increase of ethnonational conflict since World War II (Saideman, 1997). The ills that nationalism brings can be subdivided into how we relate to others and the lack of fit between states and nations.

FIGURE
Increased
Ethnonational
Conflict since 1945

How We Relate to Others

By definition, nationalism is feeling a kinship with the other "like" people who make up the nation. Differentiating ourselves from others is not intrinsically bad, but it is only a small step from the salutary effects of positively valuing our "we-group" to the negative effects of devaluing the "they-group." The most passive product of negative nationalism is a lack of concern for others.

The negativism of this feeling pales, however, when compared to active dislike of others. One too-frequent product of nationalism is **xenophobia**, the suspicion, dislike, or fear of other nationalities. Negative nationalism also often spawns feelings of national superiority and superpatriotism, and these lead to internal oppression and external aggression. It is this reality that moved Voltaire to lament in 1764 that "it is sad that being a good patriot often means being the enemy of the rest of mankind."[3]

Feelings of hatred between groups are especially apt to be intense if there is a history of conflict or oppression. Past injuries inflicted "by another ethnic group [are] remembered mythically as though the past were the present," according to one scholar.[4] This creation of heroic lore is well illustrated by the most symbolic of all paintings for Serbs, *The Maiden of Kosovo* by Uros Predic. It commemorates the battle of Kosovo in 1389, in which the Ottoman Turks defeated Serbia's Prince Lazar, thus beginning five centuries of Muslim domination. The painting features a beautiful and kind maiden giving a last drink to a handsome, but dying, Serb warrior amid a field of slain Turks. The battle, according to one commentary, is "venerated among the Serbs in the same way Texans remember the Alamo." Adds Serb historian Dejan Medakovic, "Our morals, ethics, mythology were created at that moment, when we were overrun by the Turks. The Kosovo cycle, the Kosovo myth is something that has permeated the Serbian people."[5]

It is a tragic irony that the symbol of the battle of Kosovo and its maiden is now entwined with the future of Kosovo Province in Yugoslavia. As a result of the ethnic ebb and flow in the region over the centuries, 90 percent of Kosovo Province is made up of ethnic Albanians, who are mostly Muslims, rather than the predominantly Christian Orthodox Serbs.

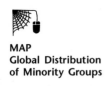

MAP
Global Distribution
of Minority Groups

Internal Oppression   The xenophobia that negative nationalism can breed leads to internal oppression because, as one scholar puts it, "Nationalism is a scavenger [that] feeds upon the pre-existing sense of nationhood" in an effort "to destroy heterogeneity by squeezing" diverse ethnic groups "into the Nation," by trying to suppress the culture of minority groups, or by driving them out of the country (Keane, 1994:175). The "ethnic cleansing" frenzy in Bosnia-Herzegovina, more recently in Kosovo, and the genocidal attacks on the Tutsis by the Hutus in Rwanda are the most horrific recent examples of xenophobia, but there are many others. When, for instance, Indonesia's economy convulsed as part of the general Asian economic crisis that erupted in 1998, the Chinese minority population in that country was widely attacked by crowds reacting to the image that the Chinese were the rich, commercial exploiters of the majority.

External Aggression   This sense of superiority and devaluing of other people, which is so often part of fervent nationalism, can also become an excuse for the conquest and domination of neighbors. Underneath its ideological trappings, the Soviet Union was a classic multiethnic empire built on territories seized by centuries of czarist Russian expansion and furthered by Soviet arms. From its beginning 500 years ago as the 15,000-square-mile Duchy of Moscovy (half the size of Maine), Russia, and then the USSR, ultimately grew to be the world's largest country. This expansion is shown in the map on the Web site.

MAP
Five Hundred Years
of Russian Expansion

Those territories have been lost, but there are strong suspicions that a rejuvenated Russia will try to reclaim them. Such concerns were heightened when Russia's parliament, the Duma, passed, by a vote of 250 to 98, a resolution in 1996 expressing the view that the dissolution of the Soviet Union had been illegal and, by inference, that all the now-independent FSRs should once again come under Moscow's control. Russia's president, Boris N. Yeltsin, has usually avoided such worrisome gestures, but even he has sometimes raised the image of Russian ambitions. Speaking before the UN General Assembly, he maintained that "the main peacekeeping burden in the territory of the former Soviet Union lies upon the Russian Federation." One adviser explained that Yeltsin did not welcome the burden but felt that "it's a dirty job that someone has to do," while another aide observed more candidly that "spheres of influence are a fact of life."[6]

For now Russia's economic and other travails mean that it is not in a position to even consider trying to reassert the earlier domination of its neighbors that it had in the days of czars and comrades. Indeed, old-fashioned imperialism may have become too costly economically and diplomatically to pursue in the future. Yet there is gnawing concern that the German theoretician Karl Marx was prescient when he warned long ago that "the policy of Russia is changeless. Its methods, its tactics, its maneuvers may change, but the polar star of its policy—world domination—is a fixed star."[7]

Lack of Concern for Others   The mildest, albeit still troubling, trait of negative nationalism is a lack of concern for others. Because we identify with ourselves as the we-group, we tend to consider the they-group as aliens. Our sense of responsibility—of even human caring—for the "theys" is limited. People in most countries accept the principle that they have a responsibility to assist the least fortunate citizens of their national we-group. All of the economically developed countries (EDCs) have extensive social welfare budgets, and the people in those countries engage in countless acts of charity, from donating blood to distributing toys for tots. The key is that we not only want to help others in our we-group, we feel that we have a duty to do so.

Internationally, most of us feel much less responsible. Horrendous conditions and events can occur in other countries that evoke little notice relative to the outraged reaction that would be forthcoming if they happened in our own country. For example, the 1.3 billion humans that the UN classifies as "people in absolute poverty," those who live on incomes of less than $1 a day, constitute about 23 percent of the world's population yet possess a scant 1.1 percent of the world's income. The grueling lives of these people stand in stark contrast to what life is like for the wealthiest 15 percent, who have 80 percent of the globe's wealth (UNDP, 1997). The wealthy countries conduct massive public efforts to assist their own poor. International efforts pale in comparison. Chapter 12 will discuss foreign aid in detail, but the bottom line is that in 1996 the EDCs through bilateral aid and through international organizations donated $58.5 billion in aid to LDCs. That is a laudable figure, but it is less stellar when you consider that the amount equaled only about one-half of one percent (0.005) of their collective GDPs. The $9.3 billion U.S. effort, compared to its wealth, was especially dismal and, at 0.0012 of the GDP, placed last among EDCs. Indeed, compared to a per capita U.S. foreign aid expenditure of $35.74, Americans each spent $277 per person on alcoholic beverages, almost 8 times as much as they spend on the world's poor.

The lack of fit between nations and states is nowhere more pronounced than in Kosovo and many other regions of Yugoslavia. This photo shows Albanian citizens leaving home to join their ethnic brethren to fight against the Serbs in Albanian-dominated, Serbian-controlled Kosovo.

The Lack of Fit between Nations and States

The spaces occupied by nations and states often do not coincide. Therefore, the concept of a nation-state in which ethnic and political boundaries are the same is more ideal than real. In fact, most states are not ethnically unified, and many nations exist in more than one state. This lack of "fit" between nations and states is a significant source of international (and domestic) tension and conflict. There are four basic disruptive patterns: (1) one state, multiple nations; (2) one nation, multiple states; (3) one nation, no state; (4) multiple nations, multiple states.

One State, Multiple Nations   The number of **multinational states** far exceeds that of nationally unified states. One study found that only 9.2 percent of all countries truly fit the nation-state concept, as Figure 4.2 shows. The rest of the countries fall short of the ideal by at least some degree, with, at the extreme, 29.5 percent having no national majority.

Canada is one of the many countries whose national divisions are a continuing divisive issue. About 27 percent of Canada's 29 million people are ethnically French (French Canadians) who identify French as their "mother tongue" and first language (Francophones). The majority of this group reside

Figure 4.2

Percentages of Match between States and Nations

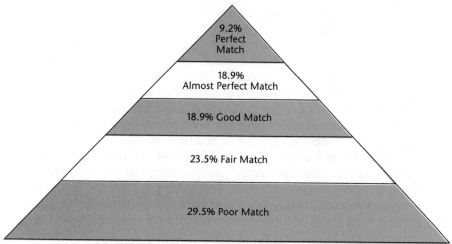

9.2% Perfect Match

18.9% Almost Perfect Match

18.9% Good Match

23.5% Fair Match

29.5% Poor Match

Perfect match = Largest nationality is 100% of the population.
Almost perfect match = Largest nationality is 90%–99% of the population.
Good match = Largest nationality is 75%–89% of the population.
Fair match = Largest nationality is 50%–74% of the population.
Poor match = Largest nationality is 0%–49% of the population.

Data source: Connor (1979).

Ideally the coincidence (match) between nationality and the total population of a state would be 100%. As this graph shows, however, this is true in only 9.2% of the states. More than 90% of states have two or more nationalities, and the largest nationality is less than a majority of the population in 29.5% of the states.

in the province of Quebec, a political subdivision rather like (but politically more autonomous than) an American state. Quebec is very French. Of the province's 7.2 million people, 83 percent are Francophones, Catholic, and French culturally.

This growing nationalist sentiment in the province gave rise to the separatist Parti Québécois and to a series of efforts to obtain autonomy, even independence, for the province. The first formal move occurred in a 1980 referendum that asked voters if they favored the "sovereignty-association" of Quebec with the rest of Canada (Rourke, Hiskes, & Zirakzadeh, 1992). This was rejected by 60 percent of the voters in Quebec. There have been several attempts to agree to constitutional changes to defuse Quebec's nationalist sentiment, but each has failed. For example, one set of amendments was defeated in a 1992 referendum, with 54.4 percent of all Canadians voting "no." Fifty-five percent of Quebec's citizens voted "no" because they felt the package gave too little; people in other provinces voted "no" because they thought the amendments gave too much.

These failures have only served to strengthen Québécois sentiment, and in 1994 the Parti Québécois became the majority party in Quebec's parliament (Fisher & Vengroff, 1995). The provincial government held a new referendum in 1995 on separation. Once again, the voters in Quebec rejected independence, but this time with only a razor-thin majority of 50.6 percent voting *non* to sovereignty and 49.4 percent voting *oui*.

It is too early to tell when, or even if, another referendum will occur. What is certain is that nationalist feelings continue strongly in Quebec. If there is a new vote, however, the narrow margin by which the voters rejected independence in 1995 could well mean that there could indeed be two sovereign countries, not just one, to the north of the United States (Young, 1995).

Many multinational states have not been as fortunate as Canada, which has largely avoided bloodshed over its national division. Other states have suffered extraordinary violence. In Rwanda in 1994, the death and destruction spawned by clashing ethnonationalist groups was given voice by Prime Minister Agathe Uwilingiyamana, when the killing began: "There is shooting. People are being terrorized. People are inside their homes lying on the floor. We are suffering," she said in a broadcast appeal for help from the capital, Kigali.[8] Those were her last public words; soon after, she was dragged from her refuge in a UN compound and murdered by marauding Hutus.

**MAP
Flashpoints,
Year 2000**

One Nation, Multiple States   A second departure from the nation-state ideal involves **multistate nationalities**. These result when nations overlap the borders of two or more states. When this occurs, nationalist sentiments create strong pressures to join the politically separate nation within one state. This impulse has frequently played a role in recent international politics when a nation was divided into two states, as indicated by the examples of North and South Vietnam, North and South Korea, East and West Germany, and the two Yemens. Ireland and Northern Ireland provide another possible example, although the Scottish heritage of many of the Protestants in the North makes the existence of a single Irish nationality in two states controversial. In any case, a single nation that dominates two states has an urge to unite the states and, thus, itself, and today only Korea (and arguably Ireland) remains as an example of such a division. But there is often conflict over union, a tension that led to fighting in four of the examples (Vietnam, Korea, Ireland, and Yemen).

Another recipe for trouble is where members of a nation that has its own state also live as a minority population in one or more surrounding states. This creates conflict when the members of the nation who live across the border in the neighboring state wish to join the motherland or when the motherland claims the area in which they live. This demand is called *irredentism*. Even if a nation-state is not (yet) seeking to incorporate all the members of the nation, surrounding states with minority segments of that nationality may react with worried hostility.

The long-standing instability in the southern Balkans is based in large part on such overlapping ethnonational and state boundaries. One reason for concern about the fighting in Kosovo Province between its majority Albanian population and the Serb-dominated government of Yugoslavia is that neighboring Albania might be drawn into the conflict on the side of the Kosovar Albanians. The urge for a greater Albanian state that includes all the region's Albanians could also destabilize neighboring Macedonia, which is about 22 percent Albanian. The threat of conflict spilling over into neighboring countries is one of the primary reasons NATO became involved in both "peace-making" and "peace-keeping" in Kosovo. NATO provided a stabilizing presence that helped avoid further escalation and involvement of other actors in the crisis.

One Nation, No State   A third pattern where the state and nation are not congruent occurs when a national group is a minority in one or more states, does not have a nation-state of its own, and wants one. The Palestinians are a familiar example of a *non-state nation;* their status is detailed on the Web site in A Further Note: Palestinians: A Nation without a State. The Hindu Tamils split between India and Sri Lanka are also a people without their own country, and the Sri Lankan Tamils have fought a long, bloody guerrilla war against the Buddhist Sinhalese majority there.

Yet another stateless nation is that of the Kurds, an ancient, non-Arab people of the Mesopotamian region, who are mostly Sunni Muslims. The most famous of all Kurds was Saladin, the great defender of Islam who captured Jerusalem from the Christians (1187) and who then defended it successfully against England's King Richard I (the Lion-Heart) and the other invading Christians during the Third Crusade (1189–1192). Estimates of the Kurdish population range between 14 million and 28 million. About half the Kurds are in Turkey; Iran and Iraq each have another 20 to 25 percent; and smaller numbers reside in Syria and Armenia. Sporadic and continuing attempts to establish an independent Kurdistan have caused conflicts with the countries in which the Kurds live. These disputes also sometimes involve outside countries, such as when the United States launched cruise missile attacks on Iraq in September 1996 after Baghdad's forces attacked one of the Kurdish groups in northern Iraq.

A FURTHER NOTE
Palestinians:
A Nation
without
a State

Overall, then, the lack of fit between nations and states has been and is a major source of conflict. Given the rampant nationalism that still exists, it is likely to continue as a problem. India is so divided by various religious, ethnic, language, and social groups that it is a wonder that the country exists at all. Africa is such a patchwork quilt of nations and states that the Organization of African Unity has refused to give aid to secessionist movements. As President Julius K. Nyerere of Tanzania put it, "African boundaries are so absurd that they need to be recognized as sacrosanct" (Jensen, 1982:58). That may be good policy for existing states, but it will surely be challenged by nations that desire self-determination.

Multiple Nations, Multiple States   When one begins to inspect the global demographic and political map closely, it becomes clear that the most common pattern is a complex one in which several states and nations overlap. This labyrinth of people and places is well illustrated by the ethnonational composition of many of the former Soviet republics.

To begin with, only about half the people in the Soviet Union were Slavic Russians. Twenty percent were related Slavic peoples, and another 20 percent were Turkic and other traditionally Muslim peoples ethnically related to the peoples in nearby countries such as Turkey, Iran, and Afghanistan. Caucasus-region Indo-Europeans, Balts, and Finno-Karelian people each constituted about 3 percent of the population, and the Romanian-related Moldovans were about 1 percent. In all, the USSR contained 58 ethnic/national groups of 100,000 or more people.

For a variety of reasons, people of many nationalities, especially Russians, had come to live in other nationalities' traditional homelands. In 1990 almost 20 percent of all Soviet citizens were living outside their home republics. About 40 million of these expatriates were members of nations that had come to have their own states. There has been considerable migration since 1990, but the ethnic mix remains highly heterogeneous.

The national hodgepodge within the FSRs is a volatile mix (Mirsky, 1997). The most widely reported conflict occurred when the approximately 1 million Muslim Chechen people in southern Russia revolted in 1991. Moscow reacted violently, and bitter fighting raged on and off until 1996, when the two sides reached an uncertain truce that, in effect, creates an autonomous Chechnya. In addition to this struggle, Armenians (Christian Orthodox) and Azerbaijanis (Muslim) fought bitterly over the territory of Nagorno-Karabakh, a predominantly Armenian enclave that was placed entirely within Azerbaijan by Moscow in 1923. The Armenians won, but at great cost to both sides. Georgians (Christian Orthodox) fought with the Abkhazians after that Muslim group declared their independence from Georgia. The Moldovans are eager for close ties, perhaps unification, with their ethnic kin in Romania. This possibility caused the almost 1 million Ukrainians and Russians living in northeast Moldova to attempt to secede. Russians in the Crimea section of Ukraine have asserted their independence and have won a level of autonomy from Kiev.

Another potential problem that could arise from the demographic hodgepodge in the former FSRs is intervention by Moscow on behalf of Russians who are being maltreated or who Moscow, for its own purposes, claims are being injured. Such a pretext took Germany into Czechoslovakia's German-populated Sudetenland in 1938, and it could be used by Russia as an excuse to move against, dominate, and perhaps reincorporate one or more FSRs. This has not yet occurred, but there have been threats, and President Yeltsin has cautioned that "it is our duty" to pay "close attention to the problems of [Russians] living in neighboring states."[9]

Nationalism and the Future

Now that we have seen the benign and malevolent faces of nationalism past and present, we can turn to the future of nationalism. One way to think about nationalism as it may develop is to consider whether or not to support the numerous unfulfilled national aspirations that exist around the world. If we take pride in our own patriotism, if we revere our founding patriots who fought and won independence, and if we value our own national distinctiveness, then does it not follow that we should support the right of self-determination for others? Another way to think about the future of nationalism is to ask whether the earlier predictions of its demise were wrong or merely premature. Whatever we may think of it, we should ask ourselves, "Does nationalism have a future in the world?"

Self-Determination as a Goal

One way to examine your feelings about nationalism is to extend the concept to every group that wishes to be sovereign (Moore, 1997). If being a proud member of a nation is good, and if the nationalistic urge of your people to govern itself in its own nation-state is laudable, then should not that privilege—or perhaps right—be extended to everyone? Americans, for one, asserted in 1776 that their nation had a right to have its own state, and they have fiercely defended it ever since.

Although it is impossible to determine exactly where the ultimate limits of national identification are, one study estimates that "there are over 5,000 ethnic minorities in the world" (Carment, 1994:551). Each of these groups has the potential to develop a national consciousness and to seek independence. Before dismissing such an idea as absurd, recall that political scientists widely recognize the existence of Barber's (1995) Jihad tendency: the urge to break away from current political arrangements and, often, to form into smaller units. World politics in the 1990s has been marked by strong nationalist movements (Musgrave, 1997). Many of these have waged bloody campaigns of separation, and the incidence of protest, rebellion, and communal conflict has risen steadily since 1945 (Gurr & Haxton, 1996).

There are numerous good reasons to support self-determination. In addition to the benefits of nationalism noted earlier, self-determination would end many of the abuses that stem from ethnic oppression. If all ethnic groups were allowed to found their own sovereign units or join those of their ethnic brethren, then the tragedies of Bosnia, Chechnya, Rwanda, and many other strife-torn peoples and countries would not have occurred.

There are also, however, numerous problems associated with the unlimited extension of self-determination. *Untangling groups* is one problem. This stems from the fact that in many places various nations are intermingled. Bosnia is such a place; Bosnian Muslims, Croats, and Serbs often lived in the same cities, on the same streets, in the same apartment buildings. How does one disentangle these groups and assign them territory when each wants to declare its independence or join with its ethnic kin in an existing country?

The *dissolution of existing states* is a second problem that the principle of self-determination raises for many states, ranging from Canada about Quebec, through Great Britain about Scotland, to Spain about Catalonia (Keating, 1996).

Irish nationalism is not the only challenge to London's control in the British Isles. Here, a member of the Scottish Nationalist Party is waving a Scottish flag in support of Scottish independence from Britain. Although the party did not win the May 6, 1999, election, the Scots voted that day for their first parliament since 1707—a tentative step toward greater Scottish autonomy.

Americans also need to ponder this problem. They have long advocated the theory of a right of self-determination. The Declaration of Independence asserts just this when it declares that "When in the course of human events, it becomes necessary for one people to dissolve the political bands which have connected them with another" and to assume "separate and equal" status, then it is the "right of the people to alter or to abolish [the old government] and to institute [a] new government." President Woodrow Wilson made much the same claim when he told Congress in 1918 that "self-determinism is not a mere phrase. It is an imperative principle of action."[10] One has to wonder, however, how Wilson would have applied this principle to national minorities in the United States. Do, for instance, Wilsonian principles mean that all Americans should support those native Hawaiians who claim correctly that they were subjugated by Americans a century ago and who want to reestablish an independent Hawaii?

Microstates present a third problem related to self-determination. The rapidly growing number of independent countries, many of which have a marginal ability to survive on their own, raises the issue of the wisdom of allowing the formation of what have been called **microstates**. These are countries with tiny populations, territories, and/or economies. Such countries have long existed, with Andorra, Monaco, and San Marino serving as examples. But in recent years, as colonialism has become discredited, more of these microstates have become established.

Table 4.1

Characteristics of a Microstate, a U.S. State, and a U.S. City

	The Republic of Kiribati	Rhode Island	Dayton
Population	79,500	990,225	178,540
Territory (sq. mi.)	226	1,545	55
Per Capita Wealth*	920	22,765	23,238

*Per capita GDP for Kiribati; per capita personal income for Rhode Island and Dayton, Ohio.

Data sources: CIA (1997); *World Almanac* (1998).

Some analysts worry about instability associated with the limited ability of microstates to sustain themselves economically or to defend themselves. The sovereign state of Kiribati is smaller in most ways than the geographically smallest U.S. state, Rhode Island, and the U.S. city with only the one-hundredth largest population.

Many microstates lack the economic or political ability to stand as truly sovereign states. One set of measures can be seen in Table 4.1's comparison of a tiny Western Pacific island country, the smallest U.S. state, and the one-hundredth most populous U.S. city. There are 40 microstates, more than one-fifth of all the world's countries, with populations of less than 1 million. In fact, if you added up all their populations, they would amount to just 10 million people, smaller than Belgium's population, about 84 percent that of Tokyo, the world's most populous city, and only 31 percent of California's population.

In this context, microstates with minimal defense capabilities and marginal economies sometimes invite outside interference by and clashes between stronger powers and create macropolitical havoc. Furthermore, the problem is apt to multiply under the disintegrative pressures that are currently besetting the international system and its main actors, the states. There are at least another 30 colonial dependencies or stateless nations that have potential for national unrest, and beyond these, there are the aforementioned 5,000 or so ethnic groups. What does one do when 1 or all 5,000-plus groups ask for what we have—independence?

Thus the exigencies of the real world suggest that some standard has to be applied to independence movements. Which should be favored? Which should not? At one end of the spectrum of opinion, there are critics of self-determination who charge that "liberalism's embrace of national self-determination [has] raised more questions than it [has] answered" (Hoffmann, 1995:163). Or, as another scholar puts it, "Self-determination movements . . . have largely exhausted their legitimacy. . . . It is time to withdraw moral approval from most of the movements and see them for what they mainly are—destructive" (Etzioni, 1993:21).

At the other end of the range of opinions, there are some commentators who advocate broad support of self-determination, which one analyst calls "the most powerful idea in the contemporary world" (Lind, 1994:88). In the middle of the spectrum of opinion, many seek a set of standards by which to judge whether or not a claim to the right of secession is legitimate. One such commonly cited standard is whether a minority people is being discriminated against by a majority population. Perhaps it would be wiser for the international community to guarantee human and political rights for minority cultural groups than to support self-determination to the point of *reductio ad absurdum*. Whatever the standard though, it is certain that applying the principle of self-determination is difficult in a complex world.

Nationalism: Will the Curtain Fall?

A critical question in the future of nationalism, and indeed the course of world politics, is whether nationalism will significantly weaken or even die out. The answer is unclear. The existence of divergent identities based on language and other cultural differences extends as far back into time as we can see. The point is that diverse cultural identities are ancient and, some analysts would say, important, perhaps inherent, traits of humans that stem from their urge to have the psychological security of belonging to a we-group. One scholar contends, for example, that being a member of a nation both "enables an individual to find a place . . . in the world [in] which he or she lives" and, also, to find "redemption from personal oblivion" through a sense of being part of "an uninterrupted chain of being" (Tamir, 1995:432).

Yet it must also be said that group identification and nationalism are not synonymous. The sense of sovereignty attached to cultural identification is relatively modern. "Nationalism and nations have not been permanent features of human history," as one scholar puts it (O'Leary, 1997:221). Therefore, nationalism, having not always been, will not necessarily always be the world's principal form of political orientation. Still, whether nationalism will vanish or become greatly diminished and, if so, what will follow are the subject of great controversy (Ishiyama & Breuning, 1998; Eley & Suny, 1996).

Those at the "nationalism-will-persist" end of the spectrum of opinion believe that modern conditions are an "ideal breeding ground" for nationalism, and, therefore, the world can "expect nationalism . . . to grow in intensity" (Motyl, 1992:322). Toward the middle of the spectrum, there are "nationalism-as-one-of-many-identities" scholars, who believe that nationalism will persist but it will compete with other demographic factors (such as region, religion, or even gender) as the primary political identity of individuals. Finally, scholars at the "nationalism-is-doomed" end of the spectrum contend, in the words of one, that whatever "shape the political map of the world will take in the twenty-first century," economic interdependence, changing political values, and other conditions "suggest that state sovereignty is unlikely to be the distinguishing principle of political organization" (Camilleri, 1990:39).

Yet another group of scholars rejects predicting the persistence or demise of nationalism by arguing that a sense of global nationalism could emerge based on the similarities among all humans and their common experiences,

This Middle Eastern desert scene is an apt image of the common global culture that crisscrosses through nations at the end of the twentieth century.

needs, and goals (Wendt, 1994). One study suggests, for instance, that "a nation coextensive with humanity is in no way a contradiction in terms. [The people of a] United States of the World . . . would be a nation in the strict sense of the word within the framework of nationalism" (Greenfeld, 1992:7). It may be that humankind will one day come together as a nation and even create a global government. Nevertheless, having a sense of primary political identification with the global village—to feel first and foremost that you are a citizen of the world—would be so different from the sense of difference and narrow loyalty that now characterizes nationalism that it may be stretching the definition of nationalism beyond its meaning to apply it to both phenomena.

What can we conclude from this scholarly disagreement? Will nationalism persist "until the last syllable of recorded time," to borrow words from Shakespeare's *Macbeth?* The answer is that the script for tomorrow's drama on the world stage is still being written by the world's political playwrights. If we think it important, each of us should lend a hand to establishing the plot, casting the actors, and writing the dialogue.

Chapter Summary

1. Nationalism is one of the most important factors in international politics. It defines where we put our primary political loyalty, and

that is in the nation-state. Today the world is divided and defined by nationalism and nation-states.

2. Nations, nation-states, and nationalism are all key concepts that must be carefully defined and clearly differentiated and understood.

3. The political focus on nationalism has evolved over the last five centuries.

4. After World War II, some predicted an end to nationalism, but they were wrong. Today nationalism is stronger, and the independence of Afro-Asian countries, the former Soviet republics, and other states has made it even more inclusive.

5. Nationalism has both positive and negative aspects.

6. On the positive side, nationalism has promoted democracy, self-government, economic growth, and social/political/economic diversity and experimentation.

7. On the negative side, nationalism has led to isolationism, feelings of superiority, suspicion of others, and messianism. Nationalism can also cause instability when there is a lack of fit between states and nations. Domestic instability and foreign intervention are often the result of such national instability. Nationalism has also led to a multiplicity of microstates.

8. There are many ethnonational groups that are seeking or may seek independence. Among other considerations, this could lead to the further multiplicity of microstates.

9. In a world of transnational global forces and problems, many condemn nationalism as outmoded and perilous. Some even predict its decline and demise. Such predictions are, however, highly speculative, and nationalism will remain a key element and powerful force in the foreseeable future.

CONNECTEXT

Chapter 5

Transnationalism: The Alternative Orientation

A speedier course than lingering languishment
Must we pursue, and I have found the path.

Shakespeare, *Titus Andronicus*

An invasion of armies can be resisted, but not an idea whose time has come.

Victor Hugo, *Histoire d'un Crime*, 1852

A recent essay on the rapid changes in the world heralded the end of the cold war "standoff between history's two most frightening military establishments" and looked forward to a "new beginning," a new opportunity for the world to address the "plethora of long neglected, nommilitary threats," such as environmental decay and the grinding poverty of much of humanity (Kreml & Kegley, 1996:123, 132).

Such sentiments are not new. We humans have often chafed at the world in which we live and have yearned to change it. "Had I been present at the creation, I would have given some useful hints for the better ordering of the universe," a dismayed King Alfonso the Wise (1221–1284) of Castile and León (in what is now Spain) once mused with near blasphemy. One suggestion heard often over the millennia of human history is that people take a broader, more inclusive view of humanity. This call for change reflects frustration with the traditional way that we humans organize ourselves politically along

Chapter Outline

ethnonational lines. Whether that political organization is the modern nation-state or some earlier form, such as the city-state, there have been critics who urge that we look beyond such territorially bounded structures. These critics urge us to adopt transnational affiliations as an alternative to traditional identification with and loyalty to the nation-state.

The Origins and Impact of Transnationalism

The concept of **transnationalism** includes a range of loyalties, activities, and other phenomena that connect humans *across nations and national boundaries.* Transnationalist thought and activity therefore are inherently counternationalist in that they undermine nationalism (and its tangible manifestation, the national state) through common political efforts by people of different nations and by raising the possibility of having a sense of primary political identification that does not focus on the nation-state.

This chapter will explore the bases and evidence of transnationalism in the world. Although the origins of transnationalist thought are ancient, transnationalism today, more than in the past, is a real process rather than just a philosophical perspective. As this chapter will make clear, transnationalism is multifaceted; it is potentially unifying and divisive; it is both praised and vilified.

Some streams of transnational thought are referred to as globalism, cosmopolitanism, or other such encompassing words. The globalist school of thought is closely associated with the idealist approach to politics, discussed in chapter 1, and is the primary focus of this chapter. There are, however, other transnational movements that may merely rearrange the conflictive political landscape by creating new parochial political identifications. The recent rise of so-called fundamentalist religious movements is an example. Then there are some powerful transnational movements, such as the mobilization of women, which are unlikely to result in parallel political structures but which, nevertheless, are creating new and powerful political identifications and, thus, are both transforming and undermining the state. For all their diversity, what these transnational beliefs and activities have in common is that they offer alternative political orientations to the traditional orientation of nationalism. Thus, this chapter surveys part of the political road less traveled by.

The development of transnationalism springs from two sources. Global interaction is one of these sources. The degree to which economic interdependence, mass communications, rapid travel, and other modern factors are intertwining the lives of people around the world is a constant theme of this book. Human thought, as we will see in our discussions of transnational feminism and transnational religion later in this chapter, is the second source of transnationalism. The philosopher René Descartes argued in *Discourse on Method* (1637) that intellect is the essence of being human. "I think, therefore

I am," he wrote. People can think abstractly, can conceive of what they have not experienced, and can group ideas together to try to explain existence and to chart courses of action. No other living thing can.

Transnational Interaction

Whatever we may wish, transnationalism is occurring. Its existence is more than a matter of intellect; it stems from myriad interactions across national borders. Such contacts have certainly always existed, but what is important here is that they have grown at an explosive rate during this century, especially its latter half. What is even more significant is that the scope and level of international interaction and interdependence will continue to expand exponentially in the foreseeable future. The expansion of transnational interaction is being driven by or made possible by a range of factors—economics, communications, transportation, and organizations. You will see, among other things, that each of these factors tends to both promote and be dependent on the others.

INTERACTIVE
EXERCISE
A Transnational
Personal Inventory

Transnational Economics

Economic interchange between people and culture is bringing the world together in many ways. The very intensifying reality of economic interdependence was addressed in chapter 1 and, thus, need not be taken up here beyond iterating two basic points. The first is that the international economy affects our jobs; what we pay for the goods and services we consume; the interest rates we pay on loans for school, cars, and mortgages; the performance of the stock and bond funds in which our college's endowment, our employer's retirement funds, and our personal savings are invested; and a comprehensive array of other economic aspects of our lives. Second, as economically intertwined as we are today, there is every prospect that the connections will grow even more complex and comprehensive.

What is important to see here is that economic interchange has a transnational impact that extends beyond dollars and cents. Many analysts believe that economic interchange is bringing people together transnationally through a familiarity with each other and each other's products. Some of these contacts are interpersonal; more have to do with the role of international economics in narrowing cultural differences and creating a sense of identification with trading partners. This is illustrated by Japan, which in 1997 sent 84 percent of its exports to Western industrialized countries and received 71 percent of its imports from them. The impact of this trade flow on Japan's sense of identity was evident in one recent study. It found that when Japanese were asked whether they felt Japan to be part of a group of Asian countries or Western countries, 40.1 percent replied "Western countries," compared to 33.7 percent who replied "Asian countries," and 26.2 percent who were divided or unsure. When those who answered "Western countries" were asked why they identified that way, 89 percent said it was because of "economic interaction" (Namkung, 1998:46).

Some integrative changes occur because of such technical matters as the need to standardize products so that, in a sense, one size fits all countries. Despite determined resistance, for instance, Americans are gradually being edged toward adopting the metric measure system used by most of the rest of the world. Americans now commonly buy 2-liter bottles of soda rather than half-gallons; it is hard to fix a car these days without a metric socket wrench set. The pressure to adopt the metric system is based on more than the fact that it is a more logical, 10-based measurement system. The impetus for change also stems from the rigors of economic competition. As one U.S. senator wrote to President Clinton, urging him to promote adopting the metric system, "In order for this nation's business to be truly competitive with the rest of the world, we must play by the same rules."[1]

For each such change that results from pressure despite our predilections, many more occur because people willingly adopt the products and styles of other cultures. Inasmuch as the globalization of culture is the product of not only economic interchange but the revolution in international communications and transportation as well, we will address that topic in a later section. The degree to which we are absorbing each other's products, however, is evident in Figure 5.1, which shows the increased amount of the wealth that Americans produce that is spent on imported goods and services.

Transnational Communications

It is almost impossible to overstate the impact that modern communications have had on international relations (Deibert, 1997; Alleyne, 1995). In only a century and a half, communications have undergone a spectacular progression of advances, beginning with the telegraph, then adding photographs, followed by radio, the ability to film events, telephones, photocopying, television, satellite communications, faxes, and now computer-based Internet contacts and information through e-mail and the World Wide Web. There were 35 million Internet users in 1994, and this number is expected to reach 180 million in 2000.

One of the impacts of global communications is to undermine authoritarian governments. As such, the rapid mass communications that are taken for granted in the industrialized democracies are still greeted with suspicion by authoritarian governments. China has long fought opening itself to uncensored outside communications, but it is proving to be a losing battle. China first allowed some citizens global Internet access in 1994. By 1996, about 40,000 Chinese were on the Internet; by late 1997 an estimated 690,000 Chinese were using the Web and receiving e-mail. The government in 1996 ordered all users to register with the police in order to "promote the healthy development of the country's information industry," one official explained.[2]

Figure 5.1

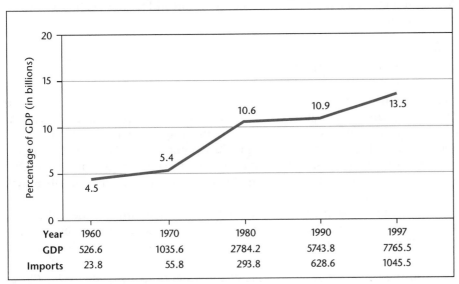

U.S. Imports as a Percentage of GDP

Year	1960	1970	1980	1990	1997
GDP	526.6	1035.6	2784.2	5743.8	7765.5
Imports	23.8	55.8	293.8	628.6	1045.5

Data source: Bureau of the Census (1997); IMF (1998).

This figure shows that an increasing percentage of the wealth produced in the United States (GDP) is spent on imports, which means that more and more of what we own and consume comes from abroad. The mounting expenditures on imports are a part of the impact of transnational economic interdependence on the globalization process.

Among other regulations, Chinese law calls for "criminal punishments and fines of up to $1,800 for the use of the Internet to "split the country" (air dissent). This is necessary, explains one official, because the Internet "connection has brought about some security problems, including manufacturing and publicizing harmful information, as well as leaking state secrets through the Internet."[3] Whatever Beijing's hopes are to control "leaks" in and out of the country, they are probably roughly akin to Peter trying to hold back the sea by putting his finger in the dike.

Global communications are also serving to promote a common culture, as will be discussed in a later section, to create changing attitudes about many aspects of international politics. The images from Kosovo, Somalia, Bosnia, and elsewhere of starving, slain, brutalized fellow humans have helped create pressures on other countries and on international organizations, such as the UN and NATO, to intervene. It is also the case that more and more people around the globe are getting their news from the same sources. The most obvious omnisource is CNN, which now reaches virtually every country in the world.

Modern communications are also bringing the gruesome realities of war into people's living rooms and the earlier sanitized, even sometimes heroic, image is largely a thing of the past. While televised pictures of gaunt Somalis helped propel U.S. troops into Somalia, later-televised images of a slain, nearly naked U.S. soldier being dragged by a rope through the dusty streets of Mogadishu created a public uproar that soon forced President Clinton to withdraw the troops.

Transnational Transportation

Just as transnational communication rapidly transmits our images and thoughts across national borders, transnational transportation carries our products and even our physical selves with a speed that would have been incomprehensible not very long ago. This point about the advent of rapid, mass transnational transportation makes it worth considering briefly how dramatically things have changed in the life of Sarah Clark Knauss of Allentown, Pennsylvania, who was born in 1880.

One thing that modern transportation has done during the life of Ms. Knauss is to make the world more familiar and interdependent by creating the ability to move huge amounts of what we produce across borders and oceans.

During the 1850s, a famous merchant vessel of its time, the *Flying Cloud,* weighed only 1,782 tons, and the then-immense *Great Eastern* weighed 22,000 tons and could carry 15,000 tons of cargo. By contrast, the modern tanker *Seawise Giant,* at 1,504 feet long (almost one-third of a mile) and 226 feet wide, is so large that crew members often use bicycles to travel from one point to another on the ship. This ship is part of the world merchant fleet that is made up of almost 27,000 freighters and tankers, which have a total capacity to carry, at any one moment, over 532 million tons of goods in some 434 million cubic feet of space. American ports alone handle over 2.6 billion tons of goods annually.

Air transportation also brings what we make to other countries and our national products to one another; it is even more important as a way of carrying people between countries. When Sarah Clark Knauss was 15 years old, Lord Kelvin, president of the Royal Society, Great Britain's leading scientific advisory organization, dismissed as "impossible" the idea of "heavier-than-air flying machines."[4] Just eight years later, in 1903, Orville and Wilbur Wright accomplished at Kitty Hawk, North Carolina, what Lord Kelvin had thought to be impossible. Now international air travel has become almost routine, each year rapidly carrying hundreds of millions of travelers between countries. Caracas, Venezuela, is closer to New York than is Los Angeles, and London is not much farther. In 1995 about 19 million Americans flew overseas, and about 20 million people flew in the opposite direction. It strains the imagination, but given the speed of the supersonic transport (SST) and the time-zone differences, it is possible to fly across the Atlantic from London to New York, and when you land the local time in New York will be earlier than the time in London when you took off.

Transnational Organizations

The growth in the number and activities of private transnational organizations, called nongovernmental organizations (NGOs), was introduced in chapter 3. What is important here about NGOs is that many of them reflect a disenchantment with existing political organizations based in or dominated by states. "Stifled by the unwillingness of nations and international organizations to share decision making, and frustrated by the failure of political institutions to bring about reform," one study explains, "political activists began to form their own cross-border coalitions in the 1970s and 1980s" (Lopez, Smith, & Pagnucco, 1995:36). These coalitions born of frustration led to an upsurge in the founding of NGOs to act as the organizational arm of transnational social movements, such as those that promote women's rights, nuclear disarmament, or environmental protection.

These NGOs promote transnationalism in numerous ways (Risse-Kappen, 1995). One source of NGO influence "is earned by taking up causes [that] states ignore or contravene" (Clark, 1995:524). The advances that women have made internationally, for instance, have not generally come at the initiative of national governments. Instead, the place of women's issues on the international political agenda is largely the result of women's groups pressing governments and international organizations to address their concerns.

Second, NGOs facilitate the building of networks of contacts and interaction across borders. This networking function was one of the valuable benefits for the approximately 30,000 mostly female delegates from some 2,000 NGOs who met in Huairou, China. The meeting paralleled the UN's Fourth World Conference on Women, which met in Beijing in 1995. "The real action here," said Sri Lankan delegate Hema Goonatilake, "is hearing and learning, forming networks."[5]

Third, NGOs bring pressure on governments to support the NGOs' various transnational programs. Reviewing the impact of the successive World Conferences on Women in Beijing and elsewhere, the New York-based Women's Environment and Development Organization (WEDO) reported in 1998 that 70 percent of the world's national governments have now drawn up plans to advance women's rights, and 66 countries have established national offices of women's affairs. "What's happened . . . could not have happened without Beijing," one scholar notes. "The energy, the activity of Beijing has not gone away."[6]

Modern transnational trade, communications, transportation, and organizations would not be relevant here if they merely brought people into contact and had no political impact. The fact is, though, that these transnational phenomena are important politically. They facilitate links among people that transcend state boundaries and help establish identifications that supplement or sometimes even take the place of nationalism. Some of these connections are global; others are narrower. But they are all transnational and are creating a different political mind-set. To explore these transnational links further, we can look at transnational feminism, transnational religion, and transnational culture.

Figure 5.2

The Human Development and Gender-Related Development Indexes

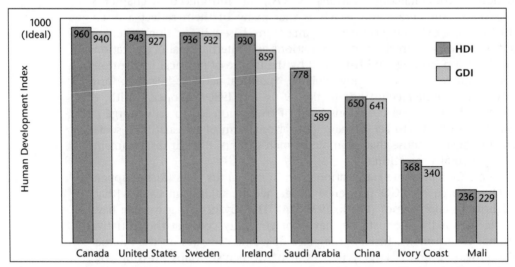

*The United Nations Development Programme's overall human development index (HDI) is based on several health, educational, and economic criteria for each country. The UNDP also calculates a gender-related development index (GDI), shown in the figure above, which is based on comparing data for males and females for the same criteria.

Data source: UNDP (1997).

This figure shows the relative socioeconomic conditions of individuals in eight countries. The HDI figures show the overall conditions of citizens in the country, while the GDI values reflect the status of gender equality. The relatively lower values of GDI versus HDI in each country indicate that in all the countries shown women are somewhat worse off than men.

Transnational Feminism

An important modern trend in international relations is the growth of transnational movements and organizations that are concerned with global issues. Some of these concerns, such as nuclear weapons and environmental degradation, are themselves relatively modern, at least in their scope. Other concerns are a continuing part of human history. What has changed for this latter group of issues is that modern communications and other factors have raised our awareness of them and have galvanized many people to try to rectify the problems.

Gender is one such transnational issue. It strains the obvious to point out that women have been and remain second-class citizens economically, politically, and socially. Historical data is scant, but there are stark current statistics. As Figure 5.2 illustrates, no country has achieved socioeconomic or political gender equality. There are relative differences between countries, with the gap between men and women generally greater in less developed countries (LDCs) than in economically developed countries (EDCs). Still, the

Women's rights are coming to the foreground around the world, and the conflict between tradition and newly sought freedom is widely manifest. In the Muslim society of Indonesia, where strict rules apply to women's daily lives, a woman was a front-runner for president in 1999.

country-to-country differences are social as well. Notice, for example, that while the overall Human Development Index (HDI) for Sweden and Ireland are nearly the same, females in Sweden have a much higher HDI than do Irish females. Similarly Saudi Arabia's HDI is higher than that of China; yet females in China fare better than females in Saudi Arabia. Socioeconomic gender differences, using somewhat different criteria, are also represented in the Web site map.

Life for women is, on average, not only hard and poorly compensated; it is dangerous. "The most painful devaluation of women," the UN reports starkly, "is the physical and psychological violence that stalks them from cradle to grave" (UNDP, 1995:7). Among other signs of violence against women are the fact that about 80 percent of the world's refugees are women and their children, and statistics show, the report continues, that annually an estimated 1 million children, mostly girls in Asia, are forced into prostitution. And an estimated 2 million girls suffer genital mutilation.

Such economic, social, and political abuses of women are not new. What has changed is women's ability to see their common status in global terms through transnational communication and transportation. What is also new is the focused determination of women and the males who support the cause of gender equality to work together through transnational NGOs to address these issues. As the UNDP report (p. 1) points out, "Moving toward gender equality is not a technocratic goal—it is a political process."

MAP
The Gender Gap:
Inequalities in
Education and
Employment

The global feminist movement is the driving force in this political process. We can examine this effort by looking first at the feminist philosophy and goals, then turning to feminist efforts, and reviewing in the Web site box, Madam Secretary, the dynamic leadership of some twentieth-century women.

Feminist Philosophy and Goals

The first thing to say about feminism is to repeat a point made in the first chapter: Feminism is a diverse movement whose adherents share some common views, but which also contains rich variances of thought. Thus, any statement about feminist thought, as with any other complex phenomenon, is necessarily a generalization. Having said that, it is still possible to highlight a number of common points in feminist thought about world politics.

First, feminists feel left out of not only the process but even the conceptualization of world politics. Feminist scholars maintain that the definition of what is relevant to the study of international relations, as presented in textbooks and most other scholarship written by men, is a product of the male point of view and ignores or underrepresents the role of women, their concerns, and their perspectives (Scott, 1996). The problem, feminists say, is that the scholarly definition of international relations has "excluded from that conception, quite comprehensively, . . . the [lives] of most women," who "experience societies and their interactions differently" than do men (Grant & Newland, 1991:1).

Concepts such as peace and security are prime examples of how, according to feminists, men and women perceive issues differently. One feminist scholar suggests that "from the masculine perspective, peace for the most part has meant the absence of war and the prevention of armed conflict" (Reardon, 1990:137). She terms this "negative peace." By contrast, Reardon (p. 138) continues, women think more in terms of "positive peace," which includes "conditions of social justice, economic equity and ecological balance." Women, more than men, are also apt to see international security as wider than just a military concept; as also including security from sexism, poverty, and other factors that assail women. Women favor this more inclusive view of security because, according to another study, "the need for human security through development is critical to women whose lives often epitomize the insecurity and disparities that plague the world order" (Bunch & Carillo, 1998:230). Physical violence is a particular concern, and feminists believe that violence at every level of human existence is related to such root causes as power hierarchies (social-economic-political inequality), with those in power devaluing "others" (those of different gender, race, or nation). As the study continues (p. 30), "The experience and fear of violence is an underlying thread in women's lives that intertwines with their most basic human security needs at all levels—personal, community, economic, and political."

A second central point about feminist philosophy is that it is normative and includes an agenda for change. One obvious feminist goal is to increase the participation of women in the political process and the positions they hold at all levels. In 1998 only four women were serving as the presidents or prime ministers of their countries. International organizations are no less gender skewed. No woman has ever headed the UN, the International Monetary Fund (IMF), the World Trade Organization (WTO), or the World Bank. Moreover, an average of just 11 percent of the senior management positions and 30 percent of the lower-level professional positions in the leading IGOs are held by women (Prügel, 1996). Like male political leaders, some females have been successful in office; others have not. Yet, as the long-time (1980–1996) president of Iceland, Vigdis Finnbogadottir, has remarked, the stereotype remains that "women are not competitive enough or women do not understand economics." "If you do something wrong," she warned other women at a conference, "you will be attacked with the strongest weapon—mockery."[7] The best answer to such derision and to skepticism about the ability of women to handle any political position with skill and determination, of course, is to guage the skill and determination of women who have achieved high office. As the Web site box Madam Secretary suggests, the reality is at odds with the negative stereotypes.

Feminist concerns extend beyond sexism's deleterious effect on a woman's opportunities to have an impact on global politics and includes the impact of discrimination on the entire society. Feminists point out correctly that keeping women illiterate retards the entire economic and social development of a society. It is not a coincidence, for example, that the percentage of women in the paid workforce is lowest in those countries where the gap between male and female literacy is the highest. Educating these illiterate women would increase the number of ways that they could contribute to their countries' economic and social growth. Beyond this, there is a correlation between the educational level of women and their percentage of the wage-earning workforce, on the one hand, and restrained population growth, on the other. In other words, one good path to population control is the achievement of a society of fully educated men and women who are employed equally in wage-earning occupations.

Feminist Programs and Progress

Feminists, both women and the men who support gender equity, are making progress. There is certainly a long way to go, but it is important to remember that just 30 years or so ago, gender equality was not even a prominent political issue in the various countries, much less on the world stage. Inasmuch as chapter 13 of this book will spend considerable time discussing the progress that women are making in the area of human rights, we will focus in this section on political advances that women are making.

Women have been active through national and transnational organizations that number at least in the hundreds. The organizations and their members have interacted transnationally at many levels ranging from the Internet

A SITE TO SURF
Institute for Global
Communications:
WomensNet

through global conferences. Individually, women with Internet access can now, for instance, find out more about their common concerns through such sites as the WomensNet home page. Collectively, women are now frequently gathering in such global forums as the UN Conference on Population and Development (UNCPD), held in Cairo in 1994, and the Fourth World Conference on Women (WCW), held in Beijing in 1995. Beyond the substantive proceedings of such conferences, they facilitate transnational contacts among women. Parma Khastgir, a Supreme Court justice in India and a delegate to the WCW, stressed this contribution in her observation that "what appealed to me most [about the WCW] was that people overcame their ethnic barriers and were able to discuss universal problems. They showed solidarity."[8]

One standard by which to judge the impact of the transnational feminist movement is the advancement of women in politics. "Never before have so many women held so much power," writes one scholar. "The growing participation and representation of women in politics is one of the most remarkable developments of the late twentieth century" (Jaquette, 1997:23). Both these statements are certainly factual, but it is also the case that progress is slow and that women are a distinct political minority. As former Norwegian prime minister (1981, 1986–1989, 1990–1996) Gro Harlem Brundtland commented dryly, "I was the first woman in 1,000 years [to head Norway's government]. Things are evolving gradually."[9] To add a bit of historical perspective: women only began to be able to vote in national elections a little more than a century ago. In 1893 New Zealand was the first country to recognize the right of women to vote. Other countries followed suit slowly. Switzerland in 1971 was the last EDC to allow female suffrage. Now, almost all countries do, although there are a few, such as Kuwait, that do not.

Voting was a significant political step for women, but access to political office has come more slowly. For example, it took 26 years after New Zealand acknowledged the right of women to vote before the first woman was elected to that country's national parliament. Since then the proportion of national legislative seats held by women has risen to only about 13 percent, and about 7 percent of the national cabinet ministers are women. Women are also gradually adding titles such as president and prime minister to their résumés, as is evident in the map of female heads of state or government on the Web site in chapter 3.

The path to political power in international organizations has also been an uphill climb. The UN Charter pledges equal opportunity for men and women. The reality a half century after the Charter was adopted is that women hold just 15 percent of all top UN administrative posts. "We are a collection of all the world's chauvinisms," another UN staff member has commented bluntly.[10] Still, progress is being made. The secretary-general has appointed a number of women to high UN posts. Most notably, Kofi Annan in 1998 named Canadian diplomat Louise Fréchette as deputy secretary-general, the UN's second highest post. Other recent additions to the ranks of women in top UN posts include Carol Bellamy (former U.S. Peace Corps director, now director of the UN Children's Fund, or UNICEF); Gro Harlem Brundtland (former prime minister of Norway, now director general of the World Health Organization); and Mary B. Robinson (former president of Ireland, now UN High Commissioner for Human Rights). Thus things are changing. Nafis Sadik has recalled that in the 1970s, when she first came to work at the UN Population Fund (UNFPA), "Western men saw me as an Asian woman; very decorative, but I couldn't possibly have any ideas."[11] As it turned out, she is not an adornment; Director Sadik now heads the UNFPA.

The accomplishments of these women have been, of course, personal. Many of the other advances of women have been made through national efforts. It is also the case, however, that the progress of women almost everywhere has been facilitated by and, in turn, has contributed to, the transnational feminist movement. Women have begun to think of themselves politically not as only American, or Canadian, or Zimbabwean women, but as women. This is both transforming national politics and weakening the hold of nationalism.

Transnational Religion

Most of the world's great religions have a strong transnational element. At its most expansive, religion can assert universalistic claims. More modestly, religion creates an urge to unite all the members of the religion or, failing that, to support coreligionists in other countries. Religions are not political ideologies in the strictest sense. Nevertheless, many religions have all the characteristics of an ideology and have an impact on the secular world as well as on spiritual life. This is particularly true when the adherents of a spiritual concept actively apply their beliefs to secular political goals, such as Pan-Islamic pride and solidarity.

MAP
Members of the
Organization of the
Islamic Conference

Religion and World Politics

"You're constantly blindsided if you consider religion neutral or outside world politics," cautions the Reverend J. Bryan Hehir of the Harvard Center for International Affairs. It is "better to understand the place that religion holds in the wider international framework," the Roman Catholic priest observes wisely.[12]

Religion has played many roles in world politics (Johnston & Sampson, 1995). Certainly, it has often been and continues to be the source of peace, humanitarian concern, and pacifism. It is also true, though, that religion has been at the center of many bloody wars. The establishment and expansion of Islam beginning late in the sixth century and the reaction of Christian Europe set off a series of clashes, including the eight Crusades (1095–1291), between the equally combative Islamic and Christian worlds. The Protestant Reformation (1517) divided Christianity, and the resulting rivalry between Protestants and Catholics was one cause of the Thirty Years' War (1618–1648) and other conflicts. Religion also played a role in the imperial era. Catholic and Protestant missionaries were early European explorers and colonizers. Whatever the missionary

It is hard to believe that the members of this Fulan Gong exercise class could be seen as a threat to anyone. But the Chinese government is worried that the adherents to this movement, a combination of Buddhism, meditation, and Chinese exercise, might evolve into a political movement centered on the exiled founder of Fulan Gong, Li Hongzhi.

movement's good intent and works were, it also often promoted and legitimized the political, economic, and cultural subjugation of local people by outsiders.

Religion-based political conflict continues. It is an element of the conflict between Israelis, who are mostly Jewish, and Arabs, who are mostly Muslim. When Great Britain gave up its colonial control of the Indian subcontinent in 1947, that area was divided between the Hindus and the Muslims. Countless members of each faith were killed in the ensuing conflict and in the subsequent wars between India and the newly created state of Pakistan. That tension continues, with a particular focus on India's predominantly Muslim border territory of Kashmir.

Religion also causes or exacerbates conflict within countries. What was Yugoslavia disintegrated in part along religious lines. The people living in Bosnia-Herzegovina were of the same Slavic stock and spoke the same Serbo-Croatian language, but being Catholic Croats, Muslim Bosnians, and Eastern Orthodox Serbs divided them into fratricidal factions. More recently, religion plays a role in the cultural divide between Serbs and Muslim Albanians in Kosovo Province. Yet another example is the long struggle between the 650,000 Roman Catholics and 950,000 Protestants of Northern Ireland that killed over 3,000 people since 1969 until the recent establishment of a hopefully permanent, but still uncertain, peace.

Organized religion also plays a range of intermediate roles as a transnational actor, projecting its values through a range of intergovernmental organizations (IGOs). Among the Christians, the World Evangelical Alliance, founded in 1846, is an early example of a Protestant NGO. The Roman Catholic Church is by far the largest and most influential of current religion-based NGOs. The Vatican itself is a state, and the pope is a secular as well as a spiritual leader. The political influence of Roman Catholicism, however, extends far beyond the Vatican. Under the first Polish-born pope, John Paul II, the Church was active both internationally and within Poland in trying to topple the communist government there and dissuading the Soviet Union from intervening. Many years ago, when a subordinate cautioned Joseph Stalin about risking the displeasure of the Church, the Soviet leader reportedly dismissed the Church's influence with the sarcastic question, "How many [army] divisions does the pope have?" The Soviet and Polish communists found out that the pope may have few divisions but that his legions are many.

More recently, the Church sparked international controversy when it opposed pro-abortion rights language at UN conferences on women held in Egypt in 1994 and in China in 1995. A Church representative claimed that the language was "a United Nations plan to destroy the family" by seeking to legitimize "abortion on demand, sexual promiscuity, and distorted notions of the family."[13] Not unexpectedly, many women at the conferences disagreed. Sally Ethelson of Population Action International, for one, accused the pontiff and his cardinals of insensitivity and argued that "women should not die or suffer irreparable physical harm as a result of unsafe abortions because of [the opposition of] a group of 114 celibate men."[14] Nevertheless, backed by some Catholic countries and in alliance with delegations from some Muslim countries, the Church was able to prevent language that specifically advocated abortions, homosexual unions, or other practices to which the Church objected.

In another important initiative, the pope traveled to Cuba in early 1998. The trip was designed to simultaneously put pressure on the communist, authoritarian government of President Fidel Castro to relax its internal restraints and to press the United States to ease or end its long-standing economic sanctions and other measures to isolate Cuba. "May Cuba . . . open itself up to the world, and may the world open itself up to Cuba so that . . . [we] may look to the future with hope," he told Castro, the awaiting throng at Havana airport, and many millions watching the event in Cuba, the United States, and elsewhere.[15] Certainly no celestial burst of enlightenment immediately changed the entrenched attitudes of the Cuban and U.S. governments, but the pope's voice was a powerful addition to the chorus that is calling on both Havana and Washington to reexamine their respective policies.

The Upsurge of Religious Fundamentalism

One aspect of religion that appears to be gaining strength in many areas of the world is fundamentalism. This phenomenon is also called religious

Even in Cuba, one of the last bastions of communism, the pope was given a warm welcome by the population of the island nation. The pope's international influence also meant that Fidel Castro was at least implicitly obligated to visit with the pontiff.

**A SITE TO SURF
The Center for
Middle Eastern
Studies**

traditionalism and religious nationalism. At least in the way that it is used here, a religious fundamentalist is someone who holds conservative religious values and wishes to incorporate those values into otherwise secular political activities, such as making laws that would apply not only to the faithful who agree with them, but to everyone. There is also a transnational element to some fundamentalists, who believe that loyalty to the religion should supersede patriotism and that all adherents of their religion should be united politically. That may mean bringing people together across borders; it may also mean driving out people of other or no faith or suppressing their freedoms within borders.

There is considerable debate over whether the rise of fundamentalism is a series of isolated events or related to a larger global trend. Taking the latter view are scholars who believe that at least part of the increase in the political stridency of religion is based on two factors: first, the mounting failure of states to meet the interests of their people, and, second, a resistance to the cultural blending that has come with modern trade, communications, and transportation. This leads people to seek a new source of primary political identification. Frequently, that is with their religion and with their coreligionists across national borders.

As part of this process, political conservatism, religious fundamentalism, and avid nationalism often become intertwined. For example, the election of Likud Party candidate Benjamin Netanyahu as prime minister of Israel in 1996 was partly due to strong support from the most orthodox Jewish groups. In addition, his coalition government needed the support of the 23 members of Israel's parliament who represent religious parties and constitute more than 20 percent of the legislature. The religious parties pressed the Netanyahu government to limit travel on Saturday, the Jewish Sabbath, and to implement other regulations based on orthodox Jewish observances. The religious right in Israel also claims that the West Bank and the Golan Heights are part of the ancient land given in perpetuity to the Jewish nation by God.

India has also seen the rise of religious traditionalism. A Hindu nationalist party, the Bharatiya Janata Party (BJP), came briefly to power in 1996, then lost power when its coalition government collapsed, only to regain power in 1998 and lose it again in 1999. Thus although the BJP's political fortunes have gone up and down, their continuing prominence shows the influence of religious traditionalism in the world's second-largest country. Unlike some of the religions being discussed here, the vast majority of Hindus live in India. Indeed, tiny Nepal is the only other country with a Hindu majority. As such, the Hindu traditionalism of the BJP has a strong nationalist content and is part of the fragmentation, Jihad tendency that is struggling against the McWorld impulse. This will be discussed later in this chapter. There we will see, among other things, that the resurgence of religious traditionalism in India played a role in its decision in 1998 to test nuclear weapons.

Transnational Culture

Having examined the transnational aspects of the specific identifications of gender and religion, we can now turn our attention to the transnationalization of a more amorphous identification: culture (Iriye, 1997). The idea of culture is difficult to deal with for several reasons. First, different cultures surely exist, but the often-seen phrase "distinct culture" is misleading. Cultures evolve, intermingle, and sometimes even merge. Also, since culture is an amalgam of many components (such as language, religion, and a common history), it is impossible to discuss culture without overlapping discussions of its component parts. You will see in the following discussion, for example, that the Pan-Arab culture impulse is closely related to the Muslim faith that most Arabs share and that the various Eastern Orthodox denominations are very much part of Pan-Slavism, which we address later. Moreover, you will see that transnational acculturation is moving the world in two divergent directions. One is associated with Barber's (1995) concept of McWorld. It is too early to speak of a world uniculture, but we have in the last half century moved quickly and substantially in that direction. The other culture direction relates to Barber's concept of Jihad. There is substantial resistance to McWorld. Furthermore, some observers believe that the world is moving to reorder itself away from the state and toward a world of cultural clash.

The Culture of McWorld

Discussions of the evolution of an amalgamated global culture inevitably include a great deal about McDonald's, basketball, rock music, e-mail, and other such aspects of pop culture as well as commentary about more overtly political transnational phenomena such as the global reach of CNN. It would be an error to suppose that such a discussion of the impact of burgers and the Chicago Bulls on global culture is an attempt to trivialize the subject. Indeed, the potential impact of common culture on cooperation set off a series of columns in the *New York Times* entitled "Big Mac I" and "Big Mac II." The columnist formulated a quasi-tongue-in-cheek "Golden Arches Theory of Conflict Prevention" based on the observation that no two countries which had McDonald's had ever fought a war. Not all analysts, it should be noted, agreed with the theory. Scholar Francis Fukuyama, for one, commented that "I would not be surprised if in the next 10 years several of these McDonald's countries go to war with each other."[16]

More substantively, there is a long line of political theory that argues that the world will come together through myriad microinteractions rather than through such macroforces of political integration as the United Nations. This school of thought believes that political communities are built by social communities and that those social communities come together through a process of interaction, familiarization, and amalgamation of diverse existing communities. Recently, former Pakistani prime minister Benazir Bhutto suggested that such a process if promoted in South Asia would help decrease tensions between India and Pakistan. She argues that structuring negotiations to focus on common ground first will help reduce conflict. As she puts it, "we cannot afford to allow a South Asian armageddon to take place. India and Pakistan, like Jordan and Israel [have done in recent years], must discover that they have more in common than in divergence and that mutual trust and cooperation will avoid war and build a peace that makes both parties more secure and prosperous."[17]

The Spread of Common Culture

There is significant evidence of cultural amalgamation in the world. The leaders of China once wore "Mao suits"; now they wear Western-style business suits, like most political leaders. When dressing informally, people in Shanghai, Lagos, and Mexico City are more apt to wear jeans, T-shirts, and sneakers than their country's traditional dress. A young person in Kyoto is more likely to be listening to The Smashing Pumpkins than to traditional Japanese music. Big Macs and Cokes are consumed around the world.

Before looking further at the evidence, one caution is in order. You will see that a great deal of what is becoming world culture is Western, especially American, in its origins. That does not imply that Western culture is superior; its impact is a function of the economic and political strength of Western Europe and the United States. Nor does the preponderance of Western culture in the integration process mean that the flow is one way. The West is being influenced by material things and philosophical values from other parts of the world. The United States, for example, is influenced by many "imports," ranging from pasta through increasingly popular soccer to Zen Buddhist meditation.

Language is one of the most important aspects of converging culture. English is becoming the common language of business, diplomacy, communications, and even culture. President Jiang Zemin of China and many other national leaders can converse in English. Indeed, a number of them, including Jacques Chirac of France, Alberto Fujimori of Peru, and Ernesto Zedillo Ponce de Léon of Mexico learned or improved their English while enrolled at U.S. universities. UN secretary-general Kofi Annan received his B.A. and M.S. degrees from U.S. universities.[18] Some foreign leaders even grew up, all or in part, in the United States. Just one example is former president Gonzalo Sánchez de Lozada of Bolivia, who speaks Spanish with an American accent.

Modern communications are one driving force in the spread of English. Whether you watch CNN in Cairo or Chicago, it is broadcast in English. There are certainly sites on the World Wide Web in many languages, but most of the software, the search engines, and information in the vast majority of Web sites are all in English. One estimate is that 90 percent of all Internet traffic is in English. As the Webmaster at one site in Russia comments, "It is far easier for a Russian . . . to download the works of Dostoyevsky translated in English to read than it is for him to get [it] in his own language."

Business is also a significant factor in the global growth of English-speaking ability. The United States is the world's largest exporter and importer of goods and services, and it is far more common for foreign businesspeople to learn the language of Americans than it is for Americans to learn Chinese, German, Japanese, and other languages. In a related way, the current ascendancy of capitalism on the world stage is bringing vastly increased numbers of foreign students to the United States to study business. Applications for admission to the MBA program from Latin America alone "have been growing at a rate of 20 percent a year for the last 5 years," notes the head of the University of Pennsylvania's Wharton school.[19] In fact, the U.S. higher education system attracts many foreign students and helps spread English and the American culture. Some 45,000 Japanese are now studying in the United States; only 1,700 Americans are enrolled in Japanese schools.

Consumer products are another major factor in narrowing cultural gaps. American movies are popular throughout much of the world. During the first week of June 1998, for example, seven of the top ten movies in Japan were American releases: 1. *Titanic,* 5. *Alien Resurrection,* 6. *Blues Brothers 2000,* 7. *As Good as It Gets,* 8. *Sphere,* 9. *I Know What You Did Last Summer,* and 10. *Desperate Measures.* Older American movies are available, among other places, through the more than 1,000 stores that Blockbuster Video has in 27 countries outside the United States. And if a European or Asian wants to look authentic at an American movie, he or she can get a pair of jeans at any of Levi's hundreds of stores on those continents, from which Levi Strauss derived about one-third of its $6.9 billion gross annual sales for 1997. Even if the product is not Western, often the style is. Kuwaiti radio now airs a call-in show called *Love Line.* Host Talal al-Yagout tells listeners in a soothing voice that "we get to talk about love, broken hearts, getting married."[20] This is not a translation from Arabic; the host and his callers converse in English. Chinese culture has also succumbed to many things American, as related in the Web site box And Never the Twain Shall Meet: Until Now.

A FURTHER NOTE
And Never the
Twain Shall Meet:
Until Now

To return to and reemphasize the main point here, there is a distinct and important intermingling and amalgamation of cultures under way. For good or ill, Western, particularly American, culture is at the forefront of the beginning of a common world culture. The observation of Frederico Mayor Zaragoza, the director-general of UNESCO, that "America's main role in the new world order is not as a military superpower, but as a multicultural superpower" is probably an overstatement, but it captures some of what is occurring (Iyer, 1996:263).

What is most important is not the specific source of common culture. Rather it is the important potential consequences of cultural amalgamation. There are, as noted, analysts who welcome it as a positive force that will bring people and, eventually, political units together. There are other people who see transnational culture as a danger to desirable diversity.

The Resistance to a Common Culture

Those who celebrate cultural diversity in the world worry about what Barber (1995) refers to as the "yawn" of cultural homogeneity—McWorld—that may accompany globalization. Consider, for example, the plight of France as it struggles to preserve its cherished and concededly glorious culture in the face of the engulfing tide of foreign culture. The dilemma, comments a French sociologist, is that "we have not found the way to modernize while preserving our imagined community."[21] Some French fret about cultural pollution, especially of Anglo-Saxon origin, and point to the fact that it is possible in Paris to walk just a hundred yards down the great Avenue des Champs-Elysées from the Arc de Triomphe and dine at *le fast food* outlet Burger King on a Whopper. Similarly, one critic labeled the presence of the Euro Disney theme park, 20 miles east of Paris, a "cultural Chernobyl."[22] The French language is also under siege, and French president Chirac has condemned the rising English-language domination of the Internet and other forms of international communication as a "major risk for humanity" through "linguistic uniformity and thus cultural uniformity."[23] French music is also falling to the enemy, ranging from rock to *le rap.* "We're too invaded by Anglo-Saxon music," a French stalwart complained. "Radios should make more room for our music, which has beautiful words and melodies."[24] All is not lost yet, though, for French traditionalists have fought back. France has amended its constitution to declare: "The language of the republic is French."[25] In a related move to protect France

Ronald McDonald is everywhere! But then so are many other Western cultural icons. Even these diehard Chinese cyclists can't avoid the larger-than-life presence of the West. Are such cultural icons an indication of growing transnationalism and the appeal of capitalism throughout the world?

from LL Cool J and other musical marauders, the government decreed in 1996 that at least 40 percent of the music on radio stations must be in French. There are even those guardians of all that is French who view the invasion of alien Whoppers, words, and rappers as more than a simple assault on their glorious culture. "The use of a foreign language is not innocent," France's minister of culture, Jacques Toubon, has warned. In reality, he has declared, it is part of the "considerable efforts" to infiltrate French culture by the "Anglo-Saxons" as part of their "hegemonic drive."[26]

The sense of cultural pride and protectionism is not limited to France. It exists broadly. People in various countries believe that their proud heritage and their values are being eroded by what they see as less desirable cultural standards. This concern was evident in the comment of one Russian that the English-dominated Internet is "the ultimate act of intellectual colonialism."[27] Often, as in politics, the United States and Americans are blamed for both real and imagined ills. After three Israeli teenagers died in a stampede at a rock music festival in their country, President Ezer Weizman charged that such things occurred because "the Israeli people are infected with Americanization. We must be wary of McDonald's; we must be wary of Michael Jackson. We must be wary of Madonna."[28]

The Culture of Jihad

There is another, nearly antithetical negative image of transnational culture that envisions a world divided and in conflict along cultural lines. The best-known thesis of this view is Samuel P. Huntington's (1996, 1993) image of a coming "clash of civilizations." Huntington's (1993:22) thesis is that "the fundamental source of conflict" in the future will "be cultural" and that "the battle lines of the future" will pit "different civilizations" against one another. He projects (p. 25) that world politics will be driven by the "interactions among seven or eight major civilizations," including "Western, Confucian, Japanese, Islamic, Hindu, Slavic-Orthodox, Latin American, and possibly African."

Like many analysts, Huntington (p. 26) believes that various modern forces work to "weaken the nation-state as a source of identity" and that new cultural identifications will emerge "to fill this gap" and to group countries into cultural blocs. His prediction for such alignments is dark. "Over the centuries," according to Huntington (pp. 25–27), "differences among civilizations have generated the most prolonged and the most violent conflicts," because "cultural characteristics and differences are less mutable and hence less easily compromised and resolved than political and economic ones."

A FURTHER NOTE
Hindutva and the Bomb

What should we make of this image of a future world torn asunder by the clash of civilizations? One unsettling sign that Huntington's theory is not totally unthinkable is the coming together of Hinduism and nationalism in India. That development is related in the Web site box *Hindutva* and the Bomb.

On a different front, evidence of potential cultural clash may be apparent in what some observers see as a rebirth of "Slavophilism," or the support of Slavic-Orthodox culture to which Huntington refers. This impulse helped set off World War I when Slavic Russia sided with Slavic Serbia against Austria-Hungary. More recently, Russia was more sympathetic to the Serbs than were most other countries during the fighting in the Balkans. This pro-Serbian orientation significantly strained ties between the Russians and other Western countries. As U.S. national security adviser Sandy Berger put it, "There has been a kind of elephant in the room" when negotiating with the Russians because of their political stance in Kosovo. Whether viewed as Slavic brotherhood or as an effort to cling to the country's waning influence in Europe in the wake of significant domestic political and economic turmoil, the political strain caused by the Russian stance was widely evident during 1999. Berger went on to state at the June 1999 G-8 summit, "With that elephant gone . . . [it will] be possible . . . to deal with a series of issues [such as help for the Russian economy] that are extraordinarily important." [29]

Whether such evidence presages a future that fits with Huntington's prediction is highly speculative. Numerous other analysts published responses to Huntington's article that challenged his conclusions (Rubenstein & Crocker, 1994). Some pointed out that while racism, ethnic and religious intolerance, and other forms of culturalism are unsettling, they have persisted throughout human history and, thus, do not augur increased cultural clashes. Other analysts believe that the forces that are bringing the world together will overcome those that are driving it apart. Another scholar contends that "the real clash of civilizations will not be between the West and one or more of the Rest," but will occur within Western civilization as it struggles with itself over the postmodernist tendency toward "marginalizing Western civilization" as the work of "dead white European males" and other "boring clichés of the deconstructionists" (Kurth, 1994:14–15).

One bit of good advice comes from Kishore Mahbubani, a diplomat from Singapore. "Huntington was right," Mahbubani (1994:10) writes, insofar as he realized that "power is shifting among civilizations." What worries the Singaporean is that in response to the reemergence of non-Western cultures, a "siege mentality is developing" in the West. What is best, he argues (p. 14) is for those in the West to dispense with the "hubris" that assumes Western values are the best and to adopt some of the values of other civilizations, just as they have adopted some of the positive values of Western culture.

Transnationalism Tomorrow

It is impossible to predict how far transnationalism will progress. It is not wildly irresponsible to project that a century from now humans will share a common culture and perhaps even a common government. That is, however, far from certain. There are those who doubt that the trend of today toward transculturalism will continue into the future. Some analysts believe, for example, that English will cease to be the common language of the Internet as more and more non-English-speaking people gain access. "Be careful of turning astute observations about the current state of the Web into implications for the future," one observer cautions wisely.[30]

Moreover, nationalism, as we saw in the last chapter, is proving to be a very resilient barrier to globalization and to such transnational movements as Islam. Whether it is based on political nationalism or on simple cultural familiarity, there is also strong resistance to cultural homogenization. However rational it might be to use the metric system, the bulk of Americans still seem to agree with the publisher of the anti-metric newsletter *Footprint,* who rejects "the folly of adopting faddish European units of measure."[31]

It is also very evident, however, that nationalism organized in the nation-state is under assault. One direction of attack is from the various jihad movements, secular and religious. Nation-states are splintering as people increasingly identify with smaller national units, ethnic groups, religions, and other demographic units. From the opposite direction, the forces of globalization press nations to assimilate with one another economically, socially, and politically. "We have to learn to push our politics in two directions at once: upward beyond the nation-state and downward below the nation-state," writes one scholar who advocates diminished nationalism. "For purposes of dealing with global issues [such as the environment], we need to inspire a large sense of global citizenship, because these are global problems with only global solutions." He adds, though, that people are seeking smaller units of political reference because they realize that "the planet is no substitute for a neighborhood," and that it is only in associations smaller than states, much less the globe, that "people can have a direct hand in exercising responsibility for their communities."[32]

Chapter Summary

1. This chapter explores the bases and evidence of transnationalism in the world. Transnationalism includes a range of loyalties, activities, and other phenomena that connect humans across nations and national boundaries.

2. Some streams of transnational thought are referred to as globalism, cosmopolitanism, or some other such encompassing word. Other transnational movements, such as religion and gender, have a more limited focus.

3. The development of transnationalism springs from two sources: human thought and global interaction.

4. Transnational interaction is increasing, as evident in changes in economics, communications, transportation, and organizations. International economic interdependence, mass communications, the ease of travel across borders, and the growth of transnational organizations are all helping to break down national barriers.

5. An important modern trend in international relations is the growth of transnational movements and organizations that are concerned with global issues. This includes transnational feminism and its associated organizations.

6. Transnational feminist philosophy and goals center on the idea that women around the world should cooperate to promote gender equality and to transform the way we think about and conduct politics at every level, including the international level. Feminist transnational thought reflects elements of postmodernism and idealism.

7. Most religions have a strong transnational element. Religion has played many roles in world politics. The roles have been both positive and negative. There is a current rise in religious fundamentalism in many areas of the world that is worrisome.

8. Transnational culture is both bringing the world together and dividing it. The movement of goods, ideas, and people across national boundaries is helping to create what is perhaps the beginning of a common global culture. Some people see this as a positive development; others oppose it.

9. Some observers believe that we are not moving toward a common culture but, instead, toward a future in which people will identify with and politically organize themselves around one or another of several antagonistic cultures or so-called civilizations.

CONNECTEXT

chapter 6

National States: The Traditional Structure

Something is rotten in the state of Denmark.

Shakespeare, *Hamlet*

Who saves his country, saves himself, saves all things, and all things saved do bless him! Who lets his country die, lets all things die, dies himself ignobly, and all things dying curse him!

Senator Benjamin H. Hill Jr., 1893

This chapter is the first of two that examine two roads that we can take toward organizing ourselves politically on the world stage. This chapter will take up the traditional organization: the state. Then, chapter 7 will examine the alternative type of organization: international governmental organizations.

The Nature and Origins of the State

In considering states, it is important, first, to understand how their existence as sovereign actors affects world politics and, second, what their political future is. Discussing these matters, however, requires that we first establish a foundation of knowledge about what states are and how they came into being and have evolved.

Chapter Outline

The State Defined

States are territorially defined political units that exercise ultimate internal authority and that recognize no legitimate external authority over them. States are the most recognized and revered of our political organizations. When an Olympian steps atop the ceremonial stands to receive his or her gold medal, the flag of the victor's country is raised and its anthem is played. States are also the most powerful of all political actors. Some huge companies approach or even exceed the wealth of some poorer countries, but no individual, company, group, or international organization approaches the coercive power wielded by most states. Whether large or small, rich or poor, populous or not, states share all or most of six characteristics: sovereignty, territory, population, diplomatic recognition, internal organization, and domestic support.

Sovereignty

The most important political characteristic of a state is **sovereignty**. This term means that the sovereign actor (the state) does not recognize as legitimate any higher authority. Sovereignty also includes the idea of legal equality among states (Cronin, 1994). As we shall presently discuss further, sovereign states developed late in the Middle Ages (ca. 500–1350), as the rulers of Europe broke away from the secular domination of the Holy Roman Empire and the theological authority of the pope and simultaneously consolidated authority within their realms over feudal estates and other competing local political organizations. The new states exercised *supreme authority* over their territory and citizens; they owed neither allegiance nor obedience to any higher authority.

It is important to note that sovereignty, a legal and theoretical term, differs from independence, a political and applied term. Independence also means freedom from outside control, and in an ideal law-abiding world, sovereignty and independence would be synonymous. In the real world, however, where power is important, independence is not absolute. Sometimes a small country is so dominated by a powerful neighbor that its independence is dubious at best. Especially in terms of their foreign and defense policies, Bhutan (dominated by India), the Marshall Islands (dominated by the United States), Monaco (dominated by France), and other such countries can be described as having only circumscribed sovereignty.

Sovereignty also implies legal *equality* among states. That theory is applied in the UN General Assembly and many other international assemblies, where each member-state has one vote. Are all states really equal, though? Compare San Marino and China (Table 6.1). San Marino lies entirely within Italy and is the world's oldest republic, dating back to the fourth century A.D. After years of self-imposed nonparticipation, the San Marinese decided to seek membership in the UN. "The fact of sitting around the table with the most important states in the world is a reaffirmation of sovereignty," explained Giovanni Zangoli, the country's foreign minister.[1] The General Assembly seated San Marino in 1992 as a sovereign equal. Nevertheless, it is

Table 6.1

San Marino and China: Sovereign Equals

	San Marino	China
Territory (sq. mi.)	24	3,600,607
Population	24,714	1,221,591,778
GDP ($ millions)	380	3,500,000
Military Personnel	0	2,300,000
Vote in UN General Assembly	1	1

China includes data for Hong Kong. San Marino has a police force with an annual budget of about $3.7 million.

Data sources: World Almanac (1998); CIA (1997).

The legal concept of sovereign equality is very different from more tangible measures of equality, as is evident in this comparison of two countries: San Marino and China.

obvious that whatever sovereignty may mean legally, in many ways the two states are not equal.

Territory

A second characteristic of a state is territory. It would seem obvious that a state must have physical boundaries, and most states do. On closer examination, though, the question of territory becomes more complex. There are numerous international disputes over borders; territorial boundaries can expand, contract, or shift dramatically; and it is even possible to have a state without territory. Many states recognize what they call Palestine as sovereign, yet the Palestinians are scattered in other countries such as Jordan. An accord that the Israelis and Palestinians signed in 1994 gave the Palestinians a measure of autonomy in Gaza (a region between Israel and Egypt) and in parts of the West Bank. Nevertheless, limited self-rule is not sovereignty. Therefore, depending on one's viewpoint, the Palestinians either have no territory or have been expelled from the territory now occupied by Israel. It is also possible to maintain, as the United States and most other countries currently do, that the Palestinians still have no state of their own.

MAP
Sovereign States:
Duration of
Independence

Population

People are an obvious requirement of any state. The populations of states range from the 850 inhabitants of the Holy See (popularly referred to as the Vatican) to China's more than 1 billion people, but all states count this characteristic as a minimum requirement.

What is becoming less clear in the shifting loyalties of the evolving international system is exactly where the population of a country begins and ends. Citizenship has become a bit more fluid than it was not long ago. For example, a national of one European Union (EU) country who resides in another EU country can now vote in local elections and even hold local office in the country in which he or she resides. Similarly, a reform accord reached

Even though the Palestinians do not yet have a true homeland, their leader, Yasir Arafat, was accorded equal status with other state leaders, including Bill Clinton of the United States, Hosni Mubarak of Egypt, and Ali Abdullah Saleh of Yemen, at the funeral of King Hussein of Jordan in February 1999.

in 1996 by the political parties of Mexico will allow Mexicans who have emigrated to the United States to vote in future Mexican presidential elections.

TABLE
World Countries:
Area, Population,
and Population
Density, 1998

Diplomatic Recognition

A classic rhetorical question is: If a tree fell in the forest and no one heard it, did it make a sound? The same question governs the issue of statehood and the recognition by others. If a political entity declares its independence and no other country grants it diplomatic recognition, is it really a state? The answer seems to be, No.

Yet the standard of external recognition remains hazy, and it may even be that a political entity that has little or no external recognition may constitute a state. For example, countries were slow to recognize the Communist government of Mao Zedong in China after it took power in 1949. U.S. recognition was withheld until 1979. Did that mean that the rechristened People's Republic of China did not exist for a time? Clearly that is not the case because, as one scholar comments, "power capabilities are equally or more important than outside recognition" in establishing the existence of a state (Thompson, 1995:220).

Despite the inexactitude of diplomatic recognition, it remains an important factor in the international system. Notice that the practice of making a political unit's status as a state dependent on the recognition of other states makes this group of actors something like a club that can accept or reject new members or even, in extreme cases, expel a member. This factor, one analyst comments, makes the modern state system "unique in that its members recognize one another as equal authority claimants" (Thomson, 1995:219). This point is important because it allows existing states to perpetuate their own status and authority by making entry into or continued membership in the club dependent generally on playing by the existing rules of the system.

Internal Organization

States must normally have some level of political and economic structure. Most states have a government, but statehood continues during periods of severe turmoil, even anarchy. Afghanistan, Liberia, Somalia, and some other existing states dissolved into chaos during the 1990s, and to speak of a government in any of them stretches the definition of the word beyond useful meaning. Yet each of these and other "failed states" continues to exist legally. Each, for instance, sits as a sovereign equal, with an equal vote in the UN General Assembly.

A FURTHER NOTE
The Dalai Lama
in Dharamsala

An associated issue arises when what once was and what still claims to be the government of a generally recognized or formerly recognized state exists outside the territory that the exiled government claims as its own. There is a long history of recognizing governments-in-exile. The most common instances have occurred when a sitting government is forced by invaders to flee. Several European governments-in-exile operated in London during World War II until their countries were liberated from the Germans by the Allies. After Vladimir Ilyich Lenin in November 1917 toppled the Russian government of President Aleksandr F. Kerensky (which had come to power after the czar abdicated the previous March), Washington and many other capitals continued to recognize Kerensky's government even though the deposed president lived in Paris and then California. A current and troubling example of what claims to be a government-in-exile involves Tibet, as explained in the Web site box, The Dalai Lama in Dharamsala.

Domestic Support

The final characteristic of a state is domestic support. At its most active, this implies that a state's population is loyal (patriotism) to it and grants it the authority to make rules and to govern (legitimacy). At its most passive, the

The Dalai Lama continues to be viewed as the leader of Tibet, even though he has been in exile for many years, after China overran the mountain region. The Chinese government has not succeeded in eroding the exiled leader's popularity among supporters of the Tibet cause in the West.

population grudgingly accepts the authority of the government. For all the coercive power that a state usually possesses, it is difficult for any state to survive without at least the passive acquiescence of its people. The dissolution of Czechoslovakia, the Soviet Union, and Yugoslavia (and, in turn, Bosnia) are illustrations of multinational states collapsing in the face of the separatist impulses of disaffected nationalities.

The Origins of the State

A SITE TO SURF
Internet Modern
History Sourcebook

In the last chapter we noted the decline of the Greek city-states as the center of political organization in the West and the eventual domination of the universalistic Roman Empire. After more than five centuries as the hub of the known Western world, Rome fell in 476. Thereafter, secular political power in the West was wielded for almost a millennium by two levels of authority—one universal, the other local. On the universalistic *macrolevel,* international organizational authority existed in the form of the Roman Catholic Church. Christianity as interpreted by the Catholic Church and its pope served as the integrating force in several ways. The Church kept Latin alive, which provided a common language among intellectuals. Christian doctrine underlay the developing concepts of rights, justice, and other political norms. Even kings were theoretically (and often substantially) subordinate to the pope. It was, for example, Pope Leo III who crowned Charlemagne "Emperor of the Romans" in 800. Charlemagne's empire did not last, but the idea of a new Christian-Roman universal state was established, and was strengthened further when in 936 Otto I was crowned head of what became known as the Holy Roman Empire.

Centuries later, the overarching authority of the Catholic Church was supplemented and, in some cases, supplanted, by great, multiethnic empires. These political conglomerations came to exercise control over many different peoples. The Austro-Hungarian, British, Chinese, Dutch, French, German, Ottoman, Russian, Spanish, and other empires controlled people in their immediate continental areas and on other continents. Most of the people within these empires did not feel a strong political identification with or an emotional attachment to them. Many of these empires lasted into this century; but the collapse of the Soviet Union, which had inherited the Russian empire, marked the end of the last of the great multiethnic empires that had provided an earlier degree of macrolevel integration.

The local, *microlevel* of authority centered on political units that were smaller than the states that would one day evolve. Principalities, dukedoms, baronies, and other such fiefdoms were ruled by minor royalty that provided local defense. This warrior elite was largely autonomous, even though individual nobles were theoretically vassals of a king or an emperor.

To sum up this brief survey of the founding and evolution of the state, we can note that during the several centuries that followed the Peace of Westphalia (1648), the genesis of national states continued as economic and social interaction grew, and monarchs such as Louis XIV of France (1643–1715), Frederick II of Prussia (1740–1786), and Peter the Great of Russia (1682–1725) consolidated their core domains and even expanded them into empires. In the development of the modern national state, however, one key element was yet to come. Missing was the concept that the state is an embodiment of the nation (the people). Kings claimed to rule and even own their realms by "divine right"; thus France's Louis XIV could proclaim, "*L'état, c'est moi*" (I am the state). Perhaps it was so then, but in 1793 another French king, Louis XVI, lost his head over this presumption, and the people claimed the state for themselves.

The coming of democracy, exemplified by the American (1776) and French (1789) Revolutions promoted the creation of the national state. The fixed territory of modern states and their sense of sovereign singularity had already begun to create a spirit of nationalism in England and elsewhere. Still, the attachment of most individuals to the state was limited by the theory that the state was the property of the monarch and the people were the crown's subjects. Democracy changed the theory of who owns the state from monarch to citizen, and that solidified nationalism. Now the state was the possession of the people, who, therefore, were obliged to support it emotionally and materially.

Once this occurred, all the basic parameters for the modern state that exist today were in place. Certainly, states continued to evolve into being as older systems slowly disintegrated. Important states like Germany and Italy did not exist a century and a half ago; other states like Vietnam did not exist 50 years ago; still other states like Ukraine did not exist a decade ago. The idea that people own and are tied to their countries also continued to evolve. A century ago, kings ruled nearly everywhere. Now they rule almost nowhere, and even authoritarian governments claim power in the name of the people.

The State as the Core Political Organization

Having explored the evolution of states, our next task is to look at the state as our primary political organization. We have already discussed the role and structure of states. The chapter on levels of analysis made the central point that the organization of the anarchical nature of the international system stems from the fact that the sovereign state is the key actor in the system. Later in that chapter, when discussing state-level analysis, we looked inside the state to illuminate the foreign policy–making process. What we can add here are examinations of differing theories of governance and of national and other interests.

Theories of Governance

It is possible to divide theories of governance into two broad categories. One includes authoritarian types of governments, which allow little or no participation in decision making by individuals and groups outside the upper reaches of the government. The second category includes democratic governments, which allow much broader and more meaningful participation. As with many things we discuss, the line between authoritarian and democratic is not precise. Instead, using broad and meaningful participation as the standard, there is a scale that runs from one-person rule to full, direct democracy (or even, according to some, to anarchism).

Authoritarian Theories of Governance

The world has witnessed the coming, dominance, and the passing of a number of nondemocratic political theories about how societies should be organized and governed. The idea of *theocratic rule* by spiritual leaders is ancient. Now, however, it has almost disappeared, although there are some elements of theocratic rule left in the popular, if not the legal, status of Japan's emperor, Thailand's king, and (most strongly) Tibet's exiled Dalai Lama. Iran also contains an element of theocratic government, and the increased strength of religious fundamentalism in many places means that it is not unthinkable that a rejuvenation of theocracy might occur. Similarly, strong *monarchism*, resting on the theory of the divine right of kings, is as old as human organization. But it has also declined almost to the point of extinction, with only a few strong monarchs (such as Saudi Arabia's king) scattered among a larger number of constitutional monarchies that severely restrict the monarch's power.

Communism as it originated in the works of Friedrich Engels and Karl Marx is essentially an economic theory. As applied, however, by Vladimir Lenin and Joseph Stalin in the USSR, by Mao Zedong in China, and by other Communist leaders in those countries and elsewhere, communism also falls squarely within the spectrum of authoritarian governance. Even Marx expected that a "dictatorship of the proletariat" over the bourgeoisie would follow communist revolutions and prevail during a transitional socialist period between capitalism and communism. Lenin institutionalized this view. His concept of dictatorship meant, in the words of one study, "the dictatorship of the Communist Party over the proletariat, since [Lenin] had little faith that the working class had the political understanding or spontaneous organizational ability to secure the existence and expansion of a communist state" (Ebenstein, Ebenstein, & Fogelman, 1994:125). Stalin even further concentrated political authority in his person and in a small group of associates. Even the Communist Party lost its control, and, another study explains, "After 1930, not a single protest was raised; not a single dissenting voice or vote expressed" any difference with what Stalin decided (Macridis & Hulliung, 1996:117). Indeed the encompassing social, economic, and political control that Stalin claimed was termed "totalitarian."

Fascism is another authoritarian political philosophy that in some of its manifestations embraces totalitarianism (Griffin, 1995). The term fascism is often used loosely to describe almost anyone far to the right. That approach is wrong, for the term should be used with some precision. Modern fascism can be traced to Italy and the ideas of Benito Mussolini and to a variant, National Socialism and Adolf Hitler and his Nazi followers, in Germany. There were some differences between Italian Fascism and German Nazism, but they were similar enough so that, one study commented, "It is not too difficult to state the basic elements of the fascist outlook" (Ebenstein, Ebenstein, & Fogelman, 1994:87). These include (1) a rejection of rationality and a reliance on emotion to govern; (2) a belief (especially for Nazis) in the superiority of some groups and the inferiority of others; (3) advocacy of the legitimacy of subjugating countries of "inferior" people; (4) a rejection of the rights of individuals in favor of a "corporatist" view that people are "workers" in the state; (5) gearing all economic activity to the support of the corporatist state; (6) an anthropomorphic view of the state as a living thing (the organic state theory); (7) belief that the individual's highest expression is in the people (*volk* in German); and (8) belief that the highest expression of the volk (and, by extension, the individual) is in the leader (*führer* in German, *duce* in Italian), who rules as a totalitarian dictator.

Perhaps the scariest threat of fascist stirrings in the 1990s is led by Vladimir Zhirinovsky of Russia. Like earlier fascists, Zhirinovsky's approach to political reform is draconian. "I may have to shoot 100,000 people," he says, "but the other 300 million will live peacefully."[2] He also sometimes takes on the trappings of earlier führers and duces, surrounding himself with "Zhirinovsky's Falcons," described as "young men in blue uniforms and black boots, some wearing dark glasses, all with sidearms strapped to their waists."[3]

As we approach the year 2000, it is possible to give only a mixed report on the prospects for the end of authoritarian government. It is true that fascists have fallen far short of electoral victory, as Zhirinovsky did in the 1996 Russian presidential race. Yet, it is also the case that the decline of authoritarian government has stalled. The collapse of authoritarian governments in the USSR, Eastern Europe, and elsewhere in the early 1990s led to predictions that democracy was about to become the governing political philosophy of the world. At least for now, as Figure 6.1 shows, that has not occurred. Only 41 percent of the world's countries are unequivocally democratic. Furthermore, as one analysis forecasts gloomily, "ideologies often go through a process of ebb and flow. Right-wing extremism and authoritarianism have deep roots, and it is not at all unlikely that . . . they may surface again" (Macridis & Hulliung, 1996:183).

Democratic Theories of Governance

The practice of democracy (which is derived from the Greek word *demos,* meaning "the citizenry") dates from the ancient Greek city-states circa 500 B.C. For more than 2,000 years, however, democracy existed only sporadically and usually in isolated locations. The gradual rise of English democracy, then the American and French Revolutions in the late eighteenth century, marked the change of democracy from a mere curiosity to an important national and transnational political idea. Still, the spread of democracy continued slowly. Then, during the late 1980s and early 1990s, dictatorship fell on hard times, and many observers have tentatively heralded the coming of a democratic age. This view was captured by Francis Fukuyama's (1989:3) essay, "The End of History?" in which he suggests that we may have come to "the end of mankind's

Figure 6.1

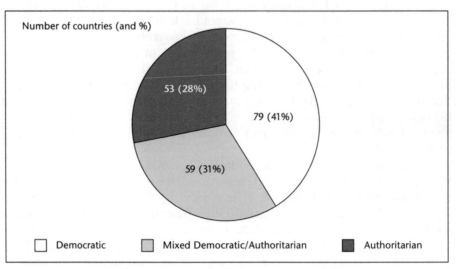

Democracy in the World

Number of countries (and %)

53 (28%)

79 (41%)

59 (31%)

☐ Democratic   ▨ Mixed Democratic/Authoritarian   ■ Authoritarian

Percentages do not equal 100 because of rounding. Status as democratic, mixed democratic/authoritarian, and authoritarian is based on evaluations of 191 countries by the organization Freedom House using a scale of 1 to 7 to designate the degree of political rights in those countries. Countries scored 1 or 2 by Freedom House are counted here as democratic; countries scoring 3, 4, or 5 are categorized as mixed; countries scoring 6 or 7 are labeled authoritarian.

Data source: Freedom House (1997).

Despite progress, democracy is not as fully rooted or as widespread as we might wish. Only about 4 in 10 countries are fully democratic. About 1 in 4 countries is still strongly authoritarian; and the rest are mixed systems with some democratic and some authoritarian aspects.

A SITE TO SURF
Freedom House

ideological evolution and the universalization of Western liberal democracy as the final form of government." Other observers are less optimistic about democracy's strength or the future spread of democracy (Attali, 1997; Burns, 1994). Certainly the spread of democracy has stalled. One study that is conducted annually shows that the number of democracies increased dramatically between 1985 and 1992 to about 79 countries and remains at that number. At the other end of the spectrum, the number of authoritarian countries at first declined during the same period by almost one-third but then returned to its earlier level, about 53 countries (Freedom House, 1997).

Standards of Democracy There are a number of ramifications of democracy that make it of interest to us here. One of these is that some countries, such as the United States, use democracy as a standard to judge other governments. That practice has spread and, in the estimate of some scholars, democratic governance is becoming a global standard that will be favored and, in some

Thinking that they are entering a raffle for a new car, these Mexican voters have been lured into this building so that members of the governing party can get information from their voting credentials. Such practices raise questions about the nature of democracy in many countries around the world.

cases, insisted on by the international community. Perhaps, but the fact remains that the world is still far from establishing a guarantee, backed by force if necessary, of democracy. Still, the norms of the international system have moved in that direction, as evidenced by the UN Security Council's authorization for action against the military government in Haiti in order to restore democracy there in the mid-1990s (Diamond, 1994).

There are, however, several difficulties with insisting that countries be democratic. One issue is that it is not always clear what is democratic and what is not. There are, for example, standards of *procedural democracy* and *substantive democracy*. Americans, Canadians, Western Europeans, and some others tend to equate democracy with procedure. If citizens periodically choose among competing candidates and follow other such procedures, then there is democracy. Many other cultures in the world view democracy as a substantive product associated with equality. Critics of American-style democracy comment, for example, about the gulf between standards of living in places such as Hollywood and the Watts section of Los Angeles, just a few miles away. Critics suggest that you have failed democratically if, despite meeting procedural requisites, your democracy produces a perpetual racial, ethnic, or gender socioeconomic underclass. Such a system, they contend, goes through the motions of democracy while, in the end, denying the most important part of democracy: the substantive human right to equality. Critics further argue that a system, such as capitalism, of vastly different economic circumstances is inherently undemocratic because the theory of free speech or the right to petition the government for the redress of grievances is undercut by the ability of wealthy individuals, groups, and corporations to spend large sums to hire professional lobbyists, to wage public relations campaigns, to donate money to electoral campaigns, to pay attorneys to sue opponents in court, and otherwise to use economic muscle unavailable to most citizens. This, the critics say, makes the contest unfair and undemocratic, no matter what the theory may be.

Possibility and Desirability of Democracy   Yet another conundrum when considering enforcing democracy as a norm in the international system involves the *possibility of democracy*. A democratic-theory issue is whether democracy is always possible. In most of the West, where democracy has existed the longest and seems the most stable, it evolved slowly and often fitfully. More recently, other parts of the world have experienced increased degrees of democratization. Some scholars argue that democracy is spread according to a "contagion theory," but other analysts find that internal factors are most closely associated with whether or not a country is democratic (Ray, 1995). Prosperity is one such domestic factor. Democracy is not inextricably connected to economic development, but there is a correlation between democracy and the level to which a country's people are well educated and can maintain a reasonable standard of living. These circumstances, however, do not exist in many countries. This may mean that attempts to promote full-fledged democracy in these countries are tantamount to trying to impose an alien political system on a socioeconomic system that is not ready for it.

Indeed, there are some who doubt the constant *desirability of democracy*. Some scholars believe that some democratizing states are prone to "belligerent nationalism, making them more bellicose than more stable, if less democratic, countries."[4] Other observers argue that it may be counterproductive to try to institute democracy before a country has established a civil society as a foundation. From this point of view, trying to impose democracy on a country before it is ready can only serve to increase the chance of internal turmoil and decrease the chance for economic development.

To this contention, those who support the spread of democracy respond that any bloodshed that it brings pales when compared to the brutality inflicted by authoritarian regimes. One study of "democide," the killing of unarmed residents by governments, demonstrates that the degree to which a government is totalitarian "largely accounts for the magnitude and intensity of genocide and mass murder" committed by that government. Therefore, the study reasons, "the best assurances against democide are democratic openness, political competition, leaders responsible to their people and limited government. In other words, power kills, and absolute power kills absolutely" (Rummel, 1995:25).

National and Other Interests

Whatever the system of governance of any state, a key factor that governs its affairs and interactions on the global stage is its interests. The concept of national interest is used almost universally to argue for or against any given policy (Clinton, 1994). Most political leaders and citizens still argue that it is paramount. Certainly, most Russians thought it laudable when President Boris Yeltsin proclaimed that "the main goal of our foreign policy is consistent promotion of Russia's national interests."[5] Indeed, it is hard to imagine a national leader announcing that he or she had taken an important action that was counter to the national interest but in the world's interest. Even if such an aberration occurred, it is improbable that the leader would remain in office much longer.

National Interest as a Standard of Conduct

The idea of using national interest as a cornerstone of foreign policy is a key element of the road more traveled by in world politics. Realists contend that it is a wise basis for foreign policy. Henry Kissinger (1994a:37), for one, regrets what he sees as the current U.S. "distrust of America's power, a preference for multilateral solutions and a reluctance to think in terms of national interest. All these impulses," Kissinger believes, "inhibit a realistic response to a world of multiple power centers and diverse conflicts."[6]

Realpolitik nationalists further contend that we live in a Darwinian political world, where people who do not promote their own interests will become prey for those who do. Nationalists further worry about alternative schemes of global governance. One such critic of globalism notes that in intellectual circles "anyone who is skeptical about international commitments today is apt to be dismissed as an isolationist crank." Nevertheless, he continues, globalization should be approached with great caution because "it holds out the prospect of an even more chaotic set of authorities, presiding over an even more chaotic world, at a greater remove from the issues that concern us here in the United States" (Rabkin, 1994:41, 47).

There are other analysts who reject the use of national interest as a guide for foreign policy. The first criticism is that there is no such thing as an objective national interest (Kimura & Welch, 1998). Instead, these critics say, what is in the national interest is totally subjective and exists entirely in the eye of the beholder. Analysts can accurately point out that national interest has been used to describe every sort of good and evil. As used by decision makers, it is a projection of the perceptions of a particular regime or even a single political leader in a given international or domestic environment. Consider again the 1994 U.S. invasion of Haiti. President Clinton told the American people that what happens in Haiti "affects our national security interests" and it was therefore imperative that "we must act now" to "protect our interests."[7] A majority of the American people disagreed with Clinton. A survey just before Clinton's speech found that only 13 percent of respondents believed that "U.S. interests are threatened" and that only 34 percent favored U.S. participation in a multinational invasion. Not only that, but some people thought the invasion of Haiti had more to do with the interests of Bill Clinton than with those of the United States. Of those polled, 32 percent said they thought the motive behind the invasion was that "Clinton will have political problems if he doesn't carry out his threat to invade."[8]

A second criticism of using national interest as a basis of policy is that it incorrectly assumes that there is a common interest. The contention here is that every society is a collection of diverse subgroups, each of which has its own set of interests. Furthermore, the concept of national interest inherently includes the assumption that if a collective interest can be determined, then that interest takes precedence over the interests of subgroups and individuals. Writing from the feminist perspective, for example, one scholar noted that "the presumption of a similarity of interests between the sexes is an assumption" that cannot be taken for granted because "a growing body of scholarly work argues that . . . the political attitudes of men and women differ significantly" (Brandes, 1994:21).

A third difficulty with the idea of national interest is the charge that operating according to one's self-defined, inherently selfish national interest inevitably leads to conflict and inequity on the world stage. The logic is simple. If you and I both pursue our national interests and those objectives are incompatible, then one likely possibility is that we will clash. Another possibility is that the interest of whichever of us is the more powerful will prevail. That is, power, not justice, will win out. Certainly, we might negotiate and compromise, as countries often do. But in an anarchical international system that emphasizes self-interest and self-help, the chances of a peaceful and equitable resolution are less than in a hierarchical domestic system that restrains the contending actors and offers institutions (such as courts) that can decide disputes if negotiation fails.

A fourth common charge is that the way that national interest is applied frequently involves double standards. This is a political golden-rule principle, at least for idealists, that holds that a country should do unto other countries what it would have done unto itself. In other words, what a state does must also be right or wrong for other actors in similar circumstances. For example, the United States has enacted a series of laws that penalize foreign companies for doing business with one or another country that the U.S. government opposes. One such law, the Helms-Burton Act, punishes those who do business with Cuba. Typical of most foreign reaction, the European Union stated that it is "firmly opposed to the extraterritoral nature" of such legislation.[9] Some critics argue that the United States is using a double standard by applying extraterritorial jurisdiction to others, when, some years ago, Americans were outraged when Arab countries applied sanctions to U.S. companies that had commercial relations with Israel. Americans, of course, see a difference between the two matters. But many others do not and wonder whether Americans can remember the old maxim that what is good for the goose ought also to be good for the gander.

A fifth objection to national interest and the way that it is applied contends that it is too often short-sighted. Concerned with their immediate, domestic needs, for example, most economically developed countries (EDCs) give precious little of their wealth to less developed countries (LDCs) in the form of foreign aid. This is short-sighted, some analysts contend, because in the long run the EDCs will become even more prosperous if the LDCs also become wealthy and can buy more goods and services from the EDCs. Furthermore, the argument goes, helping the LDCs now may avoid furthering the seething instability and violence born of poverty. "As images of life lived anywhere on our globe become available to all, so will the contrast between the rich and the poor" become a "force impelling the deprived to demand a better life from the powers that be," then-president Nelson Mandela of South Africa warned a joint session of the U.S. Congress in 1994.[10] He might also have added another old maxim: Avoid being "penny wise and pound foolish."

Alternatives to National Interest

One alternative to national interest is to adopt a standard of global interest. Proponents of this standard contend that the world would be better served if people defined themselves politically as citizens of the world along with, or perhaps in place of, their sense of national political identification. Writes one such advocate, "The apparent vast disjunction between what humankind must do to survive on the planet in a reasonably decent condition . . . and the way world society has typically worked throughout history . . . points to the need . . . for substantial evolution of world society in the direction of world community" (Brown, 1992:167).

A significant point in this internationalist argument is that its advocates claim that they do not reject national interest as such. Instead, they reject national interest in the short-sighted, narrowly self-interested way that the globalists think it is usually construed. In the long run, globalists argue, a more enlightened view of interests sees that the nation will be more secure and more prosperous if it helps everyone become more secure and prosperous. This approach suggests that national interests and human interests are closely related, perhaps even synonymous. For example, one scholar calls for "international communitarianism" to become the new agenda of world politics. "The primary moral tenet of communitarianism," he urges, "is that states should pursue their interest responsibly, that is, with attention to the consequences for other states" (Haas, 1994:7). What this means is that leaders should consider the consequences of a proposed action on the global village as well as on their own state.

Individual interests are another alternative to national interest. Virtually all individuals are rightly concerned with their own welfare. To consider your own interests could be construed as the ultimate narrow-mindedness, but it also may be liberating. It may be that your interests, even your political identification, may shift from issue to issue. As one scholar puts it, "I may identify with the United States on military defense but with the planet on the environment. In any given situation, . . . it is the nature of identification that determines how the boundaries of the self are drawn" (Wendt, 1994).

It is appropriate to ask, then, whether your individual interests, your nation's interests, and your world's interests are the same, mutually exclusive, or a mixed bag of congruencies and divergences. Only you, of course, can determine where your interests lie.

States and the Future

Sovereign, territorially defined states have not always existed, as we have noted. Therefore, they will not necessarily persist in the future. The questions are, Will they? Should they? The future of the state is one of the most hotly debated topics among scholars of international relations. The subject is very much related to the issue of the future of nationalism as detailed in chapter 4, and so a quick review of that material before proceeding here might be helpful.

In their efforts to assert their independence from Serbia and, more broadly, Yugoslavia, Albanians have toppled this statue of King Dusan, a Serbian ruler during the fourteenth century. Does this make him an icon of a fallen greater Serbia?

The State: Predictions of Diminishment and Demise

In rough division, there are two main lines of reasoning by those scholars who foresee or advocate the decline, perhaps the demise, of states as principal actors on the world stage. One contention is that states are obsolete; a second normative argument is that states are destructive (Lugo, 1996; Guéhnno, 1995).

The argument that states are obsolete and even counterproductive begins with the premise that they were created as utilitarian political organizations to meet economic, security, and other specific needs. "The nation-state is a rough and ready mechanism for furnishing a set of real services," one scholar writes. The problem, he continues, is that "the relation between what a state is supposed to do and what it actually does is increasingly slack" (Dunn, 1995:9).

There is an interesting line of reasoning that suggests that states are too large to do the small things people want and need and too little to do the big things. On the one hand, some scholars believe that one cause of the weakening of the state's claim to be sole legitimate international representative of its citizens is the feeling of many people that their interests are ignored or subverted by states and other mega-organizations of the modern world. This sense of loss of individual power in the face of increasingly larger organizations—big government, big corporations—and people's concern about their diversity being homogenized into a bland monoculture intensify when talk about world or regional government, international law, and a uniculture in the global village begins. This may lead to the Jihad tendency and propel people to join or identify with movements or organizations that are more accessible and that share common values.

On the other hand, it may be that states are too limited to deal with the greatest problems facing humankind. As one study puts it, "the separate nation-states have become ever more impotent in dealing on their own . . . with material and political realities that are increasingly threatening the safety and well-being of their citizens" (Brown, 1998:3).

All these limitations, many analysts believe, mean that the state has outlived much of its usefulness as provider and protector. That, these analysts contend, is why the world is witnessing the rapid growth of intergovernmental organizations (IGOs), such as the World Trade Organization (WTO), to deal with international issues, such as global trade. Each such effort toward establishing necessary international order inevitably diminishes the sovereignty of states and moves them just slightly farther away from the footlights at the front of the world stage.

The State: Predictions of Persistence and Prescriptions for Reform

While those who predict the diminishment or demise of the state as a primary political organization are able to make a strong case, it is hardly a foregone conclusion that what they foresee will come to pass. As we noted in chapter 4, nationalism has proven resilient, and its political vehicle, the state, still has many resources at its disposal. This leads some analysts to doubt the substantial weakening, much less the disappearance, of states as sovereign actors. As two such scholars write, "Reports of its demise notwithstanding, sovereignty appears to us to be prospering, not declining, as the twentieth century draws to a close. It still serves as an indispensable component of international politics" (Fowler & Bunck, 1995:163). "Although the evidence is not decisive," another scholar writes, "I am skeptical that state sovereignty has eroded" (Thomson, 1995:231).

Can States Cooperate?

A question related to continuance of the state as the primary international actor is whether the state is inherently a self-centered structure that pursues its interests aggressively or a political structure that can adjust to the new systemic realities by learning to cooperate and live in peace with other countries. There are some analysts, such as the neoidealists discussed in chapter 1, who believe that countries can learn to cooperate and that the increasing creation of and membership in numerous IGOs, like the WTO, is evidence that states are willing to give up some of their sovereignty in return for the benefits provided by free trade and other transnational interactions.

Neorealists, also discussed in chapter 1, reply that states join IGOs to dominate them, not to use them for cooperation. A related neorealist contention, as one study puts it, is that "states increasingly exercise sovereignty in multilateral, international institutions which are distant from societal control" (Thomson, 1995:230). The import of this argument is that the leaders of national governments try to follow their conceptions of the national interest by using the IGOs to shield the leaders from domestic political pressures and legal and constitutional restrictions. One good example is that U.S. presidents now contend that if the UN Security Council, NATO, or some other IGO has authorized action in Iraq, Haiti, the Balkans, or some other place, the president does not have to seek authorization from Congress to send U.S. troops into action. This connection between presidential power and the UN was first made by President George Bush when he told an audience, "I have the inherent power to commit our forces to battle [against Iraq] after the UN resolution [authorizing action] (Rourke, Carter, & Boyer, 1996:175).

INTERACTIVE EXERCISE
McDonald's or Democracy: What Builds World Peace?

Can States Remain at Peace?

Another impetus to change toward greater cooperation among states involves the spread of democratic governance. The basic argument is that if all states became democracies, the chance of war would decrease to near zero.

The German philosopher Immanuel Kant argued in *Perpetual Peace* (1795) that the spread of democracy would change the world by eliminating war. This would result, Kant reasoned, because "if the consent of the citizens is required in order to decide that war should be declared . . . , nothing is more natural than that they would be very cautious in commencing such a poor game, decreeing for themselves all the calamities of war." Modern scholarship has taken up this question of whether democratic regimes are more peaceful, especially with one another (Chan, 1997; Elman, 1997; Brown, Lynn-Jones, & Miller, 1996).

Using empirical methods, contemporary scholars have established "what has become regarded as a bedrock of findings that suggest that democratic states rarely, if ever, fight other democratic states" (Thompson & Tucker, 1997:428). One that looked in part at relations between countries that share borders (and, thus, are most likely to go to war) found, as shown in Figure 6.2, that of various possible combinations, contiguous democracies were the least likely to go to war.

There are several explanations proffered as to why democracies are less bellicose than autocracies. These explanations can be broadly divided into three groups: institutional explanations, normative explanations, and interest explanations.

Institutional explanations focus on how the way that democracies operate (open criticism, elections, legislative action) positively affects peace. Many scholars believe that democratic leaders are often restrained from going to war because they fear that conflict might harm their electoral chances. As one

Figure 6.2

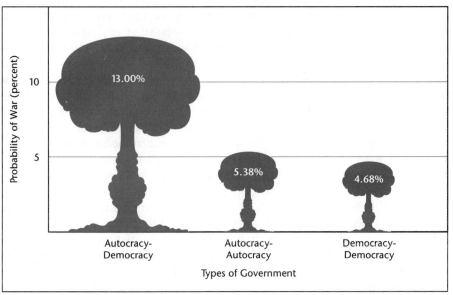

The Probability of War between Contiguous States (1950–1985)

The probability of war in any given year between any two contiguous states during the period 1950–1985.

Data source: Oneal & Russett (1996); also, see Oneal, Oneal, Maoz, & Russett (1996).

During the cold war, the most peaceful possibility between two contiguous states was when they were both democratic. The most volatile combination was when one state was autocratic and the other was democratic.

scholar puts it, "Democratic states are probably quite likely to avoid wars against one another for reasons ultimately based on the desire of their elected leaders to keep themselves in power" (Ray, 1997:60). A related argument is that, fearing loss in a war and ensuing personal political defeat, democratic leaders faced with conflict are "more inclined to sift extra resources into the war effort than are autocrats. . . . This makes democrats unattractive targets." (Bueno de Mesquita, et al., 1998).

Normative explanations hold that democracies both become allies of one another and are less likely to fight one another because they share similar values and, therefore, share benign images of each other (Gaubatz, 1996). It may also be that democratic societies and leaders, which are used to settling domestic differences peacefully, are more likely to settle international disputes in the same way (Hermann & Kegley, 1995; Raymond, 1994).

Yet another normative explanation about domestic democracy and external war is based on the view that violence is pervasive. As such, countries that are repressive internally are more apt to be violent externally. In fact, there are some scholars who take this idea even further and argue that societies, not just governments, that are violent (with, for example, prevalent family violence and murder and assaults), make for both violent domestic regimes and bellicose foreign policies. This idea goes back as far as Aristotle (384–322 B.C.), who warned in *Politics* that a citizen "trained for victory in war and the subjugation of neighboring regimes" may also be disposed "to capture the government of his own city." The idea that violence at any level breeds violence at every level is a very strong element in, among other places, feminist international relations theory.

Interest explanations attribute the democratic peace phenomenon to the fact that democracies and their citizens tend to be "satisfied." They are neither interested in upsetting the established order nor willing to accept the risks of doing so. Since there is some relationship between a country's level of economic development and the likelihood of that country being a democracy, it arguably follows that those who are relatively satisfied economically (and who have more to lose) are less bellicose than poorer, less democratic countries (Lemke & Reed, 1996; Rousseau, et al., 1996).

Not all scholars agree with the theory of democratic peace (Caprioli, 1998; Gowa, 1995). Some analysts are skeptical that the absence of war between democracies is anything more than a statistical or historical anomaly that may not persist in the future (Gartzke, 1998; Oren, 1995). This argument would disagree with, for instance, the findings shown in Figure 6.2 by suggesting that the cold war was an atypical period during which most of the democracies were in one bloc and the other bloc was made up mostly of nondemocracies. One such view contends that "the evidence . . . [shows] that the democratic peace is of relatively recent origins." The study doubts whether peace will persist because the "strong common interests among a relatively large number of states" that marked the cold war have weakened in the post–cold war period (Farber & Gowa, 1995:145).

Yet other scholars point out that democracy is not always a force for peace (James & Hristoulas, 1994). Some analysts maintain, and others dispute, that as countries transition to democracy, they may be more unstable and aggressive than either when they were clearly autocratic or than they will be when they become established democracies (Ward & Gleditsch, 1998; Gleditsch & Hegre, 1997). There is also some evidence that the behavior of democracies can become more aggressive under certain internal conditions, such as economic hardship. Other studies find that public pressure sometimes pushes democratic leaders toward war rather than away from it. One such study concludes, for example, that governments "assured of reelection" and those with "no prospect of reelection" are relatively peaceful but that "when the voters' evaluation of foreign policy outcome could have an effect on election results, then governments are biased toward violent, adventurous foreign policy projects" (Smith, 1996:133). For example, President Lyndon Johnson took the United States to war in Vietnam in part to forestall any possible partisan accusations that he had not been sufficiently anticommunist. What occurred, one scholar wrote, is that Johnson "*followed* public opinion by *leading* it into a war that neither he nor the public wanted" (Zaller, 1994:250).

The debate over whether democracy can be equated with international peace is far from over. Scholars are finding that the likelihood of war is most predictable when levels of democracy or autocracy are combined with other factors, such as the degree of trade interdependence or the degree to which countries are satisfied with their territorial status quo (Kacowicz, 1995). There is also evidence that the relationship between democracy and war is reinforcing. Not only does democracy promote peace but peace promotes democratic development (Midlarsky, 1995).

To return to the main point, some scholars believe that the sovereign state can both persist as the principal actor on the world stage and do so peacefully and cooperatively if the spread of democracy continues. "Our findings support a favorable prognosis for international relations," one study reports:

> There has been a dramatic increase in the number of democracies.... If they continue to proliferate, even societies that retain some traditional institutions of government may increasingly adopt structure and norms conducive to peace. Interdependence, too, has grown [and] the technologies that facilitate international communication and transportation continue to advance.... [All this gives] more reason than ever ... to believe that Hobbesian anarchy is being reconstructed to reflect liberal values. This is not [naive]. As Kant observed, peace does not depend upon our becoming angels as long as even devils calculate. (Oneal, Oneal, Maoz, & Russett, 1996:28)

Chapter Summary

1. States are the most important political actors. States as political organizations are defined by having sovereignty, territory, population, diplomatic recognition, internal organization, and domestic support.
2. The sovereign territorial state is a relatively modern form of political organization. States emerged in the West in the aftermath of the decline of the local authority of the feudal system and the universalistic authority of the Roman Catholic Church and the Holy Roman Empire.
3. There are various authoritarian and democratic theories of governance that shape the state as a core political organization.
4. Monarchism, communism as applied politically, and fascism are three forms of authoritarian governance. The percentage of countries ruled by authoritarian regimes has declined, but dictatorial governments are still common. Some analysts fear the democratization process has halted and even that a reverse trend might occur.

5. Democracy is a complex concept. There are different procedural and substantive standards of what determines whether or not a political system is democratic.

6. There are also disputes over when it is possible or advisable to press all countries to quickly adopt democratic forms of government.

7. There are many types of interests—national, state, governmental, global, and individual—and it is important to distinguish among them. National interest has been and is the traditional approach to determining international activity, but there are some people who contend that national interest is synonymous with destructive self-promotion and should be diminished or even abandoned.

8. The future of the state is a hotly debated topic among scholars of international relations.

9. Some analysts predict the demise of states as principal actors, claiming that states are obsolete and destructive.

10. Other analysts of nationalism contend that the state is durable and has many resources at its disposal. These analysts doubt that the states will weaken substantially or disappear as sovereign actors.

11. One key question that will help determine the fate of states is whether they can cooperate in the future to address global problems, such as environmental degradation.

12. A second key question that will help determine the fate of states is whether they can remain at peace in an era of nuclear arms and other weapons of mass destruction that have increased the severity of war manyfold.

CONNECTEXT

Chapter 7

International Organization: The Alternative Structure

Friendly counsel cuts off many foes.

Shakespeare, *Henry VI, Part 1*

[The United Nations is] group therapy for the world.

Antonio Montiero, Portuguese ambassador to the UN

The sovereign state has been the primary actor in world politics and the essential building block of the state-based international system. Indeed, it is hard to conceive of any other form of organizing and conducting international relations. Yet there are alternatives.

International organization is one of these alternatives (Diehl, 1996). As we have seen, there are many drawbacks to basing global relations on self-interested states operating in an anarchical international system. Many observers believe that global, regional, and specialized international organizations can and should begin authoritatively to regulate the behavior of often-conflicting

Chapter Outline

states. Advocates of strengthened international organization believe that it is time to address world problems by working toward global solutions through global organizations. Those who take this view would join in the counsel given by Shakespeare in *Henry VI, Part III:* "Now join your hands, and with your hands your hearts." Such advice may be right. It is just possible that ongoing organizations will serve as prototypes or building blocks for a future, higher form of political loyalty and activity.

It is all too easy to dismiss the notion of international organizations as idealistic dreaming. But there was also a time when we believed that the world was the center of the universe. We now know that the Sun does not turn around the Earth; perhaps we can learn that the national state need not be the center of the political cosmos. Surrendering some of your country's sovereignty to an international organization may seem unsettling. But it is neither inherently wrong, nor unheard of in today's world. In fact, the growth in the number, functions, and authority of international organizations is one of the most important trends in international relations. To explore this change in governance, this chapter will take up international organizations as they currently exist and as they might operate in the future with expanded roles and authority. The primary focus will be the United Nations, but many other such organizations will be discussed to illustrate what is and what might be. The European Union, in particular, will provide us with an example of a regional organization with the potential of evolving into a true international government. Shakespeare tells us in *Hamlet* that "we know what we are, but not what we can be." Perhaps he was correct in saying that we cannot know for sure what we can be, but we surely can imagine what we *might* be if we keep our minds open to new ideas.

The Nature and Development of International Organization

The concept of international organization is not a new one, although the practice of having a continuous international organization is a relatively recent advance in the conduct of international relations. Now there are a growing number of permanent international organizations whose size and scope vary greatly, ranging from multipurpose, nearly universal organizations like the United Nations to single-purpose organizations with very few member countries.

Types of International Organizations

The term *international organization* tends to bring the United Nations to mind. There are many more, however. They can be divided geographically into global or regional organizations and grouped by functions into general or specialized international organizations, as shown in Table 7.1. Whatever their specifics, though, all the organizations that we will discuss in this chapter share the fact that their memberships consist of national governments. Therefore, they

Table 7.1

Types and Examples of IGOs

| | Purpose | |
Geography	General	Specialized
Global	United Nations	World Trade Organization
Regional	European Union	Arab Monetary Fund

International organizations (IGOs) can be classified according to whether they are general purpose, dealing with many issues, or specialized, dealing with a specific concern. Another way of dividing IGOs is into global and regional organizations.

are termed international **intergovernmental organizations (IGOs)** to distinguish them from the transnational (or international) **nongovernmental organizations (NGOs)** discussed in several other chapters.

The Roots of International Organization

International organization is primarily a modern phenomenon. One thing that you can note about IGOs is that nearly all of them were created in the last 50 years or so. It is also true, though, that the origins of international organizations extend far back in history. Three main root systems have nourished the current growth of international organizations.

Belief in a Community of Humankind

The first branch of the root system is the universal concern for improving the condition of humanity. The idea that humans share a common bond is not new. Philosophers, including William Penn, the Abbé de Sainte-Pierre, and Immanuel Kant, argued that the way to accomplish this end was through general international organizations (Pagden, 1998; Bohman & Lutz-Bachmann, 1997).

The *United Nations* is the latest, and most advanced, developmental stage of universal concern with the human condition. Like the **League of Nations** founded immediately following World War I, the UN was established mainly to maintain peace. Nevertheless, it has increasingly become involved in a broad range of issues that encompasses almost all the world's concerns. In addition, the UN and its predecessor, the League, represent the coming together of all the root systems of international organizations. They are more properly seen as the emergent saplings of extensive cooperation and integration.

Big-Power Peacekeeping

The second branch of the root system is the idea that the big powers have a special responsibility to cooperate and preserve peace. When the United Nations succeeded the League of Nations, the special status and responsibilities of the big powers in the League's council were transferred to the UN Security Council (UNSC). Like its predecessor, the UNSC is the main peacekeeping

These technicians are servicing an American aircraft that is based in Italy and is being used for the NATO peacekeeping mission in Kosovo. Even though intergovernmental organizations such as the UN are implicitly and explicitly based on the notion of collective security, this scene is testament to the need for big-power involvement in peacekeeping at least for the foreseeable future.

organ and includes permanent membership for five major powers (China, France, Great Britain, Russia, and the United States). We will further explore the Security Council, but for now we should notice that a conceptual descendant of the Concert of Europe is alive and well in the UNSC.

Functional Cooperation

The third branch of our root system is composed of the specialized agencies that deal with specific economic and social problems. The six-member Central Commission for the Navigation of the Rhine, established in 1815, is the oldest surviving IGO, and the International Telegraphic (now Telecommunications) Union (1865) and the Universal Postal Union (1874) are the oldest surviving IGOs with global membership. As detailed below, the growth of specialized IGOs and NGOs has been phenomenal. This aspect of international activity is also reflected in the UN through the 20 specialized agencies associated with the world body.

The Expansion of IGOs

An important phenomenon of the twentieth century is the rapid growth in the number, activities, and importance of intergovernmental and nongovernmental organizations.

Figure 7.1

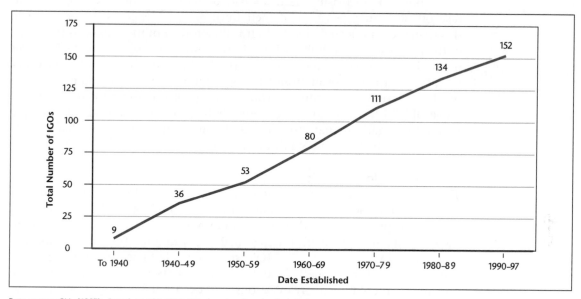

The Establishment of IGOs

Data source: CIA (1997). Based on 152 IGOs listed and authors' calculations.

The growth of IGOs is primarily a modern trend. You can see here, based on one source's list of 152 IGOs, that most were established in the last half century. In fact, these 152 IGOs have been in existence an average of only 30 years. That makes them only slightly younger on average than Americans, whose average age in 1997 was 34.

Quantitative Expansion

This century has seen rapid growth in the number of countries and an even faster percentage growth of all types of IGOs. Figure 7.1 highlights this rapid expansion. This figure also gives us an important perspective to remember when evaluating the evolution of IGOs. That perspective is the relative "youthfulness" of the average IGO. Using what one source considers the 110 most important IGOs, it is possible to calculate that in 1997 the average age of these IGOs was 30, some four years younger than the age of the average American.

Expansion of Roles

Even more important than the growing number of IGOs is the expanding roles that they play. There are several aspects to this. First, more and more common governmental functions are being dealt with by IGOs. If you reviewed the major departments and ministries of your national government and the subjects they address, it is almost certain that you would be able to find one or more IGOs that deal with the same subjects on the international level. Second, some of these expanding roles are dealt with by creating new IGOs. For example, the development of satellites and the ability to communicate through them and the need to coordinate this capability led to the establishment of the International Telecommunications Satellite Organization (INTELSAT) in 1971.

Third, the increasing need for IGO activity is leading existing IGOs to take on new functions beyond their initial roles. Few IGOs better illustrate this than the European Union (EU). It is the product of the expanded functions of the European Community, which, in turn, was the result of the 1967 merger of the European Economic Community, the European Coal and Steel Community, and the European Atomic Energy Community. Furthermore, the scope of EU activities is expanding beyond its original economic focus to a wider range of political and social concerns. It is also developing an increasingly important organizational structure, and some Europeans hope that the EU will evolve into a United States of Europe.

Reasons for Expansion

This century's rapid growth of international organizations, both in number and in scope of activity, is the result of a number of forces. Those forces will be detailed presently, but they were summarized by two scholars who examined why states act through international organizations. Their conclusion was that "by taking advantage . . . of IO's, states are able to achieve goals that they cannot accomplish [alone]" (Abbot & Snidal, 1998:29). In other words, the growth of international organizations has occurred because countries have found that they need them and that they work.

Increased international contact is one cause of expansion. The revolutions in communications and transportation technologies have brought the states of the world into much closer contact. These interchanges need organizational structures in order to become routine and regulated. The International Telegraphic Union, founded over a century ago, has been joined in more modern times by the INTELSAT and almost 300 others.

The world's *increased interdependence,* particularly in the economic sphere, has fostered a variety of IGOs designed to deal with this phenomenon (Diehl, 1997). The International Monetary Fund (IMF) and the World Bank are just two examples. Regional trade and monetary organizations, cartels, and, to a degree, multinational corporations are other examples. A third cause of the growth of international organizations is the *expansion of transnational problems* that affect many states and require solutions that are beyond the resources of any single state. One such issue (and its associated IGO) is nuclear proliferation (International Atomic Energy Agency).

A fourth incentive for the expansion of IGOs is the *failure of the current state-centered system* to provide security. The agony of two world wars, for instance, convinced many that peace was not safe in the hands of nation-states. The United Nations is the latest attempt to organize for the preservation of peace. The continuing problems in health, food, human rights, and other areas have also spurred the creation of IGOs.

A fifth factor is the *effort of small states to gain strength through joint action.* The concentration of military and economic power in a handful of countries has led less powerful actors to join coalitions in an attempt to influence events. Sixth and last, the existence and successes of international organizations provide *role models* that have generated still other IGOs and NGOs. People and countries have learned that they can sometimes work together internationally, and this has encouraged them to try new ventures in international organization and cooperation.

Goals of International Organization

There is no doubt that the number and importance of international organizations have grown in this century. We should, therefore, ask ourselves, What is it that we want international organizations to accomplish ultimately? This question is especially important for the most significant and strongest IGOs. The various ideas about the proper and possible goals of IGOs can be grouped into two broad categories. One category includes relatively limited and traditional goals. The second category is much more far-reaching and foresees international organizations moving toward assuming the roles of regional governments or even of a global government.

The roles of intergovernmental organizations, to date in their evolution, have been defined mostly in limited, traditional ways. There are, however, a range of more far-reaching activities that some people believe IGOs can and should take up. It is possible to arrange these roles along a scale that measures how close each is to the traditional road or the alternative road of international politics. Starting at the traditional end of the scale and moving toward the alternative end, the four roles are: interactive arena, creator and center of cooperation, independent international actor, and supranational organization.

Before moving to these four roles, it should be noted that they are evaluated quite differently by realists and idealists. *Realists* believe that there are only two roles that IGOs can play. One is as an interactive arena in which each country pursues its narrow national interests. The second role is that of promoting limited, pragmatic cooperation when that goal works to each state's advantage. As one realist scholar puts it, IGOs "are basically a reflection of the distribution of power in the world. They are based on the self-interested calculations of the great powers, . . . have no independent effect on state behavior, . . . [and] therefore . . . are not an important cause of peace" (Mearsheimer, 1995:7).

Idealists have a very different view (Majeski & Fricks, 1995). They reject the realist analysis of IGOs as "incomplete and logically unsound" because, in part, it does not offer "a plausible account of the investments that states have made in such international institutions as the EU, NATO, GATT, and the regional trading organizations." Furthermore, and looking toward the future, idealists contend that IGOs are "essential if states are to have any hope of sustained cooperation" and that "international institutions . . . will be components of any lasting peace" (Keohane & Martin, 1995:47, 50).

INTERACTIVE EXERCISE
Searching for International Organizations: Roles and Resources

Interactive Arena

The most common use of IGOs is to provide an interactive arena in which member-states pursue their individual national interests (Krause & Knight, 1995). The IGO itself is technically neutral, but members or coalitions of members often try to use it to further their goals. This approach is rarely stated openly, but it is obvious in the struggles within the UN and other IGOs, where countries and blocs of countries wage political struggles with a vengeance. During the Persian Gulf crisis of 1990–1991 and since, for instance, the United States used the UN to provide legitimacy for the U.S. desire to expel Iraq from Kuwait and, subsequently, to use sanctions (especially preventing Iraq from selling oil) to prevent any rebuilding of Iraqi military might. This does not imply that Washington has used Machiavellian maneuvers to manipulate an unwilling UN membership. Rather, it means that the United States was and is determined to defeat any Iraqi threat to the source of the oil that fuels the industrialized countries. It is probable that the United States would have forced Iraq from Kuwait and then sought to weaken the Iraqi regime in any case, but securing UN support for the military campaign and sanctions has helped defuse any charge that a superpower was and is picking on an LDC or a non-Western country.

The use of supposedly integrative international organizations to gain national advantage is somewhat contradictory to the purpose of these organizations and has disadvantages. One negative factor is that it sometimes transforms these organizations into another scene of struggle rather than utilizing them to enhance cooperation. Furthermore, countries are apt to reduce or withdraw their support from an international organization that does not serve their narrow national interests. Still, the use of IGOs as interactive arenas does not necessarily imply a corruption of the intent of the organizations. There is a theory of international integration called intergovernmentalism that argues that integration can advance even when IGOs are the arena for self-interested national interaction with each country's policy preference determined in part by domestic politics. The reasoning is that even when realpolitik is the starting point, the process that occurs in an IGO fosters the habit of cooperation and compromise (Huelshoff, 1994).

The interactive arenas aspect of IGOs has other advantages. Sometimes, as in the case of reversing Iraq's aggression, using the IGO makes it politically easier to take needed action. Also, debate and diplomatic maneuver may even provide a forum for diplomatic struggle. This role of providing an alternative to the battlefield may promote the resolution of disputes without violence. As Winston Churchill put it once, "To jaw-jaw is better than to war-war."[1]

Creator and Center of Cooperation

A second role that IGOs perform is to promote and facilitate cooperation among states and other international actors. This type of activity is called **functionalism**. The term represents the idea that the way to global cooperation is through a "bottom up," evolutionary approach that begins with limited, pragmatic cooperation on narrow, nonpolitical issues, and uses each such instance of cooperation as a building block to achieve broader cooperation on more and more politically sensitive issues.

International regimes are one-way stations along that path (Hasenclever & Mayer, 1997). A regime is not a single organization. Instead, a **regime** is a collective noun that designates a complex of stated and understood principles, norms, rules, processes, and organizations that, in sum, help to govern the behavior of states and other international actors in an area of international concern such as the use and protection of international bodies of water.

The idea of regimes is based on the theory that comprehensive cooperation will evolve through a process that gradually merges the initially separate rules of international law and treaties; the activities of IGOs and NGOs; the patterns of compliant behavior by states and other actors; and the expectations of the international actors and the people of the world into a unified whole—a regime (Cortell & Davis, 1996). Some regimes may encompass cooperative relations within a region (Solingen, 1994). Other regimes like the UN Convention on the Law of the Sea are global, and provide rules for the use of the world's oceans and seas (Young & Osherenko, 1993).

Independent International Actor

The third of the existing and possible IGO roles is that of an independent international actor. This role is located distinctly toward the alternative end of the traditional-alternative scale of IGO activities. Technically, what any IGO does is controlled by the wishes and votes of its members. In reality, many IGOs develop strong, relatively permanent administrative staffs. These individuals often identify with the organization and try to increase its authority and role. The views of staff members may differ from the views of the IGO's member-countries. Global expectations—such as "the UN should do something"—add to the sense that an IGO may be a force unto itself. Soon, to use an old phrase, the whole (of the IGO) becomes more than the sum of its (member-country) parts. We will explore this role more fully when we discuss the United Nations later in the chapter. But insofar as IGOs do play an independent role, proponents of this approach argue that it should be one mainly of mediation and conciliation rather than coercion. The object is to teach and allow, not to force, states to work together.

To a degree, organizational independence is intended and established in the charters of various IGOs. The International Court of Justice (ICJ) was created to act independently. The UN Charter directs that the secretary-general and his or her staff "shall not seek or receive instructions from any government or from any other authority external to the organization." And the European Parliament is a unique example of an IGO assembly whose representatives are popularly elected rather than appointed and directed by national governments.

Independence is also a product of the assertiveness of the international bureaucracies. As we will see later in this chapter, the assertive leadership of

FIGURE
Regimes for
Oceans and Seas

A SITE TO SURF
Oceans and the
Law of the Sea

numerous chief executive officers of IGOs, such as European Commission President Jacques Delors of the EU or UN secretaries-general Dag Hammarskjöld, Boutros Boutros-Ghali, and Kofi Annan have helped give their organizations a vision and will that are more than mere reflections of the desires of the member-states.

Supranational Organization

It may also be possible for IGOs to play a fourth role: **supranational organization**. This means that the international organization has authority over its members, which, therefore, are subordinate units. Theoretically, some IGOs possess a degree of supranationalism and can obligate members to take certain actions. In reality, supranationalism is extremely limited. Few states concede any significant part of their sovereignty to any international body. But there are some signs that the dogged independence of states is giving way to limited acceptance of international authority. As we will see in chapter 9 on international law, for instance, countries normally abide by some aspects of international law, even at times when it conflicts with their domestic law or their immediate interests.

The extreme limits on supranationalism that now prevail do not mean, however, that the authority of IGOs cannot expand. There is a vision held by some proponents of international organization that goes far beyond the roles discussed in the preceding sections. There are many people who believe that it is time to move toward a more established form of international government. Such supranational government could be **regional** or global, federal or confederal in scope and could manifest itself in a variety of the ways discussed throughout this chapter.

There is a strong critique of the potential for growing supranationalism. Critics argue that, first, there are *practical barriers* to the ultimate form of supranationalism, **world government.** The assumption here is that nationalism has too strong a hold and that neither political leaders nor masses would be willing to surrender independence to a universal body. Are we ready to "pledge allegiance to the United States of the World"? Critics of the world government movement also pose political objections. They worry about the concentration of power that would be necessary to enforce international law and to address the world's monumental economic and social problems. Critics further doubt that any such government, even given unprecedented power, could succeed in solving world problems any better than less (potentially) authoritarian alternatives. Some skeptics further argue that centralization would inevitably diminish desirable cultural diversity and political experimentation in the world. Another criticism of the world government movement is that it diverts attention from more reasonable avenues of international cooperation, such as the United Nations and other existing IGOs.

Whatever one's views about whether international governance should occur at the regional or global level—or at all, for that matter—the reality is that there is movement toward supranational organization. Many observers see this shift as the natural outcome of a process of adjusting political structure to human needs. There are others, however, such as the members of the John Birch Society, who believe that the move toward greater international government is a plot of **elites** to strip away the rights and benefits associated with national citizenship.

To further explore the current and expanding roles of IGOs, we can break them down into two groups: regional IGOs and global IGOs. There are many organizations at each level, and many of these will be touched upon in the following pages of this chapter or explored in detail in later chapters. For now, though, it will be most instructive to focus on the most prominent regional IGO, the European Union, and the most important global IGO, the United Nations.

Regional IGOs: Focus on the European Union

The growth of regional IGOs has been striking (Mace & Therien, 1996). Prior to World War II there were no prominent regional IGOs. Now there are many. Most of these are relatively specialized, with regional economic IGOs, such as the Arab Cooperation Council, the most numerous. There are, however, other specialized regional IGOs, such as the Agency for the Prohibition of Nuclear Weapons in Latin America and the Caribbean. Other regional IGOs are general purpose and deal with a range of issues. These include, for example, the Organization of African Unity (OAU) and the Organization of American States (OAS).

One noteworthy development regarding regional IGOs is that some of them are transitioning from specialized to general purpose organizations. The Association of Southeast Asian Nations (ASEAN) was founded in 1967 to promote regional economic cooperation. More recently, though, ASEAN has begun to take on a stronger political tinge, and, in particular, may serve as a political and defensive counterweight to China in the region. A more obvious change in role is evident for the Economic Community of West African States (ECOWAS). It was established in 1975 to facilitate economic interchange, but in the 1990s ECOWAS took on a very different function when it intervened in the multisided civil war raging in Liberia. Approximately 8,000 troops from member countries Gambia, Ghana, Guinea, Nigeria, and Sierra Leone moved to end the fighting that had turned almost half of Liberia's 2.3 million people into refugees in neighboring countries. Hampered by very limited funds and personnel, the ECOWAS force did not try to dominate militarily, but it did provide enough stability to lead to an ECOWAS-sponsored demobilization of the armed factions in January 1997.

Beyond any of these examples of regional IGOs, the best example of what is possible is the regionalism in Europe (Dinan, 1994). There, the European Union, an IGO of 15 member countries, has moved toward full economic integration. It has also traveled in the direction of considerable political cooperation.

The Origins and Evolution of the European Union

The **European Union (EU)** has evolved through several stages. One early impetus for European economic cooperation came in 1947 when the United States demanded that Europe make joint requests for and plans to use U.S. aid provided by the European Recovery Program, also known as the Marshall Plan. Within Europe, France's foreign minister, Robert Schuman, proposed in 1950 that the continent's coal and steel production be placed under a single authority. He is considered by some to be the father of modern Europe because of his vision of a united Europe. The Schuman Plan soon came to fruition, and from this beginning European economic and political integration has evolved considerably. Some people believe that one day the French leader's vision will be fulfilled, and that a United States of Europe will come into being.

One way to keep track of the changes in the structure and purpose of the EU described in the following paragraphs is to note the changes in the names of the successive organizations. "What's in a name?" you might ask, echoing Shakespeare's heroine in *Romeo and Juliet*. As she discovered, the names Capulet and Montague proved important. So too, the name changes leading up to the current EU are important in the tale they tell.

Economic Integration

The genesis of the EU dates back to 1952 when Belgium, France, (West) Germany, Italy, Luxembourg, and the Netherlands joined together to create a common market for coal, iron, and steel products called the European Coal and Steel Community (ECSC). It proved so successful that in 1957 the six countries signed the Treaties of Rome that created the **European Economic Community (EEC)** to facilitate trade in many additional areas and the European Atomic Energy Community (EURATOM) to coordinate matters in that realm. Both new communities came into being on January 1, 1958.

Interchange among the 6 countries expanded rapidly, and they soon felt that they should coordinate their activities even further. This led to their creating the European Communities (EC), which went into operation in 1967. Each of the 3 preexisting organizations maintained a legal identity, but they gradually turned their individual activities over to the EC's policy-making and judicial institutions. The membership and the level of integration of the EC continued to expand. Denmark, Ireland, and Great Britain were admitted in 1973, bringing membership to 9. Greece became the 10th member in 1981; Spain and Portugal's admission in 1986 brought the EC's membership to 12. The most recent expansion came on January 1, 1995, when 3 new countries (Austria, Finland, and Sweden) joined the (by then) EU, bringing its membership to 15. The EU in 1997 extended membership invitations to 6 countries: Cyprus, the Czech Republic, Estonia, Hungary, Poland, and Slovenia. Several others, including Bulgaria, Latvia, Lithuania, Romania, and Slovakia, are also seeking membership, although the EU's Agenda 2000 report released in 1997 indicated that those countries would have to make further democratic or economic reforms before they could hope to join the EU. The eventual, if not quite stated, goal of the EU is to encompass all the region's countries. Jacques Santer, the president of the European Commission, insists that no country that meets the EU economic and political standards should be kept out. "There will be no such things as 'in countries' and 'out countries'; rather there will be 'ins' and 'pre-ins'," he has said.[2]

For about 30 years, the integrative process in Europe focused on economics. Members of the EC grew even more interdependent as economic barriers were eliminated. The EEC had established a common agricultural policy (CAP) in 1964 governing such issues as crop subsidies. In 1968 the members of the EC abolished the last tariffs on manufactured goods among themselves and established a common EC external tariff. The EC also began to bargain as a whole with other countries in trade negotiations. The EC also signed the Lomé Convention (1975), establishing mutually preferential trade relations with 46 African, Caribbean, and Pacific (ACP) countries and coordinated aid by EC members to the LDCs. The EC was further strengthened in 1970 when its members agreed to fund it with a virtually independent revenue source by giving it a share of each country's value-added tax (VAT, similar to a sales tax) and all customs duties collected on imports from non–EC countries.

The next major step in the EU's evolution toward economic integration came in 1987 when the Single European Act (SEA) went into effect. Passed by the European Council, the SEA amended the basic EC agreement and committed the EC to becoming a fully integrated economic unit by the end of 1992. This planned integration was given the sobriquet "Europe 1992" to symbolize the goal of the complete elimination of all internal barriers to the movement of trade, capital, workers, and services. That goal was not quite reached, but by 1993 the EC had achieved the most advanced level of regional economic integration in history.

A SITE TO SURF
The European Union

Political Integration

There comes a point in economic integration when pressure builds to take steps toward political integration. One reason this occurs is that it is impossible to reach full economic integration among sovereign states whose domestic and foreign political policies are sometimes in conflict. Moreover, as the people become one economically, it becomes less bizarre to think of becoming one politically.

The current and more political phase of Europe's integrative evolution is reflected in the name European Union. It came into existence on November 1, 1993, the day that the far-reaching Treaty on European Union (commonly called the **Maastricht Treaty**) went into effect. Among the treaty's important economic provisions are calls for monetary integration, the coordination of social policies (such as labor conditions and benefits), and other steps to increase economic integration further.

Of even potentially greater importance are the political changes included in the treaty. The concept of European citizenship has been expanded. Citizens of EU countries can travel on either an EU or a national passport, and citizens of any EU country can vote in local and European Parliament elections in another EU country in which they live. There is a growing number of joint European enterprises, such as the European Space Agency, the various multilateral efforts to mediate conflictual disputes, such as those in the Balkans, and even the eventual movement toward a common security policy.

Yet another indication of the political, as well as economic, integration of Europe is the emergence of an ever larger and more active and powerful EU infrastructure. The EU's administrative staff has almost quintupled from a little over 5,000 in 1970 to about 25,000 today. The number of EU regulations, decisions, and directives from one or the other EU body has risen from an annual 345 in 1970 to over 600 a year. The annual EU budget is about $87 billion, raised from tariff revenues and from part of each member's VAT. The future evolution of the EU is not set, of course, but we would do well to examine what may be the prototype of the government of Europe.

The Government of Europe: A Prototype

FIGURE
Membership and Organizational Structure of the European Union

The EU's organizational structure is extremely complex, but a brief look at it is important to illustrate the extent to which a regional government has been created. The figure on the Web site gives a brief overview of this structure. The EU's government can be divided for analysis into the political leadership, the bureaucracy, the legislature, and the judiciary (Richardson, 1997).

Political Leadership

Political decision making occurs within the *Council of Ministers*. Some confusion occurs in nomenclature, because when the Council of Ministers meets with the prime ministers and other heads of government in attendance, it is commonly called the *European Council*. This more august council meets twice a year and decides on the most important policy directions for the EU. Its work is supplemented by the regular Council of Ministers meetings, which occur as often as twice a week. Most sessions are held in Brussels, Belgium, which is the principal site of the EU administrative element. The ministers are normally the foreign ministers, but other ministers (such as agricultural ministers) also represent their countries, depending on the matters to be discussed. Both councils were originally designed to reflect the individual views of the member-states on an equal basis. As such, each country originally had one vote. This was changed by the Single European Act in 1986, and now voting on many measures is by a weighted-vote plan (termed "qualified majority voting"). Under this plan the larger EU countries have more votes on some matters. There are a total of 87 votes, with each country's allocation ranging from 10 votes for Germany to 2 votes for Luxembourg. Unanimity is required for most important measures, but some issues related to markets and taxation within the EU can be passed by 62 votes.

The importance of the European Council as a central decision-making body was underlined in 1996 during the confrontation between Great Britain and the rest of the EU members after the EU banned the importation of

Are these two men (former European Commission president Jacques Delors [left] and current president Jacques Santer) leaders of one the most powerful political entities in the world? Given that they attend the G-8 summits each year and exercise significant control over the politics and economics of all 15 EU countries, one could certainly answer, "yes."

British beef because of the discovery that some of it carried mad cow disease, which is fatal to humans. British prime minister John Major claimed that the EU had overreacted, and used the necessity for unanimity on many questions to block the ability of the EU's political leadership to make any decisions until a compromise was reached.

Bureaucracy

Bureaucracy in the EU is organized within the *European Commission*. The 20-member commission was established to administer policy adopted by the council. Individual commissioners are selected from the member-states on the basis of two each from France, Germany, Great Britain, Italy, and Spain and one commissioner from each of the other members. The commissioners are not, however, supposed to represent the viewpoint of their country. The commissioners serve five-year terms and act as a cabinet for the EU, with each commissioner overseeing an area of administrative activity. One of the commissioners is selected by the Council of Europe to be the commission president. This official serves as the EU's administrative head and is the overall director of the EU bureaucracy headquartered in Brussels (Cini, 1997; Nugent, 1997).

The post of president of the commission has evolved into one of the most significant in the EU. It may be that organizations tend to focus on a single head, but whatever the cause, the commission's president has arguably begun to evolve into something like a president of the European Union. A great deal of that evolution can also be attributed to Jacques Delors, a French national who served as president from 1985 through 1994 and who became known as "Mr. Europe" because of his strong advocacy of European integration (Ross, 1995a). Delors and his staff created a core structure, informally referred to as "Eurocrats," which has a European point of view, rather than a national orientation.

The growing importance of the post of president of Europe and the Eurocracy over which that individual presides was also evident in the sharp battle that occurred within the European Council over a successor to Delors. This struggle is discussed in the Web site box Much Ado about Something, which examines that and other conflicts over the heads of various IGOs. The essence of the EU controversy was the insistence of the British and some others that the EU's bureaucracy and its president needed to be more restrained. To accomplish that, the Council of Europe finally named Luxembourg's prime minister, Jacques Santer, as the new president of the European Commission; he was confirmed by the European Parliament with a vote of 416 to 103 (with 59 abstentions) in January 1995. Prime Minister Major described the Luxembourger as a "decentralizer," and true to this description, Santer has taken a lower profile than did Delors.[3] Nevertheless, the size and power of the EU bureaucracy mean that anyone serving as its president will be a person of significant influence.

A FURTHER NOTE
Much Ado
about Something

Legislative Branch

The *European Parliament* serves as the EU's legislative branch and meets in Strasbourg, France. It has 626 members, apportioned among the EU countries on a modified population basis and elected to five-year terms. As the most populous country, Germany has 99 seats; the least populous country (Luxembourg) has 6 seats. Unlike most international congresses, such as the UN General Assembly, the European Parliament's (EP) members are elected by voters in their respective countries. Furthermore, instead of organizing themselves within the parliament by country, the representatives have tended to group themselves by political persuasion. The 1994 elections, for example, resulted in nine identifiable groupings of legislators, ranging from the small, 13-member, communist-leaning Left Unity coalition to the also tiny 14-member, right-wing European Right coalition. The largest two groups were the Socialist Party (199 members) and the moderately conservative European People's Party (148 members).

The mostly advisory authority of the EP is still only a shadow of that of national legislatures such as Canada's Parliament or the U.S. Congress. But the EP is struggling to carve out a more authoritative role. It can, for instance, veto some regulations issued by the commission and by the two councils. A key power, albeit one that is so far little used, is the EP's ability to accept or reject the EU budget proposed by the commission. The EP can also pass resolutions that put it on record regarding specific matters. It voiced its displeasure with progress in Bosnia, for example, by calling on the council to fire the EU's chief negotiator in the Balkans. This ability to speak out is increasing the EP's ability to help set the political agenda, that is, to determine what is being debated in Europe (Tsebelis, 1994).

Judicial Branch

The *Court of Justice* is the main element of the judicial branch of the EU (Alter, 1998; Garrett, Kelemen, & Schulz, 1998; Mattli & Slaughter, 1998). The 13-member court hears disputes that arise under the treaties that govern the structures and processes of the EU. These treaties are the EU's "constitution." The court is also gaining authority. In 1988, for instance, it ruled that certain VAT exemptions in Great Britain violated EU treaties and would have to be eliminated. The ruling prompted some members of the British Parliament to grumble that it was the first time since Charles I's reign (1625–1649) that the House of Commons had been compelled to raise taxes. One bit of evidence of the mounting influence of the court is that its workload became so heavy that the EU created a new, lower court, the Court of First Instance, with jurisdiction over antitrust and other matters. The judicial branch also includes the Court of Auditors, which monitors budget spending, and is supplemented by the European Court of Human Rights.

The Future of the EU

In the euphoric days that followed the signing of the Maastricht Treaty, German chancellor Helmut Kohl called it the "fulfillment of a dream" and predicted that "further integration is now inevitable. The course is irreversible."[4] Perhaps, but whether or not that is true, the next steps toward integration will be even more difficult than the earlier ones, and some European leaders are worried that momentum has been lost. "If we do not act now" to achieve further integration, a concerned Kohl remarked, "the ship of Europe will go adrift."[5]

Obstacles to Further EU Integration

There is considerable resistance to further integration of the EU (Gabel, 1998; Cafruny & Lankowski, 1997; Landau & Whitman, 1997). When voters in several countries were asked to ratify the Maastricht Treaty, the French in 1992 voted *oui,* but only by a narrow 1 percent margin. The Danes rejected the treaty by a slim 1.4 percent margin before reversing themselves and accepting it the following year after some changes were made in Denmark's favor. Then, in 1994, when offered a chance for their country to join the EU, Norwegian voters rejected membership by a margin of 53 percent to 47 percent.

There are a number of factors that contribute to this resistance. *Dissatisfaction with the EU government* in Brussels is one factor. Some European voters oppose expansion of EU functions because of their sense that so-called

A FURTHER NOTE
When Is
a Banana
a Banana?

Eurotaxes are too high and that the EU bureaucracy, the "Eurocracy," is too powerful and unresponsive. Some of the numerous tales of Eurocratic excess that circulate are related in the Web site box When Is a Banana a Banana?

The upshot of such stories was evident in one poll that found only 22 percent of respondents saying that they were satisfied with the EU's performance. Fifty-three percent said they were dissatisfied, and 25 percent were unsure.[6] Giving voice to these percentages, one Norwegian explained why he was voting against EU membership: "Already our government is big enough. Why make it bigger? Oslo is already far away—why go all the way to Brussels?"[7]

Nationalism is a second factor hindering greater EU political integration. There are some analysts who conclude that Europeans have entered a "post-nationalistic phase" in which nationalism "no longer appears as a basic characteristic" and "aspiring to supranational cooperation" is the primary political impulse (Rhodes & Mazey, 1995; Dogan, 1994:281). Such evaluations may be overly optimistic. One Danish political analyst contends that his country's "no" vote in 1992 reflected "Danish nationalism, but not directed at anyone, just a sense that we need to protect our culture."[8] Nationalism-based resistance is especially evident in the newer EU members, where polls show that support for European integration is weaker than it is in the original six EU members that signed the Treaties of Rome in 1957. Perhaps because of their physical separation from the continent by the English Channel, the British seem especially wary of what Prime Minister John Major called "centralist Europe."[9] His successor, Prime Minister Tony Blair, is less overtly suspicious of EU centralization, but Blair's Labour government has not rushed to embrace the plan for a European currency or other steps toward further integration.

Concern about German domination is a third factor troubling the future of European integration. Germany accounts for 21 percent of the EU's population, 25 percent of the GNP, and 27 percent of total EU merchandise exports. The moves toward eventually integrating national military forces are especially unnerving to some people who remember past German aggressiveness. Many signs indicate that Germany no longer poses a threat to its neighbors (Meiers, 1995). There are constitutional restrictions on the use of German forces, and the Kohl government has pledged to limit German troop strength to 370,000. Also, antimilitarism is a strong sentiment in Germany. It is not uncommon, for example, that in any given year, more German youth will choose the option of a 13-month stint in public service, rather than a 10-month stint in the German military.

Economic disparity among EU members is a fourth factor hampering integration. The original six members were relatively close in their economic circumstances. The addition of new countries has and will continue to change that. As it stands, the average annual per capita incomes of EU countries range from Denmark's nearly $29,900 to Greece's $8,200. Adding East European countries, such as Poland ($2,900 per capita GDP), which have been invited or wish to join the EU, will further complicate integrating the EU's diverse economies.

Concern about the economic impact of further integration is, for example, undermining support of the EU among Germans. The German government has been, along with France, at the forefront of the integration drive, but Germans are worried that monetary integration will destabilize their currency. "The citizens' mistrust [of monetary union] could very quickly turn against the European idea," worried Chancellor Kohl.[10] Germany's inflation rate in 1995 was 1.8 percent, compared to 3.1 percent for the rest of the EU. While that difference is not huge, it unsettles Germans, who recall the hyperinflation that ruined them in the 1920s. A recent poll showed that of those Germans with an opinion, a majority favor EU membership and the Maastricht Treaty, but a majority also opposed introducing a European currency and abolishing the German mark.[11]

Indications of Momentum in EU Integration

For all these and other difficulties, there are also many signs that the EU will continue to become more integrated and will perhaps one day become the United States of Europe. This possibility may seem far-fetched to some, but the strength of the European movement should not be underestimated. Most economic barriers among the countries of the EU have vanished, and political integration, while still in its infancy, has progressed further than many imagined possible not long ago.

During the unpredictable years to come, the great test for EU integration may well be its ability to integrate its currencies (Overturf, 1997). It will be impossible to achieve full economic integration or move much further toward political integration as long as the business of the EU is conducted with 15 different currencies. The EU took a significant step toward financial integration in 1999 when on January 1 the EU countries began using the euro for some banking and financial transactions. The currency will be in full use by 2002, according to EU officials. The introduction of the euro was felt quickly because of its use as a method of payment for electronic commerce, or e-commerce. As Hugo Lunardelly, Microsoft's European marketing manager, put it, "Without the Internet, the euro wouldn't have had as big of an impact." This suggests, then, that the information and technological revolution is having an accelerating effect on political-economic integration.[12]

Global IGOs: Focus on the United Nations

The growing level and importance of IGO activity and organization at the regional level is paralleled by IGOs at the global level. Of these, the United Nations is by far the best known and most influential. Therefore, we will focus in this section on the UN, both as a generalized study of the operation of IGOs and as a specific study of the most prominent member of their ranks (Tessitore & Woolfson, 1997; Mingst & Karns, 1995).

IGO Organization and Related Issues

Many people assume that the study of organizational structure is dry and meaningless, but the contrary is true. Constitutions, rules of procedure, finance,

Figure 7.2

The Structure of the United Nations

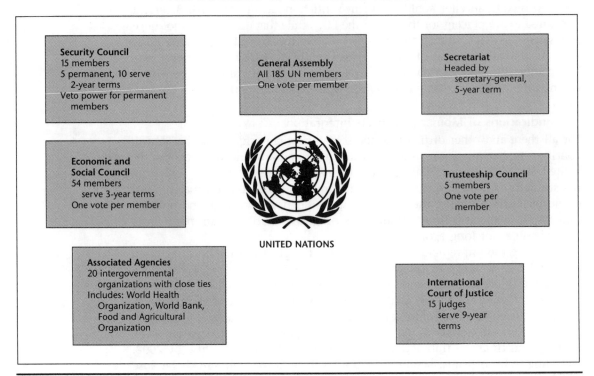

Security Council
15 members
5 permanent, 10 serve
  2-year terms
Veto power for permanent
  members

General Assembly
All 185 UN members
One vote per member

Secretariat
Headed by
  secretary-general,
  5-year term

**Economic and
Social Council**
54 members
  serve 3-year terms
One vote per member

Trusteeship Council
5 members
One vote per
  member

UNITED NATIONS

Associated Agencies
20 intergovernmental
  organizations with close ties
Includes: World Health
  Organization, World Bank,
  Food and Agricultural
  Organization

**International
Court of Justice**
15 judges
  serve 9-year
  terms

The United Nations is a complex organization. It has 6 major organs and 20 associated agencies.

organization charts, and other administrative details are often crucial in determining political outcomes. An outline of the UN's structure is depicted in Figure 7.2. The following discussion of the structure of IGOs and related issues will take up matters such as general membership, the structure of representative bodies, voting formulas, the authority of executive leadership, and the bureaucracy. Then we will turn to the matter of IGO finance.

General Membership

Theoretically, membership in most IGOs is open to any state that is both within the geographic and/or functional scope of that organization and subscribes to the principles and practices of that organization. In practice, a third standard, politics, often becomes a heavy consideration in membership questions. Today the UN has nearly universal membership, but that was not always the case. One point of occasional controversy is the standards for *admitting new members*. During the UN's first decade of operation, for example, the United States and the Soviet Union each blocked the admission of states

Figure 7.3

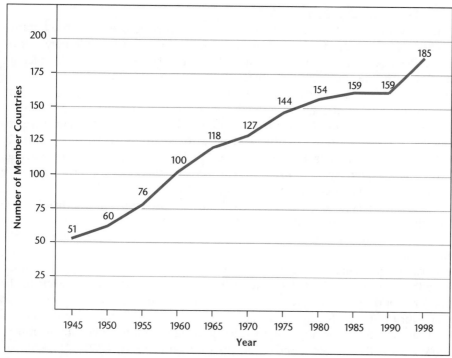

UN Membership, 1945–1998

Data source: Riggs & Plano (1994); authors.

The number of countries in the United Nations has risen rapidly, especially as newly independent countries have joined the world organization. The 263 percent rise in UN membership is an indication of the increased number of states in existence and also of the UN approach to nearly universal membership.

sympathetic to the other superpower. Since then UN membership has expanded quickly to its current total of 185, as Figure 7.3 shows.

Politics can, however, still play a role in admissions. A very sensitive membership question that the UN may have to face in the near future involves the possibility of the Palestinians declaring statehood and asking for admission. A preliminary skirmish occurred in mid-1998 when the General Assembly voted by an overwhelming margin of 124 to 4 (with others abstaining or not voting) to give the Palestinians what amounts to an informal associate membership. Only the Marshall Islands, Micronesia, and the United States joined Israel on the losing side. The Palestinians will not have the right to vote, but they will have the ability to take part in debates in the UN and perform other functions heretofore reserved to states. Nassar al-Kidwa, the head of the Palestinian delegation, told the General Assembly, "A small victory was achieved for Palestine today, and we thank you for that. . . . However, . . . it is our hope that our reliance on this resolution passed today will not last for a long time, as we hope that the United Nations will accept Palestine as a member state in the near future."[13]

Representative Bodies

There are important issues that relate to how to structure the representative bodies of international organizations. Most IGOs have a **plenary representative body** that includes all members. The theoretical basis for plenary bodies is the mutual responsibility of all members for the organization and its policies. The UN **General Assembly (UNGA)** is the UN's plenary organ, but in other IGOs it may be termed a council, a conference, a commission, or even a parliament. These plenary bodies normally have the authority to involve themselves in virtually all aspects of their organizations. Thus, in theory, they are the most powerful elements of their organizations. In practice, however, the plenary organization may be secondary to the administrative structure or some other part of the organization.

A second type of representative body is based on *limited membership*. The theory here is that some members have a greater stake, responsibility, or capacity in a particular area of concern. The UN **Security Council (UNSC)** has 15 members. Ten are chosen by the UNGA for limited terms, but five are permanent members (Barber, 1996). These five (China, France, Russia, the United Kingdom, and the United States) were the five leading victorious powers at the end of World War II and were thought to have a special peacekeeping role to play. During the UN's more than 50 years, these five countries served continuously as permanent members on the Security Council. Of the other 180 members, more than half have never served on the Council (Russett, 1997).

This special status enjoyed by the five permanent members of the UNSC, compared to the occasional role played by most other UN members, has become a simmering issue in the UN. The most common argument against the arrangement is that the existing membership has never been fully realistic and is becoming less so as time goes by. Many global and regional powers that do not have permanent seats are beginning to press for change. Japan's prime minister has declared his country "ready to take up the challenge" of a permanent seat, while adding in a very Japanese way, "We will not press our way through. We will not conduct a campaign."[14] Similarly, if no less subtly, Germany's foreign minister has avowed that "Germany is . . . prepared to assume responsibility as a permanent member of the Security Council."[15] India's delegate to the UN has said that when a new formula is reached to determine which powerful countries should have permanent seats, "We believe that India will be among them."[16]

Less powerful countries are also urging reform. The president of Sri Lanka, for one, has called on the UNSC to "become more representative and more responsible to the general membership of the United Nations." Similarly, the president of Zambia has declared that the Council "can no longer be maintained like the sanctuary of the Holy of Holies with only the original members acting as high priests, deciding on issues for the rest of the world who cannot be admitted."[17] Dissatisfaction with the Security Council has spawned many plans to revise it, but none has achieved any reform to date. Whatever eventual reform plan takes hold, change will be hard to achieve and certainly the result of a long and arduous international political process.

Voting Formulas

One of the difficult issues to face any international organization is the formula for allocating votes. Three major alternatives as they exist today are majoritarianism, weighted voting, and unilateral negative voting.

Majoritarianism is the most common voting formula used in IGOs. This system has two main components: (1) each member casts one equal vote, and (2) the issue is carried by either a simple majority (50 percent plus one vote) or, in some cases, an extraordinary majority (commonly two-thirds). The theory of majoritarianism springs from the concept of sovereign equality and the democratic notion that the will of the majority should prevail. The UNGA and most other UN bodies operate on this principle.

The problem with the idea of equality among states is that it does not reflect some standards of reality. Should Costa Rica, with no army, cast an equal vote with the powerful United States? Should San Marino, with a population of thousands, cast the same vote as China, with its more than one billion people? It might be noted, for example, that in the UNGA, states with less than 15 percent of the world's population account for two-thirds of the vote. By contrast, the 10 countries with populations over 100 million (Bangladesh, Brazil, China, India, Indonesia, Japan, Nigeria, Pakistan, Russia, and the United States), which combine for about 60 percent of the world's population, have less than 6 percent of the votes in the General Assembly. One impact of the one-country-one-vote formula in the UNGA has been a marked change in the voting power of regions and blocs. When the UN began operation, for example, Europe and four other predominantly Eurowhite countries (Australia, Canada, New Zealand, and the United States) held 37 percent of the UNGA vote. These countries now command only 24 percent of the vote. By contrast, Africa's vote, which stood at 8 percent in 1945, is now 28 percent of the UNGA total, and the percentage of votes wielded by the Asian-Pacific countries has increased from 16 percent to 28 percent.

Weighted voting, or a system that allocates unequal voting power on the basis of a formula, is a second voting scheme. Two possible criteria are population and wealth. As noted earlier, the European Parliament provides an example of an international representative body based in part on population. A number of international monetary organizations base voting on financial contributions. Voting in the World Bank and the International Monetary Fund is based on member contributions. The United States alone commands about 18 percent of the votes in the IMF, and it and France, Germany, Great Britain, and Japan together can cast almost 39 percent of the votes in that IGO. This "wealth-weighted" voting is especially offensive to LDC states, which contend that it continues the system of imperial domination by the industrialized countries.

Figure 7.4

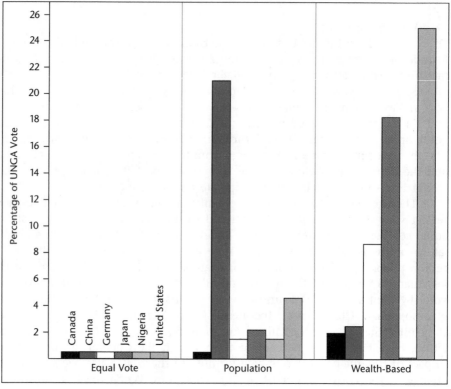

Equal, Population-Based, and Wealth-Based Voting Formulas

Data source: World Bank (1997).

Voting schemes are a crucial issue for international parliamentary assemblies. This figure shows the varying voting strengths that six countries would have in the United Nations General Assembly if voting were based on equality, population, or wealth.

Unanimity constitutes a third voting scheme. This system allows any member to block action unilaterally. The Organization for Economic Cooperation and Development (OECD) and some other IGOs operate on that principle. Unanimity preserves the concept of sovereignty but can easily lead to stalemate.

The voting formula in the UNSC by which some countries can **veto** proposals that others cannot is an unusual variation on the unanimity scheme. In the UN Security Council, any of the 5 permanent members can, by its single vote, veto a resolution favored by the other 14 members (O'Neill, 1997). Between 1946 and 1990, the veto was cast 264 times, with each of the members using its special prerogative to protect its interests. Since then, only a few vetoes have been cast, but the veto power and the threat of its use remains important.

As dry as they may seem, the formulas for deciding vote allocation have a major impact on who will be powerful, who will not, and what policies will be adopted (Holloway & Tomlinson, 1995). Furthermore, how to apportion representation in the parliamentary bodies of such IGOs as the UN will become increasingly important and contentious as the IGOs become more powerful, especially if and when they begin to have true supranational power to compel states to act in certain ways. One way to think further about the ramifications of various voting schemes is to examine Figure 7.4. It shows the percentage of the vote in the current UNGA that various countries would have, based on the present equal vote or on other possible formulas using population or wealth as the voting determinant. Certainly, the political stakes of different formulas raise difficult issues. They are not intractable, however. Numerous countries, including the United States and (more recently) Canada, have had to deal with the issue as part of their development, and they have successfully done so.

Political Leadership

It is difficult for any organization to function without a single administrative leader, and virtually all IGOs have one officer who is the chief executive officer (CEO). The UN's administrative structure is called the **Secretariat**, and the secretary-general is the chief administrator. In this section we will take up the selection and role of the UN secretary-general and other CEOs of IGOs. Then, in the next section, we will address the bureaucratic understructure of IGO secretariats.

Selection   In the UN, the secretary-general is nominated by the UNSC, then elected by the General Assembly for a five-year term. This simple fact does not, however, adequately emphasize the political considerations that govern the appointment of administrators (Urquhart, 1995). One sign of the importance of IGOs is that who will head them has often been, and seems increasingly to be, the subject of intense struggle among member-countries. This is taken up in the Web site box Much Ado about Something.

Role: Activism versus Restraint   An issue that swirls around IGO executives is their proper role. The role orientations of the UN secretary-general and other IGO leaders can range between activism and restraint. For the most part, the documents that established IGOs anticipated a restrained role. In the UN Charter, for example, the Secretariat is the last major organ discussed. That placement indicates the limited role that the document's drafters intended for the secretary-general. Although the Charter allows the secretary-general to bring peace-threatening situations before the UNSC, the position was meant to be largely administrative.

Whatever was intended, the first secretary-general, Trygve Lie of Norway (1946–1953), and his immediate successor, Dag Hammarskjöld of Sweden (1953–1961), were activists who steadily expanded the role of their office. Hammarskjöld believed that he had a "responsibility" to act to uphold the peace even if the UNGA and UNSC would not or could not and, he said, "irrespective of the views and wishes of the various member governments" (Archer, 1983:148).

The height of Hammarskjöld's power came during the crisis that followed the independence of the Belgian Congo in 1960 (Zaire, 1971–1997). The secretary-general used UN military forces to avert outside intervention, to suppress the attempt by Katanga Province to secede, and to restore peace. It is somehow sadly fitting that he died when his plane crashed during a personal mission to the area in 1961. It is widely thought that Hammarskjöld's plane was shot down by mercenaries hired by American and European owners of Katangan copper mines who had incited the Katanga rebellion out of fear that the left-leaning government of the newly independent Congo would take over the mines.

Hammarskjöld's independence was not appreciated by other big powers either. The Soviets were so upset at his activism and what they saw as a pro-Western stance of Hammarskjöld that in 1961 they proposed a "Troika" plan to divide the office into three parts. He fended off these efforts, but the uproar led his successors to be less assertive, although each has been active in important ways. Javier Pérez de Cuéllar also became a significant, independent diplomat during his ten years in office. His successor, Boutros Boutros-Ghali (1992–1996) also set his own course that frequently put him at odds with the United States and other powerful UN members. His independence was one factor in his inability to win a second term in office. It is not yet clear how assertive Kofi Annan will be in the coming years, though his effectiveness as a mediator in such tense situations as those surrounding Iraq's refusal to allow UNSCOM weapons inspections in 1997 and 1998 have won praise from many diplomats, including those in the United States (Starkey, Boyer, & Wilkenfeld, 1999).

Bureaucracy

The staff of IGOs, in the way of all governmental organizations, has tended to expand numerically. And, as also exists with governments at all levels, complaints about the size and supposed inefficiency and unresponsiveness of bureaucracies have made them a lightning rod for discontent with government. We have already reviewed the criticism of the EU's bureaucracy. Much the same discontent besets the UN and its staff.

The secretary-general appoints the other principal officials of the Secretariat, but there are numerous restraints on who is selected. Several principal positions are, in practice, reserved for and named by one big power or another. The UN and other IGOs also distribute positions on a regional basis. The UN has 2,608 important posts subject to geographic allotment. The "desirable range" of appointees from each region results in Western Europe, the United States, and Canada holding about 40 percent of the posts, compared, for example, to Asia with about 16 percent. This set of standards reflects power more than population, and it is subject to the criticism that it disproportionately favors predominantly Eurowhite countries over other countries. Also, the Secretariat is subject to charges of gender bias in its appointment practices.

The very size and efficiency of the staffs of the UN headquarters in New York, UN regional offices, and other IGOs have been a focal point of considerable criticism in recent years. The charge that Secretary-General Boutros-Ghali had not reformed and trimmed the bureaucracy was a major line of attack on his leadership by the United States and some other countries. Certainly, as with almost any bureaucracy, it is possible to find horror stories about the size and activities of IGO staffs. It is also the case, however, that the charges that the UN and its associated agencies are a bureaucratic swamp need to be put in perspective.

One point to note is that the UN is trimming its staff. The Secretariat staff, which had peaked at about 12,000 in 1985, declined to 10,000 in 1995, and fell further to 8,850 in 1998. Some perspective on such data can be gained by comparing UN bureaucrats to local governments and to companies. The city of Milwaukee, for instance, employs more people (9,000) than does the UN. Even if one were to count all 51,484 employees of the UN and its many affiliated agencies (like the World Health Organization) they would only be roughly equal in number to the municipal employees of Los Angeles. Many corporations are also larger than the UN. General Motors has about 700,000 employees and Wal-Mart workers number 649,000. Indeed, with some 183,000 em-

Many people question the power of the UN in world affairs. But as President Clinton's presence signifies, much time and effort is paid to courting UN members' support on issues of global concern. Even if the UN's operational power is questioned, one cannot deny the symbolic and agenda-setting power of this universal international organization.

ployees, McDonald's has 358 percent more people devoted to serving the world hamburgers, french fries, and shakes than the UN has people devoted to trying to supply the world with peace, health, dignity, and prosperity.

Also, it is often hard to trim IGO bureaucracies because they represent a presence and power for many member-countries. Therefore it is the members, not the IGO leaders, who resist reform. "I wrote twice to the [General] Assembly asking it to abolish the Trusteeship Council and still it has not been abolished," exclaimed a frustrated Boutros-Ghali at one point.[18]

IGO Financing and Related Issues

All IGOs face the problem of obtaining sufficient funds to conduct their operations. National governments must also address this issue, but they have the power to impose and legally collect taxes. By contrast, IGOs have very little authority to compel member-countries to support them.

The United Nations is no exception, and it is beset by severe and controversial financial problems. There are several elements to the extended UN budget. The first is the *core budget* for headquarters operations and the regular programs of the major UN organs. Second, there is the *peacekeeping budget* to meet the expenses of operations being conducted by the Security Council. These two budgets amounted to $2.583 billion in FY1999, a drop from $2.632 billion in FY1995. Supporting the UN budget cost each American $2.71—or would have if the United States fully paid its share of UN costs. The third budget element is called the *voluntary contributions budget,* which funds 13 UN agencies such as the United Nations Children's Fund (UNICEF) and the United Nations Environment Program (UNEP). The combined expenditures of these 13 agencies are about $5.8 billion.

The UN is almost entirely dependent on the assessment it levies on member-countries to pay its core and peacekeeping budgets. This assessment is fixed by the UNGA based on a complicated formula that reflects the ability to pay. According to the UN Charter, which is a valid treaty binding on all signatories, members are required to meet these assessments and may have their voting privilege in the General Assembly suspended if they are seriously in arrears. There are eight countries that have assessments of 2 percent of the budget or higher. They and their percentages of the 1998 budget assessment are: the United States (25.0 percent), Japan (15.6 percent), Germany (9.1 percent), France (6.4 percent), Great Britain (5.3 percent), Italy (5.3 percent), Russia (4.3 percent), and Canada (3.1 percent). Together, these eight contribute almost three-quarters of the UN regular budget. At the other end of the financial scale, there are a large number of countries that pay very little, with 30 UN members paying the minimum assessment of 0.001 percent (1/1000 of 1 percent, or as little as $13,000) based on a new assessment schedule enacted by the UNGA in 1997. The "target" voluntary budget payments are the same as the core budget. Because of their special responsibility (and their special privilege, the veto), permanent Security Council members pay a somewhat higher assessment for peacekeeping, with the U.S. share at 31 percent.

The assessment scheme is criticized by some on the grounds that while the eight countries with assessments of 3 percent or higher collectively pay 73.7 percent of the UN budget, they cast just less than 4.3 percent of the votes in the UNGA. The countries with a 0.01 percent assessment account for less than 1 percent of the UN budget, but they command 49.0 percent of the votes in the General Assembly. One result of the gap between contributions and voting power has been disenchantment with the organization by a number of large-contributor countries who sometimes find themselves in the minority on votes in the UNGA.

Such numbers are something of a fiction, however, because some countries do not pay their assessment. In mid-1998, member-states were in arrears by $2.53 billion. The United States was the largest debtor. It owed $1.54 billion to the UN, accounting for 61 percent of the UN deficit. Various U.S. administrations have made some effort to pay their country's bills, but Congress has stolidly refused to appropriate sufficient funds to erase the U.S. debt.

As a result the UN is in a state of fiscal crisis at the very time it is being asked to do more and more to provide protection and help meet other humanitarian and social needs. "It is," said a frustrated Boutros-Ghali just before he stepped down, "as though the town fire department were being dispatched to put out fires raging in several places at once while a collection was being taken to raise money for the fire-fighting equipment."[19] The analogy between the UN's budget and firefighting and other municipal budgets is hardly hyperbole. At $2.9 billion, Boston's budget is larger than the UN's. The $1 billion that the UN will spend on peacekeeping during FY1999 is less than half of the $2.1 billion that New York City spends on its police force and only a little more than the $784 million the city budgets for fire protection.

The unwillingness of the U.S. Congress to fund the U.S. assessment, particularly combined with the criticism of the UN heard in the United States, has opened the floodgates to a torrent of criticism from even staunch U.S. allies. "We are growing tired of UN bashing," growled Prime Minister Jean Chrétien of Canada, "and it is especially irritating when it comes from those who are not paying their bills." And, in a line that British diplomats had been waiting for over 200 years to deliver, British foreign secretary Malcolm Rifkind said the American presence in the UN was tantamount to "representation without taxation."[20]

IGO Activities and Related Issues

The most important aspects of any international organization are what it does, how well this corresponds to the functions we wish it to perform, and how well it is performing its roles. The following pages will begin to explore these aspects by examining the scope of IGO activity, with an emphasis on the UN. Much of this discussion will only begin to touch on these activities, and many of them receive more attention in other chapters.

Promoting International Peace and Security

The United Nations is among the many IGOs that strive to prevent international conflict, to limit its severity, and to restore the peace when violence occurs. This role for the UN is symbolized by the opening words of the Charter. They dedicate the organization to saving "succeeding generations from the scourge of war, which . . . has brought untold sorrow to mankind." The UN attempts to fulfill this goal by creating norms against violence, by providing debate as an alternative to fighting, by intervening diplomatically to avert the outbreak of warfare or to help restore peace once violence occurs, by instituting diplomatic and economic sanctions, by dispatching UN military forces to repel aggression or to act as a buffer between warring countries, and by promoting arms control and disarmament. Note that the following individual consideration of each of these six approaches to avoiding and resolving conflict does not imply that they are used in isolation. Often just the opposite is true: the UN will pursue several approaches at once.

Creating Norms against Violence   One way that the United Nations helps promote international peace and security is by creating norms (beliefs about what is proper) against aggression and other forms of violence. To accomplish this, the UN works in such areas as promoting the concept of nuclear nonproliferation through the International Atomic Energy Agency, limiting chemical and biological weapons, and promoting rules for the restrained conduct of war when it occurs.

There is a growing acknowledgment, as found in the UN Charter and elsewhere, that using military force except in self-defense is unacceptable. Countries that sign the Charter pledge to accept the principle "that armed force shall not be used, save in the common interest" and further agree to "settle their international disputes by peaceful means," to "refrain in their international relations from the threat or the use of force" except in self-defense, and to "refrain from giving assistance to any state against which the United Nations is taking preventive or enforcement action." Reaffirming the Charter's ideas, the UN (and other IGOs) have condemned Iraq's invasion of Kuwait, Serbian aggression against its neighbors, and other such actions. These denunciations and the slowly developing norm against aggression have not halted violence, but they have created an increasing onus on countries that strike the first blow. When, for example, the United States decided in 1989 to depose the regime of Panama's strongman, General Manuel Noriega, it acted unilaterally. Noriega was toppled, but Washington's action was condemned by both the UN and the OAS. Five years later, Washington again decided to overthrow the regime of a small country to its south. But before U.S. troops landed in Haiti, Washington took care to win UN support for its action.

Providing a Debate Alternative   A second peace-enhancing role for the United Nations and some other IGOs is serving as a passive forum in which members publicly air their points of view and privately negotiate their differences. The UN thus acts like a safety valve, or perhaps a sound stage where the world drama can be played out without the dire consequences that could occur if another "shooting locale" were chosen. This grand-debate approach to peace involves denouncing your opponents, defending your actions, trying to influence world opinion, and winning symbolic victories. The British ambassador to the UN has characterized it as "a great clearing house for foreign policy," a place where "We talk to people . . . whom we don't talk to elsewhere because we have fraught relations with them."[21]

Diplomatic Intervention   International organizations also regularly play a direct role in assisting and encouraging countries to settle their disputes peacefully. Ideally this occurs before hostilities, but it can take place even after fighting has started. The United Nations and other IGOs perform the following functions: (1) *Inquiry:* Fact-finding by neutral investigators; (2) *Good Offices:* Encouraging parties to negotiate; acting as a neutral setting for negotiations; (3) *Mediation:* Making suggestions about possible solutions; acting as an intermediary between two parties; (4) *Arbitration:* Using a special panel to find a solution that all parties agree in advance to accept; and (5) *Adjudication:* Submitting disputes to an international court such as the ICJ. These activities do not often capture the headlines, but they are a vital part of maintaining or restoring the peace.

It is possible, even probable, that renewed fighting between Iraq and the United States and some other countries was averted in early 1998 because of Secretary-General Annan's personal mediation and his ability to fashion a solution acceptable to all. According to UN ambassador Bill Richardson, "Annan's personal diplomacy coupled with a formula that only he, through his stature, could sell to the Iraqis" was the difference between war and peace.[22]

Sanctions   The increased interdependence of the world has heightened the impact of diplomatic and economic sanctions. In recent years, these have been applied by the UN, the OAS, and other IGOs on such countries as Haiti, Iraq, Libya, South Africa, and Yugoslavia. Success has varied. Sanctions against South Africa helped ease apartheid there. Economic sanctions have forced Iraq grudgingly to give up some of its hidden remaining arms and arms production facilities and to allow UN military inspectors to search for other violations of the agreements that ended the war in 1991. Other sanctions have not worked as well. The recurrent problems the United States and other countries have had with Saddam Hussein over weapons proliferation, despite the use of economic sanctions against Iraq, demonstrates the difficulty often experienced in implementing sanctions effectively.

Peacekeeping   The United Nations additionally has a limited ability to intervene militarily in a dispute. There is also a limited history of other IGOs, such as the OAS, undertaking collective military action. In the UN, this process is often called peacekeeping. It is normally conducted under the auspices of the UNSC, although the UNGA has sometimes authorized action. The following paragraphs will sketch the record of UN peacekeeping, but the bulk of our discussion on this topic and other international security efforts by the UN and other IGOs can be found in chapter 10 on the alternative path to pursuing peace.

The United Nations was founded with the lofty goal of securing the peace. It has not been able to accomplish that, at least not yet. That does not mean that UN efforts to provide international security have failed. What the UN has been able to do is to mount a number of military missions that have often provided relief and sometimes even permanent peace for war-weary people in many places (Esman & Telhami, 1995).

Through 1999, the United Nations has mounted 49 peacekeeping operations (including observer missions) that have utilized over 750,000 military and police personnel from a substantial number of troops or police forces from more than 75 countries. Never before have international forces been so active as they are now. The number of UN peacekeeping operations has risen markedly in the post–cold war era, as shown in Figure 7.5. In mid-1999, there were 15 active UN peacekeeping operations with forces of varying sizes in the field at locations throughout the world. These forces totaled 13,386 soldiers. As the UN took on more missions, the cost of maintaining peacekeeping

A SITE TO SURF
UN Peacekeeping
Operations

Figure 7.5

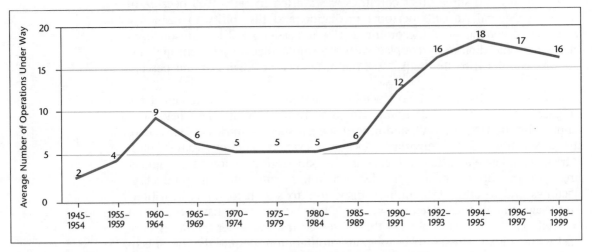

The Growth of UN Peacekeeping Operations

Data source: UN, Department of Peacekeeping Web site, http://www.org/depts/dpko/, September, 1999.

The end of the cold war and its standoff in the Security Council between the United States and the Soviet Union has allowed the UN to mount a significantly increased number of peacekeeping operations in the 1990s.

missions rose sharply from $235 million in FY1987 to about $3.5 billion for FY1996. From there it has fallen off to approximately $1 billion in 1998. The end or curtailing of the UN role in a number of hot spots, especially Bosnia, accounts for the drop in the peacekeeping budget.

United Nations forces have generally acted as neutral buffers between conflicting parties. With a few exceptions, peacekeeping forces have not conducted active military operations. Instead they have usually positioned themselves between the combatants. At times this provides an excuse to stop fighting for two combat-weary foes who are otherwise unable to find a way to disengage. A variation on this peacekeeping role is when UN forces take up positions to try to prevent a spread of the fighting. The most recent deployment of peacekeepers in this mode is in East Timor, where 7,500 peacekeepers were put in place in the summer and fall of 1999 to help end the bloody conflict on the Indonesian-occupied island. Only time will tell if the UN effort will achieve its goals, as the Indonesian government and guerrilla forces continue to struggle for control.

United Nations peacekeeping, then, seldom involves a stern international enforcer smiting aggressors with powerful blows. Few countries are willing to give any IGO much power and independence. Rather, UN peacekeeping is a "coming between," a positioning of a neutral force that creates space and is intended to help defuse an explosive situation. This in no way lessens the valuable role that the UN has played. In the early 1960s, UN troops kept the Congo from exploding into a cold war battlefield, and UN forces were an important factor in allowing the disengagement of Egyptian and Israeli troops in 1973. After many years of violence, the people of Cyprus live in peace under the watch of UN forces there.

United Nations peacekeepers alone could not stop the killing in Bosnia, but many fewer died than would have been the case without a UN presence. Fortunately, UN peacekeeping forces have suffered relatively few casualties, but almost 1,500 have died in world service. For these sacrifices and contributions to world order, the UN peacekeeping forces were awarded the 1988 Nobel Peace Prize.

Arms Control and Disarmament   Promoting arms control and disarmament is another international security function of IGOs. They are not only involved in individual conflicts but are concerned with conflict in general. Consequently, they are active in several efforts to regulate or eliminate the weapons of war. The visit of Secretary-General Boutros-Ghali to North Korea in December 1993 was followed by an easing of Pyongyang's confrontational stance on its nuclear program. That allowed international negotiations to resume, which led to an agreement in October 1994 that resolved the simmering crisis. It may well be that the UN can also help promote nuclear arms restraint or disarmament in other areas of the world.

Social, Economic, Environmental, and Other Roles

In addition to maintaining and restoring the peace, IGOs engage in a wide variety of other activities. These are only briefly noted below because they receive much greater attention in other chapters. Chapter 9 on international law, for example, examines the roles of the ICJ and other international law-adjudicating and lawmaking bodies in establishing and interpreting international law. Chapter 12 will detail the wide variety of UN and other IGO activities designed to enhance economic development and cooperation. And chapters 13 and 14 will review the extensive efforts of international organizations to promote human rights and social welfare and to protect the environment.

During the early years of the United Nations, the emphasis of the organization's efforts was on security. This concern has not abated. In fact, peacekeeping efforts have grown, as we have seen. Security concerns have increasingly been joined, however, by social, economic, environmental, and other nonmilitary security concerns. The increase in the number of LDC member-countries, whose concerns often had little to do with the cold war, began the trend. Now with the cold war ended, the concern with a variety of nonmilitary security issues will surely increase. "The real problem of the next 10 years," Secretary-General Boutros-Ghali commented when he took office in 1992, "will be mainly in the countries of the Third World." These problems, he said, will not only be "military confrontations" but the problems of "refugees, hunger, drought. So many problems."[23] His prediction proved generally accurate.

Given the influx of LDCs into the UN and their rise in power in that body, it is important to consider their view of and role in the UN and other IGOs. Some LDC commentators have portrayed the UN, at least historically, as a vehicle for neocolonial Western domination. The veto-dominated Security Council has been especially suspect. The growing assertiveness of the LDCs and the changing balance of power in their favor, in the General Assembly, the Economic and Social Council, and elsewhere, have led to a changing orientation. Now the UN and other IGOs are increasingly being used by the LDCs to band together and assert their demands for political, social, and economic equity. In a generally power-politics world, the UN and other IGOs provide a ready forum for LDC complaints against the larger powers. Also, insofar as there is majoritarian voting, the UN gives the LDCs a vehicle for giving substance to its proposals and criticisms by passing resolutions. As such, IGOs are a primary arena of the North-South struggle.

In addition to the issues of particular interest to the South, the UN and other IGOs are active on a variety of fronts. One of these is promoting *laws and norms.* An important and increasing role of international organizations is defining and expanding international law and international norms of cooperation. International courts associated with IGOs help establish legal precedent. Also, the signatories to the UN Charter and other IGO constitutions incur obligations to obey the principles of these documents. International organizations additionally sponsor multinational treaties, which may establish the assumption of law. As one scholar sees the norm-building function of IGOs, "The procedures and rules of international institutions create information structures. They determine what principles are acceptable as a basis for reducing conflicts and whether governmental actions are legitimate or illegitimate. Consequently, they help shape actors' expectations" (Keohane, 1998:91).

International organizations also *promote the quality of human existence.* A wide variety of IGOs and NGOs devote their energies to problems of the environment, humanitarian causes, economic progress, and social concerns such as health, nutrition, and literacy. For example, UNICEF, WHO, and other agencies have undertaken a $150 million program to develop a multi-immunization vaccine. This vaccine program will increase the number of children—estimated now to be 2 million—who will survive because of such international medical assistance. The Food and Agriculture Organization (FAO) has launched a program to identify, preserve, and strengthen through new genetic techniques domestic animals that might prove especially beneficial to LDCs. Western breeds of pigs, for example, usually produce only about 10 piglets a litter; the Taihu pig of China manages 15 to 20. The FAO hopes to use the latter and other appropriate animals to increase protein availability in the LDCs.

The UN and other international organizations have also improved the quality of life through their efforts to *protect human rights.* One scholar calls the UN "an agent of change" in human rights and other fields, and comments that much of the current "stress on the preservation and promotion of human rights can be traced to the debates and actions of the UN" (Rosenau, 1992:59).

Yet another role of IGOs has been to *encourage national self-determination.* The UN Trusteeship Council once monitored numerous colonial dependencies, but the wave of independence in recent decades steadily lessened its number of charges. Then, in October 1994, the United States and Palau notified the

As this photo demonstrates, the UN's impact is widespread and important to many people of the world, particularly in its role of helping to alleviate basic human needs problems. Here, an ethnic Albanian man in Kosovo is carrying food supplies that he has obtained from the UN High Commission on Refugees (UNHCR). They will be used to help his family weather the severe personal disruptions caused by the war in Kosovo.

council that, as Kuniwo Nakamura, Palau's president, put it, "we have made our own decision that we are ready to embark on the journey of independence with confidence."[24] Inasmuch as Palau was the last trust territory, the announcement meant that the Trusteeship Council's mission was fulfilled and its business concluded.

Promoting other international organizations and integration is one more role of the UN that deserves mention. The United Nations operates in association with a variety of other regional and specialized IGOs, and it also grants consultative status to nearly 700 NGOs. Thus, international organizations of all types cooperate to encourage and strengthen one another (Anderson, 1994).

Evaluating IGOs and Their Future

The United Nations has now been in operation for more than fifty years. What it has accomplished, or not accomplished, is important, but an even larger question is the UN's future. It is easy to be skeptical. International organization certainly has many doubters and critics. Given the continued conflicts in the world and the ongoing economic and social misery, it is all too easy to get discouraged or to dismiss international organization as inadequate, misguided, and impossibly idealistic. Even those who support the UN and the idea of greater global governance recognize that the organization must adapt to the rapidly changing international scene.

There are several ways to evaluate IGOs. Some of these have been touched on already. Surely we must ask that IGOs make progress in meeting their goals and do so efficiently. It is incorrect to assume that all calls for budgetary and administrative reform are signs of dangerous isolationism by those demanding change. Yet it is inappropriate for the U.S. government or any other critic to hold IGOs to standards, such as cutting bureaucracy and spending, that it itself cannot accomplish to the satisfaction of all. It is also important to evaluate IGOs in comparative perspective. The size and cost of IGOs are dwarfed by the employees and budgets of many governments and even corporations.

Furthermore, insofar as the UN does not meet our expectations, we need to ask whether it is a flaw of the organization or the product of the unwillingness of member-states to live up to the standards that countries accept when they ratify the Charter. Simply paying their assessments is one thing more countries could do. Congress refuses to do that because it says the UN does not work very well. Many Americans have the same opinion of Congress, but they may not withhold their taxes. The UN will also work better if countries try to make it effective. It is a truism, as Egyptian scholar Ali Dessouki put it, that "when the big powers are in agreement, the UN performs. When they aren't, the UN is paralyzed."[25] In short, sometimes the UN does not work because its members will not let it.

It is also important when evaluating the UN and other IGOs to consider the successes as well as the failures. That is the standard Kofi Annan appeals for when he implores people to "Judge us rightly . . . by the relief and refuge that we provide to the poor, to the hungry, the sick and threatened: the peoples of the world whom the United Nations exists to serve."[26] Between its 40th and 50th anniversaries, the United Nations surpassed all previous marks in terms of numbers of simultaneous peacekeeping missions, peacekeeping troops deployed, and other international security efforts. Such UN–sponsored conferences as those on environment (Rio de Janeiro in 1992), human rights (Vienna, 1993), population (Cairo, 1994), women's issues (Beijing, 1995), social needs (Stockholm, 1995), and food (Rome, 1996) have all focused attention on global problems and have made some contribution to advancing our knowledge of and enhancing our attempts to deal seriously with a wide range of economic, social, and environmental global challenges. The UN and other IGOs have made a contribution.

One must also ask what the alternative is to the UN and other international organizations fostering greater international cooperation. Can the warring, uncaring world continue unchanged in the face of nuclear weapons, persistent poverty, an exploding population, periodic mass starvation, continued widespread human rights violations, resource depletion, and environmental degradation? Somehow the world has survived these plagues, but one of the realities that this book hopes to make clear is that we are hurtling toward our destiny at an ever-increasing, now exponential speed. In a rapidly changing system, doing things the old way may be inadequate and may even take us down a road, although familiar, that will lead the world to cataclysm. At the very least, as Secretary of State Madeleine Albright notes, "The United Nations gives the good guys—the peacemakers, the freedom fighters, the people who believe in human rights, those committed to human development—an organized vehicle for achieving gains."[27] To return to the question, If not the UN, then what? there may be considerable truth in the reply of the British ambassador to the UN. Amid all sorts of "disasters and problems," and despite the UN's limitations, the ambassador opined, the reality is "that it's the UN, with all its warts, or it's the law of the jungle."[28] It is through this jungle that the road more familiar has passed, and following it into the future may bring what Shakespeare was perhaps imagining when he wrote in *Hamlet* of a tale that would "harrow up thy soul, [and] freeze thy young blood."

To repeat an important point, the UN and other IGOs are, in the end, only what we make them. They do possess some independence, but it is limited. Mostly their successes and failures reflect the willingness or disinclination of member-countries to cooperate and use them to further joint efforts. Kofi Annan urged support of the UN by quoting what Winston Churchill said to Franklin Roosevelt, "Give us the tools and we will do the job."[29] In the same vein, Dag Hammarskjöld aptly predicted, "Everything will be all right—you know when? When people, just people, stop thinking of the United Nations as a weird Picasso abstraction and see it as a drawing they made themselves."[30]

Whether that occurs is uncertain. What is clear is that critics of IGOs are too often narrowly negative. They disparage the organizations without noting their contributions or suggesting improvements. IGOs hold one hope for the future, and those who would denigrate them should make other, positive suggestions rather than implicitly advocate a maintenance of the status quo. There is a last bit of Shakespeare's wisdom, found in *Julius Caesar*, that is worth pondering. The playwright counsels us that:

> There is a tide in the affairs of men
> Which, taken at the flood, leads on to fortune;
> Omitted, all the voyage of their life
> Is bound in shallows and in miseries.

Chapter Summary

1. One sign of the changing international system is this century's rapid rise in the number of intergovernmental organizations (IGOs).
2. There are many classifications of international organizations, the most basic distinction being between IGOs that are global and regional on one dimension and specialized and general on another dimension.
3. Current international organization is the product of three lines of development: the idea that humans should live in peace and mutual support, the idea that the big powers have a special responsibility for maintaining order, and the growth of specialized international organizations to deal with narrow nonpolitical issues.

4. The rapid growth of all types of international organizations stems from increased international contact among states and people, increased economic interdependence, the growing importance of transnational issues and political movements, and the inadequacy of the state-centered system for dealing with world problems.

5. There are significant differences among views on the best role for international organizations.

6. Some observers argue that international organizations are best suited to promoting cooperation among states rather than trying to replace the state-centered system. Still others contend that international organizations should concentrate on performing limited functional activities with the hope of creating a habit of cooperation and trust that can later be built upon. Finally, many view international organizations as vehicles that should be manipulated to gain one's country's individual political goals. The UN serves as an example of how current IGOs are organized and operate.

7. Some observers favor moving toward a system of supranational organization, in which some form of world government, or perhaps regional governments, would replace or substantially modify the present state-centered system.

8. The EU provides an example of the development, structure, and roles of a regional IGO. The EU has evolved considerably along the path of economic integration. The movement toward political integration is more recent and is proving more difficult than economic integration.

9. The United Nations provides an example of the development, structure, and roles of a global IGO.

10. There are several important issues related to the structure of international organizations. One group of questions relates to membership.

11. Another group of questions involve membership criteria.

12. Voting schemes to be used in such bodies are another important issue. Current international organizations use a variety of voting schemes that include majority voting, weighted voting, and negative voting.

13. Another group of questions concerns the administration of international organizations, including the role of the political leaders and the size and efficiency of IGO bureaucracies. The source of IGO revenue and the size of IGO budgets are a related concern.

14. There are also a number of significant issues that relate to the general role of international organizations. Peacekeeping is one important role.

15. Other roles for the UN and other international organizations include promoting international law, promoting arms control, bettering the human condition, promoting self-government, and furthering international cooperation.

16. However one defines the best purpose of international organization, it is important to be careful of standards of evaluation. The most fruitful standard is judging an organization by what is possible, rather than setting inevitably frustrating ideal goals.

Chapter **8**

National Power and Diplomacy: The Traditional Approach

Then, everything includes itself in power,
Power into will, will into appetite.

Shakespeare, *Troilus and Cressida*

All politicians make their decisions on the basis of national or
political interest and explain them in terms of altruism.

Former Israeli diplomat Abba Eban, 1996

Once upon a time," began a fable told by the great British diplomat and prime minister Winston Churchill, "all the animals in the zoo decided that they would disarm." To accomplish that laudable goal, the animals convened a diplomatic conference, where, Churchill's tale went:

> The Rhinoceros said when he opened the proceeding that the use of teeth was barbarous and horrible and ought to be strictly prohibited by general consent. Horns, which were mainly defensive weapons, would, of course, have to be allowed. The Buffalo, the Stag, the Porcupine, and even the little Hedgehog all said they would vote with the Rhino, but the Lion and

Chapter Outline

the Tiger took a different view. They defended teeth and even claws, which they described as honourable weapons of immemorial antiquity. The Panther, the Leopard, the Puma, and the whole tribe of small cats all supported the Lion and the Tiger. Then the Bear spoke. He proposed that both teeth and horns should be banned and never used again for fighting by animals. It would be quite enough if animals were allowed to give each other a good hug when they quarreled. No one could object to that. It was so fraternal, and that would be a great step toward peace. However, all the other animals were very offended by the Bear, and the Turkey fell into a perfect panic. The discussion got so hot and angry, and all those animals began thinking so much about horns and teeth and hugging when they argued about the peaceful intentions that had brought them together, that they began to look at one another in a very nasty way. Luckily the keepers were able to calm them down and persuade them to go back quietly to their cages, and they began to feel quite friendly with one another again.[1]

In addition to being colorfully entertaining, Sir Winston's allegory is instructive. It contains glimpses of many of the points about diplomacy that we will discuss in this chapter. We will begin by looking at *power*. This is an appropriate place to start because power remains the essential element of diplomacy in a system in which countries for the most part pursue goals that are in their self-interest. Depending on the situation, there is a variety of potential or real rewards and punishments that actors can utilize to influence other actors. The rhino and the lion were both powerful, and each might have used its strength to press its position if the negotiations had continued. The turkey had little tangible strength and would have had to rely on its guile and other intangible diplomatic skills to persuade the other animals to eliminate claws, horns, and even hugs. When the zookeepers became involved, they had assets too and may have offered the animals economic incentives, such as food, to get them to return to their cages.

Having established the power foundations of diplomacy, we will turn to the general *nature of diplomacy*. This involves the overall system, the setting in which modern diplomacy occurs. In Churchill's story, the zoo is the system in which diplomacy among the animals took place. One must assume that the system in which they lived was based on self-interest more than on anarchical cooperation because various groups of animals selected goals that were advantageous to themselves with little thought to how they affected others. The zoo system also apparently allowed some potential for fighting and thus based success in part on the Darwinian law of the jungle. Yet it is also the case that the animals were also partly constrained by the zookeepers with, perhaps, some protection afforded by cages.

The third part of this chapter will examine the conduct of diplomacy. We will begin by examining the characteristics of *modern diplomacy* and by looking at how it has evolved. Multilateral diplomacy, for example, has become a much more prominent part of diplomacy than it once was. In Churchill's story, the animals conducted multisided negotiations instead of bilateral diplomacy between, say, just the rhino and the tiger. Those two animals might have made a bilateral agreement that both horns and fangs were acceptable;

once hedgehogs, turkeys, and others became involved, the diplomatic dynamic changed considerably. In such a circumstance, diplomatic coalition building is one aspect of support gathering. It may well have been that, before the conference, the rhino had met with the buffalo, stag, porcupine, and hedgehog to convince them that they should support the rhino's position that horns were defensive weapons, while teeth and claws were offensive weapons.

Finally, we will turn explore various diplomatic options. Direct negotiation is one method, and the animals were engaged in that. Signaling is another method. This occurred when the animals "began to look at one another in a very nasty way." Public diplomacy to win the support of public opinion is another diplomatic method, and it is possible to see in Churchill's story how a clever diplomatic proposal can create an advantage. One can imagine the bear's proposal emblazoned in the *Zoo News* headline the next day: "Bear Proposes Eliminating All Weapons. Suggests Hugging as Alternative to Fighting." World opinion might have rallied to the bear; this would have put pressure on the other negotiators to accede to a seemingly benign proposal to usher in a new world order based on peace, love, and hugging.

Before proceeding, we should take a moment to put this chapter in context. It is the first of two chapters that look at the traditional and the alternative bases for establishing what policies will prevail in the world. The traditional approach involves countries practicing national diplomacy by applying power in the pursuit of their self-interest. This approach does not mean that might makes right, but it surely means that might usually makes success. The alternative approach, discussed in chapter 9, is to apply the standards of international law and justice to the conduct of international relations so that right, rather than who is mightiest, will more often determine who prevails.

National Power: The Foundation of National Diplomacy

"Until human nature changes, power and force will remain at the heart of international relations," a top foreign policy adviser in the Clinton administration once commented.[2] Not everyone would agree with such a gloomy realpolitik assessment, but it underlines the crucial role that power plays in diplomacy. When the goals and interests of states conflict, states often struggle to determine whose interests will prevail. The resolution rests frequently on who has the most power. It is impossible to tell for sure what China would have done in 1996 if neither Taiwan nor the United States had possessed formidable military forces. But that was not the case. Taiwan has a well-armed military and the United States is a superpower.

The Nature of Power

Social scientists struggle to define and measure power and to describe exactly how it works. Harvard University dean Joseph Nye (1990:178) has suggested that "power in international politics is like the weather. Everyone talks about it, but few understand it." Alluding to an even greater mystery, Nye confides that power is "like love . . . easier to experience than to define or measure." He also warns that if we always dominate others with our strength, "we may be as mistaken about our power as was the fox who thought he was hurting Brer Rabbit when he threw him into the briar patch." Weather, love, briar patches? Yes, power is perplexing! If its intricacies can throw a Harvard dean into such a morass of mixed metaphors and similes, then how can we understand power? The first step is to define the way this text uses the word, so that we can proceed from a common point.

Power as an Asset

The term **power** can be understood to equal national capabilities. Power is a political resource, which encompasses the sum of the various elements that allow one country to have its interests prevail over the interests of another country. Power is multifaceted. It includes tangible elements, such as numbers of weapons; it also includes intangible elements, such as public morale. In short, national power is the sum of the attributes of a state that enable it to achieve its goals even when they clash with the goals of other international actors.

One way to comprehend power is to think about *power as money*, as a sort of political currency. Equating power and money is helpful because both are assets that can be used to acquire things. Money buys things; power causes things to happen. Like money, power is sometimes used in a charitable way. But also like money, power is more often used for self-interest. It is also true that acquiring money and power both often require sacrifices. Furthermore, those who use their financial or power assets imprudently may lose more than they gain. As with any analogy, however, you should be wary of overusing the comparison. There are differences between money and power. One is that political power is less liquid than money; it is harder to convert into things that you want. A second difference is that power, unlike money, has no standard measurement that allows all parties to agree on the amount involved.

As with money, one of the confusions about power is whether it is an asset (an end, goal) that you try to acquire and maintain or a tool (a means, instrument) that you use. It is both. Countries seek both to acquire power and to use it in international politics. While this chapter concentrates on power as an asset, it is important to realize that countries sometimes treat power as a goal.

One important issue about any asset is, "How much is enough?" If you think about money as a physical object, it is pretty useless. It is inedible, you cannot build anything useful out of money, and it will not even burn very well if you need to keep warm. Yet some people become obsessed with having money for its own sake. For them, acquiring money is an end in itself. Literature is full of such stories, ranging from Molière's *The Miser* to Dickens's classic *A Christmas Carol* and its tragic tale of Ebenezer Scrooge. The misers give up love, friendships, and other pleasures to get and keep money only to discover, in the end, that their money becomes a burden. Similarly, some people believe that countries can become fixated on acquiring power, especially military power, beyond what is prudently needed to meet possible exigencies. This, critics say, is unwise because power is expensive, it creates a temptation to use it, and it spawns insecurity in others.

Measuring Power

At a general level, it is possible to measure or at least estimate power. There can be no doubt, for example, that China is more powerful than Mongolia. Beyond such broad judgments, however, it must be said candidly that scholars and policy makers have not been successful at anything approaching precise measurements of power. This was well illustrated by a study that reviewed four attempts by various scholars to devise formulas to measure national power (Taber, 1989). At the most general level, all four studies agreed that the United States, the (still in existence) Soviet Union, China, Japan, Great Britain, France, and Germany were among the world's ten most powerful countries. Beyond that consensus, however, there were numerous disagreements based on the imprecise ability to measure power. Two of the studies rated the Soviet Union the most powerful. One each rated the United States and China most powerful. One ranked China only seventh. Brazil ranked number three in one study and India ranked number four in another study; yet two studies did not place either country in the top ten. The list need not go on to make the point that different calculations about measuring power yielded very different results.

The difficulty of precisely measuring power is a result of the fact that many aspects of power are difficult to quantify. Gathering data on some aspects of power (such as number of guns, GDP, or population) is easy. Quantifying other aspects of power, such as leadership, borders on the impossible.

Does this mean that trying to estimate national power is a fool's quest? No, it does not. To repeat a point, there are clearly differences in national power. Ignoring them would be foolish, but it would also be a mistake to ignore the complexity and fluidity of power and to underestimate or overestimate the power of others based on one or more simple calculations.

Characteristics of Power

Power is not a simple and stable phenomenon. Indeed, it is very much a political chameleon, constantly changing even while it remains the same. The last task of this section is to explore the impact of the various characteristics of power.

Power Is Dynamic   As the fate of the Soviet Union indicates, power is a dynamic phenomenon. Even simple measurements show that power is constantly in flux. Economies prosper or lag, arms are modernized or become outmoded, resources are discovered or are depleted, and populations rally behind or lose faith in their governments.

Not only can the specific power of a country change, but some scholars believe that the very nature of power is changing. They contend that military and other assets that contribute to *coercive power* (the ability to make another country do or not do something) are declining in importance as military force and economic sanctions become more costly and less effective. Simultaneously, according to this view, *persuasive power* and the factors, such as moral authority or technological excellence, that enhance a country's image of leadership are increasing in importance (Hall, 1999).

Some scholars even believe that war has become so destructive that it is a fading phenomenon, especially among economically developed countries (EDCs). That thought is given some credence by the fact that the 1990s were not a time of interstate warfare, with the major exception of Iraq's invasion of Kuwait and a few relatively minor border clashes. Perhaps coercive diplomacy will sometime become a relic of humankind's barbaric past, but that day, if it comes at all, is probably far in the future for two reasons. First, as one study notes, in the 1990s violence continues, and intrastate (internal) warfare, such as the conflicts in the Balkans and in Rwanda, "constitutes a growth industry" (Bloomfield & Moulton, 1997:34). Second, there are still times when force or the threat of force is needed to resolve an international crisis. After an agreement that averted war in 1998 over Iraq's refusal to allow continued UN arms inspections, Iraqi foreign minister Tarik Aziz and UN secretary-general Kofi Annan held a joint press conference to review the settlement. Aziz contended that it was "diplomacy that reached this agreement, not the saber-rattling." To which Annan chimed in, "You can do a lot with diplomacy, but of course you can do a lot more with diplomacy backed up by firmness and force."[3]

Power Is Both Objective and Subjective   We have seen on several occasions that international politics is influenced both by what is true and by what others perceive to be true. *Objective power* consists of assets that you objectively possess and that you have both the capacity and the will to use. As such, it is a major factor in determining whose interests prevail, as Iraq found out in 1991 in its war with the U.S.–led coalition of forces.

Subjective power is also important. It is common to hear politicians argue that their country cannot back down in a crisis or get out of an ill-conceived military action because the country's reputation will be damaged. Research shows that concern to be overdrawn (Mercer, 1996). Still, a country's power is to a degree based on others' perceptions of its current or potential power or its reputation for being willing (or not willing) to use the power it has. Sometimes the perception that a country is not currently powerful can tempt another country. When asked for his evaluation of the U.S. military in 1917, a German admiral replied, "Zero, zero, zero." Based on this perception of U.S. power, Germany resumed the submarine warfare against U.S. merchant shipping, a move that soon led to war with the United States.

Power Is Relative   Power does not exist in a vacuum. Since power is about the ability to persuade or make another actor do or not do something, calculating power is of limited use except to measure it against the power of the other side. When assessing capabilities, then, **relative power**, or the comparative

We usually think of the United States as a very powerful country. But even a powerful country cannot prevent everything it wants to stop from happening. This Cuban refugee has reached shore in Florida—his ultimate goal, as most who reach shore are allowed to stay in the United States. Those who are stopped in the water are usually deported. So even the powerful United States has difficulty preventing a single individual from breaching the absolute security of its border.

power of national actors, must be considered. We cannot, for example, say that China is powerful unless we specify *in comparison to whom*. Whatever Beijing's power resources may be, China's relative power compared to another major power, such as Japan, is less than is China's relative power compared to a smaller neighbor, such as Vietnam.

Power Is Situational   A country's power varies according to the situation, or context, in which it is being applied. A country's **situational power** is often less than the total inventory of its capabilities. Military power provides a good example. There are times when using military force is beyond imagination. The United States and Canada have serious disputes occasionally, but it is hard to imagine the countries clashing militarily. At other times, military power is virtually useless. During the Iranian hostage crisis, American military power had little value, given the goal of getting the hostages out alive.

Power Is Multidimensional   Power is multifaceted. Therefore, to analyze power well it is important to consider *all* the dimensions of power *and* to place them in their proper relative and situational contexts. Only then can we begin to answer the question of who is powerful and who is not. To help with that process, our next step is to identify the various determinants of national power.

INTERACTIVE EXERCISE
Winning Wars
Isn't Simple

The Elements of Power

There are many ways to categorize the multitudinous elements of power. One common way that we have already mentioned is to distinguish between objective (easily measurable, tangible) elements of power and subjective (hard-to-measure, intangible) facets of power. Another approach is to group both the tangible and the intangible power assets into various functional categories. Two such categories, the national core and the national infrastructure, are central to the power of all countries because they serve as a foundation for the more utilitarian categories of national power, specifically military power and economic power. We will, in the following sections, analyze these two central categories of national power; military and economic power will be discussed in chapters 10 and 12 respectively.

INTERACTIVE EXERCISE
Creating Your Own International Power Index

The National Core

The national state forms the basis of this element of national power. The essence of a state can be roughly divided into three elements: national geography, people, and government.

National Geography

The *location* of a country, particularly in relation to other countries, is significant. The Chinese army's significance as a power factor is different for the country's relations with the United States and with Russia. The huge Chinese army can do little to threaten the United States, far across the Pacific Ocean. By contrast, Russia and China share a border, and the People's Liberation Army could march into Siberia. Location can be an advantage or a disadvantage. Spain was able to avoid involvement in either world war partly because of its relative isolation from the rest of Europe. Poland, sandwiched between Germany and Russia, and Korea, stuck between China and Japan, each has a distinctly unfortunate location. The Israelis would almost certainly be better off if their promised land were somewhere—almost anywhere—else. And the Kuwaitis probably would not mind moving either, providing they could take their oil fields with them.

A country's *topography*—its mountains, rivers, and plains—is also important. The Alps have helped protect Switzerland from its larger European neighbors and spared the Swiss the ravages of both world wars. Topography can also work against a country. The broad European plain that extends from Germany's Rhine River to the Ural Mountains in central Russia has been an easy invasion avenue along which the armies of Napoleon, Kaiser Wilhelm II, and Hitler have marched.

A country's *size* is important. Bigger is often better. The immense expanse of Russia, for example, has repeatedly saved it from invasion. Although sometimes overwhelmed at first, the Russian armies have been able to retreat into the interior and buy time in exchange for geography while regrouping. By contrast, Israel's small size gives it no room to retreat.

A country's *climate* can also play a power role (Eichengreen, 1998). The tropical climate of Vietnam, with its heavy monsoon rains and its dense vegetation, made it difficult for the Americans to use effectively much of the superior weaponry they possessed. At the other extreme, the bone-chilling Russian winter has allied itself with Russia's geographic size to form a formidable defensive barrier. Many of Napoleon's soldiers literally froze to death during the French army's retreat from Moscow, and 133 years later Germany's army, the Wehrmacht, was decimated by cold and ice during the sieges of Leningrad and Stalingrad. In fact, the Russian winter has proved so formidable that Czar Nicholas I commented, "Russia has two generals we can trust, General January and General February."

People

A second element of the national core is a country's human characteristics. Tangible demographic subcategories include number of people, age distribution, and such quantitative factors as health and education. There are also intangible population factors such as morale.

Population   As is true for geographic size, the size of a country's population can be a positive or a negative factor. Because a large population supplies military personnel and industrial workers, sheer numbers of people are a positive power factor. It is unlikely, for instance, that Tonga (pop. 104,000) will ever achieve great-power status. A large population may be disadvantageous, however, if it is not in balance with resources. India (pop. 929 million) has the world's second largest population, yet because of the country's poverty ($340 per capita GDP), it must spend much of its energy and resources merely feeding its people.

Age Distribution   It is an advantage for a country to have a large number and percentage of its population in the productive years (15–65 by international reporting standards). Some countries with booming populations have a heavy percentage of children who must be supported. In other countries with limited life expectancy, many people die before they complete their productive years. Finally, some countries are "aging," with a geriatric population segment that consumes more resources than it produces.

Health and Education   An educated, healthy population is important to national power. There are health and education variations among all countries, but LDCs are especially disadvantaged compared to EDCs, as illustrated in Table 8.1, which contrasts Canada and Mozambique. It will be hard, for example, for LDCs to make up the gap in scientists and engineers. As a percentage of their populations, the EDCs have 13 times more of these professionals than does Latin America, 26 times more than Asia (excluding Japan), and 50 times more than Africa. It should be noted, however, that for some LDCs, the disparity is beginning to ease. China, for one, now has over 150,000 students in graduate school, an increase of more than 600 percent since 1980.

MAP
Illiteracy Rates

Table 8.1

Health and Education in Canada and Mozambique

Country	Spending ($) on Health and Education	Life Expectancy	Infant Mortality	Population per Physician	Daily Calorie Supply	Adult Literacy (%)
Canada	2,296	79	0.13	446	3,058	99
Mozambique	9	46	27.50	33,333	1,680	40

Public spending for health and education and calorie supply figures are per capita; infant mortality is the percentage of children who die before age 5.

Data source: World Bank (1997); UNDP (1997); *World Resources* (1998).

Canada's relatively educated and healthy population is more of a power asset than is Mozambique's relatively disadvantaged population.

Health problems can also sap a country's power. The health data shown in Table 8.1 can be supplemented by such information as the specific health problems that some countries face. AIDS is a world scourge, but it is particularly devastating in Africa. Data released by the UN in 1998 indicates that 70 percent of the world's 30 million HIV-infected people live in Africa, and the virus has infected at least 10 percent of the adult population in 13 countries. In one of these, Zimbabwe, 1 of every 4 adults is HIV positive.

Morale   A final factor that affects the population element of national power is the morale of a country's citizens. World War II demonstrated the power of strong civilian morale. Early in the war, Great Britain and the Soviet Union reeled under tremendous assaults by the Nazi forces. Yet the Allies hung on. Winston Churchill proclaimed in Parliament on October 9, 1940, during the darkest days of the war, that for the British people "Death and sorrow will be the companions of our journey; hardship our garment; constancy and valor our only shield. We must be united, we must be undaunted, we must be inflexible." The British answered Sir Winston's call. They remained undaunted; they held; they prevailed.

Conversely, the collapse of national morale can bring about civil unrest and even the fall of governments. The end of the USSR in 1991 provides an example. Polls in 1990 showed that 90 percent of Soviets believed that the country's economic situation was bad or critical, and 57 percent had no confidence in the future. Soviet president Mikhail Gorbachev may have won the 1990 Nobel Peace Prize, but as one member of the legislature grumbled about Gorbachev, "Let's be honest, he would never win the Nobel Prize for Economics."[4] Soon Gorbachev could not govern because no one would follow, and the Soviet Union faded away.

The impact of an individual leader is often a key component of international power. Yasir Arafat has remained at the pinnacle of Palestinian leadership for 30 years and over that time has played many different roles in the Middle East conflict and peace process. Ehud Barak's impact, as the new Israeli leader, is expected to be significant as he steers toward a course of reconciliation with the Palestinians that had been taken off-track by his predecessor.

Government

The quality of a country's government is a third power element associated with the national core. The issue is not what form of government, such as a democracy or an authoritarian system, a country has. Instead the issue is *administrative competence:* whether a state has a well-organized and effective administrative structure to utilize its power potential fully. The collapse of the Soviet Union stemmed in part from its massive and inefficient bureaucratic structure. "The management of the state is failing fast. Ministries are completely paralyzed," one top Soviet official complained in 1990. "We have brought the motherland to an awful state, turning it from an empire admired throughout the world to a state with an inglorious present and an indefinite future," agreed a Soviet diplomat.[5]

Leadership skill also adds to a government's strength. Leadership is one of the most intangible elements of national power. Yet it can be critical, especially in times of crisis. For example, Prime Minister Winston Churchill's sturdy image and his inspiring rhetoric well served the British people during World War II. By contrast, the ill health of President Boris Yeltsin, which includes heart problems and reported bouts of depression complicated by alcohol abuse, has often made for an unsteady hand at the helm of Russian affairs during the country's difficult times.

The National Infrastructure

Another group of the elements of power that form the foundation of state power is related to a country's infrastructure. The infrastructure of a state might roughly be equated with the skeleton of a human body. For a building, the infrastructure would be the foundation and the framing or girders. To examine the infrastructure of the state as an element of national power, the following sections will discuss technological sophistication, transportation systems, and information and communications capabilities. Each of these factors strongly affects any country's capacity in the other elements of power.

Technology

"Everything that can be invented has been invented," intoned Charles H. Duell, commissioner of the U.S. Office of Patents in 1988.[6] Commissioner Duell was obviously both in error and in the wrong job. Most of the technology that undergirds a great deal of contemporary national power has been invented since his short-sighted assessment. Air conditioning modifies the impact of weather, computers revolutionize education, robotics speed industry, synthetic fertilizers expand agriculture, new drilling techniques allow for undersea oil exploration, fiber optics speed information, and lasers bring the military to the edge of the Luke Skywalker era. Thus, technology is an overarching factor and will be discussed as part of all the tangible elements.

Transportation Systems

The ability to move people, raw materials, finished products, and sometimes the military throughout its territory is another part of a country's power equation. The collapse of public support for the Soviet Union and its subsequent demise was partly a result of the lack of enough affordable food. Just before the USSR ceased to exist, its official news agency, Tass, reported that 29 million tons of grain, 1 million tons of meat, and 25 percent of vegetables were lost between farm and table. Tass also reported that 1,700 trains were stalled because of lack of fuel or repair parts. The same sort of discouraging figures also applied to the country's trucks. Thus, one major hurdle that the FSRs face to restore their economic vitality is repairing and expanding their relatively limited transportation system. As one standard, for every 1,000 square miles of its territory, Russia has but 84 miles of paved roads and 14 miles of railroad track. The United States has 1,049 miles of paved roads and 45 miles of railroad track for the same amount of territory. Inadequate transportation systems are also a problem for less developed countries (LDCs). Nigeria, for one, has just 213 miles of paved roadway and only 6 miles of railroad track for each 1,000 square miles.

Information and Communications Systems

A country's information and communications capabilities are becoming increasingly important (Rothkopf, 1998). The advent of satellites and computers has accelerated the revolution begun with radio and television. Photocopying machines, then fax machines, and now the Internet have dramatically changed communications. Enhanced communications technology increases the ability of a society to communicate within itself and remain cohesive. It also increases efficiency and effectiveness in industry, finance, and the military. The EDCs have a wide advantage in this area; many other countries are struggling to enter the microchip age.

The Nature of Diplomacy

Now that we have explored the core and infrastructure elements of the power foundation on which much of national diplomacy rests, we can turn to the conduct of national diplomacy. To provide a level of continuity in our discussion of diplomacy, this chapter will make frequent, although not exclusive, use of illustrations from three diplomatic events.

The U.S.–North Korea nuclear crisis of 1993 and 1994 is one of the events. This occurred when the United States moved to force North Korea (the Democratic People's Republic of Korea, DPRK) to give up its alleged nuclear weapons program. Alarm that North Korea was developing a nuclear bomb rang out in 1993 when North Korea announced its withdrawal from the Nuclear Non-Proliferation Treaty (NPT) and the press reported that the CIA believed that the DPRK probably had one or two nuclear weapons. The image of a nuclear-armed North Korea created grave concerns because of the possibility of a nuclear nightmare occurring on the ever-tense Korean peninsula and because, in the estimate of former U.S. defense secretary Harold Brown, "A few nuclear weapons in North Korea could have a significant effect on the possibility of nuclear programs in Japan, South Korea, and Taiwan."[7]

What followed was a series of diplomatic moves and countermoves during a 19-month-long confrontation that focused on persuading North Korea (1) to allow the resumption of inspections by the UN–associated International Atomic Energy Agency (IAEA) and (2) to dismantle those nuclear reactors that the DPRK had or was building that were capable of producing nuclear weapons–grade uranium or plutonium. The confrontation escalated to the point that between April and June 1994 there were dire threats, military moves, and an open discussion of the possibility of war in the capitals of Pyongyang, North Korea, Seoul, South Korea, and Washington, D.C.

Then diplomacy lowered the flame of crisis. All the parties eased their stands to facilitate agreement. North Korea agreed to suspend work on the nuclear reactors it had under construction, to dismantle its current nuclear energy program over 10 years, and to allow the IAEA inspections to resume. The United States and its allies pledged that they—principally Japan and South Korea—would spend approximately $4 billion to build in North Korea two nuclear reactors that were not capable of producing plutonium for bomb building. The West also agreed to help meet North Korea's energy needs by annually supplying it with about 138 million gallons of petroleum until new reactors are on line. The issue resurfaced in 1998 when U.S. intelligence agencies discovered what, they charged, was a massive effort by North Korea to build an underground nuclear facility, so this tale of diplomacy may not yet be over.

The Taiwan Strait crisis of 1996 is the second event that will be used to illustrate various aspects of diplomacy. This event, which featured diplomatic interplay between China and the United States during the period just before Taiwan's presidential election in 1996, is detailed in the Web site box To Be or Not to Be.

A FURTHER NOTE
To Be or Not to Be

The U.S.–Iraq inspection crisis of 1997–1998 is the third diplomatic event used extensively in the discussion of diplomacy that follows. Iraq had agreed in the aftermath of the Persian Gulf War of 1991 to allow UN inspectors to ensure that the Iraqis had destroyed all their nuclear, biological, and chemical weapons capabilities. Over the years there was frequent friction between Iraq and the UN inspection team, and this escalated to crisis level when, in late 1997, Iraq refused to allow the inspectors access to large facilities that Baghdad claimed were presidential palaces.

Like the crisis on the Korean peninsula four years before, the confrontation with Iraq teetered on the edge of war. Finally, however, the diplomatic maneuvering again avoided war. The crisis subsided after a trip by UN secretary-general Kofi Annan to Baghdad, where he negotiated an agreement acceptable to both sides. Among other things, Saddam Hussein agreed to let the UN inspectors enter the supposed presidential palaces and Annan held out the hope that the long-standing economic sanctions on Iraq would be eased, perhaps even ended. As with the North Korean nuclear issue and many other sagas of diplomacy, the agreement in early 1998 was not the end of the story. Later in the year, perhaps trying to take advantage of President Clinton's embroilment in the Monica Lewinsky affair, Iraq again defied UN inspectors. Once again the world sought a solution somewhere between acquiescence and war.

The Functions of Diplomacy

As it has traditionally been practiced, diplomacy has focused on the national interest. Writing in the 1400s in one of the first treatises on diplomacy, Emalao Barbaro asserted that "the first duty of an ambassador is . . . to do, say, advise, and think whatever may best serve the preservation and aggrandizement of his own state" (Craig & George, 1995). More sardonically, Sir Henry Wotton, the English ambassador to Venice, wrote in *Reliquae Wottonianae* (1651) that "an ambassador is an honest man sent to lie abroad for the commonwealth [state]." Whether it is conducted with honor or deceit, diplomacy is carried on by officials with a variety of titles such as president, prime minister, ambassador, or special envoy, and it is worthwhile to explore the roles that these officials and other diplomats play in promoting the national interest.

Observer and reporter is one role. A primary diplomatic role has always been to gather information and impressions and to analyze and report these back to the home office. This mostly includes routine activity, such as reading

The diplomatic maneuverings of UN secretary-general Kofi Annan played an important role in obtaining an agreement from Saddam Hussein during the 1997–98 UNSCOM weapons inspection crisis. Without Annan's diplomatic finesse, war might have been the ultimate outcome.

newspapers and reporting observations. Many embassies also contain a considerable contingent of intelligence officers who are technically attached to the diplomatic service but who are in reality a part of their country's intelligence service. Whatever the method, it is important for policy makers to know both the facts and the mood of foreign capitals, and the embassy is a primary source.

The value of this function is especially evident when it is absent. The internal politics and international intentions of North Korea, for example, are largely shrouded from outside view. Many countries, including the United States, do not have embassies in Pyongyang, and those diplomats who are there are generally restricted in their travel and contacts in North Korea. One U.S. official noted that "compared with North Korea, the Soviet Union was a duck-soup intelligence target."[8] This lack of good information was particularly worrisome during the events of 1993 and 1994 that involved North Korea's nuclear program. "The fact of the matter is that we don't really understand what they are doing," a U.S. official commented at one point.[9]

Negotiator is a second important role of a diplomat. Negotiation is a combination of art and technical skill that attempts to find a common ground among two or more divergent positions (Hopmann, 1996). For all of the public attention given to meetings between national leaders, the vast bulk of negotiating is done by ambassadors and other such personnel. The early negotiations between U.S. and North Korean diplomats resembled two boxers feeling each other out in the early rounds. "The whole idea is to test the proposition that the North Koreans are willing to deal," observed the chief American negotiator, Assistant Secretary of State Robert L. Gallucci. "And I always put it

A FURTHER NOTE
United States–North
Korea Agreed
Framework

in terms of 'test the proposition' because I don't have . . . high confidence that we actually can resolve this through negotiations."[10]

Substantive and symbolic representative is a third role of a diplomat. Substantive representation includes explaining and defending the policies of the diplomat's country. Misperception is dangerous in world politics, and the role that diplomats play in explaining their countries' actions and statements to friends and foes alike is vital to accurate communications. Diplomats, to a degree, also personify, and thus symbolically represent, their countries. For example, ambassadors who have historical ties to the country to which they are accredited are apt to be received enthusiastically, enhancing the image of their country. Reverse characteristics can alienate people. The appointment in 1997 of Felix Rohatyn, who speaks fluent French and was awarded the Legion of Honor by France, as U.S. ambassador to Paris was warmly greeted by the French. Whatever the other fine qualifications of Ambassador Daniel Kurtzer, many Egyptians were dismayed when in 1998 President Clinton named him the first Jewish U.S. ambassador to an Arab country. "A Rabbi in the Robes of a Diplomat," grumbled the headline of one Egyptian news magazine.[11] Other Egyptians sprang to Ambassador Kurtzer's defense and the imbroglio eventually died down. A few diplomats, however, have managed to offend nearly everyone in their host country. Few Italians were able to appreciate the American humor of President Bush's ambassador to Italy, who joked before going to Rome that the modern Italian navy had to have glass-bottom boats "so they can see the old Italian navy."[12]

Diplomats can sometimes *intervene* to tell a weaker country what to do. When, in 1972, South Vietnam resisted the U.S.–negotiated settlement, President Nixon cabled President Thieu that "all military and economic aid will be cut off . . . if an agreement is not reached" and that "I have . . . irrevocably decided to proceed . . . to sign [the agreement]. I will do so, if necessary, alone [and] explain that your government obstructs peace." As the United States' chief diplomat, Nixon was being distinctly undiplomatic. "Brutality is nothing," he told Kissinger. "You have never seen it if this son-of-a-bitch doesn't go along, believe me" (Kissinger, 1979:1420, 1469). Thieu went along.

Finally, diplomacy is also sometimes conducted for its *propaganda value*. Even where there is little hope for settlement, it may benefit a country's image to appear reasonable or to make opponents seem stubborn. As Soviet leader Nikita Khrushchev told a diplomat, "Never forget the appeal that the idea of disarmament has to the outside world. All you have to say is 'I'm in favor of it,' and it pays big dividends" (Shevchenko, 1985:246).

The Diplomatic Setting

The nature of diplomacy and how it is carried out are also affected by its setting (Starkey, Boyer, & Wilkenfeld, 1999). The setting can be roughly divided into three parts: the international system, the diplomatic environment, and the domestic connection.

The International System

One aspect of the setting is the system. As we have noted many times, the nature of the anarchical international system creates a setting in which self-interested actors pursue their diplomatic goals by, if necessary, using power to ensure that their goals prevail over the goals of others. That emphasis on national interest is why this chapter discusses national diplomacy and national power.

Moreover, there are no authoritative outside actors to resolve disputes in the system among the main actors, the states. What is important to see about the system is that there was no supranational force to unravel the complex situations, such as the one in which China, Taiwan, and the United States found themselves during the crisis that arose over China's attempt to influence Taiwan's 1996 presidential election. Taipei and Washington could only look to themselves to forestall any military attempt by Beijing to reincorporate Taiwan. China was similarly limited to self-reliance. In the current system, the only recourse for China if Taiwan had announced its independence would have been to try to reincorporate Taiwan militarily. Thus, when a tense issue occurred, all the actors had little choice but to rely on their own power to protect their divergent national interests.

The Diplomatic Environment

A second part of the diplomatic setting is determined by the relationships among the various actors who are involved in a particular matter. This part of the setting can be subdivided into four diplomatic environments: hostile, adversarial, coalition, and mediation diplomacy.

Hostile Diplomacy   Where one or more countries are engaged in armed clashes or when there is a substantial possibility that fighting could result, diplomacy is conducted in a hostile environment. The maneuvering surrounding the U.S.–Iraq inspection crisis of 1997–1998 fell distinctly within the range of hostile diplomacy. The United States increased its firepower in the region to include 300 warplanes in Saudi Arabia, Kuwait, and Bahrain and the aircraft carriers USS *Nimitz* and USS *George Washington* in the Persian Gulf. The U.S. fleet in the Gulf was joined by a British aircraft carrier HMS *Invincible* and included nine ships able to fire Tomahawk cruise missiles deep into Iraq. To underline the possibilities, U.S. secretary of defense William Cohen told reporters that "If one

Unfortunately, diplomacy often becomes hostile in international affairs and that hostility may be accompanied by military action or its threat. These Indian weapons are being readied for use (or threatened use) in May 1999, in the recurrent Indo-Pakistani conflict over the territory of Kashmir.

has to resort to military options . . . they will be substantial. They are something that Saddam Hussein should understand, and something a great deal more than any pinprick that might have been delivered in the past."[13]

Adversarial Diplomacy   An environment of adversarial diplomacy occurs at a less confrontational level when two or more countries' interests clash but when there is little or no chance of armed conflict. A great deal of diplomacy involving economic issues occurs in adversarial circumstances as countries press other countries to accede to their wishes. During the 1990s, for example, there has been a more adversarial—but not hostile—relationship between Japan and the United States over Washington's efforts to get Tokyo to lower its trade barriers and stimulate its lagging economy so that the Japanese will buy more American exports. The thought of either Tokyo or Washington threatening to use force, much less actually doing so, is inconceivable in the foreseeable future. Yet relations between the two capitals have often been tense; stated and, more often, implied threats of economic sanctions and other forms of coercive diplomatic action have sometimes volleyed back and forth across the Pacific. For example, during one struggle in 1995 in which the United States was trying to force Japan to agree to further open its markets, Washington threatened to impose a 100 percent tariff on imported Japanese luxury cars. To ensure that Japan got the point, Vice President Al Gore used the imagery that once governed the cold war's eyeball-to-eyeball confrontations with the Soviet Union to warn, "We're not going to blink."[14]

Coalition Diplomacy   When a number of countries have similar interests, often in opposition to the interest of one or more other countries, then coalition diplomacy becomes a significant aspect of international activity (Hampson & Hart, 1995). National leaders spend a good deal of time and effort to build coalitions that will support the foreign policy initiatives of their country or of other international actors that they support. When, for instance, Iraq invaded Kuwait in August 1990, President George Bush spent much time and effort in rounding up international support for military action against Iraq. During the first four days of the crisis, Bush made 23 phone calls to a dozen foreign leaders and personally flew to Colorado to consult with British prime minister Margaret Thatcher, who was coincidentally speaking at a conference there.

Bush and his advisers also rallied support against Iraq under the auspices of the United Nations. The UN Security Council passed a series of resolutions approving economic sanctions and the deployment of military forces in the Gulf region. The Security Council later approved the action taken in January and February by the American-led coalition forces to push Iraq out of Kuwait. These efforts did more than just build multinational support for the U.S. goal of ousting Iraq from Kuwait. The use of multilateral organizations also lent an air of legitimacy to a war that, if the United States had waged it unilaterally, would have created much more furor than was the case as a UN-sponsored operation.

Mediation Diplomacy   Unlike hostile, adversarial, or coalition diplomacy, mediation diplomacy occurs when a country that is not involved directly as one of the parties tries to help countries in conflict resolve their differences. The peace in Northern Ireland is far from secure, but the mediation of the United States has given Catholic and Protestant Irish their best chance in decades to live without terror. The accords that were reached among the two religious groups and the British and Irish governments in April 1998, and subsequently ratified by Northern Irish voters in a referendum, were achieved through a long peace conference presided over by former U.S. Senate majority leader George J. Mitchell. Moreover, when the talks appeared to stall at a critical stage, President Clinton made several calls beginning at 3:15 A.M. EST to British prime minister Tony Blair, Irish prime minister Bertie Ahern, Sinn Fein president Gerry Adams, and Protestant Ulster Unionist Party head David Trimble. By most accounts, the president's efforts helped tip the balance in favor of peace. By the end of the day there was an agreement. It was a positive outcome facilitated, according to one of the participants, by "the strong support we have had from President Clinton in the peace process. . . . He made clear to me that if we reach an agreement, he will give us any assistance, particularly in the economic field, that we seek."[15]

The Domestic Connection

Domestic politics provide the third part of the diplomatic setting. What is known as "two-level game theory" holds that a country's diplomats must find a solution that is acceptable to both the other country at the international level and, at the domestic level, to the political actors (legislators, public opinion, interest groups) in the diplomat's own country. From this perspective, the diplomatic setting exists at the domestic as well as at the international level, and is influenced by the interplay of the two levels when leaders try to pursue policies that satisfy the actors at both levels (Boyer, 1999; Trumbore, 1998; Peterson, 1996; Putnam, 1998).

During the Taiwan crisis, the leaders of China and the United States not only had to find a point of agreement between themselves, they also had to fend off domestic forces that were pushing to escalate the crisis (Ross, 1995). A significant point of Chinese political culture is their drive to regain their "lost territories." It is so powerful that President Jiang Zemin told the U.S. ambassador, "Any leader who let this pass [Taiwan's independence] would be overthrown."[16]

President Clinton also had to deal with strong domestic forces. The House Republican Policy Committee urged Clinton to commit the United States "to the defense of Taiwan."[17] Perhaps even more telling, Clinton also came under fire from members of his own Democratic Party. "It was one thing to normalize [relations] with China when both Beijing and Taiwan had authoritarian regimes," said Democratic House member Nancy Pelosi. "The fact is, Taiwan is now a democracy, and that makes all the difference in the world."[18]

The Conduct of Diplomacy

Diplomacy is a complex game of maneuver in which the goal is to get other players to do what you want them to do. The players can number from two, in **bilateral diplomacy**, to many, in multilateral diplomacy. The rules of diplomacy are, at best, loose. The norms of the system set down some guidelines to diplomacy, but they are ever-evolving and even the ones that exist are not always followed. The unilateral, aggressive use of force, for instance, is now widely considered a violation of the rules. Yet players still sometimes employ it, and the penalties for rules violations are uncertain (Morgan, 1994).

Another factor that adds to the complexity of the often multisided, loosely constrained diplomatic game is that it is multidimensional. There is not just one mode of play. Instead, like all the most fascinating games, diplomacy is intricate and involves considerable strategy that can be employed in several ways. Thus, while diplomacy is often portrayed by an image of somber negotiations over highly polished wooden tables in ornate rooms, it is much more than that. Modern diplomacy is a far-ranging communications process. In the following pages, we will first discuss some of the evolving characteristics of modern diplomacy. Then we will move on to a brief discussion of the basic rules of diplomatic operations and close this chapter with an examination of the various options diplomats have available to them in their negotiations.

Modern Diplomacy

Although diplomatic practice has evolved slowly, the World War I (1914–1918) era serves as a benchmark in the transition to modern diplomacy. It was the beginning of the end of European world dominance. It also marked the fall of the German, Austrian, Ottoman, and Russian emperors. Nationalistic self-determination stirred strongly in Europe and other parts of the world. New powers—the United States, Japan, and China—began to assert themselves and they joined or replaced the declining European countries as world powers. The "old diplomacy" did not vanish, but it changed substantially. The "new diplomacy" includes seven characteristics: expanded geographic scope, multilateral diplomacy, parliamentarianism, democratization, open diplomacy, leader-to-leader diplomacy, and public diplomacy. These new practices have been greeted as "reforms," but many also have drawbacks.

Expansion of Geographic Scope

The diplomacy of the twentieth century has been marked by expansion of its geographic scope. The two Hague Conferences (1899, 1907) on peace, particularly the second, with its 44 participants, included countries outside the European sphere. President Wilson's call for national self-determination foreshadowed a world of almost 200 countries. Today, the United Nations, with its nearly universal membership, symbolizes the truly global scope of diplomacy.

Multilateral Diplomacy

Although conferences involving a number of nations occurred during the nineteenth century, that practice has expanded greatly in the modern era. Woodrow Wilson's call for a League of Nations symbolizes the rise of **multilateral diplomacy**. There are now a number of permanent world and regional international organizations. Ad hoc conferences and treaties are also more apt to be multilateral. Before 1900, for example, the United States attended an average of one multilateral conference per year. Now, the United States is a member of scores of international organizations and American diplomats participate daily in multilateral negotiations.

Multilateral diplomacy has increased for several reasons. Technological progress is one. Advances in travel and communications technology allow faster and more frequent contacts among countries. Second, multilateral diplomacy has increased because more countries and leaders recognize that many global concerns, such as the environment, cannot be solved by any one country or through traditional bilateral diplomacy alone. Instead, global cooperation and solutions are required. Third, diplomacy through multilateral organizations is attractive to smaller countries as a method of influencing world politics beyond their individual power.

A fourth factor promoting multilateral diplomacy is the rise of expectations that important international actions, especially the use of military force, will be taken within the framework of a multilateral organization. An important point to make about multilateral diplomacy is that participation in a global setting does not mean that countries pursue policies for the global good. Instead, as we saw in the preceding chapter, countries most often try to achieve their self-interests by manipulating multilateral organizations and conferences.

Parliamentary Diplomacy

Another modern practice is **parliamentary diplomacy**. This includes debate and voting in international organizations and sometimes supplants negotiation and compromise.

The maneuvering involved in parliamentary diplomacy was strongly evident in the UN with regard to North Korea during 1993 and 1994. The United States had to proceed cautiously with threats of UN–endorsed sanctions against North Korea because both China and Russia were averse to sanctions and each possessed a veto. "What will the Chinese do?" Assistant Secretary Gallucci rhetorically asked reporters at a briefing. "Will you be able to pass a sanctions resolution? If there is anybody in this room who knows things they know, if they are willing to give me odds, and I do not care in which direction, I'll take them. I do not know what the Chinese are going to do."[19]

Despite the reluctance of China and Russia to act, parliamentary diplomacy did eventually play a role in putting pressure on North Korea. In late May 1994, the five permanent members of the Security Council issued a joint statement calling on North Korea to provide evidence that it was not reprocessing spent nuclear reactor fuel rods into plutonium for weapons. Among other benefits, this statement signaled to Pyongyang that the so-called Big Five were united in opposition to a North Korean nuclear weapons capability and that even Chinese and Russian patience was not inexhaustible.

Democratization

The elite and executive-dominant character of diplomacy has changed in several ways. One is that diplomats are now drawn from a wider segment of society. This has the advantage of making diplomats more representative of their nations. It also means, though, that diplomats have lost the common frame of reference once provided by their similar cosmopolitan, elite backgrounds. Diplomats now have their attitudes rooted in their national cultures and are more apt to suffer from the antagonisms and misperceptions that nationalistic stereotyping causes.

A second democratic change is the rise of the roles of legislatures, interest groups, and public opinion. Executive leaders still dominate the foreign policy–making process, but it is no longer their exclusive domain. Now, as discussed in the earlier section on the domestic setting, national executives often must conduct two-level diplomacy by negotiating with domestic actors as well as other countries to find a mutually agreeable solution to outstanding issues.

The democratization of diplomacy means, among other things, that diplomats conduct public diplomacy aimed at influencing not just leaders, but also the legislatures, interest groups, and public opinion in other countries. As an aide has quoted UN secretary-general Kofi Annan as explaining it, "If I can't get the support of governments, then I'll get the support of the people. People move governments."[20]

Open Diplomacy

Of Woodrow Wilson's Fourteen Points, his call for "open covenants, openly arrived at" is the best remembered. As such, Wilson would have approved of the fact that, much more than before, diplomacy and even international agreements are widely reported and documented. One advantage of **open diplomacy** is that it fits with the idea of democracy. Secret diplomacy more often than not is used by leaders to "mislead the populations of their own countries" rather than to keep information from international opponents (Gibbs, 1995:213).

There are, however, advantages to secret diplomacy. Most scholars and practitioners agree that public negotiations are difficult. Early disclosure of your bargaining strategy will compromise your ability to win concessions. Public negotiations are also more likely to lead diplomats to posture for public consumption. Concessions may be difficult to make amid popular criticism. In sum, it is difficult to negotiate (or to play chess) with someone kibitzing over your shoulder. Indeed, domestic opposition to dealing with an adversary may be so intense that it may be impossible to negotiate at all. The impact that domestic support for and opposition to negotiation can have on the process is amply illustrated in A Further Note: Palestinians: A Nation without

A FURTHER NOTE
Palestinians: A
Nation without
a State

a State that was cited on the Web site for chapter 4. You may want to review that now in the context of our diplomatic discussions.

Leader-to-Leader Diplomacy

Modern transportation and communications have spawned an upsurge of high-level diplomacy (Dunn, 1996). National leaders regularly hold bilateral or multilateral summit conferences, and foreign ministers and other ranking diplomats jet between countries, conducting shuttle diplomacy. One hundred thirty years of American history passed before a president (Woodrow Wilson) traveled overseas while in office. Richard Nixon departed on his first state visit to Europe only 33 days after his inauguration, and each president has surpassed his predecessor's record of foreign travel. When, in May 1997, Bill Clinton visited his 36th country while president, he surpassed George Bush's previous presidential record of 35. Since that time, trips by Clinton to Africa and China have taken his total to over 40 countries. The once-rare instances of meetings between heads of state have become so common that in some cases they have become routine. For example, the leaders of the Group of Eight (G-8), comprising the seven largest industrialized countries plus Russia, meet annually; the leaders of the European Union's countries meet at least twice a year.

The advent of globe-trotting, leader-to-leader diplomacy, or **summitry**, and the increased frequency of telecommunications diplomacy are mixed blessings. There are several *advantages*. The first is that leaders can sometimes make dramatic breakthroughs. The 1978 Camp David Accords, which began the process of normalizing Egyptian-Israeli relations after decades of hostility and three wars, were produced after President Carter, Egyptian president Sadat, and Israeli prime minister Begin isolated themselves at the presidential retreat in Maryland. Second, rapid diplomacy can help dispel false information and stereotypes. President Bush has argued that the telephone helped avoid specific misunderstandings. "I want to be sure [that U.S.–USSR agreements are] real and they're based on fact, not misunderstanding," the president explained. "If [another leader] knows the heartbeat a little bit from talking [with me], there's less apt to be misunderstanding."[21]

A third advantage of personal contact among leaders is that mutual confidence or even friendships may develop. It would be an overstatement to say that President Clinton and President Jiang Zemin of China have become friends, but they have established a level of ease with one another in the more than a half dozen meetings they have had. As one U.S. aide put it during Jiang's trip to the United States in 1997, "I think there has developed over these . . . meetings a bond. I think when Jiang talks about 'my friend Bill Clinton' and having met with him five times, he's doing more than going through the motions."[22] Indeed, there are many things to be gained from summit diplomacy, as explained in the Web site box Expansion: The Price of Diplomatic Gains.

Clear vision and good feelings are laudable, but there are also several potential *disadvantages* to leader-to-leader diplomacy. One problem is that

A FURTHER NOTE
Expansion:
The Price of
Diplomatic Gains

President Bill Clinton and President Jiang Zemin of China are sharing a laugh at a tense political time. One of the advantages of personal diplomacy is that leaders of adversarial or hostile states can use their personal relationships as anchors for stabilizing rocky state-to-state relationships.

summits may lead to ill-conceived agreements. According to Kissinger (1979:142), "Some of the debacles of our diplomatic history have been perpetrated by Presidents who fancied themselves negotiators." An irony of modern diplomacy is that the interdependent and technical natures of global issues are making them increasingly complex at the very time when leader-to-leader diplomacy is becoming more frequent. There is, one Bush administration official worried, a tendency to oversimplify problems: "We assume five or six people can do anything, and it makes it a lot easier." "But," the official warned, "if we push the experts aside, we suffer in the end."[23]

A second problem with leader-to-leader diplomacy is that it may lead to misunderstandings. There are numerous instances where leaders have made and reached what each thought was a mutual understanding, only to find to their equally mutual surprise and anger that they had misunderstood one another. Furthermore, as tricky as personal contacts may be, the telephone may present even greater difficulties. Henry Kissinger, for example, argues that "the telephone is generally made for misunderstanding. It is difficult to make a good record. You can't see the other side's expressions or body language."[24] And as e-diplomacy becomes increasingly important, leaders must also beware of the Internet problems of flaring (escalating tensions through e-mail misunderstandings) and other communications problems endemic to indirect nonverbal communications.

Third, while mistakes made by lower-ranking officials can be disavowed by their superiors, a leader's commitments, even if not well thought out, cannot be easily retracted. "When Presidents become negotiators no escape routes are left," Kissinger (1979:12) warns. "Concessions are irrevocable without dishonor."

Fourth, specific misunderstanding and general chemistry can work to damage working relations between leaders instead of improving them. Kissinger (1979:142), who should know, has observed that most world leaders are characterized by a "healthy dose of ego," and when two such egos collide, "negotiations can rapidly deteriorate from intractability to confrontation."

Public Diplomacy

The communications revolution has placed leaders and other diplomats in public view more than ever before, and their actions have an impact on world opinion that is often distinct from their negotiating positions. Among other things, this means that diplomacy is often conducted under the glare of television lights and almost everything that officials say in public is heard or read by others (Fortner, 1994; Manheim, 1994). Additionally, a country's overall image and the image of its leaders have become more important because of the democratization of the foreign policy process discussed above.

These changes have meant that international relations are also increasingly conducted through **public diplomacy**. The concept of public diplomacy can be defined as a process of creating an overall international image that enhances a country's ability to achieve diplomatic success. This is akin to propaganda.

Public diplomacy includes traditional propaganda, but goes beyond that to include what is actually said and done by political figures and their practices of national self-promotion. In essence, public diplomacy is much the same as advertising and other forms of public relations that are utilized by business. In practice, as we shall see, propaganda and public diplomacy overlap substantially. One scholar's concept of public diplomacy envisions a "theater of power" that is a "metaphor for the repertoire of visual and symbolic tools used by statesmen and diplomats." As players in the theater of power, leaders "must be sensitive to the impression they make on observers. . . . They surely [are] subject to the same sort of 'dramatic,' if not aesthetic, criticism of other kinds of public performances" (Cohen, 1987:i–ii).

A SITE TO SURF
Public Diplomacy
Forum

The Rules of Effective Diplomacy

Diplomacy as a communications process has three elements: negotiation, signaling, and public diplomacy. Delineating the three modes of diplomatic communications is easy. Utilizing them effectively is hard (Zartman, 1995). There is no set formula that will ensure victory. There are, however, several considerations that affect the chances of diplomatic success. We can examine some of these considerations by looking, in this section, at the rules of effective diplomacy, then, in the next section, by turning to the various options available for playing the great game of diplomacy. Some basic rules of effective diplomacy are:

- *Be realistic.* It is important to have goals that match your ability to achieve them. "The test of a statesman," Kissinger (1970:47) has pointed out, "is his ability to recognize the real relationship of forces." Being realistic also means remembering that the other side, like yours, has domestic opponents.
- *Be careful about what you say.* The experienced diplomat plans out and weighs words carefully.
- *Seek common ground.* Disputes begin negotiations; finding common ground ends them successfully. Almost any negotiation will involve some concessions, so it is important to maintain a degree of flexibility. Most diplomats counsel that it is important to distinguish your central from your peripheral values. Intransigence over a minor point, when a concession can bring a counterconcession on an issue important to you, is folly. There is some research indicating that concessions, even unilateral ones, are likely to engender positive responses. Other research concludes that finding common cause cannot end rivalry but can create cooperation (Bennett, 1996).
- *Understand the other side.* There are several aspects to understanding the other side. One is to appreciate an opponent's perspective even if you do not agree with it. Just four months after Ronald Reagan was inaugurated and began an arms buildup, the Soviet leader, Leonid Brezhnev, wrote his American counterpart to protest the military expansion "aimed against our country." "Try, Mr. President," Brezhnev asked Reagan, "to see what is going on through our eyes" (Kriesberg, 1992:12). It was good advice. As a corollary, it is also wise to make sure that thine enemy knows thee. Errors that result from misperceptions based on cultural differences and the lack of or wrong information are a major cause of conflict.
- *Be patient.* It is also important to bide your time. Being overly anxious can lead to concessions that are unwise and may convey weakness to an opponent. As a corollary, it is poor practice to set deadlines, for yourself or others, unless you are in a very strong position or you do not really want an agreement.
- *Leave avenues of retreat open.* It is axiomatic that even a rat will fight if trapped in a corner. The same is often true for countries. Call it honor, saving face, or prestige; it is important to leave yourself and your opponent an "out." During the crisis with North Korea, a former U.S. ambassador to Seoul argued that the leaders in Pyongyang wanted "a face-saving way out of the corner into which they have painted themselves."[25] The Clinton administration agreed, and followed a strategy of issuing repeated public assurances that, as President Clinton said, the North Koreans could ease the situation at any time by being willing to "crawl back off this ledge they are on."[26]

Options for Conducting Diplomacy

While the above rules are solid guidelines to effective diplomacy, the practice is still more art than science. Therefore, effective diplomacy must tailor its approach to the situation and the opponent. To do this, diplomats must make choices about the channel, level, visibility, type of inducement, degree of precision, method of communication, and extent of linkage that they will use (Feron, 1997).

Direct or Indirect Negotiations

One issue that diplomats face is whether to negotiate directly with each other or indirectly through an intermediary. *Direct negotiations* have the advantage of avoiding the misinterpretations that an intermediary third party might cause. As in the old game of "Gossip," messages can get garbled. Direct negotiations are also quicker. An additional plus is that they can act as a symbol.

Indirect negotiations, sometimes called "two-track diplomacy," may also be advisable (Rasmussen, 1997). Direct contact symbolizes a level of legitimacy that a country may not wish to convey. Israel, for instance, long refused to recognize or openly and directly negotiate with the PLO. Indirect diplomacy can also avoid the embarrassment of a public rebuff by the other side. During the opening moves between the United States and China, oral messages were sent through the "good offices" (friendly intermediaries) of Pakistan and Romania, and written messages were exchanged on photocopy paper with no letterheads or signatures.

A SITE TO SURF
The Institute
for Multitrack
Diplomacy

High-Level or Low-Level Diplomacy

The higher the level of contact or the higher the level of the official making a statement, the more seriously will a message be taken. It implies a greater commitment, and there will be a greater reaction. Therefore, a diplomat must decide whether to communicate on a high or a low level.

A *high level of diplomacy* has its advantages. Verbal and written statements by heads of government are noted seriously in other capitals. At one point in 1998 during the confrontation with Iraq, President Clinton personally and publicly commented on a UN Security Council resolution stating that Iraq faced "severest consequences" if it continued to block arms control inspections. "The government of Iraq should be under no illusion," Clinton said. "The meaning of severest consequences is clear. It provides [the United States and other countries] authority to act" if Iraq does not reverse its policy. Just in case Baghdad had any doubts, a State Department spokesman defined severest to mean, "There is no more severe consequence, which makes quite clear that what we're talking about here is military force."[27]

There are other times when *low-level communications* are wiser. Low-level communications avoid overreaction and maintain flexibility. Dire threats can be issued as "trial balloons" by cabinet officers or generals and then, if later thought unwise, disavowed by higher political officers. During the Taiwan crisis of 1996, the principal leaders tended to avoid military threats, leaving that role to lesser officials. For example, Tang Shubei, as deputy director of Beijing's Taiwan Affairs Office, was far enough down the official ladder to warn provocatively that "we would not hesitate to use all means, including military means, to achieve reunification of the motherland" without truly committing China to do so.[28] From a position safely distant from the pinnacle of U.S. authority in the Oval Office, Secretary of Defense William Perry growled back that China too should beware because "America has the best damned navy in the world."[29]

Sometimes it is even prudent to use a representative who is not in the government at all. An unofficial representative helped Clinton resolve the gnarly issue of U.S. representation at the 1996 inauguration of President Lee of Taiwan. Dispatching an official representative would have outraged Beijing; sending no one would have offended Taipei. So Clinton sent Vernon Jordan, who is widely recognized as one of the closest of all the so-called FOBs (friends of Bill).

Using Coercion or Rewards to Gain Agreement

Yet another diplomatic choice is whether to brandish coercive sticks or proffer tempting carrots. To induce an opponent to react as you wish, is it better to offer rewards or to threaten punishment?

Coercive diplomacy can be effective when you have the power, will, and credibility to back it up. Verbal threats and military maneuvering were central to the diplomatic interplay among the United States, North Korea, and the other countries embroiled in the 1993–1994 confrontation. Perhaps because it was the weaker side, North Korea was particularly bombastic. Its main newspaper, *Rodong Sinmum,* declared that if "war breaks out," the "reactionaries" would be "digging their own grave."[30] Given the long and bloody Korean War (1950–1953) and North Korea's considerable military might, such rhetoric was believable. There was a consensus, one Pentagon source put it, that "it's going to be a bloody, bloody mess if [war] happens. A real tragedy."[31]

The United States and its allies also practiced coercive diplomacy. They threatened economic sanctions and at least refused to rule out military action. After Pyongyang refused to allow inspections, a stern U.S. official announced, "This time the North went too far. There are no more carrots."[32]

There are also a number of drawbacks to coercive diplomacy. If it does not work, then those who have threatened force face an unhappy choice. On the one hand, not carrying out threats creates an image of weakness that may well embolden the opponent in the crisis at hand. Opponents in other ongoing and future confrontations may also be encouraged. On the other hand, putting one's military might and money where one's mouth has been costs lives and dollars and is not necessarily successful either. Even if coercion does work, it may entail a long-term commitment that was not originally planned or desired. The war with Iraq ended in February 1991, but U.S. forces have remained enmeshed in the region, have been on the verge of using force against Iraq on several occasions, and have spent many billions of dollars patrolling the region.

There are many times when *offers of rewards* may be a more powerful inducement than coercion. Threats may lead to war, with high costs and uncertain results. It may also be possible to "buy" what you cannot "win." One song in the movie *Mary Poppins* includes the wisdom that "a spoonful of sugar helps the medicine go down," and an increase in aid, a trade concession, a state visit, or some other tangible or symbolic reward may induce agreement. The incentive approach was evident during the negotiations with Iraq in 1998. In February 1998 the UN Security Council agreed to allow Iraq to increase the amount of oil it could sell every six months to pay for food and medical care to $5.2 billion. Secretary-General Annan also appealed to Iraq and its president, Saddam Hussein, through positive statements. Annan publicly praised the Iraqi leadership for its "courage, wisdom, flexibility." It was "homage to Saddam," according to one UN diplomat, and it brought down a torrent of criticism on the secretary-general from those who favored a hard-line approach.[33] Still, in the end, the carrots that Annan offered played a role in resolving the immediate crisis peacefully.

Often, the best diplomacy mixes carrots and sticks (O'Reilly, 1997). In contrast to the mixture of carrots and sticks that resolved the crisis with Iraq in 1998, U.S. diplomacy during the 1990–1991 Persian Gulf crisis offered virtually no positive incentives to Iraq. President Bush declared that "Iraq will not be permitted to annex Kuwait. That's not a threat, not a boast. That's just the way it's going to be." Some commentators criticized what they saw as a one-sided approach. In an article entitled "For Saddam, Where's the Carrot?" Roger Fisher, coauthor of the book on bargaining, *Getting to Yes,* argued that coercion was "barely half" of what was needed to resolve the crisis. He maintained that the United States should be "building a golden bridge for Saddam's retreat" and contended that Bush had erred by increasing the level of threat without providing simultaneous positive signs of what would happen if Iraq withdrew.[34]

Being Precise or Being Intentionally Vague

Most diplomatic experts stress the importance of being precise when communicating. There are times, however, when purposeful vagueness may be in order.

Precision is a hallmark of diplomacy. Being precise in both written and verbal communications helps avoid misunderstandings. It can also indicate true commitment, especially if it comes from the national leader. At times, however, *vagueness* may be a better strategy. Being vague may paper over irreconcilable differences. "The Saudis have a nice way of doing things" when they do not wish to agree, says one U.S. official. "They say, 'we'll consider it.' It is not their style to say no."[35] Lack of precision also can allow a country to retreat if necessary or permit it to avoid being too provocative. During the Taiwan election, the United States accomplished both goals by refusing to say exactly what it would do if China attacked Taiwan. When a reporter asked Secretary of State Christopher what would occur, he pushed aside the possibility of a Sino-American war as mere "operational details."[36]

Communicating by Word or Deed

Diplomacy utilizes both words and actions to communicate. Each method has its advantages. *Oral and written communications,* either direct or through public diplomacy, are appropriate for negotiations and also can be a good signaling strategy. They can establish positions at a minimum cost and are more apt to maintain flexibility than active signaling.

Signaling by action is often more dramatic than verbal signaling and it has its uses. Some signals can be fairly low level. The Clinton administration signaled its displeasure with China's threat against Taiwan by, among other things, putting a freeze on government financial backing of U.S. business investments in China and canceling a scheduled visit of China's defense minister to Washington. "A large-scale official visit is not appropriate in the current climate," U.S. defense secretary William Perry announced laconically; Beijing understood the message.[37] Various military actions, ranging from alerting forces, through deploying them, to limited demonstrations of force, can also be effective (albeit perilous) signals.

Linking Issues or Treating Them Separately

A persistent dispute is whether a country should deal with other countries on an issue-by-issue basis or link issues together as a basis for a general orientation toward the other country. Advocates of *linking issues* argue that it is inappropriate to have normal relations on some matters with regimes that are hostile and repressive. Those who favor *treating issues separately* claim that doing so allows progress on some issues and keeps channels of communications and influence open.

A major, ongoing linkage issue in U.S. foreign policy is whether most-favored-nation (MFN) trade status for China and other expressions of normal U.S.-China relations should be tied to Beijing's changing certain policies, such as its internal oppression, that Americans do not like. Since becoming president, Bill Clinton has consistently argued that issues regarding China should not be linked. In part he contends that regular interaction will be a "force for change in China, exposing China to our ideas and ideals." He also argued just before his trip to China in 1998 that "our engagement with China serves American interests . . . [by promoting] stability in Asia, preventing the spread of weapons of mass destruction, combating international crime and drug trafficking, [and] protecting the environment."[38] Not mentioned, but a factor, were the many billions of dollars in U.S. exports and investments that go to China.

Maximizing or Minimizing a Dispute

Diplomats face a choice over whether to put a confrontation in a broad or narrow context. The advantage of maximizing a dispute by invoking national survival, world peace, or some other major principle is that it increases credibility. During the Taiwan Strait crisis, China maximized the stakes by having the country's second-ranking official, Premier Li Peng, publicly depict the matter as a "core principle" involving China's "territorial integrity and the cause of reunification."[39]

Yet the advantages of *minimizing a dispute* were also evident in the Taiwan crisis. To avoid unwanted war or a serious diplomatic disruption, China stressed that it was not about to try to forcefully reincorporate Taiwan. Instead, Beijing said its intent was limited to only forestalling "the separatist activities on

Taiwan and the forces working for Taiwan's independence."[40] The United States also took great efforts to minimize the confrontation. Most importantly, Washington took pains to assure China that it would not support a declaration of independence by Taiwan. "We want to make clear, against indications of some in Beijing who are thinking of using force, that we are committed to a one-China policy, but in the context of peaceful unification," a Clinton administration official said.[41] Taiwan contributed to minimizing the stakes by somewhat disingenuously declaring itself "adamant in its pursuit of national reunification and [in] strong opposition to Taiwan independence."[42] Washington was also careful to downplay any U.S. military threat to China. "Our decision to deploy naval forces to the region was one with the intent to defuse tension, not to raise tension," a senior White House official publicly assured China and the world.[43]

A final note is that despite the recitation of diplomatic rules and analysis of the advantages and disadvantages of various diplomatic options in the preceding two sections, there is no substitute for skill and wisdom. Understanding how the game ought to be played does not always produce a win on the playing field of sports or a success at the negotiating table of diplomacy. Certainly you are advantaged if you know the fundamentals, but beyond that, individual capacity and field savvy provide the margin of victory.

Chapter Summary

1. National diplomacy is the process of trying to advance a country's national interest by applying power assets to attempt to persuade other countries to give way.

2. Power is the foundation of diplomacy in a conflictual world. National power is the sum of a country's assets that enhance its ability to get its way even when opposed by others with different interests and goals.

3. Measuring power is especially difficult. The efforts to do so have not been very successful, but they do help us see many of the complexities of analyzing the characteristics of power.

4. These characteristics include the facts that power is dynamic, both objective and subjective, relative, situational, and multifaceted.

5. The major elements of a country's power can be roughly categorized as those that constitute (1) its national core, (2) its national infrastructure, (3) its national economy, and (4) its military. The core and infrastructure are discussed here and form the basis for economic and military power, which are analyzed in later chapters.

6. The national core consists of a country's geography, its people, and its government.

7. The national infrastructure consists of a country's technological sophistication, its transportation system, and its information and communications capabilities.

8. Diplomacy is a communication process that has three main elements. The first is negotiating through direct or indirect discussions between two or more countries. The second is signaling. The third is public diplomacy.

9. The functions of diplomacy include advancing the national interest through such methods as reporting, negotiating, symbolically representing, and intervening.

10. Diplomacy does not occur in a vacuum. Instead it is set in the international system, in a specific diplomatic environment (hostile, adversarial, coalition, and mediation diplomacy), and in a domestic context.

11. Good diplomacy is an art, but it is not totally freestyle, and there are general rules that increase the chances for diplomatic success.

12. There are also a wide variety of approaches or options in diplomacy. Whether contacts should be direct or indirect, what level of contact they should involve, what rewards or coercion should be offered, how precise or vague messages should be, whether to communicate by message or deed, whether issues should be linked or dealt with separately, and the wisdom of maximizing or minimizing a dispute are all questions that require careful consideration.

International Law and Morality: The Alternative Approach

The law hath not been dead, though it hath slept.

Shakespeare, *Hamlet*

Power not ruled by law is a menace.

Arthur J. Goldberg, U.S. Supreme Court justice

The focus of this chapter is on the notion that world politics can be conducted with a greater emphasis on following international law and attempting to ensure justice. This is an alternative approach to national diplomacy and its power-based pursuit of self-interest discussed in the last chapter. It would be naive to think that the actors in any system would not be motivated in significant part by what is good for themselves. Most individuals and groups in domestic political systems emphasize their own welfare, just as states do in the international system. There are differences, however, in how domestic and international systems work. What is of interest here is the way domestic systems, compared to the international system, restrain the pursuit of self-interest.

Legal systems are one thing that helps limit the role of pure power in a domestic system. The Fourteenth Amendment to the U.S. Constitution, for example, establishes "the equal protection of the laws" as a fundamental principle. Certainly, powerful individuals and groups have distinct advantages in

Chapter Outline

every domestic system. Rules are broken and the guilty, especially if they can afford a high-priced attorney, sometimes escape punishment. Still, in the United States, laws cannot overtly discriminate and an attorney is provided to indigent defendants in criminal cases. Thus, the law evens the playing field, at least sometimes.

Morality is a second thing that restrains the role of power in domestic systems. We are discussing what is "right" here, not just what is legal. Whether the word is moral, ethical, fair, or just, there is a greater sense in domestic systems than there is in the international system that appropriate codes of conduct exist, that the ends do not always justify the means, and that those who violate the norms should suffer penalties. Surely, there is no domestic system in which everyone acts morally toward everyone else. Yet the sense of morality and justice that citizens in stable domestic systems have does have an impact on their behavior.

Most importantly, what all this means is that politics does not have to work just one way. There are alternatives. Idealists envision and prescribe a system of international law that covers more and more aspects of international interchange and that contains strong mechanisms to resolve disputes and enforce the law. *Realists* do not believe that this goal is attainable and suspect that national states will follow the dictates of national interest, ignore the law, and act in a self-serving way, especially on national security and other vital matters. Idealists reply that they are not so foolish as to imagine a perfect world, only a better one.

Fundamentals of International Law and Morality

What actors may and may not legitimately do is based in both international and domestic law systems on a combination of expectations, rules, and practices that help govern behavior. We explore the fundamental nature of these legal systems and moral codes by looking first at the primitive nature, growth, and current status of international law; then by turning to issues of morality.

Primitive Nature of International Law

No legal systems, domestic or international, emerge full blown. They grow, advancing from a primitive level to ever more sophisticated levels. As such, all legal systems can be placed on an evolutionary scale ranging from primitive on one end to modern on the other. Note that modern does not mean finished; people in the future may shake their heads in disbelief over how rudimentary current legal systems are. This is speculative, but what is certain is that the concept of a *primitive but evolving legal system* is important to the understanding of international law.

The current international legal system falls toward the primitive end of the evolutionary scale of legal systems. First, as in all primitive law systems, the international system does not have a formal rule-making, or legislative, process. Instead, codes of behavior are derived from custom or from explicit agreements among two or more societal members or groups. Second, there is little or no authority in any formal government to judge or punish violations of law. Primitive societies, domestic or international, have no police or courts. Moreover, a primitive society is often made up of self-defined units (such as kinship groups), is territorially based, primarily governs itself, and resorts to violent "self-help" in relations with other groups.

Viewing international law as a primitive legal system has two benefits. One is that we can see that international law does exist, even if it is not as developed as we might wish. The second benefit is that it encourages us with the thought that international society and its law may evolve to a higher order (D'Amato, 1994).

Growth of International Law

The beginning of international law coincides with the origins of the state. As sovereign, territorial states arose, they needed to define and protect their status and to order their relations. Gradually, along with the state-based political system, elements of ancient Jewish, Greek, and Roman practice combined with newer Christian concepts and also with custom and practice to form most of the rudiments of the prevailing international system of law (Van Dervort, 1997).

A number of important theorists built on this foundation. The most famous of these was the Dutch thinker Hugo Grotius (1583–1645), whose study *De Jure Belli et Pacis* (On the Law of War and Peace) earned him the title "father of international law." Grotius and others discussed and debated the sources of international law, its role in regulating the relations of states, and its application to specific circumstances such as the justification and conduct of war and the treatment of subjugated peoples. From this base, international law expanded and changed slowly over the intervening centuries, as the interactions between the states grew and the expectations of the international community became more sophisticated.

It is the twentieth century, however, that has marked the most rapid expansion by far of concern with international law and its practical importance. Increasing international interaction and interdependence have significantly expanded the need for rules to govern a host of functional areas such as trade, finance, travel, and communications. Similarly, our awareness of our ability to destroy ourselves and our environment and of the suffering of victims of human rights abuses has led to lawmaking treaties on such subjects as genocide, nuclear testing, use of the oceans, and human rights. Even the most political of all activities, war and other aspects of national security, have increasingly become the subject of international law. Aggressive war, for example, is outside the pale of the law. The response of the UN authorizing sanctions, then force against Iraq after it invaded Kuwait reflected, in part, a genuine global rejection of aggression.

These Kosovar volunteers are exhuming the bodies of 97 ethnic Albanians reputedly killed by Serbian guards in August 1999. While it might be relatively easy to uncover evidence of war crimes, it is much more difficult to use international law to arrest and prosecute the alleged criminals.

The Practice of International Law

One of the charges that realists make against faith in international law is that it exists only in theory, not in practice. As evidence, critics cite ongoing, largely unpunished examples of "lawlessness" such as war and human rights abuses. The flaw in this argument is that it does not prove its point. In the first place, international law *is* effective in many areas. Furthermore, the fact that law does not cover *all* problem areas and that it is not *always* followed does not disprove its existence (Higgins, 1994). There is, after all, a substantial crime rate in the United States, but does that mean there is no law?

International law is *most effective* in governing the rapidly expanding range of transnational **functional relations** that have been rapidly increasing. Functional interactions are those that involve "low politics," a term that designates such things as trade, diplomatic rules, and communications.

International law is *least effective* when applied to "high-politics" issues such as national security relations between sovereign states. When vital interests are involved, governments still regularly bend international law to justify their actions rather than alter their actions to conform to the law.

This does not mean, however, that the law never influences political decisions. To the contrary, there is a growing sensitivity to international legal standards, especially insofar as they reflect prevailing international norms. Both international law and world values, for instance, are strongly opposed to states unilaterally resorting to war except in self-defense. Violations such as Iraq's invasion of Kuwait still occur, but they are met with mounting global condemnation and even counterforce. Now even countries as powerful as the United States regularly seek UN authorization to act when, in cases such as Haiti in 1994, they might not long ago have acted on their own initiative (Brilmayer, 1994).

The Fundamentals of International Morality

As with international law, it would be equally erroneous to overestimate the impact of morality on the conduct of states or to dismiss the part that morality plays. As one scholar notes, "Contrary to what the skeptics assert, norms do indeed matter. But norms do not necessarily matter in the ways or often to the extent that their proponents have argued" (Legro, 1997:31).

Concepts of moral behavior may stem from religious beliefs, from secular ideologies or philosophies, from the standard of equity (what is fair), or from the practice of a society. We will see in our discussion of roots of international law that what a society considers moral behavior sometimes becomes law. At other times, legal standards are gradually adopted by a society as moral standards. Insofar as moral behavior remains an imperative of conscience rather than law, we can consider morality in a broad sense. There are distinctions that can be made between moral, ethical, and humanitarian standards and behavior, but for our purposes here, the three terms—morals, ethics, and humanitarianism—are used interchangeably.

It is madness—given recurring war, gnawing human deprivation, persistent human rights violations, and debilitating environmental abuse—to imagine that morality is a predominant global force. Yet moral considerations do play a role in world politics (Frost, 1996). Even more important, as discussed throughout this book, there is a growing body of ethical norms that help determine the nature of the international system. Progress is slow and inconsistent, but it exists. The UN-authorized force did not drop nuclear weapons on Iraq in 1991, even though it arguably could have saved time, money, and the lives of Americans and their allies by doing so. Many countries give foreign aid to less developed countries. National leaders, not just philosophers and clergy, regularly discuss and sometimes even make decisions based on human rights. Consumers have rallied to the environmentalist cause to protect dolphins by purchasing only cans of tuna on which dolphin-safe logos are featured.

As appealing as this call to righteous action may be, applying moral principles to the exigencies of world politics is difficult. One fruitful way to consider morality in world politics is by addressing several challenging questions.

The International Legal System

International law, like any legal system, is based on four critical considerations: the philosophical roots of law, how laws are made, when and why the law is obeyed (adherence), and how legal disputes are decided (adjudication).

The Philosophical Roots of Law

Before considering the mechanics of the legal system, it is important to inquire into the roots of law. Ideas about what is right and what should be the law governing any community do not spring from thin air. Rather, they are derived from sources both external and internal to the society that they regulate.

External Sources Some laws come from sources external to a society. The idea here is that some higher, metaphysical standard of conduct should govern the affairs of humankind. An important ramification of this position is that there is or ought to be one single system of law that governs all people.

Those who believe in the external sources can be subdivided into two schools. One relies on **ideological or theological principle**. This school of thought holds that law is derived from an overarching ideology or theology. For instance, a substantial part of international legal theory extends back to early Western proponents of international law who relied on Christian doctrine for their standards. The writings of Saint Augustine and Saint Thomas Aquinas on the law of war are examples. There are also elements of long-standing Islamic, Buddhist, and other religions' law and scholarship that serve as a foundation for just international conduct.

The **naturalist** school is a second school of external-source thought. This view holds that humans, by nature, have certain rights and obligations. The English philosopher, John Locke, argued in *Two Treatises of Government* (1690) that there is "a law of nature" that "teaches all mankind, who will but consult it, that all [people] being equal and independent [in the state of nature], no one ought to harm another in his life, health, liberty, or possessions." Since countries are collectives of individuals, and the world community is a collective of states and individuals, natural law's rights and obligations also apply to the global stage and form the basis for international law.

Critics of the theory of external sources of law contend that standards based on theology (**divine principle**) lead to religious oppression. The problems with natural law, critics charge, are both that it is vague and that it contains such an emphasis on individualism that it almost precludes any sense of communitarian welfare. If a person's property is protected by natural law, then, for instance, it is hard to justify taking any individual's property through taxes levied by the government without the individual's explicit agreement.

Internal Sources Some legal scholars reject the idea of divine or naturalist roots and, instead, focus on the customs and practices of society. This is the **positivist** school. Positivists believe that law reflects society and the way people want that society to operate. Therefore, law is and ought to be the product of the codification or formalization of a society's standards.

Critics condemn the positivist approach as amoral and sometimes immoral, in that it may legitimize immoral, albeit common, beliefs and behavior of a society as a whole or of its dominant class. These critics would say, for instance, that slavery was once widespread and widely believed proper, but it was never moral or lawful, by the standards of either divine principle or natural law.

How International Law is Made

Countries usually make their domestic law through a constitution (constitutional law) or by a legislative body (statutory law). In practice, law is also established through judicial decisions (interpretation), which set guidelines (precedent) for later decisions by the courts. Less influential sources of law are custom (common law), and what is fair (equity).

Compared to its domestic equivalent, modern international lawmaking differs markedly in that it is much more decentralized. There are, according to the Statute of the International Court of Justice, four sources of law: international treaties, international custom, the general principles of law, and judicial decisions and scholarly legal writing. Some students of international law would tentatively add a fifth source: resolutions and other pronouncements of the UN General Assembly. These five rely primarily on the positivist approach but, like domestic law, include elements of both external and internal sources of law.

International Treaties   Treaties are the primary source of international law. A primary advantage of treaties is that they **codify**, or write down, the law. Agreements between states are binding according to the doctrine of **pacta sunt servanda** (treaties are to be served/carried out). All treaties are lawmaking for their signatories, but it is possible to argue that some treaties are even applicable to nonsignatories. Multilateral treaties, those signed by more than two states, are an increasingly important source of international law. When a large number of states agree to a principle, the norm begins to take on system-wide legitimacy. The 1948 Convention on the Prevention and Punishment of the Crime of Genocide, for example, has been ratified by most states. Some would argue, therefore, that genocide has been "recognized" and "codified" as a violation of international law and that this standard of conduct is binding on all states regardless of whether or not they have formally agreed to the treaty.

International Custom   The second most important source of international law is custom. The old, and now supplanted, rule that territorial waters extend three miles from the shore grew from the distance a cannon could fire. If you were outside the range of land-based artillery, then you were in international

The judges that sit on the International Court of Justice take decisions on a wide range of international legal disputes. Here ICJ president Mohammed Bedjaoui of Algeria makes some opening remarks on hearings about the legality of the use of nuclear weapons. These hearings were requested by the World Health Organization (WHO).

waters. Maritime rules of the road and diplomatic practice are two other important areas of law that grew out of custom. Sometimes, long-standing custom is eventually codified in treaties. An example is the Vienna Convention on Diplomatic Relations of 1961, which codified many existing rules of diplomatic standing and practice.

General Principles of Law   By this standard, the International Court of Justice (ICJ) applies "the general principles of law recognized by civilized nations." Although such language is vague, it has its benefits. It allows "external" sources of law, such as "morality," to be considered. More than any other standard, it was these general principles that Iraq's aggression in 1990 violated. Even if he was being hyperbolic, U.S. secretary of state James Baker's worry that "if might is to make right, then the world will be plunged into a new dark age" catches something of the international reaction.[1] The principle of "equity," what is fair when no legal standard exists, also has some application under general principles.

Judicial Decisions and Scholarly Writing   In many domestic systems, legal interpretations by courts set precedent according to the doctrine of *stare decisis* (let the decision stand). This doctrine is specifically rejected in Article 59 of the Statute of the International Court of Justice (ICJ), but as one scholar points out, "The fact is that all courts . . . rely upon and cite each other [as precedent] abundantly in their decisions" (Levi, 1991:50). Thus, the rulings of the ICJ, other international tribunals, and even domestic courts when they apply international law help shape the body of law that exists. Another possible role of international judicial bodies, and one that is exercised by many domestic courts, is judicial review. This is a court's authority to rule on whether the actions of the executive and legislative branches violate the constitution or other charter under which the court operates. The European Court of Justice has exercised that authority, and some scholars believe that the ICJ is moving cautiously toward a similar stand.

International Representative Assemblies   The preceding four sources of international law are generally recognized. The idea that laws can come from the UN General Assembly or any other international representative assembly is much more controversial. Clearly, to date, international law is nonlegislative. The General Assembly cannot legislate international law the way that a national legislature does. Yet, UN members are bound by treaty to abide by some of the decisions of the General Assembly and the Security Council, which makes these bodies quasi-legislative. Some scholars contend that those resolutions that are approved by overwhelming majorities of the General Assembly's nearly universal membership constitute international law. The reasoning here is that such votes reflect international custom and/or the general principles of law and, therefore, they subtly enter the stream of international law. We may, then, be seeing the beginnings of legislated international law, but, at best, it is in its genesis. Certainly, UN resolutions and mandates are often not followed, but some would argue that this means that the law is being violated rather than that the law does not exist.

INTERACTIVE EXERCISE
Statistics of the European Court of Justice (ECJ)

Adherence to the Law

Adherence to the law is a third essential element of any legal system. What makes the law effective in any legal system is a mixture of compliance and enforcement. As Figure 9.1 represents, people obey the law because of a mixture of voluntary and coerced compliance, and they enforce the law through a mixture of enforcement by central authorities and enforcement through self-help.

Compliance   Obedience in any legal system—whether it is international or domestic, primitive or sophisticated—is based on a mix of voluntary compliance and coercion. *Voluntary compliance* occurs when the subjects obey the law because they accept its legitimacy. This means that people abide by rules

Figure 9.1

Factors in Adherence to the Law

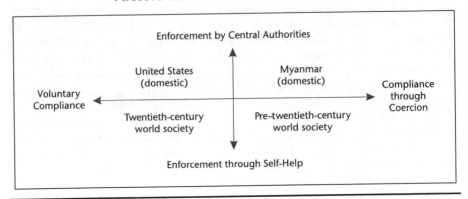

Two crucial factors in international law are how the law is enforced and what encourages compliance. These factors differ over time and for different societies.

because the people accept the authority of the institution that made the rules (say, a legislature or a court) and/or agree that the rules are necessary to the reasonable conduct of society. *Coercion* is the process of gaining compliance through threats of violence, imprisonment, economic sanction, or other punishment.

The overall degree of compliance to the law is lower in the international system than in most domestic systems, but insofar as adherence to international law has grown, it has been based more on voluntary compliance than on coercion. Legitimacy based primarily on pragmatism is the key to international voluntary compliance. Countries recognize the need for a system that is made predictable by adherence to laws.

Enforcement   In all legal systems, enforcement relies on a combination of *enforcement by central authorities* and *enforcement through self-help.* In more sophisticated legal systems, most enforcement relies on a central authority such as the police. Still, even the most sophisticated legal system recognizes the legitimacy of such self-help doctrines as self-defense. Primitive societies rely primarily on self-help and mediation to enforce laws and norms. As a primitive society evolves, it begins to develop enforcement authorities. Domestic systems have done this, and the international system is now just beginning to take this evolutionary path.

In the primitive international legal system, enforcement by central authorities has been slow to develop. Domestic societies rely on central authorities to provide law enforcement organizations (usually the police) and sanctions (fines, prison) to compel compliance with the law. Neither law enforcement organizations nor sanctions are well developed at the international level, but both have begun to evolve. International law continues to rely mainly on self-help to enforce adherence, as reflected in the UN Charter's recognition of national self-defense. There have been, however, instances of enforcement and the number is growing. War criminals were punished after World War II, and indictments have been handed down for war crimes in Bosnia. Economic and diplomatic sanctions are becoming more frequent and are sometimes successful. Armed enforcement by central authorities is even less common and sophisticated. The UN–authorized military actions against Iraq (1991) and Haiti (1994) were more akin to an Old West sheriff authorizing posses to chase the outlaws than true police actions, but they did represent a step toward enforcement of international law by central authorities.

Adjudication of the Law

How a political system resolves disputes between its actors is a key element in its standing along the primitive-to-modern evolutionary scale. As primitive legal systems become more sophisticated, the method of settling disputes evolves from (1) primary reliance on bargaining between adversaries, through (2) mediation/conciliation by neutral parties, to (3) **adjudication** (and the closely related process of arbitration) by neutral parties. The international system of law is in the early stages of this developmental process and is just now developing the institutions and attitudes necessary for adjudication.

International Courts   There are a number of international courts in the world today. The genesis of these tribunals extends back less than a century to the Permanent Court of International Arbitration established by the Hague Conference at the turn of the century. In 1922 the Permanent Court of International Justice (PCIJ) was created as part of the League of Nations, and in 1946 the current **International Court of Justice (ICJ)**, which is associated with the UN, evolved from the PCIJ. The ICJ, or so-called World Court, sits in The Hague, the Netherlands, and consists of 15 judges, who are elected to nine-year terms through a complex voting system in the UN. By tradition, each of the five permanent members of the UN Security Council has one judge on the ICJ, and the others are elected to provide regional representation.

    In addition to the ICJ, there are a few regional courts of varying authority and levels of activity, including the European Court of Justice (ECJ), the European Court of Human Rights, the Inter-American Court of Human Rights, the Central American Court of Justice, and the Community Tribunal of the Economic Community of West African States. None of these has the authority of domestic courts, but like the ICJ, the regional courts are gaining more credibility. In 1997, for example, the ECJ, in a ruling that sets legal precedent for the national courts in all 15 EU countries, upheld a German law that gave women preference for public sector jobs. The court found historic discrimination against women in hiring and promotion stemming "from deep-rooted prejudices and from stereotypes" and reasoned the contested German law was a legitimate way to "restore the balance."[2]

MAP
The International Court of Justice (ICJ)

Jurisdiction   Although the creation of international tribunals during this century indicates progress, the concept of sovereignty remains a potent barrier to adjudication. The authority of the ICJ extends in theory to all international legal disputes. There are two ways that cases come before the ICJ. One is when states submit contentious issues between them. The second is when one of the organs or agencies of the UN asks the ICJ for an advisory opinion.

From 1946 through the present, the court has annually taken up only about two new contentious cases submitted by states or advisory cases involving issues submitted by organs of the United Nations. This is obviously relatively few cases, given the ICJ's broad jurisdiction and the number of issues facing the world and its countries. More than any other factor, the gap between the court's jurisdiction and its actual role is a matter of the willingness of states to submit to decisions of the ICJ. First, states must agree to be subject to the ICJ. Although all UN member countries are technically parties to the ICJ statute, they must also sign the so-called *optional clause* agreeing to be subject to the compulsory jurisdiction of the ICJ. Many countries have not done so. For example, in the mid-1990s the court had to dismiss a case brought by Portugal against Indonesia because Jakarta is not a signatory of the optional clause.

Second, irrespective of their agreement to accept ICJ jurisdiction, countries can reject it or the court's decisions in specific cases. When, in 1984, Nicaragua filed a case with the ICJ charging that U.S. support of the Contra rebels and its mining of Nicaraguan harbors violated international law, the United States argued that the charges were political and, therefore, that the court had no jurisdiction. When the ICJ rejected the U.S. objections and decided to hear the case, the United States terminated its agreement to submit to the compulsory jurisdiction of the ICJ.

Third, even if countries are signatories of the optional clause, they can attach "reservations" to their agreement. While the United States was a party to the optional clause, for example, it reserved the right to reject ICJ jurisdiction in any "domestic matter . . . as determined by the United States." This is an extremely broad disclaimer and, in effect, means that the United States can reject ICJ jurisdiction on virtually any issue.

Fourth, in addition to jurisdiction, it is important to note that the ICJ has little power to enforce its decisions. While domestic courts rely heavily on the willingness of those within its jurisdiction to comply voluntarily, the courts are also usually backed up by powerful executive branches that can enforce decisions when necessary. By contrast, with the UN Secretariat as its executive branch, the ICJ does not have a source of strong support to back up its decisions.

Use and Effectiveness of International Courts   Given the real limits on the jurisdiction of the ICJ and other international courts, it is tempting to write them off as of little more than symbolic value. Such a judgment would be in error (Bodie, 1995; Jennings, 1995). The ICJ, for instance, does play a valuable role. Its rulings help define and advance international law. Furthermore, the

Canada and Spain clashed in 1995 when the Canadians seized the Spanish fishing ship *Estai*, which refused to recognize Canada's claimed authority to regulate fishing in the open seas off its coast. The patrol vessel *Sir Wilfred Templeman* is escorting the captured *Estai* (right) into the Newfoundland port of St. John's in this photograph. The two countries were able to submit their disagreement to the International Court of Justice and to agree that international law, not military might, should determine which country is right.

court can contribute to countries that want to settle a dispute peacefully but that are having difficulty compromising because of domestic pressures. One example occurred when a dispute arose between Spain and Canada after Ottawa limited fishing in an area off Canada's coast. When the Spanish boat *Estai* refused to comply, Canadian patrols seized the boat and arrested its captain. In an earlier era, the Canadian and Spanish navies might have settled the dispute. Fortunately, the ICJ was available as an alternative dispute resolution mechanism, and Spain brought its case before the court, where it was heard in June 1998. Ironically, the ICJ rejected Spain's case in December 1998. In a 12-5 vote, the court decided that it had no jurisdiction to rule in the fishing dispute, thus siding with Canada. Canada had defended the seizing of the ship by citing domestic law that allows it to protect fish stocks. Canadian officials had argued that the ICJ lacked the power to overrule domestic fishing law, having filed a so-called reservation to this effect with the court in 1994. The Canadian document excluded laws on fish stocks from the court's reach. Thus in a sense, by making an authoritative ruling and establishing legal precedent in the process, the ICJ also maintained the primacy of Canadian domestic law in this issue area.

Even when countries reject ICJ jurisdiction, the court's decisions may have some effect. In the Nicaragua versus United States case, discussed earlier, the court heard the case anyway and ruled in Nicaragua's favor. This decision gave a black eye to the United States in the court of world opinion and strengthened the U.S. domestic opponents of the Reagan administration's policy. The United States stopped mining Nicaragua's harbors.

The ICJ's advisory opinions also help resolve issues between IGOs and may even help establish general international law. In separate actions, the UN General Assembly and the World Health Organization separately asked the ICJ to rule on the legality of using nuclear weapons (Matheson, 1997). The court ruled in 1996 that "the threat or use of nuclear weapons would generally be contrary to the rules of international law applicable in armed conflict," but went on to say that it was unable to "conclude definitively whether the threat or use of nuclear weapons would be lawful or unlawful in an extreme circumstance of self-defense, in which the very survival of a state would be at stake."[3] While the ICJ's ruling was not as all-encompassing as some antinuclear advocates hoped, the decision does put any leader considering the use of nuclear weapons except in extremis on notice that he or she could wind up the defendant in some future war crimes trial.

Finally, there is evidence that the willingness of countries to utilize the ICJ, the ECJ, and other international courts and to accept their decisions is slowly growing. The Web site map (see page 239) and cases discussed in the interactive exercise Surf the World Court show that countries around the world serve on the court and are party to its cases. Now more than 50 countries, including Canada and the United Kingdom, adhere to the optional clause giving the ICJ compulsory jurisdiction over their international legal disputes. It is true that the international judicial system is still primitive, but each of the more than 150 opinions issued by the PCIJ and the ICJ in this century is one more than the zero instances of international adjudication in the last century.

**INTERACTIVE
EXERCISE**
Surf the
World Court

Applying International Law and Morality

Law and morality are easy to support in the abstract, but it is much more difficult to agree on how to apply them. To examine this, we will look at issues of cultural perspective, issues of applying international law and standards of morality equally to states and individuals, and issues of prudence.

Law and Morality: Issues of Cultural Perspective

As primitive political systems evolve and expand to incorporate diverse peoples, one problem that such legal systems encounter is the "fit" between differing culturally based concepts of law and morality. The evolving international system of law faces the same difficulty. Most of the international law and many of the international standards of morality that currently exist and influence world politics are based on the concepts and practices of the West. This is a result of U.S. and European dominance, though, and does not mean that Western concepts are superior to those held in other parts of the world. Now, in a changing international system, Africans, Asians, Latin Americans, and other non-Westerners are questioning and sometimes rejecting law based on Western culture.

Western and Non-Western Perspectives

There are numerous points on which Western and non-Western precepts of law and morality differ. The *Western view* of law is based on principles designed to protect the long-dominant power of this bloc of states. Order is a primary point, as is sovereignty. Closely related is the theory of property, which holds that individuals (and states) have a "right" to accumulate and maintain property (wealth). This is a major philosophical underpinning of capitalism. Western law also relies heavily on the process and substance of law rather than on equity. Thus, there is an emphasis on courts and what the law is rather than on what is fair.

The *non-Western view* of international law is influenced by the different cultural heritage of non-Western states, by the recent independence of those states, and by the history of exploitation their people have often suffered at the hands of the West. The newer, mostly non-Western, and mostly less developed countries (LDCs) claim that since they had little or no role in determining the rules that govern the international system, they are not bound by preexisting agreements, principles, or practices that work to their disadvantage. These countries support sovereignty and reject aspects of international law that they claim are imperialistic abridgments of their sovereignty. They insist on noninterference. They support, for example, the "Calvo clause," by which Western-based multinational corporations (MNCs) agree that their home governments have no right to interfere in host countries to protect the MNCs' property. The LDCs also reject weighted decision-making schemes, such as those in the Security Council and the International Monetary Fund, that favor the rich and powerful. The LDCs often emphasize equity over the substance and process of law. For them, the important standard is fairness, especially in terms of economic maldistribution.

Moreover, Western and non-Western law and morality differ considerably on the *rights of the individual* versus *the rights of the community*. Imagine a scale that ranges, on one end, from a value system in which the rights of an individual are always more important than those of the community to, at the other end, a value system where the good of the community always take precedent over the good of the individual. Western states would generally fall toward the individualistic end of the scale; non-Western states would generally fall farther toward the communitarian end of the scale.

We have already noted, for example, that Western individualism strongly supports the idea of individual property rights, even in the face of widespread societal poverty; that is a core principle of capitalism. Preserving order, especially where criminal acts are alleged, is another major point where individualism and communitarianism diverge. There is a long list of rights that are afforded in the United States to individuals accused and even convicted of crimes. Non-Western cultures tend to think this practice gives the society too little protection; they therefore favor a more communitarian approach to ordering their society. That perspective was expressed succinctly by Singapore's foreign minister, Shanmugam Jayakumar, who defended what Americans might see as draconian laws by explaining, "We believe that the legal system must give maximum protection to the majority of our people. We make no apology for clearly tilting our laws and policy in favor of the majority."[4]

Is a Universal Standard of Law and Morality Possible and Desirable?

Given the differences in perspective that we have just noted, two questions arise. The first is whether universal law and morality is possible. In the realm of human rights, for example, the debate focuses substantially on the conflicting views of *positivists* and *universalists*. Positivists, as explained in the earlier section on the sources of law, hold that there are many systems of law and morality based on divergent cultural customs. Therefore, no single stan-dard does (or, they suspect, can) exist, at least not without global cultural homogenization. Universalists rely on the tenets of ideology, theology, natural law, or some other overarching philosophy to argue that universal law and standards of morality are possible. Representing this view, President Clinton told his hosts while he was in China in 1998 that he was "convinced that certain rights are universal. I believe that everywhere, people have a right to be treated with dignity, to give voice to their opinions, to choose their own leaders, to associate with who they wish, to worship how, when, and where they want."[5]

Law and Morality: Issues of Application to States and Individuals

Within the international system, both international law and the debate over moral behavior have focused primarily on states. Individual actions have more recently become the subject of international law and of the discourse over moral behavior. The first thing to address is whether states and individuals can be held to the same standards of law and morality. Then we can look at the specific issues of law and morality as they relate to states and to individuals.

Do Standards of Law and Morality Apply Equally to States and Individuals?

It is common for states to act legitimately in ways that would be reprehensible for individuals. If you are in your country's air force and shoot down five enemy pilots, you are an "ace"; if you, as an individual, shoot five people, you are a mass murderer. Of course, we recognize differences between justifiable and inexcusable actions, but where do you draw the line? Some have argued that the state cannot be held to individual moral standards. Realist philosopher and statesman Niccolò Machiavelli wrote in *The Prince* (1517) that a ruler "cannot observe all those things which are considered good in men, being often obliged, in order to maintain the state, to act against faith and charity, against humanity, and against religion."

Proponents of state morality disagree and argue that neither national interest nor sovereignty legitimizes immoral actions. A philosopher and statesman who took this view was Thomas Jefferson. While secretary of state, Jefferson once argued that since a society is but a collection of individuals, "the moral duties which exist between individual and individual" also form "the duties of that society toward any other; so that between society and society the same moral duties exist as between the individuals composing them" (Graebner, 1964:55).

States and the Standards of Law and Morality

Traditionally, international law has concerned itself with the actions and status of states. Some of the most prominent issues are sovereignty, war, the biosphere, and human rights.

Issues of Sovereignty   Sovereignty continues to be a cornerstone of the state system, but sovereignty is no longer a legal absolute. Instead, it is being chipped away by a growing number of law-creating treaties that limit action. Sovereignty is also being slowly restricted by the international communities' growing intolerance of human rights abuses and other ills inflicted by governments on their people. One example was the successful demand by the UN, supported by most of the world's countries, that South Africa end apartheid and give political power to its nonwhite citizens. The idea of a right to democracy that supersedes sovereignty was enforced when the UN authorized the international military overthrow of the military junta in Haiti.

Issues of War   Most of the early writing in international law was concerned with the law of war, and this issue continues to be a primary focus of legal development. In addition to issues of traditional state-versus-state warfare, international law now attempts also to regulate revolutionary and internal warfare and terrorism (Howard, Andreopoulos, & Shulman, 1994; Arend & Beck, 1994).

To illustrate these diverse concerns, we can focus on the long debate on when and how war can morally and legally be fought. "Just war" theory has two parts: the cause of war and the conduct of war. Western tradition has believed in *jus ad bellum* (just cause of war) in cases where the war is (1) a last resort, (2) declared by legitimate authority, (3) waged in self-defense or to establish/restore justice, and (4) fought to bring about peace. The same line of thought maintains that *jus in bello* (just conduct of war) includes the standards of proportionality and discrimination. Proportionality means that the amount of force used must be proportionate to the threat. Discrimination means that force must not make noncombatants intentional targets.

As laudable as limitations on legitimate warfare may seem, they present problems. One difficulty is that the standards of when to go to war and how to fight it are rooted in Western-Christian tradition. The parameters of jus in bello and jus ad bellum extend back to Aristotle's *Politics* (ca. 340 B.C.) and are especially associated with the writings of Christian theological philosophers Saint Augustine (Aurelius Augustinus, A.D. 354–430) and Saint Thomas Aquinas

(1226–1274). As a doctrine based on Western culture and religion, not all the restrictions on war are the same as those derived from some of the other great cultural-religious traditions, including Buddhism and Islam.

Another difficulty with the standards of just war, even if you try to abide by them, is that they are vague. What, for example, is proportionally in line with jus in bello? Almost everyone would agree, for instance, that Great Britain would not have been justified in using nuclear weapons against Argentina during the 1982 Falkland Islands War. But what if Iraq had used chemical weapons against coalition forces in the 1991 war? Would the British, French, and Americans have been justified if they had retaliated with nuclear weapons? Some people even argue that using nuclear weapons under any conditions would violate the rule of discrimination and thus be immoral.

The jus in bello standard of discrimination also involves matters of degree rather than clear lines. During World War II, for example, American and British planes leveled dozens of German cities, killed some 600,000 civilians, wounded 1 million, and left perhaps 20 million homeless; 55,000 allied airmen also died carrying out the assaults. In a single raid during February 1945, with the war nearly over, Allied warplanes dropped 2,960 tons of explosives on Dresden. The resulting firestorm lasted seven days and reached temperatures of 1,000 degrees Fahrenheit, killing at least 30,000 civilians by blast, incineration, and suffocation. That is about as many people killed in one raid as were killed by Luftwaffe bombs in London during the entire war. Royal Air Force (RAF) general Sir Arthur "Bomber" Harris, who commanded the British bomber forces during World War II, characterized his task as bringing "the horror of fire" to German cities and "to bring the masonry crashing down on top of the Boche, to kill Boche, and to terrify Boche."[6] That he did, and as for the ethics of bombing cities, he explained that "I would not regard the whole of the remaining cities of Germany as worth the bones of one British grenadier."[7] How do you evaluate the air raid strategy of Great Britain and the United States? Was it jus in bello?

Issues of the Biosphere   Another important and growing area of international law addresses the obligation of states and individuals to use the biosphere responsibly on the theory that it belongs to no one individually and to everyone collectively. This area of law is aptly illustrated by the law of the sea.

The status of the world's oceans is a long-standing subject of international law. The international maritime rules of the road for ships have long had general acceptance. The extension of a state's territorial limits to 3 miles into the ocean was another widely acknowledged standard based, as noted, on international custom.

In recent years, the resource value of the seas has grown because of more sophisticated harvesting and extraction technology, and this has created uncertainty and change. Undersea oil exploration, in particular, is the source of serious dispute among a number of countries. As early as 1945, the United States claimed control of the resources on or under its continental shelf. In 1960 the Soviet Union proclaimed the extension of its territorial waters out to 12 miles, a policy that has been imitated by others, including the United States as of 1988. Several Latin American countries claimed a 200-mile territorial zone, and the United States not only established a 200-mile "conservation zone" in 1977 to control fishing but in 1983 extended that control to all economic resources within the 200-mile limit.

In an ambitious attempt to settle and regulate many of these issues, the Law of the Sea Convention defines coastal zones, establishes an International Seabed Authority to regulate nonterritorial seabed mining, and provides for the sharing of revenue from such efforts. After it was opened for signature and ratification in 1982, it took a decade for the treaty to receive the ratification by 60 countries that was required for it to take effect. Many states, especially the economically developed countries (EDCs), which possess most of the financial and technical capability to exploit the seas, feared that their interests would be harmed by the convention's provisions regarding control of territorial waters or coastal resources. These countries were also concerned that the voting formula in the governing body might allow the LDCs to dominate decisions to the detriment of the coastal and/or industrialized powers that are able to exploit seabed mining and ocean fishing areas. Much of this opposition has ended. Under President Bill Clinton, the United States changed its earlier opposition and agreed to the Law of the Sea Treaty. That agreement came with important national protections, and it has often been and remains the case that the struggle over control of the seas is one of sovereign self-interest versus international common interest.

Issues of Human Rights   International law is developing affirmatively in the area of defining human rights. International attention to the law of human rights has grown because of many factors, including the horror of the images of abuses that television reveals, the expanding efforts of individuals and organizations that promote human rights, and the growing awareness that human rights violations are a major source of international instability.

The UN Charter supports basic rights in a number of its provisions. This language was expanded in 1948 when the UN General Assembly passed the Universal Declaration of Human Rights. No country voted against the declaration, although a few did abstain. Since then, the growth of global human rights has also been enhanced by a number of important global multilateral treaties. The most important of these treaties are listed in Table 9.1. In addition to global treaties, there have been a number of regional multilateral treaties such as the Helsinki Accords (1977) that address European human rights and the African Charter on Human and Peoples' Rights (1990).

Much, however, remains to be done. Canada and several other countries have signed all the human rights treaties found in Table 9.1, but many countries have not. There are also many countries, including the United States, whose legislatures have not ratified some of the treaties because of fears that they might be used as platforms for interfering in domestic affairs or for pressing demands for certain international policy changes, such as a redistribution of world economic resources.

Table 9.1

Eight Important Multilateral Human Rights Treaties

Multilateral Treaty	Year	Signatories (1997)
Convention on the Prevention and the Punishment of the Crime of Genocide	1949	120
Convention Relating to the Status of Refugees	1951	125
International Convention on the Elimination of All Forms of Racial Discrimination	1965	148
International Covenant on Civil and Political Rights	1976	136
International Covenant on Economic, Social, and Cultural Rights	1976	135
Convention on the Elimination of All Forms of Discrimination against Women	1979	153
Convention against Torture and Other Cruel, Inhuman, or Degrading Treatment or Punishment	1984	102
Convention on the Rights of the Child	1989	190

Data source: UNDP (1997).

Most countries have signed a variety of multilateral treaties, thereby agreeing to abide by the treaties' various human rights standards. Even though not all countries have signed, and there have also been numerous violations, many analysts argue that such treaties take on the characteristic of international law once they have been signed by the preponderance of the world's states. As such, the standards set in these treaties may be used in a number of ways, including through international courts and tribunals, to judge cases of states and individuals.

The gap between existing legal standards and their application is the area of greatest concern. Gross violations of the principles set down in the multilateral treaties continue to occur. And the record of international reaction to violation of the standards and enforcement of them through sanctions and other means is very sporadic and often weak. "We have not traveled as far or as fast as we had hoped," UN deputy secretary-general Margaret J. Anstee has commented on the convention to protect women (Cook, 1994).[8] To varying degrees, this could be said about all human rights treaties. Yet their existence provides a constant reminder that most of the world considers certain actions to be reprehensible. The treaties also serve, in the view of many, as a standard of international law and conduct for which states and individuals can be held accountable. Thus, the growth of human rights law has just begun. The acceptance of the concept of human rights has gained a good deal more rhetorical support than practical application, and enforcement continues to be largely in the hands of individual states with a mixed record of adherence. For all these shortcomings, though, human rights obligations are now widely discussed, and world opinion is increasingly critical of violations.

Individuals and the Standards of Law and Morality

International law has long addressed the treatment of individuals, but it is only recently that international law has begun to deal with the actions of individuals. A series of precedents in this century have marked this change. In the Nuremberg and Tokyo war crimes trials after World War II, German and Japanese military and civilian leaders were tried, convicted, imprisoned, and in some cases executed for waging aggressive war, for war crimes, and for crimes against humanity. The trial (and execution) of Japanese general Tomoyuki Yamashita established the "Yamashita precedent" that commanders were responsible for the actions of their troops. There were no subsequent war crimes tribunals through the 1980s. Now, separate international judicial tribunals have been established to deal with the Holocaust-like events in Bosnia and the genocidal massacres in Rwanda. As the Web site box Global Crime and Punishment indicates, however, progress on prosecution of war criminals has been slow, and the prospects for bringing those most responsible for the atrocities to international justice are problematic at best.

A FURTHER NOTE
Global Crime and
Punishment

Another set of issues regarding the application of international law to individuals involves cases where single countries apprehend and try suspects. Where those individuals are being tried for crimes in the country that has accused them, the cases fall squarely under international law. But a growing phenomenon is for countries to capture and try accused international criminals for crimes that did not occur within the country taking action.

The application of international law to individuals for heinous crimes brings some satisfaction. It is easy to argue that international borders should not be barriers to justice. And, indeed, limits on the right of a country to use its sovereignty to refuse to extradite an individual accused of international crimes were recently affirmed by the World Court. Libya brought a suit in the ICJ claiming that the UN sanctions imposed on it for refusing to surrender the men accused of international terrorism were a violation of Libya's sovereignty. The ICJ rejected Libya's assertion, and the government in Tripoli began negotiations to extradite the two suspects. Several countries have arrested and turned over to international tribunals individuals accused of war crimes in the Balkans and in Rwanda.

The taking of people from one country by another country without going through proper extradition procedures sets a risky example that could haunt those who feel justified in practicing it when their sensibilities are outraged. For example, during the Vietnam War the United States dropped tons of a herbicide,

War criminal or freedom fighter? Kurdish rebel leader Abdullah Ocalan asserts that Turkey has violated his rights and that he is merely fighting for the right of self-rule for the Kurds. The Turkish government, however, views him as a criminal and has imprisoned him on the island of Imrali, near Istanbul.

Agent Orange, which has been traced to a high rate of disease in those exposed to it and to birth malformations of their children. It is a tragic irony that one of the senior U.S. military officers in the war effort, Admiral Elmo Zumwalt, attributes the birth defects of his grandchild and the later death of his son to the fact that the younger Zumwalt was exposed to the carcinogen while serving in Vietnam. One has to wonder how Americans would respond if Admiral Zumwalt, former secretary of defense Robert McNamara, and other ranking officials from that time were spirited to Hanoi to stand trial as accused war criminals.

One way to avoid the problems of trying foreign nationals for violations of the law in the country that is bringing the accusation and, perhaps, some of the difficulties of legally extraditing or illegally apprehending people would be to establish a permanent International Criminal Court (ICC). That is exactly what the world community is trying to do in the proposed ICC.

Law and Morality: Issues of Prudent Judgment and Application

In a perfect world, everyone would act morally, obey the law, and insist that others conduct themselves in the same way. Moreover, what is legal and what is not, and what is moral and what is not, would be clear. Finally, our choices would be between good and evil. In our imperfect world, standards and choices are often much murkier, which leads to several questions regarding the prudence of applying our standards of law and morality.

INTERACTIVE EXERCISE
You Be the Judge

Can Ends Justify Means? One conundrum is whether an act that, by itself, is evil can be justified if it is done for a good cause. There are those who believe that ends never justify means. The great eighteenth-century philosopher Immanuel Kant took a position of moral absolutism in his *Groundwork on the Metaphysics of Morals* (1785) and argued that ends never justify means. He therefore urged us to "do what is right though the world should perish."

In practice, the primitive international political system can make applying strong moral principles strictly, adhering to international law, and other such altruistic acts unwise and even dangerous. Clearly, most of us do not adhere to such an absolute position. Most of us explicitly or implicitly accept capital punishment, or the atomic bombings of Hiroshima and Nagasaki, as somehow justified as retaliation or even as an unfortunate necessity to a better end (Beres, 1995). The problem, again, is where to draw the line. How about assassination? Think about the atrocities waged by Adolf Hitler and his Nazi machine. What if you had a time machine? Given what you know of World War II and of the genocide of 6 million Jews, would you be justified in traveling back to 1932 and assassinating Hitler?

Should We Judge Others by Our Own Standards? The issue about whether to judge others morally rests on two controversies. The first, which we have already addressed, is whether there is a universal morality. Those who deny that there is contend that a country that attempts to require others to live up to its version of what is right is guilty of **cultural imperialism**. Chinese scholar Li Zhongcheng (1994:1) has, for instance, criticized the UN's Universal Declaration of Human Rights (1948) as a document that has only "affirmed the traditional dominant status of the basic Western liberalist concepts" and given "priority to [individual] civil and political rights" while ignoring collective "social and economic rights." Many human rights advocates reject such claims as poor attempts to justify the unjustifiable. President Chandrika Kumaratunga of Sri Lanka, for one, has expressed the opinion that "of course, every country has its own national ethos, but . . . when people talk about a conflict of values, I think it is an excuse that can be used to cover a multitude of sins" (Franck, 1997:627).

The second objection to applying morality is that for one country to insist on its form of moral behavior violates other states' sovereignty. Many Americans have few qualms about criticizing the human rights record of other countries, but they can become outraged when others find American standards lacking. Capital punishment is legal and on the rise in most U.S. states, but many other countries find the practice abhorrent. Therefore they refuse to extradite accused criminals to the United States if there is a possibility of capital punishment. The opposition to capital punishment is intensified by the belief that there are demographic injustices in who gets executed. The UN Commission on Human Rights (UNCHR) passed a resolution in 1998 calling for a moratorium on executions because, in part, of a UNCHR report that found that in the United States "race, ethnic origin and economic status appear to be key determinants of who will and will not receive a sentence of death."[9]

What If Moral and Legal Standards Clash?   Another dilemma occurs when two choices, both of which we can define as desirable, clash. Or, what does one do when the choice you face is not between good and bad, but, from your point of view, between bad and worse?

Consider Algeria. In 1990, after more than two decades of one-party rule, Algeria held free elections and the opposition party gained control of the national legislature. Democracy clearly was working. Good! Well, perhaps. The coalition of groups that won formed the Front for Islamic Salvation (FIS), an Islamic fundamentalist movement. It campaigned on the platform of instituting the *shari'ah,* the law of the Koran. Among other things, such a change would have severely restricted the freedom of women. One Algerian woman objected that the fundamentalists are "not democrats interested in dialogue," but "little fascists" and a bunch of "bearded, sexually frustrated men" who wanted to take away the freedom that Algerian women had gained under the more secular, but less democratic, government that had preceded the fundamentalists.[10] What happened was that the military staged a coup, and the brief experiment with democracy ended. Some women's rights were preserved, but democracy was short-circuited (Bova, 1997). What should policy be in such circumstances?

Is It Prudent to Apply Moral and Legal Standards?   Another objection to trying to apply moral principles is based on self-interest. Recall that realists maintain that national interest sometimes precludes the application of otherwise laudable moral principles, and that the primary function of the state is to promote the national interest, not to further abstract standards of morality. To do the latter, it is possible to argue, casts a person as a perpetual Don Quixote, a pseudo knight-errant whose world is not real, whose quest is unfulfillable, and whose wish "to dream the impossible dream," while appealing romantically, may even be dangerous. The dangers are that you waste your reputation, your wealth, and your human resources trying to do the impossible, and that because not all states act morally, those who do are at a disadvantage: "Nice guys finish last."

Those who disagree with this line of reasoning contend that it fails the test of courageously standing up for what is right. They might even recall the remonstration of President John Kennedy, who, evoking Dante Alighieri's *The Divine Comedy* (1321), commented, "Dante once said that the hottest places in hell are reserved for those who in a period of moral crisis maintain their neutrality."[11]

More pragmatically, advocates of applying principles of law and morality contend that greater justice is necessary for world survival. This argument deals, for example, with resource distribution. It contends that it is immoral to maintain a large part of the world both impoverished and without self-development possibilities. The inevitable result, according to this view, will be a world crisis that will destroy order as countries fight for every declining resource.

One way out of the dilemma about when and how great a degree of law, morality, and other principles to apply to foreign policy may be to begin with the observation that you do not have to choose between being unswervingly principled and attempting to maintain one standard or the other—morality or amorality. There is a middle ground that relies on prudence as a guiding principle. There is a well-known prayer that asks for the courage to change what wrongs one can, the patience to accept the wrongs that one cannot change, and the wisdom to know the difference. From this perspective, a decision maker must ask, first, whether any tangible good is likely to result and, second, whether the good will outweigh negative collateral consequences. By the first standard, taking high-flown principled stands when it is impossible or unlikely that you will affect the situation is quixotic. By the second standard, applying morality when the overall consequences will be vastly more negative also fails the test of prudence.

The Future of International Law and Morality

The often anarchic and inequitable world makes it easy to dismiss talk of conducting international relations according to standards of international law and morality as idealistic prattling. This view, however, was probably never valid and certainly is not true now. An irreversible trend in world affairs is the rapid acceleration of states and people interacting in almost all areas of endeavor. As these interactions have grown, so has the need for regularized behavior and for rules to prescribe that behavior. For very pragmatic reasons then, many people have come to believe, as one international lawyer notes, that "most issues of transnational concern are best addressed through legal frameworks that render the behavior of global actors more predictable and induce compliance from potential or actual violators" (Ratner, 1998:78). The growth of these rules in functional international interactions has been on the leading edge of the development of international law. Advances in political and military areas have been slower, but here too there has been progress. Thus, as with the United Nations, the pessimist may decry the glass as only half full, whereas, in reality, it is encouraging that there is more and more water in the previously almost empty glass.

All the signs point to increasing respect for international law and a greater emphasis on adhering to at least rudimentary standards of morality. Violations of international standards are now more likely to draw criticism from the world community. It is probable, therefore, that international law will continue to develop and to expand its areas of application. So too will the moral discourse increase in its impact on the actions of the international actors. There will certainly be areas where growth is painfully slow, and there will also be those who violate the principles of law and morality and who sometimes get away with their unlawful and immoral acts. But, just as surely, there will be progress.

Chapter Summary

1. International law can be best understood as a primitive system of law in comparison with much more developed domestic law. There are only the most rudimentary procedures and institutions for making, adjudicating, and enforcing international law. This does not mean, however, that international law is impotent, only that it is in an earlier stage of development than domestic law.

2. As a developing phenomenon, international law is dynamic and has been growing since the earliest periods of civilization. This growth has accelerated in the twentieth century because the increasing level of international interaction and interdependence requires many new rules to govern and regularize contacts in trade, finance, travel, communication, and other areas. The possible consequences of war have also spurred the development of international law.

3. Thus far, international law is most effective when it governs functional international relations. International law works least well in areas that touch on the vital interests of the sovereign states. Even in those areas, though, international law is gradually becoming more effective.

4. Morality is another factor in establishing the rules of the international system. It acts as a guide to action and as the basis for some international law.

5. The international legal system has four essential elements: its philosophical roots, lawmaking, adherence, and adjudication.

6. The roots of law for any legal system may come from external sources, such as natural law, or from within the society, such as custom.

7. Regarding lawmaking, international law can be argued to spring from a number of sources, including divine principle, the nature of humankind, societal custom and practices, and lawmaking documents passed or agreed to by states. As in most primitive legal systems, international lawmaking is still heavily nonlegislative and decentralized, but it is slowly taking on those more advanced characteristics.

8. Regarding adherence, international law, again like primitive law, relies mainly on voluntary compliance and self-help. Here again, though, there are early and still-uncertain examples of enforcement by third parties, a feature that characterizes more advanced systems.

9. The fourth essential element of a legal system, adjudication, is also in the primitive stage in international law. But the application of international law by domestic courts and, even more important, the existence of the International Court of Justice and other such international judicial bodies represent an increasing sophistication of international law in this area as well.

10. In a still culturally diverse world, standards of international law and morality have encountered problems of fit with different cultures. Most current international law and many concepts of morality, such as the stress on individualism, are based on Western ideas and practices, and many states from the South object to certain aspects of international law as it exists.

11. The changes in the world system in this century have created a number of important issues related to international law. Among these are the status of sovereignty, the legality of war and the conduct of war, rules for governing the biosphere, and observing and protecting human rights.

12. International law has been interpreted as applying to states. Now it is also concerned with individuals. Primarily, it applies to the treatment of individuals by states, but it also has some application to the actions of individuals. Thus people, as well as countries, are coming to have obligations, as well as rights, under international law.

13. It is not always possible to insist on strict adherence to international law and to high moral standards, yet they cannot be ignored. One middle way is to apply principles prudently.

Chapter **10**

Managing National and International Security

He's mad that trusts in the tameness of a wolf.

Shakespeare, *King Lear*

An eye for an eye only winds up making the whole world blind.

Mohandas K. (Mahatma) Gandhi

Security is the enduring yet elusive quest. "I would give all my fame for a pot of ale, and safety," a frightened boy cries out before a battle in Shakespeare's *King Henry V.* The battle was joined in Shakespeare's play and peace perished. Today most of us similarly seek security. Yet we are tempered by the reality that while humans have sought safety throughout history, they have usually failed to achieve that goal for long.

Thinking about Security

Perhaps one reason that security from armed attack has been elusive is that we humans have sought it in the wrong way. The traditional path has emphasized national self-defense by amassing arms to deter aggression. Alternative

Chapter Outline

paths have been given little attention and fewer resources. From 1948 through 1997, for example, the world states have spent 1,700 times as much on their national military budgets (about $34 trillion) as on UN peacekeeping operations (about $22 billion). It just may be, then, that the first secretary-general of the United Nations, Trygve Lie, was onto something when he suggested that "wars occur because people prepare for conflict, rather than for peace."[1]

The aim of this chapter is to think anew about security from armed aggression in light of humankind's failed effort to find it. Because the traditional path has not brought us to a consistently secure place, it is only prudent to consider alternative, less-traveled-by, paths to security. These possible approaches include limiting or even abandoning our weapons altogether, creating international security forces, and even adopting the standards of pacifism.

Before proceeding with our examination of security, it bears mentioning that our focus in this chapter is exclusively on security from armed attack. In a broader sense, one study argues correctly, "security involves more than protection against military attack." Therefore, "human security cannot be measured by [just] preparation for war." It must also include protection from poverty, disease, environmental degradation, interpersonal violence, and oppression. "When human rights and the environment are protected," the study concludes, "people's lives and identities are likely to be secure; where they are not protected, people are not secure, regardless of the military capacity of that state under which they live" (Klare & Thomas, 1994:4). These other aspects of security will be addressed in chapters 11 through 14.

A Tale of Insecurity

One way to think about how to increase security is to ponder the origins of insecurity. To do that, let us go back in time to the hypothetical origins of insecurity. Our vehicle is a parable. Insecurity may not have started exactly like this, but it might have.

A Drama and Dialogue of Insecurity

It was a sunny, yet somehow foreboding, autumn day many millennia ago. Og, a caveman of the South Tribe, was searching for food. It had been a poor season for hunting and gathering, and Og fretted about the coming winter and his family. The urge to provide security from hunger for his family carried Og northward out of the South Tribe's usual territory and into the next valley.

It was the valley of Ug of the North Tribe. The same motivations that drove Og also urged Ug on, but he had been luckier. He had just killed a large antelope. Ug, then, was feeling prosperous as he used his large knife to clean his kill. At that moment, Og, hunting spear in hand, happened out of the forest and came upon Ug. Both hunters were startled, and they exchanged cautious greetings. Ug was troubled by the lean and hungry look of the spear-carrying stranger. Unconsciously, Ug grasped his knife more tightly. The tensing of his ample muscles alarmed Og, who instinctively dropped his spear point to a defensive position. Fear was the common denominator. Neither wanted a confrontation, but they were trapped. Their disengagement negotiation went something like this (translated):

Ug: You are eyeing my antelope and pointing your spear at me.

Og: And your knife glints menacingly in the sunlight. But this is crazy. I mean you no harm; your antelope is yours. Still, my family is needy and it would be good if you shared your kill.

Ug: Of course I am sympathetic, and I want to be friends. But this is an antelope from the North Tribe's valley. If there is any meat left over, I'll even give you a little. But first, why don't you put down your spear so we can talk more easily?

Og: A fine idea, Ug, and I'll be glad to put down my spear, but why don't you lay down that fearful knife first? Then we can be friends.

Ug: Spears can fly through the air farther. . . . *You should be first.*

Og: Knives can strike more accurately. . . . *You should be first.*

And so the confrontation continued, with Og and Ug equally unsure of the other's intentions, with each sincerely proclaiming his peaceful purpose, but with each unable to convince the other to lay his weapon aside first.

Critiquing the Drama

Think about the web of insecurity that entangled Og and Ug. Each was insecure about providing for himself and his family in the harsh winter that was approaching. Security extends further than just being safe from armed attacks. Ug was a "have" and Og was a "have-not." Ug had a legitimate claim to his antelope; Og had a legitimate need to find sustenance. Territoriality and tribal differences added to the building tension. Ug was in "his" valley; Og could not understand why unequal resource distribution meant that some should prosper while others were deprived. The gutting knife and the spear also played a role. But did the weapons cause tension or, perhaps, did Ug's knife protect him from a raid by Og?

We should also ask what could have provided the security to get Og and Ug out of their confrontation. If Og's valley had been full of game, he would not have been driven to the next valley. Or if the region's food had been shared by all, Og would not have needed Ug's antelope. Knowing this, Ug might have been less defensive. Assuming, for a moment, that Og was dangerous—as hunger sometimes drives people to be—then Ug might have been more secure if somehow he could have signaled the equivalent of today's 911 distress call and summoned the region's peacekeeping force, dispatched by the area's intertribal council. The council might even have been able to aid

Og with some food and skins to ease his distress and to quell the anger he felt when he compared his ill fortune with the prosperity of Ug.

The analysis of our parable could go on and be made more complex. Og and Ug might have spoken different languages, worshipped different deities, or had differently colored faces. That, however, would not change the fundamental questions regarding security. Why were Og and Ug insecure? More important, once insecurity existed, what could have been done to restore harmony?

Conflict and Insecurity

The dilemmas faced by Ug and Og continue to perplex world leaders today. As we will see in the first portion of this chapter, insecurity, conflict, and war continue to permeate the international landscape. But there are a number of ways to move beyond persistent insecurity as the latter portion of this chapter will examine. In that portion of the chapter we will discuss a variety of methods for managing national and international security in the contemporary world system. But first, we turn to a discussion of the roots of conflict in the international system and the forms it takes in the contemporary world.

War and World Politics

Whether one considers war a tale of tragedy or a saga of heroism, there is resonance to scholar Max Weber's (1864–1920) classic observation: "The decisive means for politics is violence. Anyone who fails to see this is . . . a political infant" (Porter, 1994:303). Realists would agree that war is an inherent part of politics. Idealists would rejoin that humans can learn to live without war. Whoever is right, though, the fact for now is that countries continue to rely on themselves for protection and sometimes use threats and violence to further their interests. Thus, it is important to grasp the role of force to understand the conduct of international politics.

War: The Human Record

War is as ancient as humanity (Cioffi-Revilla, 1996). There are varying estimates of the number of wars that have occurred throughout history, but there can be little doubt that the number is high. One reasonable number, as shown in Figure 10.1, is that there have been almost 1,000 wars during the current millennium. Looking even farther back, it is possible to estimate that the world has been totally free of significant interstate, colonial, or civil war in only about 1 out of every 12 years in all of recorded human history.

The data also shows that war is not a tragic anachronism waged by our less civilized ancestors. To the contrary, political violence continues. Two ways to gauge this are frequency and severity. *Frequency*, depending on how is it measured, provides either bad or not so bad news. If the number of wars is

Figure 10.1

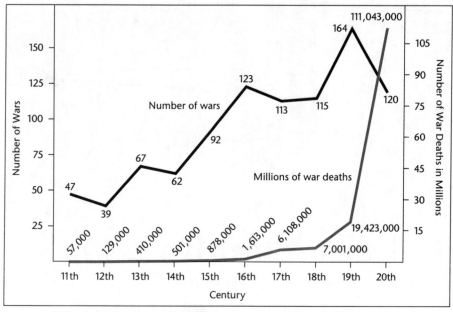

890 Years of War and Death, 1110–1998

Data sources: Eckhardt (1991); authors. Eckhardt defines a war as a conflict that (1) involves a government on at least one side and (2) accounts for at least 1,000 deaths per year of the conflict.

This figure shows the long-term trend in the rise of both the frequency and severity of war. Beginning in the year 1000, the number of wars in each century has usually increased. The soaring death toll of this century's wars, which account for 75 percent of the millennium's total, is a truly alarming figure.

measured, the bad news, as Figure 10.1 shows, is that of all the wars over the last ten centuries some 30 percent have occurred in the last two centuries. The not-so-bad news is that since the end of the Napoleonic era (1816), the annual number of new wars between countries has declined somewhat. Moreover, since there are many more countries than there once were, the chance that a country will be at war in any given year is less than it once was. It is also the case, though, that the number of civil wars has increased, which means that the overall incidence of interstate and intrastate warfare remains relatively steady (Pickering & Thompson, 1998; Wallensteen & Sollenberg, 1995).

Severity is the truly awful news. Again, as Figure 10.1 shows, over 147 million people have died during wars since the year 1000. Of the dead, an astounding 75 percent have perished in this century and 89 percent since 1800. Not only are we much more efficient at killing soldiers, we also now kill larger numbers of civilians as part of the war effort. During World War I, 8.4 million soldiers and 1.4 million civilians died. World War II killed 16.9 million troops and 34.3 million civilians, for a staggering 8.5 million deaths

No matter the strength of the political cause, there is no escaping the fact that war and other armed conflicts produce death. These Colombian soldiers are mourning the loss of 15 comrades who were killed by a leftist rebel group in July 1999.

per year. The worst news may lie ahead. President John F. Kennedy told the United Nations in 1961 that "mankind must put an end to war, or war will put an end to mankind." A general nuclear exchange between two countries with extensive arsenals would escalate the casualty count from millions per year to millions per minute, and Kennedy's cataclysmic characterization might literally come to pass.

The Causes of War: Three Levels of Analysis

Why war? This question has challenged investigators over the centuries (Geller & Singer, 1998). Philosophers, world leaders, and social scientists have many theories. It may be that further research can identify a single root cause of war, but it is more likely that the inability of so many fine minds to agree on what that cause might be means that there is no single reason why people fight. Moreover, some wars result from a culmination of causes, rather than from one single issue.

Given all this, one way to discuss the multiple causes of war is to classify them according to the three levels of analysis as outlined in chapter 3. You may want to go back and review that chapter and think about how each level of analysis provides ways for us to understand the causes of conflict in our world. System-level analysts might focus on power imbalances among major actors; state-level analysts might focus on the competitive efforts of states to seek and maintain power relative to other states; and individual-level analysts

A FURTHER NOTE
War Is Hell!

might focus on the personal ambitions of particular leaders as causes of conflict. You may also wish to take some time to examine the Web site box War Is Hell! to get a more striking analysis of war and its effects.

Force as a Political Instrument

It may be that future social scientists will be able to write of war in the past tense, but for the present we must recognize conflict as a fact of international politics. For this reason, having discussed the human record and causes of war, we should also consider levels of violence, the effectiveness of force, the changing nature of warfare, and the classification of wars. One of the things you might gain from this discussion is that the possession of arms and the threat of violence have important *psychological* and *diplomatic impacts* in addition to their strictly military role. Before delving into those topics, however, it is appropriate first to consider the nature of military power that provides the sword for policy makers to wield.

For good or ill, military power adds to a country's ability to prevail in international disputes. Military power is based on an array of tangible factors, such as spending and weapons levels, and intangible factors, such as leadership, morale, and reputation. Military power is not free, though. To the contrary, acquiring it and using it can be costly in many direct and indirect ways.

But given the importance of military power as a tool of national defense and diplomacy, it is not uncommon for people to assume that the phrase "too much military power" must be an oxymoron. Exactly how much is enough is a complex question, but it is certain that there are clear dangers associated with overemphasizing military power. Three such perils deserve special mention. They are insecurity, temptation, and expense.

Military power creates insecurity. One result of power acquisition is the "spiral of insecurity." This means that our attempts to amass power to achieve security or gain other such ends are frequently perceived by others as a danger to them. They then seek to acquire offsetting power, which we see as threatening, causing us to acquire even more power . . . then them . . . then us, *ad infinitum,* in an escalating spiral. As we will see later in this chapter's review of disarmament, the arms race is a complex phenomenon, but the interaction of one country's power and other countries' insecurity is an important factor in world politics.

Military power creates temptation. A second peril that the accumulation of power creates is the temptation to use it. Merely having global power sometimes means that a country may try to project itself into an area that is of peripheral interest. The United States went to war in Vietnam despite the fact that President Lyndon Johnson derided it as a "raggedy-ass fourth-rate country." One reason Americans intervened in Vietnam was because of a so-called arrogance of power. Had U.S. military power been more modest, the United States might have emphasized diplomacy or maybe even acquiesced to the reunification of North and South Vietnam. One can never be sure, but it is certain that it is hard to shoot someone if you do not own a gun.

TABLE
Defense
Expenditures,
Armed Forces,
Refugees, and
the Arms Trade

MAPS
Nations with
Nuclear Weapons

Military
Expenditures as
Percent of Gross
Domestic Product

Size of Armed Forces

Military power is expensive. A third problem with acquiring power for its own sake is that it is extremely expensive. Beyond short-term budget decisions about spending (domestic or defense programs) and how to pay the bills (taxes or deficits), there is a more general, longer-range concern. This is the argument that amassing and using military resources in the pursuit of hegemony saps a great power's strength and eventually leads to its decline. One scholar who studied the decline of great powers between 1500 and the 1980s concluded that "imperial overstretch" was the cause of their degeneration (Kennedy, 1988). In a thesis labeled "declinism," Kennedy contends that superpowers of the past have poured so many resources into military power that, ironically, they have weakened the country's strength by siphoning off resources that should have been devoted to maintaining and improving the country's infrastructure. Kennedy's study did not include the Soviet Union, but it is arguable that the collapse of the USSR followed the pattern of overspending on the military, thereby enervating the country's economic core. Declinists warn that the United States is also guilty of imperial overstretch and could go the way of other great powers that rose, dominated, then fell from the pinnacle of power (Lundestad, 1994; Rasler & Thompson, 1994).

The declinist thesis has many critics. At the strategic level, some critics argue that there is far more danger posed by a "lax Americana" than by any effort to create a "pax Americana" because if the United States does not exercise certain leadership as hegemon, then the international system is in danger of falling into disorder.[2] In the same vein, some scholars warn that a rush to peace is only slightly less foolish than a rush to war. One study reviews the sharp cuts in U.S. military spending after World War II, the Korean War, and the Vietnam War and concludes, "In each case the savings proved only temporary, as declining defense budgets eroded military readiness and necessitated a rush to rearm in the face of new dangers abroad" (Thies, 1998:176).

At the economic level, critics of declinism contend that there is no direct connection between levels of military and domestic spending. They question the common conjecture that more military spending means less domestic spending and vice versa. Moreover, the critics say, Kennedy was wrong about the economic cause of decline. These critics agree with Kennedy that overconsumption (spending that depletes assets faster than the economy can replace them) at the expense of reinvestment (spending that creates infrastructure assets) causes decline. Whereas Kennedy argues that excessive military spending causes overconsumption, his critics say that the villain is too much social spending or "social overstretch." "Whether in the form of bread and circuses in the ancient world or medical care for the lower classes and social security for the aged in the modern world," the argument goes, it is social spending on the least productive elements of a society that financially drains a society (Gilpin, 1981:164). It is a harsh judgment, but its advocates believe that the economic reality is that such altruistic programs may leave our spirits enriched but our coffers depleted. Consider, for example, Figure 10.2. It shows that U.S. military spending has declined while spending on social programs has increased steadily as a percentage of the U.S. budget. It

Figure 10.2

Changes in U.S. Military and Social Program Spending

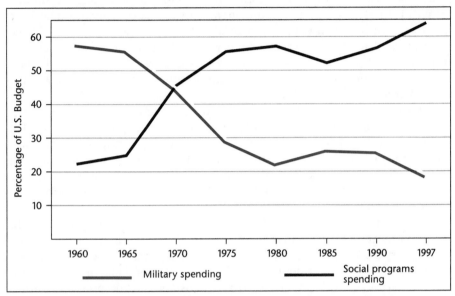

Social spending does not include education. Military spending includes Department of Defense, Department of Energy nuclear weapons programs, and veterans' programs.

Data source: U.S. Bureau of the Census (1997).

Many analysts agree that a country's power declines if it does not invest in its infrastructure, but they disagree about what diverts funds from that investment. Military-spending declinists argue that defense spending is the drain; social-spending declinists contend that appropriations for welfare, old-age care, and other such programs are sapping the U.S. economy. This figure shows the relative changes in U.S. military and social spending, but it does not answer whether either or both are too high, too low, or about right.

is also the case, however, that U.S. military spending accounts for about one-third of all military spending in the world. Which, if either, category would you cut to increase spending on education, transportation, communications, and other infrastructure programs?

Levels of Violence: From Intimidation to Attack

A country's military power may be used in several escalating ways: (1) as a diplomatic backdrop that creates perceived power through military potential; (2) as a source of supply to another government or an insurgency group; (3) by explicitly threatening its use against an opponent; (4) through limited demonstrations of violence; and (5) by direct use of military forces to defeat an opponent. It also should be noted that the options provided by the five levels of violence form a *multiple menu.* That is, they are often exercised concurrently.

Military power does not have to be used, supplied, or even overtly threatened to be effective. Its very existence establishes a *diplomatic backdrop* that influences other countries. "Diplomacy without force is like baseball without a bat," one U.S. diplomat has commented.[3] One obvious role of military strength is to persuade potential opponents not to risk confrontation. Military power also influences friends and neutrals. One reason why the United States has been, and remains, a leader of the West is because massive U.S. conventional and nuclear military power creates a psychological assumption by both holder and beholder that the country with dominant military power will play a strong role.

Another way to use military power without actually having to fight is to serve as *a source of supply to another government or an insurgency group*. This approach is utilized in two related ways. One way is to supply an ally with arms during times of peace in order to strengthen a mutual position. The United States, for example, is a major supplier of arms to Israel. Arms are also regularly supplied overtly or covertly to a government or insurgent group that is embroiled in a war.

A step up the escalation ladder is *overtly threatening* an opponent. This may be done verbally, or it may involve shifts in the readiness or deployment of a country's armed forces. As the crisis with Iraq over UN arms inspections peaked in early 1998, President Clinton warned, "Either Saddam acts [to allow inspections] or we will have to."[4] To give substance to the president's threat the Pentagon leaked the outlines of the planned Operation Desert Thunder, which included a salvo of about 300 sea-based and 100 air-launched cruise missiles, and a round-the-clock campaign 1,200 combat sorties against Iraq over four days to be carried out by Air Force and Navy carrier-based warplanes.

Limited demonstration of your capability and commitment is a third military option. This involves actual combat use of the military but in a way that is aimed at intimidating or harassing rather than defeating an opponent. One way to do this is by covert action such as hit-and-run guerrilla-style attacks or terrorism. A second method is using very limited forces in an overt way. American threats were sufficient in 1998, but actual force in a limited demonstration was used in September 1996 when the United States attacked Iraqi military installations with about 30 cruise missiles in an effort to persuade Baghdad to end its military operations against Kurdish areas in the northern part of Iraq.

Direct action is the most violent option and involves using full-scale force to attempt to defeat an opponent. Within this context, the level of violence can range from highly constrained conventional conflict to unrestricted nuclear war.

The Effectiveness of Force

Another aspect of the threat and use of force is the question of whether or not it works in a utilitarian way. It does, and one of the reasons that weapons and war persist in the international system is that they are sometimes successful. The threat of violence may successfully deter an enemy from attacking you or an ally. The actual use of force also sometimes accomplishes intended goals. Given these realities, we should ask ourselves how to determine if force will be effective by utilitarian standards. Answering this question necessitates looking at measurements and conditions for success.

Measurement   There are two ways of measuring the effectiveness of war. One is by trying to apply *cost/benefit analysis*. War is very expensive. There is no accurate count of the deaths in the Persian Gulf War, but 100,000 is a reasonable estimate. The UN-coalition countries spent $60 billion to oust Iraq from Kuwait. Estimates of the costs to both sides (including the physical destruction and lost oil revenues) are as high as $620 billion. Were the results worth the loss of life, human anguish, and economic destruction? Although such trade-offs are made in reality, it is impossible to arrive at any objective standards that can equate the worth of a human life or political freedom with dollars spent or territory lost.

The second way to judge the effectiveness of force is in terms of *goal attainment*. The issue is whether the accumulation and use of military power achieve the desired results. Wars are often caused by specific issues and fought with specific goals. Furthermore, the choice for war is not irrational because leaders usually calculate, accurately or not, their probability of success (Nevin, 1996; Fearon, 1995). This calculation is called the *expected utility* of war. In the words of one study, "Initiators [of war] act as predators and are likely to attack [only] target states they know they can defeat" (Gartner & Siverson, 1996:4; Smith, 1995). An interesting related finding that helps to explain the different pattern of war exhibited by democratic countries compared to authoritarian countries is that "democratic leaders select wars to participate in that have a lower risk of defeat than is true for their authoritarian counterparts." The reason democratic leaders are more war averse, two scholars say, is because they fear that defeat will result in losing their office, thereby threatening "the very essence of the office-holding *homo politicus*" (Bueno de Mesquita & Siverson, 1995:852; Bennett & Stam, 1996).

Conditions for Success   The next question, then, is: When does force succeed and when does it fail to accomplish its goals? There is no precise answer, but it is possible to synthesize the findings of a variety of studies and the views of military practitioners (see the Technical Explanation and Matters of Terminology section on p. 433) to arrive at some rudimentary rules for the successful use of military force, especially in cases of intervention when a country has not been directly attacked. In cases of intervention, success is most likely when:

1. A country takes action in areas where it has a clearly defined, preferably long-standing, and previously demonstrated commitment.
2. Government leaders are strongly committed to military action and have said so publicly.
3. Military force is used to counter other military force rather than to try to control political events.

4. Military force is used early and decisively (with sufficient force), rather than through extended threatening and slow escalation.

5. Goals are clearly established and adhered to, even if success seems to open other possibilities.

6. Use of military action and the announced goals both enjoy widespread domestic support.

These correlations between military action, political circumstances, and success are only preliminary and do not guarantee success. They do, however, indicate some of the factors that contribute to successful use of the military instrument.

The Changing Nature of War

The scope and strategy of war have changed greatly over the centuries (Weltman, 1995). Two factors are responsible: technology and nationalism.

High-tech versus low-tech weapons. . . a choice every country must make. The choice would seem obvious if your country has sufficient resources for the best, but here a Serbian child celebrates on top of an American stealth fighter brought down over Serbia in March 1999 by low-tech tactics.

It goes without saying that the *technological ability to kill* has escalated rapidly. Successive "advances" in the ability to deliver weapons at a distance (hand-held, then thrown, then bow and arrow, then rifle, then cannon, then plane, then missile) and in killing power (individuals, then gunpowder, then TNT, then nuclear weapons) have resulted in mounting casualties, both absolutely and as a percentage of soldiers and civilians of the countries at war.

Nationalism has also changed the nature of war. Before the nineteenth century, wars were generally fought between noble houses with limited armies. The French Revolution changed that. War began to be fought between nations, with increases in intensity and in numbers involved. France's Grand Army was the first to rely on a mass draft and the first to number more than a million men.

As a result of technology and nationalism, the *scope* of war has expanded. Entire nations have become increasingly involved in wars. Before 1800, no more than 3 of 1,000 people of a country participated in a war. By World War I, the European powers called 1 of 7 people to arms. Technology increased the need to mobilize the population for industrial production and also increased the capacity for, and the rationality of, striking at civilians. Nationalism made war a movement of the masses, increasing their stake and also giving justification for attacking the enemy nation. Thus, the lines between military and civilian targets have blurred.

Finally, the *strategy* of war has changed. Two concepts, the power to defeat and the power to hurt, are key here. The **power to defeat** is the ability to seize territory or overcome enemy military forces and is the classic goal of war. The **power to hurt**, or coercive violence, is the ability to inflict pain outside the immediate military sphere. It means hurting some so that the resistance of others will crumble. The power to hurt has become increasingly important to all aspects of warfare because the war effort depends on a country's economic effort and, often, the morale of its citizens. Perhaps the first military leader to understand the importance of the power to hurt in modern warfare was General William Tecumseh Sherman during the U.S. Civil War. "My aim was to whip the rebels, to humble their pride, to follow them to their inmost recesses, and [to] make them fear and dread us," the general wrote in his memoirs.[5]

Traditionally wars were fought with little reference to hurting. Even when hurting was used, it depended on the ability to attack civilians by first defeating the enemy's military forces. During the American Revolution, for example, the British could have utilized their power to hurt—to kill civilians in the major cities they controlled—and they might have won the war. Instead they concentrated on defeating the American army (which at first they could not catch, then which grew stronger), and they lost.

In the modern era, the power to defeat has declined in importance relative to the power to hurt. Guerrilla and nuclear warfare both rely extensively on terror to accomplish their ends. Even conventional warfare sometimes uses terror tactics to sap an opponent's morale. The use of strategic bombing to blast German cities during World War II is an example.

Classifying Wars

The changing nature of war, the increased power of weapons, and the shifts in tactics have all made classifying wars more difficult. Studies of war and other uses of political violence divide these acts into a variety of categories. Whatever the criteria for these categories, though, the exact boundaries between various types of wars or other political phenomena are imprecise. Therefore, you should be concerned mostly with the issues involved in planning for and fighting wars. With recognition of their limits, this chapter will rely on a mix of geographical scope and weaponry to divide international conflict into three categories: local conflict, regional conflict, and strategic nuclear conflict.

TABLE
Armed Conflict
in the 1990s

Local Conflict

Of our three categories of international conflict, the one that has the most limited geographical scope and involves the least powerful weapons is local conflict involving, at most, a very few countries. It is possible to use a variety of the instruments of violence at this level. Three ways for an outside country to apply its military power in local conflict are through (1) arms transfers, (2) covert operations and terrorism, and (3) direct and overt military intervention.

Arms Transfers

The international supply of arms is big business, involving tens of billions of dollars annually. There are several motivations to export arms that we will explore. Whatever the cause, however, the global flow of arms can be properly considered as a form of intervention because, whether intended or not, it has an impact on events within countries and between countries (other than the supplier). This is particularly true where the exports are to LDCs.

Arms Transfers: Destinations and Sources   The export and import of arms has long been important economically and politically, but it reached new heights during the cold war as the two hostile superpowers struggled for influence. World arms exports during the 1980s alone totaled $490 billion. The arms that flowed in the world came largely from the EDCs. Of all arms exported during the last half of the 1980s, the Soviet Union was the largest supplier, accounting for 37 percent of transfers, and the United States was a close second with 33 percent of transfers. The LDCs were the destination of about two-thirds of the flow of weaponry.

More recently, the end of the cold war, the drop in military aid, and the easing of tensions in the Middle East have combined to decrease the arms trade. Overall, annual world arms transfers (sales and military aid) have dropped from $41 billion in 1987 to $23 billion in 1996. Still, the movement of arms that continues is substantial. Figure 10.3 shows the current percentage of arms imports of various global regions. At 48.1 percent, Asia is particularly worrisome, especially since this represents a sharp increase from the 25 percent of imports that Asia received in 1987.

As far as arms exports go, the EDCs remain the dominant exporters, with 94 percent of the market. And of all countries, the United States is the world's leading arms merchant, selling $15.2 billion worth of arms in 1997, for 44 percent of the world market; France and Russia are tied for second with nearly 20 percent, and China is a close fourth (Keller, 1995).

Arms Transfers: Motives and Dangers   There are several motives that prompt countries to sell and give weapons to other countries or to insurgent groups (Sanjian, 1998). One motive is to *supply allies* with arms during peacetime. A second reason countries supply weapons is to *intervene in a conflict*. The rebellious ethnic Albanians in Yugoslavia's Kosovo Province had no heavy weapons and little money to buy them, yet as the conflict continued throughout 1998 the quality and quantity of weapons in the hands of the Kosovars increased steadily. Some of the weapons or the funds to buy them from arms dealers came from Albania, from ethnic Albanians abroad, and from Muslim countries wishing to support their coreligionists in Kosovo.

Figure 10.3

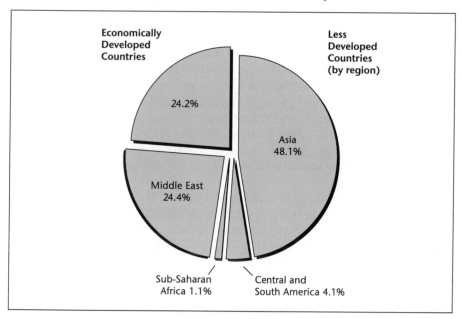

Percentage of World Arms Imports

Economically Developed Countries — 24.2%

Less Developed Countries (by region):
- Asia 48.1%
- Middle East 24.4%
- Sub-Saharan Africa 1.1%
- Central and South America 4.1%

Data source: SIPRI (1997). Percentages do not add to 100 because of rounding.

World arms imports in 1996 amounted to $23 billion. LDCs are the largest importers, with Asia far ahead of other regions.

A third motive for supplying arms is that the supplier country hopes to *gain diplomatic influence* over the recipient by befriending it or by creating a dependency relationship. While this may work, it is far from certain that supplying arms will increase the supplying country's influence over the recipient country. Sometimes the strategy works, but often it does not. As one study of U.S. policy between 1950 and 1992 notes, the search for influence through the arms trade has been most successful when the approach was positive (selling rather than withholding), when the issue was foreign (rather than promoting democracy or human rights), when the other government was civilian, and earlier in the 42-year period when the United States exercised greater hegemonic power (Sislin, 1994).

Preserving the defense production infrastructure is a fourth motive to sell weapons. Officials in the United States and elsewhere worry that declining military budgets will lead to the closing of defense plants in their country and the movement of scientists, engineers, and skilled plant workers into other fields. This loss of capacity, they fear, will be difficult to replace if it is needed in the future, especially if it is needed quickly. One way to have both a low defense budget and continued weapons production capability is to keep the weapons industry and its workers busy making arms for other countries and groups.

National economic benefit is a fifth, and now perhaps the predominant, motive behind arms exports. Weapons production keeps workers on the job, taxes from their incomes flowing to the government, and profits from sales rolling in to corporations and their investors. When, in May 1998, the United Arab Emirates announced that it would buy 80 U.S. F-16 fighters for $7 billion, the deal was hailed personally by Vice President Al Gore and meant that the plane's manufacturer, Lockheed Martin, could reverse its plan to lay off 2,000 of the 11,000 workers at its Forth Worth plant and, instead, add 2,000 workers. Further illustrating the importance of foreign sales is that in 1995, for the first time ever, U.S defense plants built more warplanes for foreign recipients (97 aircraft) than for the U.S. military (92 aircraft).

It is worth belaboring the obvious to point out that selling or giving arms to other countries is not like other trade and aid transfers. There can be little doubt that countries have legitimate defense needs and that sometimes arms transfers help stabilize situations. It is also true, however, that the massive flow of arms entails dangers to both the importing and to the exporting countries. These dangers include but are not limited to the following:

- One danger of the weapons trade is cost. Countries, especially poorer ones, face classic "guns or butter" budget decisions about whether to spend on defense or domestic programs. At least some of the more than $16 billion a year in weapons that LDCs import could be devoted to domestic infrastructure or social programs.
- A second danger is that the arms flow has increased the level and perhaps frequency and intensity of violence between countries and within countries. This is especially true for LDCs that do not produce most of their own weapons (Kinsella & Tillema, 1995; Brzoska & Pearson, 1994).
- A third peril of the weapons trade, according to some critics, is that supplying weapons for others to kill with brings moral corruption to the supplier. One of several especially troubling ramifications of the arms trade is the merciless maiming and death caused by land mines, as discussed in the Web site box The Killing Fields.
- A fourth danger in the arms trade is that the country supplying the weapons begins to be identified with the recipient country or rebel group. If things begin to go badly for the recipient, and even more and more powerful weapons do not reverse the tide, then the supplier may be tempted to send advisers, engage in limited combat support, and, finally, commit to a full-scale military intervention with its own troops. This is how the United States waded ever deeper into the quagmire in Vietnam and how the Soviet Union fell into the abyss in Afghanistan.

A FURTHER NOTE
The Killing Fields

- A fifth danger, and one that faces the supplier, is that it may eventually find itself facing its own weapons. This possibility became starkly evident during the Persian Gulf War. In the decade before its invasion of Kuwait, Iraq bought fighter aircraft from Egypt and France; various aircraft and armor missiles from Egypt, France, and Italy; tanks from Egypt and Kuwait; armored personnel carriers from France and Great Britain; artillery from Egypt, France, and Saudi Arabia; and bombs from Saudi Arabia.
- A sixth problem with the arms trade is that, however laudable you think your goals are, it is hard to persuade others not to do what you are doing. For instance, the massive U.S. arms sales, says one analyst, "give a green light to other weapons sellers in the world."[6] Moreover, the U.S. contention that it sells arms to only responsible recipients strikes others as patently self-serving. One effort by Washington to prevent the sale of weapons to Iran left a Czech official fuming that the Americans "are preaching that we drink water while they drink wine. I consider it hypocritical."[7]

Covert Operations and Terrorism

A second form of intervention involves supporting dissident forces in another country or directly intervening through special operations, such as guerrilla forces, intelligence operatives, or other clandestine agents. When such covert activities extend beyond attacking a certain range of clearly military targets—and the line is thin—the operations move into the realm of terrorism. Acts of terrorism can affect international relations in many ways. Domestic terrorism can take the life of a national leader or even destabilize and topple a government. Transnational terrorist groups, such as Hamas in the Middle East, can strike out around the globe in an effort to advance their cause.

What concerns us most here is **state terrorism**. This is terrorism carried out directly by, or specifically encouraged and funded by, an established government. The State Department's annual terrorist report has, at various times, accused Cuba, Iran, Iraq, Libya, North Korea, Sudan, Syria, and other countries of state terrorism.

The Record of Covert Operations and Terrorism   The use of covert military intervention by countries has increased in recent decades for several reasons. First, there has been an increase in civil strife within countries. Second, attempts to topple governments or to create separatist states are now usually waged using guerrilla tactics, rather than conventional tactics, as occurred during the U.S. Civil War. More than any single reason, this change in tactics has occurred because the preponderance of high-tech weapons available to government forces makes it nearly suicidal for opposition forces to try to fight conventionally. Third, covert intervention avoids the avalanche of international and, often, domestic criticism that overt interventions set off. Fourth, clandestine

Even though progress has been made in the British-Irish peace process, terrorism, such as the explosion in Lurgan, Northern Ireland, pictured here, still sometimes characterizes the relationship in this decades-old conflict. How to combat terrorism is a significant problem for political units, which are equipped for preventing large-scale violence, but less so for random political violence.

operations allow the initiating country to more easily disengage if it wishes than would be possible if it overtly committed regular military forces.

There are different estimates of the number of covert military operations, but it is safe to say that the number of paramilitary operations has been extensive since World War II. The United States and, while it existed, the Soviet Union stand first in the ranks of countries that have participated in such activities, but many countries have sent military special operations forces or intelligence operatives into other countries.

International terrorism has also become a regular occurrence. The number of attacks rose from 165 in 1968 to peak at 666 in 1987. Since then the trend has been downward, with the 304 acts of international terrorism in 1997 one of the lowest annual totals since the early 1970s. Approximately 9,500 people have died from terrorist attacks, and another 24,000 have been wounded during the last three decades. The number of casualties in 1997 was 221 dead and 393 wounded, substantial reductions from the previous year. The grim figures for 1998 are not yet finalized, but the simultaneous attacks on the U.S. embassies in Kenya and Tanzania (killing nearly 300 and wounding over 1,000 people), the bombing in Omagh, Northern Ireland (killing 28 and wounding more than 200), and other terrorist attacks certainly made 1998 one of the bloodiest years on record in terms of those killed and maimed by terrorists.

Geographically, international terrorism has been widespread, with all regions other than North America suffering frequent terrorist attacks. International terrorists have perpetrated some attacks in the United States, such as the spectacular bombing of the World Trade Center in New York City that killed six people in 1993. A much greater danger, however, has been domestic terrorists, such as the militia zealots who bombed the Oklahoma City federal building in 1995, killing 168 people.

What defenses can countries throw up against such terrorist attacks? The answer, John M. Deutch, the CIA director, told Congress in 1996, is that "the ability of our country, or, I might say, any other country in the developed world to protect their infrastructure from a terrorist attack based on nuclear, chemical, and biological weapons is very, very small indeed."[8] To test its ability to respond, the government conducted a mock biological attack in early 1997. In the exercise a supposed genetically engineered virus mix of smallpox and Marburg viruses (a combination that rendered the resulting disease invulnerable to existing cures), was spread along the U.S.–Mexico frontier. "You could make such a virus today," said a leading expert on genetic engineering. "Any trained molecular virologist with a really good lab can do it."[9] The results of the exercise remain secret, but they reportedly confirm CIA director Deutch's earlier statement that the country was unprepared.

In the end, terrorism, like most forms of violence, exists because terror tactics sometimes do accomplish their goals. However much one may condemn the acts themselves, it is also accurate to say that over the years Palestinian terrorists almost certainly played a role in increasing the willingness of Israel to deal with them, in enhancing global awareness of and concern with the Palestinian cause, and in bringing pressure on Israel by the international community to reach an agreement with them (Sederberg, 1995).

Direct Military Intervention

The most overt form of coercive intervention in a localized area of operation is for a country to dispatch its own forces to another country. The junctures where military aid becomes military intervention and where limited military intervention becomes full-scale war are debatable. What is implied here, though, is the direct but limited use of military personnel on one side or the other of another country's internal conflict.

Beyond the cost in lives and wealth to the intervening country, there is the danger that direct military intervention will fail or that it will escalate into a full-scale war that, in turn, may itself fail. The U.S. experience in Vietnam is an example of an intervention that both escalated and failed, as is the long, and ultimately unsuccessful, Soviet involvement in Afghanistan throughout most of the 1980s.

The legitimacy of intervention is also controversial. Panama provides a good case in point. General Manuel Noriega was abhorrent by almost any political or ethical standard. The U.S. intervention ended his rule, and Panama is well rid of him. Does this legitimize the U.S. intervention? Certainly President Bush thought so, and others agreed. Yet intervening in the internal affairs of another country is troubling. It may well be, as Senator Edward M. Kennedy observed, that "the United States [or anyone else] does not have the right under international law . . . to roam the hemisphere to bring dictators to justice or . . . to impose democracy by the barrel of a gun on Panama or any other nation."[10]

Regional Conflict

As the geographical scope expands and, usually, as the killing capacity of weapons increases, entire regions become involved. Geographically, even the two conflicts labeled world war in this century were, in a sense, regional conflicts. The vast majority of the fighting in World War I took place in Europe and its surrounding waters. The theater of combat in World War II was broader, but the conflict can also be seen as two great regional wars. One, in Europe and North Africa, primarily pitted the Germans and the Italians against the Americans, British, French, and Russians. The second, in Asia, was mostly a struggle between the Americans, British, and Chinese on one side and the Japanese on the other. Other regions remained largely unscathed.

Regional conflicts often include the use of more and more powerful weapons. Such wars used to be called "conventional wars" or "traditional wars" to distinguish them, in part, from "nuclear wars." That distinction makes less sense to some observers now because a few countries possess an array of tactical (battlefield) nuclear weapons. The availability of chemical and biological weapons and the ongoing development of electronic and other weapons that, not long ago, were the stuff of science fiction also render inadequate the use of the adjectives *conventional* or *traditional* to describe regional wars.

Most wars are fought within limits. **Escalation** occurs when the rules are changed and the level of combat increases (Carlson, 1995). The dangers of escalation and the prudence of keeping wars limited make it important to understand how to avoid unchecked escalation. As with most things political, there is no set formula. There are, however, a few useful standards.

Keep lines of communication open. The basic principle is that escalation (or de-escalation) should be a deliberate strategy used to signal a political message to the enemy. Accordingly, it is also important to send signals through diplomatic or public channels so that the opponent will not mistake the escalation as an angry spasm of violence or the de-escalation as a weakening of resolve.

Limit goals. Unlimited goals by one side may evoke unlimited resistance by the other, so limiting goals is another way to avoid unchecked escalation. It is usually appropriate, for instance, that a goal should fall short of eliminating the opponent as a sovereign state! Even where unconditional victory is the aim, obliteration of the enemy population is not an appropriate goal.

Restrict geographical scope. It is often wise to limit conflict to as narrow a geographical area as possible. American forces refrained from invading China during the Korean War. Similarly, the Soviets passed up the temptation to blockade Berlin in 1962 in response to the U.S. blockade of Cuba.

Observe target restrictions. Regional wars can be controlled by limiting targets. Despite their close proximity, the Arabs and Israelis have never tried to bomb each other's capitals. Iraq's launch of Scud missiles against Tel Aviv and other Israeli cities in 1991 was, by contrast, a serious escalation.

Limit weapons. Yet another way to keep war limited is to adhere to the principle that the level of force used should be no greater than the minimum necessary to accomplish war aims. The stricture on weapons has become even more important in an era when there is such a great potential for the use of limited, on-the-battlefield nuclear, biological, and chemical (NBC) weapons. Although some people argue that a weapon is a weapon and it makes no difference what kills you, the horror with which NBC weapons are regarded probably means that even their limited use would set off a serious escalation that could lead to strategic nuclear war. Even if that were avoided, using NBC weapons would almost surely entail devastating costs far beyond the worth of the original goals of a war. Moreover, the power of conventional weapons should not be underestimated. The spreading availability to countries of weapons systems (especially missiles) capable of accurately delivering extremely powerful explosives over a long range strains the outer boundary of traditional warfare.

Strategic Nuclear War

The Bible's Book of Revelation speaks of an apocalyptic end to the world: a "hail of fire mixed with blood fell upon the earth; and . . . the earth was burnt up. . . . The sea became blood . . . and from the shaft rose smoke like the smoke of a great furnace and the sun and the air were darkened." Revelation laments, "Woe, woe, woe to those who dwell on earth," for many will die a fiery death, and the survivors "will seek death and will not find it; they will long to die, and death will fly from them." Whatever your religious beliefs, such a prophecy is sobering. We now have the capability to sound "the blast of the trumpets" that will kill the living and make those that remain wish to die.

The world joined in a collective sigh of relief when the Soviet Union collapsed and the cold war between the two great nuclear powers ended. Almost overnight, worry about the threat of nuclear war virtually disappeared from the media and general political discussion. Unfortunately, the hard numbers belie the perception of significantly greater safety. It is certainly true that the number of strategic nuclear weapons has declined since the end of the cold war. Nevertheless, there remains a huge number of extremely powerful nuclear weapons.

The United States and Russia remain the nuclear Goliaths. At the beginning of 1998, the U.S. strategic (intercontinental-range) arsenal included 7,250 nuclear warheads and bombs and 1,074 missiles and bombers to carry them to destinations anywhere in the world. Russia's strategic inventory was 6,240 weapons and 1,205 delivery vehicles. Each country can also count several thousand tactical nuclear weapons in their arsenals. China, France, Great Britain, India, and Pakistan all openly have nuclear weapons, and Israel and (perhaps) North Korea have undeclared nuclear weapons, adding another 1,100 or so nuclear devices to the volatile mix of over 21,000 tactical and strategic nuclear devices. The largest of the warheads has an explosive power up to 50 times that of the bombs dropped on Japan in 1945. Additionally, several countries have or are suspected of having nuclear weapons development programs, and another 30 countries have the technology base needed to build nuclear weapons. Thus, nuclear weapons proliferation is a global concern.

Given this reality, it would be unwise to discount the continuing impact of nuclear weapons on world politics. One role that nuclear weapons play is to be a part of the "backdrop" of power and influence. There can be little doubt that the massive nuclear capability of the United States is part of what makes it a superpower. Similarly, the continuing importance of Russia, despite its tremendous travails, rests in part on its still immense nuclear arsenal. Second, nuclear weapons are part of direct deterrence. Whether or not nuclear weapons will always deter conventional or nuclear attack is uncertain, but they have at least sometimes been and remain a restraining factor that deters an opponent from attacking in the first place or that limits an opponent's weapons or tactics (Lebow & Stein, 1995). It is not unreasonable to conjecture, for instance, that the nuclear option that the United States, France, and Great Britain all had in the Persian Gulf War may have helped deter Saddam Hussein from using his chemical weapons. Finally, the atomic attacks on Hiroshima and Nagasaki demonstrate that humans have the ability and the will to use weapons of mass destruction. Therefore, it is naive to imagine that nuclear war cannot happen. To the contrary, there are several ways that a nuclear war could break out.

How a Nuclear War Might Start

For all its potential horror, nuclear war is within the realm of possibility. Strategic analysts envision many possible scenarios, including (1) an accident, (2) an irrational leader in control of the nuclear launch codes, (3) an unprovoked attack, (4) a last-gasp defense by a state on the verge of defeat, (5) an inadvertent error in judgment, and (6) an escalation. Two points to note are that, firstly, these scenarios are not equally likely. Inadvertent war and escalation, for instance, are much more likely than an accident. Secondly, the six are not necessarily mutually exclusive. They may combine into *multipath scenarios.* For example, a crisis on the China-Russia border with the possibility of escalation to war could lead to a partial release of nuclear weapons safety controls, thereby increasing the chances of accidental war. You should also take time to do the Web site exercise It's Your Call, Mr./Madam President, which lays out one possible scenario and asks you to decide the outcome.

INTERACTIVE EXERCISE
It's Your Call, Mr./Madam President

Strategic Nuclear Weapons and Strategy

The fact that nuclear weapons exist and remain a factor in international politics, the unsettling reality that nuclear war could start, and the impact that nuclear weapons would have make it important that we briefly examine strategic nuclear weapons and strategy. There are issues of what a country's nuclear arsenal and doctrines should be that seldom enter the public debate, but that are crucial to an effective and stable arsenal. Furthermore, the post–cold war changes have brought on new challenges in strategic planning. As one expert has noted, within the declared nuclear weapons countries, it "is clear that there is a great debate . . . over who is the enemy and what is the target."[11] Within the debate, the two main issues are (1) how to minimize the chance of nuclear war and (2) how to maximize the chance of survival if a nuclear exchange does occur. It is not possible here to review all the factors that impinge on these issues, but we can illustrate the various concerns by examining deterrence and then several specific issues about weapons systems and strategy.

Deterrence The concept of deterrence has been and remains at the center of the strategy of all the nuclear powers. **Deterrence** is persuading an enemy that attacking you will not be worth any potential gain. Deterrence is based on two factors: capability and credibility.

Capability. Effective deterrence requires that you have the capacity to respond to an attack or impending attack on your forces. This capability is what India claimed it was seeking when it openly tested nuclear weapons in mid-1998. "Our problem is China," said an Indian official. "We are not seeking [nuclear] parity with China. . . . What we are seeking is a minimum deterrent."[12] Just having weapons, however, is not enough. Since there is no way to defend effectively against a missile attack once it is launched, deterrence requires that you have enough weapons that are relatively invulnerable to enemy destruction so that you can be assured that some will survive for a counterattack. Submarine-launched ballistic missiles (SLBMs) are the least vulnerable; fixed-site, land-based intercontinental ballistic missiles (ICBMs) are the most vulnerable. Air-launched (bombs, short-range missiles) and mobile ICBMS (such as the Russian SS-25) are in the midrange of vulnerability.

Credibility. It is also necessary for other states to believe that you will actually use your weapons. Perception is a key factor. The operational reality will be determined by what the other side believes rather than by what you intend. We will see, for example, that some analysts believe that relying on a second-strike capability may not always be credible.

This two-part equation for deterrence sounds simple enough on the surface, but the question is how to achieve it. The debate can be roughly divided into two schools of nuclear strategy. They are characterized by the bizarrely colorful acronyms of **MAD** (Mutual Assured Destruction) and **NUT** (Nuclear Utilization Theory).

Those who favor the mutual assured destruction strategy (the MADs) believe that deterrence is best achieved if each nuclear power's capabilities include (1) a sufficient number of weapons that are (2) capable of surviving a nuclear attack by an opponent and then (3) delivering a second-strike retaliatory attack that will destroy that opponent. MADs believe, in other words, in *deterrence through punishment*. If each nuclear power has these three capabilities, then a mutual checkmate is achieved. The result, MAD theory holds, is that no power will start a nuclear war because doing so will lead to its own destruction (even if it destroys its enemy).

Those who favor nuclear utilization theory (the NUTs) contend that the MAD strategy is a mad gamble because it relies on rationality and clear-sightedness when, in reality, there are other scenarios (discussed earlier in the section "How a Nuclear War Might Start") that could lead to nuclear war. Therefore, NUTs prefer to base deterrence partly on *deterrence through damage denial* (or limitation), in contrast to the punishment strategy of MADs. This means that NUTs want to be able to destroy enemy weapons before the weapons explode on one's own territory and forces. One way to do this is to destroy the weapons before they are launched.

Managing Insecurity: Approaches and Standards of Evaluation

Think back for a moment to our drama about Ug and Og at the beginning of this chapter and the stalemate that ensued between the protagonists at the end the story. Now bring your minds from the past to the present, from primordial cave dwellers to yourself. Think about contemporary international security. The easiest matter is determining what our goal should be. How to do that is, of course, a much more challenging question.

There are, in essence, four possible approaches to securing peace. The basic parameters of each is shown in Table 10.1. As with many, even most, matters in this book, which approach is best is part of the realist-idealist debate.

Unlimited self-defense, the first of the four approaches, is the traditional approach of each country being responsible for its own defense and amassing weapons it wishes for that defense. The thinking behind this approach rests on the classic realist assumption that humans have an inherent element of greed and aggressiveness that promotes individual and collective violence. This makes the international system, from the realists' perspective, a place of danger where each state must fend for itself or face the perils of domination or destruction by other states.

Beyond the traditional approach to security, there are three alternative approaches: *limited self-defense* (arms limitations), *international security* (regional and world security forces), and *abolition of war* (complete disarmament and pacifism). Each of these will be examined in the pages that follow. Realists do not oppose arms control or even international peacekeeping under the right circumstances. Most realists, for instance, are willing to concede that the huge arsenals of weapons that countries possess are dangerous. These realists are, therefore, willing to admit also that there can be merit in carefully negotiated, truly verifiable arms accords. But because the three alternative approaches all involve some level of trust and depend on the triumph of the spirit of human cooperation over human avarice and power-seeking, they are all more attractive to idealists than to realists.

Table 10.1

Four Approaches to Security

Security Approach	Sources of Insecurity	World Political System	Armaments Strategy	Primary Peacekeeping Mechanism	Standard
Unlimited Self-Defense	Many; probably inherent in humans	State-based; national interests and rivalries; fear	Have many and all types to guard against threats	Armed states, deterrence, alliances, balance of power	Peace through strength
Limited Self-Defense	Many; perhaps inherent, but weapons intensify	State-based; limited coop-eration based on mutual interests	Limit amount and types to reduce capabilities, damage, tension	Armed states; defensive ca-pabilities, lack of offensive capabilities	Peace through limited offensive ability
International Security	Anarchical world system; lack of law or common security mechanisms	International political inte-gration; regional or world government	Transfer weapons and authority to international force	International peacekeeping/peacemaking force	Peace through law and universal collective defense
Abolition of War	Weapons; personal and national greed and insecurity	Various options from pacifistic states to liber-tarian global village model	Eliminate weapons	Lack of ability; lack of fear; individual and collective pacifism	Peace through being peaceful

Concept source: Rapoport (1992).

The path to peace has long been debated. The four approaches outlined here provide some basic alternatives that help structure this chapter on security.

To evaluate the approaches to security, begin by considering the college community that you are living in while taking the course for which this book is being used. The next time you are in class, look around you. Is anyone carrying a gun? Are you? Probably not. Think about why you are not doing so. The answer is that you feel relatively secure.

The word "relatively" is important here. There are, of course, dangerous people in your community who might steal your property, attack you, and perhaps even kill you. There were 19,645 killings, 95,769 reported rapes, and 1,566,742 other violent crimes in the United States during 1996. Criminals committed another 11,701,300 burglaries, car thefts, and other property crimes. These statistics demonstrate clearly that you are not absolutely secure. Yet most of us feel secure enough to forgo carrying firearms.

The important thing to consider is why you feel secure enough not to carry a gun despite the fact that you could be murdered, raped, beaten up, or have your property stolen. There are many reasons. *Domestic norms* against violence and stealing are one reason. Most people around you are peaceful

INTERACTIVE EXERCISE
What Would You Spend for Your Security?

and honest and are unlikely, even if angry or covetous, to attack you or steal your property. Established *domestic collective security forces* are a second part of feeling secure. The police are on patrol to deter criminals, and if anyone does attack you or steal your property, you can call 911; criminal courts and prisons deal with convicted felons. *Domestic disarmament* is a third contributor to your sense of security. Most domestic societies have disarmed substantially, shun the routine of carrying weapons, and have turned the legitimate use of domestic force beyond immediate self-defense over to their police. *Established domestic conflict-resolution mechanisms* are a fourth contributor to security. There are ways to settle disputes without violence. Lawsuits get filed, and judges make decisions. Indeed, some crimes against persons and property are avoided because most domestic political systems provide some level of social services to meet human needs.

To return to our stress on relative security, it is important to see that for all the protections and dispute-resolution procedures provided by your domestic system, and for all the sense of security that you usually feel, you are not fully secure in your domestic society. Nor are you secure in the global system. For that matter, neither are you likely to achieve absolute security through any of the methods offered in this chapter or anywhere else. Therefore, the most reasonable standard by which to evaluate any approach to security is whether or not it improves your relative security. If the global community follows the path of arms control, of collective security, or of pacifism, will it enhance security? Or are we better off keeping to the traditional path of heavily armed self-reliance?

These are very challenging questions. When thinking about the various approaches, keep relative safety in mind and beware of one-sided critics. There are critics of the alternative path to security who ignore the perils of the traditional approach and merely point to possible dangers on the alternative road. Similarly, some of those who advocate taking the nontraditional path feel that it is only necessary to point to the almost countless wars that have occurred while using the traditional approach and to assume that the road less traveled by will be better. Neither of these one-sided arguments provides much understanding. Instead, and inasmuch as absolute security is not a realistic goal, the traditional and alternative roads should each be examined with an eye to deciding which of them offers the greatest degree of relative safety.

Limited Self-Defense through Arms Control

The first alternative approach to achieving security involves limiting the numbers and types of weapons that countries possess. This approach, commonly called **arms control**, aims at lessening military (especially offensive) capabilities and lessening the damage even if war begins. Additionally, arms control advocates believe that the decline in the number and power of weapons systems will ease political tensions, thereby making further arms agreements possible (Gallagher, 1998).

Methods of Achieving Arms Control

Within the general arms control approach, there are two somewhat different strategies. One of these is *arms limitations*. This means preventing an increase in the quantities of weapons that countries possess. The second arms control strategy is *arms reductions*. This means reducing quantities and types of weapons that you and others already possess. Ultimately, arms reductions might achieve complete disarmament. That possibility is, however, distinct from mere arms control and will be dealt with in a separate section later in this chapter. A third arms control strategy is **nonproliferation**. This strategy aims at preventing countries without certain types of weapons from acquiring them. Nonproliferation commonly refers to nuclear weapons, but in a broader sense it also means preventing the spread of weapons capability at any level—nuclear, biological, chemical, and conventional (NBC)—especially through foreign help (Feaver & Niou, 1996).

There are a number of methods of arms control that are applicable to arms limitations, arms reductions, or both strategies. These include numerical restrictions; research, development, and deployment restrictions; categorical restrictions; and transfer restrictions. Several of the arms control agreements that will be used to illustrate the restrictions are detailed in the following section on the history of arms control, but to familiarize yourself with them quickly, it would be wise to peruse the agreements listed in Table 10.2 and also to examine in detail the Web site box The End or the Beginning?, which recounts the problems of controlling arms in South Asia.

A FURTHER NOTE
The End or the Beginning?

Numerical Restrictions   Placing numerical limits on existing weapons, or weapons that might be developed, is the most common approach to arms control. This approach specifies the number or capacity of weapons and/or troops that each side may possess. In some cases the numerical limits may be at or higher than current levels. For example, both the first and second Strategic Arms Limitations Talks (**SALT I** and **SALT II**) Treaties listed in Table 10.2 relied heavily on numerical limits to cap future expansion rather than to reduce existing levels.

Numerical limits may also be lower than existing arsenals. The two Strategic Arms Reduction Talks (**START I** and **START II**) Treaties significantly reduced the number of American and Russian nuclear weapons.

Development, Testing, and Deployment Restrictions   A second method of arms limitation involves restricting the development of new weapons and the testing of existing ones, and constraining the deployment of new or existing systems. One example of this approach is the Antiballistic Missile (ABM) Treaty of 1971 that put stringent limits on U.S. and Soviet efforts to build a ballistic missile defense (BMD) system. The attempt to implement a Comprehensive Test Ban Treaty (CTBT), signed in 1996, is a more recent attempt of this type. Although signed by 154 countries, the CTBT will not go into force for the moment, as the U.S. Senate voted against it in October 1999. Citing the treaty as "fatally flawed" primarily because of problems with verification and with the treaty's ability to deal with existing nuclear violators, Senate Republicans were almost uniformly opposed to it, while Democrats vowed to make the

(Continued on page 283)

Table 10.2

Arms Control Treaties

Treaty	Provisions	Date Signed	Number of Signatories
Geneva Protocol	Bans the use of gas or bacteriological weapons	1925	125
Antarctic Treaty	Internationalizes and demilitarizes the continent	1959	42
Limited Test Ban	Bans nuclear tests in the atmosphere, outer space, or under water	1963	123
Outer Space Treaty	Internationalizes and demilitarizes space, the moon, and other celestial bodies	1967	94
Non-Proliferation Treaty (NPT)	Prohibits selling, giving, or receiving nuclear weapons, materials, or technology for weapons	1968	178
Seabed Arms Control	Bans placing nuclear weapons in or under the seabed	1971	92
Biological Weapons	Bans the production and possession of biological weapons	1972	131
Strategic Arms Limitation Talks Treaty (SALT I)	Limits the number and types of U.S. and USSR strategic weapons (expired 1977)	1972	2
ABM Treaty	U.S.–USSR pact limits antiballistic missile testing and deployment	1972	2
Threshold Test Ban	Limits U.S. and USSR underground tests to 150 kt	1974	2
Environmental Modification	Bans environmental modification as a form of warfare	1977	62
SALT II	Limits the number and types of USSR and U.S. strategic weapons	1979	2
Intermediate-Range Nuclear Forces (INF)	Eliminates all U.S. and Soviet missiles with ranges between 500 km and 5,500 km	1987	2
Missile Technology Control Regime (MTCR)	Limits transfer of missiles or missile technology	1987	25
Conventional Forces in Europe Treaty (CFE)	Reduces conventional forces in Europe. Nonbinding protocol in 1992 covers troops	1990–1992	20 30
Strategic Arms Reduction Talks Treaty (START I)	Reduces strategic nuclear forces between the United States and the USSR/Belarus, Kazakhstan, Russia, and Ukraine	1991–1992	2 5
START II	Reduces U.S. and Russian strategic nuclear forces	1993	2
Chemical Weapons Convention (CWC)	Bans the possession of chemical weapons after 2005	1993	157
Comprehensive Test Ban Treaty (CTBT)	Bans all nuclear weapons tests	1996	154

SALT II was never ratified. START II has not been ratified by Russia.
The MTCR is not a treaty, as such, but rather a negotiated understanding. The NPT was renewed and made permanent in 1996. The CTBT is open for ratification.

Data sources: SIPRI 1998; various news sources.

The progress toward controlling arms has been slow and often unsteady, but each agreement in this table represents an improvement in the international political system.

treaty's defeat a high-profile issue in the 2000 election campaign. Supporters argued that the U.S. public overwhelmingly favored treaty ratification and that not signing would hurt the American position as a world leader, especially as the United States is the only nuclear power to reject it.

Categorical Restrictions   A third approach to arms control involves limiting or eliminating certain types of weapons. The Intermediate-Range Nuclear Forces (INF) Treaty eliminated an entire class of weapons—intermediate-range nuclear missiles. The START II Treaty will erase multiple-independent-reentry-vehicle (MIRV) warhead ICBMs from the nuclear arsenals. The new Anti-Personnel Mine (APM) Treaty will make it safer to walk the Earth.

Transfer Restrictions   A fourth method of arms control is to prohibit or limit the flow of weapons and weapons technology across international borders. The NPT, for example, pledges countries with nuclear weapons or nuclear weapons technology not to supply the weapons or technology to nonnuclear states.

Limiting the transfer of missile technology and missiles capable of attacking distant points is another arms control area that focuses on transfer restrictions. The primary effort to stem missile proliferation centers on an informal 1987 agreement, styled the **Missile Technology Control Regime (MTCR)**.

The MTCR has not halted missile proliferation, which is alarming even if the missiles are only coupled with conventional warheads. India, Japan, and a few other countries have developed missiles capable of launching satellites that, as a side effect, have intercontinental capability. Just one step down, there are a number of countries with nuclear weapons or with current or recent nuclear pretensions that have also developed or purchased long-range missiles. These countries include, among others, Argentina, Brazil, Iran, Iraq, Israel, Libya, North Korea, Pakistan, and South Africa.

The Barriers to Arms Control

Limiting or reducing arms is an idea that most people favor. Yet arms control has proceeded slowly and sometimes not at all. The devil is in the details, as the old maxim goes, and it is important to review the continuing debate over arms control to understand its history and current status. None of the factors that we are about to discuss is the main culprit impeding arms control. Nor is any one of them insurmountable. Indeed, important advances are being made on a number of fronts. But together, these factors form a tenacious resistance to arms control.

Security Barriers   Perhaps the most formidable barrier to arms control is thrown up by security concerns. Those who hold to the realist school of thought have strong doubts about whether countries can maintain adequate security if they disarm totally or substantially. Realists are cautious about the current political scene and about the claimed contributions of arms control.

Realists are not persuaded that the end of the cold war necessarily means that national security systems can or should be dismantled substantially. One concern is that the relaxation of tensions between the two military super-powers and their present and former allies in Europe cannot be confidently predicted to continue. Russia has been severely weakened, and the fighting ability of its conventional forces is highly suspect. Yet Moscow's nuclear force remains awesome. "They can do nothing much in Moscow, but they can wipe out New York," says one Russian defense correspondent about Russia's lead-ers.[13] Moreover, the severe economic and social turmoil that continues to beset Russia leads observers to worry about the country's future political stability or direction.

Arms control skeptics also worry about China. While other military budgets have been dropping in the 1990s, China's has been growing. Some analysts even question how much authority the civilian leadership in Beijing has over the People's Liberation Army. Among other worries, China's nuclear force continues to grow in number, power, and ability to strike accurately over long distances (Lewis & Xue, 1994).

Beyond the threat possibly posed by Russia and China, realists worry about the growing military capability of many other countries, including the LDCs. The proliferation of nuclear, chemical, and very powerful conventional weapons has made these countries formidable potential military opponents. Iran, for example, has bought diesel submarines and Su-24 and MiG-29 war-planes from Russia. The Iranians almost certainly have chemical weapons and may also have embarked on biological and nuclear weapons programs. There are also strong allegations that Tehran has purchased large, surface-to-surface M-9 or M-11 missiles from China, Rodung medium-range missiles from North Korea, and missile technology from Russia. Iran appears to be also using these systems as models to develop its own missile production capability, and in July 1998 it tested what is believed to have been an Iranian-produced Shahab-3 missile, with an approximate range of 800 miles. Among other places, this would bring Israel within range of the Shahab-3 (Arnett, 1997).

Realists also have doubts about arms control because they are skeptical of many of the arguments that idealists make to support reducing or elimi-nating arms. Realists doubt that arms races occur, that reducing arms will increase security, or that arms talks represent progress.

Realists *doubt that arms set off an arms race.* Instead, a classic tenet of realpolitik is that humans arm themselves and fight because the world is dangerous, as represented by Theory A in Figure 10.4. Given this view, realists believe that political settlements should be achieved before arms reductions are negotiated. Idealists, by contrast, agree with Homer's observation in the *Odyssey* (ca. 700 B.C.) that "the blade itself incites to violence." This is repre-sented by Theory B in Figure 10.4.

While the logic of arms races seems obvious, and indeed occurs in some specific cases, it is also true that empirical research has not confirmed the arms race model as an overall phenomenon (Li, 1996; Weede, 1995; Travis, 1994). Similarly, it is not clear whether arms decreases cause or are caused by periods of improved international relations (Koubi, 1994). Instead, a host of domestic and international factors influence a country's level of armaments.

Figure 10.4

Three Theories about the Relationship between Arms, Tension, and War

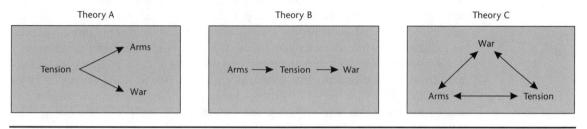

Theory A approximates the realist view. Theory B fits the idealist view of the causal relationship between arms, tension, and use. Theory C suggests that there is a complex causal interrelationship between arms, tension, and war in which each of the three factors affects the other two.

What this means is that the most probable answer to the chicken-and-egg debate about which should come first, political agreements or arms control, lies in a combination of these theories.

Many arms control skeptics also *doubt that arms control increases security.* There is no doubt that the number of nuclear weapons has dropped significantly since the 1980s, when they peaked at 69,490. By the beginning of 1998, that number had dropped by 48 percent to 36,110. Moreover, only about 13,700 of these were mounted in active weapons systems, with the rest in retirement, in reserve, or awaiting dismantlement. Does this make the world safer? Many arms control advocates take it as a given that fewer nuclear weapons make the world more secure. Realists take the opposite view and argue that without political agreements, arms reductions only serve to make one more vulnerable.

There are even some analysts who believe that arms, especially nuclear arms, have increased security. Early in the atomic age, Winston Churchill observed that "it may be that we shall by a process of sublime irony" come to a point "where safety will be the sturdy child of terror and survival the twin brother of annihilation" (Nogee & Spanier, 1988:5). His point was that nuclear weapons may have made both nuclear war and large-scale conventional war between nuclear powers too dangerous to fight. There are also scholars whose work supports this view. One study suggests that where great-power interests conflict, "peace . . . may depend on the maintenance of credible deterrent policies. . . . Consequently, the great powers such as the United States should not allow their pursuit of [defense cuts] to undermine the potency of their nuclear deterrent" (Huth, Gelpi, & Bennett, 1993:619). Similarly, another study concludes that without proportionate decreases by all nuclear powers, "U.S. and Russian force reductions below 1,000 warheads are [only] ambiguously stable" (Cimbala, 1995:165). If such views are correct, then eliminating or perhaps even substantially reducing nuclear weapons levels could make war more possible and decrease security.

While these realist doubts merit consideration, you should be chary of too easily accepting them. One caution is that such conclusions are disputed by other studies (Rotblat, Steinberger, & Udgaonkar, 1993). It is also important to be wary of the implication that idealists who advocate arms control are confined to academia and other places outside the "real" realm of the military and policy-making professions. That is not true. For example, General George Lee Butler, a former commander of the U.S. Strategic Command, with overall responsibility for U.S. nuclear forces, and 56 other retired generals and admirals from the various nuclear weapons countries issued a manifesto in 1996, which declared that nuclear weapons are now "of sharply reduced utility"; it called for "substantially reducing their numbers," and proclaimed that "the ultimate objective of phased reduction should be the complete elimination of nuclear weapons from all nations" (Schultz & Isenberg, 1997:87).

Technical Barriers   The complexity of weapons creates many technical barriers to arms control. *How to compare weapons systems* is one problem. Numbers alone mean little in arms negotiations because similar weapons have varying quality, capability, capacity, and vulnerability characteristics. When reducing ICBMs, for example, how does one equate a fixed-site U.S. Minuteman III with 3 MIRVED 170 kiloton warheads versus a road-mobile Russian SS-25 with a single 550 kiloton warhead? If you were a U.S. negotiator, would you eliminate one of your Minuteman IIIs for each SS-25 the Russians scrapped?

Verification difficulties pose another technical barrier to arms control. Countries suspect that others will cheat. A favorite phrase of Ronald Reagan's was "trust, but verify." Possible cheating can be divided into two levels: *break-out cheating* and *creep-out cheating*. A violation significant enough by itself to endanger your security would constitute a break-out. This possibility worries skeptics of arms control. Some are also hesitant about arms control because of what they believe would be the reluctance of democracies to respond to creep-out cheating. In this scenario, no single violation would be serious enough by itself to create a crisis or warrant termination of the treaty. Yet the impact of successive and progressive violations might seriously upset the balance of forces.

There have been great advances in verification procedures and technologies. The most important recent procedural advance is increased **on-site inspection (OSI)**. Countries are increasingly willing to allow others to inspect their facilities. In most cases, OSI has become part of recent arms control agreements. Yet as the problems UN inspectors have had in Iraq illustrate, even OSI is not foolproof, especially if the other side is not cooperative. National technical means (NTM) of verification using satellites, seismic measuring devices, and other equipment have also advanced rapidly. These have been substantially offset, however, by other technologies that make NTM verification more difficult. Nuclear warheads, for example, have been miniaturized to the point where ten or more can fit on one missile and could literally be hidden in the back of a pickup truck or even in a good-sized closet. Therefore, in the last analysis, virtually no amount of OSI and NTM can ensure *absolute verification*.

Because absolute verification is impossible, the real issue is which course is more dangerous: (1) coming to an agreement when there is at least some chance that the other side might be able to cheat or (2) failing to agree and living in a world of unrestrained and increasing nuclear weapons growth? Sometimes, the answer may be number 2. Taking this view while testifying before the U.S. Senate about the pending Chemical Weapons Convention, former secretary of state James A. Baker III counseled, "The Bush administration never expected the treaty to be completely verifiable and had always expected there would be rogue states that would not participate." Nevertheless, Baker urged ratification on the grounds that "the more countries we can get behind responsible behavior around the world . . . , the better it is for us."[14]

Domestic Barriers   Presidents and prime ministers are not kings. Especially in democratic countries, leaders have numerous other powerful domestic political actors that they must work with or, perhaps, overcome in the policy-making process. Some of the opposition that leaders face when they try to restrain or reduce arms comes from the ideological differences and policy doubts expressed above. In addition to these security and technical issues, other domestic opposition to arms control often stems from national pride and from the interrelationship among military spending, the economy, and politics.

National Pride   The Book of Proverbs tells us that "pride goeth before destruction," and this statement is equally applicable to modern arms acquisitions. Whether we are dealing with conventional or nuclear arms, national pride is a primary drive behind their acquisition. For many countries, arms represent a tangible symbol of strength and sovereign equality. EXPLOSION OF SELF-ESTEEM read one newspaper headline in India after that country's nuclear tests in 1998.[15] LONG LIVE NUCLEAR PAKISTAN read a Pakistani newspaper headline soon thereafter. "Five nuclear blasts have instantly transformed an extremely demoralized nation into a self-respecting proud nation . . . having full faith in their destiny," the accompanying article explained.[16]

Military Spending, the Economy, and Politics   President Dwight D. Eisenhower once told Americans that "every gun that is made, every warship launched, every rocket fired signifies, in the final sense, a threat to those who hunger and are not fed, those who are cold and are not clothed."[17] The trouble with this charge is that for all its stirring emotion, it may not be true.

Critics and supporters of defense spending have long argued over whether it harms or contributes to the economic health of the world and its individual countries. Critics charge that because military expenditures are in capital-intensive industries (require large sums of money but employ relatively few people to produce relatively few products), they create fewer jobs per dollar spent than more labor-intensive enterprises, such as education or construction.

Such arguments about the negative impact of arms spending have an element of truth. Still, they should be accepted only with caution. The relationship between defense spending and the overall economy is extremely complex, and scholars differ widely on specific impacts (Mintz & Stevenson, 1995; Graham, 1994). First, lower defense expenditures do not necessarily mean higher budget funds for nondefense programs. Nor is it always true that increased defense spending leads to cuts in domestic programs. It is more accurate to say that defense spending may affect domestic spending but that the impact is inconsistent, both over time and among programs.

Moreover, whatever the objective truth may be, it is perceptions and politics that often dominate the arms control debate within countries. Economically, arms are big business, and economic *interest groups* pressure their governments to build and to sell weapons and associated technology (Keller & Nolan, 1997). American industry, its workers, the cities and towns in which they reside, for example, have been prime supporters of military spending and foreign sales. Additionally, there are often *bureaucratic* elements in alliance with the defense industry and its workers. Finally, both interest groups and bureaucratic actors receive support from *legislators* who represent the districts and states that benefit from military spending. For example, part of the U.S. FY1999 budget passed by Congress included more $22 million C-130 transports than the Clinton administration wanted. The extra planes had the support of the Lockheed workers who produce them, the Air Force that will get them, and the legislators in whose districts the planes are either made or will be subsequently stationed. Indeed, the symbiotic linkage between these three domestic elements makes it probable that Eisenhower's concern about the military-industrial complex should be expanded to the military-industrial-congressional complex.

International Security Forces

The idea of forming international security forces to supplement or replace national military forces is a second approach to seeking security on the road less traveled by. This approach would enhance, not compete with, the first approach, arms control. Organizing for international security would emphasize international organizations and deemphasize national defense forces. Thus, the creation of international security forces and the first approach, arms control, are mutually supportive.

International Security Forces: Theory and Practice

The idea of seeking security through an international organization is not new. Immanuel Kant foresaw the possibility over two centuries ago in *Idea for a Universal History from a Cosmopolitan Point of View* (1784). "Through war, through the taxing and never-ending accumulation of armament . . . after devastations, revolutions, and even complete exhaustion," Kant predicted, human nature would bring people "to that which reason could have told them in the beginning": that humankind must "step from the lawless condition of savages into a league of nations" to secure the peace. These ideas have evolved into attempts to secure the peace through such international structures as the

Concert of Europe, the League of Nations, and the United Nations. An increased UN peacekeeping role has been especially evident, and other international organizations also have occasionally been involved in international security missions (Roberts, 1996; Sutterlin, 1995). The far-reaching language in the UN Charter related to peacekeeping can be found in the Web site box The UN Charter and International Security.

An important point is that while our discussion here will focus on the UN as a global organization, much of what is said is also applicable to regional intergovernmental organizations (IGOs) and their security forces. Most recently, the North Atlantic Treaty Organization (NATO) is providing international security forces in Kosovo. Also in Europe, the **Organization for Security and Cooperation in Europe (OSCE)** shows signs of evolving into a regional security structure. Established in 1973, the OSCE now has 54 members (including almost all the countries of Europe as well as Canada and the United States) and it has begun so-far limited efforts to send monitors and other personnel to try to resolve differences in several places, especially in the former Soviet republics. OSCE missions have operated in Albania, Bosnia, Croatia, Estonia, Georgia, Latvia, Macedonia, Moldova, Tajikistan, Ukraine, and several trouble spots within Russia, such as Chechnya. The largest OSCE peacekeeping effort involved the dispatch of 6,000 troops from eight countries to Albania in April 1997 when that country's political system collapsed into anarchy amid factional fighting. Beyond Europe, troops from the Economic Community of West African States (ECOWAS) helped return Liberia to some semblance of normalcy after a particularly horrendous civil war (Love, 1996). Nigerian-led ECOWAS forces were also instrumental in 1998 in ousting a military junta that had taken over in Sierra Leone and restoring the civilian government. And in the Western Hemisphere, the Organization of American States (OAS) has been active in trying to secure democracy in Haiti, to settle the border dispute between Ecuador and Peru, in demining efforts in Central America, and also in counterterrorism in the region.

To organize our discussion of global and regional international security forces, we can examine the theory and practice of their use according to three essential concepts: collective security, peacekeeping, and peacemaking.

Collective Security   One theory behind use of international security forces through the UN and other IGOs is the concept of **collective security**. This idea was first embodied in the Covenant of the League of Nations and is also reflected in the Charter of the United Nations. Collective security is based on four basic tenets. First, all countries forswear the use of force except in self-defense. Second, all agree that the peace is indivisible. An attack on one is an attack on all. Third, all pledge to unite to halt aggression and restore the peace, and all agree to supply whatever materiel or personnel resources are necessary to form a collective security force associated with the UN or some other IGO to defeat aggressors and restore the peace.

Collective security, then, is not only an appealing idea but one that works—domestically, that is. It has not been a general success on the international

A FURTHER NOTE
The UN Charter
and International
Security

A SITE TO SURF
Peacekeeping
and NATO

scene. In part, applying collective security is limited by problems such as how, in some cases, to tell the aggressor from the victim. But these uncertainties also exist domestically and are resolved. The more important reason that collective security fails is the unwillingness of countries to subordinate their sovereign interests to collective action. Thus far, governments have generally maintained their right to view conflict in terms of their national interests and to support or oppose UN action based on their nationalistic points of view. Collective security, therefore, exists mostly as a goal, not as a general practice. Only the UN intervention in Korea (1950–1953) and in the Persian Gulf (1990–1991) came close to fulfilling the idea of UN-authorized collective security.

Peacekeeping   What the United Nations has been able to do more often is implement a process commonly called **peacekeeping**. Apart from using military force, peacekeeping is quite different from collective security. The latter identifies an aggressor and employs military force to defeat the attacker. Peacekeeping takes another approach and deploys an international military force under the aegis of an international organization such as the UN to prevent fighting, usually by acting as a buffer between combatants. The international force is neutral between the combatants and must have been invited to be present by at least one of the combatants.

MAP
United Nations
Peacekeeping and
Collective Security
Operations

Some of the data regarding the use of UN peacekeeping forces and observer groups to help restore and maintain the peace were given in chapter 7 but bear repeating briefly here. During its first 52 years (1945-through early 1997), the United Nations sent over 750,000 soldiers, police officers, and unarmed observers from more than 111 countries to conduct 48 peacekeeping or truce observation missions. Over 1,550 of these individuals have died in UN service. The frequency of such UN missions has risen sharply, as we discussed at length in chapter 7. In 1998 there were 16 different armed UN forces of varying size, totaling 29,000 troops, in the field in Africa, Asia, the Caribbean, Europe, and the Middle East. The cost of these operations peaked at about $3.5 billion for FY1996, but has since declined to about $1 billion annually.

Several characteristics of UN peacekeeping actions can be noted. First, most have occurred in LDC locations, as evident in the Web site map. Second, UN forces have generally utilized military contingents from smaller or non-aligned powers. Canada has been the most frequent contributor, sending troops to assist the United Nations in 80 percent of the crises. The Scandinavian countries and Ireland have also been especially frequent participants. The end of the cold war has made it possible for the troops of larger powers to take a greater part in international security missions, and in mid-1998, 619 American and 253 Russian troops were in the field as UN peacekeepers.

Peacemaking   For all the contributions that UN peacekeeping efforts have made, they have sometimes been unable to halt fighting quickly (or even at all) or to keep the peace permanently. The numerous reasons for the limited effectiveness of UN forces can be boiled down to two fundamental and related problems: The first problem is that countries frequently do not support UN

After eight years of conflict, the two sides in Sierra Leone's bloody civil war signed a peace agreement in July 1999. It will be monitored by a UN observer force for the foreseeable future.

forces politically or financially. It is often difficult to get the self-interested UN Security Council members, especially the five, veto-wielding permanent members, to agree to authorize a UN mission. Even when the mission is authorized, it is often given a very narrow scope of authority to act and few troops. When the UN initially sent forces to the Balkans, the secretary-general asked for 35,000 peacekeepers. He got only 7,000, and their lack of heavy weapons and lack of authority to take strong action led, at one point, to UN troops being taken hostage and chained to potential targets to deter threatened action by NATO forces.

One response to the frustration with the inability of the UN to achieve greater success in preserving and restoring the peace has been an increasing number of calls for a more active UN military role called **peacemaking**. This new role would involve heavily armed UN forces with the authority to restore and maintain the peace. Such UN units would not only intervene where fighting had already broken out. They could also be deployed to imperiled countries before trouble has started, thereby putting an aggressor in the uncomfortable position of attacking UN forces as well as national defense forces.

International Security and the Future

What does the future hold for international security? While there are certainly many impediments on the path to international security, it would be foolish to dismiss the idea as impossible. First, it is in almost everyone's interest to prevent or contain crises, and there is a growing recognition that cooperation through the use of an international security force may often be a more effective way to maintain or restore peace than is continued reliance on unlimited national self-defense in a world capable of producing and using nuclear, biological, and chemical weapons (Cusack & Stoll, 1994). As such, the existence of peacekeeping has been largely a functional response to an international problem, and the increased number of missions, whether by the UN or one of the regional organizations, is evidence that the international security efforts are necessary and almost certainly have become a permanent part of world politics.

Second, it is important to see that many of the shortcomings of previous international security missions have not been due to an inherent failure of the UN (Wesley, 1997). Certainly the UN has problems, as any large political and bureaucratized organization does. The central problem, at least in Kofi Annan's view, is that the UN has "been asked to do too much with too little."[18]

Efforts to create the nucleus of a UN ready force continue but remain controversial (Rosenblatt & Thompson, 1998; Ratner, 1996; Haynes & Stanley, 1995). For the immediate future the approach may be to distinguish types of international security efforts, including peacekeeping and peacemaking missions, and to handle them differently (Diehl, Druckman, & Wall, 1998). Bernard Miyet, the undersecretary-general for peacekeeping contends that "peace enforcement and serious peace restoration campaigns will . . . be the responsibility of a coalition of interested countries using their own forces but with a green light from the Council." This model is much like the one of the NATO-led intervention in Bosnia in 1995. By contrast, according to Miyet, the UN would be responsible for "peacekeeping and light peace-restoration efforts."[19] A similar model is being employed in Kosovo.

Whatever the model, talk of an international security force may sound outlandish, but this is one of those junctures when it is important to remember the events during the life of Sarah Clark Knauss, who was born in 1880 and lives in Pennsylvania. When this centenarian was born, the Hague Conferences, the League of Nations, and the United Nations were all in the future. When she was of college age in the late 1890s, talk of international peacekeeping forces in Bosnia, Cyprus, Haiti, and other far-flung places would have been greeted with incredulous shakes of the head. Yet all these things exist today. The world needed them. Some say the world also needs an international security force.

Abolition of War

The last of the four approaches to security that we will examine in this chapter looks toward the abolition of war. For our purposes, we will divide the discussion into two parts: complete disarmament and pacifism.

Complete Disarmament

The most sweeping approach to arms control is simply to disarm. The principal argument in favor of disarmament is, as noted, the idea that without weapons people will not fight. This rests in part on sheer inability. **General** and complete disarmament (GCD) might be accomplished either through unilateral disarmament or through multilateral negotiated disarmament.

In the case of *unilateral disarmament,* a country would dismantle its arms. Its safety, in theory, would be secured by its nonthreatening posture, which would prevent aggression, and its example would lead other countries to disarm also. Unilateral disarmament draws heavily on the idea of pacifism, or a moral and resolute refusal to fight. The unilateral approach also relies on the belief that it is arms that cause tension rather than vice versa.

Negotiated disarmament between two or more countries is a more limited approach. Advocates of this path share the unilateralists' conviction about the danger of war. They are less likely to be true pacifists, however, and they believe one-sided disarmament would expose the peace pioneer to unacceptable risk.

The GCD approach has few strong advocates among today's political leaders. Even those who do subscribe to the ideal also search for intermediate arms limitation steps. Still, the quest goes on. The UN Disarmament Committee has called for GCD, and the ideal is often a valuable standard by which to judge progress as "real."

Pacifism

The second war-avoidance approach, pacifism, relies on individuals. As such, it very much fits in with the idea that people count and that you can affect world politics if you try. Unlike other approaches to security, pacifism is a bottom-up approach that focuses on what people do rather than a top-down approach that stresses government action.

Pacifism begins with the belief that it is wrong to kill (Norman, 1995). Leo Tolstoy, the Russian novelist and pacifist, told the Swedish Peace Conference in 1909 that "The truth is so simple, so clear, so evident . . . that it is only necessary to speak it out completely for its full significance to be irresistible." That truth, Tolstoy went on, "lies in what was said thousands of years ago in four words: *Thou Shalt Not Kill.*"

Beyond this starting point, pacifists have varying approaches. There are *universal pacifists,* who oppose all violence; *private pacifists,* who oppose personal violence but who would support as a last resort the use of police or military force to counter criminals or aggressors; and *antiwar pacifists,* who oppose political violence but would use violence as a last resort for personal self-defense.

The obvious argument against pacifism is that it is likely to get one killed or conquered. Those who support pacifism make several countercontentions. One is that there is a history of pacifism's being effective. As one scholar points out, "Nonviolence is as old as the history of religious leaders and movements." The analyst goes on to explain that "traditions embodied by Buddha and Christ have inspired successful modern political movements and leaders [such as] . . . "the Indian struggle for independence under the leadership of [Mohandas K.] Gandhi [in India] and the struggle of the American

Blacks for greater equality under the leadership of Martin Luther King Jr."
(Beer, 1990:16).

Gandhi was the great Indian spiritual leader (Burrowes, 1996). He began his career as an attorney trained in London, who earned what was then an immense sum of £5,000 annually practicing in Bombay. Soon, however, he went to South Africa, where, earning £50 a year, he defended Indian expatriates against white legal oppression. Gandhi returned to India in 1915 to work for its independence. He gave up Western ways for a life of abstinence and spirituality. Gandhi believed that the force of the soul focused on, to use the Hindi, *satyagraha* (truth seeking), and *ahimsa* (nonviolent soul) could accomplish what a resort to arms could not. He developed techniques such as unarmed marches, sit-downs by masses of people, work stoppages, boycotts, and what might today be called "pray-ins," whereby truth seekers *(satyagrahi)* could confront the British nonviolently. "The sword of the *satyagrahi* is love," he counseled the Indian people (Lackey, 1989:14). Gandhi became known as Mahatma (great soul) and was the single most powerful force behind Great Britain's granting of independence to India in 1947. The Mahatma then turned his soul toward ending the hatred and violence between Hindus and Muslims in independent India. For this, a Hindu fanatic, who objected to Gandhi's tolerance, assassinated him in 1948. Earlier, after the United States had dropped atomic bombs on Japan, Gandhi was moved to write that "mankind has to get out of violence only through nonviolence. Hatred can be overcome only by love. Counter-hatred only increases the surface as well as the depth of hatred." One has to suspect that had he been able to, Gandhi would have repeated this to the man who shot him.

Pacifists, especially antiwar pacifists, would also make a moral case against the massive, collective violence that is war. They would say that no gain is worth the loss. This view, pacifists would argue, has become infinitely more compelling in the nuclear age. Consider the description of Nagasaki filed by the first reporter who flew over the city after a U.S. bomber dropped an atomic bomb, killing at least 60,000 people. "Burned, blasted, and scarred," the reporter wrote, "Nagasaki looked like a city of death." It was a scene, he continued, of "destruction of a sort never before imagined by a man and therefore is almost indescribable. The area where the bomb hit is absolutely flat and only the markings of the building foundations provide a clue as to what may have been in the area before the energy of the universe was turned loose" (Lackey, 1989:112). Pacifists contend that even by the standards of just war conduct *(jus in bello)* adopted by nonpacifists, any nuclear attack would be unconscionable.

A final point about pacifism is that it is not an irrelevant exercise in idealist philosophy (Wehr, Burgess, & Burgess, 1994). There are some countries, such as Japan, where at least limited pacifism represents a reasonably strong political force. Moreover, in a changing world, public opinion, economic measures, and other nonviolent instruments may create what is sometimes called a "civilian-based defense." Indeed, there are efforts, such as the Program on Nonviolent Sanctions in Conflict and Defense at Harvard University's Center for International Affairs, which are working to show that those who favor nonviolence should not be considered "token pacifists" who are "tolerated as necessary to fill out the full spectrum of alternatives, with nonviolent means given serious considerations only for use in noncritical situations" (Bond, 1992:2). Instead, advocates of this approach believe that the successes of Gandhi, King, and others demonstrate that proactive techniques, including nonviolent protest and persuasion, noncooperation, and nonviolent intervention (such as sit-ins), can be successful.

It is true that pacifists are unlikely to be able to reverse world conflict by themselves. They are a tiny minority everywhere. Instead, pacifism may be part of a series of so-called peace creation actions. It is an idea worth contemplating.

Chapter Summary

1. War is the organized killing of other human beings. Virtually everyone is against that. Yet war continues to be a part of the human condition, and its incidence has not significantly abated.
2. The study of force involves several major questions. When and why does war occur? When it does happen, how effective is it, what conditions govern success or failure, and what options exist in structuring the use of force? The final question is how can we prevent war? This may be the most important question, but it is not the only question.
3. Although much valuable research has been done about the causes of war, about the best we can do is to say that war is a complex phenomenon that seems to have many causes. Some of these stem from the nature of our species, some from the existence of nation-states, and some from the nature and dynamics of the world political system.
4. Miltary power is both tangible and intangible. Tangible elements of power, such as tanks, are relatively easy to visualize and measure. Intangible elements of military power, such as morale and reputation, are much more difficult to operationalize.
5. Acquiring military power also has drawbacks. It creates the temptation to use it; makes others insecure; is costly. Some people argue, and others disagree, that spending too many resources on military power is a major factor in the decline of once-mighty countries.
6. Force can be used, threatened, or merely exist as an unspoken possibility. When it is used, its success requires much planning and skill. If force is to be used, it should be employed as a means, or tool, rather than, as sometimes happens, as an end in itself.
7. The nature of war is changing. Technology has enhanced killing power; nationalism has made war a patriotic cause; entire populaces,

instead of just armies, have become engaged; and the power to hurt has equaled or supplanted the power to defeat as a goal of conflict.

8. Force does not have to be used to have an impact. The possession of military power creates a backdrop to diplomacy, and the overt threat of force increases the psychological pressure even more.

9. The tools of force can be applied through arms sales and other methods of intervention.

10. When it is used, force can range from a very limited demonstration to a full-scale nuclear attack.

11. To look at the conduct of war, we examined intervention, traditional warfare, limited nuclear-biological-chemical (NBC) war, and strategic nuclear war. For each of the types of conflicts examined in this chapter, we looked at a variety of factors such as weapons and strategy. The MAD versus NUT debate, for instance, involves how to structure nuclear weapons systems and doctrines. We also saw that the ability to conduct war is continuing to change as new technology develops new weapons.

12. Security is not necessarily synonymous with either massive armaments or with disarmament. There are four approaches to security: unlimited self-defense, limited self-defense, international security, and avoidance of war.

13. From the standpoint of pure rationality, arms control, or the lack of it, is one of the hardest aspects of international politics to understand. Virtually everyone is against arms; virtually everyone is for arms control; yet there are virtually no restraints on the explosive arms escalation in which we are all trapped. It is a story that dates back far into our history, but unless progress is made, we may not have a limitless future to look forward to.

14. There are some people who believe that, because of the nature of humans and the nature of the international system, unlimited self-defense is the prudent policy. Advocates of this approach are suspicious of arms control.

15. People who favor limited self-defense would accomplish their goals through various methods of arms control.

16. There are many powerful arguments against continuation of the arms race. Arms are very costly, in direct dollars and in indirect impact on the economy. Arms are also very dangerous and add to the tensions that sometimes erupt in violence.

17. For all the possibilities, arms control historically has not been highly successful. There have been some important successes, though, such as the ban on atmospheric nuclear testing and the INF Treaty.

18. There are a number of ways to implement approaches to arms control, including arms reductions, limits on the expansion of arms inventories, and prohibitions against conventional arms transfers and nuclear proliferation.

19. There are also a number of junctures at which arms control can be applied, including the research and development and deployment stages. It is also possible to impose categorical limits to armaments, such as banning offensive weapons.

20. Despite the widespread agreement that something needs to be done, there are formidable political, technical, and other barriers to arms control.

21. There are heavy domestic pressures from the military-industrial complex and sometimes from the public against arms control.

22. Some people favor trying to achieve security through various international security schemes. The most likely focus of this approach would be the United Nations with a greatly strengthened security mandate and with security forces sufficient to engage in peacemaking, rather than just peacekeeping.

23. Avoidance of war is a fourth approach to security. One way to avoid war is to disarm. This makes violence difficult and may also ease tensions that lead to violence.

24. Individual and collective pacifism is another way to avoid violence. Pacifists believe that the way to start the world toward peace is to practice nonviolence individually and in ever-larger groups.

CONNECTEXT

Chapter 11

The International Economy:
A Global Road Map

O, behold, the riches of the ship is come onshore.

Shakespeare, *Othello*

If we make the average of mankind comfortable and secure, their prosperity will rise through the ranks.

Franklin D. Roosevelt

Given the degree to which this text has already discussed the interplay of politics and economics, you have already probably concluded correctly that, to a significant extent, economics is politics and vice versa. This chapter and the following one will continue to explicate how economics and politics intertwine. The subject of this chapter is the general nature of the international political economy (IPE), including IPE theories, and the situation of the economically developed countries (EDCs) of the North and the less developed countries (LDCs) of the South. Then chapter 12 will examine the traditional political path of national economic competition and also the alternative path of international economic cooperation.

It is important before delving into the subject to familiarize yourself with the distinctions between gross national product (GNP) and gross domestic

Chapter Outline

product (GDP), between either of those adjusted for purchasing power parity (GNP/PPP, GDP/PPP), and between **current dollars** and **real dollars**. It is also important that you understand how to read graphs (including 100-as-baseline graphs) and that you gain a sense of the origin and reliability of economic statistics. To do so, go to the section toward the end of the book entitled Technical Explanations and Matters of Terminology on page 433, and review the part on "Economics: Technical Terms and Sources."

Theories of International Political Economy

Before getting into the details of current global economic conditions, it is appropriate to examine the broad theories about the connection between economics and politics (Burch & Denemark, 1997; Pettman, 1996). As chapter 1 discussed, there are many scholars who believe that economic forces and conditions are the key determinants of the course of world politics. We also noted in chapter 1 that there are a variety of approaches to **International Political Economy (IPE)** and that they can be roughly divided into mercantilism, liberalism, and structuralism.

All of the three approaches are descriptive, in that they all purport to describe how and why conditions occur. As one scholar observes, "Clearly, a state perceives its international economic interests on the basis of a set of ideas or beliefs about how the world economy works and what opportunities exist within it" (Woods, 1995:161). The three approaches are also prescriptive, in that they make arguments about how policy should be conducted. These descriptions and prescriptions are summarized in Table 11.1. You should further note that economic nationalism is a realpolitik school of IPE, while economic internationalism and, especially, economic structuralism are idealist schools.

Economic Nationalism

The core of the economic nationalist doctrine is the belief that the state should use its economic strength to further national interests. By extension, economic nationalists also advocate using a state's power to build its economic strength. This approach is also called *economic statecraft* and, classically, *mercantilism*. Economic nationalists are realists who believe that conflict characterizes international economic relations and, therefore, that the international economy is a zero-sum game in which one side can gain only if another loses. From the economic nationalist perspective, political goals should govern economic policy because the aim is to maximize state power in order to secure state interests.

To accomplish their ends, economic nationalists rely on a number of political-economic strategies. These include:

Imperialism and neoimperialism are one set of practices of economic nationalism. Imperialism is the direct control of another land and its people for

(Continued on page 301)

Table 11.1

Approaches to International Political Economy

	Economic Nationalism	Economic Internationalism	Economic Structuralism
Associated terms	Mercantilism, economic statecraft	Liberalism, free trade, free economic interchange, capitalism, laissez-faire	Marxism, dependencia, neo-Marxism, neo-imperialism, neo-colonialism
Primary economic actors	States; alliances	Individuals, multinational corporations, IGOs	Economic classes (domestic and state)
Current economic relations	National-based conflictual; all countries compete with all other countries; zero-sum game	National conflict but cooperation increasing; non–zero-sum game	Structural conflict based on classes of countries; wealthy states exploit poor ones; zero-sum game
Goal for future	Preserve/expand state power, secure national interests	Increase global prosperity	Eliminate internal and international classes
Prescription for future	Follow economic policies that build national power; use political power to build national economy	Eliminate/minimize role of politics in economics; use politics	Radically reform system to end divisions in wealth and power between wealthy and poor countries
Desired relationship of politics and economics	Politics controls economic policy	Politics used only to promote domestic free markets and international free economic interchange	Politics should be eliminated by destruction of class system
View of states	Favorable; augment state power	Mixed; eliminate states as primary economic policy makers	Negative; radically reform states; perhaps eliminate states
Estimation of possibility of cooperation	Impossible; humans and states inherently seek advantage and dominance	Possible through reforms within a modified state-based system	Only possible through radical reform; revolution may be necessary

Conceptual sources: Balaam & Veseth (1996); Gilpin (1996); authors.

Analysts take very different approaches in describing how the international political economy works and in prescribing how it should work.

national economic gain. It was this motive that propelled Europeans outward to conquer the great colonial empires that dominated so much of the world until recent decades. Direct colonial control has largely died out, but many observers charge that neoimperialism (indirect control) continues to be a prime characteristic of the relationship that exists, or that EDCs try to achieve, between themselves and LDCs.

Economic incentives and disincentives provide a second set of economic nationalist practices. Countries that offer economic carrots, such as foreign aid and favorable trade policies, or that use economic sticks, such as sanctions, to promote the state's national interests are practicing economic nationalism. For example, the U.S. imposition in 1996 of economic sanctions on foreign companies that invest in Libya or Iran was explained by a supportive U.S. senator in pure economic nationalist terms: "This bill will cut the economic lifeline of Iran and Libya by stopping foreign investment in their energy industry."[1]

Protectionism and domestic economic support are a third set of tools that economic nationalists believe should be used to promote national power. "I use not porter [ale] or cheese in my family, but such as is made in America," George Washington once avowed.[2] From this perspective, economic nationalists are suspicious of economic interdependence on the grounds that it undermines state sovereignty and weakens the national economic strength. Economic nationalists would prefer that their respective countries use trade barriers, economic subsidies, and other

U.S. economic sanctions against Cuba have been in place since the early 1960s to help force political change in that country, but few of us ever think about the everyday impact they have on life in Cuba. Pictured here is Sergio Morales, the owner of a Harley-Davidson repair shop in Havana. The sanctions make it exceedingly difficult for him to find spare parts for the American-made motorcycle. And as he puts it, "Harleys are pure, unlike politics. For us it is about the bike itself, not where it comes from."

policies to protect national industries, especially those with military value.

Although the rationale is often muted, it is important to realize that economic nationalism has been and remains very much part of the policies of all countries. National leaders most often make decisions based on what is good for their country in the short run. It is also worth noting that while economic nationalists in the United States and many other countries are apt to describe themselves as believers in capitalism (free enterprise, a free-market economy), that self-image is inaccurate because economic nationalism requires government manipulation of the economy. Such interference violates the principles of the theory of capitalism, which hold that business should proceed largely or completely unimpeded by government.

Economic Internationalism

A second major theoretical and policy approach to IPE is economic internationalism. This approach is also associated with such terms as capitalism, laissez-faire, economic liberalism, and free trade. Economic internationalists are idealists. They believe that international economic relations should and can be conducted cooperatively because, in their view, the international economy is a non–zero-sum game in which prosperity is available to all.

Economic internationalists contend that the best way to create prosperity is by freeing economic interchange from political restrictions. Therefore, economic internationalists, in contrast to economic nationalists, oppose the use of national power to dominate other countries, the use of tariff barriers or domestic supports to distort the free flow of trade and investment, and the use of economic sanctions or incentives as policy tools.

The origins of economic liberalism lie in the roots of capitalism. In one of the early expositions of capitalist theory, *The Wealth of Nations* (1776), Adam Smith wrote that "it is not from the benevolence of the butcher, the brewer, or the baker, that we expect our dinner, but from their regard to their own interest." Smith believed that this self-interest constituted an "invisible hand" of competition that created the most efficient economies. Therefore, he opposed any political interference with the operation of the invisible hand, warning, "The statesman, who should attempt to direct private people in what manner they ought to employ their [finances] would assume an authority which . . . would nowhere be so dangerous as in the hands of a man who had folly and presumption enough to fancy himself fit to exercise it."

The pure capitalism advocated by Smith has few adherents today. Instead, most modern economic liberals favor using the state to modify the worst abuses of capitalism by ensuring that monopolies do not form and by taking other steps to ensure that the competition and unequal distribution of wealth inherent in capitalism is not overly brutal. Writing in the 1930s, the British economist John Maynard Keynes found classic capitalism "in many ways objectionable" but believed that "capitalism, wisely managed, can probably be made more efficient for attaining economic ends than any alternative system." What Keynes suggested was "to work out a social organization which shall be as efficient as possible without offending our notions of a satisfactory way of life" (Balaam & Veseth, 1996:49).

At the international level, Keynesian economics has influenced economic internationalists and the changes they advocate to traditional economic nationalist policies. They are moderate reforms, though, which would alter, but not radically change, either capitalism or the state-based international system. For example, the efforts in the 1940s to set up organizations such as the International Monetary Fund (IMF) and to promote trade through the General Agreement on Tariffs and Trade (GATT) reflect the Keynesian idea of using intergovernmental organizations (IGOs) and agreements to promote and, when necessary, to regulate international economic interchange. Modern liberals also favor such government interference as foreign aid and, sometimes, concessionary trade agreements or loan terms to assist LDCs to develop.

Still, modern liberals are capitalists, albeit modified ones, who are willing to use IGOs to promote the capitalism that they believe is the best engine of economic prosperity. The IMF, for example, presses countries to adopt capitalism in exchange for loans to help stabilize their currencies. Russia and the other former communist countries are among those who have found this to be true. In the words of Michel Camdessus, the IMF's managing director, "the stronger the program [of capitalist reform], the stronger the financing will be."[3]

In sum, modern economic liberals generally believe in eliminating political interference in the international economy. They also favor, however, using IGO and national government programs for two ends: (1) to ensure that countries adopt capitalism and free trade and (2) to ease the worst inequities in the system so that future competition can be fairer and current LDCs can have a chance to achieve prosperity. Thus economic liberals do not want to overturn the current political and economic international system. This support of a modified status quo is quite different from the more far-reaching changes advocated by economic structuralists.

A SITE TO SURF
The Role of the
Contemporary IMF

Economic Structuralism

The third major approach to IPE is called economic structuralism. Like the other two approaches, economic structuralism has both descriptive and prescriptive elements.

Economic structuralists believe that economic structure determines politics. That is, the conduct of world politics is based on the way that the world is organized economically. Structuralists contend that the world is divided between have and have-not countries and that the "haves" (the EDCs) work to keep the "have nots" (LDCs) weak and poor in order to exploit them. To change this, economic structuralists favor a radical restructuring of the economic system designed to end the uneven distribution of wealth and power.

The main variant of structuralist thought is the **dependencia theory**, which is also referred to as neo-Marxist theory and economic radical theory. Dependencia theorists argue that the exploitation of the LDCs by the EDCs is exercised through indirect control and is driven by the EDCs' need for cheap primary resources, external markets, profitable investment opportunities, and low-wage labor. The South produces low-cost, low-profit **primary products** such as agricultural products and raw materials. These support the EDCs' production of high-priced, high-profit manufactured goods, some of which are sold to the LDCs. It is, therefore, in the interest of capitalist exploiters to keep LDCs dependent. Therefore, economic structuralists say, **neocolonialism** (neoimperialism), which operates without colonies but is nevertheless imperialistic, has created a hierarchical structure in which the rich states in the center of the world economic system dominate the LDCs on the periphery of the system. The dependency of LDCs is maintained in a number of ways, such as structuring the rules and practices of international economics to benefit the North. The economic structuralists further contend that neoimperial powers corrupt and co-opt the local elite in LDCs by allowing them personal wealth in return for the governing of their countries in a way that benefits the North.

An economic radical would argue, for example, that the U.S. role in the Persian Gulf region dating back to World War II epitomizes neoimperialism. The devil's bargain, in the view of structuralists, is this: The United States protects or tries to protect the power of obscenely rich, profoundly undemocratic kings of oil-rich states. These would include, among others, the king of Saudi Arabia, the emir of Kuwait, the sultan of Oman, and (until he was toppled in 1979) the shah of Iran. For economic radicals, the U.S.-led intervention to restore the emir of Kuwait in 1991 and the continued presence of the U.S. military in the Persian Gulf region are just the latest examples of U.S. protection of the rich and undemocratic. The other half of the bargain is what the United States gets in return: cheap oil. Dependencia theorists say that the oil potentates pay back the United States for its protection of their lives of marble palaces, Rolls Royces, and Swiss bank accounts by ensuring that the price of petroleum stays low. This ensures the continued prosperity of the economy of the United States and the other EDCs. There can be little doubt that petroleum is a relative bargain, selling in 1999 at only 65 percent of its price in 1990. It is possible to argue that the decline in prices has been based on supply and demand, but structuralists would argue that those market forces have been manipulated through a greedy conspiracy between capitalist oil consumers and despotic oil producers.

Two Economic Worlds: North and South

Whether or not you subscribe to economic structuralist theory, it cannot be denied that the world is generally divided into two economic spheres: a wealthy North made up of EDCs and a less wealthy South composed of LDCs. The two geographical designations result from the fact that most EDCs lie to the north in North America and Europe and most LDCs are farther to the south in Africa, Asia, and Central and South America. There are exceptions, however, and what is important is that the North and the South are distinguished from each other by economic and political factors more than by their geographical position.

Two Economic Worlds: Analyzing the Data

The economic factor is the most objective distinction between North and South. The North is much wealthier than the South, as can be ascertained by examining countries (and the 1998 per capita GDP of each). That year the 24 wealthiest countries had an average per capita GDP of $25,510; the South's average per capita GDP was $1,250. The structure of the economy is another

Though we often think of Russia as a developed economy, it also exhibits many characteristics of a developing economy. This impoverished Russian pensioner must cope with extremely high rates of inflation, meager pension payments, and squalid living conditions. She is not alone; many others struggle with Russia's economic woes.

factor that generally differentiates EDCs from LDCs. The countries of the North tend to have more diverse economic bases that rely for their income on the production of a wide variety of manufactured products and the provision of diverse and sophisticated services. The countries of the South usually depend on fewer products for their income; these are often agricultural produce or raw materials, such as minerals. In 1994, for example, agriculture accounted for 14 percent of the GDPs of the South and only 2 percent of the GDPs of the North.

It is important to note that these two classifications and the overall numbers contain some difficulties. One is that, as with most attempts to categorize the world's political and economic divisions, the classifications are imprecise and subject to change. On the sole basis of annual per capita GDP, for example, the World Bank divides countries into four economic groups: low-income ($765 or less), lower-middle-income ($766–$3,035), upper-middle-income ($3,036–$9,385), and high-income (more than $9,386). These groupings are illustrated in the accompanying Web site map.

A second problem is that while the North is normally construed to be the high-income group, Greece (which is usually classified as part of the North) falls into the upper-middle-income group. Conversely, five countries (Israel, Kuwait, Singapore, South Korea, and the United Arab Emirates), which are usually classified as part of the South, fall into the high-income group. It is also important to note that some LDCs have moved a significant distance toward achieving a modern economic base. The **newly industrializing countries (NICs)**

MAP
GNP Per Capita

are still usually placed in the South by analysts, but countries such as South Korea ($9,700) and Israel ($15,920) could be classified as developed market economies. The NICs are also sometimes referred to as NIEs (newly industrializing economies) to accommodate the inclusion of Taiwan ($13,510).

A third issue of classifying countries economically relates to how to treat Russia, the other former Soviet republics (FSRs), and the former communist region of Eastern Europe. Some of these countries have a reasonable industrial base, although all of them have experienced significant economic difficulties during the transition. There are a few East European countries, such as Hungary ($4,120) that fall into the upper-middle-income group, but most former communist countries, including Russia ($2,240), are in the lower-middle-income group, and five of the Asian FSRs have per capita GDPs under $765, putting them in the World Bank's low-income category. Of this group of FSRs, Tajikistan ($340) is the poorest. Given the economic data, all these countries are treated here as LDCs.

A fourth concern centers on the difficulty of measuring and reporting economic data. All the statistics are only an approximation. If, for instance, you have ever had an odd job babysitting or raking leaves, have been paid for it, and have not reported your income to the government, then the GDP for your country is slightly lower than it should be. All countries, especially LDCs, have significant unrecorded economic activity. For this reason, major differences in economic circumstances, economic trends, and other macroeconomic indicators are more important than specific dollar figures.

A FURTHER NOTE
GDP–PPP: The Big
Mac Standard

Fifth, the cost of many items varies tremendously from country to country, undermining part of the relevance of some data, such as GDP. This issue is explored in the Web site box, GDP–PPP: The Big Mac Standard.

For all of these difficulties, the classification of the world into a North and a South is still useful. One reason is that the existence of a few exceptions should not disguise the fact that as a rule the countries of the South are poorer and less industrialized than those of the North. The data can be dry to read, but the reality behind that data is that, on average, the conditions of life for the citizens in the countries of the industrialized North are dramatically different from the living standards of those people who reside in the countries of the underdeveloped South. The North is a zone of relative plenty; the South is a scene of widespread deprivation.

Economic vulnerability is a second factor that unites most of the South and distinguishes it from the North. Even many upper-middle-income countries of the South have a shaky economic base that relies on one or a few products. For example, those LDCs that rely on petroleum production and export are at substantial risk when, as it has over the past few years, the price of oil declines.

Common political experiences of the LDCs are a third reason that the North-South distinction continues to be applicable. Most LDCs share a history of being directly or indirectly dominated by the EDCs of Europe and North America or, in the case of the former communist countries, by Russia.

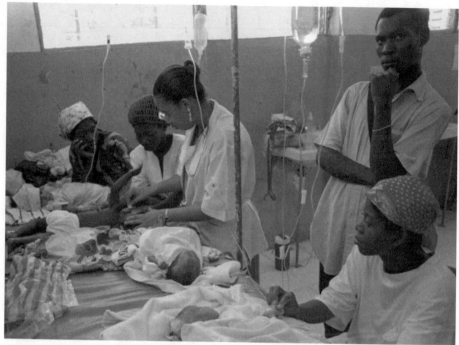

Although people in EDCs often take good health care for granted, most in LDCs cannot and do not. This hospital in Port-au-Prince, Haiti, is witness to the crowding and poor conditions characteristic of medical care in LDCs.

Two Economic Worlds: Human Conditions

Sensationalism is not the aim of this book. Still, it is hard to recount conditions of impoverishment in neutral, academic terms. Approximately 84 percent of the world's people live in the South, yet they produce only 19 percent of the global GDP. Far outpacing the fortunes of those who reside in LDCs, the 16 percent of the people who are fortunate enough to reside in the North produce 81 percent of the world's measurable GDP. Another telling calculation is that the richest 16 percent of the world's citizens produce $58 for every $1 produced by the 56 percent of the world's population who live in the low-income countries. Perhaps worse, that 58:1 ratio is up from a 30:1 ratio in 1960. As stark as these statistics are, their true meaning is in their social impacts. On average, compared with those who live in an EDC, people who live in an LDC are:

- 36 percent more likely to be illiterate if adults.
- 49 percent less likely to get a high school education.
- 5 times more likely to die before age 5.
- 38 percent less likely to have access to safe drinking water.
- 15 times more likely to die during childbirth.
- Dead 12 years earlier.

Figure 11.1

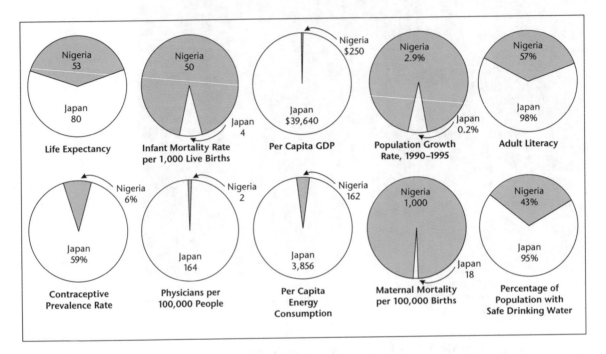

Life in the North and South: Japan and Nigeria

Data sources: UNDP (1997); World Bank (1997). Infant mortality measures deaths before age 5 per 1,000 live births; maternal mortality measures deaths during childbirth; per capita energy consumption is measured by kilograms of oil consumption or equivalents; contraceptive prevalence rate is the percentage of couples using any form of contraceptive practice. Each pie chart reflects each country's relative share of the sum of both numbers/percentages.

By most measures, life is vastly better in EDCs like Japan than in LDCs like Nigeria. These pie charts show the relative deprivation of Nigerians compared to Japanese, but no statistical representation can capture human realities. Just one example is that Nigerian children are 13 times more likely to die before age 5 than are Japanese children.

MAP
The Index
of Human
Development

The scope of the deprivation that many in the South suffer also boggles the mind when the total number of humans affected is calculated. Some 1.3 billion people live on less than $1 a day. Literacy and education are beyond the dreams of many. There are 842 million illiterate adults and 80 million children in the South who are not in school. The perils to health are everywhere. Some 1.2 billion people do not have access to safe drinking water. For every dollar spent on health care in the South, $46 are spent on health care in the North. Even those medical facilities that do exist in the South are overwhelmed. Each physician in the South is responsible for 5,833 people, compared to only 350 people for a physician in the North; 766 million people in the South have no access to any kind of health care. These conditions lead to disease and death on a wide scale. Some 158 million children in the South are malnourished; more than 12 million toddlers die each year. One-third of the people born in the South do not live to age 40.

Beyond the overall North-South statistics, it is also instructive to compare lives in two countries: Japan of the North and Nigeria of the South. The two countries have approximately equal populations, yet the statistical comparison of the two reflects a life of advantage for the Japanese and of disadvantage for the Nigerians, as shown in Figure 11.1.

Nor is the future bright for many in the South. Some indicators, such as literacy rate, physicians per capita, and life expectancy, show advances in absolute conditions in the South. Overall, though, the economic gap between North and South is widening. In 1990 the per capita GDPs of the South ($840) and the North ($19,590) left a gap of $18,750. That gap—"gulf" is a better word—had spread to $24,260 in 1998 between the North ($25,510) and the South ($1,250).

The worst news is that conditions are declining in some countries. One-third of the low-income economies (often referred to as **least developed countries, LLDCs**) have had their per capita GDPs decline over the last 25 years. Sub-Saharan Africa is a particularly depressed region. The combined GDP of the region's countries declined by 20 percent between 1980 and 1994. Even though the United States and sub-Saharan Africa have approximately equal populations, the U.S. total GDP is 23 times larger than that of sub-Saharan Africa. The region has the world's highest birthrate, and the rapidly rising population is overwhelming agriculture. Per capita food production declined in 82 percent of the region's countries since 1980. Only 51 percent of the region's population has access to clean drinking water; there is but one physician for every 18,514 people; adult illiteracy is 43 percent; life expectancy is only 50 years. It is unnecessary to recite more grim statistics in order to document that—relatively speaking and, in some cases, absolutely— the rich are getting richer and the poor are getting poorer.

Two Economic Worlds: Approaches to North-South Relations

Documenting the plight of the South is easier than agreeing on the causes or the remedies. An initial question is: Why did the gap between North and South develop? One factor was circumstance. The industrial revolution came first to Europe and, by extension, to North America. Industrialization brought the North both wealth and technology that, in part, could be turned into sophisticated weapons that overpowered the more rudimentarily armed people of the South. The need for primary products to fuel the North's factories and the search for markets in which to sell those products led to increased direct colonization and indirect domination. Nationalism intensified this process as countries also sought colonies to symbolize their major-power status. As a result of all these factors, Asians, Africans, Latin Americans, and others were exploited to benefit the industrialized, imperialist countries. This pattern existed for a century and in some cases much longer. Politically, most of the LDCs achieved independence in the decades following World War II. Economically, though, the South remains disadvantaged in its relationship with the North. In many ways that we will explore later, the international economic system remains stacked against the LDCs. What should and can be done? More specifically, what can and should the countries of the North do to assist the countries of the South?

The Economic Nationalist Approach

Economic nationalists operate from a realpolitik orientation and believe that each country should look out for itself first and foremost. Therefore, economic nationalists argue that an EDC should be governed by its own national interest when formulating trade, investment, and aid policies toward the South. Furthermore, economic nationalists suspect that the South's calls for greater equity are, in essence, attempts to change the rules so that the LDCs can acquire political power for themselves.

Economic nationalists view the political economy as a zero-sum game in which gains made by some players inevitably mean losses for other players. It is a perspective that leads economic nationalists to worry that extensive aid to LDCs may be counterproductive for both the donor and the recipient. This reasoning often uses a *lifeboat analogy*. This image depicts the world as a lifeboat that can support only so many passengers. The people of the EDCs are in the boat. The billions of poor are in the sea, in peril of drowning and clamoring to get aboard. The dilemma is that the lifeboat is incapable of supporting everyone because there are not enough resources. Therefore, if everyone gets in, the lifeboat will sink and all will perish. The answer, then, is to sail off with a sad but resolute sigh, saving the few at the expense of the many in the interest of common sense. An extension of this logic, economic nationalists suggest, is that providing food and medicine to the already overpopulated LDCs only encourages more childbearing, decreases infant mortality, and increases longevity, and thereby worsens the situation by creating more people to flounder and drown in the impoverished sea.

The Economic Internationalist Approach

Economic internationalist theorists believe that development can be achieved within the existing international economic structure. This belief is related to the idealist approach to general world politics. Economic internationalists believe that the major impediments to the South's development are its weakness in acquiring capital, its shortage of skilled labor, and some of its domestic economic policies, such as centralized planning and protectionism. These difficulties can be overcome through free trade and foreign investment supplemented by loans and foreign aid and through reduced government interference in the economy. Such policies, economic internationalists believe, will allow unimpeded international economic exchange among states, which will eventually create prosperity for all. Thus, for economic internationalists, the global economy is a non–zero-sum game. They look to integrate LDCs into the world economic system by eliminating imperfections in the current system while maintaining the system's basic structure and stability.

As for the lifeboat analogy, economic internationalists contend that we are not in (or out of) a lifeboat at all. Instead, they say, we are all inescapably sailing on the same vessel, perhaps the SS *World*, to a common destiny. From this perspective, we can all reach the home port of prosperity, or we can all suffer the fate of the *Titanic*, which struck an iceberg and sank in the North Atlantic in 1912. The 1,513 passengers who drowned came from both luxurious first-class and steerage accommodations, but they found in death the equality inherent in all humans. Commenting in this vein about Brazil, one reformer noted that the country, with its gulf between rich and poor, "is like a huge ocean liner that has been slowly sinking. The elite are in the top cabins, so they haven't been noticing as the rest of us have been going under water. But now the water is beginning to tickle their feet and they see that they're on the same sinking ship."[4]

The Economic Structuralist Approach

Structuralist scholars believe that the political-economic organization of the world patterns of production and trade must be radically altered for the LDCs to develop. In terms of the lifeboat analogy, economic structuralists believe that not only should the poor be allowed into the boat but that they should also at least share command with, and perhaps supplant, the wealthy captains who have been sailing the vessel in their own interests and at the expense of others. Marxists would not shun a peaceful change of command if that were possible, but they are not averse to a mutiny if necessary.

It is obvious that the three different IPE approaches to the general conduct of global economic affairs and to North-South relations present markedly different descriptions of, and even more dramatically different prescriptions for, the conduct of political-economic relations. To help decide which of the three contains the greatest element of truth, it is appropriate to turn to an examination of the history of the international political economy.

The Growth and Extent of the International Political Economy

Economic interchange between politically separate people predates written history. Trading records extend back to almost 3000 B.C., and archaeologists have uncovered evidence of trade in the New Stone Age, or Neolithic period (9000–8000 B.C.). Since then, economics has become an ever more important aspect of international relations. This is evident in expanding trade and the resulting increased interrelationship between international economic activity and domestic economic circumstances. We can see this by examining trade, investment, and monetary exchanges and by looking at both the general expansion of each of these factors and the uneven pattern of each.

Trade

Before beginning our discussion of the historical growth and current extent of trade, it is necessary to note the two elements that compose trade: goods and services. **Merchandise trade** is what people most frequently associate with imports and exports. These goods are tangible items and are subdivided into two main categories: primary goods (raw materials) and manufactured goods. **Services trade** is less well known but also important. Services include things that you do for others. When American architects receive pay for designing foreign buildings, when U.S. insurance companies earn premiums for insuring foreign assets or people, when American movies and other intellectual properties earn royalties abroad, when U.S. trucks carry goods in Mexico or Canada, the revenue they generate is payment for the export of services. These services are a major source of income for countries, amounting in 1997 to $1.3 billion, or 20 percent of the entire flow of goods and services across international borders.

The trade in services can also have a significant impact on a country's balance of trade. The United States in 1997 had a merchandise-trade deficit of $197 billion. To the U.S. advantage, this was somewhat offset by an $87 billion services-trade surplus, which reduced the overall trade deficit to $110 billion. It is also worth pointing out that exported services do not have to be performed overseas. American colleges and universities, for example, are the country's fifth largest exporter of services. More than 454,000 foreign students spent over $6 billion for tuition, room, and board at U.S. institutions of higher learning and at least another $3 billion on other aspects of college life ranging from textbooks to pepperoni pizzas.

A General Pattern of Expanding Trade

Trade is booming in the twentieth century, and the international flow of goods and services is a vital concern to all world states (Moon, 1996). In 1913 the entire flow of goods in world commerce totaled only $20 billion. In 1997 world trade stood at over $6.4 trillion. Even considering inflation, this represents a tremendous jump in world commerce. Figure 11.2 depicts the rise in the dollar volume of trade. Trade growth has been especially rapid during the post–World War II era of significant tariff reductions. During the 1913 to 1948 period of world wars, depression, and trade protectionism, trade increased at an average annual rate of only 0.8 percent. The postwar period has seen average annual increases at a rate of approximately 9 percent. The rapid growth of trade has been caused by a number of factors, including productive technology, resource requirements, materialism, transportation, and free trade philosophy.

Productive Technology   The industrial revolution, which began in eighteenth-century Europe, is one factor behind increased trade. As productivity increased, so did the supply of goods. From 1705 to 1780, prior to industrialization, world industrial production increased only slowly at an annual rate of only 1.5 percent, and trade increased at only about 1 percent a

(Continued on page 313)

Figure 11.2

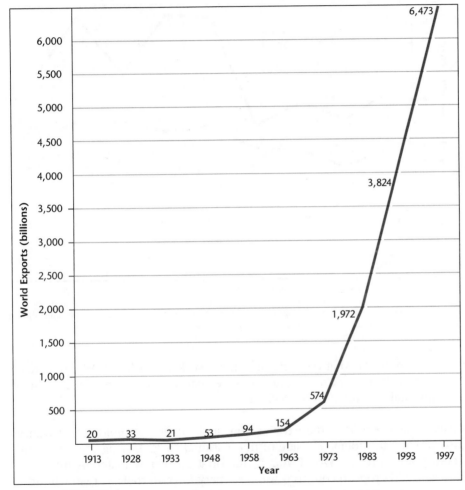

Increasing World Trade (in Billion Dollars)

Data source: IMF (1998).

Trade, measured here in current dollar exports, has grown meteorically during recent decades. This growth is one sign of the vastly increased importance of international economic relations to the health of individual countries and their citizens.

year. In the years that followed industrialization, productivity rapidly increased and so did the volume of trade.

This pattern of increases in both industrial output and trade has generally continued to the present, as you can see in Figure 11.3. The figure demonstrates that trade growth helps drive economic expansion by comparing the growth of two inflation-adjusted measures: the volume of trade (exports) and real GDP. Again, the importance of these numbers is that trade consumed

Figure 11.3

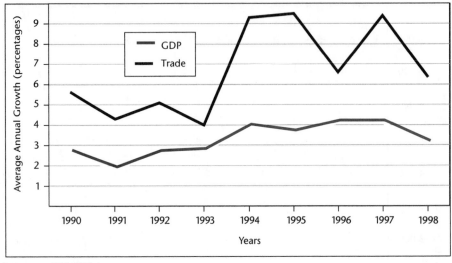

The Growth of World Trade Volume and Real GDP

Data source: IMF (1998a).

Trade volume is a measure of inflation, exchange rates, and unit prices. The years 1997 and 1998 are IMF estimates. During the 1990s, the growth of trade has continued to outpace the growth of national economies. This means that more and more of what countries produce is sold abroad and, therefore, national economic health is ever more dependent on trade.

more and more of what countries and their workers produced. Without trade, then, or with a marked decline in trade, national economies would slow, perhaps stall, or might even decline.

Resource Requirements Industrialization and other technological advances also affected the "demand" side of international trade. During the nineteenth century and through World War II, importation of raw materials by the industrialized European countries was a primary force in trade as manufacturing needs both increased demand for raw materials and outstripped domestic resource availability. During the late 1800s, for example, raw materials accounted for 97 percent of all French and 89 percent of all German imports.

In the post-1945 world economy, primary resources have declined both as a percentage of total world trade and as a percentage of the imports of the EDCs. With respect to merchandise trade, primary resources decreased from one-half of all countries' imports in 1960 to only about one-fifth in the late 1990s. In 1996, for instance, 87 percent of all U.S. imported goods were manufactured products, while only 13 percent were agricultural and mineral products. This is due to increased trade in manufactured goods, however, rather than to a decline in the demand for primary resources, which over the long term has remained strong, if often unstable.

**MAPS
Energy
Requirements
Per Capita**

**Production of
Crucial Materials**

Materialism   The rise in the world's standard of living, especially in the industrialized countries, has also contributed to "demand" pressure on international trade. More workers entered the wage-producing sector, and their "real" (after inflation) wages went up. The real wages of English craftspersons held relatively steady between 1300 and 1800, for instance, but then, beginning in 1800, after the industrial revolution, more than doubled by the 1950s.

Here again, the trend has continued into the current era. The workers of the wealthier countries have especially enjoyed increased real wages. The average real wage in the industrialized countries, for example, rose 1.8 percent annually between 1980 and 1997. This strengthens demand because individuals have more wealth with which to purchase domestic and imported goods.

Transportation   Technology has also increased our ability to transport goods. The development of railroads and improvements in maritime shipping were particular spurs to trade. They both increased the volume of trade that was possible and decreased per unit transportation costs. Less than two centuries ago, all products had to be carried abroad in sailing ships and distributed by wagon. Now foreign commerce is carried around the world by more than 25,000 oceangoing merchant vessels capable of carrying 252 million tons of cargo and, in just the United States, delivered by almost 2 million tractor-trailer trucks and by more than 18,000 locomotives (each with an average of 2.7 million horsepower) pulling almost 1.2 million freight cars.

Free Trade Philosophy   The 1930s and early 1940s were a period of global trauma, marked first by great economic depression and then by World War II. One cause for these miseries, it was said, was the high tariffs that had restricted trade and divided nations. To avoid a recurrence, the United States took the lead in reducing barriers to international trade. The General Agreement on Tariffs and Trade (GATT) came into being in 1947 when countries accounting for 80 percent of world commerce agreed to work to reduce international trade barriers. As a result of this and a series of related efforts, world tariff barriers dropped dramatically. American import duties, for example, dropped from an average of 60 percent in 1934, to 25 percent in 1945, to a current level of less than 4 percent. Other industrialized countries' tariffs have similarly dropped. Tariffs, as we will soon see, are not the only trade barrier, but their sharp reductions have greatly reduced the cost of imported goods and have strongly stimulated trade. Established by the most recent GATT round of negotiations, the World Trade Organization (WTO) was created in 1993 to provide a stronger mechanism to oversee world trade in the years ahead. The WTO will be discussed in more detail in the next chapter.

Uneven Patterns of Trade: North and South

The historical growth of trade, it is important to note, has not occurred evenly throughout the world. Instead, three facts about the patterns of international commerce stand out. First, as depicted in Figure 11.4, trade is overwhelmingly dominated by the EDCs in the North. These countries amass almost 77 percent

A SITE TO SURF
E-Commerce
and the WTO

Figure 11.4

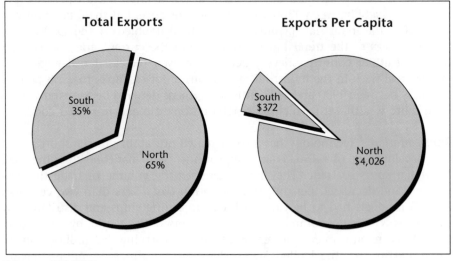

Share of Export Trade of the North and South

Total Exports

South 35%

North 65%

Exports Per Capita

South $372

North $4,026

Data source: IMF (1996).

The pattern of world trade is very uneven. The North dominates the export market, from which countries earn profits.

MAP
Exports of Primary Products

of the exports in goods and services and 67 percent of the merchandise exports. The percentage of world trade shared by the LDCs is relatively small, especially in per capita figures.

A second, and related, pattern of world trade is that only a small percentage of global commerce occurs among LDCs. Trade among LDCs in 1997 accounted for a scant 15 percent of all world trade. Moreover, the EDCs provided 60 percent of the LDCs' imports and bought 54 percent of their exports. This pattern of trade leaves the LDCs heavily dependent on the EDCs for export earnings and, thus, in a vulnerable position.

A third important trade pattern involves types of exports. EDCs predominantly export manufactured and processed products. LDCs export mostly primary products, such as food, fibers, fuels, and minerals. The United States and Chile provide a good comparison. Of all U.S. goods exported, manufactured products account for 82 percent and primary products for 18 percent. Chile's exports are just the opposite, with manufactured goods at 18 percent and primary products at 82 percent. To make matters worse, half the value of Chile's exported primary products come from just one commodity: copper. This dependence on primary products for export earnings leaves the LDCs in a disadvantaged position because the prices of primary products expand more slowly than those of manufactured goods and because world demand for primary products is highly volatile.

International Investment

Trade has not been the only form of international economic activity that has grown rapidly. There also has been a parallel expansion of international financial ties. This flow of investments can be examined by reviewing types of foreign investments and multinational corporations.

Foreign Direct and Portfolio Investment

One aspect of increased financial ties is the growth of investment in other countries. When Americans invest in British or Nigerian companies, or when Canadians invest in U.S. corporations, a web of financial interdependency is begun. Such international investment has long existed but has accelerated greatly since World War II. In 1950 U.S. direct investment abroad was $11.8 billion. That figure grew to $78.1 billion in 1970 and in 1996 stood at $796 billion, based on current value. Investors in other industrialized countries and a few investors from LDCs have added to the international flow of investment capital. Total world **foreign direct investment (FDI)**, involving a major stake in foreign companies or real estate, is well over $2 trillion, including $630 billion in direct investments in the United States. **Foreign portfolio investment (FPI)** in stocks and bonds that does not involve the control of companies and real estate is measured in the trillions. For the United States alone, foreign investors hold just over $2.4 trillion in U.S. assets, and Americans own over $1.5 trillion in foreign portfolio investment.

Like most areas of international economics, the movement of investment in the world is not evenly distributed. Since few investors are from the South, the flow of profits from investment mostly benefits the North. Certainly, the flow of investment capital has benefits for recipient countries, but even here the distribution is mixed. About two-thirds of all FDI, and an even greater percentage of FPI, is made in EDCs. The one-third of the FDI that now flows into LDCs is a significant jump. Here again, though, the flow is highly uneven. China takes in about 82 percent and India another 6 percent of the investment that goes to the 49 poorest countries (LLDCs), leaving relatively little funding available to the other 47 LLDCs.

International Investment and Multinational Corporations

To understand the flow of international investment, it is especially important to analyze the growth and practices of **multinational corporations (MNCs)**. These firms, also called transnational corporations (TNCs), are at the forefront of the international movement of investment capital and private loans among countries.

An MNC is a private enterprise that includes subsidiaries operating in more than one state. This means more than merely international trading. Rather, it implies ownership of manufacturing plants and/or resource extraction and processing operations in a variety of countries. Additionally, MNCs conduct business abroad that supply services, such as banking, insurance, and transportation. Many observers therefore contend that MNCs are transnational organizations with operations that transcend national boundaries (Pauly & Reich, 1997).

There are now tens of thousands of MNCs operating in more than one country. Not only are MNCs numerous, they also pack enormous economic muscle. Just the top 50 world corporations in 1997 had combined assets of $8.8 trillion, a combined gross corporate product (GCP) of $2.7 trillion, and over 7.1 million workers. Moreover, the size of some individual MNCs is immense. Using a company's revenue (GCP) as a standard, the biggest manufacturing MNC in 1997 was General Motors with a GCP of $161.3 billion. About 30 percent of GM's GCP came from foreign sales, and over a quarter of GM's $257 billion in assets were located outside the United States. And if GM's GCP counted as its GDP, the company would have been the world's twenty-second largest economy. Its workforce of 628,000 is larger than the populations of many small countries.

A SITE TO SURF
1999 Fortune
Global 5 Hundred

It is also worth noting that the MNCs are overwhelmingly based in the North. Therefore they contribute to the wealth and economic power of the EDCs at, some analysts would say, the expense of the South. All of the top 50 MNCs are headquartered in an EDC, with the majority (58 percent) based in the United States. Of the top 500 MNCs, 175 are American and 112 are Japanese, for 57 percent of the total. The remaining EDCs combine for another 181 of the top 500. Thus, 95 percent of the top 500 are based in the North. Only 25 of the biggest corporations are in LDCs. Even these are concentrated, though, with just two countries, South Korea (13 MNCs) and Brazil (7 MNCs), accounting for most of the top 500 MNCs headquartered in an LDC.

Monetary Relations

The increased flow of trade and capital means that **monetary relations**, including exchange rates, interest rates, and other monetary considerations, have become an increasingly significant factor in both international and domestic economic health. This has always been true, but as trade and other economic relations have expanded, the importance of monetary interchange has increased proportionately. To begin to explore the complex area of monetary relations here and in later the next chapter, we can look at the increasing globalization of the money system, how exchange rates work, and the calculation and impact of the balance of payments (Kirshner, 1995).

The Globalization of Money

Increased trade, investment, and other factors have set off a torrent of money moving in international channels. The amount of currency exchange has reached such a point that it is impossible to calculate very accurately, but it is not unreasonable to estimate that the currency flow is $1.5 trillion a day, or $548 trillion a year. About two-thirds of this moves through the banking centers in just four countries: Germany, Japan, the United Kingdom, and the

United States. With just these four leading banking centers exchanging at least $954 billion a day, this represents a phenomenal increase from the 1989 levels of $550 billion a day, or $200.8 trillion a year in currency exchanges. Central banks use their monetary reserves (foreign currencies and gold) to try to control exchange rates by buying or selling currency. The rapid rise in the rate of currency exchange means, however, that with the combined total reserves in 1995 of the world's countries and the IMF at $899 billion, the ability to control currency fluctuations is inadequate. This endangers monetary exchange stability and, by extension, economic prosperity.

To accommodate the globalization of money, there has been a parallel globalization of banking and other financial services. In a relatively short period of time, banks have grown from hometown to national to international enterprises. Another indicator of increased international financial ties is the level of international lending by private banks. Commercial banks in 1995 held approximately $9 trillion in foreign deposits and had about the same amount in outstanding international loans. Another aspect of the growth of global financial services is the merging of heretofore separate banking, insurance, stock and bond brokerage houses, and other financial enterprises into huge, multipurpose financial service conglomerates. The merger in 1998 of Citicorp and Travelers Group into Citigroup created a global giant with $698 billion in assets. Citicorp subsidiaries include Citibank, the second largest U.S. bank, which operates in nearly 100 countries, and Global Consumer Business, the world's largest issuer of credit cards (about 60 million). The Travelers Group offers a wide range of insurance products around the world, and it also controls subsidiaries such as Primerica Financial Services, and the now-merged major brokerage houses, Salomon Brothers and Smith Barney.

As with most other sources of economic power, the control of money and banking is largely dominated by the North and little influenced by the South. The 13 percent of the countries that are EDCs hold 53 percent of all foreign reserves. With the exception of a few offshore banking havens controlled by the North, the banks of the LDCs hold only 5 percent of all foreign deposits and have made only about 3 percent of all foreign loans.

Exchange Rates

Of all the facets of international economic relations, the least understood is the importance of the ebb and flow of the world's currencies. **Exchange rates** are, very simply, the values of two currencies in relation to each other—for example, how many U.S. dollars per Japanese yen and vice versa. The exchange rate is important because it affects several aspects of the balance of payments and the health of domestic economies. Fundamentally, a decline in the exchange rate of your country's currency in relation to another country's currency means that things you buy in or from that country will be more expensive and things that the other country buys in or from you will be less expensive. If your country's currency increases in value, things you buy in or from that country will be less expensive and things that the other country

These Brazilian stock traders are trying to cope with the volatility of their stock market in the aftermath of a Brazilian currency devaluation in January 1999. The devaluation sent shock waves throughout the world financial community and is evidence of the interdependence that exists across global financial centers.

buys in or from you will be more expensive. For a fuller explanation of this, see the entry "How Exchange Rates Work" in Technical Explanations and Matters of Methodology on page 433.

One example of the dramatic change in the value of a currency involves the exchange rate of the U.S. dollar versus Japan's yen (¥) since 1985. In January of that year, one dollar was worth 258 yen ($1 = ¥258). Then the dollar's value began to decline, dropping 70 percent at its low of $1 = ¥80 in mid-1995. Japan's economic woes reversed that trend, with the yen falling from its 1995 rate by 32 percent to $1 = ¥106 in September 1999. The normal way of discussing this change would be to say that the U.S. dollar in 1995 was significantly weaker than it was in 1985 versus the yen and in 1999 significantly stronger. Does weak equal bad and strong equal good, though? That depends.

If you are an American, the dollar's rally against the yen between 1995 and 1999 is good news if you are going to buy a Japanese automobile. It will cost less. Traveling in Japan will also be less costly because your dollar will be worth more there. On a more general level, if your national currency is strengthening, inflation will probably go down in your country because the foreign products you buy will be less expensive. Also, your standard of living may go up because you can by more imported goods to improve your material well-being.

If, on the other hand, you are a U.S. manufacturer trying to sell something to the Japanese, the dollar's rise is bad news because your product's price will rise in those countries and you will probably export less. A declining currency, then, benefits businesses that export, and this may translate into more jobs as factories expand to meet new orders.

Balance of Payments

A SITE TO SURF
Currency
Conversion Lessons

Along with exchange rates, another complicated aspect of the international political economy that is central to understanding a country's overall health in the global economy is that country's balance of payments. Many of the matters that we have already discussed, including exports and imports, the ebb and flow of investment capital and investment returns, and international borrowing and other financial flows, combine to determine a country's **balance of payments**, a figure that represents the entire flow of money into and out of a country—that is, credits minus debits.

Credits (Money Entering the Country)	Debits (Money Leaving the Country)
1. Export of goods	1. Import of goods
2. Export of services	2. Import of services
3. Foreign visitors (military, tourists)	3. Citizens' travel abroad
4. Foreign aid received	4. Foreign aid given
5. Inflows of capital (loans, investments)	5. Outflows of capital
6. Profits and interest earned from foreign investments	6. Profits and interest paid to foreigners
7. Government receipts from abroad	7. Government overseas expenditures

Understanding the components of the overall balance of payments is important in determining whether a country has a net inflow or a net outflow of financing. The United States has since 1989, when it had a balance-of-payments surplus of $15.3 billion, steadily amassed larger and larger balance-of-payments deficits, reaching $113.0 billion in 1997. The primary cause has been the mounting U.S. merchandise trade deficit, which grew from $101 billion in 1990 to 170 billion in 1996. Payments on the national debt are a second factor in the growing U.S. balance-of-payments deficit. With an accumulated federal debt over $5 trillion, the annual interest payment for FY1996 came to $344 billion. Of that, 29 percent ($100 billion) went to foreign bondholders.

The dollar amounts of the deficit seem huge, but so is the U.S. economy. A relative comparative standard shows us that the U.S. deficit was a not-too-worrisome 1.8 percent of the U.S. GDP in 1990, but there has been an inching upward, with the deficit at 2.2 percent of the U.S. GDP in 1996. It is the trend rather than the specific amounts that are the cause of most concern, with the IMF estimating that the U.S. deficit will reach $228 billion (2.6 percent of GDP) in 1999.

It is also worth noting that a positive balance-of-payments does not automatically mean prosperity. Beset by lagging domestic demand, poor banking practices, and other problems, Japan's economy was stagnant through most of the mid-1990s, despite an average balance-of-payments surplus (1994–1997) of $80.2 billion, equal to 1.7 percent of GDP. Still, a chronic deficit or one that is a high percentage of GDP (such as Russia's: 6.4 percent in 1996) eventually depletes a country's financial strength.

The Impact of Expanded Economic Interchange

The expansion of world trade and investment has profoundly affected countries and their citizens. Economic interdependence has inexorably intertwined national and international economic health.

Increased Economic Interdependence

One result of increased international trade, financial, and monetary interchange is that the subjects of national economic health and international economics have become increasingly enmeshed (El-Agraa, 1997; Macesich, 1997). Domestic economics, employment, inflation, and overall growth is heavily dependent on foreign markets, imports of resources, currency exchange rates, capital flows, and other international economic factors. The rise in trade is both a cause and a result of this increased international economic **interdependence**.

The impact of already-extensive and continuously growing economic interdependence has been repeatedly discussed in chapter 1, earlier in this chapter, and elsewhere in this book. It will suffice, therefore, to recount briefly the main ways that the global economy affects almost all of us at one point or another.

Trade is the most obvious, but far from the only, way that national prosperity and the international economy are connected. We need many foreign goods, such as oil. Others, such as toys and clothes, are often cheaper if imported. Exports create jobs; imports sometimes threaten jobs.

Foreign investment in U.S. government debt instruments helps keep interest rates down by increasing demand for those instruments. Without that demand, interest rates would rise, harming business expansion and the standard of living of many individuals. For example, on a $100,000, 30-year mortgage, an increase of just 1 percent in the interest rate increases the yearly payment by $897 and would put a home out of the reach of some potential buyers.

Exchange rates are also a significant determinant of domestic economic circumstances in an interdependent world. We have already noted the impact of exchange rates on prices, on trade and, therefore, on employment. There are numerous other examples. A strong currency, for instance, makes it more expensive for foreign tourists to visit. The strengthening of the U.S. dollar versus the Japanese yen between 1995 and 1999 means that if you are in the tourist business you will be hurt, because fewer Japanese visitors will come to the United States and spend their money. Japanese visitors spent more than $13 billion in the United States in 1996; they will spend much less in 1999.

Foreign direct investment also influences the domestic economy. The global flow of investment capital affects you in more ways than you probably imagine. Many familiar U.S. companies are owned by foreign investors, and the product and marketing decisions they make have a wide impact. For example, the Burger King chain is owned by British investors, Gerber's foods are produced by a Swiss-owned company, and the A&P food chain is controlled by German investors. Some resent foreign control, but the infusion of foreign capital sometimes keeps foundering U.S. companies in business and U.S. workers on the job. In other cases, foreign investors make investments that create jobs for Americans. There are tens of thousands of Americans who make Nissan automobiles in Tennessee, Hondas in Ohio, Toyotas in Kentucky, Mitsubishis in Illinois, and other foreign brand name products in U.S. plants. These American workers all owe their jobs to foreign investment.

Foreign portfolio investments are another part of the skein of international economic interdependence. Americans in 1996 owned $876 billion in foreign stocks and bonds, and the earnings from those investments amounted to many billions of dollars.

Domestic portfolio investments and the money they earn or lose for Americans are also related strongly to the international economy. About 43 percent

INTERACTIVE EXERCISE
Free Trade or Fair Trade: You Make the Decision

of all adult Americans own stock through the purchase of individual equities or mutual funds or through individual retirement plans. Companies that make up the Standard & Poor's 500, one of the key indices of the U.S. stock market, do 40 percent of their business overseas. When the world economy is good, the profits they earn result in part in dividends and capital gains for Americans, either directly or through such vehicles as retirement funds.

The list of ways that the domestic and international economies intertwine could go on almost forever! That is not necessary, though, to stress the point that the idea of **autarky**, the notion of any country's being truly economically independent, has long since ceased to be a realistic concept. The strength and weakness of the international economy have a significant impact on national economies. By the same token, the strength and weakness of the individual major EDCs and, collectively, of the smaller EDCs and the LDCs, affect the prosperity of the international economy and, by extension, one another. Most important, when all is said and done, how prosperously or poorly each of us lives is determined in significant part by the state of the global economy.

Chapter Summary

1. Economics and politics are closely intertwined aspects of international relations. Each is a part of and affects the other. This interrelationship has become even more important in recent history. Economics has become more important internationally because of dramatically increased trade levels, ever-tightening economic interdependence between countries, and the growing impact of international economics on domestic economics.

2. The study of the international political economy (IPE) examines the interaction between politics and economics.

3. There are many technical aspects to explaining and understanding the international political economy, and those not familiar with economic terms and methods should review the section "Economics: Technical Terms and Sources" found in Technical Explanations and Matters of Terminology on page 433.

4. The approaches to IPE can be roughly divided into three groups: economic nationalism (mercantilism), economic internationalism (liberalism), and economic structuralism.

5. The core of the economic nationalist doctrine is the realist idea that the state should harness and use national economic strength to further national interest. Therefore, the state should shape the country's economy and its foreign economic policy to enhance state power.

6. Economic internationalists are idealists who believe that international economic relations should and can be harmonious because prosperity is available to all and is most likely to be achieved and preserved through cooperation. The main thrust of economic

internationalism is to separate politics from economics, to create prosperity by freeing economic interchange from political restrictions.

7. Economic structuralists hold that world politics is based on the division of the world into have and have-not countries, with the EDCs keeping the LDCs weak and poor in order to exploit them. There are two types of economic structuralists. Marxists believe that the entire capitalist-based system must be replaced with domestic and international socialist systems before economic equity can be achieved. Less radical economic structuralists stress reform of the current market system by ending the system of dependencia.

8. Whether or not you subscribe to economic structuralist theory, it is clear that the world is generally divided into two economic spheres: a wealthy North and a much less wealthy South. There are some overlaps between the two spheres, but in general the vast majority of the people and countries of the South are much less wealthy and industrially developed than the countries of the North and their people. The South also has a history of direct and indirect colonial control by countries of the North.

9. Economic nationalists, economic internationalists, and economic structuralists all offer different explanations of why the relative deprivation of the South exists. The three schools of thought also have varying prescriptions about what, if anything, to do to remedy the North-South gap in economic development.

10. The history of international economics is ancient, but a change that has occurred in the second half of this century is that the level of economic interchange (trade, investments and other capital flows, and monetary exchange) has increased at an exponential rate.

11. Within the overall expansion of the international economy, there is, however, a pattern in which most of the trade, investment, and other aspects of the international political economy are dominated by the North and work to its advantage.

12. Trade in goods and services is booming, having grown 2,600 percent from $20 billion in 1913 to over $5.2 trillion in 1995.

13. There has also been a rapid expansion of international financial ties. This flow of investment can be examined by reviewing types of foreign investments and multinational corporations.

14. The increased flow of trade and capital means that monetary relations, including exchange rates, interest rates, and other monetary considerations, are a significant economic factor. It is not unreasonable to estimate that the daily currency flow is $1.5 trillion, or some $548 trillion a year.

15. The expansion of world trade and investment has profoundly affected countries and their citizens. Economic interdependence has inexorably intertwined national and international economic health.

CONNECTEXT

chapter 12

International Economic Competition and Cooperation

The gods sent not Corn for the rich men only.

Shakespeare, *Coriolanus*

As the images of life lived anywhere on our globe become available to all, so will the contrast between the rich and the poor become a force impelling the deprived to demand a better life from the powers that be.

Nelson Mandela, to a joint session of the U.S. Congress, October 7, 1994

Throughout this book we have seen that many forces work at cross-cutting purposes in the international system. There was our discussion of integration versus disintegration of political units as discussed in chapter 2; our discussion of nationalism versus transnationalism in chapters 4 and 5; the forces of sovereignty versus supranationalism as discussed in chapters 8 and 9 and elsewhere. This chapter discusses yet another dueling set of tendencies: national economic competition versus international economic cooperation.

Chapter Outline

National Economic Competition: The Traditional Road

Economic nationalism—the state-centric approach to the international political economy—is the traditional road that countries have long followed. While it is true that there has been considerable movement toward liberalizing international economic relations in recent decades, economic nationalism remains the dominant practice in global economic affairs for two reasons: First, states remain the principal actors on the world stage. Second, these states most often use economic tools and formulate economic policy to benefit themselves, not the global community. This chapter will explore the economic nationalist approach, including discussions of national economic power assets and the ways that countries utilize their economic power (Milner, 1998).

National Economic Power: Assets and Utilization

t is axiomatic that to pursue economic statecraft effectively, a country needs to possess considerable economic power. Chapter 8 has already reviewed the national infrastructure (technical sophistication, transportation systems, information and communications capabilities) that provides part of the basis for building a powerful economy. To these factors this chapter will add an understanding of how the national economy determines national power, by discussing financial position, natural resources, industrial output, agricultural output, and international competitiveness.

But you must also recognize that these economic aspects of power—a country's financial position, natural resources, industrial output, agricultural output, and international competitiveness—impact upon its ability to pursue and achieve its foreign policy goals in the world. As this suggests, states possess a variety of economic tools, and several of these are explored in detail below. These instruments are divided into economic incentives and economic sanctions.

Economic Incentives

States regularly offer economic incentives to induce other states to act in a desired way. Incentives include providing foreign aid, giving direct loans or credits, guaranteeing loans by commercial sources, reducing tariffs and other trade barriers, selling or licensing the sale of sensitive technology, and a variety of other techniques. Not all incentives are successful in changing another country's behavior, but they certainly do work some of the time (Crumm, 1995). For example, the United States in 1998 offered the Russians (and they seemed to accept) more opportunities to get involved with the lucrative satellite launching business, if Moscow agreed to stop supplying Iran with missile technology. "We are prepared to go forward and enhance cooperation in this area [satellite launches], but we cannot do it in the absence of progress on the Iran ballistic missile front," a senior U.S. official told reporters. Understanding the message, a top Russian official commented, "The increase of the quota [of launches] is an important and necessary issue for us."[1]

Other attempts to use incentives have been less successful. The details are still hazy, but it is clear that the United States supplied money and perhaps even arms to Iraq during the late 1980s. The U.S. rationale, according to the presidential directive that authorized the aid, was that it would serve as a "means of developing access to and influence with" Iraq and that "normal relations between the U.S. and Iraq would serve our longer-term interests and promote stability in both the [Persian] gulf and the Middle East."[2] Iraq's invasion of Kuwait in 1990 and the ensuing Persian Gulf War signaled the clear failure of the U.S. strategy.

Economic Sanctions

Countries and alliances can use their economic power in a negative way by applying sanctions. Methods include raising trade barriers, cutting off aid, trying to undermine another country's currency, and even instituting blockades.

The Effectiveness of Sanctions   Economic sanctions are a blunt instrument that attempts to economically bludgeon a target country into changing some specific behavior. As such, the effectiveness of sanctions is mixed. Sometimes they can be effective. Sanctions cost South Africa tens of billions of dollars and helped push the country's white leadership to end the apartheid system.

It is also the case, though, that, more often than not, sanctions fail to accomplish their goal, with some analysts placing their success rate as low as 5 percent (Elliott, 1998; Pape, 1997). And even when they do succeed, it often takes a long time to achieve the goal. For example, the UN imposed sanctions on Libya for its refusal to extradite two Libyans accused of complicity in planting a bomb in 1988. It destroyed Pan-American Flight 103 over Lockerbie, Scotland, killing 259 people on board and 11 others on the ground. Despite the sanctions, the government of Muammar Qaddafi did not agree to hand over the two suspects until mid-1998, almost a decade after the bombing took place. Under the deal struck between the U.S. Justice Department, Scottish, and Libyan officials, the two prisoners will be tried in the Netherlands under Scottish law with the case being heard by a three-judge panel, and not by a jury, as is customary under Scottish law. But even though it appears that justice may in fact be finally served for this crime, many involved feel that the conditions granted Libya in return for the extradition of the accused terrorists still belie true justice. "I think the Scottish government and [the U.S.] government are trying to put the best face on what I feel was a very politically motivated compromise," stated Stephanie Bernstein, whose husband died in the 1988 crash.[3] Many victims' families want those who *ordered* the bombing also brought to justice.

Since studies generally concur that sanctions fail more often than they are successful, a reasonable question is, When do they accomplish their goals? Sanctions are most likely to be effective in certain circumstances (Brawley,

These Buddhists are protesting in front of the U.S. Capitol in July 1999 to urge Congress to impose sanctions against the Chinese government for its repression of Tibet. Although the United States and other countries have used economic sanctions in recent years to help change policy in countries such as South Africa and Libya, the U.S. government has yet to impose sanctions against China for its Tibet policies.

SITES TO SURF
Fourth Freedom Forum: Sanctions and Incentives

Institute for International Economics: Economic Sanctions Reconsidered

1996; Shambaugh, 1996; Cortright & Lopez, 1996). These include instances where (1) "the goal is relatively modest," thereby minimizing the need for multilateral cooperation; (2) "the target is politically unstable, much smaller than the country imposing sanctions, and economically weak"; (3) "the sender and target are friendly toward one another and conduct substantial trade"; (4) "the sanctions are imposed quickly and decisively to maximize impact"; and (5) "the sender avoids high costs to itself," such as the loss of substantial export revenue (Elliott, 1993:34).

Still, sanctions remain a regular tool, especially used by the United States. "Therein is the great paradox," says one expert on sanctions. "While unilateral embargoes are less and less of an effective force in an integrated world economy, American enthusiasm for them has not diminished."[4] There are a number of possible explanations for this paradox. One is that such measures of concrete success are not the only standard by which to measure sanctions. There is also a symbolic value in sanctions that has nothing to do with whether they actually result in another country changing its behavior. Simply put, just as you might choose not to deal with an immoral person, so too, countries can express their moral indignation by reducing or severing their interactions with an abhorrent regime.

The Drawbacks of Sanctions   Especially given the high failure rate of sanctions, countries that apply them must be wary of the negative impact of sanctions on unintended victims. One such difficulty is that sanctions may harm economic interests other than those of the intended target. The UN sanctions imposed on Iraqi oil exports have cost Jordan and Turkey many millions of dollars by way of lost revenues that they would have earned for the use of pipelines that run through them and on to ports from which the oil is shipped.

Another drawback is that threatening or implementing sanctions can damage those who impose them. For instance, calls for U.S. sanctions on China in response to its alleged human rights abuses and other objectionable practices have been rejected in part because, explains a top presidential adviser, "the main victim [of sanctions] is U.S. business, and China doesn't suffer."[5] In one case, amid a flurry of threatened U.S. sanctions, Beijing used Boeing Aircraft as an example of what could occur, by choosing unexpectedly to place a $1.5 billion aircraft order with Airbus Industrie, the European consortium, rather than with Boeing. "There's no doubt we are being punished," said a dejected Ronald B. Woodard, president of Boeing Commercial Airplane Group. In fact, Woodard continued, he had been warned by a top Chinese official that if "your government constantly chooses to kick us and harass us, many, many business opportunities that should go to the U.S. [could go] elsewhere."[6]

A third criticism of sanctions is that they are often the tool used by economically developed countries (EDCs) to continue their dominance of less developed countries (LDCs). Of the 71 incidents of sanctions applied during the 1970s and 1980s, 49 of the cases (69 percent) involved EDCs placing sanctions on LDCs (Rothgeb, 1993). A fourth charge against sanctions is that they can also work to harm relations with other countries that do not support them. Recent U.S. sanctions against Cuba and some other countries have proven particularly offensive to many U.S. allies.

A fifth criticism of sanctions is that they often harm the very people whom you want to assist. President Fidel Castro of Cuba had called sanctions "noiseless atomic bombs" that "cause the death of men, women, and children."[7] Iraq provides a good example of Castro's point. There, persistent UN sanctions and a defiant government in Baghdad had a brutal impact, resulting in hardships such as scant supplies of food and medicine for the civilian population. A United Nations Children's Fund (UNICEF) report issued in 1997 estimated that 1 million Iraqi children were malnourished, and an earlier report, released in 1995 by a Harvard University School of Public Health team that visited Iraq, indicated that as many as 576,000 Iraqi children had died as a result of the sanctions. The sanctions have been relaxed in recent years to allow Iraq to begin selling some oil and, under supervision, to use the proceeds to buy food and medicine.

Now, having reviewed national economic assets and the use of the economic instrument, we can turn to specific national economic concerns and policies. This discussion will be divided into two parts: the national economic issues and policies of the North and the national economic issues and policies of the South.

The North and the International Political Economy

By many standards, the economic position of the North is enviable. Its 1997 per capita GDP was $23,999 compared to $1,280 each for the people of the South. Between 1980 and 1995, the combined GDPs of the EDCs jumped from $7.7 trillion to $22.5 trillion. That was monumental compared with a rise in the combined GDPs of the LDCs from $3.2 trillion to $5.4 trillion. Yet all is not well in the North.

The National Economies of the North

The fundamental cause of concern among EDCs is that the North's economic growth rate has slowed considerably from the high levels it had sustained earlier. The average annual real GDP growth rate of the EDCs during the 1970s was 3.2 percent; during the 1980s that declined to 3.0 percent and in the 1990s (to 1998) slipped even further to 2.0 percent. Per capita GDP, which had risen 2.3 percent annually in the 1980s, went up by only 1.6 percent a year in the 1990s. Unemployment in the EDCs, which averaged 6.8 percent in the 1980s, has crept up to an average 7.1 percent in the 1990s. The number of new jobs being created in the North increased an annual average of 1.3 percent in the 1980s; during the 1990s average job growth was but 0.8 percent.

There are many reasons for the deceleration of the North's economy. One is that economic production has entered a period that some call the *postindustrial economy*. What this means is that, through the use of robotics and other techniques, fewer and fewer workers are needed to produce more and more manufactured goods. Companies need to reduce their workforces to stay competitive internationally. Downsizing is a new, and unwelcome, word in the economic vocabulary of the North. The displaced workers are either unemployed or find jobs in the usually lower-paying service sector. The drop in defense spending has also slowed economies. Furthermore, there is the beginning of industrial competition from a few newly industrializing countries in the South. None of this means that the North is in danger of plunging into a full-scale depression. This is always a possibility, but current indicators do not presage any immediate danger. On the other hand, there is little to indicate a quick return to the moderate growth rates of the late 1980s, much less to the robust growth rates of the 1960s.

National Economic Issues and Policies of the North

Because they make up such an overwhelming percentage of the world's economic enterprise, the economic issues and policies of the North are a key determinant of the course of the global economy. For an extended period after World War II, the EDCs enjoyed good growth and were generally united politically with the United States and under its leadership. Now, with both economic and political factors changing, tensions among the EDCs are increasing.

Changes in the Economic and Political Climate in the North The 1990s have been a time of significant shifts in the international economic relations and policies of the countries of the North. There are several causes of this shift in relations. One, as noted, is the decline in the economic fortunes of the North. During the decades of booming prosperity following World War II, the rapidly expanding international economy minimized any pressures for economic rivalry among the developed countries. Now, in a less robust economic climate, there is increased protectionist sentiment. The refusal of Congress in 1997 to renew President Clinton's fast-track trade negotiation authority is one example of this shift in sentiment.

A second factor has been the end of the cold war. The resulting changes in the international system have lessened the need for strategic cooperation among the industrialized Western allies. With no common enemy to bind them together, the long-standing trade disputes among the **trilateral countries** (Japan, the United States/Canada, Western Europe) that had once been suppressed in the name of allied unity have become more acrimonious.

A third and related factor that has further complicated matters is that central direction has declined in the North. The United States once provided that direction. But with an upsurge in economic rivalries among the EDCs and with the American people less willing to support U.S. internationalism, Washington has lost some of its ability to lead. The seven most economically powerful Western countries (Canada, France, Germany, Great Britain, Italy, Japan, and the United States) have met annually since 1975 as an informal economic directorate called the **Group of Seven (G-7)**. Yet, the economic summits among the G-7 leaders have not been able to achieve effective economic coordination. Meetings of the G-7 were once major news stories; the most recent G-7 summits have accomplished little of substance and have been far from front-page news. Symbolic of that, or perhaps of the confusion that will now occur, the *New York Times* reported only on page 8 that the G-7 had in 1998 officially become the G-8, at least sometimes. The G-7 leaders' 1998 meeting in Birmingham, Great Britain, added Russia as a member and changed their name to reflect that. The 1999 summit in Köln, Germany, continued to include Russia in the elite group. In some sense, however, the G-7 will continue to exist, as the original seven agreed that they would continue to hold discussions on many financial issues, such as what to do about the Russian economy, without the Russian president. All this will bedevil students of international economics in the years to come and led some critics to dub the group the G-7½.

Whatever the cause, the result is that the EDCs have acted with a sort of dual personality in the realm of international economic affairs. There is one set of forces within most EDCs that has pressed with significant success

INTERACTIVE EXERCISE
G-8 or G-7 + 1?

for the continued expansion of **free trade** and other forms of financial inter-change among nations. The European Union (EU) has continued to integrate; much of the Northern Hemisphere joined together in the North American Free Trade Agreement (NAFTA); and the world extended and enhanced the General Agreement on Tariffs and Trade (GATT) and created the World Trade Organization (WTO) to administer it. All these efforts in the 1990s toward economic cooperation will be discussed later in this chapter.

Simultaneously, however, **protectionism** remains a powerful countervailing force, and there has been increased pressure within countries to follow economic nationalist policies. This pressure has been occasioned by the sagging economies of the North, by the increase of economic competition not only from other EDCs but also from newly industrializing countries (NICs), and by a gnawing sense of economic insecurity among many people of the North. When Americans were presented with a list of policy options and asked which they thought were important, 89 percent said that "protecting the jobs of American workers should be a very important U.S. foreign policy goal" (Rielly, 1995). Such attitudes have pushed national leaders to follow policies of economic nationalism. The result of these countervailing internationalist and nationalist economic pressures creates something of a schizophrenic pattern to the foreign economic policies in the North's EDCs. They profess support of the further internationalization of the world economy while at the same time trying to promote and protect their own national economies.

Economic Disputes among the EDCs   Amid the importance of the balance of payments to every country's economic health, trade relations among the EDCs have become more difficult in the past decade. One source of tension is that some countries have chronic trade surpluses, while other countries regularly run trade deficits. A particular point of friction during much of the first half of the 1990s was U.S.-Japan trade relations. While Japan accumulated a trade surplus during the years 1990–1996 of $726 billion, the United States amassed a $557 billion deficit. The greatest source of Japan's surplus and of the U.S. deficit has been the bilateral merchandise trade between the two countries. In 1996, for instance, the $50.4 billion U.S. merchandise deficit with Japan accounted for 30 percent of the overall U.S. merchandise trade deficit.

Tension over trade between the United States and Japan has risen and fallen in the past few years, and in 1999 seemed to have stabilized for the moment. The downturn in the economies of Asia's LDCs in 1997 further weakened Japan's moribund economy, for which exports to the Asian LDCs are very important. As a result, the Japanese reduced imports from the United States, exacerbating the drop in U.S. exports caused by the troubles in the Asian LDCs. This led U.S. leaders to press Japan to spend billions of yen on domestic programs in an attempt to stimulate Japan's economy and to take other steps that would promote consumer spending by the Japanese on, in part, imported U.S. products. The Japanese government, in turn, resented what it saw as U.S. meddling, and tension continued just below the surface. Still, no specific points of conflict, such as the 1996 auto dispute, loom on the immediate horizon.

The South and the International Political Economy

The economic goals of the North and South are both very much alike and very different. They are alike in that both the EDCs' and the LDCs' goals have to do with prosperity. They are different in that the North's goal is to preserve and enhance it; the South's goal is to achieve it.

To further understand the economic position, goals, and policies of the LDCs, the following sections will examine economic development by looking first at the LDCs' sources of development capital and then by turning to the perspective of the LDCs on development issues. Before taking up these matters, though, it is important to look at the status of LDC development.

Development in the South: Status

There can be little doubt that on many statistical bases there has been improvement in the socioeconomic development of the South. Over the last two or three decades, the infant mortality rate has been cut by one-third; the percentage of people with access to potable water has grown 70 percent; the adult literacy rate is up 35 percent; and people live an average of 43 percent longer. Between 1978 and 1995, the real GDP of the South grew an annual average of 4.4 percent. Annual real per capita GDP growth was a slower 2.6 percent, but it did advance (Dickson, 1997; Hoogvelt, 1997). But in certain cases, it is still difficult to classify the level of economic development of some states, as the Web site box, China: LDC, NIC, or EDC? suggests.

What these averages for the South disguise, though, is a highly variegated pattern of development. The progress has had its drawbacks, and there is a diverse pattern of development in the South. The disparity in development has occurred both between and within countries. As discussed in chapter 11, there exists wide *disparity between countries* in terms of levels of economic development. *Disparity within countries* is a second characteristic of LDC economic development. Economic class, sometimes based on race or ethnicity, is one division. Within the South there are cities with sparkling skyscrapers and luxuriant suburbs populated by well-to-do local entrepreneurs who drive Mercedes-Benzes and splash in marble pools. For each such scene, however, there are many more of open sewers, contaminated drinking water, distended bellies, and other symptoms of rural and urban human blight.

In addition to its more traditional woes, the South also suffers many negative side effects from the process of modernization. Medical advances have led to decreased infant mortality and increased longevity, but one result has been an *explosive population growth*. The population of sub-Saharan Africa, for instance, climbed over 280 percent from 210 million in 1960 to about 600 million in 1999 and is expected to increase to 1.23 billion by 2025.

A FURTHER NOTE
China: LDC,
NIC, or EDC?

Amid the prosperity that is evident throughout Hong Kong, many people have not yet become part of the rising economic tide. Although city scenes such as this woman carrying her worldly belongings in boxes can be found in the EDCs, the disparities between rich and poor are even more striking in LDC cities.

Economic change has also brought *rapid urbanization* as the hope of finding jobs and better health, sanitation, and other social services has set off a mass migration from rural areas to cities in the South. Between 1965 and 1995 the percentage of the South's population living in urban areas grew from 22 to 39 percent, and it is projected to reach 53 percent in the year 2020. There are now a total of approximately 175 cities in LDCs with populations that are over 1 million. São Paulo, Brazil, is the world's most populous city, with 16.7 million inhabitants.

Development has also brought *industrial and environmental dangers*. The impact of development on the environment will be detailed in chapter 14, but a brief note of the dangers is appropriate here. One problem is deforestation. This is especially critical in the South, where increased demand for wood, expanding farm and ranch acreage, and general urban growth are rapidly depleting the forests. Loss of these forests increases soil erosion, decreases oxygenation of the air, lessens rainfall, and has numerous other deleterious effects. It is also the case that LDC industrial development is adding to air, water, and soil pollution. This is a problem of industrialization in general, but pollution growth is especially acute in developing countries, which often cannot afford the expensive processes to cleanse emissions and dispose of waste.

Development in the South: Capital Needs

Whatever the problems and drawbacks of industrialization, the LDCs are justifiably determined to increase their development. Because of their poor economic base, most LDCs find it difficult to raise capital internally. Incomes are so low in India, for example, that less than 1 percent of the country's people pay income taxes. Many things can be accomplished with domestic resources and drive, but the LDCs have massive **capital needs** in order to obtain the resources required for development. "Uganda needs just two things," says its president, Yoweri Museveni. "We need infrastructure and we need foreign investment. That is what we need. The rest we shall do ourselves."[8]

In trying to obtain these resources, LDCs are constrained by their limited financial reserves, especially **hard currency**. American dollars are the standard

TABLE
World Countries:
Basic Economic
Indicators, 1997

currency of international exchange. Others, such as British pounds, German marks, Swiss or French francs, and Japanese yen, are also widely convertible. Guatemalan quetzals, Iraqi dinars, Malaysian ringgits, and Nigerian nairas are another story. They and most LDC currencies are not accepted in international economic transactions. Since more than 80 percent of all hard-currency reserves are concentrated in the industrialized countries, the LDCs struggle to purchase needed imports.

A primary issue for LDCs, then, is the acquisition of hard-currency development funds. Four main sources of convertible currencies are available: loans, investment, trade, and aid. Unfortunately, as we shall see in our discussion of these sources, there are limitations and drawbacks to each. No single source is sufficient to meet the LDCs' enormous and complex needs. As with other factors in LDC economics, the flow of capital is highly variable. A few NICs have recently had healthy inflows of capital, although even for those the Asian financial turmoil and its negative impact on almost all LDC economies has caused a new outflow. For many LDCs, there has been a continuous struggle to attract sufficient capital to develop. Also, there are numerous drawbacks to the various capital sources. These will be explored fully in the sections that follow.

Loans   One source of hard currency is loans extended by private or government sources. Based on a number of economic factors, the LDCs in the 1970s moved to finance their development needs by borrowing heavily from EDC banks, other private lenders, national governments, and international organizations. The upshot was that by 1982 LDC international debt had skyrocketed to $849 billion, and a debt crisis ensued when LDC economies suffered downturns in the late 1980s. While the rate of increase has eased, the total debt owed by the LDCs has continued to grow and stood at $2.07 trillion in 1994. Banks, mostly located in the EDCs, and other private institutional and individual bondholders are the largest creditors, holding 59 percent of the LDC debt. Governments (18 percent) and international organizations (23 percent), such as the IMF and the World Bank, hold the rest of the LDC debt.

The LDC Debt Crisis   The mutual danger of the debt crisis of the 1980s to both the North and the South led them to search for solutions. The details are complex, but a plan proposed in 1989 by U.S. secretary of the treasury Nicholas Brady began to ease the crisis. Under the Brady Plan during the 1990s, banks have forgiven over $100 billion of what the LDCs owed, lowered interest rates, and made new loans. In return, the governments of the EDCs, the IMF, and the World Bank have guaranteed the financed loans and have increased their own lending to the LDCs. The Brady Plan has also required that the LDCs meet fiscal reform requirements negotiated with the IMF and other lenders.

The immediate LDC debt crisis has abated, but its ebb may prove to be only a lull in the storm because of several factors. One is that the LDCs still have a towering debt. The debt as a percentage of the South's combined GDP was 41 percent at the peak of the crisis in 1987 and in 1995 was still at almost 40 percent. The debt dropped as a percentage of export earnings to 151 percent, but that is still a burdensome level. Among other things, it means that in 1997 the LDCs paid out $278 billion (22 percent of their annual export earnings) to meet the principal and interest charges.

Moreover, there remain signs of trouble and future shifts that could once again intensify the problem to a crisis level. The financial crisis that broke out in Asia in late 1997 continued throughout 1998 and spread to Latin America and other LDC regions. Events in 1999 showed some improvement, but high levels of uncertainty still remain. The collapse of the Russian ruble and that country's financial crisis beginning in August 1998 unsettled the world economy, and the economies of the EDCs began to feel the pinch of these events. The specter of LDCs not being able to pay their debts and the damage that would cause in the EDCs reemerged. German banks, for instance, hold $27 billion in Russian debt, and American banks have $65 billion in outstanding loans to South Korea, Thailand, and other troubled Asian economies. Moreover, worries about export markets, further currency devaluations by the LDCs, and other financial perils led the U.S. stock market to plummet, including a one-day loss of over 500 points on the Dow Jones Industrial Average in September 1998.

Private Investment   A second source of capital for LDCs is private investment through foreign direct investment (FDI) and foreign portfolio investment (FPI), terms that are explained in the last chapter. The flows of FDI and FPI are growing in importance as capital sources for the LDCs. Figure 12.1 shows that from 1984 through 1997, the net FDI and FPI in the LDCs has skyrocketed. Another upward trend in capital investment in LDCs is the proportion of global FDI that they receive. While it is still a minority, with most funds being invested in EDCs, the LDCs' proportion has increased from only one-sixth in 1990 to one-third in 1996.

Trade   Export earnings are a third possible source of development capital. In light of the vast size of the world market, and because earnings from trade can be utilized by LDCs according to their own wishes, trade is theoretically the optimal source of hard currency for LDCs. Yet, in reality, the LDCs are severely disadvantaged by the pattern and terms of international trade.

Product instability is one factor that imperils LDCs that rely on primary products for export. Countries that rely on fish and other marine foodstuffs for export are endangered by the declining fish stocks in the world's oceans. When a freeze damages Colombia's coffee crop, a drought devastates the groundnut crops that West Africa relies on, or floods wipe out the Bangladesh jute crop, then trade suffers greatly.

Market and price weaknesses are also common for primary products. A downturn in world demand can decimate markets. During the past decades, world trade in products such as cotton, sisal, jute, wool, and other fibers has been harmed by the development of synthetics. Sugar sales have been harmed

Figure 12.1

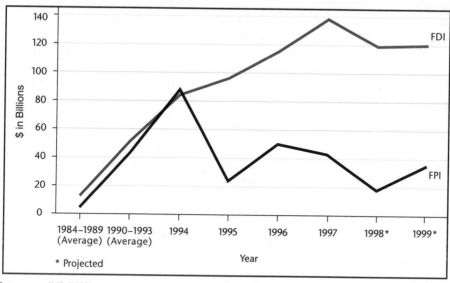

Average Annual Net Private Investment in LDCs

Data source: IMF (1998).

Foreign direct and portfolio investment is a rapidly expanding source of development capital for LDCs. Notice that FPI is relatively unstable.

by artificial substitutes and also by dietary changes. Minerals such as tin and lead have also experienced market declines. Oil is perhaps the best illustration of the havoc that changing market conditions can wreak on exporting countries. Conservation and the development of alternative energy sources in the industrialized countries, development of new petroleum fields, and overproduction by oil producers have turned what was once called "black gold" into a "black glut." Taxes and inflation are the real cause of the seemingly unending escalation of gasoline prices in the United States, Canada, and elsewhere. In real dollars, petroleum prices at the wellhead were in 1999 only about 35 percent of what they were in 1980.

The use of trade, then, to acquire capital and to improve economic conditions has not been highly effective for most LDCs. Their pattern of merchandise trade deficits, export dependence on primary products, and market and price weaknesses all disadvantage the LDCs in their trade relations with the EDCs.

Foreign Aid   A fourth possible external source of capital for LDCs is foreign aid (Hook, 1996). In some ways the flow of official development assistance (ODA) to LDCs has been impressive, amounting to over half a trillion dollars since World War II. Official ODA for 1997 was $48.3 billion. Currently, almost

A SITE TO SURF
The OECD's
Development
Assistance
Committee

all foreign aid that is given comes from the 21 (of 27) EDCs in the Organization for Economic Cooperation and Development (OECD), which are members of the OECD's Development Assistance Committee (DAC). Most of this assistance is extended through **bilateral aid** (country to country), with a smaller amount being channeled through **multilateral aid** (several countries) agencies, such as the United Nations and the World Bank.

Without disparaging the value or intent of the past or current aid effort, aid is neither a story of undisguised generosity nor one of unblemished success (Schraeder, Hook, & Taylor, 1998). Factors that reduce the impact of aid include political considerations, the military content of aid, recipient per capita aid, donor aid relative to wealth, and aid application.

Political considerations are one factor that limits the effectiveness of aid. The bilateral aid that makes up the bulk of all foreign aid is often given more on the basis of political-military interest than to meet economic needs or to promote human rights (Poe & Meernik, 1995; Hook, 1994). Amounts of aid are also affected by domestic opposition to what is often labeled "foreign giveaways" in donor countries (Katada & McKeown, 1998). About 59 percent of all U.S. bilateral foreign aid in 1997 went to just two countries: Egypt ($700 million) and Israel ($1.15 billion). By contrast, all the countries in sub-Saharan Africa received only $1.5 billion. Most other countries also give aid selectively. Great Britain and France have a special interest in their former colonies. Japan focuses on Asia and elsewhere where it has special economic interests. It should also be pointed out, however, that national interest of the donor is not the only criteria for giving aid. Democracy, human rights, and other such standards have also influenced foreign aid giving, and, according to one study, these goals have, to a degree, been promoted successfully by the aid policies of the United States and other countries (Gangadharan & Mngomezulu, 1994).

Military content is another factor that limits the impact of the aid figures that are sometimes reported. Egypt certainly needs development assistance, but of the total U.S. aid for FY1996, 57 percent was military aid. Indeed, 25 percent of all American bilateral assistance that year was military aid.

Measuring recipient per capita aid, rather than gross aid, is also useful to gain a truer picture of the impact of foreign aid. In 1997 LDCs received only about $10 per capita, and that fell to just $3.74 per person for the LLDCs, excluding China.

Donor aid relative to wealth is another analytical approach that lessens the seeming significance of aid figures. This compares aid given to the donor's wealth. Overall, aid as a percentage of EDCs' total GDP has been steadily declining for a quarter century. In 1965 aid equaled 0.47 percent of the OECD's total GDP. That percentage declined to 0.22 in 1997.

The way aid is applied is a final factor that limits its impact. Too often aid has been used to fund highly symbolic but economically unwise projects such as airports and sports arenas. Inefficiency and corruption have also sometimes drained off aid. There is criticism, too, on the grounds that aid is used to maintain the local elite, does not reach the truly poor, and, therefore, continues the dependencia relationship between North and South. In fact,

This Turkish mosque remains standing while almost everything around it was demolished by the August 1999 earthquake. Economic aid for recovery has been and will continue to be forthcoming, but disasters such as this hit LDCs very hard, as their economies are much more sensitive to disruptions than those of EDCs.

some critics argue that aid can actually retard growth, contending, for example, that giving poor people food reduces their incentive to farm. These charges are not universally accurate, but aid donors and recipients have moved to address problems that do exist. Among other changes, donors are now working to ensure that the aid is used wisely. "For too long development cooperation has focused on the economy and not the polity," the head of United Nations Development Programme (UNDP) has conceded. "Without a functioning political system and effective governance, the best-lain economic plans are not going to succeed."[9] To address this issue, aid is now being aimed at what is called "capacity building." This means creating a political and business structure to use aid more effectively to build a recipient's economic infrastructure.

Development in the South: LDC Perspectives and Policies

While the gap in wealth between the North and South has long existed, relations between the two economic spheres have not been static. The LDCs are now asserting with mounting intensity the proposition that they have a right to share in the world's economic wealth. They have acted on a number of fronts to enhance their own economic situations and to pressure the EDCs to redistribute part of their wealth. We will examine these views and efforts in terms of the LDCs' expectations, organizational movement, demands, and actions.

Rising Expectations   One of the most important developments in the last half century has been the independence movement among LDCs. Dozens of colonies in Africa and Asia demanded and won political sovereignty. Even after independence, though, many LDCs remained in an economically subservient and disadvantaged position in relation to their former colonial masters or to other dominant EDCs. Most people in LDCs are not willing to accept such manipulation. The resistance to a dependencia relationship with the North is the result of a number of factors, including the impact of nationalism on LDC negotiations with EDCs, increased moral rhetoric from many international organizations and nongovernmental organizations (NGOs) about responsibility for LDC development, and transnational ideologies such as Marxism that point to the continued possibility of exploitation of the LDCs by the EDCs.

Development of the LDC Movement   The developing identity of the South first took the form of *political nonalignment.* In 1955, 29 African and Asian countries convened the Bandung Conference in Indonesia to discuss how to hasten the independence of colonial territories and how to be nonaligned in the cold war. Most of the colonies are now independent, and the cold war is over. But the Bandung Conference remains an important mark of the ongoing sense of identity among the LDCs.

The South's concerns soon also turned to economic development. Political demands for an end to colonialism provided a role model for similar economic assertiveness. A coalition of disadvantaged countries, the **Group of 77**, emerged and called for the first United Nations Conference on Trade and Development (UNCTAD), which met in Geneva in 1964. This conference and the Group of 77 (which has grown to 132 members) evolved into an ongoing UNCTAD organization, which has also met every three or four years. UNCTAD has served as a vehicle for the LDCs to discuss their needs and to press demands on the North.

UNCTAD and the Group of 77 have also promoted many other discussions of the South's economic position. The first formal meeting between North and South occurred in a 1981 meeting at Cancún, Mexico. Fourteen states representing the Group of 77 met with eight EDCs representing the Organization for Economic Cooperation and Development (OECD), an organization that serves to promote economic coordination among the industrialized countries. Little of substantive importance was accomplished at Cancún, although the meeting did serve as a symbolic admission by the North that it has a stake in the South and that North-South economic relations are subject to negotiation between the two spheres.

More recently, the 1990s have witnessed several global conferences that have brought the EDCs and LDCs together in a formal setting. The results have generally been the same. For instance, at the UN–sponsored conference on the environment held in Rio de Janeiro, Brazil, in 1992, the LDCs pressed for significantly increased financial aid and other forms of assistance to help them develop while also protecting the environment. This challenge will be discussed further in chapter 14, but, as in Cancún, the North refused to increase funds dramatically.

LDC Demands The development of LDC consciousness and assertiveness has led to a series of demands on the industrialized North. These calls for reform are collectively known as the **New International Economic Order (NIEO)**. More than any other single document, the Declaration on the Establishment of a New International Economic Order outlines and symbolizes the South's view of, and its calls for reform of, the "old" international economic order. This declaration, adopted as a resolution by the UN General Assembly in 1974, begins by protesting the North's domination of the existing economic structure and the maldistribution of wealth. To remedy this situation, the NIEO declaration calls for a number of reforms:

1. *Trade reforms.* The NIEO envisions improved and stabilized markets for primary products. This would include removal of trade barriers and the regulation of prices and supplies.
2. *Monetary reforms.* Reforms in monetary relations include stabilization of inflation and exchange rates and increased funding from the IMF and other international monetary agencies. The NIEO also includes demands for greater LDC participation in the decision making of the IMF and other such international agencies.
3. *Industrialization.* The 1974 resolution also calls on the North to assist the South in gaining technology and in increasing industrial production.
4. *Economic sovereignty.* The South asserts its right to control its own resources and to regulate the activities of MNCs.
5. *Economic aid.* Finally, the LDCs have called on the EDCs to increase economic aid to at least be equivalent to 0.7 percent of their respective GDPs. Only four EDCs now meet that standard. There are also calls for more nonpolitical multilateral aid to be given through the World Bank and other such IGOs.

LDC Action The LDCs have not waited passively for the EDCs to respond to their demands. They have instead taken action on a number of fronts. Not all these moves have succeeded, but they indicate the South's growing assertiveness.

Establishing cartels was a second tactic that LDCs tried initially. A **cartel** is an international trading agreement among producers who hope to control the supply and price of a primary product. The first cartel was established in 1933 to regulate tea, but the decade of the 1960s was the apex of cartel formation, when 18 came into existence. They ranged in importance from the Organization of Petroleum Exporting Countries (OPEC) to the Asian and Pacific Coconut Community.

Cartels, however, have proven generally unsuccessful, as illustrated by the limited impact of even one as significant as OPEC. During the 1970s OPEC seemed almost invincible. With its 12 members in control of most of the oil needed by the seemingly insatiable EDCs, OPEC manipulated supplies and prices, which sent the cost of a barrel of oil from $1.35 (or 3.2 cents per gallon) sky-rocketing 2,500 percent to $34 per barrel in 1981. Money poured into the OPEC treasuries as black gold flowed out. During the 1970s more than $1 trillion was accumulated, and the OPEC countries' balance-of-payments surplus peaked at an annual $109 billion in 1980.

The dominance of OPEC was, however, only temporary. The high price of oil sparked massive quests to find new sources of oil. With new discoveries in the North Sea, the Gulf of Mexico, and elsewhere, the supply of oil increased. Also a greater percentage of oil came from non–OPEC countries. On the demand side, the high price of oil encouraged conservation and alternative energy measures and drove down oil consumption. The result of increased supply and decreased demand weakened prices, which dropped 23 percent in real dollars by 1985. Since then oil prices have sunk even further, averaging a miniscule $14.50 a barrel (34.5 cents a gallon) in 1998.

The upshot is that although OPEC continues to supply about 41 percent of the world's petroleum, and while OPEC members possess approximately 78 percent of the world's proven oil reserves, the cartel has not been successful in increasing oil prices because of the continuing oversupply of oil compared to demand and because there have been numerous political strains among the OPEC members. The Persian Gulf War, which involved Iraq, Kuwait, and Saudi Arabia among other OPEC members, is the most obvious symbol of the inability of OPEC to act with unity (Spar, 1994).

Protectionism was a third, and now also rapidly declining, thrust of early LDC activity. The temptation and domestic political pressure for developing countries to use tariff and nontariff barriers to protect infant industries are strong and may, in the earliest stages, even have some merit. It is also understandable, given the common fear, as one Indian economist explains, "that the foreigners will exploit, dominate, and control us."[10] Protectionist policies, however, have numerous drawbacks. Most important, there is evidence that for LDCs protectionism does not work and that economic growth is positively associated with eliminating trade impediments. Moreover, whether protectionism works or not, EDCs are less willing to tolerate it and have used a variety of approaches to entice or coerce the LDCs to open their markets.

The Future of National Economic Policy

There can be no doubt that the economic story of the last half century has been a steady movement toward ever greater economic interdependence based on an increasingly free exchange of trade, investment, and other financial activity. An array of statistics presented in this and the preceding chapter show conclusively that the movement of goods, services, investment capital, and currencies across borders has expanded exponentially. Furthermore, as we shall take up later in this chapter, the international system has created the

EU, IMF, NAFTA, World Bank, WTO, and numerous global and regional organizations and arrangements to facilitate and promote free international economic interchange.

For all this evidence, it would be erroneous to conclude that the world is on a path to inevitable economic integration and the eclipse of economic nationalism. Indeed, there are powerful arguments against and forces opposed to globalization. "We have sunlight, but we have shadows, too," Renato Ruggiero, head of the WTO, has commented.[11] Those shadows are cast, according to one analyst, by the fact that "today many people think that globalization is going to destroy their life as they know it. We have gotten used to the idea that globalization will inevitably succeed, but I am not so sure anymore."[12]

The trend toward free economic interchange and the opposing powerful forces of economic nationalism mean that one of the coming century's critical debates will be whether to continue, halt, or even reverse economic integration. We will explore that debate by looking at the arguments for and against free economic interchange. First, however, it is appropriate to review the barriers that countries can and do erect to affect the flow of goods, services, and capital.

Barriers to Free Economic Interchange

Some years ago, Paul Simon recorded a song in which the refrain was, "There must be 50 ways to leave your lover." Insofar as countries are increasingly bound together economically—for richer, for poorer; for better, for worse—there are at least 50 ways to get out of, or perhaps cheat on, that relationship.

Barriers to Merchandise Trade   There are numerous ways that countries can restrict the trade in goods.

- **Tariffs** are the most familiar trade barrier. While these are generally low, tariff hikes are still occasionally either threatened or used. Most often this occurs over economic issues. The United States has threatened to impose 100 percent tariffs on some Chinese goods if Beijing does not end the piracy of U.S. intellectual property by Chinese manufacturers.
- **Nontariff barriers (NTBs)** are a less well known but more common and important way of restricting trade. These NTBs are sometimes reasonable regulations based on health, safety, or other considerations. More often they are simply protectionist.
  - *Quotas* that limit the number of units that can be shipped are one form of NTB. Some quotas are imposed by importing countries; others are self-imposed by exporting countries in preference to facing imposed restrictions. The EU has imposed quotas on the importation of Japanese vehicles, limiting them to about 10 percent of the EU market.
  - *Pricing limits* are another way to restrain trade. During the 1996 election campaign, President Clinton pleased Florida tomato farmers by successfully pressuring the Mexican government to agree not to export tomatoes to the United States for less than 20.86 cents per pound.

- *Technical restrictions,* such as health and safety regulations, are sometimes really meant to bar imports or increase their cost considerably.
- *Subsidization* allows a domestic producer to undersell foreign competition at home. Many governments, for instance, heavily subsidize agricultural production. Efforts during the most recent round of world trade negotiations met with fierce domestic resistance in France, Japan and elsewhere.
- *Dumping* is yet another variant of an NTB. The tactic is prohibited by GATT rules, but there are frequent charges that it happens. Dumping occurs when a company sells its goods abroad at a price lower than what it sells them for at home.
- *Licensing requirements* are one way to make it difficult for foreign professionals and companies to provide services in another country. Many countries license architects, engineers, insurance agents, stock and bond traders, and other professionals.
- *Majority ownership requirements* are a way to bar the foreign ownership of businesses within a country. India, for example, requires that all companies located in India have at least 51 percent Indian ownership.

Free Economic Interchange: The Debate

There is a crucial debate being held across the world in government councils, academic circles, the media, and elsewhere about the advantages and disadvantages of economic globalization. The clash between the forces that favor the advancement of free economic interchange and those that oppose it will be one of the most pivotal struggles in the years ahead. Economic nationalism, the traditional path in world politics, remains the prevailing approach to the global economy. But there has also been great change. The countries of the world have adopted a vast array of policies, have concluded numerous economic agreements, and have created many international organizations to promote and facilitate free economic interchange. These policies, agreements, and organizations all represent an alternative approach to the international political economy, and it is to this newer path that we will turn our attention for the remainder of this chapter.

International Economic Cooperation: The Alternative Road

Economic nationalism persists and, in some aspects, is on the rise. It may even eventually provide prosperity to all states and peoples. Yet there is a gnawing doubt about the harvest that we will reap from this economic strategy. There are numerous scholars, political leaders, and others who maintain that economic nationalism underlies many of the current economic difficulties and tensions discussed in this chapter and the last one. As we have noted, however, economic internationalism also faces its own challenges and detractors.

These sharp disagreements between economic nationalists and their critics are one aspect of the overarching reality that the world is at the juncture of two political roads that diverge. One path is national self-interest, the other is international cooperation. Whatever may come, it is clear that the degree to which countries cooperate economically, or even integrate their economies, is going to be a pivotal determinant of future international relations. This is true whether the issue is relations among the economic titans of the developed North, the struggle of the less developed countries of the South to improve their lot, or the willingness of the North to help the South develop. Having reviewed the traditional road of economic nationalism thus far in this chapter, we will now examine economic internationalism and the cooperative international economic policies and organizations that this school of thought favors.

The Origins of Economic Cooperation

While economic nationalism as a sovereign state-based international system has long been the prevailing economic reality, it is also true that economic cooperation and regulation have become increasingly commonplace, albeit still limited, elements of national and international economics. The liberal idea of creating an international political economy based on free economic interchange and interdependence dates back over two centuries, as discussed in chapter 11, to Adam Smith, who wrote *The Wealth of Nations* (1776), and the French capitalist philosophers called *les Économistes*. Their views also found adherents on the other side of the Atlantic, such as Benjamin Franklin, who wrote in "Thoughts on Commercial Subjects" (1780) that "no nation was ever ruined by trade." This view was slow to take hold, though, and did not begin to shape international economic relations to any great extent until the 1930s and 1940s. A combination of the strife that had marked the twentieth century to that point and the Great Depression that was gripping the world in the 1930s led an increasing number of leaders to agree with the view of the longest-serving U.S. secretary of state (1933–1944), Cordell Hull, that "international commerce is not only calculated to aid materially in the restoration of prosperity everywhere, but it is the greatest civilizer and peacemaker in the experience of the human race" (Paterson, Clifford, & Hagan, 1995:143).

While the tensions that led to World War II kept international economic reform on the political back burner for a decade, the war added to the impetus to change the structure and course of world politics. With the United States as, first, the dominant power in the anti-Axis alliance, then as the leader of the anticommunist West, the capitalist EDCs moved during the years 1943–1948 to create the foundation for a new international economic order. The EDCs reached several accords, such as the General Agreement on Tariffs and Trade (GATT), to reduce national economic barriers. The EDCs also created a number of global and regional intergovernmental organizations (IGOs) to handle a range of economic interactions across national boundaries. The most prominent of these IGOs are the World Bank, the International Monetary Fund (IMF), and the United Nations, with its numerous economic agencies and responsibilities.

Thus began the current era of global and regional economic cooperation. Many of the changes that Hull and others anticipated came to pass. Trade and the flow of international capital flourished. These successes and the need to regulate the increased financial flows led to new agreements and to new IGOs dedicated to still further reductions of national economic barriers. The European Union (EU), the World Trade Organization (WTO), and the North American Free Trade Agreement (NAFTA) are just three of the more recent IGOs or treaties that facilitate and further the free flow of goods, services, and capital. We will examine these agreements and organizations by first taking up global efforts, then by turning to regional ones.

Global Economic Cooperation

The effort to create global economic cooperation led to two types of IGOs. One type addresses a wide range of economic and, sometimes, other issues. The UN is the best example and was discussed extensively in chapter 7, so only UN–sponsored international cooperation on development issues will be discussed here. The second type is specialized and focuses on just one aspect of international economics. The WTO, which concentrates on the trade of goods and services, is one such specialized economic IGO.

The UN and the Economic Development of the South

The second focus of UN economic activity has been on the economic development of the LDCs. Many of the UN's programs began during the mid-1960s in response to the decolonization of much of the South and the needs and demands of the new countries. The UN's attempts to foster international cooperation to advance the economic fortunes of the LDCs also reflect the organization's mission, as stated in the preamble to the UN Charter, "to employ international machinery for the promotion of the economic and social advancements of all people." This statement of values was high-flown rhetoric in 1945 and mostly still is. There is, however, a substantial and growing number of people in the North and South who contend that aiding the South to develop is not just a matter of humanitarianism.

Pragmatic Factors Urging UN Development Assistance to the South   In addition to the humanitarian reasons for assisting the South, there are a number of pragmatic concerns that motivate the UN to try to help the LDCs develop economically. *Decreased international violence* is one way that the North will benefit from increased prosperity in the South, according to aid advocates. This view contends that the poor are becoming increasingly hostile toward the wealthy. We have earlier noted that modern communications have heightened the South's sense of relative deprivation—the awareness of a deprived person (group, country) of the gap between his or her circumstances and the relatively better position of others. Research shows that seeing another's prosperity and knowing that there are alternatives to your own impoverished condition cause frustration and a sense of being cheated that often lead to resentment and sometimes to violence. Africans and others among the world's poor are "bound to wonder why it should be that poverty still prevails [over] the greater part of the globe," President Nelson Mandela warned the UN General Assembly, and was known to be angered by the fact that "many in positions of power and privilege pursue cold-hearted philosophies which terrifyingly proclaim, 'I am not your brother's keeper.' "[13]

Increased economic prosperity for the EDCs is another benefit that many analysts believe will result from the betterment of the LDCs. This view maintains that it is in the North's long-term economic interest to aid the South's development. After World War II, the United States launched the Marshall Plan, which gave billions of dollars to Europe. One motivation was the U.S. realization that it needed an economically revitalized Europe with which to trade and in which to invest. Europe recovered, and its growth helped drive the strong growth of the American economy. In the same way, according to many analysts, helping the South toward prosperity would require an immense investment by the North. In the long run, though, that investment would create a world in which many of the 1.2 billion Chinese could purchase Fords, more of India's 890 million people could afford to travel in Boeing airplanes, and a majority of the 98 million Nigerians could buy IBM personal computers. It is true that a developed South will compete economically with the North, but economic history demonstrates that increased production and competition bring more, better, and cheaper products that increase the standard of living for all.

The North: The Recalcitrant Rich   Whatever the logic of the pragmatic benefits of increasing LDC prosperity may seem, the North has been slow to respond to the development needs of the South. Traditional narrow self-interest has been strengthened recently by the rising global economic competition among, and economic uncertainty within, the EDCs. One indication of this trend, as we have noted, is that bilateral foreign economic aid–giving by the EDCs has dropped off both in real dollars and as a percentage of the EDCs' cumulative GDPs.

Efforts to bring the North and South together directly to marshal resources and coordinate programs have also shown very limited results. The initial UN–sponsored meeting, which was held in 1981 at Cancún, Mexico, yielded little of financial substance. Subsequent global meetings, such as the 1992 conference on the environment in Rio de Janeiro, the 1994 conference on population in Cairo, and the 1995 conference on social development in Copenhagen, also have not moved the North to loosen its purse strings. For example, the last of the UN's planned global conferences of the 1990s, the 1996 World Food Summit in Rome, ended, according to one press report, "on

Figure 12.2

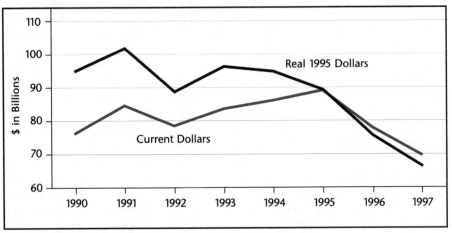

Economic Development Aid

Data source: OECD DAC Statistics at http://www.oecd.org/dac/htm/table1.htm

Somewhat different perspectives are gained by using current and real dollars as measures of total official development assistance (DA) from the North to the South through both bilateral and multilateral programs, such as the UN and IMF. The aid flow in current dollars trends upward during the 1990s to 1995, then drops off. The aid flow in real dollars (1995 = 100) shows that there has been a downward trend in the value of economic aid throughout the 1990s. The recalcitrant North has become steadily more averse to parting with government funds to assist the economic development of the South.

familiar notes: a vague pledge to do better, sharp words from poor nations against rich ones, . . . and American reservations about the internationally recognized right to be fed." The conference set down a goal to cut in half by the year 2015 the 840 million people who are malnourished, and it reaffirmed the standard that EDCs should contribute at least 0.7 percent of their GDPs to economic development. Typical of the reactions of the North to such goals and standards, the Clinton administration declared that the United States considered providing adequate nutrition for the world's poor as only "a goal or aspiration" that "does not give rise to any international obligations."[14] Indeed it is possible to argue that the recalcitrance of the rich is hardening, as Figure 12.2 demonstrates.

UN Development Programs Given the South's vast development needs and the North's limited response, the UN has provided a vital vehicle to supply information, to help obtain what funds there are, and to coordinate programs for the economic development of the LDCs.

The General Assembly, for example, combined a number of older programs and, by expanding them, created the **UN Development Programme (UNDP)** in 1965 to provide both technical assistance (such as planning) and development funds to LDCs. The UNDP's 1997 budget was approximately $2.1

billion, obtained through voluntary contributions from the member-countries of the UN and its affiliated agencies. The UNDP especially focuses on grass-roots economic development, such as promoting entrepreneurship, supporting the Development Fund for Women, and transferring technology and management skills from EDCs to LDCs.

Focusing on macroeconomic development, the **UN Industrial Development Organization (UNIDO)** promotes the growth of industry in LDCs. The suspicion of many in the South that the dependencia-minded North has little true interest in their development was heightened when, in 1967, the LDCs in the UN General Assembly had to overcome considerable opposition by many EDCs in order to create UNIDO. The doubts harbored by the LDCs could not help but be deepened by the announcements in 1995 and 1996 of Australia, Great Britain, and the United States that they were withdrawing from UNIDO. Each of these EDCs argued that its withdrawal was based on inefficiency by UNIDO, but the organization's director-general, Mauricio de Maria y Campos, undoubtedly voiced the view of many in the South when he argued that an "isolationist malaise as regards development assistance is becoming contagious at the multilateral level." This was especially troubling, he said, in light of the fact that "the fruits of globalization have not been equally distributed and poor countries are becoming increasingly marginalized."[15] Other EDCs, such as Germany, declared their intention to remain in UNIDO, and the British eventually decided not to quit the organization. Still, the departure of two important EDCs and the funds they contributed to UNIDO's budget does not bode well for the organization's future.

Another important UN organization, the **United Nations Conference on Trade and Development (UNCTAD)**, was founded in 1964 to address the economic concerns of the LDCs. While UNCTAD itself includes all the members of the UN plus some nonmembers and addresses general issues of trade and LDC development, the organization spun off a closely associated bloc called the Group of 77 (G-77) after the LDCs that issued the Joint Declaration of the Seventy-Seven Countries at the end of the first UNCTAD conference. Since then the G-77 has expanded to include all 185 UN members plus the Holy See, Switzerland, and Tonga. The G-77 meets every four years, with its next scheduled meeting to be held in Thailand in 2000. The organization was a primary vehicle for the formation and expression of LDC demands for a New International Economic Order (NIEO) discussed earlier. The assertive position of the Group of 77 and the bloc's domination of voting in many of the UN's subsidiary bodies caused discord at times with some of the developed nations. For example, this domination led the United States and a few other countries to withdraw from the United Nations Educational, Scientific, and Cultural Organization (UNESCO) on the ground that it had become a mere forum for belaboring the Western industrialized powers. More recently, however, the majority of the G-77 members have been taking a moderate stance, all the EDCs are members of UNCTAD, and the organization has become more mainstream and is not a focus of North-South tensions.

General Economic Cooperation: Other IGOs and Processes

The UN is the best known and most far-reaching of the IGOs promoting general economic cooperation, but it is not the only one. Another such organization is the **Organization for Economic Cooperation and Development (OECD)**. It was originally created by several European countries as the Organization for European Economic Cooperation in 1948 to coordinate the foreign aid that the United States extended to Europe under the European Recovery Plan (the Marshall Plan). In 1960, the member-countries agreed to ask the United States and Canada to join the organization, to change its name to OECD, and to reorient its mission to coordinating economic policy among the Western EDCs. This led to the subsequent admission of Japan and most other EDCs and to the OECD's becoming known as a "rich man's club." This has begun to change slightly. In 1994 Mexico became the first new country to be invited to join the OECD in 21 years. Mexico's admission came in light of its link to the United States and Canada under NAFTA. Since then, the Czech Republic, Hungary, Poland, and South Korea have also been admitted to the OECD, and other countries will also almost certainly soon become members. Thus it is possible to argue that the OECD is once again changing, or at least expanding, its mission to include the exchange of information and economic policy coordination among some newly industrializing countries (NICs) and some **countries in transition (CITs)** from communism to capitalism as well as among the established EDCs.

If the OECD is something of an exclusive club of the prosperous, the Group of Seven (G-7) is equivalent to the executive board. The G-7 does not have a formal connection to the OECD, but it does represent the pinnacle of economic power. As discussed earlier, the G-7, the seven most economically powerful Western countries (Canada, France, Germany, Great Britain, Italy, Japan, and the United States) have met annually beginning in 1975 as an informal economic directorate. In 1997, at the annual G-7 summit, which that year was held in Denver, Colorado, the membership was expanded for political matters to include Russia. This created what was styled a "Summit of Eight," which the press quickly labeled the G-8. The original G-7 members, however, also continued to meet separately on economic matters. This will create confusion and, to make matters worse, the president of the EU has also attended the G-7 meetings on an informal basis in recent years, leading some analysts to talk of a G-7½ and now G-8½.

Whether the G-number is 7, 8, or 8½, the most important issue is the impact of the process. Most analysts conclude that the annual summit plays a positive, if not always clear-cut role. As one scholar writes, the member-countries "do comply modestly with the decisions and consensus generated [at the annual economic summit meetings]. Compliance is particularly high in regard to agreements on international trade and energy." The analyst also points out that the meetings provide "an important occasion for busy leaders to discuss major, often complex international issues, and to develop the personal relations that help them" both to "respond in an effective fashion to sudden crises or shocks" and to "shape the international [economic] order more generally."[16]

These finance ministers of Western EDCs appear relatively relaxed at their Washington, D.C., meeting in April 1999. But in recent years they have had to help the world cope with a series of significant economic crises. From the recurrent Russian economic upheavals to downturns throughout Asia and Latin America, global financial problems require the intervention of the G-7 countries to broker international solutions.

The 1999 G-8 meeting in Köln, Germany, for example, focused on the crisis in Kosovo, debt relief for LDCs, and on the development of methods to control the $1 trillion in currency trade and stock investments that take place across the globe each day. The volatility of financial flows has been at the center of the various regional financial crises that have occurred in recent years. The debt issue also obtained some international nongovernmental attention at the 1999 summit as Irish rock singer Bono and Bishop Rodriguez of Honduras handed over a petition to the summit members demanding that the G-8 eliminate Third World debt by the year 2000. On a cooperative note, U.S.–Japan relations showed signs of warming at the summit as President Clinton praised Japan's success in turning around its economic slump and stated that the progress is "a tribute to the steadfast economic reform program of . . . prime minister [Keizo Obuchi]."[17]

Trade Cooperation: GATT and the WTO

While the UN addresses the broad range of global economic issues, there are a number of IGOs that focus on one or another specific area of economic interchange. One of the most prominent of these specialized economic IGOs on the global level is the **General Agreement on Tariffs and Trade (GATT)**. It was founded in 1947 to promote free trade, and for most of its existence, the name GATT was the source of considerable confusion because it was both the name of a treaty and the name of the organization headquartered in Geneva, Switzerland, that coordinated treaty implementation and conducted other functions. That confusion has now ended. The latest revision of GATT, discussed below, created the **World Trade Organization**, which superseded the GATT organization as of January 1, 1995. Therefore, references to the organization (even in its historical, pre–WTO years) will use WTO; the treaty will be referred to as GATT. Whatever its name, the organization's initial membership was 23 countries, but it has now expanded to 127 members and 30 additional governments have sought membership. The trade of the full members accounts for more than 85 percent of all world trade. GATT has played an important role in promoting the meteoric expansion of international trade. The organization has sponsored a series of trade negotiations that have greatly reduced tariffs and nontariff barriers (NTBs), such as import quotas.

The Latest Revisions of GATT: The Uruguay Round   The eighth, and latest, round of negotiations to revise GATT in order to further reduce trade barriers was convened in Punta del Este, Uruguay, in 1986. The **Uruguay Round** proved to be the most difficult in GATT history. When, in April 1994, the members of GATT finally gathered in Marrakech, Morocco, to sign an agreement, they broke into thunderous applause. The head of GATT, Peter Sutherland of Ireland, gleefully admitted that he was "tempted" to do "an Irish jig on the table."[18] From Washington, President Clinton hailed the pact as promoting a "vision of economic renewal" for the United States and the rest of the world.[19]

Not everyone shared Clinton's rosy view of the agreement. Some businesses that would face increased international competition were unhappy. "I consider this [GATT] to be just a complete sellout of this [the U.S. textile] industry," objected the president of Fruit of the Loom.[20] Other critics focused on the loss of sovereignty that abiding by the treaty necessarily imposes on all signatories. American commentator Patrick J. Buchanan, for one, depicted the GATT agreement as "a wholesale surrender of American sovereignty and states' rights."[21] Still other U.S. critics warned that the new GATT rules would undermine environmental protection, health and safety, and other liberal goals. These concerns have been confirmed, in the view of some, by such events as a WTO ruling in 1998 that the U.S. law that banned shrimp imports from countries whose shrimp nets failed to protect sea turtles was a violation of GATT rules. "This is the clearest slap at environmental protection to come out of the WTO to date," protested the head of one environmental group.[22]

What is important, though, is that, overall, the countries that signed the Uruguay Round document agreed to reduce their tariffs over a 10-year period by an average of one-third. According to U.S. estimates, these cuts will reduce tariffs globally by $744 billion over 10 years. Agricultural tariffs were included in GATT for the first time, and the agreement also further reduced or barred many NTBs. Japan will have to end its ban on rice imports, for example; the United States will have to end its import quotas on peanuts, dairy products, sugar, textiles, and apparel. The signatories also agreed that by 1999 they would institute effective protection of intellectual property such as patents, copyrights, trade secrets, and trademarks within five years.

Some outstanding economic issues remain outside of the GATT rules because negotiators in the Uruguay Round put them aside when they failed to reach an agreement. Because of its fear of becoming culturally Americanized, Europe, especially France, would not agree to permit unlimited distribution of movies, music, or other cultural products. Fear of losing financial control left many countries, both North and South, opposed to opening completely their insurance, banking, and brokerage service industries. National regulation and protection of the shipping, steel, and telecommunications industries were also largely exempted from GATT provisions.

Another unresolved issue for GATT involves China's adherence to the treaty and its possible membership in the WTO. China has sought membership under the rules that govern LDCs. These rules give the LDCs some advantages, such as allowing them to keep tariffs somewhat higher or somewhat longer to protect infant industries from foreign competition.

The United States has blocked China's entry into the WTO on the grounds that China's total industrial output is so large that it should not be accorded the extra protections. The rising U.S. trade deficit with China has served to intensify the American position. The projected U.S. trade deficit with China for 1998 came to about $52 billion, just slightly below the approximate $62 billion deficit with Japan. Negotiations have continued and were part of the discussions between President Bill Clinton and President Jiang Zemin when they met in Beijing in 1998. The negotiations have not, however, resolved the outstanding issues. Furthermore, the resolve of the Clinton administration has been further stiffened by the insistence of Congress that pressure be brought to bear on China. As one influential senator said, "The administration must insist that China enter under terms that are fair to the American people."[23]

The Structure and Role of the WTO　To deal with the complexities of GATT and to deal with the disputes that will inevitably arise, the Uruguay Round also created the World Trade Organization. Headquartered in Geneva, Switzerland, and currently headed by Director-General Renato Ruggiero of Italy, the WTO has the power to enforce the provisions of GATT and to assess trade penalties against countries that violate the accord. While any country can withdraw from the WTO by giving six months' notice, that country would suffer significant economic perils because its products would no longer be subject to the reciprocal low tariffs and other advantages WTO members accord one another. When one country charges another with a trade violation, a three-judge panel under the WTO hears the complaints. If the panel finds a violation, the WTO may impose sanctions on the offending country. Each country will have one vote in the WTO, and sanctions may be imposed by a two-thirds vote. This means, among other things, that domestic laws may be disallowed by the WTO if they are found to be de facto trade barriers.

Despite grumbling by critics about the loss of sovereignty, the WTO judicial process has gotten off to a good start. From 1995 through mid-1998, the WTO handled 131 cases. The United States was the country most frequently involved in the process, bringing 49 complaints to the WTO and having to answer 23 complaints by other countries. Many of these issues are settled "out of court," but of the cases actually decided by the WTO through mid-1998, the United States prevailed nine times and lost in four instances. Some, such as the ruling overturning an EU ban on U.S. beef from cattle injected with hormones, cheered interested Americans; others, such as a WTO ruling dismissing the U.S. complaint that Japan was discriminating against Kodak film, dismayed interested Americans.

When it has lost, however, Washington has so far quietly given way. What remains to be seen, however, is U.S. reaction when a highly sensitive case is brought before the WTO. The attempts by the United States through the Helms-Burton Act and other legislation to punish foreign companies that do business with Cuba, Iran, Libya, and some other countries sparked considerable anger in many countries, and in 1996 the European Union announced it would challenge the legality of these sanctions by bringing the matter before the WTO. When in 1997 the WTO moved to appoint a panel of judges to hear the case, a senior U.S. official said the WTO "has no competence to proceed" and declared, "We will not show up" at the hearing.[24] What could have been a WTO-destroying confrontation, however, was avoided when, in April 1998, the EU withdrew its complaint on the tacit understanding that President Clinton would continue to use his power to temporarily waive the provisions of the Helms-Burton law and would negotiate a resolution of the dispute with Europe.

Monetary Cooperation: The IMF

As trade and the level of other international financial transactions have increased, the need to cooperate internationally to facilitate and stabilize the flow of dollars, marks, yen, pounds, and other currencies has become vital. To meet this need, a number of organizations have been founded. The most important of these is the **International Monetary Fund (IMF)**.

A SITE TO SURF
The International
Monetary Fund

Early Monetary Regulation   The formation of the IMF stemmed in part from the belief of many analysts that the Great Depression of the 1930s and World War II were partly caused by the near international monetary chaos that characterized the years between 1919 and 1939. Wild inflation struck some countries. Many countries suspended the convertibility of their currencies, and the North broke up into rival American, British, and French monetary blocs. Other countries, such as Germany, abandoned convertibility altogether and adopted protectionist monetary and trade policies. It was a period of open economic warfare—a prelude to the military hostilities that followed.

As part of postwar planning, the Allies met in 1944 at Bretton Woods, New Hampshire, to establish a new monetary order. The **Bretton Woods system** operated on the basis of "fixed convertibility into gold." The system relied on the strength of the U.S. dollar, which was set at a rate of $35 per ounce of gold.

The delegates at Bretton Woods also established the IMF and several other institutions to help promote and regulate the world economy. Thus, like GATT, the IMF was created by the West, with the United States in the lead, as part of the liberalization of international economic interchange. The specific role of the IMF in attempting to provide stability will be discussed in the next section.

The Bretton Woods system worked reasonably well as long as the American economy was strong, international confidence in it remained high, and countries accepted and held dollars on a basis of their being "as good as gold."

The Role of the IMF   The IMF's primary function is to help maintain exchange-rate stability by making short-term loans to countries with international balance-of-payments problems because of trade deficits, heavy loan payments, or other factors. In such times, the IMF extends a country a line of credit that the country can use to draw upon IMF funds in order to help meet debt payments, to buy back its own currency (thus maintaining exchange-rate stability by balancing supply and demand), or take other financial steps.

The IMF receives its funds from reserves ($65.6 billion in 1998) placed at its disposal by wealthier member-countries and from earnings that it derives from interest on loans made to countries that draw on those reserves. To help countries stabilize their currencies, the IMF has created **Special Drawing Rights (SDRs)** as reserves that central banks of needy countries can draw on. SDR value is based on an average value, or market basket, of several currencies, and SDRs are acceptable as payment at central banks. In mid-1999, one SDR equaled about 1.36 U.S. dollars. Countries facing unacceptable declines in their currencies can borrow SDRs from the IMF and use them in addition to their own reserves to counter the price change. In mid-1998, the IMF had $77.1 billion in outstanding loans and credit lines to 97 countries. The growth of total outstanding IMF lending during this decade through 1998 is shown in Figure 12.3.

While SDRs have helped, they have not always been sufficient to halt instability. One problem is that the funds at the IMF's command are paltry compared to the immense daily flow of about $1.5 trillion in currency trading. Also, monetary regulation is difficult because countries often work at odds with one another.

Over the last two decades, the IMF has especially concentrated on loans to LDCs and to CITs. The IMF typically loans countries money to support their currency or to stabilize their financial situation by refinancing their debt. Representative of this focus, all $77.1 billion of the IMF's outstanding loans in mid-1998 were to LDCs and CITs, especially Russia. Indeed, of all countries, Russia had the largest outstanding loan ($13.7 billion) from the IMF.

Mexico was second, with its $9.0 billion outstanding loan stemming from the peso crisis. The flow of support to Mexico became necessary when

Figure 12.3

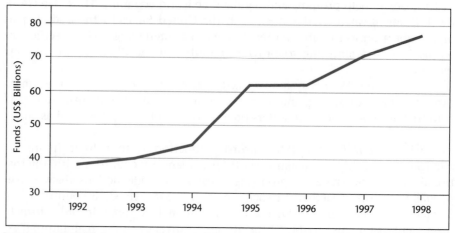

Total IMF Credit and Loans Outstanding, 1992–1998

Data source: IMF (1998). Source expresses data in SDRs; conversion to dollars by author using average SDR rate for each year. Data for 1998 is as of August.

The need to keep currencies stable in a free-floating exchange rate environment has lead to increasing importance for the IMF. The significant jump in IMF funding between 1994 and 1995 largely reflects loans to Mexico and to Russia; the jumps in 1997 and 1998 reflect the crises in Asia and Russia.

in December 1994 the foreign exchange value of the Mexican peso collapsed after several years of too-rapid expansion, intensive foreign speculation in Mexican financial securities, worry about Mexico's political stability and corruption, and some mismanagement by the Mexican treasury. Within six weeks the value of the peso plunged 45 percent from one peso equaling 28.9 U.S. cents to one peso equaling 15.9 cents.

To prevent further economic, and perhaps political, chaos in Mexico, and to protect its own substantial economic interests in a prosperous Mexican economy, the United States led an international financial rescue effort that included a $50 billion credit line, with the United States ($20 billion) and the IMF ($18 billion) by far the largest backers. The Clinton administration believed, almost certainly correctly, that the peso crisis threatened the U.S. economy. "In the end there is no choice," said one Clinton administration official; "Mexico has become an integral part of the North American market. . . . The two economies are intertwined in trade, in commerce, in the movement of people. And in the end, the bigger need is to have a stable country on our border."[25]

The IMF and the Asian Financial Crisis   The most recent round of economic crises—those in Asia and Russia—have led the EDCs and the IMF to develop new mechanisms for the disbursement of IMF financial assistance. In particular, in April 1999, the IMF Executive Board approved a U.S. proposal that would allow the international organization to better anticipate crises and send financial assistance to countries before their economies devolve into economic chaos. During the recent rounds of global economic problems, the IMF disbursed over $100 billion in rescue packages worldwide, but only after IMF conditions pushed the recipient economies deeply into recession and their currencies crashed on international markets. Trying to put the best face on still difficult economic times, IMF managing director, Michel Camdessus, said that he is "confident that this [new approach] will be an important contribution for the world to be better prepared for future crises."

But the IMF reforms may be too late, as the damage of the 1997 and 1998 economic shocks continue to be felt in Asia and Russia. In Asia, the currencies and economies of the Pacific Rim LDCs and NICs—especially Indonesia, Malaysia, South Korea, and Thailand—nose-dived in 1997 and 1998. The flow of outside investment capital into these countries dropped from a net inflow of about $90 billion in 1995 to a net outflow of −$9 billion in 1997. After years of strong growth, the GDP growth of Indonesia, Malaysia, South Korea, and Thailand all fell to near zero in 1997 and all declined in 1998. Indonesia was the worst hit, with a nearly 20 percent GDP decline in 1998.

This economic implosion led to a massive international effort, with the IMF at the forefront, to help stabilize and restart those economies. During the period extending from mid-1997 through mid-1998, the Pacific Rim countries were the largest borrowers from the IMF. Some $37 billion in IMF loans went to these countries, as part of an overall international financial assistance package of $82 billion.

The international effort was spurred by the threat posed to the world's interdependent economy by the economic destabilization of Asia. The United States, for example, exports 27 percent of its merchandise to the countries of the Pacific Rim. That region's troubles caused U.S. exports to Indonesia, Malaysia, South Korea, and Thailand to drop 44 percent from $27.8 billion during the first six months of 1997 to $15.9 billion during the first six months of 1998. The impact of this seemingly dry statistic was felt in many American homes. When, for example, United Technologies, headquartered in East Hartford, Connecticut, announced that it was laying off 1,000 workers, the company cited the decrease in aircraft jet engine orders from Asia as a primary cause.

The IMF and the Russian Financial Crisis   In addition to its assistance to the LDCs, the second main thrust of the IMF's recent efforts, and indeed its program throughout the 1990s, has been to extend assistance to the CITs in their attempts to reorient toward a market economy. In addition to the outstanding loans to Russia of $13.7 billion at the beginning of 1998, the other former Soviet republics (FSR) and CITs of Eastern Europe had outstanding loans of $7.2 billion. In total, about 29 percent of the IMF's outstanding loans in 1998 were to these countries.

As with the LDCs, the IMF's assistance to the CITs is dependent in part on the recipients' instituting market economy–oriented changes approved by the IMF. Also, just as with the LDCs, these strings attached to the IMF loans and lines of credit are controversial. It is also the case that the IMF and its managing director have responded to political as well as financial considerations in extending assistance to Russia and other CITs. The United States very much wanted to see President Boris Yeltsin reelected in 1996, and there can be little doubt that Washington's thinking helped influence the decision of the IMF to give Yeltsin a strong boost amid the Russian presidential campaign by announcing a further credit line of $10.2 billion for Russia.

These funds, it turned out, were not enough. A new, intense economic crisis broke out in mid-1998 when the inability of the Russian government to pay its bills sparked a precipitous drop in the ruble, from an exchange rate of 6 rubles = $1 to 14 rubles = $1 during July. The IMF responded to Russia's rapidly deteriorating financial instability, and to worries that this could lead to political turmoil, by approving $11.2 billion to help Moscow try to defend the ruble and to prevent a collapse of Russia's monetary and economic systems. In return, the IMF demanded that Russia continue to institute economic reforms, the most important of which was increasing tax revenues through better enforcement of existing tax laws. The IMF loans to Russia also helped set the stage for the World Bank and other lenders to advance up to another $17 billion to Russia.

The future of the Russian economy and the IMF credit line remains unclear. The financial crisis led President Yeltsin, after firing one prime minister and failing to get his replacement confirmed by the parliament, to name foreign minister Yevgeny Primakov to the post. A ranking diplomat in the communist government, Primakov indicated that he might revert to more government controls of the economy, rather than press for reforms that the IMF and the West desire. To compound worries about his posture, Primakov soon replaced most Western-oriented reformers in the government with a combination of former Communist Party officials and stronger nationalists who are critical of what they see as IMF interference in Russia's affairs. These actions could lead to policies that the IMF and its backers will find unacceptable and to a refusal by the IMF to continue its loans.

Controversy about the IMF Although the IMF has played a valuable role, it has not been above criticism. Indeed, in recent years the IMF has been one focus of struggle between the North and the South. This discord stems from two facts. First, voting on the IMF board of directors is based on the level of each member's contribution to the fund's resources. This formula gives EDCs 61 percent of the votes. Just five EDCs, the United States (18 percent), Germany and Japan (6 percent each), and France and Great Britain (5 percent each) have more votes than all the LDCs and CITs put together, which control only 39 percent of the votes. This apportionment has led to LDC charges that the fund is controlled by the North and is being used as a tool to dominate the LDCs.

The second criticism of the IMF is that it imposes unfair and unwise conditions on countries that use its financial resources. Most loans granted by the IMF to LDCs are subject to **conditionality**. This refers to requirements that the borrowing country take steps to remedy the situations that caused its balance-of-payments deficit. The IMF is also instrumental in securing new commercial loans or in the renegotiation of existing loans for LDCs, and, here again, the IMF bases its recommendations on whether these countries follow fiscal policies that the IMF considers prudent. The IMF's conditions press the LDCs to move toward a capitalist economy by such steps as privatizing state-run enterprises, reducing barriers to trade and to the flow of capital (thus promoting foreign ownership of domestic businesses), reducing domestic programs in order to cut government budget deficits, ending domestic subsidies or laws that artificially suppress prices, and devaluing currencies (which increase exports and make imports more expensive).

On the surface such conditions sound prudent, but in reality they have their drawbacks. First, LDCs charge that the IMF interferes in their sovereign domestic processes. Second, some argue that implementation of some of the reforms may destabilize countries. Those who object to conditionality claim that it harms the quality of life of LDC residents by reducing economic growth and by forcing governments to cut social services in order to maintain a balanced budget. Often it is the poorest people that are hurt the most, and civil unrest is not uncommon. When, for example, Jordan, under conditionality pressures in 1996, ended its subsidy of bread, the price of that staple food shot up overnight by 117 percent. In a country where one-third of the population lives below the poverty line, this price increase caused real hardship and sparked riots in Amman and other cities. Critics of conditionality worry that such political instability may threaten governments, particularly the new, still-tenuous democratic governments in some countries. Indeed, critics charge that the IMF asks LDCs to follow policies, such as balanced budgets and reduced imports, that countries in the North, especially the United States, cannot accomplish!

Third, some critics have contended that conditionality is aimed at maintaining the dependencia relationship. Reacting to the conditions laid down by the IMF in 1997 and 1998 to assist Asia's faltering economies, *Matichon,* a daily newspaper in Thailand, editorialized that the conditions amounted to "economic colonialism" and denounced the "financial and economic wars" that the paper said the EDCs were waging to humble the region.[26] From the same perspective, a South Korean newspaper, *Dong-A Ilbo,* wrote, "It is not desirable that [the EDCs] made use of our desperate situation for their own gains."[27]

Here we return to the importance of perceptions. Whether or not conditionality is economically or politically oppressive, and whether, even if it is neoimperialist, the IMF and others are doing it inadvertently or with intent to dominate, the reality is that many in the LDCs believe it to be so. Thus, not only is the level of current lending available from private and public sources insufficient to meet the capital needs of the LDCs, but the conditions attached to the loans and the strain of repaying huge amounts add to the tension along the North-South Axis.

The IMF and the conditionality requirements attached to its loans are also a source of contention with Russia and the other CITs. The IMF has not been subtle about its desire to push these countries to adopt capitalist economies.

In the words of the IMF's managing director, "the stronger the program [of capitalist reform], the stronger the financing will be."[28]

A SITE TO SURF
The World
Bank Group

Development Cooperation: The World Bank Group

A third type of multilateral economic cooperation involves granting loans and aid for the economic development of LDCs. The most significant development agency today is the **World Bank Group**. The group has four agencies. Two of them, the International Bank for Reconstruction and Development (IBRD) and the International Development Association (IDA), are collectively referred to as the World Bank. The larger World Bank Group also includes the International Finance Corporation (IFC) and the Multilateral Investment Guarantee Agency (MIGA).

Of the four World Bank Group agencies, the IBRD, which was founded in 1946, is the oldest and, with 180 members, the largest. All four agencies get their funds from money subscribed by their member-governments, from money the agencies borrow, and from interest paid on the loans they make.

The *International Bank for Reconstruction and Development*, of the four, is the agency whose lending policies most closely resemble those of a commercial bank. The bank applies standards of creditworthiness to recipients and the projects they wish to fund, and, like private banks, charges interest rates based on what it costs the bank to borrow money plus a relatively thin "margin" of 0.5 percent. In 1997, the IBRD made loans of $14.5 billion to fund 141 projects. The average interest the IBRD charged was 5.01 percent, and it had a net income of $1.3 billion.

Not all of the IBRD's programs, however, are determined by strict economic criteria. For example, in 1996 the bank established programs to help shattered Bosnia. The bank also set up a program to create jobs in the West Bank and Gaza to try to facilitate the evolving, but fragile peace between Palestinians and Israelis. In 1996, the IBRD also departed from its normal focus on funding development projects by agreeing to use part of its annual net revenue to help the IMF reduce the outstanding loan balances of the most indebted LDCs.

Like the IMF, the agencies that make up the World Bank Group do a great deal of good, but they have also been the subject of considerable controversy. One point of criticism involves the North's domination of the South. An American runs the World Bank, an Italian heads the WTO, and a Frenchman directs the IMF. Exemplifying these leaders is the ninth and current (since June 1995) head of the World Bank, James D. Wolfensohn. He holds MBA and J.D. degrees and has been an attorney, a Wall Street investment officer, and a consultant on international investing to more than 30 multinational corporations. As evidence of the North's domination, critics also point out that the World Bank Group, like the IMF, has a board of directors with a voting formula that gives the majority of the votes to the handful of EDCs. The United States has over 15 percent of the votes in both the IBRD and the IDA. France, Germany, Great Britain, and Japan collectively account for about another 28 percent of the IBRD and IDA votes, giving these five countries a cumulative total of about 43 percent of the vote in the two organizations.

A second complaint about the World Bank is simply that it provides too little funding. Figures such as $19.1 billion in total World Bank commitments to projects in 1997 sound impressive. But they are less so in light of the fact that lending has dropped off, with 1997 loan commitments $4.1 billion less than in 1993. Moreover, the bank's 1997 net disbursements (money given out minus repayments received) were just $7.5 billion.

The terms of the loans are a third sore spot. The World Bank Group is caught between the North's concentration on "businesslike," interest-bearing loans and the South's demands that more loans be unconditionally granted to the poorest countries at low rates or with no interest at all. The World Bank also demands that recipients take sometimes painful measures to correct what the bank judges to be economically damaging policies. Many in the LDCs charge that such policies violate their sovereignty and hurt more than they help. "I think the World Bank is some kind of monster," says Monique Olboudo, a lawyer in Burkina Faso. "It sits on top of Africa like an octopus, sucking us dry. It never looks to see the effects on the lives of the people. It treats us like numbers, economic agents."[29]

A fourth criticism of the World Bank is that it has paid too little attention to the human and environmental impacts of the projects it has funded. A bank study issued in 1994 found, for example, that dams and other projects that it had funded had created 2.5 million "development refugees" whose homes had been flooded or who had otherwise been displaced between 1986 and 1993, and that between 1994 and 1997 another 600,000 would join the ranks of development refugees because of projects funded by the bank.[30] Such negative impacts have led the World Bank to impose stricter environmental provisions on projects. The bank also now gives loans to support environmental projects, and these amounted to $250 million in 1997.

A fifth criticism of the World Bank Group has heated up in the post–cold war era as the World Bank Group and other financial IGOs have all allied themselves further with the U.S. desire to promote market economies, foreign direct investment, and other aspects of capitalism. Speaking about the Inter-American Development Bank (IDB), a regional equivalent of the World Bank, one former bank official commented that "the IDB shouldn't be in the business of making life easier for the capital markets. [It should be] in the business of helping development of countries, typically things like water, sanitation, health, and education, not toll roads, telecommunications, or power stations." The crux of the matter is whether the interests of foreign investors, who hope to make a profit, can be balanced with those of the host countries.

Regional Economic Cooperation

For all the far-reaching economic cooperative efforts at the global level, the degree of activity and economic cooperation and integration at the regional

Table 12.1

Regional Trade Organizations and Agreements

Name	Founded	Membership
European Union and antecedents	1958	15
Latin American Free Trade Association	1960	11
Central American Common Market	1961	5
Council of Arab Economic Unity	1964	11
Central African Customs Union	1966	6
Association of Southeast Asian Nations	1967	10
Andean Group	1969	5
Caribbean Community and Common Market	1973	14
Economic Community of West African States	1975	16
Gulf Cooperation Council	1981	6
Economic Community of Central African States	1983	10
Arab Cooperation Council	1989	4
Arab Maghreb Union	1989	5
Asia Pacific Economic Cooperation	1989	18
Black Sea Economic Cooperation Zone	1992	11
North American Free Trade Agreement	1992	3
South African Development Community	1992	12
Southern Common Market (Mercosur)	1995	5
Free Trade Area of the Americas	1995	34

The geographically diverse, growing number of regional trade organizations testifies to the belief of most countries that they are better able to achieve or preserve prosperity through relatively free trade than through protectionism.

**MAP
Regional
Trading
Groups**

level is even more advanced. There are a dozen regional development banks. In terms of loan commitments in 1996, the largest regional banks (and their assets) are the just-mentioned, 46-member IDB ($6 billion), the 57-member Asian Development Bank ($9.4 billion), and the 58-member European Bank for Reconstruction and Development ($2.5 billion), which focuses on projects in the European CITs. Many other regional banks are much more limited in their funding. The annual loans of the poorly funded Caribbean Development Bank, for example, amount to less than $100 million, despite its region's pressing needs.

There is also a large and growing number of regional organizations that promote free trade and other forms of economic interchange. Table 12.1 provides just one index of the interest in regional economic interchange. Note the global diversity of the regional organizations. Some, in truth, are little more than shell organizations that keep their goals barely alive. Yet in its founding, each organization represents the conviction of its members that, compared to standing alone, they could achieve greater economic prosperity by working together through economic cooperation or even economic integration.

Economic cooperation is a process whereby sovereign states cooperate with one another bilaterally or multilaterally through IGOs (such as the IMF) or processes (such as the G-7 meetings). *Economic integration* means such a close degree of economic intertwining that, by formal agreement or informal circumstance, the countries involved begin to surrender some degree of sovereignty and act as an economic unit. There is no precise point when economic cooperation becomes economic integration. It is more a matter of moving along a continuum ranging from economic isolation, through mercantile policy, then to economic cooperation, and finally to economic integration. The countries joined together in the EU have moved far along this continuum toward integration; the three countries of NAFTA are just beginning this journey. It is also worth noting that the process of economic integration is not the result of a single strand of activity. Rather, integration is a complex phenomenon that results from the interaction and mutual strengthening of transnational trade and finance, of intergovernmental and nongovernmental international organizations, and of transnational values and international law.

One discussion of transnational economic activity divides economic integration into five levels (Feld, 1979). These levels (ranging from the least to the most integrated) are (1) a *free trade area,* which eliminates trade barriers for goods between member-countries; (2) a *customs union,* which adds common tariff and nontariff barriers adopted against external countries; (3) a *common market,* which increases integration further by eliminating barriers among members to the free flow of labor, capital, and other aspects of economic interchange; (4) an *economic union,* which proceeds to harmonize the economic policies (such as tax and social welfare policies) of members; and (5) a *monetary union,* which adopts a common currency, a common central bank, and other aspects of financial integration. Feld (p. 272) comments that once monetary union is achieved, "the member states might be very close to political unification." He adds the caveat that this final step "might not really be possible without the unification of political institutions." This comment has proven to be the case for the EU, as we shall explore presently.

To give our discussion of economic integration additional substance, we can now turn our attention to the progress that has been made along the continuum toward integration. This will entail an examination of regional integration in North America and the Pacific region. The European Union will not be discussed here, as we dealt with it at length in chapter 7.

The Western Hemisphere

Economic cooperation in the Western Hemisphere does not yet rival the level found in Europe, but the process is under way. The origins of hemispheric distinctiveness and a U.S. consciousness of its connection to the hemisphere date back many years. The United States proclaimed the Monroe Doctrine in 1823. Often that meant gunboat diplomacy: heavy-handed, unilateral U.S.

intervention in the region, a practice that continued through the 1989 invasion of Panama. But, slowly, the idea that the United States should help and cooperate with its hemispheric neighbors took hold. The first hemispheric conference met in 1889. A U.S. proposal to establish a customs union was thwarted by the other 17 countries that attended, but they did create the first regional organization, the International Bureau of American Republics. That later became the Pan-American Union, then, by the Rio Treaty of 1948, the Organization of American States (OAS). President Franklin Delano Roosevelt announced the Good Neighbor Policy. John F. Kennedy announced the Alliance for Progress. The first summit of most of the hemisphere's heads of government occurred in Punta del Este, Uruguay, in 1967.

These events and trends have recently led to two important trade efforts. The first was the creation of the North American Free Trade Agreement. The second was a commitment by the hemisphere's countries to create a hemisphere-wide free trade area by the year 2005.

The North American Free Trade Agreement   For good or ill, the United States is the economic hegemon of the Western Hemisphere, and regional integration only truly began when the Americans moved to forge free trade agreements with other countries in the region. That effort began with the **North American Free Trade Agreement (NAFTA)**, encompassing much of the northern half of the hemisphere.

A SITE TO SURF
The North American Free Trade Agreement (NAFTA)

The Evolution and Provisions of NAFTA   The first step toward creating NAFTA was the U.S.–Canada Trade Agreement (1988) to eliminate most economic barriers between the two signatories by 1999. Four years later, Mexico was added to the free trade zone when in October 1992, the leaders of the three countries met in San Antonio, Texas, to sign the NAFTA documents. The following year, after considerable debate, especially in Canada and the United States, each of the countries' legislatures ratified NAFTA, and the treaty went into effect on January 1, 1994.

The agreement, which takes up more than 2,000 pages, established schedules for reducing tariff and nontariff barriers to trade over a 5-to-10-year period in all but a few hundred of some 20,000 product categories. By 2003, almost all U.S. and Canadian tariffs and about 92 percent of all Mexican tariffs on one another's merchandise will have vanished, with all tariffs eliminated by 2009. Also under NAFTA, many previous restrictions on foreign investments and other financial transactions among the NAFTA countries will end, and investments in financial services operations (such as advertising, banking, insurance, and telecommunications) will flow much more freely across borders. This is particularly important for Mexico, which, for example, has not heretofore allowed foreign direct investment in its petroleum industry. American banks, virtually banned from operating in Mexico before NAFTA, will be able to hold 15 percent of the Mexican market by the year 2000. Transportation will also be much easier. Truck and bus companies will have largely unimpeded access across borders, and in 2000, U.S. trucking firms will be allowed to become majority owners of Mexican trucking companies. There is a standing commission with representatives from all three countries to deal with disputes that arise under the NAFTA agreement.

The Impact of NAFTA   There are a few certainties and many uncertainties about the impact of NAFTA on the economies and people of Canada, Mexico, and the United States. NAFTA is certainly less advanced than the EU, but it is a no less portentous example of regional integration. NAFTA is an economic unit that, with 387 million people and a combined GDP of $7.8 trillion, will rival the EU.

The most obvious impact of NAFTA is that it allows a much freer flow of goods, services, and investment among the three member-countries. Trade among them was extensive even before NAFTA, and has grown even closer since then, as can be seen in Figure 12.4. Mexico is the most dependent on intra–NAFTA trade, with 88 percent of its exports going to and 77 percent of its imports coming from the United States and Canada. Canada's level of intra–NAFTA trade is not much less, with 84 percent of exports going to and 70 percent of its imports coming from its NAFTA partners. Another index of the importance of NAFTA is that total U.S.–Canada trade of $327 billion is the world's largest two-way commercial relationship. The United States is least dependent, albeit still heavily so, on NAFTA trade, with 32 percent of U.S. exports going to Canada and Mexico and 29 percent of its imports coming from them.

Beyond trade expansion, it is difficult to be precise about specific impacts. There was a vigorous debate in each of the three countries about whether NAFTA would bring boom or bust. The evidence is still coming in, and its analysis has been made especially complex by the collapse of the Mexican peso at the end of 1994. The vastly devalued peso impeded the ability of Mexicans to import suddenly much more expensive goods from the United States and Canada. By the same token, Mexican goods became much less expensive for Americans and Canadians. Thus, Mexico's imports dropped 16 percent and its exports soared 26 percent in 1995 compared to 1994 before the peso's plunge.

There have been numerous visions offered of a more prosperous future by the leaders of the three countries, and that image tends to be confirmed by most economists. Still, there are substantial reservations among some experts as well as the general public. Nationalism makes some Americans, Canadians, and Mexicans wary of NAFTA. Canadians and Mexicans are concerned about the possibility of being overwhelmed by American dollars and culture. Sharing the continent with the United States was once likened by then–Canadian prime minister Pierre Trudeau to "sleeping with an elephant. No matter how friendly and even-tempered the beast . . . one is affected by every twitch and grunt" (Duchacek, 1975:146).

It is, as noted, too early to tell what the specific impact of NAFTA will be. Some commentators predict that all countries will win. If you believe the naysayers, everyone will lose. What is probably closer to reality is that there will be winners and losers in every country. Consumers in all three countries

Figure 12.4

Expansion of Intra–NAFTA Trade

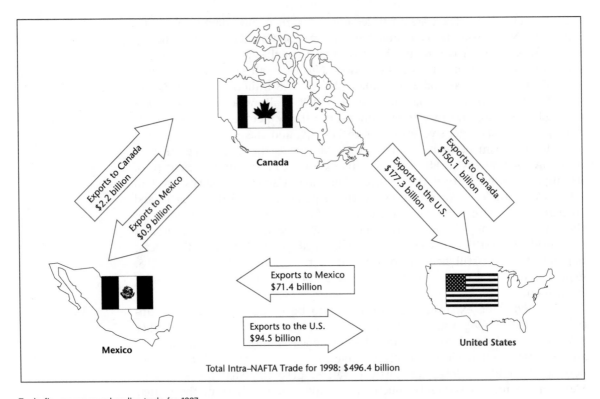

Total Intra–NAFTA Trade for 1998: $496.4 billion

Trade figures are merchandise trade for 1997.

Data source: IMF 1998.

The North American Free Trade Agreement has accounted for a rapid rise in trade among Canada, Mexico, and the United States since the treaty went into effect in 1994. There are now plans for a Western Hemisphere free trade zone, the Free Trade Area of the Americas.

will almost certainly be helped by having access to more products at lower prices due to specialization and competition. Japanese and other Asian electronics producers such as JVC, Matsushita, and Samsung have rushed to set up plants in Tijuana and other Mexican cities just across the border. These border plants, known as *maquiladoras,* have spurred an employment boom along the border and employ more than 24,000 people in Tijuana alone. The impact of NAFTA on the prosperity of the bulk of Mexico farther to the south is much less certain. The maquiladoras and, in general, freer trade with Mexico have also cost over 60,000 American jobs because of shifts of plants over the border and increased competition from Mexican products. Yet, it is also the case that the 1.5 million televisions that Samsung will be producing, employing Mexican workers at about $50 a week, will mean cheaper products for

Americans. It will also be true that as the Mexican peso and economy improve, demand for American products and services will increase.

Whatever the effect on the overall economies of each of the three participating countries may be, it is clear that some businesses and types of workers will benefit; others will be harmed. It is also clear that NAFTA reduced the sovereignty of each signatory. So do all trade agreements and, indeed, all international treaties. It is equally clear, though, that Canada and Mexico are not about to become the 51st and 52nd American states. Political integration at some point in the future is not impossible, but it will be many mañanas before that occurs, if it ever does.

The Free Trade Area of the Americas   It is possible that NAFTA may also be another step toward integration of all or most of the Western Hemisphere. Trade cooperation in the hemisphere moved toward a new higher level in 1994 with the beginning of an effort to create what has been tentatively named the **Free Trade Area of the Americas (FTAA).**

INTERACTIVE
EXERCISE
How Far Should
Western
Hemispheric Free
Trade Go? You Be
the Judge

The Origins of FTAA   Proposals for a free trade area date back to the 1880s, as noted. The reality of trade zones is more recent. Seven of the regional trade groups listed in Table 12.1 are in the Western Hemisphere, and the momentum behind trade cooperation has steadily built up during the past decade. It may be that the creation of a hemispheric trade zone will come through the addition of new members or through the merger of existing regional common markets rather than through the FTAA or some other new trade group.

The most specific precursor of the current efforts to found a hemispheric trade zone occurred in 1990 when President George Bush advocated such a goal (Hufbauer & Schott, 1994). The president said that economic advancement in the hemisphere rested on three pillars: international debt reduction, trade, and investment. Unspoken, but a fourth factor, was the continuing democratization of the hemisphere's countries. Progress was made toward each of these four goals during subsequent years. Debt reduction has proceeded slowly to less perilous, if still unsatisfactory, levels. The debt of Latin America and the Caribbean countries (measured as a percentage of their exports) fell from 384 percent in 1987 to 227 percent in 1997. Trade has grown, with the volume of exports up from an annual average of 4.5 percent during the 1980s to 9.9 percent during the 1990s. Private capital for FDI and other purposes has flowed strongly into the region south of the United States, increasing from $6.7 billion in 1990 to $22.4 billion in 1996. Democracy has spread. When the Summit of the Americas met, all but one (Cuba) of the hemisphere's countries had democratically elected governments.

The Summit of the Americas   The end result of these various efforts was the December 1994 meeting of the heads of 34 countries at the Summit of the Americas in Miami, Florida. Only Cuba was excluded. Their agreement was far-reaching. The conference agreed to aim at the creation of a free trade zone in the hemisphere within 10 years. The leaders also agreed to a series of more than 100 specific political, environmental, and economic programs and reforms. "We pushed very, very hard," said one U.S. official, to get a document in which the signatories pledged, among other things, to "strive to make our trade liberalization and environmental policies mutually supportive" and to "secure the observance and promotion of worker rights."[31]

The conference ended in near-euphoria. "The atmosphere was splendid," said José Angel Gurria, Mexico's secretary of foreign affairs. "We now have a flight plan that will keep us busy for years to come."[32] "When our work is done, the free trade area of the Americas will stretch from Alaska to Argentina," said President Clinton. "In less than a decade, if current trends continue, this hemisphere will be the world's largest market."[33]

The Future of FTAA   If it proceeds as planned, the FTAA will link the Western Hemisphere in a single market that in 2005 will have an estimated 850 million consumers buying $13 trillion worth of goods and services. The bargaining over the details will be difficult. As excited as they are about access to the U.S. markets, the hemisphere's LDCs are equally as nervous about dropping their protections and being drowned in a tidal wave of American imports, services, and purchases of local businesses and other property. Many Americans are just as sure their jobs will wind up in the hands of an underpaid Bolivian, Honduran, or perhaps Uruguayan worker. President Clinton is fond of recalling an image used often by John Kennedy in which JFK would observe, "As they say on my own Cape Cod, a rising tide lifts all boats. And a partnership, by definition, serves both partners." Another possibility, Prime Minister Owen Arthur of Barbados told President Clinton in Miami, is that "a rising tide can . . . overturn small boats."[34] Yet for all the difficulty ahead, the momentum in the direction of creating FTAA will probably carry the day. One is tempted to say that the leaders who gathered in Miami did not so much begin the task of creating a regional trade area as to recognize and organize a process that was already under way.

Yet the exact future of the FTAA remains unclear. When the second FTAA summit meeting convened in Santiago, Chile, in April 1998, the mood was a good deal more sober than it had been in Miami four years earlier. Expanding trade under U.S. leadership has faltered on several fronts. President Clinton has had increasing difficulties getting Congress to support the continued expansion of free economic exchange. For example, as discussed in the Web site box A Tale of Two Policies from chapter 3, Congress in 1997 refused to renew the president's "fast-track authority" to rapidly negotiate trade treaties. President Clinton tried to be optimistic, telling the assembled leaders, "the United States may not yet have fast-track legislation, . . . [but] I assure you that our commitment to the free-trade areas of the Americas will be in the fast lane of our concerns."[35]

The flagging American leadership has prompted one observer to compare U.S. efforts to "a guy who starts a brawl in a barroom and then slips out the backdoor."[36] In part reflecting this hiatus, Chile, which had begun negotiations to join NAFTA, turned instead toward its neighbors in South America and joined the Southern Common Market (Mercosur) instead. Chile's entry

Figure 12.5

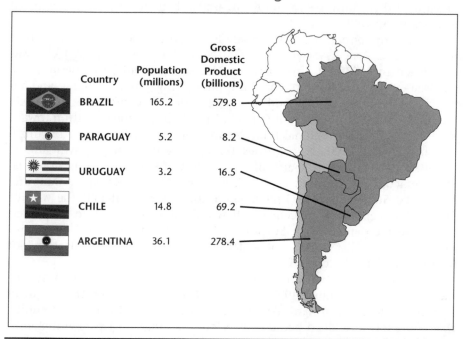

A Broader Trading Bloc

Country	Population (millions)	Gross Domestic Product (billions)
BRAZIL	165.2	579.8
PARAGUAY	5.2	8.2
URUGUAY	3.2	16.5
CHILE	14.8	69.2
ARGENTINA	36.1	278.4

The Southern Common Market (Mercosur, after its Spanish name) is an example of one of the several important and growing regional free trade organizations. A key issue for the future of the Western Hemisphere is whether it will unite into a single free trade organization, the Free Trade Area of the Americas (FTAA) or whether the hemisphere will be divided into two rival trade blocs, Mercosur and the North American Free Trade Agreement (NAFTA).

into the market with existing members Argentina, Brazil, Paraguay, and Uruguay creates a market of 225 million people with a combined GDP of $952 billion as shown in Figure 12.5. Furthermore, talks are underway to merge Mercosur with the Andean Group (Bolivia, Columbia, Ecuador, Peru, and Venezuela), which creates a trading bloc of 310 million people. "I don't want to rule out the [FTAA]," explained Argentina's president about the effort to expand Mercosur, "but charity begins at home."[37] This had led some observers to worry that an expanded Mercosur might derail the FTAA complete with NAFTA, but another analyst thought that it would be easier to form a hemispheric union after several smaller regional pacts had "ironed out" their problems. The wise advice of this analyst: "I suggest that everybody take a deep breath and calm down. A hemispheric trade agreement is going to take a while."[38]

Asia, the Pacific, and Elsewhere

The impulse for regional ties has not been confined to Europe and the Americas. Other regions have also begun to form their own groups. There are four

Arab and seven sub-Saharan African trade groups. The three Slavic FSRs (Belarus, Russia, and Ukraine) agreed in mid-1993 to negotiate cooperation agreements with an eye to a future economic union. Adding to that, Belarus and Russia agreed in April 1994 to move to unify their monetary systems based on the Russian ruble.

Even more portentous than these efforts is the trend toward regionalism in the Pacific. The Association of Southeast Asian Nations (ASEAN) was established in 1967 and now includes Brunei, Cambodia, Indonesia, Laos, Malaysia, Myanmar (Burma), the Philippines, Singapore, Thailand, and Vietnam. More recently, the oddly named series of conferences, the **Asia Pacific Economic Cooperation (APEC)**, in 1989 began the evolution toward possibly becoming a regional trade organization. The 18-member organization includes the ASEAN countries (except Vietnam, which will almost surely soon be admitted), Australia, Canada, Chile, China, Hong Kong, Japan, Mexico, New Zealand, Papua New Guinea, South Korea, Taiwan, and the United States. The APEC members account for about half the world's GDP and for about 46 percent of all world merchandise trade. APEC has a small secretariat based in Singapore, but it is symbolic of APEC's still-tentative status that it has not added a word such as "organization" or "community" to the end of its name.

INTERACTIVE EXERCISE
APEC: Realist Tool or Idealist Progress?

The first summit meeting of the APEC leaders took place in Seattle, Washington, in November 1993. The United States hoped for an agreement in principle to move toward a free trade zone, an Asia-Pacific Community. That effort was forestalled because, as Nobuo Matunaga, a Japanese diplomat, put it, "there are a variety of concerns, especially among the developing nations, that we proceed with some caution." Delegates from the other countries also doubted U.S. sincerity in light of the bruising battle in Congress over the ratification of NAFTA that was then under way. "If there was this much debate on NAFTA, imagine the debate you would have in America over a free trade area with the whole Pacific," South Korea's foreign minister, Han Sung Joo, pointed out cogently. Moreover, the delegates understood that the Americans were pushing a Pacific region trade association as a way to pressure the EU to give way during the simultaneous GATT negotiations. "We want them [the Europeans] to know that while we all want GATT, there are other options we have with Asia," a U.S. official commented.[39]

Since their initial meeting, the leaders of APEC have met annually, and foreign and finance ministers of the member-countries have met periodically. Progress toward further integration has been slow. There have been agreements in principle, for example, to achieve "free and open trade and investment" in the Asia-Pacific region. Japan and the United States are to remove all their barriers by the year 2010, with the rest of the APEC members achieving a zero-barrier level by 2020. Whether this will occur, given such factors as China's already rising trade surplus with the United States and Japan's faltering home economy, remains very unclear. Beyond this, few specific agreements have resulted from these summits, but they are part of a process of dialogue that helps keep lines of communications open.

Beyond Asia, regional trade pacts are even less developed. The various efforts to give life to them in the Middle East have fallen prey to the region's political problems, to the fact that many of the oil production–dependent economies have little to trade with one another, and other problems. Similarly, Africa's regional trade groups have languished in the face of the continent's poverty and frequent political turmoil.

The Future of Regionalism

The precise role that regional trading blocs will play on the world stage is unclear. Some observers believe that such groupings will help integrate regions, improve and strengthen the economic circumstances of the regions' countries and people, and provide a stepping-stone to world economic integration, just as the EEC was part of the genesis of the EU and just as NAFTA led to the FTAA agreement. Other analysts are worried. Economist Jagdish Bhagwati believes that "the revival of regionalism is unfortunate."[40] While regional blocs (no matter what their level of integration) must still adhere to GATT rules with respect to trade with other blocs and countries, Bhagwati is still afraid that the regions will become increasingly closed trading areas and that competition among the blocs will cause a breakdown of GATT and the construction of higher trade barriers among the blocs.

Such concerns are not far-fetched, given the impetus that is partly responsible for the current rapid regionalization that the world is undergoing. Whatever the negotiation, it is clear that part of the motivation to get together is the urge to defend against the possibility of predatory and protectionist trade practices by other economic blocs. The EU's integration is being driven in part by such fears. From Europe's point of view, competing with the United States alone is unnerving; competing with NAFTA, much less with the newly forming FTAA, is truly alarming. A modern European advocate of unity might echo Benjamin Franklin's warning to the revolutionary American colonies that if we do not all hang together, we will all hang separately, and today's equivalent of Paul Revere might gallop through the European night crying, "NAFTA is coming, NAFTA is coming!" As one Dutch scholar explained, "Even uneducated workers understand that if Europe is not strengthened, Japan and the U.S. will conquer more markets. People want a united Europe out of fear more than out of love."[41]

Similarly, NAFTA and FTAA are in part a response to the EU. "My fear," a U.S. Chamber of Commerce official told Congress, "is that, as European governments seek to balance political interests among [themselves], the legitimate interests of outsiders will be the first to be traded off. 'Fortress Europe' may not be a realistic outcome, but selected protectionism . . . will be defended as necessary" (Olmer, 1989:133). This concern led the United States to use the threat and reality of regional trade associations to pressure Europe, Japan, and others to open their markets. During the FTAA summit in Miami, Mickey Kantor, the U.S. trade representative, observed that one benefit of the meeting was that "the Europeans will be encouraged, to use a delicate word, to be more open in a number of areas we have been concerned about. And

Asians will also be encouraged to go in this direction, or they too will be left behind."[42] Like the regional trends in North America and Europe, the Southeast Asian effort is partly defensive. Explained Prime Minister Goh Chok Tong of Singapore, "Unless ASEAN can match the other regions," it will lose out. By contrast, the free trade agreement would make ASEAN a "strong player in the new world order."[43]

While these defensive reactions and counterreactions are understandable, they also contain a danger. It is that instead of promoting global economic cooperation, the regional organizations that exist or are being created may one day become centers of economic-political-military rivals that are as bitterly locked in contest as individual countries once were. There are already signs that regionalization, rather than globalization, is determining where the investors from various countries put their FDI. The majority of all American FDI in LDCs now goes to Latin America and the Caribbean. Similarly, the majority of Japan's FDI in LDCs is in East Asia and the Pacific; the French put the majority of their FDI investment in the LDCs and formerly CITs of Eastern Europe and Central Asia. There is in George Orwell's novel *1984* an image of the world divided into three hostile blocs—Eastasia, Eurasia, and Oceania—that have an unsettling geographical resemblance to a possible ASEAN-EU-FTAA tripolar system. Just as it is much too early to predict a merging of the various trade regions into a global free trade economy, so is it premature to assume an Orwellian future. The most likely path lies somewhere between the two extremes, yet either of them is possible.

Chapter Summary

1. Economics and politics are closely intertwined aspects of international relations. Each is a part of and affects the other. This interrelationship has become even more important in recent history. Economics has become more important internationally because of dramatically increased trade levels, ever-tightening economic interdependence between countries, and the growing impact of international economics on domestic economics.

2. The stronger role played by international economics means that political relations between countries have increasingly been influenced by economic relations. Conversely, politics also significantly affects economic relations. Domestic political pressures are important determinants of tariff policies and other trade regulations. Trade can also be used as a diplomatic tool.

3. Economic strength is a key element of every country's overall power. Economic power is based on financial position, natural resources, industrial output, agricultural output, and international competitiveness.

4. Countries use their economic power through a mixture of positive incentives and negative sanctions. While each approach is sometimes

successful, both incentives and, particularly, sanctions are difficult to apply successfully and have numerous drawbacks.

5. The economies of the North are prosperous compared to those of the South. With the end of the cold war and with a variety of changing economic circumstances, however, the situation has changed greatly. The EDCs are experiencing a number of economic difficulties, and economic tensions among them have increased.

6. The economies of the South are relatively weak compared to those of the North. Also, within the South there is great disparity in wealth. A few NICs have expanding and modernizing economies. There is also, in most LDCs, a small wealthy class of people and a much larger class of impoverished people.

7. The LDCs need hard currency capital to buy the goods and services that will allow them to develop their economies. There are four basic sources of hard currency: loans, foreign investment, trade, and foreign aid. There are, however, problems with each of these sources.

8. Loans are unsatisfactory because of high repayment costs. The debt crisis has eased, but LDC debt is growing once again and could threaten the global financial community.

9. Investment capital has grown in amount and importance in recent years. Still, investment capital flows mostly into just a few LDCs.

10. The Catch-22 of trade is that the primary products that LDCs mainly produce do not earn them enough capital to found industries to produce manufactured goods that would earn more money.

11. Foreign aid is minor compared with world needs and is often given on the basis of political expediency rather than economic necessity.

12. In recent years, the countries of the South have begun to make greater demands for economic equity to press the North to join in establishing a New International Economic Order.

13. There are a variety of barriers to the unimpeded international movement of trade and capital. These include such barriers as tariffs, non-tariff barriers, and licensing requirements.

14. There are significant arguments on both sides of the question of whether or not to continue to expand free international economic interchange. Advocates of doing so contend that it results in greater efficiency and lower costs and that international commerce promotes world cooperation and inhibits conflict. Opponents argue that economic barriers are needed to protect domestic industry, that overreliance on other countries is dangerous for national security reasons, and that trade can be a valuable policy tool.

15. There are a wide variety of general intergovernmental organizations (IGOs) and efforts devoted to economic cooperation. The UN maintains a number of efforts aimed at general economic development, with an emphasis on the less developed countries.

16. There are also many specialized IGOs involved in economic cooperation.

17. There is a great deal of trade cooperation, and great strides have been made through the new General Agreement on Tariffs and Trade and its administrative structure, the World Trade Organization, toward promoting free trade.

18. Among monetary institutions, the International Monetary Fund is the primary organization dedicated to stabilizing the world's monetary system. The IMF's primary role in recent years has been to assist LDCs and CITs to prosper by reducing their foreign debt. The IMF, however, attaches conditions to its assistance, and this practice has occasioned considerable criticism.

19. There are a number of international organizations established to provide developmental loans and grants to countries in need. The best-known of these is the World Bank Group, which consists of several interrelated subsidiaries. These organizations also primarily extend aid to EDCs, but, like the IMF, the conditions they attach are criticized by some analysts.

20. There are also several regional efforts aimed at economic integration. The European Union and the North American Free Trade Agreement are the most important of these.

21. The new NAFTA regional free trade area will rival the EU in population and combined GDP. The Free Trade Area of the Americas and the Asia Pacific Economic Cooperation forum are on the horizon as even larger regional organizations.

CONNECTEXT

Chapter

Preserving and Enhancing Human Rights and Dignity

The sun with one eye vieweth all the world.

Shakespeare, *Henry VI, Part 1*

Recognition of the inherent dignity and of the equal and inalienable rights of all members of the human family is the foundation of freedom, justice, and peace in the world.

Preamble to the Universal Declaration of Human Rights, 1948

As we near the end of this survey of world politics, it is appropriate to pause momentarily to remember that, amid all the sound and fury, politics ought to be about maintaining or improving the quality of life of people. We have been exploring whether the traditional state-based international system that operates on self-interested competition can best protect and enhance humanity or whether the alternative of global cooperation in an international system with reduced sovereignty will lead to a more felicitous future. This and the next chapter continue that inquiry by addressing the human rights and social dignity of the world's people and the condition of the biosphere that they inhabit. First, this chapter will address preserving and enhancing human rights and dignity by looking at efforts to provide for the human body and spirit. Then chapter 14 will take up environmental concerns and programs.

Chapter Outline

The Biosphere and Its Inhabitants: The Essence of Politics

It is important to stress that while the discussions of the human condition and the environment are divided into two chapters, the two subjects are intrinsically intertwined. The size of the globe's population and the need to feed people and supply their material needs is putting tremendous pressure on the capacity of the biosphere to provide resources and to absorb waste. Indeed, the intersection of people and their environment and the combined impact of the two on the social and economic future are so strong that the World Bank has devised a new way to measure the *comprehensive wealth* of countries. The traditional method relies exclusively on economic production measured by either per capita gross national or domestic product (GNP, GDP). The alternative method introduced by the World Bank in 1995 and dubbed "green accounting" starts with manufactured wealth (products) and adds estimates of "natural capital" and "human capital." Natural capital is divided into two subcategories. One is "land," and includes factors such as the acreage available for farming. The second is "resources," and measures available water, minerals, and other related factors. Human capital measures education, health, and other such criteria. Estimating natural and human capital is even more difficult than arriving at GDP figures, but the results are valuable. Nobel Prize–winning economist Robert M. Solow contends that the new method is more comprehensive because "what we normally measure as capital is a small part of what it takes to sustain human welfare." Therefore, adds another economist, green accounting "is a valuable thing to do even if it can only be done relatively crudely."[1]

Changing the emphasis away from mere production helps us to focus on the economic reality that any economic unit needs to add to its national core and infrastructure in order to remain prosperous. If, for example, the owner of a farm devotes all of the farm's financial and human resources to producing crops, does not take care to avoid depleting the soil and water supplies, and does not devote resources to keeping the workers healthy and to training them in the latest farm methods, then, even though production may soar in the short term, the farm's long-term prospects are not good. Similarly, countries that do not preserve and, when possible, replenish their natural and human capital may face an increasingly bleak future. As one observer put it, such "countries are [inflating] income by selling off the family jewels."[2]

The complexities of this green-accounting approach to measuring wealth should not obscure its basic message that the richness or impoverishment of the human condition is an amalgam of the human rights people enjoy or are denied and the biosphere's bounty or exhaustion.

The Nature of Human Rights

Before moving to a detailed discussion of human rights, it is important to explain the broad concept of human rights used here. We are used to thinking about human rights in terms of *individual human rights,* that is, freedom from specific abuses or restrictions, especially by governments. The American Bill of Rights, for example, prohibits (except in extreme cases) the government from abridging your right to exercise your religion or free speech, from discriminating against citizens based on race and other demographic traits, from being long-imprisoned without a trial, and from a variety of other abuses. Gradually, these constitutional prohibitions have been extended to restrict actions by U.S. state and local governments and even, in some cases, by individuals.

There is a more comprehensive concept of rights. This broader view holds that people and groups not only have the right not to be specifically abused, but that they also have *collective human rights* to a quality of life that, at minimum, does not detract from their human dignity (Felice, 1996). One scholar suggests that the most fruitful way to think about human rights is to begin with the idea that "ultimately they are supposed to serve basic human needs" (Galtung, 1994:3).

These basic human needs, which generate corresponding rights, include, among others (Galtung, 1994:72):

> "Survival needs—to avoid violence": The requisite to avoid and the right to be free from individual and collective violence.

> "Well-being needs—to avoid misery": The right to adequate nutrition and water; to movement, sleep, sex, and other biological wants, to protection from diseases, and to protection from adverse climatological and environmental impacts.

> "Identity needs—to avoid alienation": The right to self-expression; to realize your potential, to establish and maintain emotional bonds with others; to preserve cultural heritage and association; to contribute through work and other activity; and to receive information about and maintain contact with nature, global humanity, and other aspects of the biosphere.

> "Freedom needs—to avoid repression": The right to receive and express opinions, to assemble with others, to have a say in common policy; and to choose in such wide-ranging matters as jobs, spouses, where to live, and lifestyle.

Few, if any, people would argue that these rights are absolute. As the classic formulation about free speech goes, for example, freedom of speech does not include the right to shout "fire!" in a crowded theater. It is also the case that the legal rights granted and recognized by countries largely include only protections from specific abuses of individuals and groups and do not include the right to certain qualitative standards of life. But it is also arguable that the very nature of being human means that people have the right to exist in at least tolerable conditions as well as the right to be merely free from specific abuses. It is also appropriate to say a bit about the origins of human rights. Recall from chapter 9 that there is an ancient debate about the basis of human rights. One school, the *universalists*, believes that human rights are derived from one or another theological or ideological doctrine or from natural rights. This last concept holds that the fact of being human carries with it certain rights that cannot be violated or can only be violated in extremis. Universalists therefore believe that there is a single, prevailing set of standards of moral behavior on which human rights are based. The other school of thought, the *positivists*, argues that rights are the product of culture. Positivists therefore contend that in a world of diverse cultures, no single standard of human rights exists or is likely to exist short of the world becoming completely homogenized culturally. Those who believe in the cultural relativism of rights also tend to view attempts to impose standards of rights by one culture on another as cultural imperialism (Weigel, 1995).

It is not uncommon to hear those in the non-Western world argue that many of the rights asserted in such international documents as the Universal Declaration of Human Rights, which was adopted in 1948 by an overwhelming vote of the UN General Assembly, are based on the values of the politically dominant West. Positivists contend that many of these Western values, such as individualism and democracy, are not held as strongly in other cultures, and that no matter how highminded it is, Western attempts to impose them are imperialist. There are, however, leaders in non-Western cultures who reject these assertions of cultural relativism. Burmese political activist and 1991 Nobel Peace Prize winner Aung San Suu Kyi writes that claims about "the national culture can become a bizarre graft of carefully selected historical incidents and distorted social values intended to justify the policies and actions of those in power." She goes on to argue that, "It is precisely because of the cultural diversity of the world that it is necessary for different nations and peoples to agree on those basic human values which will act as a unifying factor." As for the cultural imperialism argument, Suu Kyi contends that "when democracy and human rights are said to run counter to non-Western culture, such culture is usually defined narrowly and presented as monolithic." To avoid this, she counsels, it is possible to conceive of rights "which place human worth above power and liberation above control" (Suu Kyi, 1995:14, 15, 18). The power and control she wishes to subordinate are not just those of government, but those of one ethnic group, race, religion, sex, or other societal faction over another.

It must be said that differences over what constitutes a human right are not only matters of Western and non-Western philosophies. There are also vigorous disputes between countries of similar cultural heritage. For example, Italy's Constitutional Court in 1996 by unanimous vote blocked the extradition of an Italian wanted in Florida for first-degree murder because execution is one of the possible penalties in that U.S. state. There are other countries, including Canada, that have taken the same position and will not extradite people accused of capital crimes unless assured that the death penalty will not be invoked. In the Italian case, a U.S. Department of Justice official called the court's decision "a bad omen"; Giovanni Leone, a former president of Italy, called the decision "one of historic character that does honor to Italy."[3]

The two matters of whether rights protect only against specific abuses or extend to quality of life criteria and whether rights are culture-based or

**INTERACTIVE
EXERCISE
A Global Bill
of Rights**

universal are addressed further in the Web site's interactive exercise A Global Bill of Rights. See if you agree with the range of individual and group rights that the UN General Assembly adopted.

Human Rights: Quality of Life Issues and Progress

One set of pressing problems for the world community involves preserving and enhancing human dignity by protecting and improving the physical condition of humans. These issues are, in part, economic in nature and are being addressed by the international economic cooperation efforts discussed in chapter 12. There are also, however, specific efforts to deal with such concerns as living conditions and human rights. Note that many of these issues have a strong environmental factor. It is not facile to say that how people are treated has a great deal to do with the way that they treat one another and the ecosphere they share. It is also the case that, in the view of many, food, health, and the other quality of life matters included in this section fall under the rubric of human rights (Speth, 1998). For example, the UN–sponsored World Food Summit that met in November 1996 reasserted the principle found in many international human rights documents that there is a "right to adequate food and the fundamental right of everyone to be free from hunger."[4]

Food

Some two centuries ago, Thomas Malthus predicted in *Essay on the Principle of Population* (1798) that the world's population would eventually outpace the world's agricultural carrying capacity. For the two centuries since Malthus's essay, human ingenuity has defied his predictions. The question is whether it can continue to do so, given the rapidly increasing global population.

There are two basic food problems. One is the *short-term food supply*. Regional shortages inflict real human suffering. Hunger—indeed, starvation—is most common in Africa, where more than 35 countries face a severe shortage of food. In addition to the multitudes that have died from starvation or diseases stemming from malnutrition, agricultural insufficiency has a host of negative economic impacts that range from sapping the vigor of the population to consuming development funds for food relief. The UN's Food and Agricultural Organization (FAO) estimates that around the globe there are 800 million people, one-quarter of them children under age 5, who are undernourished; some 15 million a year die from outright starvation or from diseases brought on by malnutrition.

The *long-term adequacy of the food supply* is also a significant concern. A combination of population control and agricultural development is necessary to ensure that the world's appetite does not outstrip its agriculture. There is, in essence, a race under way between demand and supply. The growing population

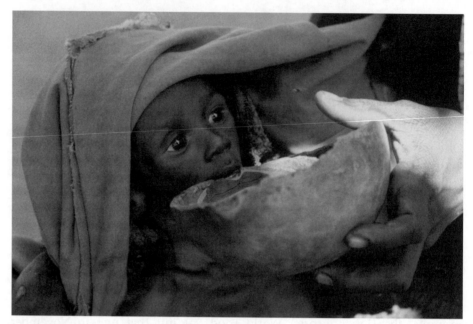

Even though enough food is produced in the world to feed the entire global population, you wouldn't know it from looking at the face of this Sudanese child. Problems of food distribution, regional conflicts, and high population growth rates make the food question a bit more complex than simply getting food to people when they need it.

and the efforts to increase the calorie, protein, and other nutrient intake of chronically underfed people is rapidly increasing demand. On the supply side, food production must rise 75 percent over the next 30 years to meet this escalating demand. Whether that standard can be met is, however, uncertain.

One critical determinant will be crop yields. On the positive side, yields have grown over 50 percent since 1970 due to the "green revolution" (the development and widespread introduction of high-yielding rice, wheat, and other grains), the increased use of fertilizers and pesticides, and other agricultural advances. On the negative side, the annual rate at which yields are increasing has been dropping steadily from about 5 percent annually in the 1970s to about 2 percent annually in the 1990s. What is worse, the FAO projects that the increase will drop to 1 percent or less in the first decade of the twenty-first century. This decline is compounded by the loss of land available for farming. Only about 11 percent of the world's land surface was ever well-suited for agriculture to begin with. Some new farmland has been added through irrigation and other methods, but even more has been lost to urbanization, to poor environmental practices that cause erosion, to soil-nutrient exhaustion, to salinization, and to other degradations. The FAO calculates that 38 percent of the world's original cropland (some 2.1 million square miles, almost two-thirds the area of the United States) has been lost to agriculture, and that a combination of increasing population and loss of farmable land has cut the world's cultivated land to six-tenths of an acre per mouth to feed.

There are several causes of hunger. *Population growth* is one. Production cannot keep up with population in many areas of the world. The result is that LDC per capita food production is barely expanding from its poverty base, and there is the constant threat of calamity. The least developed countries (LLDCs), which combine the world's highest population growth and the world's lowest economic capacity, are actually losing ground in their ability to feed their people. In the LLDCs, per capita food production declined by 6 percent between 1980 and the mid-1990s. Eighteen of these LLDCs had declines of at least 10 percent, and of those 12 had per capita food production drops of 20 percent or more.

Maldistribution of food is a second cause of hunger. For now at least, the world has the agricultural capacity to feed everyone adequately. Resources and consumption, however, are concentrated in relatively few countries. In the EDCs, daily food consumption averages a waist-expanding 3,417 calories a day, 66 percent more than the average 2,054 calories in the LLDCs. Nutritional content represents an even greater gap, with protein deficiency particularly common in the LLDCs.

Political strife is a third problem. In many countries with severe food shortages, farms have been destroyed, farmers displaced, and food transportation disrupted by internal warfare. Rwanda is one of the recent tragic examples and now produces 28 percent less food than the already-meager supply it managed to do in 1990 before it was overtaken by strife between the Hutus and Tutsis.

A number of international efforts are under way. Some deal with food aid to meet immediate needs, while others are dedicated to increasing future agricultural productivity. *Food aid* to areas with food shortages is a short-term necessity to alleviate malnutrition (Belgrad & Nachmias, 1997). Grains constitute about 95 percent of food aid. About 7 million tons of grains are donated each year. The United States is the largest supplier, annually donating over 5.7 million tons, or over 80 percent of the total. As laudable as this is, it is a drop since the mid-1980s, when aid in cereal grains annually averaged about 9 million tons (including 6.6 million tons from the United States). There are also a number of multilateral food aid efforts. The UN's World Food Program is the largest. It distributes food to needy states and maintains a reserve food stock of 500,000 tons. There are also a variety of NGOs, such as the Red Cross and the Red Crescent, that are active in food aid.

The *development of agricultural techniques and capabilities* is crucial if there is to be any hope of future self-sufficiency. On a bilateral basis, many countries' programs include agricultural development aid. There is also a multilateral effort. The oldest agricultural IGO is the FAO. It was founded in 1945, has 174 members, and has an annual budget of approximately $650 million. The FAO supplies food aid and technical assistance to LDCs. The agency has been criticized for a variety of its policies, including putting too much emphasis on short-term food aid and not enough effort into long-range agricultural growth. This, in addition to the growing recognition of the food problem, has led to the establishment of several other global food efforts.

MAPS
Gross Domestic Product: Share in Agriculture

Production of Staples: Cereals, Roots, and Tubers

Agricultural Production Per Capita

A noteworthy event in these efforts was the 1996 World Food Summit. It met at FAO headquarters in Rome and was attended by the heads of more than 80 governments. Reflecting the declining commitment of the EDCs to foreign aid, though, the leaders of most of the industrialized countries were not present. The United States, for example, was only represented by its secretary of agriculture. The tone of the meeting was set by the first plenary speaker, Pope John Paul II, who called on the world's countries to "eliminate the specter of hunger from the planet" and to "jointly seek solutions so that never again will there be hungry people living side by side with people in opulence. . . . Such contrasts between poverty and wealth cannot be tolerated."[5]

Without the strong support of the EDCs, though, there was little of immediate substance that the summit could accomplish. It did, however, establish the goal of reducing the number of undernourished people to half the present level by 2015. It also reaffirmed the UN's traditional standard that the EDCs should devote 0.7 percent of their respective GDPs to development aid, including food and agricultural assistance. Third, in a move that rankled Washington and some other capitals, the conference resolved that "food should not be used as an instrument for political and economic pressure."[6] This swipe at economic sanctions came just days after the UN General Assembly voted by 137 to 3 to urge the United States to end its 34-year embargo against Cuba.

Health

The state of medical care, sanitation, and other conditions related to health in some areas of the world is below a level imaginable by most readers of this book. The EDCs and their citizens spend on average $2,343 per citizen annually on health care. About two-thirds of that is paid for through public funds or private (usually employer-supported) health insurance. By comparison, the countries and the citizens of the South (which have scant public funds and where private health insurance is often unavailable or, for most, unaffordable) can afford to spend annually an average of just $21.22 per capita on health care. The amount for LLDCs is a mind-boggling $7.74. By another measure, there are 17 times as many physicians per person in the EDCs as there are in the LDCs. The health of the disadvantaged within developed countries and in the LDCs is an international concern because health is more than a key to personal well-being. A healthy population is vital to economic growth because healthy people are economically productive and because unhealthy people often consume more of a society's resources than they produce.

As grim as these figures are, they were once much worse. An infant born in an LDC is now 31 percent more likely to live to age 1 than an infant born in 1980. As recently as 1974, only 5 percent of all children in LDCs received any vaccinations; now 80 percent receive protection against diphtheria, whooping cough, and polio. As a result, the health of children in LDCs has improved dramatically. According to UNICEF, 90 percent of the children in LDCs live in countries that are making progress in the area of children's health. This means that about 2.5 million fewer children now die needlessly and almost a million fewer children will be disabled, blinded, crippled, or mentally handicapped than a decade ago.

A significant part of the credit for these advances belongs to the World Health Organization (WHO). Headquartered in Geneva, the UN-affiliated WHO was created in 1946, has 191 members, and has an annual budget of about $819 million from the UN and other sources. The crusade against smallpox provides a heartening example of WHO's contributions. Smallpox was a scourge throughout human history. There were over 131,000 cases worldwide in 1976 when WHO began a 10-year campaign to eradicate the disease. By 1987 smallpox was confined to a single case in Somalia; no case has been reported since 1989. Polio is another disease whose death may be imminent. The annual global incidence has been cut from 400,000 cases in 1983, to 120,00 cases in 1994, to 5,139 cases in 1997, to what WHO hopes and projects will be zero cases in 2000. As one heartened WHO official notes, the approaching eradication of polio "should be a source of pride to all of us, and it shows what can be done when everybody works together for a common cause for the benefit of mankind."[7]

Optimism based on progress is offset by continuing problems and new threats. In LDCs, 18 percent of all children born have low birth weights (less than 5.5 pounds), and the maternal mortality rate in many countries is horrendous. More than one in every 100 women who gives birth in Mali dies. That is 100 times worse than in the United States, where only about one in a thousand women dies from pregnancy complications. Also, diseases once thought to be on the decline can surge catastrophically. Tuberculosis is one such disease. WHO declared in 1993 that TB has become the leading cause of death from a single infectious agent and, in WHO's estimate, will kill more than 61,000 people a week over the next two decades.

New problems add to these old worries. The worldwide AIDS epidemic, for one, is killing many people whom medical advances had saved from other diseases. There are now at least 30 million people infected with the HIV virus, and the number of people infected is increasing by 16,000 a day. Of those infected with HIV, over 1.6 million are known to have AIDS, and that figure grew nearly 20 percent between 1997 and 1998. Even more alarming is the WHO estimate that reported AIDS cases constitute only 20 percent of all AIDS cases. So far over 7 million people, including some 2 million children, have died of AIDS. Some countries are truly devastated. More than 10 percent of the populations of Kenya, Malawi, Uganda, and Zambia are already HIV-positive, and the overall rate in sub-Saharan Africa is 5.6 percent. Children infected during gestation and birth are among the victims. More than 1 million babies have been born HIV-positive; half die immediately. Other children will fall victim to AIDS in a different way. Studies in Botswana and Uganda have found that up to 40 percent of all pregnant women are HIV-positive, and the UN estimates that by the end of the decade over 10 million children in sub-Saharan Africa alone will lose their mothers to AIDS. As one WHO physician explains the grim logic, "As more women die of AIDS, the number of orphans will rise exponentially."[8]

INTERACTIVE EXERCISE
Threats to World Health

TABLE
Mortality, Health, and Nutrition, 1997

Education

Education, like health, affects more than just the quality of life. Education is also a key to increased national and international productivity, population control, and other positive social goals. Promotion of education remains primarily a national function, but there are a number of international efforts. For one, the United Nations Educational, Scientific, and Cultural Organization (UNESCO) sponsors several programs. The national and international efforts are slowly paying off. In the 1950s less than 30 percent of all children in LDCs ever attended any school; now almost all children begin the first grade and more than half go on to begin secondary school. Overall, the level of adults with at least rudimentary literacy has increased to about 71 percent in the LDCs.

The increasing percentages should not disguise the crying needs that still exist. More than 1 billion adults are still illiterate, and their personal and societal productivity is limited. There is also a gender gap in education, especially in LDCs, where males are 18 percent more likely to be literate than females. The averages also tend to disguise regional areas of profound educational deprivation. Only 73 percent of sub-Saharan African children even begin first grade, and adult illiteracy in the region is 43 percent. The statistics showing an increase of literacy in LDCs also tend to cloud the fact that most children receive just a few years of primary education. Only about 46 percent of all children in LDCs reach secondary school; that figure is less than 10 percent in about a dozen countries. Post–secondary school education is attained by only 9 percent of LDC students, compared with 50 percent of students in EDCs. Expenditures on education also vary widely between EDCs, which annually spend $1,471 per capita, and LDCs, which can manage only $41.42 in per capita educational funding. In our technological age, the lack of advanced training is a major impediment to development. In the North there are nearly 849 scientists and technicians for each 10,000 people. For each 10,000 inhabitants of the South, there are 88 scientists and technicians; in sub-Saharan Africa there are only 10.

Human Rights Issues regarding Abuses of Individuals and Groups

The human condition depends on more than food security, level of education, and degree of health of people, individually or collectively. There is also a range of rights having to do with the treatment of specific groups or individuals within a society, whether domestic or global, that are subject to abuse. Some legal scholars distinguish between two types of such rights. *Civil rights* include positive requirements on governments to ensure that all people and groups are treated equally by the government and perhaps by everyone. The Fourteenth Amendment to the U.S. Constitution, which provides to all people in the country "the equal protection of the laws" is a quintessential statement of civil rights. *Civil liberties* are those things which the government (and perhaps anyone) cannot, or should not be able to, prevent an individual or group from doing. Freedom of religion, speech, and assembly are examples of civil liberties.

Human Rights Abuses: Diverse Discrimination and Oppression

Intolerance and the abuses that stem from it are ancient and persistent. They also are global and demographically diverse. Whether the focus is race, ethnicity, gender, sexual orientation, religious choice, or some other trait, there are few human characteristics or beliefs that have not been the target of discrimination and abuse somewhere in the world.

The hatred of other humans based on what they are, rather than on what they have done, extends as far back into history as we can see. Genocide is a modern term, but the practice is ancient. The Roman philosopher and statesman Seneca (ca. 8 B.C.–A.D. 65) wrote in *Epistles* that Romans were "mad, not only individually, but nationally" because they punished "manslaughter and isolated murders" but accepted "the much vaunted crime of slaughtering whole peoples."

In the intervening years, attitudes on racial or other forms of demographic superiority have often played a powerful, and always destructive, role in history. Many of today's divisions and problems are, for example, a legacy of the racism that combined with political and economic nationalism to rationalize oppression. The ideas of biologist Charles Darwin in *The Origin of Species* (1859) were thoroughly corrupted to allow the exploitation of the "unfit" (nonwhites) by the "fit" (whites). Whites in this context (as used here) means European-heritage whites (Eurowhites) and does not extend to Arabs, Persians, most of the people of India, and other Caucasians. Racism also joined with religion to build a case in the Western mind that subjugation was in the interest of the uncivilized and pagan—that is, nonwhite, non-Christian—societies.

This sort of bastardized **social Darwinism** also reared its head in such brutally repressive ideologies as Italian fascism and the related German credo, National Socialism. The führer proclaimed that war and conquest were "all in the natural order of things—for [they make] for the survival of the fittest." Race was a particular focus of conflict because, Hitler asserted in *Mein Kampf* (1925), "all occurrences in world history are only expressions of the races' instinct of self-preservation." This racist social theory was a key part of the Nazi *weltanschauung* (worldview) and became one of the themes of Hitler's foreign policy.

It must be added that while the genocidal attacks are often blamed on leaders who whip their former and otherwise peaceful followers up to murderous frenzy, it is also the case that ordinary common people are often all too willing to join the attacks. For example, the often-argued interpretation of the Germans' genocidal attack on the Jews and others is that Hitler and the Nazis led an overly compliant but not otherwise evil German people in history's most horrific hate campaign. To the contrary, argues Daniel Goldhagen

Recalling images of the Holocaust half a century before, these Kosovar refugees were herded onto trains by Serbian forces as part of the "ethnic cleansing" campaign. Coping with the refugee influx in spring 1999 created difficult problems for Albania and other countries in the region.

in *Hitler's Willing Executioners: Ordinary Germans and the Holocaust* (1996), "the most committed anti-Semites in history" were able to come to power and turn a grotesque "private fantasy into the core of the state," because a German culture that was "pregnant with murder" and rendered psychopathic by "hallucinatory anti-Semitism" led Germans in general to "believe [that] what they were doing to Jews was the right thing."[9]

The point is to not delude ourselves into thinking that the doctrine of superiority based on ethnic, racial, religious, or other differences died with the Third Reich or that it is always forced on unwilling populations by a few satanic leaders. Instead, hatred remains alive and well, and the many persistent forms of intolerance and oppression have been discussed earlier and will be encapsulated in the next section.

Oppression is also, of course, the tool of dictators, and the degree to which it is all too common is evident in data from one survey of political oppression and freedom that ranked countries' respect for civil liberties on a scale of 1 (best) to 7 (worst). On this scale, only 28 countries achieved a ranking of 1 or 2, while almost as many countries (23) had regimes brutal enough to garner a ranking of 6 or 7. Figure 13.1 further illustrates the degree of civil liberties available in the world (Redfern, 1995).

It is likely that you, like most of the people who read this book, live in the United States, Canada, or some other country which ranks 1 on the

Freedom House civil liberties scale and where civil rights, while far from ideal, have progressed over time. Indeed, it is hard for those of us fortunate enough to live in such countries to imagine how widespread and how harsh oppression can be. It is tempting to describe lurid tales of repression, and it would be easy to do so, for there are many. It will suffice, however, to review briefly the many types of oppression and the diversity of victims that have suffered from it by examining some of the human rights issues and violations regarding women, children, ethnic and racial groups, religious groups, indigenous people, and refugees and immigrants.

Women

In our discussion of the plight of a diversity of demographic groups, it is appropriate that we begin with the largest of all minority groups, women. Females constitute about half the world's population, but they are a distinct economic-political-social minority because of

Figure 13.1

Civil Liberties in the World

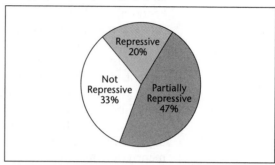

Data source: Karantnycky (1997). Data reflects the Freedom House survey's rating of civil liberties, but not political rights. Countries were ranked on a scale of 1 (least repressive) to 7 (most repressive). Ratings 1 and 2 are shown here as not repressive; ratings 3, 4, and 5 as partially repressive; and ratings 6 and 7 as repressive.

The repression of civil liberties is still common in the world. More than two-thirds of all countries are either very or partially repressive. On a scale of 1 (best) to 7 (worst), the average country ranking is 3.8.

the wide gap in societal power and resources between women and men. Compared to men, women are much less likely to have a job that pays money, are much less likely to hold a professional position, are much more likely to be illiterate, and are much more likely to be living below the poverty line (Rhein, 1998).

Moreover, women in many countries are sold or forced by poverty to go into de facto slavery in their own countries or abroad. These domestic servants are often mistreated. One Filipino diplomat in Singapore reported that during just 6 months, she heard charges by Filipino women there that included 80 physical assaults, 144 beatings, 20 rapes, 2 murders, 6 suicides, and 66 cases of withheld wages. The sale of young women and even girls (and young men and boys) into heterosexual or homosexual slavery is also relatively common in some places. Girls between 8 and 10 years old reportedly brought bids of $397 to $529 at one auction in Pakistan. According to the director of social welfare in Pakistan's Sind province, many men there believe that "since a woman is no better than a dumb, driven chattel, who cares what happens to her? She can be sold, purchased, transferred and bargained off like cows, sheep, goats or some other property."[10]

Sometimes the abuses are sanctioned by law, but more often the rights of women are ignored because male-dominated governments turn a blind eye. In some cases, there are also economic incentives for governments to ignore abuses. Prostitution is a huge business in Southeast Asia, as elsewhere, and the females—often poor girls and women who are forced or duped into sexual slavery—bring in billions of dollars. The UN estimated in 1998, for example, that Thailand's sex tourism and other aspects of the illicit sexual trade earn the country about $25 billion a year. That adds roughly 15 percent to Thailand's officially reported GDP. According to the report, "The Sex Sector: The Economic and Social Bases of Prostitution in Southeast Asia," the "revenues [the sex trade] generates are crucial to the livelihoods and earning potential of millions of workers beyond the prostitutes themselves."[11]

Most often, civil law and social strictures reinforce one another. One current place where this is so is Afghanistan. When in late 1996 a fundamentalist Muslim movement, the Taliban, took control of most of the country, the Taliban leaders decreed the *Shari'ah* (Islamic law) would be the law of the country. The Taliban interpretation of the *Shari'ah* dictates, among other things, that women should be forced to wear the burqa (a head-to-foot garment covering everything but the eyes and hands). "Some women want to show their feet and ankles," worried one Taliban leader. "They are immoral women. They want to give a hint to the opposite sex."[12] Women are also banned from working outside the home and from going to school. The Taliban also reintroduced the long-abandoned practice of stoning women, and sometimes couples, who were found to have committed adultery. In this practice, victims are buried up to their chests, then killed by people who hurl heavy stones at their heads. "Just two people, that's all, and we ended adultery [in Afghanistan] forever," one Taliban member exulted, probably naively, after one such execution. "Even 100,000 police could not have the effect that we achieved with one punishment of this kind."[13] Protests from numerous international sources, including the United Nations, were rejected by the Taliban. The Taliban minister of information and culture proclaimed that "there is no possibility of a change in Islamic principles, which have not changed in the last 1,400 years."[14]

The defense of such policies toward females on the grounds of compliance with the *Shari'ah* raises the point of cultural relativism, which is frequently used to justify the differences between how women and men are treated in some Muslim and other societies. Cultural relativism is also the crux of debate over another ancient practice—genital mutilation. The story of this African practice and the reaction of U.S. officials to a young woman who fled from Togo to avoid it is told in the Web site box Asylum.

A FURTHER NOTE
Asylum

Children

Children are not commonly considered a minority group. But insofar as they are dominated and sometimes abused by others, children fall well within the range of the groups that suffer because of their lack of economic and political power and because they are often denied rights accorded to the dominant segments of society.

Besides conditions such as lack of adequate nutrition that deny to a vast number of children any opportunity for a fulfilling life, there are a variety of abuses that children endure. Being forced to work is one of them. According to a UNICEF report released in 1996, there are 250 million children ages 5 to 14 in LDCs who go to work, not school, each day. This includes 40 percent of the children in Africa, 20 percent of the children in Asia, and 16 percent of the children in Latin America.

As detrimental as this practice is, an even more repugnant reality is the sexual exploitation of children. Precise information is difficult to gather, but the consensus among those familiar with the problem is that there is a global, multibillion-dollar sex trade, into which about 1 million children are drawn each year. UNICEF estimates that 200,000 children are being sexually exploited commercially in Thailand, 300,000 in the United States, 400,000 in India, and 650,000 in the Philippines. The estimates of children engaged in commercial sex in Brazil range between 500,000 and 2,000,000. "Brazil may be the worst in the world, but nobody really knows," says UNICEF's representative in Brazil.[15]

The treatment of children is certainly the proper concern of national governments, but it is also an international issue. It is also estimated that 10 to 12 million men travel each year internationally as "sex tourists" to exploit children. Clothes, shoes, and other products manufactured by children are sold in international trade; you may be wearing one of these products even as you read these words. The wars and civil strife that ruin the lives of boy soldiers and other children are often rooted in world affairs.

This Indian child has to work crushing rocks at a road construction site in Nepal. He is one of the 250 million children in LDCs who go to work instead of school each day.

Ethnic and Racial Groups

Strife and oppression based on ethnicity and race are still unsettlingly common. Until international pressure through economic sanctions and other actions finally compelled South African whites to surrender political power in 1994, racism persisted officially through the apartheid system that permitted 6.5 million whites to dominate the other 29 million black, Asian, and "colored" (mixed-race) people. Also in 1994 the slaughter of Tutsis by Hutus in Rwanda and the recurring violence between these two groups in Burundi and Rwanda provided a terrible example of racial/ethnic hate politics. Throughout the 1990s, various ethnic groups in what was Yugoslavia have beset one another, with the Serbs the main perpetrators, and the Muslim Bosnians and, more recently, the Muslim Kosovars, the main victims. The previous descriptions, especially in chapter 4, of these ethnic and racial tensions mean that here it is only necessary to reiterate that ethnic and racial identification are a key component of the tensions and conflict that make nationalism one of, if not the most, divisive elements of human politics.

Religious Groups

Strife and oppression based all or in part on religion is also common on the world stage, as the conflict in Northern Ireland, the conflict in Sudan between the Muslim government and non-Muslim rebels, the earlier-mentioned slaughter of Bosnian Muslims and Kosovars by Orthodox Bosnian Serbs, and other conflicts attest. There are also, as detailed in chapter 5, numerous efforts by religious fundamentalists in India, Israel, Northern Ireland, several Muslim countries, and elsewhere to align the legal codes and religious laws of their respective countries and to force everyone, regardless of their personal beliefs, to follow those theocratic laws. Even in countries where there is no move to supplant civil with theocratic law, religious intimidation is not uncommon.

Racism, anti-Semitism, and other disturbing forms of hatred are also on the rise in Europe. Russia and Eastern Europe have witnessed the reemergence of overt and not infrequent verbal and physical assaults on Jews. Gennadi Zyuganov, the leader of the political party with the most seats in Russia's parliament, has charged that Russia and the rest of Christian civilization was separated from its moral foundations by Jews who "traditionally controlled the financial life of the continent."[16] Aleksandr I. Lebed, the governor of one of Russia's largest provinces and considered a possible successor as president to Boris Yeltsin, has shown a similar anti-Semitic streak. In one instance, while meeting with a delegation of Cossacks, an ethnic group with a warrior-class tradition, he thought one of their representatives was being too meek. "You say you are a Cossack," Lebed chided the man. "Why do you speak like a Jew?"[17]

Other former communist countries in Europe are also seeing more overt anti-Semitism. A survey in Poland found that one-third of all respondents thought Jewish influence "too great" in the country, and 31 percent admitted to being somewhere between "extremely" and "slightly" anti-Semitic. When the movie *Schindler's List*, depicting the horrors in the Polish ghettos and in the concentration camps, played in Germany, some Germans charged the movie overdramatized events, and a poll found that 39 percent of the Germans surveyed agreed with the statement, "Jews are exploiting the Holocaust for their own purposes."[18]

Indigenous People

The history of the world is a story of migration and conquest that has often meant that the indigenous people of a region now find themselves a minority in national political systems imposed on their traditional tribal or other political structures. The most familiar of these groups to many readers probably are the numerous native peoples of North and South America commonly lumped together as "Indians," or more contemporarily referred to by such designations as Native Americans and Mezo-Americans. The Eskimos or Inuit of Canada and Alaska (as well as Greenland and eastern Siberia), and native Hawaiians in that U.S. state are also indigenous peoples.

The efforts of various indigenous groups in Central and South America have become increasingly well known. The unrest in the southern area of Chiapas in Mexico is associated in part with the alienation of the impoverished Mayan and other indigenous people of that region from the Mexican government. This feeling of oppression is supported by UN data that finds that on the UNDP's Human Development Index, the level of development of the Mexican people is 27 percent higher than that of the country's indigenous people. This relative poverty, even in what used to be called **Third World** countries, has led to the term **Fourth World** to designate indigenous people collectively.

One of the particular efforts of indigenous people in recent years has been their effort to protect their traditional home areas politically and environmentally from the incursion of the surrounding cultures. The spread of the people and business of Brazil into the vast interior areas of the Amazon River system has increasingly degraded the health, environment, and other aspects of the life of the indigenous people of that region. The Yanomami people, for one, are being devastated by the diseases carried by miners who have entered their region and, on occasion, by violence aimed at forcing the tribe off its lands. The number of Yanomami has shrunk to just 8,268, with 2,200 of them dying between 1988 and 1995 alone. Similarly, the 1,400 Kaipao, who live in the Brazilian Mato Grosso region in the 6.4-million-acre Xingu National Park along with 14 other tribes, are fighting a losing battle to keep outsiders (ranging from miners and loggers to ecotourists) out of their homeland.

**A SITE TO SURF
The UN
Development
Programme**

Refugees and Immigrants

Many commentators have accurately noted the rise of ethnic and racial strife, religious fundamentalism, and other xenophobic movements in recent years, but there is much less agreement about the causes. One intriguing explanation is offered by Václav Havel, who suggests that societies "tend to look for pseudo-certainties" and that people everywhere are insecure in this era of immense and rapid political, economic, and social change. One reaction for many people, Havel suggests, is "submerging themselves in a crowd, a community, and defining themselves in contrast to other communities." It is in part for this reason, the Czech president thinks, "that we are now witnessing manifestations of intolerance, xenophobia, racism, and nationalism."[19]

One clear indication of that nativist tendency is evident in the upsurge in negative feeling in many quarters of the world toward immigrants and refugees (Cornelius, Martin, & Hollifield, 1995). The post–cold war spasm of civil wars and other internal violence, added to the economic desperation of many people, has set off a flood of refugees. "Migration is the visible face of social change," as a report by the UNFPA puts it.[20] According to United Nations High Commissioner for Refugees Sadako Ogata, the refugees living outside of their native countries in 1996 stood at 13.2 million. She also estimates that there were 26 million more internally displaced persons who, while still living in their own country, had been forced to flee their homes, villages, and cities. That means that 1 out of every 147 people on this planet has been displaced.

In addition to the people who are overt refugees, there are millions of people who have legally or illegally entered other countries in order to find work. The tide of refugees and immigrants, legal and illegal, has been greeted in the EDCs with increasing resistance. The influx of Bosnians led Germany to revise its laws and begin to place much greater restrictions on political refugees, and in the national political race in 1998 both Chancellor Helmut Kohl and Gerhard Schröder, the leader of the main opposition party who succeeded Kohl after the September elections, appealed to the voters by advocating stringent restrictions on future immigration into Germany. France in 1994 changed its laws in a way that meant that many foreigners who had earlier entered France legally to work would have to leave. Most of these workers and their families came from former French colonies in Africa. Although most French people would not agree with its stridency, many would find at least some hint of truth in the view of right-wing French political leader Jean-Marie Le Pen, who portrays some parts of France as "literally gangrenous because of the foreign invasion." Beware, Le Pen warned the French of "old origin" (whites, compared to most immigrants, who are Africans), "Tomorrow the immigrants will be moving into your house, eating your food and sleeping with your wife, your daughter, or your son."[21]

Anti-immigrant and refugee opinion has also strengthened in North America. A 1995 survey of Canadians found that a majority "strongly agreed" that "there are too many immigrants coming into this country who are not adopting Canadian values" and a majority also agreed that "Canadian culture today needs to be more protected from outside influences."[22] American attitudes are similar to Canadian views. There has been broad political pressure to reduce legal immigration and illegal workers, and legislation, such as Proposition 187 in California, to deny services, including education for children, to undocumented aliens.

Coping with refugees and economically driven illegal immigrants is costing the North many billions of dollars each year in such efforts as the aid and security forces sent to the Zaire-Rwandan border in late 1996 to ease the humanitarian crisis there. Many countries are also spending vast sums on their border patrols and on other domestic programs to stem the influx of refugees and undocumented immigrants, to assist those that are admitted or who slip in, and to return some of those who do arrive to their country of origin.

Whatever the impact of programs to lessen the inflow of refugees and immigrants may be, it is certain that they are not only expensive, but that they will be unending as long as people in some countries are subject to endemic violence and poverty. The Kevin Costner movie *Field of Dreams* revolved around the line, "If you build it, they will come." To those who daily face death, disease, and hunger, the EDCs' societies of relative peace and material wealth represent a field of dreams. And people in danger and destitution will come.

One way to avoid perpetually spending vast sums on aid, immigration control, and other programs, some say, is to help the South develop quickly, to at least build a field that meets minimum needs of sustenance and safety. It is arguable that if Mexico's standard of living were to increase substantially, many of its citizens would no longer undergo the dislocation and risk the physical danger that leaving home and slipping into the United States entails. "We have a good argument now, a very concrete one," for helping the LDCs, the prime minister of Denmark told a UN conference, "which is, if you don't help the Third World . . . , then you will have these poor people in your society."[23]

The International Response to Individual and Group Human Rights Issues

It would be naive to argue that the world has even begun to come close to resolving its numerous individual and group human rights issues; it would be equally wrong to deny that a start has been made. The way to evaluate the worth of the efforts that we are about to discuss is to judge their goals and to see them as the beginnings of a process that only a few decades ago did not exist at all. Whatever country you live in, the protection of human rights has evolved over an extended period and is still far from complete. The global community has now embarked on an effort similar to your country's effort. It will, however, take time and will be subject to much controversy.

The United Nations is the most important focus of global human rights activity. The basis for UN concern is the organization's charter, which touches on human rights in several places. More specific is the Universal Declaration of Human Rights (1948), which includes numerous clauses discussed in the earlier box, Global Bill of Rights. These are proclaimed as a "common standard," an array of rights "for all peoples and all nations." Many of the rights contained in the Universal Declaration and others are also included in two other broad multilateral treaties: the International Covenant on Civil and Political Rights (1966) and the International Covenant on Economic, Social and Cultural Rights (1966). Most countries have agreed to all three of these pacts. A notable addition to these ranks came in March 1998 when China agreed to sign the treaty on civil and political rights. In addition, there are 19 other UN–sponsored covenants that address children's rights, genocide, racial discrimination, refugees, slavery, stateless persons, women's rights, and other human rights issues. These agreements and human rights in general are monitored by the UN High Commissioner on Human Rights (UNHCHR).

A SITE TO SURF
Hot Topics at
UNHCHR

There are also a number of regional conventions and IGOs that supplement the principles and efforts of the UN. The most well-developed of these are in Western Europe and include two human rights covenants (Robertson & Merrills, 1995). These are adjudicated by the European Court of Human Rights and the Commission on Human Rights. Additionally, there are a substantial number of NGOs, such as Amnesty International and Human Rights Watch, that are concerned with a broad range of human rights. These groups work independently and in cooperation with the UN and regional organizations to further human rights. They add to the swell of information about

On a 1998 tour of Africa, UN secretary-general Kofi Annan and his wife, Nane, view remains from the 1994 genocide in Rwanda. The image is a stark and stunning reminder of the cruelty that humans can and do recurrently inflict upon one another.

**INTERACTIVE
EXERCISE
Good Guys and
Bad Guys . . . Hard
to Tell the
Difference**

and criticisms of abuses. They help promote the adoption of international norms that support human rights (Clark, 1996).

The impact of IGOs and NGOs and general progress in the human rights arena have, as noted, been mixed. Political selectivity and national domestic political concerns are two of the factors that impede the growth of human rights observance and enforcement on the international stage. Both these factors were discussed in chapter 6 and, thus, merit only brief recapitulation. Political selectivity disposes all countries to be shocked when opponents transgress against human rights and to ignore abuses by themselves, by their allies, and by countries that they hope to influence. Nationalism and the standard of sovereignty continue to be used by some countries to reject outside interference of domestic abuses, and by other countries as a reason for ignoring those abuses. An associated issue is the claim that cultural standards are different, and, therefore, what is a human rights violation in one country is culturally acceptable in another.

These and other impediments should not cloud the human rights contributions of the UN, Amnesty International, and other IGOs and NGOs (Thakur, 1994). The frequency and horror of the abuses that they highlight are increasingly penetrating the international consciousness and disconcerting the global conscience. The 1993 UN–sponsored World Conference on Human Rights (WCHR) held in Vienna, Austria, provides an example. As is true for international forums on most issues, the WCHR witnessed political fissures along several lines. Some Asian, Muslim, and other countries resisted broad declarations of human rights based on what they see as Western-oriented values. This charge of cultural imperialism also led them to oppose the appointment of a high commissioner for human rights to head the United Nations Commission on Human Rights (UNCHR) and give it more impact. In the end, though, some advances were made in both defining global human rights and creating and empowering a high commissioner. To clarify human rights, the WCHR declared that "all human rights are universal and indivisible and interdependent and interrelated," while adding that "the significance of national and regional particularities and various historical, cultural, and religious backgrounds must be kept in mind" when defining rights and identifying and condemning abuses (Burk, 1994:201). Advocates of appointing a high commissioner were able to overcome the roadblocks erected at the WCHR by subsequently bringing the issue before the UN General Assembly, which created the post.

To give a bit more detail on the specific efforts of the UN, other IGOs, and NGOs in the area of human rights, we can turn to their activities with respect to women, children, ethnic and racial groups, religious groups, indigenous people, and refugees and immigrants.

Women   A great deal of the human rights attention and some of the most vigorous international human rights efforts in recent years have focused on women. The most significant progress has been made in the realm of identifying the treatment of women as a global problem, identifying some of the causes and worst abuses, and defining women's rights. This has placed the issue of women solidly on the international agenda. For example, the UN General Assembly's Third Committee, which specializes in social, cultural, and humanitarian issues, spent less than 2 percent of its time discussing women's rights from 1955 to 1965. That percentage had risen almost sevenfold by the mid-1980s, and, indeed, has now become the second most extensively discussed issue (after racial discrimination) in the committee.

A major symbolic step occurred with the UN declaration of 1975 as International Women's Year and the kickoff of a Decade for Women. Numerous conferences brought women together to document their status (Chen, 1995). Funding for projects to benefit women was begun through the establishment of such structures as the UN Fund for Women (UNIFEM, after its French initials). The adoption of the Convention on the Elimination of All Forms of Discrimination Against Women in 1979 was a pathbreaking step in defining women's rights on an international level. Not all countries, it should be noted, have ratified the convention. These countries include, as of late 1998, the United States. Progress on women's issues also occurred at the 1993 WCHR. The plan adopted by the conference urged universal adoption of the 1979 treaty and urged the UNCHR to create the post of special rapporteur on violence against women. The commission complied in early 1994, naming a Sri Lankan jurist to the post.

This rise in the level of consciousness also led to a number of other institutional changes at the UN. The organization created the Division for the

Advancement of Women, which is responsible for addressing women's issues and promoting their rights. In this role, the division administratively supports both the Commission on the Status of Women (CSW), the main UN policy-making body for women, and the Committee on the Elimination of Discrimination Against Women (CEDAW), which monitors the implementation of the 1979 convention on women's rights. The division has also organized four UN world conferences on women.

The next major step in the international women's movement came in 1995 when the fourth World Conference on Women (WCW) convened in Beijing. During the planning for the conference, its chairwoman, Gertrude Mongella, urged that "the road to Beijing must be paved with vision and commitment" (Burk, 1994:239). It was, and the story of that conference is told in the Web site box The Road to Beijing and Beyond.

A FURTHER NOTE
The Road to Beijing and Beyond

Children   Serious international efforts to protect the rights of children have only recently begun, but there have already been worthwhile steps. UNICEF is the most important single agency, but it is supported by numerous other IGOs. The efforts of UNICEF are also supported and supplemented by a wide range of NGOs, such as End Child Prostitution in Asian Tourism, which was established in 1991 by child welfare groups in several Asian countries. Their common goal, in the words of UNICEF executive director Carol Bellamy, is to "ensure that exploitive and hazardous child labor becomes as unacceptable in the next century as slavery has become in this. Children should be students in school, not slaves in factories, fields, or brothels."[24]

One noteworthy advance is the Convention on the Rights of the Child (Mower, 1997). Work on it began in 1979, which had been designated by the UN as the International Year of the Child. A draft treaty, written under the auspices of the UNCHR, was presented to and adopted unanimously by the UN General Assembly in 1989 and made available for signature and ratification by the world's countries. The convention outlines a wide range of collective and individual rights for all persons under age 18. If all countries and people abided by the convention, the sexual exploitation of children, the use of boy soldiers, the diversion of children from their education to work, and many other abuses would end.

It is a mark of hope that the convention has quickly become the most widely ratified human rights treaty in history. Indeed, as of late 1999, there were only two countries that are not party to the treaty. One is war-torn, virtually governmentless Somalia, which has not signed the treaty; the other is the United States, which has signed, but not ratified, it. Among other concerns in the United States was whether the convention would abridge the possibility in some U.S. states that minors convicted of capital crimes can be executed once they reach age 18.

A second important recent effort on behalf of children was the World Congress Against Commercial Sexual Exploitation of Children, which met in Stockholm, Sweden, during August 1996. It was attended by representatives of 122 national governments, the UN and other IGOs, and 471 NGOs. The authority of such international meetings is severely limited, but they do serve a valuable function by focusing attention on issues. As the congress's general rapporteur, Vitit Muntarbhorn of Thailand, noted, "There can be no more delusions—no one can deny that the problem of children being sold for sex exists, here and now, in almost every country in the world."[25]

Despite the near impossibility of opposing children's rights in theory, the effort to protect them in practice, like most international human rights programs, runs into the problems of nationalism and parochialism. Countries resist being told what to do, and they are better able to see what others should do than what they themselves should do. Arundhati Ghose, India's representative to the UNCHR in Geneva, reacted recently to criticism of the number of children being exploited in India by lashing out at what she called "finger pointing" by other countries. She recounted that when India had tried to garner support for a global ban on sex tourism, the effort had met resistance from Germany, Japan, Korea, and the Netherlands. While displaying ads in German magazines offering "boys of any color, size, or age," Ghose related that other countries had told her, "We are not willing to ban promotion of sex tours." What Ghose wants to do is avoid finger pointing because, she says, "If we can agree that it's nobody's fault, but it's a bad thing, then we can tackle it." But, she added, "the moment you start apportioning blame, people go on the defensive."[26]

Ethnic, Racial, and Religious Groups　Efforts to define the rights of ethnic, racial, and religious groups have been part of the major human rights documents such as the International Covenant on Economic, Social, and Cultural Rights and the Convention on the Prevention and Punishment of the Crime of Genocide. There have also been some specific agreements, such as the International Convention on the Elimination of all Forms of Racial Discrimination (1969). It is a step forward that 145 countries have been willing to agree to this document, which, among other things, proclaims that its signatories are "convinced that any doctrine of superiority based on racial differentiation is scientifically false, morally condemnable, socially unjust and dangerous, and that there is no justification for racial discrimination, in theory or in practice, anywhere."

These efforts have been supplemented by some levels of enforcement. The earlier international pressure on South Africa to end legal racism was an important step. The international tribunals investigating and trying war crimes committed in the Balkans and in Rwanda are further evidence that persecution based on ethnicity, race, or religion are increasingly considered an affront to the global conscience.

Indigenous People　The UN General Assembly proclaimed 1993 to be the International Year of the Indigenous Peoples. The following year, as part of that year's UNHRC meeting, representatives of the more than 5,000 indigenous peoples agreed to an International Covenant on the Rights of Indigenous Nations and made it available for signature and ratification by the world's countries. The efforts of indigenous people have also been furthered by numerous

NGOs, including the International Indian Treaty Council, the World Council of Indigenous Peoples, the Inuit Circumpolar Conference, and the Unrepresented Nations and Peoples' Organization. The causes of indigenous people were also furthered when the Nobel Peace Prize Committee made its 1992 award to Rigoberta Menchú of Guatemala in recognition of her efforts to advance the rights of her Mayan people in her country and to further the welfare of indigenous people globally.

Refugees and Immigrants   International efforts on behalf of refugees provide very mixed results. There have been a number of efforts to define the status and the rights of both international and internal refugees. An early effort was the 1951 Convention Relating to the Status of Refugees (1951). This document charged the UN with providing assistance to people who were being persecuted in their countries or who feared persecution if returned to their home countries of origin. The convention also defined the basic rights of refugees and minimum standards for their treatment and has served, among other things, as a foundation for subsequent efforts on behalf of refugees. It is also true, though, that it is one of the least widely ratified of the UN's major human rights treaties. Because of concerns that they might be required to open their borders to refugees or extend rights to those that managed to arrive unbidden, only 124 countries have signed and ratified it, with the United States among the countries that has not signed the treaty.

Aid to refugees, while scant compared to their need, presents a somewhat brighter picture. The effort on behalf of displaced persons in the early 1950s also led to the creation of the UN High Commissioner for Refugees (UNHCR) in 1951 with wide responsibility for refugee rights and needs. Also formed that year was the International Organization for Migration (IOM), a body specifically concerned with the movement of refugees either to new homes or back to their former homes, as appropriate. There are also any number of IGOs such as the International Red Cross and its Muslim counterpart, the International Red Crescent, that are involved in providing food, clothes, shelter, and other necessities. The immense need for such aid has been regularly evident in recent times in the refugee camps of Bosnia, along the Rwanda-Zaire border, in Albania near Kosovo Province, and elsewhere.

Chapter Summary

1. This chapter discusses two types of human rights. Individual human rights consist of freedom from specific abuses or restrictions, especially by governments. Collective human rights encompass the right to a quality of life, including adequate nutrition, reasonable health care, and educational opportunity that, at minimum, does not detract from human dignity.

2. Population growth, the underproduction of food, and the maldistribution of the food that is produced means that there are many

people who do not receive adequate nutrition. International organizations, such as the Food and Agriculture Organization, attempt to provide short-term food relief and long-term agricultural assistance to countries facing nutritional shortages.

3. Many people in LDCs face diseases and lack of medical care to degrees that boggle the minds of most people in EDCs. Some of the diseases, such as AIDS, can become a world health threat. The World Health Organization, other IGOs, and many NGOs are attempting to bring better health care to people globally.

4. The ability of individuals to achieve a higher quality of life and the ability of countries to develop economically depend in substantial part on education. More than 1 billion adults are still illiterate, many more have only the most rudimentary education, and the personal and societal productivity of these people is limited. The United Nations Educational, Scientific, and Cultural Organization is one of many international organizations working to improve education in the LDCs.

5. There are two types of individual rights. Civil rights include standards, such as equal standing in the courts, which must exist to ensure that all people and groups are treated equally. Civil liberties are those things, like exercising free speech, which individuals cannot be prevented from doing.

6. Human rights abuses are widespread. They spring from intolerance, authoritarianism, and other causes and are often rationalized by pseudoscientific theories, such as social Darwinism, and by repressive ideologies, such as fascism.

7. The discussion of human rights abuses and the efforts to ease them focuses on women, children, ethnic and racial groups, religious groups, indigenous people, and refugees and immigrants.

8. The area of human rights is one of the most difficult to work in because violations are usually politically based. Therefore, efforts to redress them are often resented and rejected by target countries. The greatest progress has been made in adopting a number of UN declarations, such as the Universal Declaration of Human Rights, and multilateral treaties that define basic human rights. The enforcement of human rights is much less well developed, but the rising level of awareness and of disapproval of violations on a global scale is having a positive impact. There are also many IGOs, such as the UN Human Rights Commission, and NGOs, such as Amnesty International, that work to improve human rights.

Chapter **14**

Preserving and Enhancing the Global Commons

Dear earth, I do salute thee with my hand.

Shakespeare, *Richard II*

Over the long haul of life on this planet, it is the ecologists, and not the bookkeepers of business, who are the ultimate accountants.

Stewart L. Udall, U.S. secretary of the interior

This chapter deals with ecological concerns and cooperation, but it is in many ways an extension of the human rights issues in chapter 13. One connection between the two chapters is the normative question, Should we care? Clearly, the view in this text is that we all should care. Self-interest compels us to attend to issues of the world's expanding population, the depletion of natural resources, the increase of chemical discharges into the environment, and the impact of these trends on the global biosphere. You will see that new approaches are needed because solutions attempted by single countries will be insufficient to solve the problems we humans face collectively. The issues discussed in this chapter are transnational problems. Therefore, their solution requires transnational programs achieved through international cooperation (Zurn, 1998; Bellany, 1997; Choucri, 1995).

Chapter Outline

Toward Sustainable Development

Before taking up specific issues, it is helpful to understand that they are related. To do this, we can discuss two overarching controversies. One debates the *ecological state of the world*. You will see presently that some analysts are truly alarmed about the future. Other observers believe that worries about the ecosphere are frequently overwrought. The second broad controversy focuses on **sustainable development**. The issue is whether (or perhaps, how) the world can continue simultaneously to sustain development and to protect its environment. An associated term of importance is **carrying capacity**, which is the largest number of humans that the Earth can sustain indefinitely at current rates of per capita consumption of natural resources.

The Ecological State of the World

There is a book, *The State of the World* (Brown, 1998), published annually.[1] Just as the U.S. president delivers an annual State of the Union address to Congress, so too should we regularly assess the ecological state of the world.

A SITE TO SURF
Worldwatch
Institute
Environmental
Alerts

Environmental pessimism aptly describes the view of one group of analysts about the state of the world. Lester Brown and the others who contribute to the annual *State of the World* volume are among this group. Brown (1998:4) writes that "the key environmental indicators are increasingly negative. Forests are shrinking, water tables are falling, soils are eroding, wetlands are disappearing, fisheries are collapsing, range lands are deteriorating, rivers are running dry, temperatures are rising, coral reefs are dying, and plants and animal species are disappearing." Brown draws a grim analogy between the ever-expanding economy and human cancer cells. Unless they are checked, such cells continually grow, consuming the resources of the body, until the cancer destroys the human who is its unwilling host. Where will this lead? Brown (p. 19) worries that "we may be accumulating a backlog of problems that will become unmanageable, undermining confidence in our political institutions, leading to their collapse and to social disintegration."

Some pessimistic analysts even foresee "environmental scarcities" as the cause of future warfare among states desperate to sustain their economies and quality of life. According to one study, scarcities of renewable resources are already causing some conflict in the world, and there may be "an upsurge of violence in the coming decades . . . that is caused or aggravated by environmental change" (Homer-Dixon, 1998:342).

Environmental optimism rejects this gloomy view of the world and its future. Indeed, some optimists believe that the pessimists resemble Chicken Little, the protagonist in a children's story who was hit on the head by a shingle that had fallen off the barn roof. Convinced that he had been struck by a piece of the sky, Chicken Little panicked and raced around the barnyard crying, "The sky is falling, the sky is falling," thereby creating unfounded pandemonium. For example, one optimist chastises the ecology movement for promoting "green guilt" by "scaring and shaming people" and falsely contending that there is "little that we in the industrial world . . . do that . . . [is not] lethal, wicked, or both."[2]

Optimists say that the sky remains safely in its traditional location and that with reasonable prudence there is no need to fear for the future. They argue that we will be able to meet our needs and continue to grow economically through conservation, population restraints, and, most importantly, technological innovation. This upbeat view has earned this group the sobriquet "technological optimists." They believe that new technology can find and develop oil fields. Synthetics can replace natural resources. Fertilizers, hybrid seeds, and mechanization can increase acreage yields. Desalinization and weather control can meet water demands. Energy can be drawn from nuclear, solar, thermal, wind, and hydroelectric sources. In sum, according to one of the best-known optimists, economist Julian Simon (1994:297), not only do the scientific facts indicate that "the current gloom-and-doom about a 'crisis' of our environment is all wrong," but "almost every economic and social change or trend points in a positive direction." In fact Simon was so sure of his view, that in 1980 he made a $1,000 bet with an equally convinced pessimist, biologist Paul Ehrlich, author of *The Population Bomb,* about the prices of five basic metal ores in 1990. Ehrlich wagered that population demands would drive the prices up; Simon bet they would not. A decade and nearly a billion people later, the prices were all down. Ehrlich sent Simon a check.

It is important to note that most optimists do not dismiss the problems that the world faces. "Progress does not come automatically," Simon wrote (p. 306); "and my message is not complacency. In this I agree with the doomsayers—that our world needs the best efforts of all humanity to improve our lot." That effort will be provided, he continued, expressing his profound optimism, by our "ultimate resource . . . people—especially skilled, spirited, and hopeful young people . . . who will exert their wills and imaginations for their own benefit, and so inevitably they will benefit not only themselves but the rest of us as well."

Sustainable Development

MAP
Air and Water
Quality

Industrialization and science have been two-edged swords in their relationship to the environment and the quality of human life. On the positive side, industrialization has vastly expanded global wealth, especially for the economically developed countries (EDCs). Science has created synthetic substances that enhance our lives; medicine has dramatically increased our chances of surviving infancy and has extended adult longevity. Yet, on the negative side, industry consumes natural resources and discharges pollutants into the air, ground, and water. Synthetic substances enter the food chain as carcinogens, refuse to degrade, and have other baleful effects. Decreased infant mortality rates and increased longevity have been major factors behind the world's skyrocketing population growth.

All these phenomena and trends, however, are part of modernization and are unlikely to be reversed. The dilemma is how to protect the biosphere and, at the same time, advance human socioeconomic development. This conundrum overarches specific issues such as population, habitat destruction, and pollution.

Pessimists would certainly see this concern as immediate and critical, but even most optimists would concede that the challenge would be vastly compounded if you were to bring the industrial-production and standard-of-living levels of the nearly 5 billion people who live in less developed countries (LDCs) in the South up to the levels enjoyed by the less than 1 billion people who reside in the North.

The Conundrum of Sustainable Development

Here is the problem you should ponder as you read the rest of this chapter. If the minority of the world's population who live in EDCs use most of the resources and create most of the pollution, how can the South develop economically without accelerating the ecological deterioration that already exists? Think about what consumption would be like if China were economically developed and the Chinese per capita consumption of petroleum and minerals and emission of CO_2 were equal to that of Americans. Given the fact that China's population is about four times that of the United States, a fully developed China with a per capita consumption equal to the United States (compared to current consumption and emissions) would increase the two countries' combined petroleum consumption by 362 percent, their combined mineral consumption by 432 percent, and their combined CO_2 emissions by 324 percent. Furthermore, if you were to bring the rest of the LDCs up to the U.S. (as an EDC) level of resource use and emissions discharge, then you would hyperaccelerate the depletion of natural resources and the creation of pollution even more. Clearly, this is not acceptable.

Options for Sustainable Development

What to do? is the question. Apart from doing little or nothing and hoping for the best, there are two options. One is to restrict or even halt economic development. The second option is to make the cooperative political and financial commitment to develop in as environmentally safe a way as is possible.

Severely Restricting Development   Preserving the environment by consuming less is the first option. What is necessary, according to one analyst, is to institute "an integrated global program to set permissible levels" for consumption and emission, to mobilize huge financial resources for resource conservation and pollution control, and to create "effective international institutions with legally binding powers . . . to enforce [the] agreed-upon standards and financial obligations" (Johansen, 1994:381).

Objections to such solutions leap to mind. Are we, for instance, to suppress LDC development? If the Chinese do not get more cars, if Indians are kept in the fields instead of in factories, and if Africans continue to swelter

This outdated Indian power plant was imploded by a joint Indian and British demolition team in June 1999. A new plant will be built by a Japanese consortium as part of an Indian effort to create a more solid infrastructure for its development efforts. Such plants are very costly and are few and far between in LDCs, often coming at significant environmental costs.

in the summer's heat without air conditioners, then accelerated resource use and pollution discharges can be partly avoided. Another possible answer is for the people of the North to use dramatically fewer resources and to take the steps needed to reduce pollution drastically. Polls show that most people favor the theory of conservation and environmental protection. Yet practice indicates that, so far, most people are also unwilling to suffer a major reduction in their conveniences or standards of living.

Paying the Price for Environmentally Responsible Development   A second option is to pay the price to create and distribute technologies that will allow for a maximum balance between economic development and environmental protection. Without modern technology and the money to pay for it, China, for example, poses a serious environmental threat. China now stands second behind the United States in terms of national production of carbon dioxide emissions. A primary reason is that China generates most of its commercial power by burning coal, which is very polluting. Moreover, the country's coal consumption is expected to more than double between what it was in 1990 and 2010, and that will increase annual carbon dioxide emissions from about 700 million tons in 1990 to 1,400 million tons in 2010.

There are options, such as generating more power by burning petroleum or utilizing hydroelectric energy. Each option, however, has trade-offs, which are often win-lose scenarios. For China, consuming more oil would require vastly expensive imports, which could affect the country's socioeconomic development. Increased oil consumption at the level China would need would also accelerate the depletion of the world's finite petroleum reserves. Moreover, the new oil fields that are being found often lie offshore, and drilling endangers the oceans.

A second option, using hydroelectricity to provide relatively nonpolluting energy, requires the construction of dams that flood the surrounding countryside, displace its residents, and spoil the pristine beauty of the river valley downstream. China, for example, is trying to ease its energy crunch and simultaneously develop clean hydroelectric power by building the massive Three Gorges dam and hydroelectric project on the Yangtze River. The engineering project rivals the Great Wall of China in scope. When completed, the project will vastly increase the availability of electric power to rural provinces by generating 18,200 megawatts of electricity without burning highly polluting coal. The dam will also help stem floods that have often caused catastrophic damage downstream. To accomplish these benefits, however, the dam will create a reservoir approximately 400 miles long, thereby flooding 425 square miles of fertile land, inundating 1,500 factories, some 160 towns, 16 archaeological sites, and submerging what many consider one of the most scenic natural places in the world. The huge reservoir also began in 1997 to force what will become an estimated 1.1 million people from their homes. Thus, the Three Gorges project is an almost perfect illustration of the difficulty of sustainable development. Even though the project will ease some environmental problems (in this case, coal burning) it will also have an adverse impact on people and on the environment.

Even if you can cut such Gordian knots, you will encounter other problems: the short-term costs of environmental protection in terms of taxes to pay for government programs; the high costs of products that are produced in an environmentally acceptable way and that are themselves environmentally safe; and the expense of disposing of waste in an ecologically responsible manner.

Moreover, since the LDCs are determined to develop economically, yet struggle to pay the costs of environmentally sound progress, the North must extend significant aid to the South to help it develop in a relatively safe way. Money is needed to create nonpolluting energy resources, to install pollution control devices in factories, and to provide many other technologies. The costs will be huge, approaching, in some estimates, $20 billion a year.

Is the North willing to pay this price? Polls show that people in many countries are concerned about global warming, ozone layer destruction, deforestation, wildlife destruction, and acid rain. Cross-national polls also regularly find that a majority of respondents say that their governments should do more to protect their country's environment and also to be involved in the global environmental effort. Yet surveys additionally find that a majority of citizens think that their tax burdens are already too heavy and are unwilling to support large expenditures on environmental programs. One illustrative poll asked Americans if they would pay $200 in extra taxes to clean up the environment. A laudable 70 percent said yes. That was the limit of the majority's financial commitment, though. When the next question raised the cleanup bill to an extra $500, only 44 percent said yes. This resistance will work against any attempt to amass the funds that need to be spent internationally to help the LDCs simultaneously develop and protect the environment.[3]

The Debate over Sustainable Development: What to Believe   "Help!" you might exclaim at this point. "Is it necessary to live in unheated tents and abandon our cars to keep the sky from falling?" Fortunately, the answer is Probably not.

There is a need, though, to consider the problems and possible solutions carefully. The answers are not easy. Indeed, sustainable development is "a Herculean task," as Canadian diplomat Maurice Strong, the secretary-general of the 1992 Earth Summit, put it.[4] Thus, we should now turn our attention to the specific issues surrounding the state of the biosphere and its inhabitants, and the possibility of achieving international cooperation toward sustainable development. We will first consider population. Then we will turn to concerns over such resources as minerals, forests, wildlife, and water. Last, the chapter will take up environmental issues, including pollution of the ground, water, air, and upper atmosphere.

Sustainable Development: Issues and Cooperation

Throughout history, humans have taken their world for granted. They have assumed that it will always be here, that it will yield the necessities of life, and that it will absorb what is discarded. For several millennia this assumption proved justifiable. The Earth was generally able to sustain its population and replenish itself.

Now, the exploding human population and technology have changed this. Not only are there five times as many people as there were just a little more than 150 years ago, but our technological progress has multiplied our per capita resource consumption and our per capita waste and pollutant production. Technological wizardry may bring solutions, as the optimists predict, but such solutions are uncertain; for now the reality is that the world faces a crisis of carrying capacity—the potential of no longer being able to sustain its population in an adequate manner or being able to absorb its waste. To put this as an equation:

Exploding population	x	Spiraling per capita resource consumption	x	Mounting waste and pollutant production	=	Potential catastrophe

Population Issues and Cooperation

Identifying the population problem is simple: There are too many of us and we are reproducing too quickly. Here are some amazing and, to most people, disturbing, statistics. Stop and think about what they mean for the future.

On or about June 16, 1999, the population of the world passed the 6 billion mark. That is a stunning number. It took all of human history to 1804 for the population to reach 1 billion. Adding the next billion people took just 123 years. Now we are expanding by 1 billion people about every 12.5 years. Of all the people who have ever lived, an incredible 25 percent are alive right now. One country, China, with its 1.2 billion inhabitants, has more people than there were humans in the entire world less than 200 years ago. And just since the birth in 1880 of the world's oldest living person, Sarah Clark Knauss of Allentown, Pennsylvania, the world population has about tripled. At its current growth rate of 80 million per year, the world is annually adding a number of people equal to the combined populations of Argentina and Egypt. In only the time it took you to take this course, assuming a 15-week semester, the world's population expansion equaled the number of people in Romania. Almost one in every three people in the world is a child (less than 16 years old). Most of these children will soon become adults and want to be parents.

Projections of future population trends are not reassuring either. According to the United Nations Population Fund (UNFPA), the world population will reach the 10.4 billion mark in the year 2100 and will not level off until it reaches about 11 billion people in 2200. Thus the population continues to expand at a rapid pace, and the 1999 milestone of 6 billion people means a doubling of the Earth population in less than 40 years. There are approximately 30 countries with a population growth rate between 3.0 percent and 4.9 percent; they will double their populations in 14 to 22 years. About another 50 countries have population growth rates between 2.0 percent and 2.9 percent; they will double their populations in 23 to 34 years. Such numbers have convinced Pakistani physician Nafis Sadik, the executive director of the UNFPA, that population growth is a "crisis" that "heightens the risk of future economic and ecological catastrophe."[5]

To the extent that anything in the UNFPA data and estimates can be considered good news, it is that the rate of growth has slowed somewhat. As recently as 1994, the population was expanding at 94 million a year, and the UN was estimating that it would reach 11.6 billion by 2150. Even this bit of good news about the decline in the overall growth rate is dampened, however, by the fact that the fastest population increases are occurring in the LDCs, especially those in Africa, which often are the least able to support their people, and whose economic development is further retarded by the burden of the increased population. Moreover, as one demographer commented about the easing of the population growth rate, "The difference is comparable to a tidal wave surging toward one of our coastal cities. Whether the tidal wave is 80 feet or 100 feet high, the impact will be similar."[6] Population increases are shown in Figure 14.1.

Causes of the Population Problem

There are several causes of the rapidly expanding population. One is fewer deaths. Infant mortality has decreased; adult longevity has increased. These two factors combine to mean that even in areas where the birthrate declines,

Figure 14.1

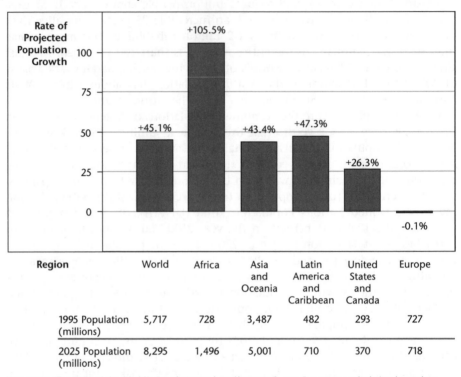

Population Growth 1998–2025

Region	World	Africa	Asia and Oceania	Latin America and Caribbean	United States and Canada	Europe
1995 Population (millions)	5,717	728	3,487	482	293	727
2025 Population (millions)	8,295	1,496	5,001	710	370	718

Data source: The State of the World's Population at http://www.unfa.org. Percentage calculation by authors.

World population growth is not even. The burden of additional people will fall most heavily on the regions with a predominance of less developed countries, which have scant resources to support their burgeoning populations.

the population growth rate sometimes continues to accelerate. Sub-Saharan Africa's birthrate declined from 47 births per 1,000 population in the early 1970s to 44 in the late 1990s, but during the same period life expectancy increased from 45 years to 50 years because of a decrease in the infant mortality rate (annual deaths per thousand children through age 5) from 135 children to a better, if still tragic, 97 children. Furthermore, the region's overall crude death rate (annual death of people per thousand) dropped from 21 to 16. The net result is that the rapidly declining death rates have more than offset the more slowly declining birthrates and resulted in an annual population growth of 2.8 percent. This means that the region's population will double between 1994 and 2019.

Another reason for the alarming population growth is the huge population base of 5.8 billion. This problem is one of mathematics. Although the global fertility rate (number of expected births per woman) has declined from

4.9 in 1970 to its current rate of 2.8 and continues to ebb, there are so many more women in their childbearing years that the number of babies born continues to go up. During the next decade, some three billion women will enter their childbearing years. At the current fertility rate, these women will have 8.4 billion children.

There is a clear relationship between poverty and birthrates. In the late 1990s, the population growth rate in EDCs is 0.3 percent. The growth rate in the LDCs is 1.7 percent, 5.7 times faster than that of the EDCs. The rate in the poorest countries is even higher. The growth rate in sub-Saharan Africa is 2.8 percent, more than 9 times the EDC rate. With a fertility rate of 3.1, India alone accounted for more than 30 percent of all the babies born in 1997, and at current rates India will surpass the population of China (fertility rate: 1.8) within a few decades.

How does one explain the link between population and poverty? One commonly held view is that overpopulation causes poverty. This view reasons that with too many people, especially in already poor countries, there are too few resources, jobs, and other forms of wealth to go around. Perhaps, but that is only part of the problem, because it is also true that poverty causes overpopulation. The least developed countries tend to have the most labor-intensive economies, which means that children are economically valuable because they help their parents farm or, when they are somewhat older, provide cheap labor in mining and manufacturing processes. As a result, cultural attitudes in many countries have come to reflect economic utility. Having a large family is also an asset in terms of social standing in many societies with limited economic opportunities.

Furthermore, women in LDCs have fewer opportunities to limit the number of children they bear. Artificial birth control methods and counseling services are less readily available in these countries. Another fact is that women in LDCs are less educated than are women in EDCs. It is therefore harder to convey birth control information, especially written information, to women in LDCs. Additionally, women in LDCs have fewer opportunities than do women in EDCs to gain paid employment and to develop status roles beyond that of motherhood. The inadequacies in financial, educational, and contraceptive opportunities for women are strongly and inversely correlated to high fertility rates, as shown in Figure 14.2.

The International Response to the Population Problem

The world has generally concluded that something must be done to stem population growth. The only option, other than letting disproportionate numbers of poor children die in infancy and allowing impoverished adults to die in their forties and fifties, is to lower the average fertility rate from its current global average of 2.8 to 2.1, which is considered the stable replacement rate. As infant mortality and crude death rates continue to drop, it may even be necessary to reach 2.0 or slightly lower to stabilize the population.

While the population problem has been building up momentum for almost two centuries, efforts to deal with the issue through international cooperation are relatively recent. The growth of cooperative efforts is symbolized

MAPS
Population
Growth Rate

Total Fertility Rate

Figure 14.2

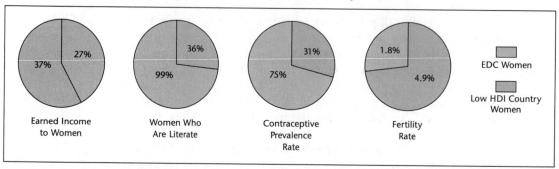

Women's Income, Educational, and Contraceptive Opportunities and Fertility Rate

Earned Income to Women: 37% / 27%
Women Who Are Literate: 99% / 36%
Contraceptive Prevalence Rate: 75% / 31%
Fertility Rate: 4.9% / 1.8%

Legend: EDC Women / Low HDI Country Women

Proportions for each circle are derived by adding the data for the two groups of women, then calculating the percentage of the sum for each group. The 48 low–human development countries are those that fell to the bottom of the UNDP's 1997 Human Development Index (HDI), which is based on a variety of social and economic data. There is a strong correlation between low HDI status and status as a least developed country (LLDC). Contraceptive prevalence rate is the percentage of married women of childbearing age who use, or whose husbands use, any form of contraception. Fertility rate is the number of children that the average woman is projected to have at current birthrates.

Data source: UNDP (1997). Proportion calculations by authors.

There is a strong relationship between the availability to women of jobs, education, and contraceptive programs and the number of children they bear. The evidence indicates that the best way to control population growth is to enhance women's opportunities.

by the establishment of numerous international governmental and nongovernmental organizations (IGOs, NGOs) concerned with the issue and by a series of world conferences on population.

Unfortunately, not all the news about the effort to constrain population growth is good. Funding to keep programs going is vital, and the downtrend in the foreign aid of many EDCs is imperiling population programs. The U.S. Congress, for example, cut or held up funding to the United Nations, the International Monetary Fund, and the U.S. Agency for International Development in an attempt to make the Clinton administration agree to include language that would bar any of the appropriated funds going to any agency that supports abortions overseas or counsels women about their availability. One of the legislators who sponsored the restrictions explained that the move was a message that if population-control organizations want funding they should be "getting out of the abortion business." The impact, according to the UNFPA director, Nafis Sadik, is that even more abortions will be performed because "17 to 18 million unwanted pregnancies are going to take place, a couple of million abortions will take place, and I'm sure that 60,000 to 80,000 women are going to die because of these abortions—and all because the money has been reduced."[7]

International Organizations and the Population Problem   The effort to control the globe's population is led appropriately by the United Nations. There are a number of associated organizations and programs within the UN's purview.

Of these, the UNFPA, a subsidiary organ of the UN General Assembly, is the largest. The agency began operations in 1969 and focuses on promoting family planning services and improving reproductive health in LDCs. During its three decades of operation, the UNFPA has provided a total of $3.7 billion to support population programs to 168 countries. The organization is funded through voluntary contributions, and in 1997 had a budget of some $309 million donated by about 95 countries. This aid currently accounts for about one-fourth of the world's population assistance to LDCs. Beyond that, the agency helps coordinate the programs of other efforts by IGOs, NGOs, and national governments.

Within the UN group of associated agencies, the work of the UNFPA is supported by the United Nations Children's Fund (UNICEF), the World Health Organization (WHO), and other IGOs. These efforts are further supplemented by and often coordinated with NGOs such as the International Planned Parenthood Federation (IPPF). This British-based organization, which was founded in 1952, operates its own international family planning programs and also links the individual planned parenthood organizations of about 150 countries. The IPPF is funded by these national organizations, by private contributions, and by donations from approximately 20 countries. Like a number of other IGOs in the population control and reproductive health area, the IPPF has consultative status with the UN.

World Population Conferences   The rapidly rising global population also led the UN to begin the World Population Conference series to focus world attention on the issue, to seek agreement on solutions, and to galvanize international cooperative efforts to address the issue. There have been three conferences, the first two of which met in Bucharest (1974) and in Mexico City (1984). The most recent of these, the 1994 **United Nations Conference on Population and Development (UNCPD)** met in Cairo, Egypt. It was organized by the UNFPA, and brought together delegates from over 170 countries and a large number of NGOs. The session focused on population control and on reproductive health. Each year, for example, about 413,000 women (99 percent of whom live in LDCs) die from complications of pregnancy and childbirth. Abortion presents a particularly emotional issue for both its supporters and opponents. Some 40 percent of all women in LDCs (outside of China) live in countries where abortion is illegal or severely restricted. Moreover, even where abortion is legal, there is often a lack of medical care. Perhaps half of the world's annual estimated 36 to 54 million abortions are performed illegally or by personnel without proper training, and in many countries, such as Nigeria and Ethiopia, over half of all maternal mortality is the result of illegal abortions.

Such harsh realities turned the attention of the conference to a third focus, which was, in the words of Nafis Sadik, "gender equality and empowering women to control their lives, especially their reproductive lives."[8] As such, an important, if informal, role of the UNCPD was to bring women together internationally and to promote a shared consciousness of gender as a transnational focus of political identity and activity. "Women have dreams at every level," commented a Pakistani delegate; "when an opportunity [such as the Cairo conference] comes, they take it." A Chinese delegate agreed that she had become more aware that "women all over the world have a lot of things in common."[9]

Whether the programs being developed are engendered by IGOs and NGOs or by global conferences such as the UNCPD, there are two basic approaches to reducing the birthrate. One is social, the other is economic.

Social Approaches to Reducing the Birthrate   One approach to reducing the birthrate involves social programs such as providing information about birth control and encouragement to practice it. The social approach also involves making birth control devices and pills, sterilization, and, in some cases, abortion programs available. At the national level, many LDCs have made strong efforts, given their limited financial resources. In Thailand, for instance, 72 percent of all couples use contraceptive practices (the contraceptive prevalence rate).

These national efforts are supported by the UNFPA, the IPPF, and other IGOs and NGOs, and their combined efforts have had an impact. During the early 1960s, the contraceptive prevalence rate in the LDCs was only 9 percent. Now about 56 percent of couples in LDCs practice birth control. This contraceptive prevalence rate falls off drastically in the least developed countries (LLDCs), where (excluding China) it is only 21 percent. There are at least 15 countries in which the rate is a mere 10 percent or less.

Economic Approaches to Reducing the Birthrate   Population growth can also be slowed through economic approaches. The evidence that poverty causes population increases means that if the poverty gap both between countries and within countries is narrowed, then declining birthrates will be among the benefits. Therefore, efforts must be made to develop the LDCs and to equalize income distribution within countries if population is to be controlled. One economic approach to population control is to improve the status of women, because women who are more fully and equally employed have fewer children.

Those who study population dynamics have found that advancing the economic and educational opportunities available to women needs to be an integral part of population control. This realization was one of the factors that led the UN to designate 1975 as International Women's Year and to kick off the Decade for Women. That year the UN also convened the first World Conference on Women. These initiatives were followed in 1976 by the establishment of the UN Development Fund for Women (UNIFEM, after its French acronym). The Fund works through 10 regional offices to improve the living standards of women in LDCs by giving them technical and financial support to improve the entry of women into business, scientific and technical careers, and other key areas. UNIFEM also strives to incorporate women into the international and national planning and administration of development programs and to ensure that the issues of particular concern to women such as food, security, human rights, and reproductive health are kept on the global agenda. The UN also established the International Research and Training Institute for the Advancement of Women with the task of carrying out research, training, and information activities related to women and the development process. Headquartered in the Dominican Republic, the institute conducts research on the barriers that impede the progress of women in social, economic, and political development.

Resource Issues and Cooperation

Recent decades have witnessed increased warnings that we are using our resources too quickly. Most studies by individual analysts, governmental commissions, and private organizations have concluded that the rate at which humans are depleting energy, mineral, forest, land, wildlife, fishery, and water resources is a matter for concern ranging from caution to serious alarm.

Petroleum, Natural Gas, and Minerals

The supply of oil, gas, and mineral resources is one area of concern. At the forefront of these worries are the cost and supply of energy resources. The energy issue has such immense economic and environmental ramifications that it set off a war when Iraq invaded Kuwait in 1990.

World energy needs are skyrocketing. Global commercial energy production increased roughly 25 percent between 1985 and 1995. The burning of fossil fuels (coal, oil, gas) accounts for about 90 percent of output. There has been a growth of geothermal and hydroelectric power generation, but together they still account for 3 percent of world energy production, with nuclear power plants producing the remaining 7 percent of all commercial energy. Of the various sources, nuclear energy production by far increased the most rapidly (+1,365 percent) over the 20-year period.

At one time the world had perhaps 2,330 billion barrels of oil beneath its surface. Roughly one-third of that has already been consumed. Projections of future use are tricky, as are estimates of future reserves, but at current levels of use (26 billion barrels in 1997, or 1.2 trillion gallons), the world's proven supply of petroleum and natural gas will be exhausted in about the year 2040 and 2058 respectively. If all estimated reserves of oil and gas can be tapped, the production of each might last another decade or so beyond that. Coal will last almost 500 years at current consumption rates, but it is a major pollutant if not controlled by expensive technology. The development of hydroelectric power is attractive in some ways, but it is expensive to develop and, as noted, placing of dams on rivers creates environmental and social problems. Nuclear power is yet another alternative, and some countries have become reliant on it. Belgium and Lithuania lead in this category, each generating 97 percent of its commercial electricity by nuclear power. There are, however, high costs and obvious hazards to nuclear power. Some people advocate developing wind, solar, geothermal, and other such sources of power.

So far, though, cost, production capacity, and other factors have limited the application of these energy sources and will continue to do so unless there are major technological breakthroughs.

Dealing with the supply and demand for energy also requires understanding of use patterns. The vast majority of all energy is used by the EDCs. Most of the growing demand for energy, by contrast, is a result of increased needs by the countries of the South. During the period 1980–1995, the energy consumption of EDCs increased 21 percent, while the LDCs' energy use increased 43 percent. Among other things, this means that LDC development without proper energy conservation and other environmental safeguards is a serious concern.

The supply of fossil fuel resources has the highest political profile, but there are also many other minerals being rapidly depleted. Based on world reserves and world use, some minerals that are in particularly short supply (and the year that the Earth's supply will be exhausted) include copper (2056), lead (2041), mercury (2077), tin (2053), and zinc (2042). Moreover, "current use" may well skyrocket as current LDCs develop, and that eventuality would considerably decrease the projected depletion years listed here.

The resource puzzle, as mentioned, is how, all at the same time, to (1) maintain the industrialized countries' economies and standards of living, (2) promote economic development (which will consume increased energy and minerals) in the South, and (3) manage the problems of resource depletion and environmental damage involved in energy and mineral production and use. If, for instance, we were able to develop the South to the same economic level as the North, if the LDCs' energy-use patterns were the same as the North's currently are, and if the same energy resource patterns that exist now persisted, then petroleum reserves would be dry soon after the turn of the century. Natural gas and many other minerals soon would follow oil into the museum of geological history.

Forests and Land

The depletion of forests and their resources concerns many analysts. Data compiled by the UN Food and Agriculture Organization (FAO) and other sources indicates that the increase in world population and, to a lesser degree, economic development are destroying the world's forests (FAO, 1995). Some 1 billion people depend on wood as an energy source, and many forests have disappeared because of such domestic needs as cooking and heating. Forests are also being cleared to make room for farms and grazing lands. Forests and woodland still cover about 25 percent of the Earth's land area. Once, however, they occupied 48 percent of the land area, and tree cover is declining by about one percent every three years. Cash-poor countries are cutting their trees and exporting the wood to earn capital to pay off their international debt and to finance economic development. Forests are also being drowned by hydroelectric projects and being strip-mined for minerals. Acid rain and other environmental attacks increase the toll on trees. Whatever the cause, the result is that some 25.6 million acres (about 40,000 sq. mi.) of forest are

MAP
Deforestation and
Desertification

being lost every year. This is a loss roughly equivalent to clear-cutting both Belgium and Ireland. Reforestation replaces only about 10 percent of the loss.

Even worse, the FAO projects that harvesting trees for fuel, paper, and wood products will increase 53 percent from 4.3 billion tons it was in 1990 to 6.6 billion tons in 2010. Clearing land for agriculture will take a further toll on the world's trees. Overall, the FAO estimates that 39 percent of the Earth's remaining relatively pristine "frontier forests" are in severe to moderate danger from agriculture, logging, mining, and other threats. It is easy to blame the LDCs for allowing their forests to be overcut, but many in those countries ask what alternative they have. "Anyone, American, Dutch or whatever, who comes in and tells us not to cut the forest has to give us another way to live," says an official of Suriname (a former Dutch colony). "And so far they haven't done that." Instead, what occurs, charges the country's president, is "eco-colonialism" by international environmental organizations trying to prevent Suriname from using its resources.[10]

Deforestation has numerous negative consequences. One is global warming, which we will discuss in a later section. Another ill effect of forest depletion is that the cost of wood needed for cooking and heating goes up and may swallow a third of a poor family's income in some African cities. In some rural areas, wood is so scarce that each family must have at least one member working nearly full-time to gather a supply for home use. The devastation of the forests is also driving many forms of life into extinction. A typical 4-square-mile section of the Amazon Basin rain forest contains some 750 species of trees, 125 kinds of mammals, 400 types of birds, 160 different kinds of reptiles and amphibians, and perhaps 300,000 insect species. The loss of biodiversity has an obvious aesthetic impact, and there are also pragmatic implications. Some 25 percent of all modern pharmaceutical products contain ingredients originally found in plants. Extracts from Madagascar's rosy periwinkle, for example, are used in drugs to treat children's leukemia and Hodgkin's disease. A drug called taxol, derived from the Pacific yew, is a promising treatment for breast and ovarian cancer. Many plants also contain natural pesticides that could provide the basis for the development of ecologically safe commercial pesticides to replace the environmental horrors (such as DDT) of the past. You may also want to explore one unusual implication of deforestation in the Web site box A World without Chocolate.

A FURTHER NOTE
A World without Chocolate

Deforestation also causes soil erosion. Tropical forests rest on thin topsoil. This land is especially unsuited for agriculture, and it becomes exhausted quickly once the forest is cut down and crops are planted or grazing takes place. With no trees to hold soil in place, runoff occurs, and silt clogs rivers and bedevils hydroelectric projects. Unchecked runoff can also significantly increase the chances of down-river floods and may result in loss of life and economic damage.

Since 1950, according to the United Nations Environmental Program (UNEP), 4.6 million square miles of land have suffered mild to extensive soil degradation. This is an area equal to about the size of India and China. At its worst, *desertification* occurs. More of the world's surface is becoming desertlike

A SITE TO SURF
United Nations
Environment
Programme

because of water scarcity, timber cutting, overgrazing, and overplanting. The desertification of land is increasing at an estimated rate of 30,600 square miles a year, turning an area the size of Austria into barren desert. Moreover, that rate of degradation could worsen, based on UNEP's estimate that 8 billion acres are in jeopardy. Some areas are in particular trouble. "All regions of the world suffer from desertification and drought," Arthur Campeau, Canada's ambassador for environment and sustainable development, points out, "but the African nations are the most vulnerable and the least able to combat these problems."[11]

Wildlife

The march of humankind has driven almost all the other creatures of the Earth into retreat and, in some cases, into extinction. Beyond the impact of deforestation, there are many other human by-products, ranging from urbanization to pollution, that destroy wildlife habitat. Whatever its cause, a decrease in the planet's wildlife will be an ineffable loss to humans. The drug Capoten, which is used to control high blood pressure, is derived from the venom of the Brazilian pit viper. And the American Heart Association has identified an anti–blood-clotting drug based on substances found in bat saliva that is effective in preventing heart attacks in humans. Many endangered species have no known immediate pragmatic value. Nevertheless, a world without giant pandas, hooded cranes, Plymouth red-bellied turtles, and Chinese river dolphins will be a less diverse, less appealing place.

Unfortunately, some species do have economic value: The trade in feathers, pelts, ivory, and other wildlife products is endangering indigo macaws, snow leopards, black rhinoceroses, and many other species. In the mid-1980s the legal trade alone of wildlife products included 192,000 wildcat skins, 472.5 tons of ivory, and 10.5 million reptile skins. Poachers added to this grisly business. During the 1980s, legal hunters and poachers seeking ivory, which sold for up to $120 per pound, slaughtered some 650,000 elephants, reducing their number by half. Rhinoceros horns and other products are in demand in Asia because of the belief in *jinbu,* the Chinese word for the notion that inadequacies ranging from poor eyesight to sterility can be remedied by eating parts of various animals. Pollution also threatens wildlife. Birds and fish, for instance, are particularly affected by insecticides that enter their systems directly and through the food they eat.

Human food requirements bring increasing pressure on the ocean's fish, mollusks, and crustaceans. The importance of marine life as food and the demands of a growing world population combined to increase the marine catch by 23 percent between 1985 and 1995, to 75.2 million metric tons. The FAO estimates that the sustainable annual yield of the oceans is somewhere between 69 and 96 million tons. Competition is fierce for this resource, and a 1998 report indicates that the world's fishing fleets have the capacity to take 155 percent more fish than can be replaced through natural reproduction.[12] This has already led, according to FAO data, to 69 percent of the commercial species of marine life being fully fished or overfished. Therefore, fishing at current fleet capacity or even continuing the current level of marine harvest will mean that fish, crustaceans, and mollusks are being taken, or soon will be taken, faster than they can replenish themselves. A decline in the marine catch could pose a health threat to countries that rely on fish for vital protein supplies. Especially imperiled would be Asia and Africa, where fish contribute 28 percent and 21 percent respectively of the protein in the diet of the regions' inhabitants.

Water

The final resource that we will examine here is perhaps the most basic of all. Along with oxygen, water is an immediate need for almost all life forms. Seventy-one percent of the Earth's surface may be covered by water, but 96.5 percent is salt water, and 2.4 percent is in the form of ice or snow. This leaves just 1.1 percent readily available for human consumption, a significant part of which is polluted, and drinking it poses serious health risks. Moreover, this scarce water supply is threatened, and the cry "Water, water, everywhere/Nor any drop to drink" of Samuel Taylor Coleridge's Ancient Mariner may foreshadow the shortages of the future. Increased agricultural and industrial use, pollution, and other factors are depleting or tainting water supplies. Fresh water use, after tripling between 1940 and 1975, has slowed its growth rate to about 2 to 3 percent a year.

The catch that these Japanese fishermen are hauling in looks like a good one. Lack of conservation in fishing grounds, however, has taken its toll around the world and has endangered many species, making such catches less frequent.

Much of this is due to population stabilization and conservation measures in the developed countries. Still, because the population is growing and rainfall is a constant, the world needs to use an additional 7.1 trillion gallons each year just to grow the extra grain needed to feed the expanding population.

Complicating matters even more, many countries, especially LDCs, have low per capita supplies of water, as you can see in the Web site map. To make matters worse, the water usage in these countries will increase as they develop their economies. These increases will either create greater pressure on the water supply or will limit a country's growth possibilities. Globally, most fresh water is used for either agriculture (65 percent) or industry (25 percent), with only 10 percent for households. Industrialized countries, however, use greater percentages for industry and more water per capita overall than LDCs. It follows then, that as the LDCs industrialize, their water needs will rise rapidly. China provides an example; water use for industry, which amounted in 1980 to 46

MAPS
Annual Water Use

Projected Per Capita Water Availability, 2000

billion cubic meters, will increase a projected 385 percent to 177 billion cubic meters in 2000.

Many analysts are worried by the projections that water shortages will increase (Engleman & LeRoy, 1995). There are currently 80 countries with 40 percent of the Earth's inhabitants that are included on the "water stress index" because they annually have less than 1,000 cubic meters of water per person available. For comparison, each American has 8,983 cubic meters of water available and annually uses 1,870 cubic meters. By the year 2025, given population increases and water usage, the combined populations of water-distressed countries will increase to at least 3.3 billion. The competition for scarce water could lead to international tensions. There are, for example, 19 countries that get 20 percent or more of their fresh water from rivers that originate outside their borders. The security of these countries would be threatened if upstream countries diverted that water for their own purposes or threatened to limit it as a political sanction. Such possibilities have led some analysts to suggest that in the not-too-distant future the access to water supplies could bring "thirsty" countries to and over the brink of war.

Resource Conservation: The Global Response

While pessimists and optimists disagree about how serious the problems are and how immediate and drastic remedies need be, it is certain that mineral, forest, wildlife, and water resources must be more carefully managed and conserved. After several millennia of unchecked resource use, people are now beginning to act with some restraint and to cooperate in conservation causes. All the various individual and organized efforts cannot be mentioned here, but a few illustrative examples will serve to demonstrate the thrust of these activities. One major step at the international level came in 1994 when the United States, after a decade of opposition, signed the UN's Law of the Sea Treaty. The treaty, which soon thereafter went into effect, gives countries full sovereignty over the seas within 12 miles of their shores and control over fishing rights and oil- and gas-exploration rights within 200 miles of their shores. That should help improve conservation in these coastal zones. Additionally, an International Seabed Authority, with its headquarters in Jamaica, has been established and will help regulate mining of the seabed in international waters and will receive royalties from those mining operations to help finance ocean-protection programs.

The international community also has begun to act to stem or reverse desertification. Meeting in Paris, some 100 countries signed the Convention on Desertification in 1994. Sri Kamal Nath, India's environment minister, commented that desertification "is as much of a threat to the planet and civil society as war, and we have to combat it with as much vigor."[13] To that end the convention created a "Global Mechanism" to coordinate efforts and to urge countries to channel money through the Global Environmental Facility (see the Web site box on the Earth Summit) to meet the $10 to $20 billion

A FURTHER NOTE
The Earth Summit
and Sustainable
Development

that the UN estimates is needed during the next two decades for land preservation and reclamation projects.

Progress is also being made in the preservation of forest and wildlife resources. Membership in environmental groups has grown dramatically. In several European countries and in the European Parliament, Green parties have become viable political forces, and in 1998 became part of the governing coalition of Chancellor Gerhard Schröder in Germany. The growing interest in flora and fauna is also increasing the so-called ecotourist trade, and many countries are beginning to realize that they can derive more economic benefit from tourists shooting pictures than from hunters shooting guns or loggers wielding chain saws.

National and international efforts are also being taken in other areas. A 64 percent decline between the mid-1980s and the mid-1990s in the catch of demersal fish (such as cod, flounder, and haddock) in the northwest Atlantic prompted both Canada and the United States to limit severely or temporarily ban catches in rich fishing grounds such as the Grand Banks and the Georges Bank off their North Atlantic coasts. Canada has also reached an agreement with the European Union to regulate fishing in and near these rich fisheries. On an even broader scale, 99 countries, including all the major fishing countries, agreed in 1995 to an international treaty that will regulate the catch of all the species of fish (such as cod, pollock, tuna, and swordfish) that migrate between national and international waters. "The freedom to fish on the high seas no longer exists as it once did. It is no longer a free-for-all situation," explained the elated chairman of the conference, Satya Nandan of Fiji.[14]

At the global level, the International Whaling Commission (IWC) regulated whaling, finally banning it in 1986 except for the taking by Japan and others of about 130 minke whales annually for (questionably, some say) scientific purposes. Since then, Japan has unilaterally increased its catch to about 540 minkes. Norway in 1993 also resumed commercial whaling in defiance of the IWC ban. That year Norway allowed its whalers to harpoon 100 minke whales, and that number has increased to 671 for 1998. Japan will take about an equal number of whales, and Iceland, which had quit the IWC in opposition to the ban, takes 200 minkes annually. At current prices (in Norway), each minke, which weighs about 7 tons, brings about $6,000, making whaling an $8.4 million industry. The good news, though, is that the resumption of limited whaling will be regulated and will be limited to minke whales, whose number may be about 900,000.

In fact, the whale controversy touches on one of the difficulties of environmentalism, which is distinguishing conservation as such from the emotional opposition of many people to killing whales or other creatures, especially those that have captured the public's sympathy. To some people, whaling is abhorrent. When the 1998 meeting of the IWC convened in Muscat, a spokesperson from Campaign Whale, an international NGO, declared that "it is time to end this obscene industry once and for all."[15]

From another perspective, the scientific committee that advises the IWC concluded that the substantial number of minke whales meant that the species

INTERACTIVE EXERCISE
What is the Environment Worth to You? Conservation and Opportunity Costs

This motorcyclist is delivering dogs to a dog-meat restaurant in Hanoi, Vietnam. Although many cultures would find eating dog meat taboo, it is commonplace in many other places and highlights the different ways cultures evaluate the value of food sources.

could tolerate controlled hunting. This evidence is cited by Iceland, Norway, and Japan in support of their decisions to allow whaling. "We cannot allow uninformed sentiment to decide on the controlled use of our natural resources," argued Norwegian prime minister Gro Harlem Brundtland.[16] Whaling countries also believe that the international pressure involves a degree of two-faced cultural imperialism. As one Japanese whaler commented, "Americans say that harpooned whales are so pitiful, but it's just a difference of diet. I can't understand why people don't feel the same way about cows or pigs."[17]

Whatever the fate of the minke may be, other species of whales are now protected. As a result the numbers of some whales and other marine mammals are recovering. For one, the Pacific gray whale population has doubled since conservation began, and it is no longer on the U.S. endangered species list. Among other marine mammals, the world's walrus population has quintupled to 280,000; Galapagos and Antarctic fur seals, both once at the edge of extinction, now have viable populations.

The world's increasing list of endangered species is also now gaining some relief through the Convention on the International Trade in Endangered Species (CITES). Elephants were added in 1989 to the CITES list of endangered species, and 87 countries meeting in Geneva banned the trade in ivory and elephant parts. This agreement did not end the ivory trade, but, in conjunction with individual bans on importation imposed by most EDCs and many other countries, it dropped ivory prices to about $6 a pound, thereby substantially undercutting the economic incentive to poach elephants for ivory. Indeed, for elephants, the protection was so successful that herds have increased substantially in several African countries. That growth, the competition of elephants with farmers, and the gain that could be reaped from selling stockpiled tusks and licensing elephant hunters led in 1997 to an agreement at the CITES meeting in Johannesburg, South Africa, to allow Botswana, Namibia, and Zimbabwe to sell $30 million worth of their stockpiled ivory to Japan. Even though the ivory came from either legal kills to prevent overpopulation or from confiscations from poachers and would be used in the main for conservation programs, the proposal was highly controversial at CITES. The United States, France, and some other countries opposed the sale.

Japan, Switzerland, and others favored it and accused opponents of trying paternally to tell Africans how to manage conservation. "It's difficult for people [outside Africa] to believe that there's any need to kill elephants," one observer at a CITES conference commented. "But they don't have to grow their food in elephant country."[18] In the end, the initial proposal to sell 150 tons was reduced to 60 tons, and the sale was limited to a one-time event. The ban on elephant products remained in place, and new measures were taken to protect tigers, sharks, and some other species that are endangered or under severe pressure.

Environmental Issues and Cooperation

The state of the biosphere is related to many of the economic and resource issues we have been examining. Like the concerns over those issues, international awareness and activity are relatively recent and are still in their early stages.

Areas of Environmental Concern

Several concerns that also have an environmental impact, such as desertification, deforestation, and biodiversity loss, have been discussed. The next sections will look at ground pollution, water pollution, air pollution, and global warming and ozone layer depletion due to atmospheric pollution.

Ground Pollution   The pollution of the land is a significant problem, but the territorial dominance of states renders this issue primarily domestic and, therefore, outside the realm of international action. Where solid waste disposal does have an international impact is through international dumping. With their disposal sites brimming and frequently dangerous, EDCs have annually shipped as much as 1.5 million tons of hazardous wastes to LDCs. Financial considerations have persuaded some countries to accept these toxic deliveries. Resistance has built, however, in response to the growing sense that, as Nigerian diplomat Saad M. Baba put it, "international dumping is the equivalent of declaring war on the people of a country."[19] Another international aspect of ground pollution is that it is often caused by waste disposal by multinational corporations (MNCs), which often set up operations in LDCs because they have fewer environmental regulations.

Water Pollution   There are two water environments: the marine (saltwater) environment and the freshwater environment. Water pollution is damaging both.
  Marine pollution has multiple sources. Spillage from shipping, ocean waste dumping, and offshore mining and oil and gas drilling activity account for 23 percent of the pollutants that are introduced into the oceans, seas, and other international waterways. Petroleum is a particular danger. Of the 940 million gallons of petroleum discharged each year into the marine environment, almost half comes from transportation spillage. Municipal and industrial waste discharges account for another 36 percent of the total. Offshore

drilling is a rising threat, with the production of petroleum from marine drilling steadily rising.

Another 44 percent of the marine pollution is carried by the rivers, which serve as highways that carry human sewage, industrial waste, pesticide and fertilizer runoff, petroleum spillage, and other pollutants into the seas. One of the worst sources are fertilizers, and their global use has grown from about 40 million tons a year in 1960 to some 140 million metric tons annually in the mid-1990s. Another major source is the exploding world population, which creates ever more intestinal waste. Many coastal cities are not served by sewage treatment facilities. Sewage is the major polluter of the Mediterranean and Caribbean Seas and the ocean regions off East Africa and Southeast Asia. Industrial waste is also common.

Freshwater pollution of lakes and rivers is an international, as well as a domestic, issue. The discharge of pollutants into lakes and rivers that form international boundaries (the Great Lakes, the Rio Grande) or that flow between countries (the Rhine River) is a source of discord. Freshwater pollution is also caused by acid rain and other contaminants that drift across borders.

Air Pollution   The world's air currents ignore national boundaries, making air pollution a major international concern (Soroos, 1997). To illustrate the many sources of and problems associated with air pollution, we will explore the acid rain issue.

Acid rain is caused by air pollutants that contaminate water resources and attack forests through rainfall. Sulfur dioxide (SO_2) and nitric acids from the burning of fossil fuels and from smelting and other industrial processes are the major deleterious components of acid rain. The damage done by acid rain has followed industrialization. The United States, Canada, and Europe were the first to suffer. Especially in the northern part of the United States and in Canada there has been extensive damage to trees and many lakes have become so acidified that most of the fish have been killed.

Europe has also suffered extensive damage. About a quarter of the continent's trees have sustained moderate to severe defoliation. The annual value of the lost lumber harvest to Europe alone is an estimated $23 billion. The tourist industry is also in danger, imperiling millions of other jobs. The death of trees and their stabilizing root systems increases soil erosion, resulting in the silting-up of lakes and rivers. The list of negative consequences could go on, but that is not necessary to make the point that acid rain is environmentally and economically devastating.

The good news is that pollution control in the EDCs has substantially reduced new air pollution. Annual EDC sulfur dioxide emissions, for instance, have declined from almost 60 million tons in 1960 to about 35 million tons in 1995. The bad news is that the improvement in the EDCs is being more than offset by spiraling levels of air pollution in the LDCs. This is particularly true in Asia. There, rapid industrialization combined with the financial inability to spend the tens of billions of dollars needed to control SO_2 emissions is expected to more than triple annual SO_2 emissions from 34 million tons in 1990 to about 115 million tons in 2020.

Global Warming   Many scientists believe that we are experiencing a gradual pattern of global warming. The reason, according to these scientists, is the *greenhouse effect*, which is caused by carbon dioxide (CO_2) from fossil fuel burning and from accumulations of other chemical gas discharges. The CO_2 accumulates in the upper atmosphere and creates a blanket effect, trapping heat and preventing the nightly cooling of the Earth. Other gases, especially methane and chlorofluorocarbons (CFCs), also contribute heavily to creating the thermal blanket. The warming blanket effect is accelerated because it causes faster evaporation and the resulting atmospheric vapor amplifies the effect.

There is controversy about the existence, causes, and impact of the greenhouse effect. We will begin with a brief synopsis of what is known and what is in dispute. Then we will turn to the key issue: What to do.

What is known includes the fact that both global CO_2 emissions and CO_2 levels in the atmosphere have increased. This increase is associated with the industrial revolution. Global CO_2 emissions have risen 278 percent since 1950. Now more than 26 billion tons of CO_2 are discharged annually, and they are joined by 270 million tons of methane and 400,000 tons of CFCs. Since these gases linger in the atmosphere for 50 to 200 years, the cumulative effect is also worth considering. Scientists estimate that at the beginning of the industrial revolution in the mid-1700s there were about 55 million tons of CO_2 in the atmosphere. Since then, an additonal 931.7 billion tons have been discharged, and a great deal of that CO_2 remains trapped in the atmosphere. About 80 percent of these emissions come from the burning of coal, gas, petroleum, and other fossil fuels during industrial activity.

MAP
Per Capita
CO_2 Emissions

What is in dispute is the impact of increased CO_2 concentrations. Scientists estimate that over the last century the Earth's average temperature rose $0.5°C/1.1°F$. But because the Earth has natural warming and cooling trends, not all scientists are convinced that CO_2–driven warming is under way. A 1995 report of the UN–sponsored Intergovernmental Panel on Climatic Change (IPCC) argued, however, that the buildup of CO_2 and the climatic changes over the last few decades are "unlikely to be entirely due to natural causes," and that "a pattern of climatic response to human activities is identifiable in the climatological record."[20] At least one result, according to many scientists, is that the average global temperature is increasing. In fact, 1997 was the warmest year in recorded history, and 1980, 1981, 1983, 1987, 1988, 1990, and 1995 were the previous seven warmest years since global record keeping began in 1856. The temperature in 1996 was just a fraction lower than it was in 1995, but 1996 was still one of the ten warmest years in recorded history. Scientists speculated that after a temporary cooling between 1991 and 1994 as a result of the atmospheric ash from the 1991 eruption of Mount Pinatubo in the Philippines and other natural phenomena, the upward trend of temperatures has resumed. This problem as it relates to the deforestation problem discussed above is examined further in the Web site box (↑Vehicles) + (↓Trees) ≠ Sustainable Development.

Most important is what emissions and their impact will be in the future. There is not a great deal of dispute about the International Energy Agency's

A FURTHER NOTE
(↑ Vehicles) +
(↓ Trees) ≠
Sustainable
Development

being correct in its estimate that if trends continue, emissions of CO_2 will in 2010 exceed the 1990 level by 30 to 40 percent. Many scientists doubt that it will be possible to stop the current trend before reaching 450 ppm or even 550 ppm by around the year 2050. This level would mean a doubling of the atmospheric CO_2 over what it was in the preindustrial era and, in the estimate of these analysts, would accelerate global warming. The UN–sponsored Intergovernmental Panel on Climatic Change (IPCC) is among the pessimists. It has concluded that, given current trends, the world's average temperature could increase 1° to 6°F by the year 2100. For comparison, the temperature increase since the last ice age is estimated to be 5° to 9°F. Rainfall, wind currents, and other climatic patterns could be dramatically, and sometimes dangerously, altered. The polar ice caps would melt more quickly, and sea levels would rise. The IPCC report estimated that up to 118 million people could be displaced over the next century. Satellite-generated sea measurements indicate, one scientist reported, that "the mean annual rise in sea level will probably be something like one or two millimeters a year."[21] This is a small annual rise, but over time it can be significant. The sea level particularly affects island countries, 37 of which have formed the Alliance of Small Island States. As a former president of Kiribati notes, "If the greenhouse effect raises sea levels by one meter, it will virtually do away with Kiribati.... In 50 or 60 years my country will not be here" (Flavin, 1996:34).

Violent weather caused by rapid evaporation, the buildup of atmospheric heat, and other factors that would create higher winds also worries the pessimists. The head of the IPCC notes that the 1980s and early 1990s were remarkable for their "frequency and intensity of extremes of weather and climate."[22] Insurance industry data shows, for example, that the number of catastrophic windstorms in the world increased from 8 in the 1960s, to 14 in the 1970s, to 29 in the 1980s. Moreover, the scientist added, floods and droughts have increased as well. If anything, the weather turned even worse in many parts of the world during 1997–1998 as the strongest El Niño in history caused torrential rains and floods in some areas, spawned tornadoes in others, and reduced rainfall to near arid levels in yet other areas.

The UN has warned that global warming "could have a wide range of impacts on human health, most of which would be adverse."[23] Scientists predict, for example, that warming could increase the number and range of mosquitoes, with a resulting annual increase of 80 million malaria cases. Cholera, dengue fever, and other hemorrhagic diseases associated with warm climates could also spread northward and southward.

Environmental optimists are less concerned. Some scientists do not believe that increases will be huge, either because they will not occur in any case or because offsetting factors, such as increased cloudiness, will ease the effect. Others believe that whatever temperature increase is occurring is from natural trends. One study labels CO_2 "an unlikely candidate for causing any significant worldwide temperature change."[24] Another analyst warns against "greenhouse anxiety" and states flatly that "there is no solid scientific evidence to support [the theory that] the Earth is warming because of man-made greenhouse gases" (Salmon, 1993:25; Beckerman & Malkin, 1994).

Optimists also predict that some could benefit and most could adapt to the changes brought on by global warming (Moore, 1998). Drought in the lower and middle latitudes would ruin some present agricultural areas, the logic goes, but new ones would be created and would prosper at higher latitudes. Farmers in colder regions might have their growing seasons and bounty increased. Moreover, a U.S. National Academy of Science study concluded that while global warming was occurring, people could adapt and that "we mustn't get into the state of mind that . . . [leads us to] think the world is going to vaporize."[25]

What to do is the key issue in the global warming debate. Economic cost is one factor. Those who recommend caution in responding to demands that global warming be halted also point out that significantly reducing CO_2 emissions will not be easy. It might well require substantial lifestyle changes in the industrialized countries. "To stabilize carbon dioxide concentrations at even twice today's levels . . . over the next 100 years can be attained only [if] emissions eventually drop substantially below the 1990 levels," the IPCC has calculated.[26] To do that "will require a degree of bureaucratic control over economic affairs previously unknown in the West," predict two scholars who oppose such a course.[27] Costs would also be enormous. The Union of Concerned Scientists, for instance, has concluded that a program to cut CO_2 emissions by 70 percent over a 40-year period would cost the U.S. economy $2.7 trillion. The organization argues, however, that the loss would be more than offset by a $5 trillion savings in fuel costs. Others have pointed to the economic stimulus that would be provided by creating alternative, environmentally safe technologies.

In the end, what can be said for certain, then, is that climatic warming is occurring, but, in the words of one scientist, "we have no means of knowing, actually" how much, if any, of that is due to atmospheric emissions.[28] Do you bet trillions in economic costs that emissions-driven global warming is occurring, or do you bet the atmosphere that it is not? Given the fact that CO_2 stays in the atmosphere for centuries and that, if it is having a climatic effect, it will take several lifetimes to begin to reverse significantly, the U.S. National Research recommends betting the money. "Despite the great uncertainties," it counsels, "greenhouse warming is a potential threat sufficient to justify action now."[29]

Ozone Layer Depletion   In contrast to the debate over global warming, there is little doubt about the depletion of the ozone layer and the damage that it causes. Atmospheric ozone (O_3) absorbs ultraviolet (UV) rays from the sun, and, without the ozone layer 10 to 30 miles above the planet, human life could not exist. The ozone layer is being attacked by the emission of chlorofluorocarbons (CFCs), a chemical group that gasifies at low temperatures, releasing chlorine atoms. These attack ozone and turn it into atmospheric oxygen (O_2), which does not block ultraviolet rays. Each chlorine atom can repeat this transformation up to 100,000 times.

Because of their low gasification point, CFCs are good refrigerants and insulators and are therefore used in refrigerators and air-conditioners and in

This newspaper vendor uses a mask to protect himself from air pollution in Mexico City. The sign behind him indicates the day's pollution levels, which have been exacerbated in recent years by brush fires around the city. Unfortunately, such scenes are not isolated to Mexico and can be found throughout the world, though most seriously in and around rapidly growing LDC cities.

products such as styrofoam. CFCs are also found in many spray can propellants, fire extinguishers, and industrial solvents. Some 400,000 metric tons are spewed into the atmosphere annually. The most dramatic depletion, according to a report by the World Meteorological Organization, is occurring over Antarctica, where a 3.86 million-square-mile hole—about the size of Europe and with as much as a 70 percent depletion of atmospheric O_3— occurs annually. Ozone levels over the rest of the world have declined less, but they are still down about 10 percent since the 1950s.

Emissions of CFCs create several problems. One is that they add to the greenhouse effect, as noted above. More to the point here, the thinning of the ozone layer increases the penetration through the atmosphere of ultraviolet-B (UV-B) rays, which cause cancers and other mutations in life forms below. Scientists estimate that each 1 percent decrease in the ozone layer will increase UV-B penetration 1.3 percent. This can increase the rate of various types of skin cancer from 1 to 3 percent. The impact of this on Americans was noted in chapter 1. Australia and New Zealand have measured temporary increases in UV-B radiation of as much as 20 percent, and light-skinned Australians have the world's highest skin cancer rate. Another possible deleterious effect of increased UV-B bombardment came to light when a study of the water surrounding Antarctica found evidence of a 6 to 12 percent decline in plankton organisms during the period of the annual ozone hole. Such losses at the bottom of the food chain could restrict the nutrition and health of fish and eventually humans farther up the food chain. Also, scientists from Oregon State University, studying the inexplicably rapid drop in the number of frogs around the world, have concluded that UV-B radiation may be killing the eggs before they hatch into mosquito larvae–consuming tadpoles.

Environmental Protection: The International Response

Like many of the other issues discussed in this chapter, environmental problems have been slowly growing for centuries. They have accelerated rapidly in this century, however, and in some cases they have reached hypervelocity growth rates. Only recently has widespread public and governmental concern been sparked. The result is that programs are just beginning. Most of the work that has been done has had a national focus, and there have been many advances. In a great part of the developed world, where the problems were most acute and where the resources to fund programs were available, water is cleaner, acid rain is being curbed, trees are being planted, toxic wastes are being dealt with better, recycling is under way, and a host of other positive programs have stemmed and have sometimes even reversed the flood tide of pollution. Because many forms of pollution spread internationally, the national programs have been beneficial.

There has also been progress at the international level (Meyer, Frank, & Tuma, 1997; Caldwell, 1996). There are many IGOs and NGOs that focus on one or more environmental programs. The UN has been involved in a number of environmental efforts (Conca, 1995). These began with the 1972 Conference on the Human Environment in Stockholm. This led to the establishment of the United Nations Environmental Programme (UNEP). The work of the many IGOs that are concerned with preserving and enhancing the biosphere is supplemented by a vast host of NGOs dedicated to the same purpose (Haas & McCabe, 1996; Wapner, 1996). It is also increasingly common for trade treaties, such as the North American Free Trade Agreement and other international pacts, to include environmental protection clauses (Audley, 1997). Additionally, there are countless local organizations and even individuals involved in international environmental activism (Lipschutz & Mayer, 1996).

Protecting the Ozone Layer   Among its other accomplishments, in 1987 the UNEP sponsored a conference in Montreal to discuss protection of the ozone layer. There, 46 countries agreed to reduce their CFC production and consumption by 50 percent before the end of the century. Subsequent amendments to the Montreal Convention at quadrennial conferences, the last of which was held in Vienna in 1995, resulted in multilateral treaties requiring a complete phaseout of CFC production by EDCs by 1996 and LDCs by 2010. Also, at Vienna, more than 100 countries agreed to phase out production and use by EDCs of the pesticide methyl bromide, which also weakens the ozone layer, by 2010 (Litfin, 1994).

As a result, there is relatively good news on ozone depletion. The annual global production of CFCs has dropped more than 70 percent from 1.1 million tons in 1986 to about 225,000 tons. The annual buildup of CFC concentrations has slowed from 5 percent in the 1980s to a current 1 percent, and scientists now estimate that CFC concentrations will begin to decrease after the year 2000. The Montreal Convention and its amendments are "a beautiful case study of environmental action," one scientist exults.[30] Furthermore, because ozone replenishes itself fairly rapidly, it is, one scientist says, "a renewable resource."[31] This means that by about the year 2020 the ozone level will have increased to about the concentration it was in 1979. "The ozone problem will correct itself," another scientist comments, "if we stick to what we plan" as far as eliminating CFC production and use.[32]

Easing Global Warming   Progress on dealing with global warming has been more limited. The reduction of CFCs will have a positive impact because of their role in global warming. The significant reduction of CO_2 discharges will be more difficult. There is increased recognition of the need to act, however, and a UNEP–sponsored World Climate Conference convened in Geneva in 1990 with the CO_2 problem as a major focus. At that meeting of 130 countries, most EDCs pledged to stabilize or reduce greenhouse gas emissions by the year 2000. The United States, however, declined to join in because of concern about the cost and the negative domestic economic impact. The global effort to reduce greenhouse gas emissions was reconfirmed in the Global Warming Convention signed at the 1992 Earth Summit. Further progress occurred when President Clinton agreed to drop the U.S. reservation to that treaty's suggested timetables for reducing emissions.

**A FURTHER NOTE
To Kyoto and
Beyond**

Progress on that treaty will, however, be difficult to put into effect. The next major effort to give practical application to the goal of easing the threat of global warming came in Kyoto, Japan, in 1997. The events leading up to the conference, its outcome, and the implications are related in the Web site box To Kyoto and Beyond.

Addressing Other Environmental Concerns   There has also been progress on a range of other environmental concerns, such as international dumping. The 1989 Convention on the Control of Transboundary Movements of Hazardous Wastes and Their Disposal (the Basel Convention), signed by 105 countries in Switzerland, limits such activity. In 1991 almost all African states signed the Bamako Convention in Mali banning the transboundary trade in hazardous wastes on their continent. The limits in the Basel Convention were stiffened further in reaction to the continued export of hazardous wastes under the guise of declaring that the materials were meant for recycling or as foreign aid in the form of recoverable materials. Great Britain alone exported 105,000 tons of such toxic foreign aid in 1993 to 65 LDCs, a practice that one British opposition leader called the "immoral . . . dumping of our environmental problems in someone else's backyard."[33] As of January 1, 1998, all such shipments for recycling and recovery purposes were banned.

Marine pollution has also been on the international agenda for some time, and progress has been made. One of the first multilateral efforts was the International Convention for the Prevention of Pollution from Ships. More recently, 43 countries, including the world's largest industrial countries, agreed in 1990 to a global ban on dumping industrial wastes in the oceans. It went into effect in 1995. The countries also agreed not to dispose of nuclear waste in the oceans.

After reading this chapter and the ones on international law, international organization, arms control, and economic cooperation, it is easy to be discouraged. The problems are immense and complex; barriers to cooperation are formidable; failure to find solutions carries potentially dire consequences. And sometimes when you begin to think that you are making progress, as the world has in recent years, a setback occurs. Still, the world must and does continue to try to preserve and improve the condition of the Earth and its people. It is true that the current level of cooperation, when compared with the problems, seems woefully inadequate, but that does not mean that we should despair.

The message here is to avoid the extremes of either unguarded optimism or hopeless pessimism. It is equally unwise to take the rosy "It's darkest before the dawn" approach or the gloom-and-doom approach represented by comedian Eddie Murphy's observation that "Sometimes it's darkest before the light goes out completely."

Don't sell the early efforts that we have discussed in this chapter and elsewhere too short. It is only during this century, and really since World War II, that the need to cooperate has penetrated our consciousness and our conscience. The intervening years have been a microsecond in human history. In that sense, much has been done. Yet, much remains to be done to secure the future, and the microseconds keep ticking by.

This book began its discussion of the alternative nationalist and internationalist approaches to world politics by using Robert Frost's poem about two roads diverging in a wood. The choice of which one to take is yours and that of the rest of humankind. Your present and, more important, your future will be determined by which road you follow. It will be hard to turn back. So, as Shakespeare tells us in *King Richard III*, "Go, tread the path that thou shalt ne'er return."

Chapter Summary

1. This chapter deals with ecological concerns and cooperation. Self-interest, some people would say self-survival, compels us to attend to issues concerning the world's expanding population, the depletion of natural resources, the increase of chemical discharges into the environment, and the impact of these trends on the global biosphere.

2. A key concept and goal is sustainable development. The question is how to continue to develop industrially and otherwise while

simultaneously protecting the environment. Given the justifiable determination of the LDCs to develop economically, the potential accelerated resource depletion and pollution production are very high.

3. There is a wide range of views about how great the environmental threats are and what can and should be done to address them.

4. Population is a significant problem facing the world, with the global population having already passed the 5 billion mark. The 1994 UN Conference on Population and Development in Cairo marked the latest step in the effort to control population and the associated attempts to improve women's reproductive and other rights. There are also numerous international organizations, such as the United Nations Population Fund, working in the area. The most effective way to control population is to improve the educational and economic status of women and to make contraceptive services widely available.

5. Growing population and industrialization have rapidly increased the use of a wide range of natural resources. It is possible, using known resources and current use rates, to project that petroleum, natural gas, and a variety of minerals will be totally depleted within the coming century. The world's forests, its supply of fresh water, and its wildlife are also under population and industrialization pressure. There are many international organizations and efforts, symbolized by the 1992 Earth Summit, to address these problems.

6. Population growth and industrialization are also responsible for mounting ground pollution, water pollution, air pollution, global warming, and ozone layer depletion due to atmospheric pollution. Other areas, such as efforts to reduce CO_2 emissions, have only just begun and are difficult because of their cost.

7. The efforts at international cooperation in the areas discussed in this chapter return us to the question of standards of judgment. It is easy to view the vast extent of the problems facing the globe, to measure the limited effort being made to resolve them, and to dismiss the entire subject of international cooperation as superficial. It is true that not nearly enough is being done. But it is also true that only a very few decades ago nothing was being done. From that zero base, the progress made since World War II is encouraging. The only question is whether or not we will continue to expand our efforts and whether or not we will do enough, soon enough.

An Epilogue to the Text/
A Prologue to the Future

Where I did begin, there I shall end.

Shakespeare, *Julius Caesar*

So here it is some months later, and we are at the end of this book and this course. Finals await, and then, praise be, vacation. That well-deserved break from your academic labors brings you to an implicit point of decision about what to do with this text, the other course readings, and the knowledge you have gained from your instructor. One option is to sell what books you can back to the bookstore and forget the rest. We can remember from our undergraduate days how attractive an idea that sometimes seems.

But then, again, is that really the best option? Probably not. We began our semester's journey with the idea that we are all inescapably part of the world drama. There may be times when we want to shout, "Stop the world, I want to get off," but we cannot. We have also seen that we are both audience and actors in the global play's progress. At the very least, we are all touched by the action in ways that range from the foreign designer jeans that we wear to, potentially, our atomized end.

We can leave it at that, shrug our shoulders, and complain and mumble at the forces that buffet us. But we also can do more than that. We do not have to be just passive victims. We can, if we want and if we try, help write the script. The plot is ongoing and improvisational. The final scene is yet unwritten. We are not even sure when it will occur. It could be well into the far distant future—or it could be tomorrow. This, more than any particular point of information, is the most important message. You are not helpless, and you owe it to yourself and your fellow humans to take an active role in your life and in the world's tomorrows.

The world is beset by great problems. War continues to kill without cessation. A billion-dollar diet industry prospers in many countries of the North due to the fact that many of its citizens are overweight, while in the

South, infants and the elderly starve to death in the dry dust. As if localized malnutrition were too slow and selective, we globally attack our environment with the waste products of our progress, and the human population tide threatens to overwhelm Earth's ability to sustain the people who live on it. Of even more immediate peril, an expanse of nuclear mushroom clouds could instantly terminate our biosphere's more evolutionary decay.

To face these problems, we have, at best, a primitive political system. Sovereignty strengthens nationalities but divides the world. Frontier justice is the rule. As in a grade-B western, most of the actors carry guns on their hips and sometimes shoot it out. The law is weak, and the marshals have more authority in theory than in practice.

There are few anymore who really try to defend the system of assertive sovereignty as adequate for the future. Clearly, it is not. What is less certain is what to do next and how to do it. Cooperation, humanitarianism, enlightenment, and other such words provide easy answers, but they are vague goals. Real answers are difficult to come by. They may involve tough choices, such as our being asked to give up some things now so that they will not be taken later, be less sovereign, curb our lifestyle, risk arms control in the hope of avoiding nuclear war, and think of the world in terms of "we."

At every step of the way there will be those who urge caution, who counsel self-preservation first, who see the world as a lifeboat. Maybe they will be right—but probably not. We *have* begun to move toward a more rational order. Our discussion has clearly shown that progress has occurred, but also that the progress is yet limited and fragile. This is where you come in. Your job is to work to make the world the place you want it to be. It is your job to consider the problems, to ponder possible solutions, to reach informed opinions, and to act on your convictions. Think? Yes, of course. But also DO!! That is what is really important.

In the end, citizens of the world would do well to heed the sage advice of the Mauryan (present-day India) emperor Asoka (269–232 B.C.). After witnessing the carnage of war, he converted to Buddhism and came to rule his vast empire based on the principles of peace rather than on those of coercion and fear. He left the following admonition that continues to resonate in today's world of struggle and conflict:

> [M]y sons and grandsons . . . should not regard it as their duty to conquer a new conquest. . . . They should take pleasure in patience and gentleness and regard as [the only true] conquest the conquest won by piety . . . because that avails for both this world and the next. (Smith, n.d.:175)

Be governed by your knowledge and proceed.

Technical Explanations And Matters Of Terminology

Page 41. **Some matters of terminology: EDC/LDC.** The use of the acronym EDC for economically developed country is not common in the literature. I am using "economically developed" here instead of simply "developed" in order to stress the economic factor and to avoid the all-too-common stereotype of the countries of the South as culturally or otherwise inferior. Indeed, the designation LDC, or less developed country, is misleading in the same way. Less economically developed country (LEDC) would be preferable, and politically and economically disadvantaged country (PEDC) would be better still, because these terms would recognize that the countries are in a relatively weak international political and economic position. The acronym LDC, however, is so common that I will continue to use it. The South is also referred to frequently as the Third World, although this term is rapidly becoming outmoded. It has been used somewhat inconsistently, but it generally has meant LDCs, especially those not aligned with either of the two superpowers in the East-West Axis. It may seem odd to refer to Third World countries when we do not refer to Second World ones, but the term has been useful to designate those countries that are not only politically and economically disadvantaged but that have invariably suffered through or are still undergoing a direct or an indirect colonial experience in this century. It would be reasonable therefore to classify many of the former Soviet republics as Third World countries. Poor, mostly Muslim Uzbekistan, for example, was until recently something of a colony of the Russian-dominated Soviet state. The point is that such countries, many of which have had unfortunate experiences with politically and militarily powerful EDCs, share similar views of EDCs and their alleged role in causing and maintaining the LDCs' unjust economic and politically disadvantaged status. Finally, some analysts have used the words "core" and "periphery" to designate, respectively, those countries with power as being at the center of the political system and those without much power on the margins. These nuances need not concern us here.

Therefore, the terms North, EDC, developed country, and core country all mean about the same thing; as do South, LDC, Third World, and periphery country.

Names in non-Western Cultures. Names in many parts of the world do not follow the format familiar to Americans, Canadians, and others whose names are most likely to follow the European tradition of a first (given) name followed by a family name (surname). In China, the Koreas, Vietnam, and many other countries in Asia, the custom is to place the surname first, followed by the given name. Thus, Zhu Rongji would be addressed formally as Premier Zhu. Given the greater formality followed in China (and most of the rest of the world) compared to the United States, only Zhu's family and very close friends would call him Rongji. Japan presents something of a twist on this practice. Like most other North and East Asian people, the Japanese in their own usage place the surname first. But the very externally oriented Japanese have long practiced putting the given name first in all communications with the outside world. Thus internally in Japanese characters, the Japanese would refer to their prime minister as Obuchi (surname) Keizo (given name). Externally in English or other languages, he would be designated Keizo Obuchi. There are also countries in which only one name is used. Najibullah is the entire name of the Soviet-backed president of Afghanistan overthrown by U.S.–backed rebels in 1992. In somewhat the same way, the familiar name of President Saddam Hussein of Iraq creates some confusion. Originally, he was given his father's name (Hussein) coupled with what could be construed as a surname, al-Takrit, after the Takrit region of his home in Iraq. The designation "Saddam" is not a name as such. Rather it is an adopted political appellation meaning "one who confronts." In this way, he is President Hussein, but his familiar name is also Hussein. Finally, Spanish-heritage surnames often have longer and shorter versions that relate to family and origin. The full name of the Mexican president inaugurated in December 1994 is Ernesto Zedillo Ponce de León, who succeeded President Carlos Salinas de Gortari. After the first long form, they would be referred to as Presidents Zedillo and Salinas. In the same way, former Costa Rican president and 1987 Nobel Peace Prize winner Oscar Arias Sanchez is President Arias.

The Spelling and Pronunciation of Chinese. The Chinese language does not have an alphabet. It uses many thousands of characters that mean whole words or can be combined to form new words. Many of the characters also have varying meanings, depending on the way they are pronounced. In written Chinese, this is indicated by accent marks. Unlike Western languages, though, the accent marks indicate tone rather than stress. Words can have an even, high tone, go up, go down, or start in a low tone and trail off. This accounts for the "sing-song" impression that Westerners have of spoken Chinese. Because of its characters, non-Western pronunciation, and other factors, translating Chinese into English has always been tricky. For many years the English Wade-Giles system of 1859 was used; in 1979 China adopted their own Pinyin (meaning "phonetic") system of romanization. By this, Mao Tse-tung became Mao Zedong; Chou En-lai became Zhou Enlai, Teng Hsiao-ping became Deng Xiaoping. For places, Beijing replaced Peking; Guangzhou replaced Canton; and Chongqing replaced Chungking. Except to maintain accuracy in a few historical references, Pinyin is used in this text. To detail pronunciation would take a great deal of space indeed. Just a few and only approximate guides are to pronounce *eng* as *ung, ian* as *en, ie* as *yeah, q* as *ch, ou* as in *bone, ua* as *ooa, uan* as *won, uai* as *why, uang* as *wong, ue* as *we, ui* as *way, un* as *oo, uo* as *woa, x* as *sh,* and *z* as *ds.*

Page 265. The Conditions for Military Success. Elements for success are those of George, Hall, and Simons (1971), which include (1) strong U.S. determination, (2) a less determined opponent, (3) clear U.S. goals, (4) a sense of urgency to accomplish these goals, (5) adequate domestic political support, (6) usable military options, (7) fear of U.S. escalation by the opponent, and (8) clarity concerning terms of the peaceful settlement. Other elements of success have been provided by Blechman and Kaplan (1978) and include (1) the opponent finds the threat credible, (2) the opponent is not yet fully committed to a course of action, (3) the goal is maintaining the authority of a particular regime abroad, (4) force is used to offset force by an opponent, (5) the goal is to have an opponent continue current behavior, that

is, to deter a change in behavior, (6) the action is consistent with prior policy, (7) there has been previous U.S. action in the area, (8) U.S. involvement begins early in the crisis, (9) military action is taken rather than threatened, and (10) strategic forces become involved, thus signaling seriousness of purpose. Caspar Weinberger's six criteria included (1) vital U.S. interests must be at stake, (2) there must be a clear intention of winning, (3) political and military objectives must be clearly defined, (4) sufficient military force must be employed to gain the objective, (5) there must be reasonable congressional and public support, and (6) combat should be a last resort. General Colin Powell's comments, made during a press interview, were not as easily enumerated as Weinberger's, but they generally agreed with the criteria of the then–secretary of defense. Powell's views can be found in the *New York Times,* September 29, 1992, p. A1.

Page 299. Economics: Technical Terms and Sources. The terms *gross national product* (GNP) and *gross domestic product* (GDP) are similar but not interchangeable. GNP measures the sum of all goods and services produced by a country's nationals whether they are in the country or abroad. Thus GNP includes data such as the profits of a country's MNCs. By the same logic, GNP does not include profits from production in one's country by foreign MNCs. GDP includes only income within a country (by both nationals and foreigners) and excludes foreign earnings of a country's nationals. In the past, GNP was the most common reporting base. Now, increasingly, GDP is replacing GNP because of the globalization of business and the feeling that (in terms of domestic economic activity) GDP is a more accurate indicator than GNP. The United States replaced GNP with GDP as its reporting base beginning in 1992. The fact that some countries report only GNP and others report only GDP creates slight statistical comparison anomalies.

The most recent change in calculating a country's production of wealth is the addition of "purchasing power parity" (PPP) to the calculation. Because GDP or GNP is expressed in a single currency, usually the U.S. dollar, it does not fully account for the difference in prices for similar goods and services in different countries. Some countries are more expensive than the United States. Refer to the box GDP–PPP on the Web site (chapter 14) for a complete explanation of GDP–PPP. There is certainly value to PPP adjustments, but this book uses unadjusted figures. Using both adjusted and unadjusted figures would created more confusion than clarity, and the reason for using the unadjusted

GDP/GNP is that since many of the industrial and technological products that LDCs wish to acquire come from abroad, the cost to the LDC is not affected by PPP. A U.S. tractor that costs $50,000, costs $50,000 whether you buy it in the United States or Kenya. Therefore, PPP masks the gap in international purchasing power between LDCs and EDCs and inflates the economic position of LDCs compared to EDCs in the world economy.

All monetary values in this book are in current U.S. dollars (US$), unless otherwise noted. There are two ways to express monetary values. One is in current dollars, which means the value of the dollar in the year reported. Because of inflation, using current dollars means that, for example, the percentage increase in *value* of exports will rise faster than the percentage increase in the *volume* of exports over any period. The second way to express monetary value is in *real dollars,* or uninflated dollars. This means that the currency is reported in terms of what it would have been worth in a stated year. In this book, monetary value is in current U.S. dollars except where noted. Therefore, you could say either that a car in 1998 cost $14,233 or that (assuming a 4 percent inflation rate) it cost $10,000 in real 1989 dollars. Note that you figure inflation by compounding the rate, that is, multiplying $10,000 by $1.04 \times 1.04 \times 1.04$. . . . The number 100 is used as a baseline in many of the figures in this and other chapters. It is used to show relative change. This number is an abstraction and has no value as such. It simply allows comparisons of later growth or decline. It is used instead of zero to avoid pluses and minuses before subsequent data. For example, if you earned $5,000 in 1989 and a friend earned $7,000, and you wished to compare later earning growth, you would make 1989 earnings for both of you equal to 100. Then, if in 1998 you earned $8,000, but your friend earned only $4,000 (using increments of 10 to equal each $1,000), your earnings would be expressed as 130 and your friend's earnings would be 70. You may find that the data, such as trade expressed in dollars, used in this book for any given year or period varies somewhat from what is cited by another source. Most of the data is based on extensive compilations and complex calculations completed by the sources cited or by the author. But the reporting organizations, such as the U.S. government, the United Nations, the IMF, the World Bank, and GATT all use slightly different assumptions and inputs in calculating their final figures. Most of the major sources used herein include careful discussion of exactly how they arrive at their conclusions. You may refer to these if you wish a detailed explanation of their methodologies. The key, then, usually is not to focus too much on specific numbers, especially if they come from different sources. Rather it is best to concentrate on patterns, such as the rate of growth or decline of trade over a period of years. Unless specifically noted, this chapter relies on the following sources for financial, trade, and other economic data: International Monetary Fund (1997–98), *Direction of Trade Statistics*, Washington, DC; IMF (1998), *International Financial Statistics*; IMF (1998), *World Economic Outlook*; IMF (1998), *IMF Survey*; U.S. Central Intelligence Agency (CIA) (1997), *The World Factbook, 1997–98*; (U.S.) Bureau of the Census and U.S. Economics and Statistics Administration (1997), *Statistical Abstract of the United States, 1997*; *World Almanac, 1997* and *1998*; World Bank (1998), *World Development Report, 1998*; World Resources Institute (1998), *World Resources, 1997–98*. In addition to these sources, four newspapers—the *Financial Times* (London), the *Hartford Courant* (Hartford, Connecticut), the *New York Times* (New York), and the *Wall Street Journal* (New York)—were used as sources herein. Several further comments on these sources are appropriate. One is that many are periodic publications. The most current year used is shown, but historical data may also be drawn from various issues in the current or earlier years. Second, some sources of historical data are not shown because of the sheer mounting volume of citation that would be necessary through multiple editions of this study. Where it is not cited herein, historical data sources are cited in earlier editions of *International Politics on the World Stage*. Third, full bibliographic citations for most of the sources listed here can be found in this volume's bibliography.

Page 319. **How Exchange Rates Work.** To begin to understand the mysteries of how exchange rates work and the impact of their fluctuation, consider the following two scenarios: the first with the dollar ($) equal to the post–World War II high of 258 yen (¥), which was the case in early 1985; and the second with the dollar equal to the current value of ¥106. For illustration, assume that one automobile costs ¥3,096,000 to manufacture in Japan and another costs $18,000 to build in Detroit. Let us further suppose that an average Japanese worker makes ¥1,806 an hour; an American makes $10 an hour. Manufacturing costs and wages are not directly affected by exchange rates and, therefore, remain constant.

Automobile Imports at a ¥258 = $1 Exchange Rate

•At ¥258 to the dollar, the equivalent cost is $12,000 for the Japanese car (¥3,096,000 ÷ ¥258) and ¥4,644,000 for the U.S. car ($18,000 × ¥258).

•It will take the Japanese worker earning ¥1,806 ($7) an hour a total of 1,714 work hours (¥3,096,00 ÷ ¥1,806) to buy the Japanese car and 2,571 work hours (¥4,644,000 ÷ ¥1,806) to buy the U.S. car. The Japanese worker will probably buy the Japanese car.

•It will take the American worker earning $10 (¥2,580) an hour a total of 1,200 work hours (¥3,096,000 ÷ ¥2,580) to buy the Japanese car and 1,800 work hours ($18,000 ÷ $10) to buy the U.S. car. The American worker will probably buy the Japanese car.

•With both the Japanese and the American worker buying Japanese cars, Japanese automobile exports to the United States will rise and U.S. exports to Japan will decline.

Automobile Imports at a ¥106 = $1 Exchange Rate

•At ¥106 per dollar, the equivalent cost is $29,200 for the Japanese car (¥3,096,000 ÷ ¥106) and ¥1,908,000 for the U.S. car ($18,000 × ¥106).

•It will take the Japanese worker earning ¥1,806 ($17) an hour a total of 1,714 work hours (¥3,096,000 ÷ ¥1,806) to buy the Japanese car and 1,056 work hours (¥1,908,000 ÷ ¥1,806) to buy the U.S. car. The Japanese worker will probably buy the U.S. car.

•It will take the American worker earning $10 (¥1,060) an hour a total of 2,920 work hours (¥3,096,000 ÷ ¥1,060) to buy the Japanese car and 1,800 work hours ($18,000 ÷ $10) to buy the U.S. car. The American worker will probably buy the U.S. car.

•With both the Japanese and the American workers buying U.S. cars, exports from Japan will decline and U.S. exports will rise.

Endnotes

CHAPTER 1

1. *New York Times,* January 12, 1998, p. A14.
2. Korb is quoted in Anthony Lewis, "The Defense Anomaly," *New York Times,* January 22, 1996, p. A15.
3. *New York Times,* May 24, 1994, p. C1.
4. *Hartford Courant,* June 9, 1996, A2.
5. *Newsweek,* March 21, 1994, p. 76.
6. *Hartford Courant,* May 18, 1992, p. A5.
7. CNN.com, analysis by Kenneth Stein, "An Israeli Election Different from All Others."
8. *New York Times,* November 28, 1995, p. A14.
9. *New York Times,* October 6, 1995, p. B10.
10. *Time,* April 13, 1992, p. 28.
11. *New York Times,* May 27, 1994, p. A8.

CHAPTER 2

1. *San Diego Union Tribune,* April 22, 1996.
2. *New York Times,* March 6, 1992, p. D2. The scholar is Shafigul Islam at the U.S.–based Council of Foreign Relations.
3. *New York Times,* March 25, 1998, p. D1.
4. *New York Times*, February 17, 1998, p. A1.
5. *Hartford Courant,* September 5, 1995, p. A1.
6. *New York Times,* April 17, 1996, p. A23. Clinton recalled the conversation to columnist Thomas L. Friedman, as related in his column "Gardening with Beijing."
7. *New York Times*, March 16, 1998, p. A6.
8. *Time,* June 1, 1992, p. 43.

CHAPTER 3

1. *Congressional Quarterly Weekly Report,* September 1, 1990, p. 2778.
2. *Time,* September 12, 1991, p. 53.

3. *New York Times,* September 17, 1995, p. A26.
4. *Hartford Courant,* October 17, 1997, p. A12. The conversation was on a tape of Nixon's conversations released in 1997.
5. Representative Jim Leach, quoted in the *New York Times,* September 26, 1993, p. A12.
6. *New York Times,* October 31, 1995, p. A3.
7. *New York Times,* January 5, 1993, p. A11.
8. *New York Times,* January 12, 1998, p. D1.
9. Pew Research Center News Interest Index, found on the Web at http://www.peoplepress.org/topten.htm.
10. *New York Times,* June 19, 1996, p. A10.
11. James A. Baker III, *The Politics of Diplomacy: Revolution, War and Peace, 1989-1992* (New York: G. P. Putnam's Sons), quoted in Philip Taubman, "The Man in the Middle," *New York Times Book Review,* October 29, 1995, p. 9.
12. *New York Times,* April 19, 1996, p. A2.
13. *New York Times,* June 1, 1998, p. S3.
14. The adviser was Arthur Goldberg, and the quote is from Robert Dallek, *Flawed Giant: Lyndon Johnson and His Times, 1961–1973* (New York: Oxford University Press, 1998) as reproduced in a review of the book, Sean Wilentz, "Lone Starr Setting," *New York Times Book Review,* April 12, 1998, p. 6.
15. *New York Times,* October 22, 1993, p. A14.
16. *New York Times,* October 2, 1993, p. A8.
17. *New York Times*, January 8, 1997, p. A3.
18. *U.S. News & World Report,* February 8, 1993, p. 39.
19. *New York Times,* April 17, 1994, p. A6.

CHAPTER 4

1. *New York Times,* October 6, 1995, p. B10.
2. *New York Times,* June 8, 1994, p. A16.

3. From "Patrie" in *Dictionnaire Philosophique*, 1764.

4. *New York Times,* August 2, 1994, p. C1. The anthropologist was Eugene Hammel.

5. *New York Times,* April 10, 1994, p. E1.

6. *Hartford Courant,* December 27, 1991, p. A1.

7. *Time,* March 12, 1990, p. 50.

8. *Hartford Courant,* April 8, 1994, p. A8.

9. *New York Times,* May 11, 1998, p. A6.

10. *New York Times,* February 25, 1994, p. A6.

11. Wilson's speech to Congress was on February 11, 1918.

CHAPTER 5

1. *New York Times,* June 4, 1996, p. C1.

2. *Hartford Courant,* February 15, 1996, p. A19.

3. *New York Times,* December 31, 1997, p. A3.

4. *Time,* June 15, 1996, p. 54.

5. *Hartford Courant,* September 10, 1995, p. A7.

6. *New York Times,* March 8, 1998, p. A15. The scholar was Charlotte Bunch, executive director, Center for Women's Global Leadership, Rutgers University.

7. *Hartford Courant,* July 10, 1992, p. A1.

8. *New York Times,* September 16, 1995, p. A5.

9. *New York Times,* January 28, 1998.

10. *New York Times,* April 10, 1995, p. A1.

11. *New York Times,* April 10, 1995, p. A1.

12. *New York Times,* August 24, 1994, p. E5.

13. *Newsweek,* June 10, 1994, p. 82.

14. *New York Times,* June 15, 1994, p. A1.

15. *New York Times,* January 22, 1998, p. A14.

16. The columns by Thomas L. Friedman and the quote by Fukuyama are from the *New York Times,* December 8, 1996, p. E15, and December 11, 1996, p. A27.

17. *New York Times,* June 8, 1999, p. A27.

18. *New York Times,* April 14, 1996, p. D1.

19. *New York Times,* December 12, 1994, p. E4.

20. *New York Times,* October 21, 1994, p. A4.

21. *New York Times,* August 24, 1997, p. E5. The sociologist was Pierre Birnbaum.

22. *Time,* April 20, 1992, p. 32.

23. *Hartford Courant,* March 7, 1996, p. E4.

24. Hartford Courant, January 2, 1996, p. B5.

25. *New York Times,* July 11, 1992, p. A3.

26. *New York Times,* March 15, 1994, p. A1.

27. *New York Times,* April 14, 1996, p. D1.

28. *Manchester Guardian Weekly,* August 13, 1995, p. 18.

29. CNN.com, June 20, 1999.

30. David Shenk of the Columbia University Freedom Forum Media Studies Center, quoted in the *New York Times,* April 14, 1996, p. D1.

31. *New York Times,* June 4, 1996, p. C1.

32. The scholar was political theorist Michael Sandel of Harvard University, quoted in the *New York Times,* March 18, 1996, p. A21.

CHAPTER 6

1. *New York Times,* February 26, 1992, p. A6.

2. *Time,* July 11, 1994, p. 42.

3. *New York Times,* April 4, 1994, p. A1.

4. Edwin D. Mansfield and Jack Snyder, quoted in the *Wall Street Journal,* June 25, 1996, p. 1.

5. *Hartford Courant,* February 25, 1994, p. A4.

6. *Newsweek,* June 6, 1994, p. 37.

7. *New York Times,* September 19, 1994, p. A10.

8. *Newsweek,* September 19, 1994, p. 37.

9. *New York Times,* July 25, 1996, p. A14.

10. *New York Times,* October 7, 1994, p. A1.

CHAPTER 7

1. Churchill made the widely quoted statement on June 26, 1954, while visiting the United States. Various papers printed it the next day.

2. *Manchester Guardian Weekly,* July 27, 1997, p. 4.

3. *New York Times,* July 16, 1995, p. A1.

4. *Time,* December 23, 1991, p. 29.

5. *New York Times,* October 17, 1995, p. A10.

6. *World Opinion Update,* August 1994.

7. *New York Times,* November 29, 1994, p. A6

8. *Hartford Courant,* June 3, 1992, p. A1.

9. *New York Times,* February 5, 1996, p. A10.

10. *New York Times,* October 17, 1995, p. A10.

11. *World Opinion Update,* January 1996, p. 11.

12. Kristi Essick, "Euro to Aid E-Commerce, Experts Say," CNN.com, March 8, 1999.

13. *New York Times,* July 8, 1998, p. A1.
14. Prime Minister Morihior Hosokawa, quoted in the *New York Times,* September 26, 1993, p. A16.
15. Foreign Minister Klaus Kinkel, quoted in the *New York Times,* September 30, 1993.
16. Sharad Pawar, quoted in the *New York Times,* November 15, 1995, p. A9.
17. President Chandrika Bandaranaike Kumaratunga of Sri Lanka and President Frederick J. T. Chiluba of Zambia, both quoted in the *New York Times,* October 23, 1995, p. A8.
18. *New York Times,* October 22, 1995, p. A1.
19. *New York Times,* September 12, 1995, p. A1.
20. *Time,* October 30, 1995, p. 74.
21. *New York Times,* December 16, 1996, p. A8.
22. James Traub, "Kofi Annan's Next Test," *New York Times Magazine,* March 29, 1998, p. 49.
23. *New York Times,* August 3, 1992, p. A1.
24. *New York Times,* November 6, 1994, p. A11.
25. *Time,* October 30, 1995, p. 74.
26. *New York Times,* July 17, 1997, p. A1.
27. *New York Times,* January 8, 1997, p. A3.
28. *New York Times,* September 18, 1994, p. A16.
29. Kofi Annan, "The Unpaid Bill That's Crippling the UN," an op-ed piece, *New York Times,* March 9, 1998, p. A19.
30. Hammarskjöld's widely quoted statement is attributed to the *New York Times,* June 27, 1955.

CHAPTER 8

1. Churchill told this story in a speech on October 24, 1928, and it can be found, among other places, in Robert Rhodes James, ed., *Winston S. Churchill: His Complete Speeches: 1897–1963,* vol. 5 (1974), p. 5421.
2. *New York Times,* March 7, 1996, p. A10.
3. *New York Times,* February 24, 1998, p. A1.
4. The quote and the poll data are from the *New York Times,* May 27, 1990, p. A10.
5. The quotes by Leningrad Communist Party chief Boris Gidaspov and diplomat Vladimir Brovikov are from *Time,* February 19, 1990, pp. 33, 35.
6. *Time,* July 15, 1996, p. 54.
7. *Time,* April 11, 1994, p. A10.
8. *Time,* June 13, 1994, p. 32.
9. *New York Times,* May 29, 1994, p. A1
10. *New York Times,* August 28, 1994, p. E7.
11. *New York Times,* April 9, 1998, p. A4.
12. *Time,* July 31, 1989, p. 17.
13. Cohen news conference on January 31, 1998, taken from the Web at http://www.fas.org/news/iraq/1998/01/index.html.
14. *New York Times,* June 30, 1995, p. D5.
15. BBC report of April 10, 1998, from the Web at: http://news.bbc.co.uk/low/english/events/northern_ireland/latest_news/newsid_76000/76778.stm.
16. The quote is Ambassador J. Stapleton Roy's recollection of what Jiang said, *New York Times,* July 3, 1995, p. E3.
17. *New York Times,* March 7, 1996, p. A1.
18. *New York Times,* March 12, 1996, p. A1.
19. *New York Times,* May 6, 1994, p. A6.
20. *New York Times,* March 3, 1998, p. E3.
21. *Time,* April 9, 1990, p. 39.
22. *New York Times,* October 30, 1997, p. A1.
23. *Washington Post,* April 13, 1990, p. A7.
24. *New York Times,* February 3, 1996, p. A11.
25. Ambassador Donald Gregg, quoted in the *Hartford Courant,* March 22, 1994, p. A1.
26. *New York Times,* December 3, 1993, p. A8.
27. *New York Times,* June 6, 1998, p. A1.
28. *New York Times,* March 7, 1996, p. A1.
29. Wen Wei Po and William Perry are quoted in the *New York Times,* March 22, 1996, p. A10.
30. *Hartford Courant,* March 17, 1994, p. A6.
31. *Time,* June 13, 1994, p. 32.
32. *New York Times,* March 17, 1994, p. A10.
33. *New York Times,* February 25, 1998, p. A1.
34. *Christian Science Monitor,* October 15, 1990, p. 18.
35. *New York Times,* October 4, 1994, p. A1. The official was Assistant Secretary of Defense Joseph Nye.
36. *USA Today,* March 11, 1996, p. A7.
37. *New York Times,* March 23, 1996, p. A5.
38. *New York Times,* June 6, 1998, p. A1.
39. *New York Times,* August 19, 1995, p. A1.
40. Foreign Minister Qian Qichen, quoted in the *New York Times,* March 26, 1996, p. A6.

41. *New York Times,* March 12, 1996, p. A1.
42. *New York Times,* March 13, 1996, p. A3.
43. Chief of Staff Leon Panetta, quoted in the *New York Times,* March 18, 1996, p. A3.

CHAPTER 9

1. *New York Times,* August 12, 1990, p. A10.
2. *New York Times,* November 12, 1997, p. A7.
3. *New York Times,* July 9, 1996, p. A6.
4. *New York Times,* May 5, 1994, p. A11.
5. *New York Times,* June 29, 1998, p. A1.
6. *Manchester Guardian Weekly,* August 14, 1994, p. 25.
7. *Washington Post,* June 1, 1992, p. B1.
8. *New York Times,* January 24, 1990, p. A1.
9. *New York Times,* April 7, 1998, p. A17.
10. *New York Times,* April 18, 1992, p. A9.
11. Kennedy's remark was on June 24, 1963, and can be found in the *Public Papers of the President of the United States: John F. Kennedy, 1963.*

CHAPTER 10

1. *Labor,* September 6, 1947.
2. Jacob Heilbrunn and Michael Lind, "The Third American Empire," an op-ed piece in the *New York Times,* January 2, 1996, p. A15.
3. The diplomat was Charles H. Thomas II, former U.S envoy to Bosnia, quoted in the *New York Times,* November 29, 1995, p. E2.
4. *New York Times,* February 21, 1998, p. A1.
5. Gary W. Gallagher, "At War with Himself," a review of Michael Fellman, *Citizen Sherman: A Life of William Tecumseh Sherman* (New York: Random House, 1995) in the *New York Times Review of Books,* October 22, 1995, p. 24.
6. *Hartford Courant,* November 16, 1994, p. F6.
7. *New York Times,* February 13, 1994, p. A12. The official was Vladimir Diouhy, Czech minister of industry and trade.
8. *New York Times,* March 21, 1996, p. A12.
9. *New York Times,* April 26, 1997, p. A1. The expert was Dr. William A. Haseltine.
10. *Congressional Record,* January 23, 1990, S12.
11. *New York Times,* October 26, 1994, p. A10.

12. New York Times, July 7, 1998, p. A7.
13. *New York Times,* September 13, 1996, p. A1.
14. *New York Times,* September 12, 1996, p. A9.
15. *Newsweek,* May 25, 1998, p. 32B.
16. *New York Times,* May 31, 1998, p. A1.
17. *New York Times,* September 13, 1996, p. A1.
18. *New York Times,* January 6, 1995, p. A3.
19. *New York Times,* May 4, 1997, p. 12.

CHAPTER 11

1. *New York Times,* July 24, 1996, p. A1.
2. Quoted in Michael Lind, "Why Buy American?" a review of Alfred E. Eckes Jr., *U.S. Foreign Trade Policy since 1776* (Chapel Hill: University of North Carolina Press, 1995) in the *New York Times Book Review,* October 29, 1995, p. 42.
3. *New York Times,* April 16, 1992, p. A1.
4. Emerson Kapaz of São Paulo, quoted in the *Wall Street Journal,* June 21, 1991, p. A11.

CHAPTER 12

1. *New York Times,* March 9, 1998, p. A1.
2. *New York Times,* May 29, 1992, p. A3.
3. Economist Gary C. Hufbauer, quoted in the *New York Times,* September 11, 1996, p. D1.
4. Stanley Roth of the National Security Council staff, quoted in the *New York Times,* February 21, 1996, p. A9.
5. *New York Times,* June 9, 1996, p. F1.
6. *New York Times,* October 23, 1995, p. A8.
7. *New York Times,* March 2, 1997, p. A39.
8. *New York Times,* April 7, 1996, p. E5.
9. *Time,* September 19, 1995, p. 92.
10. *New York Times,* June 25, 1996, p. A1.
11. Klaus Schwab, director of the Davos Forum, quoted in Thomas L. Friedman, "Revolt of the Wannabes," a column in the *New York Times,* February 7, 1996, p. A19.
12. *New York Times,* October 24, 1995, p. A10.
13. The newspaper quoted is the *New York Times,* and that quote and the U.S. reservation are from the *New York Times,* November 18, 1996, p. A3.

14. UNIDO press release (IDO/1658), December 9, 1996, taken from the Web.

15. John Kirton of the University of Toronto's G-7 Research Group, "What Is the G-7?" document on the Web on November 10, 1996, at http://unl1.library.utoronto.ca/www/g7/what_is_g7.html.

16. The Sutherland quote is from the *Hartford Courant,* April 16, 1994, p. A1.

17. The Clinton quote, said earlier at the end of negotiations, is from the *Hartford Courant,* December 16, 1993, p. D8.

18. *New York Times,* December 16, 1993, p. D8.

19. *New York Times,* November 23, 1994, p. A18.

20. *New York Times,* April 7, 1998, p. D1.

21. The quote of Senator Charles E. Grassely, chairman of the Subcommittee on Trade, is from the *New York Times,* November 21, 1996, p. A1.

22. *New York Times,* February 21, 1997, p. A1.

23. *New York Times,* January 4, 1995, p. D4.

24. *New York Times,* February 17, 1998, p. A1.

25. *Hartford Courant,* December 12, 1997, p. A11.

26. *Hartford Courant,* February 24, 1993, p. A8.

27. *New York Times,* June 20, 1994, p. A1.

28. The analyst was Louis T. Wells of the Harvard Business School, quoted in the *New York Times,* May 25, 1996, p. A1.

29. *New York Times,* December 8, 1994, p. A14.

30. *New York Times,* December 12, 1994, p. A8.

31. *New York Times,* December 11, 1994, p. A1.

32. Both quotes are from the *New York Times,* December 12, 1994, p. A8.

33. *New York Times,* April 19, 1998, p. A10.

34. The analyst was Phillip Hughes, chairman of the Council of the Americas, quoted in the *New York Times,* March 24, 1996, p. A13.

35. *New York Times,* September 18, 1997, p. A7.

36. *New York Times,* April 19, 1998, p. A10.

37. All quotes are from the *New York Times,* November 19, 1993, p. A1.

38. *New York Times,* August 23, 1992, p. F5.

39. Jans Kerkhofs of Louvain University, quoted in *Time,* December 9, 1991, p. 40.

40. *New York Times,* December 12, 1994, p. A8.

41. *New York Times,* January 29, 1992, p. D2.

CHAPTER 13

1. Both quotes, the second by Robert Repetto of the World Resources Institute, are from the *New York Times,* September 19, 1995, p. C1.

2. Paul Portney of Resources for the Future, quoted in the *New York Times,* September 19, 1995, p. C1.

3. *New York Times,* February 28, 1996, p. A3.

4. Final document of the World Food Summit, November 17, 1996, taken from the World Wide Web at http://www.fao.org/wfs/final/rde.htm.

5. CNN news item, November 13, 1996, taken from the World Wide Web.

6. Final document of the World Food Summit, November 17, 1996, taken from the World Wide Web at http://www.fao.org/wfs/final/rde.htm.

7. *Hartford Courant,* September 30, 1994, p. A8.

8. *New York Times,* November 28, 1996, p. A10.

9. The quotes are from an interview of Goldhagen, not from his book, and are found in the *New York Times,* April 1, 1996, p. C11.

10. *Hartford Courant,* December 13, 1991, p. A1.

11. *New York Times,* August 20, 1998, p. A11.

12. *New York Times,* August 29, 1997, p. A4.

13. *New York Times,* August 29, 1997, p. A4.

14. *New York Times,* October 9, 1996, p. A8.

15. Toronto *Globe and Mail,* August 26, 1996, reproduced in the *World Press Review,* November 1996, p. 10.

16. Quoted in Adrian Karatnycky, "The Real Zyuganov," an op-ed piece in the *New York Times,* March 5, 1996, p. A23.

17. *New York Times,* June 28, 1996, p. A1.

18. The poll, commissioned by the American Jewish Committee, was reported in the *Hartford Courant,* March 30, 1994, p. A11.

19. *New York Times,* December 10, 1993, p. A11.

20. *Hartford Courant,* July 7, 1993, p. A1.

21. Le Pen is quoted in Timothy Christenfeld, "Wretched Refuse Is Just the Start," *New York Times,* March 10, 1996, p. A15.

22. *The Public Perspective,* January 1996, p. 33.

23. *New York Times,* March 11, 1995, p. A5.

24. *Hartford Courant,* December 12, 1996, p. A8.

25. Report on the World Congress Against Commercial Sexual Exploitation of Children, taken in December 1996 from the UNICEF Web site at http://www.childhub.ch/webpub/csechome/.

26. Quoted in Barbara Crossette, "Snubbing Human Rights," *New York Times,* April 28, 1996, p. E3.

CHAPTER 14

1. The *State of the World* series is written and edited by Lester R. Brown and a shifting group of other analysts. Each annual edition also carries the appropriate year as part of the title. The series is published by W. W. Norton in New York and sponsored by the Worldwatch Institute, which Brown heads.

2. Theodore Roszak, "Green Guilt and Ecological Overload," an op-ed piece published in the *New York Times,* June 9, 1992, p. A27. Roszak is on the faculty of California State University, Hayward.

3. *Time,* December 12, 1990, p. 48.

4. *Time,* June 1, 1992, p. 42.

5. *New York Times,* April 30, 1992, p. A12.

6. *New York Times,* December 31, 1997, p. A6.

7. Representative Christopher Smith and Nafis Sadik are both quoted in the *New York Times,* February 16, 1996.

8. *Time,* September 5, 1994, p. 52.

9. The Pakistani delegate, Said Khawar Mumtaz of Punjab University, and the Chinese delegate, Wang Jiaxaing of Beijing Foreign Studies University, were quoted in the *New York Times,* September 2, 1994, p. A3.

10. All quotes are from the *New York Times,* September 4, 1995, p. A2.

11. *New York Times,* December 12, 1993, p. A5.

12. *New York Times,* August 23, 1998, p. A19.

13. *New York Times,* October 10, 1994, p. A4.

14. *Hartford Courant,* August 4, 1995, p. A9.

15. *New York Times,* May 17, 1998, p. A1.

16. The quote of the Icelander and Norway's prime minister are both from *Time,* August 2, 1993, p. 45.

17. *New York Times,* June 24, 1996, p. A4.

18. *Hartford Courant,* November 10, 1994, p. A1. The observer was Perran Ross of the Florida Museum of Natural History in Gainesville.

19. *Time,* January 2, 1989, p. 47.

20. *New York Times,* September 10, 1995, p. A1.

21. *New York Times,* December 20, 1994, p. C4. The scientist was R. Steven Nerem of NASA.

22. *New York Times,* May 24, 1994, p. C1. The IPCC head was John Houghton.

23. *New York Times,* July 8, 1996, p. A2.

24. *New York Times,* September 14, 1993, p. C1. The scientist was Dixy Lee Ray, author of a 1993 book, *Environmental Overkill: Whatever Happened to Common Sense?*

25. *Hartford Courant,* September 22, 1991, p. A1. Statement by Paul Waggoner, who headed the academy's study panel.

26. *Hartford Courant,* September 16, 1994, p. A8.

27. *New York Times,* September 14, 1993. The scholars are Ben W. Bolch and Harold Lyons of Rhodes College, authors of *Apocalypse Not: Science, Economics and Environmentalism.*

28. *New York Times,* May 24, 1994. This scientist was John Houghton, former head of the IPCC and author of *Global Warming: The Complete Briefing.*

29. *New York Times,* September 14, 1993, p. C1.

30. *Hartford Courant,* August 26, 1993, p. A3. The scientist was James W. Wilkins of the U.S. National Oceanic and Atmospheric Administration.

31. *Washington Post National Weekly Edition,* April 26–May 2, 1993, p. 6. The scientist was Richard Stolarski of NASA.

32. *Hartford Courant,* December 16, 1994, p. A6. The scientist was Mark Schoeberl of NASA.

33. *Manchester Guardian Weekly,* March 20, 1994, p. 10. The opposition leader was Chris Smith, environment spokesman for the Labour Party.

Glossary

Actors (international) Individuals or organizations that play a direct role in the conduct of world politics. **27**

Adjudication The legal process of deciding an issue through the courts. **239**

Anarchical political system An anarchical system is one in which there is no central authority to make rules, to enforce rules, or to resolve disputes about the actors in the political system. Many people believe that a system without central authority is inevitably one either of chaos or one in which the powerful prey on the weak. There is, however, an anarchist political philosophy that contends that the natural tendency of people to cooperate has been corrupted by artificial political, economic, or social institutions. Therefore, anarchists believe that the end of these institutions will lead to a cooperative society. Marxism, insofar as it foresees the collapse of the state once capitalism is destroyed and workers live in proletariat harmony, has elements of anarchism. **27**

Arms control A variety of approaches to the limitation of weapons. Arms control ranges from restricting the future growth in the number, types, or deployment of weapons, through the reduction of weapons, to the elimination of some types (or even all) weapons on a global or regional basis. **280**

Asia Pacific Economic Cooperation (APEC) A regional trade organization founded in 1989 and including 18 countries. **370**

Autarky Economic independence from external sources. **323**

Balance of payments A figure that represents the net flow of money into and out of a country due to trade, tourist expenditures, sale of services (such as consulting), foreign aid, profits, and so forth. **320**

Balance of power A concept that describes the degree of equilibrium (balance) or disequilibrium (imbalance) of power in the global or regional system. **53**

Bilateral diplomacy Negotiations between two countries. **216**

Bilateral (foreign) aid Foreign aid given by one country directly to another. **338**

Bretton Woods system The international monetary system that existed from the end of World War II until the early 1970s; named for an international economic conference held in Bretton Woods, New Hampshire, in 1944. **354**

Bureaucracy The bulk of the state's administrative structure that continues even when leaders change. **68**

Capital needs The requirements of all countries, and LDCs in particular, for money to expand their economies. **334**

Carrying capacity The number of people that an environment, such as Earth, can feed, provide water for, and otherwise sustain. **401**

Cartel An international agreement among producers of a commodity that attempts to control the production and pricing of that commodity. **341**

Chemical Weapons Convention (CWC) A treaty that was signed and became effective in 1995 under which signatories pledge to eliminate all chemical weapons by the year 2005; to submit to rigorous inspection; to never develop, produce, stockpile, or use chemical weapons; and to never transfer chemical weapons to another country or assist another country to acquire such weapons. **282**

Codify To write down a law in formal language. **235**

Coercive diplomacy Using threats or force as a diplomatic tactic. **224**

Cognitive decision making Making choices within the limits of what you consciously know. **74**

Collective security The original theory behind UN peacekeeping. It holds that aggression against one state is aggression against all and should be defeated by the collective action of all. **289**

Conditionality A term that refers to the policy of the International Monetary Fund, the World Bank, and some other international financial agencies to attach conditions to their loans and grants. These conditions may require recipient countries to devalue their currencies, to lift controls on prices, to cut their budgets, and to reduce barriers to trade and capital flows. Such conditions are often politically unpopular, may cause at least short-term economic pain, and are construed by critics as interference in recipient countries' sovereignty. **358**

Countries in transition (CITs) Former communist countries such as Russia whose economies are in transition from socialism to capitalism. **350**

Crisis situation A circumstance or event that is a surprise to decision makers, that evokes a sense of threat (particularly physical peril), and that must be responded to within a limited amount of time. **64**

Cultural imperialism The attempt to impose your own value system on others, including judging others by how closely they conform to your norms. **251**

Current dollars The value of the dollar in the year for which it is being reported. Sometimes called inflated dollars. Any currency can be expressed in current value. *See* **Real dollars**. **299**

Decision making The process by which humans choose which policy to pursue and which actions to take in support of policy goals. The study of decision making seeks to identify patterns in the way that humans make decisions. This includes gathering information, analyzing information, and making choices. Decision making is a complex process that relates to personality and other human traits, to the sociopolitical setting in which decision makers function, and to the organizational structures involved. **73**

Dependencia theory The belief that the industrialized North has created a neocolonial relationship with the South in which the LDCs are dependent on and disadvantaged by their economic relations with the capitalist industrial countries. **303**

Deterrence Persuading an opponent not to attack by having enough forces to disable the attack and/or launch a punishing counterattack. **277**

Direct democracy Policy making through a variety of processes, including referendums, by which citizens directly cast ballots on policy issues. **73**

Divine principle A school of thought about the origin of law that believes that theological scripture and doctrine provide the proper basis of secular law. **234**

Economically developed country (EDC) Industrialized countries, which are mainly found in the Northern Hemisphere. **41**

Elites Those individuals in a political system who exercise disproportionate control of policy either by occupying policy-making positions or by having direct access to and influence over those who do. **169**

Escalation Increasing the level of fighting. **274**

Ethnonational groups An ethnic group that feels alienated from the state in which it resides and that wishes to break away from that state to establish its own autonomous or independent political structure or to combine with its ethnic kin in another state. Many ethnic groups, such as Italian Americans, have no separatist leanings; many nations, such as Americans, are composed of many ethnic groups. **59**

European Economic Community (EEC) The regional trade and economic organization established in Western Europe by the Treaty of Rome in 1958; also known as the Common Market. **170**

European Union (EU) The Western European regional organization established in 1983 when the Maastricht Treaty went into effect. The EU encompasses the still legally existing European Community (EC). When the EC was formed in 1967, it in turn encompassed three still legally existing regional organizations formed in the 1950s: the European Coal and Steel Community (ECSC), the European Economic Community (EEC), and the European Atomic Energy Community (EURATOM). **170**

Eurowhites A term to distinguish the whites of Europe and of Australia, Canada, New Zealand, the United States, and other countries whose cultures were founded on or converted to European culture from other races and ethnic groups, including Caucasian peoples in Latin America, the Middle East, South Asia, and elsewhere. **29**

Exchange rate The values of two currencies relative to each other—for example, how many yen equal a dollar or how many lira equal a pound. **319**

Foreign direct investment (FDI) Buying stock, real estate, and other assets in another country with the aim of gaining a controlling interest in foreign economic enterprises. Different from portfolio investment, which involves investment solely to gain capital appreciation through market fluctuations. **317**

Foreign portfolio investment (FPI) Investment in the stocks and the public and private debt instruments (such as bonds) of another country below the level where the stock- or bondholder can exercise control over the policies of the stock-issuing company or the bond-issuing debtor. **317**

Fourth World A term used to designate collectively the indigenous (aboriginal, native) people of the countries of the world. **391**

Free trade The international movement of goods unrestricted by tariffs or nontariff barriers. **332**

Free Trade Area of the Americas (FTAA) The tentative name given by the 34 countries that met in December 1994 at the Summit of the Americas to the proposed Western Hemisphere free trade zone that is projected to come into existence by the year 2005. **367**

Functional relations Relations that include interaction in such usually nonpolitical areas as communication, travel, trade, and finances. **232**

Functionalism International cooperation in specific areas such as communications, trade, travel, health, or environmental protection activity. Often symbolized by the specialized agencies, such as the World Health Organization, associated with the United Nations. **166**

Gender gap The difference between males and females along any one of a number of dimensions, including foreign policy preferences. **64**

General Agreement on Tariffs and Trade (GATT) The world's primary organization promoting the expansion of free trade. Established in 1947, it has grown to a membership of over 100. **351**

General and complete disarmament (GCD) Total disarmament. **293**

General Assembly The main representative body of the United Nations, composed of all member-states. **180**

Gross domestic product (GDP) A measure of income within a country that excludes foreign earnings. **5, 50**

Gross national product (GNP) A measure of the sum of all goods and services produced by a country's nationals, whether they are in the country or abroad. **41**

Group of Seven (G-7) The seven economically largest free market countries: Canada, France, Great Britain, Italy, Japan, the United States, and Germany. 331

Group of 77 Group of 77 countries of the South that cosponsored the Joint Declaration of Developing Countries in 1963 calling for greater equity in North-South trade. This group has come to include more than 120 members and represents the interests of the less developed countries of the South. 340

Groupthink How an individual's membership in an organization/decision-making group influences his or her thinking and actions. In particular there are tendencies within a group to think alike, to avoid discordancy, and to ignore ideas or information that threaten to disrupt the consensus. 80

Hard currency Currencies, such as dollars, marks, francs, and yen, that are acceptable in private channels of international economics. 334

Idealists Analysts who reject power politics and argue that failure to follow policies based on humanitarianism and international cooperation will result in disaster. 13

Ideological or theological principles A set of related ideas in secular or religious thought, usually founded on identifiable thinkers and their works, that offers a more or less comprehensive picture of reality. 234

Incremental decision making Also incrementalism. The tendency of decision makers to treat existing policy as a given and to follow that policy ("policy inertia") or make only marginal changes in the policy. 81

Incremental policy *See* **Incremental decision making.** 81

Individual-level analysis An analytical approach that emphasizes the role of individuals as either distinct personalities or biological/psychological beings. 22

Interdependence (economic) The close interrelationship and mutual dependence of two or more domestic economies on each other. 40, 322

Intergovernmental organizations (IGOs) International/transnational actors composed of member countries. 49, 161

Intermestic The merger of *inter*national and do*mestic* concerns. 3, 65

International Court of Justice (ICJ) The world court, which sits in The Hague with 15 judges and is associated with the United Nations. 239

International Monetary Fund (IMF) The world's primary organization devoted to maintaining monetary stability by helping countries fund balance-of-payments deficits. Established in 1947, it now has 170 members. 354

International political economy (IPE) An approach to the study of international relations that is concerned with the political determinants of international economic relations and also with the economic determinants of international political relations. 22, 299

International system An abstract concept that encompasses global actors, the interactions (especially patterns of interaction) among those actors, and the factors that cause those interactions. The international system is largest of a vast number of overlapping political systems that extend downward in size to micropolitical systems at the local level. *See* **System-level analysis.** 25

Investment, foreign *See* **FDI, FPI.** 317

Issue areas Substantive categories of policy that must be considered when evaluating national interest. 64

League of Nations The first true general international organization. It existed between the end of World War I and the beginning of World War II and was the immediate predecessor of the United Nations. 161

Least developed countries (LLDCs) Those countries in the poorest of economic circumstances. In this book, this includes those countries with a per capita GNP of less than $400 in 1985 dollars. 309

Less developed countries (LDCs) Countries, located mainly in Africa, Asia, and Latin America, with economies that rely heavily on the production of agriculture and raw material and whose per capita GDP and standard of living are substantially below Western standards. 41

Levels of analysis Different perspectives (system, state, individual) from which international politics can be analyzed. 22

Maastricht Treaty The most significant agreement in the recent history of the European Union (EU). The Maastricht Treaty was signed by leaders of the EU's 12 member-countries in December 1991 and outlines steps toward further political-economic integration. 171

MAD (Mutual Assured Destruction) A situation in which each nuclear superpower has the capability of launching a devastating nuclear second strike even after an enemy has attacked it. The belief that a MAD capacity prevents nuclear war is the basis of deterrence by punishment theory. 277

Mass The nonelite element of a political society. The majority of people who do not occupy policy-making positions and who do not have direct access to those who do. 168

Merchandise trade The import and export of tangible manufactured goods and raw materials. 312

Microstate A country with a small population that cannot economically survive unaided or that is inherently so militarily weak that it is an inviting target for foreign intervention. 108

Missile Technology Control Regime (MTCR) A series of understandings that commits most of the countries capable of producing extended-range missiles to a ban on the export of ballistic missiles and related technology and that also pledges MTCR adherents to bring economic and diplomatic pressure to bear on countries that export missile-applicable technology. **283**

Monetary relations The entire scope of international money issues, such as exchange rates, interest rates, loan policies, balance of payments, and regulating institutions (for example, the International Monetary Fund). **318**

Multilateral diplomacy Negotiations among three or more countries. **217**

Multilateral (foreign) aid Foreign aid distributed by international organizations such as the United Nations. **338**

Multinational corporations (MNCs) Private enterprises that have production subsidiaries or branches in more than one country. **50, 317**

Multinational states Countries in which there are two or more significant nationalities. **102**

Multipolar system A world political system in which power primarily is held by four or more international actors. **29**

Multistate nationalities Nations whose members overlap the borders of two or more states. **104**

Munich analogy A belief among post–World War II leaders, particularly Americans, that aggression must always be met firmly and that appeasement will only encourage an aggressor. Named for the concessions made to Hitler by Great Britain and France at Munich during the 1938 Czechoslovakian crisis. **84**

Nation A group of culturally and historically similar people who feel a communal bond and who feel they should govern themselves to at least some degree. **91**

Nationalism The belief that the nation is the ultimate basis of political loyalty and that nations should have self-governing states. *See* **Nation-state**. **93**

Nation-state A politically organized territory that recognizes no higher law, and whose population politically identifies with that entity. *See* **State**. **93**

Naturalist (school) Those who believe that law springs from the rights and obligations that humans have by nature. **234**

Neocolonialism Control of less developed countries (especially in the South) by more developed countries through indirect means, such as economic dominance and coopting the local elite. **303**

New International Economic Order (NIEO) A term that refers to the goals and demands of the South for basic reforms in the international economic system. **341**

Newly industrializing countries (NICs) Less developed countries whose economies and whose trade now include significant amounts of manufactured products. As a result, these countries have a per capita GDP significantly higher than the average per capita GDP for less developed countries. **41, 305**

Nongovernmental organizations (NGOs or INGOs) International/transnational organizations with private memberships. **50, 161**

Nonproliferation A prohibition against the transfer of nuclear weapons, material, or technology from nuclear-capable to nonnuclear-capable countries. **281**

Non–status quo situations Circumstances or events that depart from the existing norm and that portend innovative policy that significantly changes established policy direction. **64**

Nontariff barrier (NTB) A nonmonetary restriction on trade, such as quotas, technical specifications, or unnecessarily lengthy quarantine and inspection procedures. **343**

Norms A principle of right action that is binding on members of a group and that serves to regulate the behavior of the members of that group. The word is based on the Latin *norma*, which means a carpenter's square or an accurate measure. Norms are based on custom and usage and may also become part of formal law. Norms are recognized in international law under the principle of *jus cogens* (just thought), which states that a standard of behavior accepted by the world community should not be violated by the actions of a state or group of states. In domestic systems, "common law" is equivalent to norms in the international system. **57**

North American Free Trade Agreement (NAFTA) An economic agreement among Canada, Mexico, and the United States that went into effect on January 1, 1994. It will eliminate most trade barriers by 2009 and will also eliminate or reduce restrictions on foreign investments and other financial transactions among the NAFTA countries. **364**

North-South Axis The growing tension between the few economically developed countries (North) and the many economically deprived countries (South). The South is demanding that the North cease economic and political domination and redistribute part of its wealth. **41**

NUT (Nuclear Utilization Theory) The belief that because nuclear war might occur, countries must be ready to fight, survive, and win a nuclear war. NUT advocates believe this posture will limit the damage if nuclear war occurs and also make nuclear war less likely by creating retaliatory options that are more credible than massive retaliation. **277**

On-site inspection (OSI) An arms control verification technique that involves stationing your or a neutral country's personnel in another country to monitor weapons or delivery vehicle manufacturing, testing, deployment, or other aspects of treaty compliance. **286**

Open diplomacy The public conduct of negotiations and the publication of agreements. **218**

Operational reality The process by which what is perceived, whether that perception is accurate or not, assumes a level of reality in the mind of the beholder and becomes the basis for making an operational decision (a decision about what to do). **86**

Organization for Economic Cooperation and Development (OECD) An organization that has existed since 1948 (and since 1960 under its present name) to facilitate the exchange of information and otherwise to promote cooperation among the economically developed countries. In recent years, the OECD has begun to accept as members a few newly industrializing and former communist countries in transition. 350

Organization for Security and Cooperation in Europe (OSCE) Series of conferences among 34 NATO, former Soviet bloc, and neutral European countries that led to permanent organization. Established by 1976 Helsinki Accords. 289

Pacta sunt servanda Translates as "treaties are to be served/carried out" and means that agreements between states are binding. 235

Parliamentary diplomacy Debate and voting in international organizations to settle diplomatic issues. 217

Peacekeeping The use of military means by an international organization such as the United Nations to prevent fighting, usually by acting as a buffer between combatants. The international force is neutral between the combatants and must have been invited to be present by at least one of the combatants. *See* **Collective security.** 290

Peacemaking The restoration of peace through, if necessary, the use of offensive military force to make one or all sides of a conflict cease their violent behavior. 291

Plenary representative body An assembly, such as the UN's General Assembly, that consists of all members of the main organization. 180

Political culture A concept that refers to a society's general, long-held, and fundamental practices and attitudes. These are based on a country's historical experience and on the values (norms) of its citizens. These attitudes are often an important part of the internal setting in which national leaders make foreign policy. 65

Political executives Those officials, usually but not always in the executive branch of a government, who are at the center of foreign policy making and whose tenures are variable and dependent on the political contest for power. 66

Popular sovereignty A political doctrine that holds that sovereign political authority resides with the citizens of a state. According to this doctrine, the citizenry grant a certain amount of authority to the state, its government, and, especially, its specific political leaders (such as monarchs, presidents, and prime ministers), but do not surrender ultimate sovereignty. 28, 95

Positivist (school) Those who believe that law reflects society and the way that people want the society to operate. 234

Power The totality of a country's international capabilities. Power is based on multiple resources, which alone or in concert allow one country to have its interests prevail in the international system. Power is especially important in enabling one state to achieve its goals when it clashes with the goals and wills of other international actors. 200

Power to defeat The ability to overcome in a traditional military sense—that is, to overcome enemy armies and capture and hold territory. 267

Power to hurt The ability to inflict pain outside the immediate battle area; sometimes called coercive violence. It is often used against civilians and is a particular hallmark of terrorism and nuclear warfare. 267

Primary products Agricultural products and raw materials, such as minerals. 303

Protectionism The use of tariffs and nontariff barriers to restrict the flow of imports into one's country. 332

Public diplomacy A process of creating an overall international image that enhances your ability to achieve diplomatic success. 221

Real dollars The value of dollars expressed in terms of a base year. This is determined by taking current value and subtracting the amount of inflation between the base year and the year being reported. Sometimes called uninflated dollars. Any currency can be valued in real terms. *See* **Current dollars.** 299

Realists Analysts who believe that countries operate in their own self-interests and that politics is a struggle for power. 13

Realpolitik Operating according to the belief that politics is based on the pursuit, possession, and application of power. 31

Regime A complex of norms, treaties, international organizations, and transnational activity that orders an area of activity such as the environment or oceans. 167

Regional government A possible middle level of governance between the prevalent national governments of today and the world government that some people favor. The regional structure that comes closest to (but still well short of) a regional government is the European Union. 168

Relative power Power measured in comparison with the power of other international actors. 202

Role How an individual's position influences his or her thinking and actions. 79

SALT I The Strategic Arms Limitation Treaty signed in 1972. 281

SALT II The Strategic Arms Limitation Treaty signed in 1979 but withdrawn by President Carter from the U.S. Senate before ratification in response to the Soviet invasion of Afghanistan. 281

Secretariat The administrative organ of the United Nations, headed by the secretary-general. In general, the administrative element of any IGO, headed by a secretary-general. 183

Security Council The main peacekeeping organ of the United Nations. The Security Council has 15 members, including 5 permanent members. 180

Services trade The purchase (import) from or sale (export) to another country of intangibles such as architectural fees; insurance premiums; royalties on movies, books, patents, and other intellectual properties; shipping services; advertising fees, and educational programs. **312**

Situational power The power that can be applied, and is reasonable, in a given situation. Not all elements of power can be applied to every situation. **203**

Social Darwinism A social theory that argues it is proper that stronger peoples will prosper and will dominate lesser peoples. **385**

Sovereignty The most essential characteristic of an international state. The term strongly implies political independence from any higher authority and also suggests at least theoretical equality. **27, 138**

Special drawing rights (SDRs) Reserves held by the International Monetary Fund that the central banks of member-countries can draw on to help manage the values of their currencies. SDR value is based on a "market-basket" of currencies, and SDRs are acceptable in transactions between central banks. **355**

State A political actor that has sovereignty and a number of characteristics, including territory, population, organization, and recognition. **138**

State terrorism Terrorism carried out directly by, or encouraged and funded by, an established government of a state (country). **271**

State-level analysis An analytical approach that emphasizes the actions of states and the internal (domestic) causes of their policies. **22**

Status quo situations Circumstances or events that conform to the existing norm and that are apt to evoke incremental policy decisions that do not significantly change basic policy direction. **64**

Strategic Arms Reduction Talks (START I) Treaty I A nuclear weapons treaty signed by the Soviet Union and the United States in 1991 and later re-signed with Belarus, Kazakhstan, Russia, and Ukraine that will limit Russia and the United States to 1,600 delivery vehicles and 6,000 strategic explosive nuclear devices each, with the other three countries destroying their nuclear weapons or transferring them to Russia. **281**

Strategic Arms Reduction Talks (START II) Treaty II A nuclear weapons treaty signed by the Soviet Union and the United States in 1993, which establishes nuclear warhead and bomb ceilings of 3,500 for the United States and 2,997 for Russia by the year 2003 and that also eliminates some types of weapons systems. To date (1999) the treaty has not been ratified by the Russian parliament and, therefore, the treaty is not legally in effect. **281**

Subnational actors Institutions and other elements of a country's political structure, including the political leadership, legislature, bureaucracy, interest groups, political opposition, and the public. **66**

Summitry Diplomatic negotiations between national leaders. **219**

Supranational organization Organization that is founded and operates, at least in part, on the idea that international organizations can or should have authority higher than individual states and that those states should be subordinate to the supranational organization. **168**

Sustainable development The ability to continue to improve the quality of life of those in the industrialized countries and, particularly, those in the less developed countries while simultaneously protecting the Earth's biosphere. **401**

System-level analysis An analytical approach that emphasizes the importance of the impact of world conditions (economics, technology, power relationships, and so forth) on the actions of states and other international actors. **22**

Tariff A tax, usually based on percentage of value, that importers must pay on items purchased abroad; also known as an import tax or import duty. **343**

Third World A term once commonly used to designate the countries of Asia, Africa, Latin America, and elsewhere that were economically less developed. The phrase is attributed to French analyst Alfred Sauvy, who in 1952 used *tiers monde* to describe neutral countries in the cold war. By inference, the U.S.-led Western bloc and the Soviet-led Eastern bloc were the other two worlds. But since most of the neutral countries were also relatively poor, the phrase had a double meaning. Sauvy used the older *tiers*, instead of the more modern *troisième*, to allude to the pre-Revolutionary (1789) third estate (*tiers état*), that is, the underprivileged class, the commoners. The nobility and the clergy were the first and second estates. Based on this second meaning, Third World came most commonly to designate the less developed countries of the world, whatever their political orientation. The phrase is less often used since the end of the cold war, although some analysts continue to employ it to designate the less developed countries. **391**

Transnational actors Organizations that operate internationally, but whose membership, unlike IGOs, is private. **50**

Transnational corporations (TNCs) A transnational corporation is a business enterprise that conducts business beyond just selling its product in more than one country. Countries with factories in several countries are TNCs, as are banks with branches in more than one country. The businesses are also referred to as multinational corporations (MNCs). The two terms are synonymous; TNC is used herein based on UN usage. **50**

Transnationalism Extension beyond the borders of a single country; applies to a political movement, issue, organization, or other phenomenon. **114**

Trilateral countries The United States and Canada, Japan, and the Western European countries. **331**

Two-level game The concept that in order to arrive at satisfactory international agreements, a country's diplomats actually have to deal with (at one level) the other country's negotiators and (at the second level) legislators, interest groups, and other domestic forces at home. **67**

UN Conference on Population and Development (UNCPD) A UN–sponsored conference that met in Cairo, Egypt, in September 1994 and was attended by delegates from more than 170 countries. The conference called for a program of action to include spending $17 billion annually by the year 2000 on international, national, and local programs to foster family planning and to improve the access of women in such areas as education. **411**

UN Conference on Trade and Development (UNC-TAD) A UN organization established in 1964 and currently consisting of all UN members plus the Holy See, Switzerland, and Tonga, that hold quadrennial meetings aimed at promoting international trade and economic development. **349**

UN Industrial Development Organization (UNIDO) A UN specialized agency established in 1967, currently having 165 members, that promotes the industrialization of economically less developed countries. **349**

UN Development Programme (UNDP) An agency of the UN established in 1965 to provide technical assistance to stimulate economic and social development in the economically less developed countries. The UNDP has 48 members selected on a rotating basis from the world's regions. **348**

Uruguay Round The eighth, and latest, round of GATT negotiations to reduce tariffs and nontariff barriers to trade. The eighth round was convened in Punta del Este, Uruguay, in 1986 and its resulting agreements were signed in Marrakesh, Morocco, in April 1994. **352**

Veto A negative vote cast in the UN Security Council by one of the five permanent members; has the effect of defeating the issue being voted on. **182**

Vietnam analogy An aversion to foreign armed intervention, especially in conflicts in less developed countries involving guerrillas. This attitude is especially common among political leaders and other individuals who were opposed to the U.S. war in Vietnam or who were otherwise influenced by the failed U.S. effort there and the domestic turmoil that resulted. **84**

West Historically, Europe and those countries and regions whose cultures were founded on or converted to European culture. Such countries would include Australia, Canada, New Zealand, and the United States. The majority of the populations in these countries are also "white," in the European, not the larger Caucasian, sense. After World War II, the term West took on two somewhat different but related meanings. One referred to the countries allied with the United States and opposed to the Soviet Union and its allies, called the East. The West also came to mean the industrial democracies, including Japan. *See* **Eurowhites 28**

World Bank Group Four associated agencies that grant loans to LDCs for economic development and other financial needs. Two of the agencies, the International Bank for Reconstruction and Development (IBRD) and the International Development Association (IDA), are collectively referred to as the World Bank. The other two agencies are the International Finance Corporation (IFC) and the Multilateral Investment Guarantee Agency (MIGA). **360**

World government The concept of a supranational world authority to which current countries would surrender some or all of their sovereign authority. **168**

World Trade Organization (WTO) The organization that replaced the General Agreement on Tariffs and Trade (GATT) organization as the body that implements GATT, the treaty. **352**

Xenophobia Fear of others, "they-groups." **99**

Abbreviations

The following abbreviations are used in the text:

ABM	Anti-Ballistic Missile
APEC	Asian Pacific Economic Cooperation Forum
ASEAN	Association of Southeast Asian Nations
ATTU	Atlantic to the Urals (region)
BIS	Bank for International Settlement
BMD	Ballistic Missile Defense
CEDAW	Committee on the Elimination of Discrimination Against Women
CFE	Conventional Forces in Europe (treaty)
CIS	Commonwealth of Independent States
CIT	Country in transition
CITES	Convention on the International Trade in Endangered Species
CSW	Commission on the State of Women
CTBT	Comprehensive Test Ban Treaty
CWC	Chemical Weapons Convention
EC	European Community
ECJ	European Court of Justice
ECOSOC	Economic and Social Council
ECOWAS	Economic Community of West African States
ECSC	European Coal and Steel Community
EDC	Economically Developed Country
EEC	European Economic Community
EMS	European Monetary System
EP	European Parliament
EPA	Environmental Protection Agency
EU	European Union
EURATOM	European Atomic Energy Community
FAO	Food and Agriculture Organization (United Nations)

FDI	Foreign Direct Investment
FIS	Front for Islamic Salvation
FPI	Foreign Portfolio Investment
FSR	Former Soviet Republic
FTAA	Free Trade Agreement Area of the Americas
GATT	General Agreement on Tariffs and Trade
GCD	General and Complete Disarmament
GCP	Gross Corporate Product
GDP	Gross Domestic Product
GNP	Gross National Product
GPS	Global Positioning System
HDI	Human Development Index
IAEA	International Atomic Energy Agency
IBRD	International Bank for Reconstruction and Development
ICBM	Intercontinental Ballistic Missile
ICJ	International Court of Justice
IDA	International Development Association
IFAD	International Fund for Agricultural Development
IFC	International Finance Corporation
IFOR	International Force
IGO	Intergovernmental Organization
ILO	International Labor Organization
IMF	International Monetary Fund
IOM	International Organization for Migration
IPCC	International Panel on Climatic Change
IPE	International Political Economy
IPPF	International Planned Parenthood Federation

JCS	Joint Chiefs of Staff
LDC	Less Developed Country
LLDC	Least Developed Country
MAD	Mutual Assured Destruction
MFN	Most-Favored-Nation
MNC	Multinational Corporation
MTCR	Missile Technology Control Regime
NAFTA	North American Free Trade Association; North American Free Trade Agreement
NATO	North Atlantic Treaty Organization
NBC	Nuclear-Biological-Chemical
NGO	Nongovernmental Organization
NIC	Newly Industrializing Country
NIEO	New International Economic Order
NPT	Non-Proliferation Treaty
NSC	National Security Council
NTB	Nontariff Barrier
NTM	National Technical Means
NUT	Nuclear Utilization Theory
OAS	Organization of American States
OAU	Organization of African Unity
ODA	Official Development Aid
OECD	Organization for Economic Cooperation and Development
OSCE	Organization for Security and Cooperation in Europe
OSI	On-Site Inspection
PCIJ	Permanent Court of International Justice
PLA	People's Liberation Army (China)
PLO	Palestine Liberation Organization
SALT	Strategic Arms Limitation Talks
SDF	Self-Defense Force (Japan)
SDI	Strategic Defense Initiative

SDR	Special Drawing Right
SLBM	Sea-Launched Ballistic Missile
START	Strategic Arms Reduction Talks
THAAD	Theater High Altitude Area Defense
TNC	Transnational Corporation
UN	United Nations
UNCED	United Nations Conference on Environment and Development
UNCHR	United Nations Commission on Human Rights
UNCPD	United Nations Conference on Population and Development
UNCTAD	United Nations Council on Trade and Development
UNDAR	Universal Declaration of Human Rights
UNDP	United Nations Development Programme
UNEP	United Nations Environment Program
UNESCO	United Nations Educational, Scientific, and Cultural Organization
UNFPA	United Nations Population Fund
UNGA	United Nations General Assembly
UNICEF	United Nations Children's Fund
UNIDO	United Nations Industrial Development Organization
UNIFEM	UN Fund for Women
UNSC	United Nations Security Council
VAT	Value-Added Tax
WCHR	World Conference on Human Rights
WCW	World Conference on Women
WEU	Western European Union
WFC	World Food Council
WHO	World Health Organization
WTO	Warsaw Treaty Organization (Warsaw Pact)

References

Abbott, Kenneth W., and Duncan Snidal. 1998. "Why States Act through Formal International Organizations." *Journal of Conflict Organization,* 42:3–32.

Alleyne, Mark D. 1995. *International Power and International Communication.* New York: Macmillan.

Alter, Karen J. 1998. "Who Are the 'Masters of the Treaty'?: European Governments and the European Court of Justice." *International Organization,* 52:121–148

Alulis, Joseph, and Vickie Sullivan, eds. 1996. *Shakespeare's Political Pageant: Essays in Politics and Literature.* Boulder, CO: Rowman & Littlefield.

Ambrose, Stephen E. 1991. *Nixon: The Triumph of a Politician, 1962–1972.* New York: Simon & Schuster.

Anderson, Robert B. 1994. "Inter-IGO Dynamics in the Post–Cold War World: The O.A.S. and the U.N." Presented at the annual meeting of the International Studies Association, Washington, DC.

Archer, Clive. 1983. *International Organizations.* London: Allen & Unwin.

Arend, Anthony Clark, and Robert J. Beck. 1994. *International Law and the Use of Force.* New York: Routledge.

Arnett, Eric. 1997. *Military Capacity and the Risk of War: China, India, Pakistan and Iran.* Oxford, UK: Oxford University Press.

Attali, Jacques. 1997. "The Clash of Western Civilization: The Limits of the Market and Democracy." *Foreign Policy,* 107:54–64.

Audley, John J. 1997. *Green Politics and Global Trade: NAFTA and the Future of Environmental Politics.* Washington, DC: Georgetown University Press.

Bacchus, William I. 1997. *The Price of American Foreign Policy: Congress, The Executive, and International Affairs Funding.* University Park: University of Pennsylvania Press.

Balaam, David N., and Michael Veseth. 1996. *Introduction to International Political Economy.* Upper Saddle River, NJ: Prentice Hall.

Barber, Benjamin R. 1995. *Jihad vs. McWorld.* New York: Times Books/Random House.

Barber, Charles T. 1996. "UN Security Council Representation: The First 50 Years and Beyond." Paper presented at the International Studies Association convention, San Diego.

Barber, James David. 1985. *Presidential Character,* 3rd ed. Englewood Cliffs, NJ: Prentice Hall.

Barkey, Karen, and Mark von Hagen, eds. 1997. *After Empire: Multi-Ethnic Societies and Nation-Building.* Boulder, CO: Westview.

Barnet, Richard J., and Cavanagh, John. 1994. *Global Dreams: Imperial Corporations and the New World Order.* Washington, DC: Institute for Policy Studies.

Barrington, Lowell W. 1997. "Nation and 'Nationalism': The Misuse of Key Concepts in Political Science." *PS: Political Science & Politics,* 30:712–724.

Bartelson, Jens. 1995. *The Genealogy of Sovereignty.* New York: Cambridge University Press.

Beckerman, Wilfred, and Jess Malkin. 1994. "How Much Does Global Warming Matter?" *Public Interest,* 114:3–16.

Beer, Francis A. 1990. "The Reduction of War and the Creation of Peace." In *A Reader in Peace Studies,* ed. Paul Smoker, Ruth Davies, and Barbara Munske. New York: Pergamon.

Beer, Francis A., and Robert Harriman, eds. 1996. *Post-Realism: The Rhetorical Turn in International Relations.* Ann Arbor: University of Michigan Press.

Belgrad, Eric A., and Nitza Nachmias. 1997. *The Politics of International Humanitarian Aid Operations.* Westport, CT: Praeger.

Bellany, Ian. 1997. *The Environment in World Politics: Exploring the Limits.* Lyme, NH: Edward Elgar.

Bennett, D. Scott. 1996. "Security, Bargaining, and the End of Interstate Rivalry." *International Studies Quarterly,* 40:157–184.

Bennett, D. Scott. 1997. "Testing Alternative Models of Alliance Duration, 1816–1984." *American Journal of Political Science,* 41:846–878.

Bennett, D. Scott, and Allan C. Stam III. 1996. "The Duration of Interstate Wars, 1816–1985." *American Political Science Review,* 90:239–257.

Beres, Louis René. 1995. "Assassination and the Law: A Policy Memorandum." *Studies in Conflict and Terrorism,* 18:299–315.

Blanton, Shannon Lindsey. 1996. "Images in Conflict: The Case of Ronald Reagan and El Salvador." *International Studies Quarterly,* 40:23–44.

Bloomfield, Lincoln P., and Allen Moulton. 1997. *Managing International Conflict: From Theory to Policy.* New York: St. Martin's Press.

Bobrow, Davis B., and Mark A. Boyer. 1998. "International System Stability and American Decline: A Case for Muted Optimism." *International Journal,* 53:285–305.

Bodie, Thomas J. 1995. *Politics and the Emergence of an Activist International Court of Justice.* Westport, CT: Praeger.

Bohlen, Charles E. 1973. *Witness to History.* New York: W. W. Norton.

Bohman, James, and Matthias Lutz-Bachmann, eds. 1997. *Perpetual Peace: Essays on Kant's Cosmopolitan Ideal.* Cambridge, MA: MIT Press.

Bond, Doug. 1992. "Introduction." In *Transforming Struggle: Strategy and the Global Experience of Nonviolent Direct Action.* Cambridge, MA: Program on Nonviolent Sanction in Conflict and Defense, Center for International Affairs, Harvard University.

Bouton, Marshall M. 1998. "India's Problem Is Not Politics." *Foreign Affairs,* 77/3:80–94.

Bova, Russell. 1997. "Democracy and Liberty: The Cultural Connection." *Journal of Democracy,* 8:112–125.

Boyer, Mark A. 1993. *International Cooperation and Public Goods: Opportunities for the Western Alliance.* Baltimore: Johns Hopkins University Press.

Boyer, Mark A. 1996. "Political System and the Logic of Two-Level Games: Moving beyond Democracies in the Study of International Negotiation." Paper presented at the International Studies Association Northeast convention, Boston.

Boyer, Mark A. 1999. "Issue Definition and Two-Level Games: An Application to the American Foreign Policy Process," *Diplomacy and Statecraft,* 10(3).

Brandes, Lisa C. O. 1993. "Who Cares? Interest, Concern, and Gender in International Security Policy." Presented at the annual meeting of the International Studies Association, Acapulco, Mexico.

Brandes, Lisa, C. O. 1994. "The Liberal Feminist State and War." Presented at the annual meeting of the American Political Science Association, New York.

Brawley, Mark. 1996. "Economic Coercion by a Power in Relative Decline: Why Sanctions May Be More Effective as Hegemonic Leadership Ebbs." Paper presented at the International Studies Association convention, San Diego.

Breuning, Marijke. 1995. "Culture, History, and Role: How the Past Shapes Foreign Policy Now." Paper presented at the International Studies Association convention, Chicago.

Breuning, Marijke. 1996. "Nationalist Parties and Foreign Policy Assistance." Paper presented at the International Studies Association convention, San Diego.

Brilmayer, Lea. 1994. *American Hegemony: Political Morality in a One-Superpower World.* New Haven, CT: Yale University Press.

Brooks, Stephen G. 1997. "Dueling Realisms." *International Organization,* 51:445–478.

Brown, Lester, ed. 1998. *State of the World 1998.* New York: W. W. Norton.

Brown, Michael E., Sean Lynn-Jones, and Steven E. Miller, eds. 1996. *Debating the Democratic Peace.* Cambridge, MA: MIT Press.

Brown, Seyom. 1988. *New Forces, Old Forces, and the Future of World Politics.* Glenville, IL: Scott, Foresman.

Brown, Seyom. 1992. *International Relations in a Changing Global System.* Boulder, CO: Westview.

Brown, Seyom. 1998. "World Interests and the Changing Dimension of Security." In *World Security: Challenges for a New Century,* 3rd ed., ed. Michael T. Klare and Yogesh Chandran. New York: St. Martin's.

Brzoska, Michael, and Frederick Pearson. 1994. *Arms and Warfare: Escalation, Deescalation, and Negotiation.* Columbia: University of South Carolina Press.

Bueno de Mesquita, Bruce J., James D. Morrow, Randolph Siverson, and Alistair Smith. 1998. "An Institutional Analysis of the Democratic Peace." Paper presented at the International Studies Association convention, Minneapolis.

Bueno de Mesquita, Bruce J., and Randolph M. Siverson. 1995. "War and the Survival of Political Leaders: A Comparative Study of Regime Types and Political Accountability." *American Political Science Review,* 89:841–855.

Bull, Hedley, and Adam Watson. 1982. *The Expansion of International Society.* London: Oxford University Press.

Bunch, Charlotte, and Roxana Carillo. 1998. "Global Violence against Women: The Challenge to Human Rights and Development." In *World Security: Challenges for a New Century,* 3rd ed., ed. Michael T. Klare and Yogesh Chandran. New York: St. Martin's.

Burch, Kurt, and Robert A. Denemark, eds. 1997. *Constituting International Political Economy: International Political Economy Yearbook, vol. 10.* Boulder, CO: Lynne Rienner.

Bureau of the Census. See (U.S.) Bureau of the Census and U.S. Economics and Statistics Administration.

Burk, Erika. 1994. "Human Rights and Social Issues." In *A Global Agenda: Issues before the 49th General Assembly,* ed. John Tessitore and Susan Woolfson. Lanham, MD: University Press of America.

Burns, Timothy, ed. 1994. *After History: Francis Fukuyama and His Critics.* Lanham, MD: Rowman & Littlefield.

Burrowes, Robert J. 1996. *The Strategy of Nonviolent Defense.* Albany: State University of New York Press.

Cafruny, Alan W., and Carl Lankowski, eds. 1997. *Europe's Ambiguous Unity: Conflict and Consensus in the Post-Maastricht Era.* Boulder,CO: Lynne Rienner.

Caldwell, Lynton Keith. 1996. *International Environmental Policy: From the Twentieth to the Twenty-First Century.* Durham, NC: Duke University Press.

Camilleri, Joseph A. 1990. "Rethinking Sovereignty in a Striking, Fragmented World." In *Contending Sovereignties: Redefining Political Community,* ed. R. B. J. Walker and Saul H. Mendlovitz. Boulder, CO: Lynne Rienner.

Caplan, Richard, and John Feffer, eds. 1996. *Europe's New Nationalism: States and Minorities in Conflict.* New York: Oxford University Press.

Caprioli, Mary. "Why Democracy?" In *Taking Sides: Clashing Views on Controversial Issues in World Politics,* 8th ed., ed. John T. Rourke. Guilford, CT: Dushkin/McGraw-Hill.

Caprioli, Mary, and Mark A. Boyer, 1999. "The Impact of Gender on International Crises: Tough Cases for Analysis?" Unpublished manuscript.

Carlson, Lisa J. 1995. "A Theory of Escalation of International Conflict." *Journal of Conflict Resolution,* 39:511–534.

Carment, David. 1994. "The Ethnic Dimension in World Politics: Theory, Policy, and Early Warning." *Third World Quarterly,* 15:551–579.

Carter, Jimmy. Speech, December 6, 1978. *Department of State Bulletin,* January 1979.

Cederman, Lars-Erik. 1997. *Emergent Actors in World Politics: How States and Nations Develop and Dissolve.* Princeton, NJ: Princeton University Press.

Central Intelligence Agency. *See* U.S. (CIA).

Chan, Steve. 1997. "In Search of Democratic Peace: Problems and Promise." *Mershon International Studies Review,* 41:59–91.

Chang, Lawrence. 1992. "The View from Washington." In *The Cuban Missile Crisis Revisited,* ed. James N. Nathan. New York: St. Martin's.

Chen, Martha Alter. 1995. "Engendering World Conferences: The International Women's Movement and the United Nations." *The Third World Quarterly,* 16:477–495.

Choucri, Nazli. 1995. *Global Accord: Environmental Challenges and International Responses.* Cambridge, MA: MIT Press.

CIA. *See* U.S. (CIA).

Cimbala, Stephen J. 1995. "Deterrence Stability with Smaller Forces: Prospects and Problems." *Journal of Peace Research,* 32:65–78.

Cini, Michelle. 1997. *The European Commission: Leadership, Organization and Culture in the EU Administration.* New York: Manchester University Press.

Cioffi-Revilla, Claudio. 1996. "Origins and Evolution of War and Politics." *International Studies Quarterly,* 40:1–22.

Clark, Ann Marie. 1995. "Non-Governmental Organizations and Their Influence on International Society." *Journal of International Affairs,* 48:507–526.

Clark, Ann Marie. 1996. "The Contribution of Non-Governmental Organizations to the Creation and Strengthening of International Human Rights Norms." Paper presented at the International Studies Association convention, San Diego.

Clinton, W. David. 1994. *The Two Faces of National Interest.* Baton Rouge: Louisiana State University Press.

Cohen, Bernard C. 1995. *Democracies and Foreign Policy: Public Participation in the United States and the Netherlands.* Madison: University of Wisconsin Press.

Conca, Ken. 1995. "Greening the United Nations: Environmental Organizations and the UN System." *Third World Quarterly,* 16:441–458.

Conley, Richard S. 1997. "Sovereignty or the Status Quo: The 1995 Pre-Referendum Debate in Québec." *The Journal of Commonwealth & Comparative Politics,* 35:67–92.

Conover, Pamela Johnston, and Virginia Sapiro. 1993. "Gender, Feminist Consciousness, and War." *American Journal of Political Science,* 37:1079–1099.

Cook, Rebecca, ed. 1994. *Human Rights of Women: National and International Perspectives.* Philadelphia: University of Pennsylvania Press.

Cornelius, Wayne A., Philip L. Martin, and James F. Hollifield, eds. 1995. *Controlling Immigration: A Global Perspective.* Stanford, CA: Stanford University Press.

Cortell, Andrew P., and James W. Davis Jr. 1996. "How Do International Institutions Matter? The Domestic Impact of International Rules and Norms." *International Studies Quarterly,* 40:451–478.

Cortright, David, and George A. Lopez, eds. 1996. *Economic Sanctions: Panacea or Peacebuilding in a Post–Cold War World?* Boulder, CO: Westview.

Cox, Robert W., ed. 1997. *The New Realism: Perspectives on Multilateralism and World Order.* New York: St. Martin's.

Craig, Gordon A., and Alexander L. George. 1995. *Force and Statecraft: Diplomatic Problems of Our Time,* 3rd ed. New York: Oxford University Press.

Cronin, Bruce. 1994. "The State and the Nation: Changing Norms and the Rules of Sovereignty in International Relations." *International Organization,* 48:107–131.

Crumm, Eileen M. 1995. "The Value of Economic Incentives in International Politics." *Journal of Peace Research,* 32:313–330.

Crystal, Jonathan. 1998. "A New Kind of Competition: How American Producers Respond to Incoming Foreign Direct Investment." *International Studies Quarterly,* 42:513–544.

Cusack, Thomas R., and Richard Stoll. 1994. "Collective Security and State Survival in the Interstate System." *International Studies Quarterly,* 38:33–59.

D'Amato, Anthony, ed. 1994. *International Law Anthology.* Cincinnati, OH: Anderson.

Deibert, Ronald. 1997. *Parchment, Printing, and Hypermedia: Communication and World Order Transformation.* New York: Columbia University Press.

Diamond, Larry. 1994. "The Global Imperative: Building a Democratic World Order." *Current History,* 93 (579):1–7.

Dickson, Anna K. 1997. *Development and International Relations: A Critical Introduction.* Cambridge, UK: Polity Press.

DiClerico, Robert E. 1979. *The American President.* Englewood Cliffs, NJ: Prentice Hall.

Diehl, Paul F., ed. 1996. *The Politics of Global Governance: International Organizations in an Interdependent World.* Boulder, CO: Lynne Rienner.

Diehl, Paul, ed. 1997. *The Politics of Global Governance: International Organizations in an Interdependent World.* Boulder, CO: Lynne Rienner.

Diehl, Paul F., Daniel Druckman, and James Wall. 1998. "International Peacekeeping and Conflict Resolution: A Taxonomic Analysis with Implications." *Journal of Conflict Resolution,* 42:33–55.

Dinan, Desmond. 1994. *Ever Closer Union? An Introduction to the European Community.* Boulder, CO: Lynne Rienner.

Dogan, Mattei. 1994. "The Decline of Nationalisms in Western Europe." *Comparative Politics,* 23:281–306.

Druckman, Daniel. 1994. "Nationalism, Patriotism and Group Loyalty: A Social Psychological Perspective." *Mershon International Studies Review,* supplement to *International Studies Quarterly,* 38:43–68.

Duchacek, Ivo D. 1975. *Nations and Men.* Hinsdale, IL: Dryden.

Dunn, David H., ed. 1996. *Diplomacy at the Highest Level: The Evolution of International Summitry.* New York: St. Martin's.

Dunn, John. 1995. "Introduction: Crisis of the Nation State?" In *Contemporary Crisis of the Nation State?* ed. John Dunn. Oxford, U.K.: Blackwell.

Ebenstein, Alan O., William Ebenstein, and Edwin Fogelman. 1994. *Today's Isms: Socialism, Capitalism, Fascism, and Communism.* Englewood Cliffs, NJ: Prentice Hall.

Eichengreen, Barry. 1998. "Geography as Destiny." *Foreign Affairs,* 77/2:128–139.

El-Agraa, Ali M., ed. 1997. *Economic Integration Worldwide.* New York: St. Martin's.

Eley, Geoff, and Ronald Grigor Suny. 1996. *Becoming National.* New York: Oxford University Press.

Elliott, Kimberly Ann. 1993. "A Look at the Record." *Bulletin of the Atomic Scientists,* November.

Elliott, Kimberly Ann. 1998. "The Sanctions Glass: Half Full or Completely Empty?" *International Security,* 23:50–65.

Elman, Colin. 1996. "Why Not Neorealist Theories of Foreign Policy?" *Security Studies,* 6:7–53.

Elman, Miriam Fendius. 1995. "The Foreign Policies of Small States: Challenging Neorealism in Its Own Backyard." *British Journal of Political Science,* 25:171–217.

Elman, Miriam Fendius, ed. 1997. *Paths to Peace: Is Democracy the Answer?* Cambridge, MA: MIT Press.

Ember, Carol R., and Melvin Ember. 1996. "War, Socialization, and Interpersonal Violence." *Journal of Conflict Resolution,* 38:620–646.

Engleman, Robert, and Pamela LeRoy. 1995. *Sustaining Water: An Update.* Washington, DC: Population Action International.

Esman, Milton J., and Shibley Telhami, eds. 1995. *International Organizations and Ethnic Conflict.* Ithaca: Cornell University Press.

Esposito, John L., ed. 1997. *Political Islam: Revolution, Radicalism, or Reform?* Boulder, CO: Lynne Rienner.

Etzioni, Amitai. 1993. "The Evils of Self-Determination." *Foreign Policy,* 89:21–35.

(FAO) Food and Agricultural Organization. 1995. "Forest Resources Assessment 1990: Global Synthesis." *FAO Forestry Paper 124.* Rome: FAO.

Farber, Henry S., and Joanne Gowa. 1995. "Polities and Peace." *International Security,* 20:123–146.

Farnen, Russell, ed. 1994. *Nationalism, Ethnicity, and Identity: Cross-National and Comparative Perspectives.* New Brunswick, NJ: Transaction.

Farnham, Barbara, ed. 1994. *Avoiding Losses/Taking Risks.* Ann Arbor: University of Michigan Press.

Fearon, James D. 1995. "Rationalist Explanations for War." *International Organization,* 49:379–414.

Feaver, Peter D., and Emerson M. S. Niou. 1996. "Managing Nuclear Proliferation: Condemn, Strike, or Assist?" *International Studies Quarterly,* 40:209–234.

Feld, Werner J. 1979. *International Relations: A Transnational Approach.* New York: Alfred Publishing.

Felice, William F. 1996. *Taking Suffering Seriously: The Importance of Collective Human Rights.* Albany: State University of New York Press.

Ferguson, Yale H. and Richard W. Mansbach. 1996. *Polities: Authority, Identities, and Change.* Columbia: University of South Carolina Press.

Feron, James D. 1997. "Signaling Foreign Policy Interests." *Journal of Conflict Resolution,* 41:68–90.

Fewsmith, Joseph. 1994. "Reform, Resistance, and the Politics of Succession." In *Chinese Politics in Historical Perspective,* ed. Brantly Womack. Englewood Cliffs, NJ: Prentice Hall.

Finn, James, ed. 1997. *Freedom in the World: The Annual Survey of Political and Civil Liberties, 1996–1997.* New York: Freedom House.

Fisher, Samuel, and Richard Vengroff. 1995. "The 1994 Quebec Provincial Elections: Party Realignment, Independence Referendum, or More of the Same." *Quebec Studies,* 19:1–15.

Fitzmaurice, John. 1995. "The 1994 Referenda on EU Membership in Austria and Scandinavia." *Electoral Studies* 14:226–231.

Flavin, Christopher. 1996. "Facing up to the Risks of Climate Change." In *State of the World 1996,* ed. Lester R. Brown. New York: W. W. Norton.

Forde, Steven. 1995. "International Realism and the Science of Politics: Thucydides, Machiavelli, and Neorealism." *International Studies Quarterly,* 39: 141–160.

Fowler, Michael Ross, and Julie Marie Bunck. 1995. *Law, Power, and the Sovereign States: The Evolution and Application of the Concept of Sovereignty.* University Park: University of Pennsylvania Press.

Foyle, Douglas C. 1997. "Public Opinion and Foreign Policy: Elite Beliefs as a Mediating Variable." *International Studies Quarterly,* 41:141–170.

Fozouni, Bahman. 1995. "Confutation of Political Realism." *International Studies Quarterly,* 39:479–510.

Franck, Thomas M. 1997. "Is Personal Freedom a Western Value?" *American Journal of International Law.* 91:593–627.

Frankel, Benjamin, ed. 1994. "Realism." Symposium issue of *National Security.*

Freedom House. 1997. *Freedom in the World: The Annual Survey of Political Rights & Civil Liberties, 1996–1997.* New Brunswick, NJ: Transaction.

Frost, Mervyn. 1996. *Ethics in International Relations.* New York: Cambridge University Press.

Fukuyama, Francis. 1989. "The End of History?" *National Interest,* 16:3–18.

Gabel, Matthew. 1998. "Public Support for European Integration: An Empirical Test of Five Theories." *Journal of Politics,* 60:333–355.

Gallagher, Nancy W., ed. 1998. *Arms Control: New Approaches to Theory and Policy.* Newbury Park, UK: Frank Cass.

Galtung, Johan. 1994. *Human Rights in Another Key.* Cambridge, UK: Polity Press.

Gangadharan, Bindu, and Charles Mngomezulu. 1994. "Economic-Military Aid Dependence on the United States and the Breakdown of Authoritarian Regimes and the Transition to Democracy in the Third World: A Cross-National Analysis." Presented at the International Studies Association convention, Washington, DC.

Ganguly, Rajat, and Ray Taras. 1998. *Understanding Ethnic Conflict.* New York: Addison, Wesley, Longman.

Garrett, Geoffrey, R. Daniel Kelemen, and Heiner Schulz. 1998. "The European Court of Justice, National Governments, and Legal Integration in the European Union." *International Organization,* 52:149–176.

Gartner, Scott Sigmund, and Randolph M. Siverson. 1996. "War Expansion and War Outcome." *Journal of Conflict Resolution,* 40:4–15.

Gartzke, Erik. 1998. "Kant We All Just Get Along? Opportunity, Willingness, and the Origins of the Democratic Peace." *American Journal of Political Science,* 42:1–27.

Gaubatz, Kurt T. 1996. "Democratic States and Commitment in International Relations." *International Organization,* 50:109–139.

Geller, Daniel S. 1993. "Power Differentials and War in Rival Dyads." *International Studies Quarterly,* 37:173–193.

Geller, Daniel S., and J. David Singer. 1998. *Nations at War: A Scientific Study of International Conflict.* Cambridge, U.K.: Cambridge University Press.

Gellner, Ernest. 1995. "Introduction." In *Notions of Nationalism,* ed. Sukumar Periwal. Budapest: Central European University Press.

George, Alexander L. 1994. "Some Guides to Bridging the Gap." *Mershon International Studies Review,* 39:171–172.

Gerner, Deborah J. 1995. "The Evolution of the Study of Foreign Policy." In *Foreign Policy Analysis,.* ed. Laura Neack, Jeane A. K. Hey, and Patrick J. Haney. Englewood Cliffs, NJ: Prentice Hall.

Geva, Hehemia, and Alex Mintz, eds. 1997. *Decisionmaking on War and Peace: The Cognitive-Rational Debate.* Boulder, CO: Lynne Rienner.

Gibbs, David N. 1995. "Secrecy and International Relations." *Journal of Peace Research,* 32:213–238.

Gilpin, Robert. 1981. *War and Change in World Politics.* Cambridge, U.K.: Cambridge University Press.

Glad, Betty. 1989. "Personality, Political and Group Process Variables in Foreign Policy Decision Making: Jimmy Carter's Handling of the Iranian Hostage Crisis." *International Political Science Review,* 10:35–61.

Gleditsch, Nils Petter, and Håvard Hegre. 1997. "Peace and Democracy: Three Levels of Analysis." *Journal of Conflict Resolution*, 41:283–310.

Gochman, Charles S., and Aaron M. Hoffman. 1996. "Peace in the Balance? A Matter of Design." *International Studies Notes*, 21/2 (Spring): 20–25.

Gordenker, Leon, and Thomas G. Weiss. 1995. "NGO Participation in the International Policy Process." *Third World Quarterly*, 16:543–556.

Gowa, Joanne. 1995. "Democratic States and International Disputes." *International Organization*, 49:511–522.

Graebner, Norman, ed. 1964. *Ideas and Diplomacy.* New York: Oxford University Press.

Graham, Norman A., ed. 1994. *Seeking Security and Development: The Impact of Military Spending and Arms Transfers.* Boulder, CO: Lynne Rienner.

Grant, Rebecca, and Kathleen Newland, eds. 1991. *Gender and International Relations.* Bloomington: Indiana University Press.

Gray, Colin S. 1994. "Force, Order, and Justice: The Ethics of Realism in Statecraft." *Global Affairs*, 14:1–17.

Greenfeld, Liah. 1992. *Nationalism: Five Roads to Modernity.* Cambridge, MA: Harvard University Press.

Greenstein, Fred. 1995. "Political Style and Political Leadership: The Case of Bill Clinton." In *The Clinton Presidency: Campaigning, Governing, and the Psychology of Leadership*, ed. Stanley Renshon. Boulder, CO: Westview.

Griffin, Roger, ed. 1995. *Fascism.* New York: Oxford University Press.

Griffiths, Martin. 1995. *Realism, Idealism, and International Politics.* New York: Routledge.

Guéhnno, Jean Marie. 1995. *The End of the Nation-State.* Translated by Victoria Elliott. Minneapolis: University of Minnesota Press.

Guibernau, Montserrat. 1996. *Nationalisms: The Nation-State and Nationalism in the Twentieth Century.* Cambridge, U.K.: Polity Press.

Gurr, Ted Robert, and Michael Haxton. 1996. "Minorities Report (1). Ethnopolitical Conflict in the 1990s: Patterns and Trends." Paper presented at the International Studies Association convention, San Diego.

Haas, Michael. 1994. "International Communitarianism." Presented at the annual meeting of the American Political Science Association, Washington, DC.

Haas, Peter M., and David McCabe. 1996. "International Institutions and Social Learning in the Management of Global Environmental Risks." Paper presented at the International Studies Association convention, San Diego.

Hall, John. 1995. "Nationalism, Classified and Explained." In *Notions of Nationalism*, ed. Sukumar Periwal. Budapest: Central European University Press.

Hall, Rodney Bruce. 1999. *National Collective Identity: Social Constructs and International Systems.* New York: Columbia University Press.

Hampson, Fen Olser, with Michael Hart. 1995. *Multilateral Negotiations: Lessons from Arms Control, Trade, and the Environment.* Baltimore, MD: Johns Hopkins University Press.

Haney, Patrick J. 1995. "Structure and Process in the Analysis of Foreign Policy Crises." In *Foreign Policy Analysis*, ed. Laura Neack, Jeane A. K. Hey, and Patrick J. Haney. Englewood Cliffs, NJ: Prentice Hall.

Hardin, Russell. 1995. *One for All: The Logic of Group Conflict.* Princeton, NJ: Princeton University Press.

Hart, Paul, and Eric K. Stern, eds. 1997. *Beyond Groupthink: Political Group Dynamics and Foreign Policy Making.* Ann Arbor: University of Michigan Press.

Hasenclever, Andreas, and Peter Mayer. 1997. *Theories of International Regimes.* Cambridge, UK: Cambridge University Press.

Haynes, Lukas, and Timothy W. Stanley. 1995. "To Create a United Nations Fire Brigade." *Comparative Strategy*, 14:7–21.

Herek, Gregory M., Irving L. Janis, and Paul Huth. 1987. "Decision-Making during International Crises: Is the Quality of Progress Related to the Outcome?" *Journal of Conflict Resolution*, 31:203–236.

Hermann, Margaret G., and Joe D. Hagan. 1998. "International Decision Making: Leadership Matters." *Foreign Policy*, No. 110 (Spring): 124–137.

Hermann, Margaret G., and Charles W. Kegley Jr. 1995. "Rethinking Democracy and International Peace: Perspective from Political Psychology." *International Studies Quarterly*, 39:511–533.

Hey, Jeanne A. K. 1995a. "Ecuadoran Foreign Policy since 1979: Ideological Cycles or a Trend toward Neoliberalism?" *Journal of Interamerican Studies*, 35/4 (Winter): 57–88.

Higgins, Rosalyn. 1994. *Problems and Process: International Law and How We Use It.* New York: Oxford University Press.

Hirst, Paul, and Grahame Thompson. 1996. *Globalization in Question: The International Economy and the Possibilities of Governance.* Cambridge, U.K.: Polity Press.

Hoffmann, Stanley. 1995. "The Crisis of Liberal Internationalism." *Foreign Policy*, 98:159–179.

Holloway, Steven K., and Rodney Tomlinson. 1995. "The New World Order and the General Assembly: Block Realignment at the UN in the Post–Cold War World." *Canadian Journal of Political Science,* 28:227–254.

Homer-Dixon, Thomas. 1998. "Environmental Scarcity and Intergroup Conflict." In *World Security: Challenges for a New Century,* 3rd ed., ed. Michael T. Klare and Yogesh Chandran. New York: St. Martin's.

Hoogvelt, Ankie. 1997. *Globalization and the Postcolonial World: The New Political Economy of Development.* Baltimore, MD: Johns Hopkins University Press.

Hook, Steven W. 1994. *National Interest and Foreign Aid.* Boulder, CO: Lynne Rienner.

Hook, Steven W. 1996. *Foreign Aid toward the Millennium.* Boulder, CO: Lynne Rienner.

Hopf, Ted. 1991. "Polarity, the Offense-Defense Balance, and War." *American Political Science Review,* 85:475–493.

Hopmann, P. Terrence. 1996. *The Negotiation Process and the Resolution of International Conflicts.* Columbia: University of South Carolina Press.

Houghton, David Patrick. 1994. "The Role of Analogical Reasoning in Novel Foreign Policy Situations." Paper presented at the American Political Science Association convention, New York.

Hout, Will. 1997. "Globalization and the Quest for Governance." *Mershon International Studies Review,* 41:99–106.

Howard, Michael, George J. Andreopoulos, and Mark R. Shulman, eds. 1994. *The Laws of War.* New Haven, CT: Yale University Press.

Hudson, Valerie M., ed. 1997. *Culture and Foreign Policy.* Boulder, CO: Lynne Rienner.

Hudson, Valerie M., and Christopher S. Vore. 1995. "Foreign Policy Analysis Yesterday, Today, and Tomorrow." *Mershon International Studies Review,* a supplement to *International Studies Quarterly,* 39/2 (October): 209–238.

Huelshoff, Michael G. 1994. "Domestic Politics and Dynamic Issue Linkage: A Reformulation of Integration Theory." *International Studies Quarterly,* 38:255–280.

Hufbauer, Gary Clyde, and Jeffrey J. Schott. 1994. *Western Hemisphere Economic Integration.* Washington, DC: Institute for International Economics.

Huntington, Samuel. 1993. "The Clash of Civilizations." *Foreign Affairs,* 72(3):56–73.

Huntington, Samuel P. 1996. *The Clash of Civilizations and the Remaking of World Order.* New York: Simon & Schuster.

Huth, Paul K., Christopher Gelpi, and D. Scott Bennett. 1993. "The Escalation of Great Power Militarized Disputes: Testing Rational Deterrence Theory and Structural Realism." *American Political Science Review,* 87:609–623.

(IMF) International Monetary Fund. 1998a. *World Economic Outlook.* May 1998. IMF: Washington, DC.

(IMF) International Monetary Fund. 1998b. *Direction of Trade Statistics.* Quarterly, January 1998. IMF: Washington, DC.

(IMF) International Monetary Fund. 1998. *International Financial Statistics.* March 1998. IMF: Washington, DC.

Iriye, Akira. 1997. *Cultural Internationalism and World Order.* Baltimore, MD: Johns Hopkins University Press.

Ishiyama, John T., and Marijke Breuning. 1998. *Ethopolitics in the "New" Europe.* Boulder, CO: Lynne Rienner.

Iyer, Pico. 1996. "The Global Village Finally Arrives." In *Annual Editions: Global Issues 96/97.* Guilford, CT: Dushkin/McGraw-Hill.

Jackman, Robert W., and Ross A. Miller. 1995. "Voter Turnout in the Industrial Democracies during the 1980s." *Comparative Political Studies,* 27:467–192.

James, Patrick, and Athanasios Hristoulas. 1994. "Domestic Politics and Foreign Policy: Evaluating a Model of Crisis Activity for the United States." *Journal of Politics,* 56:327–348.

Jaquette, Jane S. 1997. "Women in Power: From Tokenism to Critical Mass." *Foreign Policy,* 108:23–97.

Jeffreys-Jones, Rhodri. 1995. *Women and the Shaping of American Foreign Policy, 1917–1994.* New Brunswick, NJ: Rutgers University Press.

Jennings, Robert Y. 1995. "The International Court of Justice at Fifty." *American Journal of International Law,* 89:493–506.

Jensen, Lloyd. 1982. *Explaining Foreign Policy.* Englewood Cliffs, NJ: Prentice Hall.

Johansen, Robert C. 1994. "Building World Security: The Need for Strengthened International Institutions." In *World Security: Challenges for a New Century,* ed. Michael T. Klare and Daniel C. Thomas. New York: St. Martin's.

Johnston, Douglas, and Cynthia Sampson, eds. 1995. *Religion, the Missing Dimension of Statecraft.* New York: Oxford University Press.

Kacowicz, Arie M. 1995. "Explaining Zones of Peace: Democracies as Satisfied Powers?" *Journal of Peace Research,* 32:265–276.

Karatnycky, Adrian. 1997. *Freedom in the World: The Annual Survey of Political Rights & Civil Liberties.* New York: Freedom House.

Katada, Saori N., and Timothy J. McKeown. 1998. "Aid Politics and Electoral Politics: Japan, 1970–1992." *International Studies Quarterly,* 42:591–600.

Kaufman, Stuart J. 1997. "The Fragmentation and Consolidation of International Systems." *International Organization,* 51:755–776.

Keane, John. 1994. "Nations, Nationalism, and Citizens in Europe." *International Social Science Journal,* 140:169–184.

Keating, Michael. 1996. *Nations against the State: The New Politics of Nationalism in Quebec, Catalonia, and Scotland.* New York: St. Martin's.

Kedourie, Elie. 1994. *Nationalism,* 4th ed. Cambridge, MA: Blackwell.

Kegley, Charles W., and Gregory Raymond. 1994. *A Multipolar Peace: Great-Power Politics in the Twenty-First Century.* New York: St. Martin's.

Keller, William W. 1995. *Arm in Arm: The Political Economy of the Global Arms Trade.* New York: Basic Books.

Keller, William W., and Nolan, Janne E. 1997. "The Arms Trade: Business As Usual?" *Foreign Policy,* 109:113–125.

Kennedy, Paul. 1988. *The Rise and Fall of the Great Powers.* New York: Random House.

Keohane, Robert O. 1998. "International Institutions: Can Interdependence Work?" *Foreign Policy,* 110:82–96.

Keohane, Robert O., and Lisa L. Martin. 1995. "The Promise of Institutionalist Theory." *International Security,* 20/1:39–51.

Keylor, William. 1996. *The Twentieth Century World.* New York: Oxford University Press.

Kimura, Masato, and David A. Welch. 1998. "Specifying 'Interests': Japan's Claim to the Northern Territories and Its Implications for International Relations Theory." *International Studies Quarterly,* 42:213–244.

Kinsella, David, and Herbert K. Tillema. 1995. "Arms and Aggression in the Middle East: Overt Military Interventions, 1948–1991." *Journal of Conflict Resolution,* 39:306–329.

Kirshner, Jonathan. 1995. *Currency and Coercion: The Political Economy of International Monetary Power.* Princeton, NJ: Princeton University Press.

Kissinger, Henry A. 1970. "The Just and the Possible." In *Negotiation and Statecraft: A Selection of Readings,* U.S. Congress, Senate Committee on Government Operations, 91st Cong., 2nd sess.

Kissinger, Henry A. 1979. *The White House Years.* Boston: Little, Brown.

Klare, Michael T., and Daniel C. Thomas, eds. 1994. "Introduction: Thinking about World Security." In *World Security: Challenges for a New Century,* 2nd ed. New York: St. Martin's Press.

Klotz, Audie. 1997. *Norms in International Relations: The Struggle against Apartheid.* Ithaca, NY: Cornell University Press.

Kocs, Stephen A. 1995. "Territorial Disputes and Interstate War, 1945–1987." *Journal of Politics,* 57:159–175.

Korbin, Stephen. 1996. "The Architecture of Globalization: State Sovereignty in a Networked Global Economy." In *Globalization, Governments and Competition.* Oxford, UK: Oxford University Press.

Koubi, Vally. 1994. "Military Buildups and Arms Control Agreements." *International Studies Quarterly,* 38:605–622.

Krause, Keith, and W. Andy Knight, eds. 1995. *State, Society, and the UN System: Perspectives on Multilateralism.* Tokyo: United Nations University Press.

Kreml, William P., and Charles W. Kegley Jr. 1996. "A Global Political Party: The Next Step." *Alternatives,* 21:123–134.

Kriesberg, Louis. 1992. *International Conflict Resolution.* New Haven, CT: Yale University Press.

Krosnick, Jon, and Shibley Telhami. 1995. "Public Attitudes toward Israel: A Study of the Attentive and Issue Publics." *International Studies Quarterly,* 39:535–554.

Kurth, James. 1994. "The *Real* Clash." *The National Interest,* 37:3–15.

Lackey, Douglas. 1989. *The Ethics of War and Peace.* Englewood Cliffs, NJ: Prentice Hall.

Landau, Alice, and Richard Whitman, eds. 1997. *Rethinking the European Union: Institutions, Interests, and Identities.* New York: St. Martin's.

Lapid, Yosef, and Friedrich Kratochwil. 1996. *The Return of Culture and Identity in IR Theory.* Boulder, CO: Lynne Rienner.

Lebow, Richard Ned, and Janice Gross Stein. 1995. "Deterrence and the Cold War." *Political Science Quarterly,* 110: 157–182.

Lefebvre, Jeffrey A. 1994. "Historical Analogies and the Israeli-Palestinian Peace Process: Munich, Camp David, and Algeria." *Middle East Policy,* 3:84–101.

Legro, Jeffrey W. 1996. "Culture and Preferences in the International Cooperation Two-Step." *American Political Science Review,* 90:118–137.

Legro, Jeffrey W. 1997. "Which Norms Matter: Revisiting the 'Failure' of Internationalism." *International Organization,* 51:31–63.

Lemke, Douglas, and William Reed. 1996. "Regime Types and Status Quo Evaluations: Power Transition Theory and the Democratic Peace." *International Interactions,* 22:143–164.

Lemke, Douglas, and Suzanne Warner. 1996. "Power Parity, Commitment to Change, and War." *International Studies Quarterly,* 40:235–260.

Levi, Werner. 1991. *Contemporary International Law,* 2nd ed. Boulder, CO: Westview.

Lewis, John Wilson, and Xue Litai. 1994. *China's Strategic Seapower: The Politics of Force Modernization in the Nuclear Age.* Stanford, CA: Stanford University Press.

Li Chien-pin. 1996. "Fear, Greed, or Garage Sale: The Analysis of Defense Spending in East Asia." Paper presented at the International Studies Association convention, San Diego.

Li Zhongcheng. 1994. "Struggles among Different Schools of Human Rights." Presented at the Sino-American Relations Conference cosponsored by the China Institute of Contemporary International Relations and the Washington Institute for Values in Public Policy, Beijing, China.

Lind, Michael. 1994. "In Defense of Liberal Nationalism." *Foreign Affairs,* 73(3):87–99.

Lindsay, James M. 1994. "Congress, Foreign Policy, and the New Institutionalism." *International Studies Quarterly,* 38:281–304.

Lipschutz, Ronnie D., and Judith Mayer. 1996. *Global Civil Society and Global Environmental Governance: The Politics of Nature from Place to Planet.* Albany: State University of New York.

Litfin, Karen T. 1994. *Ozone Discourses: Science and Politics in Global Environmental Cooperation.* New York: Columbia University Press.

Lohmann, Susanne, and Sharyn O'Halloran. 1994. "Divided Government and U.S. Trade Policy: Theory and Evidence." *International Organization,* 48:595–632.

Lopez, George A., Jackie G. Smith, and Ron Pagnucco. 1995. "The Global Tide." *Bulletin of the Atomic Scientists,* 51/6 (July/August): 33–39.

Love, Herbert. 1996. "Lessons of Liberia: ECOMOG and Regional Peacekeeping." *International Security,* 21:145–176.

Lugo, Luis E. 1996. *Sovereignty at the Crossroads? Morality and International Politics in the Post–Cold War Era.* Lanham, MD: Rowman & Littlefield.

Lundestad, Geir. 1994. *The Fall of Great Powers: Peace, Stability, and Legitimacy.* Oxford, U.K.: Oxford University Press.

Mace, Gordon, and Jean-Philippe Therien, eds. 1996. *Foreign Policy and Regionalism in the Americas.* CO: Lynne Rienner.

Macesich, George. 1997. *World Economy at the Crossroads.* Westport, CT: Praeger.

Macridis, Roy C., and Mark L. Hulliung. 1996. *Contemporary Political Ideologies.* New York: HarperCollins.

Mahbubani, Kishore. 1994. "The Dangers of Decadence." *Foreign Affairs,* 72/4 (September/October): 10–14.

Majeski, Stephen, and Shane Fricks. 1995. "Conflict and Cooperation in International Relations." *Journal of Conflict Resolution,* 39:622–645.

Mandelbaum, Michael, ed. 1995. *Strategic Quadrangle: Russia, China, Japan and the United States in East Asia.* Washington, DC: Brookings.

Mansbach, Richard W. 1996. "Neo-This and Neo-That: Or, "Play It Sam" (Again and Again)." *Mershon International Studies Review,* 40:90–95.

Mansfield, Edward D. 1994. *Power, Trade, and War.* Princeton: Princeton University Press.

Maoz, Zeev. 1996. *Domestic Sources of Global Change.* Ann Arbor: University of Michigan Press.

Matheson, Michael J. 1997. "The Opinions of the International Court of Justice on the Threat or Use of Nuclear Weapons." *American Journal of International Law,* 91:417–436.

Mattli, Walter, and Anne-Marie Slaughter. 1998. "Revisiting the European Court of Justice." *International Organization,* 52:177–210.

May, Ernest R. 1994. "The 'Great Man' Theory of Foreign Policy." Review of Henry Kissinger. *Diplomacy. New York Times Book Review,* April 3.

McKim, Robert, and Jeff McMahan. 1997. *The Morality of Nationalism.* New York: Oxford University Press.

Mearsheimer, John J. 1995. "The False Promise of International Institutions." *International Security,* 19/3:5–49.

Meiers, Franz-Josef. 1995. "Germany: The Reluctant Power." *Survival,* 37/3 (Autumn): 82–104.

Mercer, Jonathan C. 1996. *Reputation and International Politics.* Ithaca, NY: Cornell University Press.

Metselaar, Max, and Bertjan Verbeek. 1996. "Bureau-Politics. Decisional Conflicts, and Small Group Dynamics." Paper presented at the International Studies Association convention, San Diego.

Meyer, John W., David John Frank, and Nancy Brandon Tuma. 1997. "The Structuring of a World Environmental Regime, 1870–1990." *International Organization,* 51:623–652.

Midlarsky, Manus I. 1995. "Environmental Influences on Democracy: Aridity, Warfare, and a Reversal of the Causal Arrow." *Journal of Conflict Resolution,* 39:224–262.

Miller, Benjamin. 1995. *When Opponents Cooperate: Great Power Conflict and Collaboration in World Politics.* Ann Arbor: University of Michigan Press.

Milner, Helen V. 1997. *Interests, Institutions, and Information: Domestic Politics and International Relations.* Princeton, NJ: Princeton University Press.

Milner, Helen V. 1998. "International Political Economy: Beyond Hegemonic Stability." *Foreign Policy,* 110:112–123.

Mingst, Karen A., and Margaret P. Karns. 1995. *The United Nations in the Post-Cold War Era.* Boulder, CO: Westview.

Mintz, Alex, and Randolph T. Stevenson. 1995. "Defense Expenditures, Economic Growth, and the 'Peace Dividend.'" *Journal of Conflict Resolution,* 39:283–305.

Mirsky, Georgiy I. 1997. *On Ruins of Empire: Ethnicity and Nationalism in the Former Soviet Union.* Westport, CT: Greenwood.

Mitchell, Neil J. 1995. "The Global Polity: Foreign Firms' Political Activity in the United States." *Policy,* 27:447–463.

Mo, Jongryn. 1994. "The Logic of Two-Level Games with Endogenous Domestic Coalitions." *Journal of Conflict Resolution,* 38:402–422.

Moon, Bruce E. 1996. *Dilemmas of International Trade.* Boulder, CO: Westview.

Moore, Gale. 1998. *Climate of Fear: Why We Shouldn't Worry about Global Warming.* Washington, D.C.: Cato Institute.

Moore, Margaret. 1997. "On National Self-Determination." *Political Studies,* 45:900–915.

Morgan, T. Clifton. 1994. *Untying the Knot of War: A Bargaining Theory of International Crises.* Ann Arbor: University of Michigan Press.

Morgenthau, Hans W. 1973, 1986. *Politics among Nations.* New York: Knopf. Morgenthau's text was first published in 1948 and periodically thereafter. Two sources are used herein. One is the fifth edition, published in 1973. The second is an edited abstract drawn from pp. 3–4, 10–12, 14, 27–29, and 31–35 of the third edition, published in 1960. The abstract appears in Vasquez 1986:37–41. Pages cited for Morgenthau 1986 refer to Vasquez's, not Morgenthau's, book.

Motyl, Alexander J. 1992. "The Modernity of Nationalism: Nations, States and Nation-States in the Contemporary World." *Journal of International Affairs,* 45:307–324.

Mower, A. Glenn, Jr. 1997. *The Convention of the Rights of the Child: International Law Support for Children.* Westport, CT: Greenwood.

Murray, A. J. H. 1996. "The Moral Politics of Hans Morgenthau." *The Review of Politics,* 58:81–109.

Musgrave, Thomas D. 1997. *Self-Determination and National Minorities.* Oxford, UK: Clarendon.

Namkung, Gon. 1998. *Japanese Images of the United States and Other Nations: A Comparative Study of Public Opinion and Foreign Policy.* Doctoral dissertation. Storrs, CT: University of Connecticut.

Nathan, Andrew. 1998. *China's Transition.* New York: Columbia University Press.

Neuman, Stephanie. 1998. *International Relations Theory and the Third World.* New York: St. Martin's.

Nevin, John A. 1996. "War Initiation and Selection by Consequences." *Journal of Peace Research,* 33: 99–108.

Niou, Emerson M. S., and Peter C. Ordeshook. 1994a. "'Less Filling, Tastes Great': The Realist-Neoliberal Debate." *World Politics,* 46:209–234.

Noël, Alain, and Jean-Philippe Thérien. 1996. "Political Parties, Domestic Institutions, and Foreign Aid." Paper presented at the International Studies Association convention, San Diego.

Nogee, Joseph L., and John Spanier. 1988. *Peace Impossible—War Unlikely: The Cold War between the United States and the Soviet Union.* Glenville, IL: Scott, Foresman.

Nolan, Cathal J. 1995. *Ethics and Statecraft.* Westport, CT: Greenwood.

Nolan, Stanley D., and Dennis P. Quinn. 1994. "Free Trade, Fair Trade, Strategic Trade, and Protectionism in the U.S. Congress, 1987–1988." *International Organization,* 48:491–525.

Norman, Richard. 1995. *Ethics, Killing, and War.* Cambridge, U.K.: Cambridge University Press.

Nugent, Neill, ed. 1997. *At the Heart of the Union: Studies of the European Commission.* New York: St. Martin's.

Nye, Joseph S., Jr. 1990. "The Changing Nature of World Power," *Political Science Quarterly,* 105:177–192.

O'Leary, Brendan. 1997. "On the Nature of Nationalism: An Appraisal of Ernest Gellner's Writings on Nationalism." *British Journal of Political Science,* 27:191–222.

Olmer, Lionel H. 1989. "Statement on EC 1992 and the Requirement for U.S. Industry and Government Partnership." *Europe 1992.* Hearings before the U.S. Congress, House of Representatives, Subcommittee on Trade of the Committee on Ways and Means. March 20.

Oneal, John R., Frances Oneal, Zeev Maoz, and Bruce Russett. 1996. "Interdependence, Democracy, and International Conflict, 1950–85." *Journal of Peace Research,* 33:11–28.

O'Neill, Barry O. "Power and Satisfaction in the Security Council." In *The Once and Future Security Council,* ed. Bruce Russett. New York: St. Martin's.

O'Reilly, Marc J. 1997. "Following Ike": Explaining Canadian–U.S. Co-operation during the 1956 Suez Crisis." *Journal of Commonwealth & Comparative Studies,* 35/3:75–107.

Oren, Ido. 1995. "The Subjectivity of the 'Democratic' Peace." *International Security,* 20:147–184.

Ostrom, Charles W., and H. J. Aldrich. 1978. "The Relationship between Size and Stability in the Major Power International System." *American Journal of Political Science,* 22:743–771.

Overturf, Stephen F. 1997. *Money and European Union.* New York: St. Martin's.

Pagden, Anthony. 1998. "The Genesis of 'Governance' and Enlightenment Conceptions of the Cosmopolitan World Order." *International Social Science Journal,* 50:7–16.

Papayoanou, Paul A. 1997. "Economic Interdependence and the Balance of Power." *International Studies Quarterly,* 41:113–140.

Pape, Robert A. 1997. "Why Economic Sanctions Do Not Work." *International Security,* 22:90–136.

Parenti, Michael. 1992. "U.S. Intervention: More Foul than Foolish." In *Competing Conceptions of American Foreign Policy,* ed. Stanley J. Michalak Jr. New York: HarperCollins.

Park, Bert Edward. 1994. *Ailing, Aging, Addicted: Studies of Compromised Leadership.* Lexington, KY: University Press of Kentucky.

Parsons, Karen Toombs. 1994. "Exploring the 'Two President' Phenomenon: New Evidence from the Truman Administration." *Presidential Studies Quarterly,* 24:495–514.

Paterson, Thomas G., J. Garry Clifford, and Kenneth J. Hagan. 1995. *American Foreign Relations: A History. Vol. II: Since 1895.* 4th ed. Lexington, MA: D. C. Heath.

Pauly, Louis W. and Simon Reich. 1997. "National Structures and Multinational Corporate Behavior: Enduring Differences in the Age of Globalization." *International Organization,* 51:1–30.

Peterson, Susan. 1996. *Crisis Bargain and the State: The Domestic Politics of International Conflict.* Ann Arbor: University of Michigan Press.

Pettman, Ralph, ed. 1996. *Understanding International Political Economy, with Readings for the Fatigued.* Boulder, CO: Lynne Rienner.

Phan, Chau T. 1996. "International Nongovernmental Organizations, Global Negotiations, and Global Activist Networks: The Emergence of INGOs As Partners in the Global Governance Process." *International Organization,* 51:591–622.

Pickering, Jeffrey, and William R. Thompson. 1998. "Stability in a Fragmenting World: Interstate Military Force, 1946–1988." *Political Research Quarterly,* 51:241–264.

Poe, Steven C., and James Meernik. 1995. "U.S. Military Aid in the 1980s: A Global Analysis." *Journal of Peace Research,* 32:399–411.

Pollins, Brian M. 1996. "Global Political Order, Economic Change, and Armed Conflict: Coevolving Systems and the Use of Force." *American Political Science Review,* 90:103–117.

Porter, Bruce D. 1994. *War and the Rise of the State.* New York: Free Press.

Powell, Robert. 1996. "Stability and the Distribution of Power." *World Politics,* 48:239–267.

Powlick, Philip. J. 1995. "The Sources of Public Opinion for American Foreign Policy Officials." *International Studies Quarterly,* 39:427–52.

Powlick, Philip J., and Andrew Z. Katz. 1998. "Defining the American Public Opinion/Foreign Policy Nexus." *Mershon International Studies Review,* 42/1:29–62.

Puchala, Donald J. 1995. "The Pragmatics of International History." *Mershon International Studies Review* (a supplement to *International Studies Quarterly*), 39:1–18.

Prügel, Elisabeth. 1996. "Gender in International Organization and Global Governance: A Critical Review of the Literature." *International Studies Notes,* 21/1 (Winter): 26–27.

Putnam, Robert D. 1998. "The Logic of Two-Level Games," *International Organization* 42(3): 427–460.

Rabkin, Jeremy. 1994. "Threats to U.S. Sovereignty." *Commentary,* 97(3):41–47.

Rasler, Karen A., and William R. Thompson. 1992. "Concentration, Polarity and Transitional Warfare." Presented at the International Studies Association convention, April, Atlanta, GA.

Rasler, Karen A., and William R. Thompson. 1994. *The Great Powers and the Global Struggle, 1490–1990.* Lexington: University of Kentucky Press.

Rasmussen, J. Lewis. 1997. "Peacemaking in the Twenty-First Century: New Rules, New Roles, New Actors," in I. William Zartman and J. Lewis Rasmussen, eds. *Peacemaking in International Conflict: Methods and Techniques.* Washington, DC: U.S. Institute for Peace Press, pp. 23–50.

Ratner, Steven R. 1996. *The New UN Peacekeeping: Building Peace in Lands of Conflict after the Cold War.* New York: St. Martin's.

Ray, James Lee. 1995. "Global Trends, State-Specific Factors and Regime Transitions, 1825–1993." *Journal of Peace Research,* 32:49–63.

Ray, James Lee. 1997. "The Democratic Path to Peace." *Journal of Democracy,* 8/2:49–64.

Raymond, Gregory A. 1994. "Democracies, Disputes, and Third-Party Intermediaries." *Journal of Conflict Resolution,* 38:24–42.

Reardon, Betty A. 1990. "Feminist Concepts of Peace and Security." In *A Reader in Peace Studies,* ed. Paul Smoker, Ruth Davies, and Barbara Munske. Oxford, U.K.: Pergamon Press.

Redfern, Paul. 1995. "Measuring Human Rights." In *Global Governance: Ethics and Economics of the World Order,* ed. Meghnad Desai and Paul Redfern. London: Pinter.

Rehbein, Kathleen A. 1995. "Foreign-Owned Firms' Campaign Contributions in the United States." *Policy Studies Journal,* 23:41–61.

Renan, Ernest. 1995. "Qu'est-ce Qu'une Nation?" In *Nationalism,* ed. John Hutchinson and Anthony D. Smith. New York: Oxford University Press.

Renshon, Stanley A., ed. 1993. *The Political Psychology of the Gulf War: Leaders, Publics, and the Process of Conflict.* Pittsburgh: University of Pittsburgh Press.

Renshon, Stanley A. 1995. "Character, Judgment, and Political Leadership: Promise, Problems, and Prospects of the Clinton Presidency." In *The Clinton Presidency: Campaigning, Governing, and the Psychology of Leadership,* ed. Stanley Renshon. Boulder, CO: Westview.

Rhein, Wendy. 1998. "The Feminization of Poverty: Unemployment in Russia." *Journal of International Affairs,* 52:351–367.

Rhodes, Carolyn, and Sonia Mazey. 1995. *The State of the European Union, Vol. 3: Building a European Polity.* Boulder, CO: Lynne Rienner.

Rhodes, Edward. 1994. "Do Bureaucratic Politics Matter? Some Discomforting Findings from the Case of the U.S. Navy." *World Politics,* 47:1–41.

Richards, Diana. 1993. "A Chaotic Model of Power Concentration in the International System." *International Studies Quarterly,* 37:55–72.

Richardson, Jeremy, ed. 1997. *European Union: Power and Policy-Making.* New York: Routledge.

Ripley, Brian. 1995. "Cognition, Culture, and Bureaucratic Politics." In *Foreign Policy Analysis,* ed. Laura Neack, Jeane A. K. Hey, and Patrick J. Haney. Englewood Cliffs, NJ: Prentice Hall.

Risse-Kappen, Thomas. 1991. "Public Opinion, Domestic Structure, and Foreign Policy in Liberal Democracies." *World Politics,* 43:479–512.

Risse-Kappen, Thomas, ed. 1995. *Bringing Transnational Relations Back In: Non-State Actors, Domestic Structure, and International Institutions.* New York: Cambridge University Press.

Roberts, Adam. 1996. "From San Francisco to Sarajevo: The UN and the Use of Force." *Survival,* 37/4 (Winter): 7–28.

Robertson, A. H., and J. G. Merrills. 1995. *Human Rights in Europe: A Study of the European Convention on Human Rights.* Manchester, U.K.: Manchester University Press.

Robertson, Charles L. 1997. *International Politics since World War II: A Short History.* Armonk, NY: M. E. Sharpe.

Robinson, William I. 1996. *Promoting Polyarch: Globalization, U.S. Intervention, and Hegemony.* New York: Cambridge University Press.

Rogers, J. Phillip. 1987. "The Crisis Bargaining Code Model: A Cognitive Schema Approach to Crisis Decision-Making." Presented at the International Studies Association convention, April, Washington, DC.

Rosati, Jerel A. 1995. "A Cognitive Approach to the Study of Foreign Policy." In *Foreign Policy Analysis,* ed. Laura Neack, Jeane A. K. Hey, and Patrick J. Haney. Englewood Cliffs, NJ: Prentice Hall.

Rosenau, James N. 1990. *Turbulence in World Politics: A Theory of Change and Continuity.* Princeton, NJ: Princeton University Press.

Rosenau, James N. 1992. *The United Nations in a Turbulent World.* Boulder, CO: Lynne Rienner.

Rosenau, James N. 1997. *Along the Domestic-Foreign Frontier: Exploring Governance in a Turbulent World.* Cambridge, UK: Cambridge University Press.

Rosenau, James N., and Mary Durfee. 1995. *Thinking Theory Thoroughly.* Boulder, CO: Westview.

Rosenblatt, Lionel, and Larry Thompson. 1998. "The Door of Opportunity: Creating a Permanent Peacekeeping Force." *World Policy Journal.* 15:36–47.

Ross, Robert S. 1995. *Negotiating Cooperation: The United States and China, 1969–1989.* Stanford, CA: Stanford University Press.

Rotblat, Joseph, Jack Steinberger, and Bhalchandra Udgaonkar. 1993. *A Nuclear-Weapons-Free World: Desirable? Feasible?* Boulder, CO: Westview.

Rothgeb, John M., Jr. 1993. *Defining Power: Influence and Force in the Contemporary International System.* New York: St. Martin's.

Rothkopf, David J. 1998. "Cyberpolitik: The Changing Nature of Power in the Information Age." *Journal of International Affairs.* 51:325–360.

Rourke, John T. 1990. *Making Foreign Policy: United States, Soviet Union, China.* Pacific Grove, CA: Brooks/Cole.

Rourke, John T. 1993. *Presidential Wars and American Democracy: Rally 'Round the Chief.* New York: Paragon.

Rourke, John T. 1994. "United States–China Trade: Economic, Human Rights, and Strategic Issues." *In Depth,* 4/3:135–162.

Rourke, John T., Ralph G. Carter, and Mark A. Boyer. 1996. *Making American Foreign Policy,* 2nd ed. Guilford, CT: Brown & Benchmark/Dushkin.

Rourke, John, and Richard Clark. 1998. "Making U.S. Foreign Policy toward China in the Clinton Administration." In *After the End: Making U.S. Foreign Policy in the Post-Cold War World,* ed. James M. Scott. Durham, N.C.: Duke University Press.

Rourke, John T., Richard P. Hiskes, and Cyrus Ernesto Zirakzadeh. 1992. *Direct Democracy and International Politics.* Boulder, CO: Lynne Rienner.

Rousseau, David L. Christopher Gelpi, Dan Reiter, and Paul K. Huth. 1996. Assessing the Dyadic Nature of the Democratic Peace, 1918–1988." *American Political Science Review,* 90:512–533.

Rubenstein, Richard E., and Jarle Crocker. 1994. "Challenging Huntington." *Foreign Policy,* 96:113–128.

Rummel, R. J. 1995. "Democracy, Power, Genocide, and Mass Murder." *Journal of Conflict Resolution,* 39:3–26.

Rusk, Dean, as told to Richard Rusk. 1990. *As I Saw It.* New York: W. W. Norton.

Russett, Bruce, ed. 1997. *The Once and Future Security Council.* New York: St. Martin's.

Saideman, Stephen M. 1997. "Explaining the International Relations of Secessionist Conflicts: Vulnerability versus Ethnic Ties." *International Organization,* 51:721–754

Salmon, Jeffrey. 1993. "Greenhouse Anxiety." *Commentary,* July.

Sanjian, Gregory S. 1998. "Cold War Imperatives and Quarrelsome Clients: Modeling U.S. and USSR Arms Transfers to India and Pakistan." *Journal of Conflict Resolution,* 42:97–127.

Saunders, Robert M. 1994. "History, Health and Herons: The Historiography of Woodrow Wilson's Personality and Decision-Making." *Presidential Studies Quarterly,* 24:57–77.

Schampel, James H. 1996. "A Preponderance of Conflict over Peace: A Dialogue with Charles Gochman and Aaron Hoffman." *International Studies Notes,* 21/2 (Spring): 26–27.

Schmidt, Brian C. 1997. *The Political Discourse of Anarchy.* Albany: State University of New York Press.

Schoenbaum, David. 1993. *The United States and the State of Israel.* New York: Oxford University Press.

Schraeder, Peter J., Steven W. Hook, and Bruce Taylor. 1998. "Clarifying the Foreign Aid Puzzle: A Comparison of American, Japanese, French, and Swedish Aid Flows." *World Politics,* 50:294–324.

Schrodt, Philip A. 1995. "Events Data in Foreign Policy Analysis." In *Foreign Policy Analysis,* ed. Laura Neack, Jeane A. K. Hey, and Patrick J. Haney. Englewood Cliffs, NJ: Prentice Hall.

Schubert, James N. 1993. "Realpolitik as a Male Primate Strategy." Presented at the annual meeting of the International Studies Association, Acapulco, Mexico.

Schultz, Kathryn R., and David Isenberg. 1997. "Arms Control and Disarmament." In *A Global Agenda: Issues before the 52nd General Assembly of the United Nations,* ed. John Tessitore and Susan Woolfson. Lanham, MD: Rowman & Littlefield.

Schweller, Randall L., and David Priess. 1997. "A Tale of Two Realisms: Expanding the Institutions Debate." *Mershon International Studies Review,* 41:1–32.

Scott, Catherine V. 1996. *Gender and Development: Rethinking Modernization and Dependency Theory.* Boulder, CO: Lynne Rienner.

Sederberg, Peter C. 1995. "Conciliation as Counter-Terrorist Strategy." *Journal of Peace Research,* 32:295–312.

Shambaugh, George E., IV. 1996. "Dominance, Dependence, and Political Power: Tethering Technology in the 1980s and Today." *International Studies Quarterly,* 40:559–588.

Sherill, Robert. 1979. *Why They Call It Politics.* New York: Harcourt Brace Jovanovich.

Shevchenko, Arkady. 1985. *Breaking with Moscow.* New York: Alfred A. Knopf.

Simon, Julian L. 1996. "More People, Greater Wealth, More Resources, Healthier Environment." In *Taking Sides: Clashing Views on Controversial Issues in World Politics,* 7th ed., ed. John T. Rourke. Guilford, CT: Dushkin.

Simons, Geoff. 1998. *Vietnam Syndrome: Impact on U.S. Foreign Policy.* New York: St. Martin's.

(SIPRI) Stockholm International Peace Research Institute. Annual Editions. *SIPRI Yearbook.* Oxford, U.K.: Oxford University Press.

Sislin, John. 1994. "Arms as Influence: The Determinants of Successful Influence." *Journal of Conflict Resolution,* 38:665–689.

Siverson, Randolph M., and Harvey Starr. 1994. "Regime Change and the Restructuring of Alliances." *American Journal of Political Science,* 38:145–61.

Smith, Alastair. 1995. "Alliance Formation and War." *International Studies Quarterly,* 39:405–426.

Smith, Alastair. 1996. "Diversionary Foreign Policy in Democratic Systems." *International Studies Quarterly,* 40:133–153.

Solingen, Etel. 1994. "The Domestic Sources of Regional Regimes: The Evolution of Nuclear Ambiguity in the Middle East." *International Studies Quarterly,* 38:305–338.

Somit, Albert, and Steven A. Peterson. 1997. *Darwinism, Dominance, Democracy: The Biological Bases of Authoritarianism.* Westport, CT: Greenwood.

Soroos, Marvin S. 1997. *The Endangered Atmosphere: Preserving a Global Commons.* Norman: University of Oklahoma Press.

Spanier, John, and Eric M. Uslaner. 1993. *American Foreign Policy Making and the Democratic Dilemmas,* 6th ed. New York: Macmillan.

Spar, Debora L. 1994. *The Cooperative Edge: The Internal Politics of International Cartels.* Ithaca, NY: Cornell University Press.

Spegele, Roger D. 1996. *Political Realism in International Theory.* Cambridge, U.K.: Cambridge University Press.

Speth, James Gustave. 1998. "Poverty: A Denial of Human Rights." *Journal of International Affairs,* 52:277–292.

Starkey, Brigid, Mark A. Boyer, and Jonathan Wilkenfeld. 1999. *Negotiating a Complex World.* Boulder, CO: Rowman & Littlefield.

Sterling-Folker, Jennifer. 1997. "Realist Environment, Liberal Process, and Domestic-Level Variables." *International Studies Quarterly,* 41:1–26.

Stoessinger, John G. 1998. *Why Nations Go to War,* 7th ed. New York: St. Martin's.

Strange, Susan. 1997. *The Retreat of the State: The Diffusion of Power in the World Economy.* New York: Cambridge University Press.

Sutterlin, James S. 1995. *The United Nations and the Maintenance of International Security.* Westport, CT: Praeger.

Suu Kyi, Aung San. 1995. "Freedom, Development, and Human Worth." *Journal of Democracy,* 6/2 (April): 12–19.

Taber, Charles S. 1989. "Power Capability Indexes in the Third World." In *Power in World Politics,* ed. Richard J. Stoll and Michael D. Ward. Boulder, CO: Lynne Rienner.

Tamir, Yael. 1995. "The Enigma of Nationalism." *World Politics,* 47:418–440.

Taylor, Andrew J., and John T. Rourke. 1995. "Historical Analogies in the Congressional Foreign Policy Process." *Journal of Politics,* 57:460–468.

Tessitore, John, and Susan Woolfson, eds. 1997. *A Global Agenda: Issues before the 52nd General Assembly of the United Nations.* Lanham, MD: Rowman & Littlefield.

Thakur, Ramesh. 1994. "Human Rights: Amnesty International and the United Nations." *Journal of Peace Research,* 31:143–60.

Thies, Wallace J. 1998. "Deliberate and Inadvertent War in the Post–Cold War World." In *Annual Editions, American Foreign Policy 98/99,* ed. Glenn P. Hastedt. Guilford, CT: Dushkin/McGraw-Hill.

Thompson, James C., Jr. 1989. "Historical Legacies and Bureaucratic Procedures." In *Major Problems in American Foreign Policy,* Vol. 2, ed. Thomas G. Paterson. Lexington, MA: D. C. Heath.

Thompson, Kenneth W. 1994. *Fathers of International Thought: The Legacy of Political Theory.* Baton Rouge: Louisiana State University Press.

Thompson, William R. 1995. "Principle Rivalries." *Journal of Conflict Resolution,* 39:195–223.

Thompson, William R., and Richard Tucker. 1997. "A Tale of Two Democratic Peace Critiques." *Journal of Conflict Resolution,* 41:428–454.

Thomson, Janice E. 1995. "State Sovereignty in International Relations: Bridging the Gap between Theory and Empirical Research." *International Studies Quarterly,* 39:213–233.

Tickner, J. Ann. 1997. "You Just Don't Understand: Troubled Engagements between Feminists and IR Theorists." *International Studies Quarterly,* 41:611–632.

Togeby, Lisa. 1994. "The Gender Gap in Foreign Policy Attitudes." *Journal of Peace Research,* 31:375–392.

Travis, Rick. 1994. "Military Spending in Developing Countries: A Response to One's Neighbors." Presented at the annual meeting of the International Studies Association, Washington, DC.

Trumbore, Peter. 1998. "Public Opinion as a Domestic Constraint in International Negotiations." *International Studies Quarterly,* forthcoming September 1998.

Tsebelis, George. 1994. "The Power of the European Parliament as a Conditional Agenda Setter." *American Political Science Review,* 88:128–142.

(UNDP) United Nations Development Programme. Annual editions. *Human Development Report.* New York: Oxford University Press.

(UNICEF) United Nations Children's Fund. Annual editions. *State of the World's Children 1998.* New York: Oxford University Press.

Urquhart, Brian. 1995. "Selecting the World's CEO." *Foreign Affairs,* 74/3 (May-June): 21–27.

(U.S.) Bureau of the Census. Annual editions. *Statistical Abstract of the United States.* Washington, DC.

U.S. (CIA) Central Intelligence Agency. Annual editions. *World Fact Book.* Washington: GPO.

Van Dervort, Thomas R. 1997. *International Law and Organization.* Thousand Oaks, CA: Sage.

Vandenbroucke, Lucien. 1991. *Perilous Options: Special Operations in U.S. Foreign Policy.* Unpublished dissertation, The University of Connecticut. A manuscript based on Vandenbroucke's revised dissertation was published in 1993 under the same title by Oxford University Press.

Vasquez, John A., ed. 1986. *Classics of International Relations.* Englewood Cliffs, NJ: Prentice Hall.

Vasquez, John A. 1995. "Why Do Neighbors Fight? Proximity, Interaction, or Territoriality." *Journal of Peace Research,* 32:277–293.

Vasquez, John. 1998. *The Power of Power Politics.* Cambridge: Cambridge University Press.

Verdier, Daniel. 1994. *Democracy and International Trade: Britain, France, and the United States, 1860–1990.* Princeton, NJ: Princeton University Press.

Vertzberger, Yaacov Y. I. 1994 "Collective Risk Taking: The Decisionmaking Group and Organization." Presented at the annual meeting of the International Studies Association, Washington, DC.

Wallensteen, Peter, and Margareta Sollenberg. 1995. "After the Cold War: Emerging Patterns of Armed Conflict 1989–94." *Journal of Peace Research,* 32: 345–360.

Walker, Stephen G., Mark Schafer, and Michael D. Young. 1998. "Systematic Procedures for Operational Code Analysis: Measuring and Modeling Jimmy Carter's Operational Code." *International Studies Quarterly,* 42:175–189.

Walsh, David F., Paul J. Best, and Kul B. Rai. 1995. *Governing through Turbulence: Leadership and Change in the Late Twentieth Century.* Westport, CT: Praeger.

Walt, Stephen M. 1996. "Alliances: Balancing and Bandwagoning." In *International Politics,* 4th ed., ed. Robert J. Art and Robert Jervis. New York: HarperCollins.

Wapner, Paul. 1996. *Environmental Activism and World Civic Politics.* Albany: State University of New York.

Ward, Michael D., and Kristian S. Gleditsch. 1998. "Democratizing for Peace." *American Political Science Review,* 92:51–62.

Wayman, Frank W. 1994. "Bipolarity and War: The Role of Capability of Concentration and Alliance Patterns among Major Powers, 1816–1965." *Journal of Peace Research,* 21:61–78.

Wayman, Frank W., and Paul F. Diehl, eds. 1994. "Reconstruction." In *Realpolitik.* Ann Arbor: University of Michigan Press.

Weede, Erich. 1995. "Why Nations Arm: A Reconsideration." *Journal of Peace Research,* 32:229–232.

Weigel, George. 1995. "Are Human Rights Still Universal?" *Commentary,* 99/2 (February): 41–45.

Weinstein, Edwin A. 1981. *Woodrow Wilson: A Medical and Psychological Biography.* Princeton, NJ: Princeton University Press.

Weltman, John J. 1995. *World Politics and the Evolution of War.* Baltimore, MD: Johns Hopkins University Press.

Wendt, Alexander. 1994. "Collective Identity Formation and the International State." *American Political Science Review,* 88:384–398.

Wesley, Michael. 1997. *Casualties of the New World Order: The Causes of Failure of UN Missions to Civil Wars.* New York: St. Martin's.

Woods, Ngaire. 1995. "Economic Ideas and International Relations: Beyond Rational Neglect." *International Studies,* 39:161–180.

World Almanac and Book of Facts. Annual editions. New York: Funk & Wagnalls.

World Bank. World Development Report. Annual editions. New York: Oxford University Press.

World Resources Institute. Annual editions. *World Resources.* New York: Oxford University Press.

Yavlinsky, Grigory. 1998. "Russia's Phony Capitalism." *Foreign Affairs,* 77/3:67–79.

Young, O. R., and G. Osherenko, eds. 1993. *Polar Politics: Creating International Environmental Regimes.* Ithaca, NY: Cornell University Press.

Young, Robert A. 1995. *The Secession of Quebec and the Future of Canada.* Montreal: McGill-Queen's University Press.

Zakaria, Fareed. 1993. "Is Realism Finished?" *National Interest,* 32:21–32.

Zaller, John. 1994. "Strategic Politicians, Public Opinion, and the Gulf Crisis." In *Taken by Storm: The Media, Public Opinion, and U.S. Foreign Policy in the Gulf War,* ed. W. Lance Bennett and David L. Paletz. Chicago: University of Chicago Press.

Zartman, I. William, ed. 1995. *Elusive Peace: Negotiating the End to Civil Wars.* Washington, DC: Brookings.

Zurn, Michael. 1998. "The Rise of International Environmental Politics: A Review of Current Research." *World Politics,* 50:617–649.

Index

Page numbers in **boldface** refer to glossary terms

468

Credits

Evolution of the World Political System

DARK AGES   MIDDLE AGES   RENAISSANCE

Great civilizations and empires: Egypt, the Indus Valley, Athens, Sparta, the Americas, China, Persia, Rome, and smaller political divisions	Fall of Rome	Charlemagne crowned "Emperor of the Romans"		Russia's Ivan the Great — Russian consolidation begins	Machiavelli writes *The Prince*	Reformation begins	Henry VIII breaks with pope	
	476	**570**	**800**	**1350**	**1462**	**1513**	**1517**	**1534**	**155**
		Great empire of Ghana founded	Mohammad born — Islam founded	Idea of universal Christian empire begins	Mayan civilization peaks			Beginning of the collapse of Holy Roman Empire	

MULTIPOLAR BALANCE OF POWER

Russian Revolution	World War I begins		First manned flight	Spanish-American War	Dominion of Canada established		U.S. naval squadron in Tokyo Bay demands U.S.–Japan trade
1917	**1914**	**1911**	**1903**	**1898**	**1868**	**1867**	**1853**
	Chinese Manchu emperor deposed			U.S. imperialist period	Meiji restoration begins modern era in Japan		U.S. naval squadron in Tokyo Bay demands U.S.–Japan trade

MULTIPOLAR SYSTEM DECLINES

World Depression   World War II

World War I ends	Versailles Peace Conference — League of Nations	Economic chaos in Germany	Hitler in power — Mao Zedong's Long March begins	First television broadcast	Munich crisis	Germany invades Poland	Bretton Woods Conference	United Nations founded — Atomic bomb dropped
1918	**1919**		**1934**	**1936**	**1938**	**1939**	**1944**	**194**

NEW SYSTEM EVOLVING   BIPOLAR ERA ENDS

Renewed Détente

Euro becomes common European currency	India and Pakistan conduct nuclear tests	First woman U.S. secretary of state	World Conference on Women	World Trade Organization begins	Cairo Population Conference — Chaos in Rwanda	NAFTA ratified — European Union begins	Clinton in power — Chaos in Bosnia	War in Persian Gulf	Berlin Wall opene — Tiananmen Square massac
1999	**1998**	**1997**	**1996**	**1995**	**1994**	**1993**	**1992**	**1991**	**198**
Wye River Accord implemented for Mid-East peace	Government change in Germany after 16 years	Kofi Annan becomes UN secretary-general	Peace in Bosnia	UN's 50th anniversary	Summit of the Americas	START II	Earth Summit	Soviet Union collapses — Yeltsin heads Russia	

NEW INTERNATIONAL SYSTEM EMERGING

*To Linda, Ralph, and Stephanie
and their great sibling support*

About the Authors

JOHN T. ROURKE, Ph.D., is chair of the department of political science at the University of Connecticut. He is the author of *International Politics on the World Stage*, Seventh Edition (Dushkin/McGraw-Hill, 1997) and *Presidential Wars and American Democracy: Rally 'Round the Chief* (Paragon House, 1993); coauthor with Ralph G. Carter and Mark A. Boyer of

John T. Rourke and Mark A. Boyer

Making American Foreign Policy (Dushkin Publishing Group/Brown & Benchmark, 1996) and of *Direct Democracy and International Politics: Deciding International Issues through Referendums* (Lynne Rienner, 1992); the editor of *Taking Sides: Clashing Views on Controversial Issues in World Politics*, Ninth Edition (Dushkin/McGraw-Hill, 2000); and the author of *Making Foreign Policy: United States, Soviet Union, China* (Brooks/Cole, 1990), *Congress and the Presidency in U.S. Foreign Policymaking* (Westview, 1985), and numerous articles and papers. He enjoys teaching introductory classes and does so each semester at the university's Storrs and Hartford campuses. Rourke believes that politics affect us all, and that we can affect politics. Rourke practices what he propounds; he is involved in the university's internship program, advises one of its political clubs, has served as a staff member of Connecticut's legislature, and has been involved in political campaigns on the local, state, and national levels.

MARK A. BOYER, Ph.D., is an associate professor of political science at the University of Connecticut. He is the author of *International Cooperation and Public Goods: Opportunities for the Western Alliance* (Johns Hopkins University Press, 1993), coauthor with Brigid Starkey and Jonathan Wilkenfeld of *Negotiating a Complex World* (Rowman & Littlefield, 1999), as well as author of articles in the *Journal of Conflict Resolution, Defense Economics, Review of International Political Economy, Pacific Focus, International Journal, Journal of Peace Research, Diplomacy and Statecraft*, and a number of chapters in edited volumes. In January 2000, he became the inaugural editor of the newest journal of the International Studies Association, *International Studies Perspectives*. He is a 1992–93 Pew Faculty Fellow in International Affairs and a 1986–88 SSRC-MacArthur Fellow in International Peace and Security. He directs the Connecticut Project in International Negotiation (CPIN), which conducts computer-assisted foreign policy simulations for high school students throughout the northeastern United States (visit his Web site: www.lib.uconn.edu/~mboyer/). A strong proponent of active forms of learning, Boyer employs a wide mix of teaching approaches, ranging from case teaching to various types of simulations.

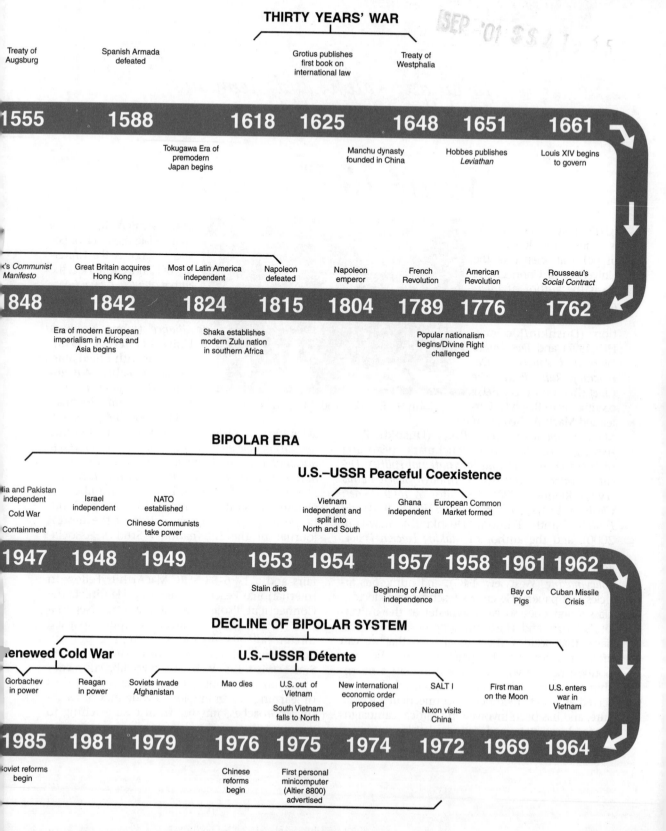

THIRTY YEARS' WAR

Treaty of
Augsburg

Spanish Armada
defeated

Grotius publishes
first book on
international law

Treaty of
Westphalia

1555 1588 1618 1625 1648 1651 1661

Tokugawa Era of
premodern
Japan begins

Manchu dynasty
founded in China

Hobbes publishes
Leviathan

Louis XIV begins
to govern

x's *Communist
Manifesto*

Great Britain acquires
Hong Kong

Most of Latin America
independent

Napoleon
defeated

Napoleon
emperor

French
Revolution

American
Revolution

Rousseau's
Social Contract

1848 1842 1824 1815 1804 1789 1776 1762

Era of modern European
imperialism in Africa and
Asia begins

Shaka establishes
modern Zulu nation
in southern Africa

Popular nationalism
begins/Divine Right
challenged

BIPOLAR ERA

U.S.–USSR Peaceful Coexistence

lia and Pakistan
independent

Cold War

Containment

Israel
independent

NATO
established

Chinese Communists
take power

Vietnam
independent and
split into
North and South

Ghana
independent

European Common
Market formed

1947 1948 1949 1953 1954 1957 1958 1961 1962

Stalin dies

Beginning of African
independence

Bay of
Pigs

Cuban Missile
Crisis

DECLINE OF BIPOLAR SYSTEM

Renewed Cold War

U.S.–USSR Détente

Gorbachev
in power

Reagan
in power

Soviets invade
Afghanistan

Mao dies

U.S. out of
Vietnam

South Vietnam
falls to North

New international
economic order
proposed

SALT I

Nixon visits
China

First man
on the Moon

U.S. enters
war in
Vietnam

1985 1981 1979 1976 1975 1974 1972 1969 1964

Soviet reforms
begin

Chinese
reforms
begin

First personal
minicomputer
(Altier 8800)
advertised